Imposter Syndrome and AI:

Navigating Human Identity in the Age of Intelligent Machines

Laeeq Razzak Janjua
https://orcid.org/0000-0002-1948-5859
WSB University, Poland

Kozma Dorottya Edina
https://orcid.org/0000-0002-4948-8815
University of Pannonia, Hungary

Bhupinder Singh
https://orcid.org/0009-0006-4779-2553
North Bangkok University, Thailand

IGI Global
Scientific Publishing
Publishing Tomorrow's Research Today

Vice President of Editorial	Melissa Wagner
Director of Acquisitions	Mikaela Felty
Director of Book Development	Jocelynn Hessler
Production Manager	Mike Brehm
Cover Design	Jose Rosado

Published in the United States of America by
IGI Global Scientific Publishing
701 East Chocolate Avenue
Hershey, PA, 17033, USA
Tel: 717-533-8845 | Fax: 717-533-7115
Website: https://www.igi-global.com E-mail: cust@igi-global.com

Library of Congress Cataloging-in-Publication Data

LCCN: 2025054458 (CIP Data Pending)
ISBN13: 9798337366180
Isbn13Softcover: 9798337366197
EISBN13: 9798337366203
British Cataloguing in Publication Data
A Cataloguing in Publication record for this book is available from the British Library.

Table of Contents

Detailed Table of Contents

Artificial intelligence has become a revolution in the vibrant subject of environmental governance since it is helping develop new ways in which people can keep track of, control, and preserve common natural resources. AI in environmental governance employs machine learning and big-data analytics alongside predictive modelling to solve some of the complicated issues associated with climate change, the lack of the biosphere, and environmental pollution. A case in point, with the help of AI software, one can analyse big data based on satellite photos, Internet of Things, and environmental sensors to track deforestation in real-time, anticipate ecological issues, or manage resources optimally as part of conservation restrictions. This integration can be characterized by a greater level of efficiency and accuracy, and therefore, the policy makers could derive their decisions using data that cannot be obtained using the traditional methods.

The legal inferences of AI-driven change of copyrighted works advance complicated questions under intellectual property and copyright law including the boundary between conversion in use or infringement. AI-generated modifications from copyrighted materials can be considered copyright infringement if they reproduce, distribute, or publicly display the original work without permission from the copyright holder. The copyright holders can exclusive use to make, distribute or create derivative works from, copies of its original expression. These rights can also be infringed upon by unauthorized derivative works that are too similar in form and design to the original work. Copyright defines a derivative work as any new material that is based upon an existing work, including modifications or adaptations.

design, algorithmic transparency, and corporate accountability to protect the dignity of children in India's fast-developing AI-driven marketplace.

Employment regulations are predicated on the idea that identity, sense of safety and social fit determine ability to work. Therefore, unemployed has an impact on a person's mental health, social identity, and self-esteem in addition to their financial loss. The concept of fairness is the foundation of employment law which also lessens the associated societal and personal costs upon emphasizing substantive the safeguards and procedural fairness. There are provisions like social security and anti-discrimination protection, these laws not only assisted people with their practical necessities but also provided working people with a feeling of fairness and self-respect. This chapter identifies and assesses the legal provisions in professional displacement enhancing imposter syndrome and identity crisis in employment because of automation and AI in industries.

Although modern technology has made accessing mental health treatment simpler, but should still respect people's privacy even if the human beings utilize AI technologies for psychoanalysis or assistance with an identity crisis. AI applications must be utilized with sensitive personal data in order to have any chance of identifying cognitive, emotional, and behavioral qualities. This brings up issues with discrimination, abuse, and prejudice in algorithms. This chapter discusses the ethical and legal considerations that must be made in order to ensure the security of mental health data while using AI-assisted diagnosis and treatment technologies. It also examines if regulations in other nations and areas, such as GDPF in Europe and HIPPA in the US, might alter the procedures for handling psychological data. The obvious human rights to consent, mental integrity and freedom of body are also covered in this chapter.

The idea of "human-centered AI" is a "naive aspiration" that entails building AI with people in mind first. This method promotes the development of AI to improve, not replace, human decision-making, and it is said to respect user autonomy, trust, and well-being. Human-centered AI uses design principles that include everyone, development methodologies that incorporate everyone, and ethical frameworks to produce systems that a wide range of people, including persons with impairments and people from marginalized groups, can use. AI systems that lessen cognitive load, offer individualized aid, and keep people in charge of life-saving decisions may help some mental health outcomes. This strategy of putting people first will make sure that AI maintains a tool for empowerment, respects human dignity and the principle of fair access, and improves quality of life while reducing any negative consequences that might happen through continual stakeholder involvement and ethical oversight.

The internet has facilitated a global pandemic of online child sexual exploitation and abuse (OCSEA), posing deep challenges to law and policy. This chapter provides a combined assessment of the international, legal, and technical responses to this crisis. It looks at the foundation international legal regimes, such as UN conventions and regional instruments like the Lanzarote Convention, which impose requirements on states to criminalize and cooperate across borders. The discussion is based on comparative national case studies of the United States, United Kingdom, and India, revealing varied but convergent legal reaction. Moreover, the chapter also critically examines technological solutions like hash-matching and AI and multi-stakeholder alliances facilitating detection and enforcement. Finally, it underlines the stark dichotomy between safeguarding children and safeguarding fundamental rights, most notably in the areas of encryption and abuse content generated by AI, calling for a proportionate, child-focused response to eliminate this evil harm.

The concept of new business models is altering who performs the work, how it gets done and its value across every sector. The lower costs of getting and sharing information have made it possible to use automation algorithms to create activities and make documents. These technology promises beg critical questions about the morality, legality and social implications of replacing or transforming economic institutions we find around us. The international shifts have been more profoundly felt in the workplace than automation and artificial intelligence. The logic of the Industrial Age is no longer valid in our workplace, which exhibits both human and machine intelligence. This rise is challenging traditional labor norms as the professional identity crises and self doubt generated by AI displacement are more and significant in nature.

Automation and artificial intelligence continue to disrupt the workforce economy, transforming industries and institutions, as well as traditional employment models. Although automation promises to improve productivity and efficiency, it poses its own problems in job displacement and skill gaps like imposter syndrome and identity crises as the replacement of human workforce to AI and rebotics. In order to cope with this transition, companies, government bodies and educational institutions need to take initiative, in the form of retraining initiatives, AI-human collaboration, labour policies etc. This discussion must also include ethical considerations, regulatory frameworks, and equitable opportunities for employment as AI continues to develop. As automation progresses the societies should shape it by augmentation of human potential instead of replacement, which could help facilitate sustainable economic growth and resilient labour workforce.

The legal world is faced with impostor syndrome and human identity crisin AI era. Technology, psychology and law are intersecting in a new way that is just beginning to appear on the horizon Properly speaking, the adaptation of AI-based technology will influence not only professional decisions but also creativity and self-perception. People are often at a loss to pin down their own worthiness or legitimacy of position in a machine-dominated world. This phenomenon--first noted by psychologists as "imposter syndrome" (because it makes people feel that they are taking up someone else's position and not deserving to be there)--has taken on fresh significance in the computer age. The outputs generated by those employing AI in offices, education systems and other creative industries make human input and machine aid into artificially merged matter.

Human identity plays a dominant role in the discourse on algorithmic bias in artificial intelligence at this very moment. It is precisely the very attributes that constitute identity- race, caste, gender, disability, class position and locational belonging which are transmuted into data points, proxy variables and risk indices in algorithmic systems, and often without the consent or even a decent understanding of the affected persons. In the field of Environmental Impact Assessment (EIA), where AI tools are increasingly the basis for decision support tools or models of pollution dispersion, health risk prediction, mitigation prioritization and ranking of project alternatives, how identity is encoded or not encoded in data-sets thus affects who is made visible as "at risk" and who is effectively excluded from environmental decision making.

AI methods for psychological assessment relied only on neuro-computational analysis and data-driven modeling, which quantified feelings and actions. The capacity of machine learning to detect cognitive distortions, diagnoses, and treatment strategies is used to assess theories. However, the ethical guidelines that regulate professional treatment sessions are often not followed by these technological techniques. However, AI systems are unable to comprehend the scenario, maintain secrets, or experience other people's emotions. The hazards go beyond data privacy to the core elements of self-perception and personal identity development when AI applications impede on issues like identity crises, emotional instability, and the handling of traumatic situations. The possibility of re-traumatization, the theft of personal narratives, or the use of mental states as commodities for behavior profiling and financial gain is increased when there is a lack of robust data governance in this domain.

The “imposter syndrome behind bars” is the feeling many prisoners have that they do not deserve personal development, educational achievements or rehabilitative accomplishments while incarcerated. In the context of jail and prison, there are many have layers of profound internalized self-doubt as a result of society’s bias against criminalized identity and the resolutely stratified nature of life behind bars. When prisoners accomplish something going to school, teaching other prisoners or taking part in therapy programs, as they can feel internally conflicted as to whether it has been real, if it is only them performing. This chapter emphasizes on that how prisoners' dissonance slips into the personal stories of society portraying them as what they did, denying their humanity and truthfulness. The also supporting environments and help much in affirming positive identity rebuilding.

Parenting in the era of algorithms requires parents to navigate strong societal forces as well as expert systems that employ technology and data to manage caring. Children who are deaf or hard of hearing and their families may benefit much from such technology, but it also brings with it the competing demands of monitoring, emotional escalation, and the constant need to improve. These frameworks stand to misselitiate diverse forms of communication and the modality that so many deaf and hard-of-hearing people's lives revolve around in ways that subsequently shape parents' experiences, activism, or other parenting within narrow bands. As a result, the use of alternative theoretical perspectives becomes necessary in order to understand the diversity that exists amongst contributions by both children and their caregivers outside canonical measures of success.

Algorithmic discrimination takes many shapes, each amplifying bias in AI-powered career platforms. AI tools used for hiring, promotions, performance ranking and workplace monitoring can inscribe and amplify instead of erasing gender and racial inequality. There is a potential for bias due to unrepresentative training data, the use of proxy variables rather than protected characteristics in decision making, design trade-offs that favour system efficiency over equity and feedback loops that keep into the data “successful” profiles from minority groups. When researchers have looked more closely at AI hiring systems, they have seen intricate interactions among multiple categories, where the model might favor some women overall while being particularly biased against certain groups of Black men or particular communities of women from a given ethnic background an insight that reveals discrimination to be not something that emerges cleanly along individual axes like gender and race.

Job skills changed when workers reorganized companies, and people's views of their professional identities changed as well. According to this essay, identity crises and self-doubt brought on by robots doing human work should be addressed in new labor legislation, as should the handling of layoffs. It would also examine the legislation protecting workers' rights and the ethical justifications for businesses' social responsibility. It holds that in order to safeguard employees' health and maintain their human dignity, labor regulations need to be modified. However, the author claims that automation still destroys a person's spirit, regardless of how beneficial technology is in everyday life. It offers a rights-based approach to preserving workers' dignity and social standing in an era when technological slaves are beginning to resemble humans. The safety and mental well-being of individuals should be considered by the government when drafting work rules.

Imposter syndrome as already prevalent in elite legal and scientific circles mutates into something even more corrosive under AI pressure. Lawyers say they have found themselves lying awake, ruminating over how the AI has bungled analyses of causation in their models, feeling feelings from shame to a visceral sense of moral failure. The expert witnesses are noticing a new practice: rehearsing their testimony under the cloud that the other side's AI probably already has stress-tested every citation and data set they will present. The ceaseless exposure to machine perfection generates a feedback loop in which human fallibility seems not just unfortunate but sinful. That cognitive tension is made worse by the ethical and interpretive opaqueness of many AI systems. As practitioners begin to feel displaced by machine-driven authority or coerced into over-aligning their arguments to the predictions of an algorithm, anxiety may increase.

Preface

The development of artificial intelligence opens humanity the door to a new era, the era marked not only by the technical power but by a significant psychological and moral self-examination. As artificial intelligences study, think and even generate, it must question previously very strong conception of expertise, authenticity and self-worth. This is an edited book on "Imposter Syndrome and AI: Navigating Human Identity in the Age of Intelligent Machines" explore the fundamental aspects between human identity and artificial abilities. Once analyzed in the concept of academia, professional life or even creativity, imposter syndrome has gained new sense of urgency in the digital era. There is an insider feeling of anxiety grabbing at the core of increasing pre-evidence of algorithms in decision-making, writing, art and research. The book is a compilation of interdisciplinary writings on concepts of merit and identity restructuring in AI augmentation by people and institutions by employing law, psychology, education, computer science, and philosophy together.

These chapters compiled here are not simply a diagnosis of a psychological phenomenon; they bring light to the socio-technical ecologies enhancing the feeling of inadequacy and displacement. They further suggest the ways to resiliency, ethical design, and inclusive innovation where technology supplements but does not impair the human potential. Such an integration of empirical inquiry, critical reflection and practical wisdom aims to enable the dialogue in this book to be both a humane and a critical examination of the same. It challenges scholars, students, professionals and technologists at large to consider the lines of the imposter syndrome as a sign of weakness but as a reflection of the dynamic relationship between human awareness and artificial intelligence.

CHAPTER OVERVIEW

Chapter 1: AI Driven Environmental Governance and the Rise of Imposter Syndrome among Legal Experts

Artificial intelligence has become a revolution in the vibrant subject of environmental governance since it is helping develop new ways in which people can keep track of, control, and preserve common natural resources. AI in environmental governance employs machine learning and big-data analytics alongside predictive modelling to solve some of the complicated issues associated with climate change, the lack of the biosphere, and environmental pollution. A case in point, with the help of AI software, one can analyse big data based on satellite photos, Internet of Things, and environmental sensors to track deforestation in real-time, anticipate ecological issues, or manage resources optimally as part of conservation restrictions. This integration can be characterized by a greater level of efficiency and accuracy, and therefore, the policy makers could derive their decisions using data that cannot be obtained using the traditional methods.

Chapter 2: AI Generated Creativity and the Law: Protecting Human Originality Amid Imposter Fears

The legal inferences of AI-driven change of copyrighted works advance complicated questions under intellectual property and copyright law including the boundary between conversion in use or infringement. AI-generated modifications from copyrighted materials can be considered copyright infringement if they reproduce, distribute, or publicly display the original work without permission from the copyright holder. The copyright holders can exclusive use to make, distribute or create derivative works from, copies of its original expression. These rights can also be infringed upon by unauthorized derivative works that are too similar in form and design to the original work. Copyright defines a derivative work as any new material that is based upon an existing work, including modifications or adaptations. This chapter focuses on the protection of human original work and imposter fears from AI-generated creativity from legal sphere.

Chapter 3: AI in Education and Skill Assessment: Enhancing Learning or Intensifying Impostor Syndrome in Students

With features like tailored learning, real-time feedback, customizable study materials, and exams that adapt to your performance, intelligent systems are revolutionizing education and skills testing. Although these advancements increase productivity and physical activity, they can have a negative impact on mental health. Constant evaluations can demoralize students, and algorithmic styling might make them doubt their skills, which can result in imposter syndrome. In AI-assisted environments, pressure to do well can be detrimental, particularly if it appears that internal validation of performance is involved. However, when applied properly, AI can benefit students by identifying their areas of strength, promoting development, and lessening prejudice. Emotional intelligence and technological know-how must be combined to ensure that AI tools benefit people rather than harm them. It must consider if we are creating more intelligent systems or more anxious pupils as schools evolve.

Chapter 4: Algorithmic Innocence and Commercial Predation Redefining Child Exploitation: Era of AI-Driven Advertising under POCSO and Digital Rights Framework

Children's interaction with algorithms is innocent, so artificial intelligence appears caring and personalised. In virtual worlds, children play, learn, and socialise, and AI increasingly powers data-driven targeting of goods and services. This chapter contends that such algorithmic places obscure the line between fun and exploitation and are an evil child manipulation. It recasts these practices within India's shifting digital governance framework based on the Protection of Children from Sexual Offences Act, 2012 (POCSO), the Digital Personal Data Protection Act, 2023 (DPDP), and other relevant consumer protection and digital rights laws. By means of behavioural profiling and emotional prediction, algorithms infringe on children's privacy, agency, and liberty of the mind. Hence, it is necessary to bolster ethical design, algorithmic transparency, and corporate accountability to protect the dignity of children in India's fast-developing AI-driven marketplace.

Chapter 5: Assessment of Legal Responses to Professional Displacement and Self-Doubt: Employment Law and the AI Identity Crisis

Employment regulations are predicated on the idea that identity, sense of safety and social fit determine ability to work. Therefore, unemployed has an impact on a person's mental health, social identity, and self-esteem in addition to their financial loss. The concept of fairness is the foundation of employment law which also lessens the associated societal and personal costs upon emphasizing substantive the safeguards and procedural fairness. There are provisions like social security and anti-discrimination protection, these laws not only assisted people with their practical necessities but also provided working people with a feeling of fairness and self-respect. This chapter identifies and assesses the legal provisions in professional displacement enhancing imposter syndrome and identity crisis in employment because of automation and AI in industries.

Chapter 6: Data Protection and Mental Health Privacy: Legal Standards for AI-Powered Psychological Assessment and Identity Crisis Intervention

Although modern technology has made accessing mental health treatment simpler, but should still respect people's privacy even if the human beings utilize AI technologies for psychoanalysis or assistance with an identity crisis. AI applications must be utilized with sensitive personal data in order to have any chance of identifying cognitive, emotional, and behavioral qualities. This brings up issues with discrimination, abuse, and prejudice in algorithms. This chapter discusses the ethical and legal considerations that must be made in order to ensure the security of mental health data while using AI-assisted diagnosis and treatment technologies. It also examines if regulations in other nations and areas, such as GDPF in Europe and HIPPA in the US, might alter the procedures for handling psychological data. The obvious human rights to consent, mental integrity and freedom of body are also covered in this chapter.

Chapter 7: Designing Human-Centered AI to Promote Confidence, Inclusivity and Mental Well-Being

The idea of "human-centered AI" is a "naive aspiration" that entails building AI with people in mind first. This method promotes the development of AI to improve, not replace, human decision-making, and it is said to respect user autonomy, trust, and well-being. Human-centered AI uses design principles that include everyone, development methodologies that incorporate everyone, and ethical frameworks to produce systems that a wide range of people, including persons with impairments and people from marginalized groups, can use. AI systems that lessen cognitive load, offer individualized aid, and keep people in charge of life-saving decisions may help some mental health outcomes. This strategy of putting people first will make sure that AI maintains a tool for empowerment, respects human dignity and the principle of fair access, and improves quality of life while reducing any negative consequences that might happen through continual stakeholder involvement and ethical oversight.

Chapter 8: Digital Vulnerability and Legal Protection of Children: Examining International Responses to AI-Driven Exploitation and Behavioral Manipulation

The internet has facilitated a global pandemic of online child sexual exploitation and abuse (OCSEA), posing deep challenges to law and policy. This chapter provides a combined assessment of the international, legal, and technical responses to this crisis. It looks at the foundation international legal regimes, such as UN conventions and regional instruments like the Lanzarote Convention, which impose requirements on states to criminalize and cooperate across borders. The discussion is based on comparative national case studies of the United States, United Kingdom, and India, revealing varied but convergent legal reaction. Moreover, the chapter also critically examines technological solutions like hash-matching and AI and multi-stakeholder alliances facilitating detection and enforcement. Finally, it underlines the stark dichotomy between safeguarding children and safeguarding fundamental rights, most notably in the areas of encryption and abuse content generated by AI, calling for a proportionate, child-focused response to eliminate this evil harm.

Chapter 9: Exploring Legal Structures for Workplace Automation Concerning Employment Law: Professional Identity Crises and Self-Doubt Generated by AI Displacement

The concept of new business models is altering who performs the work, how it gets done and its value across every sector. The lower costs of getting and sharing information have made it possible to use automation algorithms to create activities and make documents. These technology promises beg critical questions about the morality, legality and social implications of replacing or transforming economic institutions we find around us. The international shifts have been more profoundly felt in the workplace than automation and artificial intelligence. The logic of the Industrial Age is no longer valid in our workplace, which exhibits both human and machine intelligence. This rise is challenging traditional labor norms as the professional identity crises and self doubt generated by AI displacement are more and significant in nature.

Chapter 10: Future of Work in the Age of Automation in Global Scenario Navigating Imposter Syndrome and Identity Crisis: Routing AI, Job Displacement and Workforce Renovation

Automation and artificial intelligence continue to disrupt the workforce economy, transforming industries and institutions, as well as traditional employment models. Although automation promises to improve productivity and efficiency, it poses its own problems in job displacement and skill gaps like imposter syndrome and identity crises as the replacement of human workforce to AI and rebotics. In order to cope with this transition, companies, government bodies and educational institutions need to take initiative, in the form of retraining initiatives, AI-human collaboration, labour policies etc. This discussion must also include ethical considerations, regulatory frameworks, and equitable opportunities for employment as AI continues to develop. As automation progresses the societies should shape it by augmentation of human potential instead of replacement, which could help facilitate sustainable economic growth and resilient labour workforce.

Chapter 11: Global Anti-Discrimination Law and AI Concerning Imposter Syndrome and Legal Frameworks: Gender, Diversity and Intersectional Bias in Professional Advancement Technology

In the age of artificial intelligence, strong anti-discrimination laws are important for more than just following the rules. It includes social, ethical and economic issues of interest to technologists and non-technologists alike. The regulations would help reduce the chance that AI perpetuates stereotypes that limit women and other groups, based on preconceived ideas. Lost impostor syndrome, behind-the-scenes' and careers being ruined by AI-bias fuel psychological damage to self-esteem, job satisfaction, retention etc."AI bias" If "bias exits in neural networks that has emerged in the workforce," then it's best to circumvent such bias before problems arise. In that chapter, it examines how international antidiscrimination law links to AI, with examples of impostor syndrome. It also explores the intersection of this technology with global anti-discrimination laws, and in doing so, reveals significant legal and sociotechnical implications.

Chapter 12: Imposter Syndrome among Legal Professionals in an AI Augmented Judiciary

The necessity to respond to imposter syndrome in this scenario is significant, as it crosses the fundamental ethical considerations, judicial independence, and sustainable development goals, specifically SDG 16 of access to justice and SDG 8 of decent work. The litigious system of law has long required an uncompromising belief-in-self; barristers in wigs before the Supreme Court or High Courts represent authority. By changing the roles of interpretive mastery to oversight via predictive sentencing algorithms and contract made bots installed on tribunals like the National Company Law Tribunal and family courts, AI augmentation disrupts this archetype.

The outcome with the symptomatology perfectionism, overworks, and burns out shows the pervasive effect of the syndrome. The implication of sustainable legal ecosystems is conspicuous: SDG-associated judiciaries need robust maintenance sticks, but imposter syndrome is subtractive of this, as it encourages seclusion rather than cooperation, as evidenced by the unwillingness to co-author AI-aided opinions.

Chapter 13: Imposter Syndrome among Women with Disabilities: Examining Human Identity in the Era of Artificial Intelligence

Disability women with disabilities are welcomed with twin exclusion through gender bias, ableism, and technologically driven marginalisation, further intensified by the emergence of Artificial Intelligence (AI). Imposter syndrome, persistent self-doubt despite ability, becomes an inescapable challenge, breaking down their confidence and professional advancement. This study explores the intersection of gender, disability, and AI in shaping impostor experiences using doctrinal analysis of legal documents, AI ethics guidelines, and international instruments such as the UNCRPD and CEDAW. The study illustrates that AI-powered work systems, learning tests, and employment monitoring tend to write and inscribe biases and magnify identity crises. At the same time, accessible and inclusive AI technologies can fight impostor feelings. It is suggested in the article that accessibility, intersectional inclusivity, and rights-based management be employed to enable equal AI to serve empowered disabled women and uphold human identity.

Chapter 14: Impostor Syndrome in Tech Industries: A Case Study Approach to AI Developers, Data Scientists and Innovators

Impostor Syndrome in tech industry has become a widespread issue, especially among AI developers, data scientists and innovators who live under a high-pressure, fast-changing work environment. Such specialists are often plagued by self-doubt, wondering how competent they are in the face of obvious skills, credentials, and accomplishments. With technology developing at an increasingly rapid pace and the competitive need for revolutionary ideas, the mental pressure to keep up and the sense of inferiority are growing. Case study methods demonstrate that many exceptionally gifted individuals tend to explain their peers' successes by luck, rather than their talent and worry that they themselves will be unmasked as "frauds." Such structures do not only affect the mental well-being of individuals, they also stifle creativity, collaboration and productivity in organizations. Impostor Syndrome can be countered with individual interventions like mentorship, peer-support networks, and workplace cultures that value learning as much as outcomes.

Chapter 15: Legal Dimensions of Imposter Syndrome and Human Identity Crisis in the Age of Artificial Intelligence

The legal world is faced with impostor syndrome and human identity crisin AI era. Technology, psychology and law are intersecting in a new way that is just beginning to appear on the horizon Properly speaking, the adaptation of AI-based technology will influence not only professional decisions but also creativity and self-perception. People are often at a loss to pin down their own worthiness or legitimacy of position in a machine-dominated world. This phenomenon--first noted by psychologists as "imposter syndrome" (because it makes people feel that they are taking up someone else's position and not deserving to be there)--has taken on fresh significance in the computer age. The outputs generated by those employing AI in offices, education systems and other creative industries make human input and machine aid into artificially merged matter.

Chapter 16: Navigating Human Identity in AI Algorithmic Bias and Reasonable Technology Deployment in Environmental Impact Assessment: Community Protection concerning Legal Frameworks

Human identity plays a dominant role in the discourse on algorithmic bias in artificial intelligence at this very moment. It is precisely the very attributes that constitute identity- race, caste, gender, disability, class position and locational belonging which are transmuted into data points, proxy variables and risk indices in algorithmic systems, and often without the consent or even a decent understanding of the affected persons. In the field of Environmental Impact Assessment (EIA), where AI tools are increasingly the basis for decision support tools or models of pollution dispersion, health risk prediction, mitigation prioritization and ranking of project alternatives, how identity is encoded or not encoded in data-sets thus affects who is made visible as "at risk" and who is effectively excluded from environmental decision making.

Chapter 17: Privacy in Mental Healthcare by Data Protection: Exploring AI-Powered Psychological Assessment and Identity Crisis Intervention with Legal Provisions

AI methods for psychological assessment relied only on neuro-computational analysis and data-driven modeling, which quantified feelings and actions. The capacity of machine learning to detect cognitive distortions, diagnoses, and treatment strategies is used to assess theories. However, the ethical guidelines that regulate professional treatment sessions are often not followed by these technological techniques. However, AI systems are unable to comprehend the scenario, maintain secrets, or experience other people's emotions. The hazards go beyond data privacy to the core elements of self-perception and personal identity development when AI applications impede on issues like identity crises, emotional instability, and the handling of traumatic situations. The possibility of re-traumatization, the theft of personal narratives, or the use of mental states as commodities for behavior profiling and financial gain is increased when there is a lack of robust data governance in this domain.

Chapter 18: Psychology of Confinement and Intersections of Imposter Syndrome: Identity Reconstruction and Human Rights in Prisons

The "imposter syndrome behind bars" is the feeling many prisoners have that they do not deserve personal development, educational achievements or rehabilitative accomplishments while incarcerated. In the context of jail and prison, there are many have layers of profound internalized self-doubt as a result of society's bias against criminalized identity and the resolutely stratified nature of life behind bars. When prisoners accomplish something going to school, teaching other prisoners or taking part in therapy programs, as they can feel internally conflicted as to whether it has been real, if it is only them performing. This chapter emphasizes on that how prisoners' dissonance slips into the personal stories of society portraying them as what they did, denying their humanity and truthfulness. The also supporting environments and help much in affirming positive identity rebuilding.

Chapter 19: Reframing Success and Contribution in AI-Augmented Systems Challenges to Parenting Children with Hearing Impairment: Imposter Syndrome and Rethinking Human Worth

Parenting in the era of algorithms requires parents to navigate strong societal forces as well as expert systems that employ technology and data to manage caring.

Children who are deaf or hard of hearing and their families may benefit much from such technology, but it also brings with it the competing demands of monitoring, emotional escalation, and the constant need to improve. These frameworks stand to misselitiate diverse forms of communication and the modality that so many deaf and hard-of-hearing people's lives revolve around in ways that subsequently shape parents' experiences, activism, or other parenting within narrow bands. As a result, the use of alternative theoretical perspectives becomes necessary in order to understand the diversity that exists amongst contributions by both children and their caregivers outside canonical measures of success.

Chapter 20: Regulating Algorithmic Bias and Global Legal Approaches in Gender, Diversity and Intersectional Equity in AI-Driven Professional Systems

Algorithmic discrimination takes many shapes, each amplifying bias in AI-powered career platforms. AI tools used for hiring, promotions, performance ranking and workplace monitoring can inscribe and amplify instead of erasing gender and racial inequality. There is a potential for bias due to unrepresentative training data, the use of proxy variables rather than protected characteristics in decision making, design trade-offs that favour system efficiency over equity and feedback loops that keep into the data "successful" profiles from minority groups. When researchers have looked more closely at AI hiring systems, they have seen intricate interactions among multiple categories, where the model might favor some women overall while being particularly biased against certain groups of Black men or particular communities of women from a given ethnic background an insight that reveals discrimination to be not something that emerges cleanly along individual axes like gender and race.

Chapter 21: Role of Employment Law in Addressing Professional Identity Crises and Self-Doubt Triggered by AI Displacement: Legal Frameworks for Workplace Automation

Job skills changed when workers reorganized companies, and people's views of their professional identities changed as well. According to this essay, identity crises and self-doubt brought on by robots doing human work should be addressed in new labor legislation, as should the handling of layoffs. It would also examine the legislation protecting workers' rights and the ethical justifications for businesses' social responsibility. It holds that in order to safeguard employees' health and maintain their human dignity, labor regulations need to be modified. However, the author claims that automation still destroys a person's spirit, regardless of how beneficial technology is in everyday life. It offers a rights-based approach to preserving workers' dignity and social standing in an era when technological slaves are beginning to resemble humans. The safety and mental well-being of individuals should be considered by the government when drafting work rules.

Chapter 22: The Psychological Impact of AI Led Litigation Support: Algorithms, Anxiety and Imposter Syndrome in the Age of AI

Imposter syndrome as already prevalent in elite legal and scientific circles mutates into something even more corrosive under AI pressure. Lawyers say they have found themselves lying awake, ruminating over how the AI has bungled analyses of causation in their models, feeling feelings from shame to a visceral sense of moral failure. The expert witnesses are noticing a new practice: rehearsing their testimony under the cloud that the other side's AI probably already has stress-tested every citation and data set they will present. The ceaseless exposure to machine perfection generates a feedback loop in which human fallibility seems not just unfortunate but sinful. That cognitive tension is made worse by the ethical and interpretive opaqueness of many AI systems. As practitioners begin to feel displaced by machine-driven authority or coerced into over-aligning their arguments to the predictions of an algorithm, anxiety may increase.

Chapter 23: Workplace Automation Laws and the Rise of Imposter Syndrome among Employees

Workplace automation powered by artificial intelligence, robotic process automation (RPA), and advanced machine learning has shifted from back-office trial balloons to a central operational strategy . AI systems that remove routine work from manufacturing, IT services and gig platforms by no: it technological displacement clauses. This development is in line with a broader trend towards proactive measures against such practices, involving bias audits in AI hiring tools. This historical development illustrates a tension between technological determinism and worker protections. The primary legal reforms address automation risks through mandatory reskilling, compensation amendments and algorithmic accountability as India's labor codes fall short of global standards such as the ban on opaque high-risk systems in EU AI Act. The lagging regulation creates a paradox in most jurisdictions automation races ahead unconstrained by law, while employees are assured that "humans remain in the loop," fostering an ambient that fuels imposter syndrome.

Chapter 1
AI-Driven Environmental Governance and the Rise of Imposter Syndrome Among Legal Experts

Rajni Parmar
https://orcid.org/0009-0009-4305-7289
Government Law College, Alwar, India

Sadhana Parmar
Nirwan University Jaipur, India

Aradhana Parmar
https://orcid.org/0009-0009-6384-3471
Maharishi Arvind University, Jaipur, India

ABSTRACT

Artificial intelligence has become a revolution in the vibrant subject of environmental governance since it is helping develop new ways in which people can keep track of, control, and preserve common natural resources. AI in environmental governance employs machine learning and big-data analytics alongside predictive modelling to solve some of the complicated issues associated with climate change, the lack of the biosphere, and environmental pollution. A case in point, with the help of AI software, one can analyse big data based on satellite photos, Internet of Things, and environmental sensors to track deforestation in real-time, anticipate ecological issues, or manage resources optimally as part of conservation restrictions. This

DOI: 10.4018/979-8-3373-6618-0.ch001

integration can be characterized by a greater level of efficiency and accuracy, and therefore, the policy makers could derive their decisions using data that cannot be obtained using the traditional methods.

1. INTRODUCTION AND FOUNDATIONS OF AI IN ENVIRONMENTAL GOVERNANCE

The legal professionals, who traditionally spoke about environmental laws, treaties, and enforcement mechanisms as formulas on a high level, now have to make their way in the world where algorithms are more intricate and fast. Disintermediation may be particularly acute when it comes to matters like international environmental law, which involves AI software scanning contracts, anticipating a lawsuit by using historical data, and formulating regulatory texts (Grenardo, 2022). This is also found in an example of China where AI-driven evaluation of listed companies was found to positively impact green governance performance over empirical estimation using the panel data, 2009-2013, and comparison of corporate sustainability indices through automated monitoring of compliance and risk management assessment (Balan, 2024). The Asian Development Bank has also observed that AI can identify a chance to promote inclusive and visible environmental change to systemic resilience with AI enabling organisations to simulate climate events and engaging stakeholders in more participatory decision-making (Kapartziani, 2025). There are contradictions in this technological revolution, however: AI as a concept in itself has special environmental hazards, data centres are energy-consuming and produce e-waste, so organizations like the United Nations Environment Programme are urging to make AI sustainable (Mantgomery & Gerhardt, 2025). With AI in the systems of governance, where UNESCO want to apply AI fairly, to the creation of classifier machine learning models that propose the interdependence of climate action and socioeconomic factors, it confronts human concerns of legal wisdom.

1.1. Development of AI technologies in the Area of Sustainability

This kind of technology as well brings about the feeling of obsolescence of the lawyers making it harder to overcome the imposter-syndrome-the psychological aspect of people who feel that they are not as good as they are supposed to be (Coken, 2025). Recent studies show that the prevalence of imposter syndrome has already achieved high rates in the legal world, with 74% of all lawyers and 83% of junior lawyers being affected (Sweatman, 2024). The synthetic intelligence is compounding the problem of this syndrome because algorithms have the ability to engage in more complex processes, like answering whether a nation has ratified the Paris Accords or whether the environmental impact assessment is sufficient, without issue and without exhaustion, and human professionals feel obscure by comparison.

To environmental law experts and advocates dealing with multilayered issues like transboundary pollution or carbon trading regulations, AI with its natural language processing and predictive analytics capabilities is threatening to shake the pool. To illustrate, a skilled attorney in the process of preparing a case on the destruction of habitats may find the AI algorithm to be able to correlate international databases, judicial precedents, and live satellite footage to create results in a few minutes, thus questioning the perceived worth of the human expert. Such impostorization, where AI makes people feel inferior, is not exclusive to beginners but runs across the ranks, as managers and senior partners have to deal with the tools that forge expertise democracy. The syndrome can take a specialised form in AI-informed governance: sufficiently qualified legal experts will fear going against AI judgments on the grounds that their intuitive viewpoint is becoming obsolete, they might even believe the critique that AI is biased in climate governance, disadvantaged communities, and reproduce biased information (Wang & Huang, 2025).

1.2 Interconnection with Sustainable Development Goals (SDGs)

The difference between the two is stark because AI, at the same time, provides environmental stewards with management tools and transparent decision-making, it destroys the self-confidence said to be necessary in ethical usage. Governance decision-makers and boards are urged to see AI as a frontier source of climate action, a balance exists between its potential to be innovative and social pressures like the rolling out of workforce and workforce reduction (Moassefi et al., 2025). In this regard, I suggest nurturing ambivalent human-AI partnerships, which protect lawyers relying on AI as an aid instead of an adversary, and highlighting distinctly human qualities (communication) like ethical judgment, negotiation, and empathy in environmental conflicts. Improvements in training programmes can directly be brought in relation to imposter syndrome by seeking to make emergent lawyers realise that AI represents a collaborative tool to help solve risks and innovations as opposed to a destructive force. Corporate governance needs to change as well, which is to strike a balance between the environmental impact of AI, and the ability to use the technology fairly to avoid creating a world run by technologically illiterate elites (Bajorek, 2024). Finally, a balanced strategy that acknowledges the power of AI and at the same time does not reduce key human aspect is crucial.

1.3 International Case Studies in the AI Implementation

It is only reinforced by the widespread sense of imposter syndrome that legal professionals feel in the age of AI: the new social contract is unable to establish itself for the first time on the basis of the law and policy. Rather, it has to integrate technological capability and uniquely human intelligence (Al Lawati et al., 2025). With AI penetrating, detecting deepfakes in environmental reporting or detecting threats to governance, the individuals doing scrutinising and oversight of an increasingly digital decision-making process, need to establish their authority understanding that the real skill lies in interpreting AI outputs in the multidimensional context of justice, fairness and sustainability. This combination would not only reduce the self-doubt but also make AI support the environmental needs of mankind at the same time preserving the position that could not be replaced by the people who safeguard it (Almomani et al., 2025).

2. TECHNOLOGICAL APPLICATIONS IN MONITORING AND PREDICTION

Technical developments in monitoring and forecasting have transformed environmental management, allowing for advanced real-time control over ecosystems in the face of rising stressors such as climate change, pollution, and biodiversity losses. At the heart of these breakthroughs is the combination of artificial intelligence (AI) with Internet of Things (IoT) sensors, satellite remote sensing and big-data analytics, which unlocks unprecedented data acquisition and predictive capabilities (Strachan, 2022).

Low-cost sensors and field-deployable devices are ubiquitous as components of IoT networks which monitor air quality (particulate matter, ozone, heavy metals) and water parameters (pH, turbidity or dissolved oxygen) (Ochs, 2021). When combined with AI algorithms, such systems can be used to detect anomalies and trigger warnings in advance, allowing raw data to become actionable insights for pollution control. Satellite tech, coupled with machine learning, offers global-scale monitoring: NASA's MODIS and ESA's Sentinel series of platforms can observe deforestation, glacial melt and land-use shifts at the finest levels of detail. Artificial intelligence, or AI, algorithms analyze huge sets of images to detect illegal logging or habitat loss in near real time, aiding conservation work in places like the Amazon.

AI is great at forecasting and prediction: predictive modeling deep learning and hybrid physical-ML models predict pollution levels, fire spread, and climate scenarios more accurately than traditional methods. For example, neuronal networks process historical and real-time data from IoT and satellites to forecast GHG emissions, extreme weather events or biodiversity shifts that could inform disaster preparedness and policymaking. New tools such as NASA's Prithvi weather-climate base model and UNEP-funded platforms bring together multi-source data for localized forecasts, while edge computing facilitates on-site analytics to enable a swifter response. They enable the latter to work more efficiently but also make access more democratic, putting powers in the hands of stakeholders ranging from governments to citizens. Barriers also remain, such as data limitations and AI's energy needs, but progress continues to offer hope for sustainable and resilient stewardship of Earth (Decosimo, 2022).

2.1 AI for Air Quality and Pollution Forecasting with Water Resource Management and Contamination Detection

AI is revolutionizing environmental monitoring by coupling advanced algorithms with sensor networks, satellite data and big data analytics to predict air quality and pollution, and also improving water resource management and contamination tracking (Grenardo, 2024). AI in air quality and pollution forecasting AI uses ML algorithms such as Random Forest, Long Short-Term Memory (LSTM) models to predict pollutant concentrations such as PM2 with up to 98.2% accuracy. These can distil huge quantities of information from IoT sensors, weather trends and urban traffic to issue live warnings and long-term predictions; helping cities to take the most proactive approach possible in avoiding health hazards.

AI-enabled schemes refine predictions depending on evolving factors such as emissions and meteorology, one illustrative case is scalable approach classifying air quality indices for public health warnings. Collaborations between NASA and governments use AI to scrutinize satellite images in a mission to pinpoint pollution hotspots and predict patterns, thus helping redesign cities to minimize emissions levels from trains or factories. Worldwide, AI can help to mitigate urban pollution by fine-tuning traffic and industrial operations using predictive analytics tools such as dashboards that forecast the day's pollution levels like a weather report as soon as 2025. Moving to water management, AI is prefecting the use of our limited supply by processing soil moisture and weather data along with historic usage patterns to predict demand, using IoT sensors to detect leaks on-the-fly and reduce wastage in agriculture and urban systems. In contamination surveillance, AI supported sensor data and spectral analysis can quickly identify contaminants like heavy metals, bacteria, chemicals in water bodies facilitating early warning and responding for quality incidents. State-of-the-art solutions integrate remote sensing and machine learning for the monitoring of groundwater, the prediction of contamination risks under changing climate, and contribute to improve sustainable management in water-scarce areas (Fines, 2025).

Data-driven decisions for water allocation: here, UNESCO and others recognize AI applications within bibliometic-based strategies in water management (demand prediction, pollution mitigation) as tools that enable data-driven decision making to equally distribute resources. The synergy between AI applications for air and water is found in integrated environmental governance concepts, such as the consideration of how sources of air pollution influence water quality through acid deposition or run-off in integrated response models that look at multiple impacts simultaneously.

3. POLICY FRAMEWORKS AND REGULATORY CHALLENGES: LEGAL GAPS IN AI-ENABLED ENVIRONMENTAL LAWS

In the new frame of artificial-intelligence (AI) intersecting with environmental governance, policy frameworks and regulatory challenges present a number of substantial legal gaps that limit effective oversight of AI-applied rules for nature as global AI usage for surveillance, anticipation, and sanctioning on environmental matters is surging amid ecological crisis. Policy frameworks in existence, like the European Union's AI Act, policy try to work-in sustainability considerations but are loose and voluntary rather than stringent mandates, only narrowly concentrating on documentation of an energy footprint during development stages and not interference with water use and material mining across the entire lifecycle of AI systems (Zangana et al., 2025). It reads: "This Act does not classify high-environmental-footprint models within those referred to as 'high-risk,' and leaves environmental protection to a secondary role couched in the technical sandboxes and harmonized standard, that will allow enforcement of it only beginning 2028 and without any tools for public participation or accountability."

In the U.S., a bill called the Artificial Intelligence Environmental Impacts Act of 2024, would require an expansive EPA-led study into AI's environmental impacts (energy use, pollutants, water use, e-waste and lifecycle assessments), and create a voluntary reporting mechanism through NIST to help standardize measurements and increase transparency. One example of the great paradox here is that while such frameworks often take their cue from cornerstone environmental principles such as those enshrined in the Rio Declaration, environmental and AI are not joined up neatly for them; consider how e.g. the precautionary principle suggests a preclusion of measures on uncertain risks (whereas an analysis will yield that millions were trained to create a GPT-3 whose carbon footprint exceeds hundreds of transatlantic flights), yet extant laws do not compel EIA before deployment or 'sustainability by design' to ensure "trimness".

3.2 Cross-Jurisdictional Data Governance Issues

The polluter-pays principle, core to environmental law, might compel AI developers to incorporate damage costs such as data center water use forecast at six times all of Denmark's domestic use or pollution from rare earth mining, but legal gaps remain too vast (and there is not yet a liability regime quite like that proposed with the EU's Corporate Sustainability Due Diligence Directive which would cover rights and uses running out-of-control through the hands of operators of AI). Post-Chevron judicial changes limit agency deference and heighten review of AI outputs that might be based on suspect or incomplete data possibly glossing over cumulative effects or public comments, and opening up procedural failures to litigation. Destruction outside the field also takes place in international settings, where AI weaponry contributes to environmental decay by mining minerals in war zones, deploying enormous energy for training and causing collateral damage during combat; however, review of weapons is not based on explicit provisions such as those related to the environment under the rules of IHL found Article 36 of the Geneva Conventions permitting a loophole for destruction of certain areas including but not limited to deforestation, water pollution emissions. The United Nations Guiding Principles on Business and Human Rights provide non-binding guidance, but there is no specific treaty covering the lifecycle of pollution from AI to which private entities ordering the training may be held accountable for harm to the environment (Bennett, 2025).

4. ETHICAL DILEMMAS IN AI-DRIVEN SYSTEMS WITH ALGORITHMIC BIAS AND ENVIRONMENTAL JUSTICE

The emerging ethical dilemmas in AI-enabled environmental systems, especially in the intersection of algorithmic bias and environmental justice, have become particularly ethical issues in the rapidly developing field (O'Connor, 2025). Although these technological advances hold hope to solution to climate emergencies, they also fuel social inequalities and ecological destruction.

The use of AI to predict the pollution, allocate resources, and forecast climate is influenced by bias due to skewed training data that reflects historical injustices; thus, AI-based systems result in discrimination against populations that are already at risk of environmental hazards. An example of algorithmic bias is algorithmic bias due to biased data or inaccurate assumptions or being under-represented and is observed in tools that estimate the probability of illegal dumping or felling trees in cities. In such applications, the mechanisms can have discriminative effects, prioritizing low-income neighbourhoods on the basis of discriminatory enforcement data, and therefore circle credibility to similar effects as criminal-justice instruments like COMPAS do, which unfairly characterize identified groups as being at higher risk. It is not just a technical prejudice but a highly ethical one because it increases social inequalities. An illustrative example is the AI-based decision-making about the location of dangerous facilities or distribution of clean-up efforts in an environmental-justice question, scaled against privilege wealthy whiter neighbourhoods over those of colour with a comparatively stronger place in diverse pollution burdens, respectively, and unintentionally contaminating health inequalities, like high rates of respiratory disease in under-to-be-serviced groups (De Queiroz, 2025). The moral quandary deepens as one considers AI contribution to eco-justice: flawed or biased decision-making, e.g., not detecting pollution hotspots because a lack of data regarding isolated and native territories exist, propagates disparities and deprives people of equal access to clean air, water and soil that will weaken world pledges to sustainable-development targets.

4.1 Privacy of Data in Ecological Surveillance

Even the carbon footprint of AI per se brings with it significant ethical cries. Large models are energy-consuming; one system that perform natural language processing could emit the same amount of CO 2 as five vehicles during its lifespan, and in the future it has been projected that AI may consume as much energy as a whole country, thus contributing substantially to climate change despite supposed offsetting. These systems are run in data centres that use high amounts of electricity; most of it fossil-generated and water, which is needed to cool, even further creating a lack of water, thermal pollution and loss of biodiversity in arid areas. Such effects are disproportionately displayed on users in the global south who have a high reliance on local resources hence reducing the phenomenon of exploitation of the society with destruction of nature.

Ethical issues are based on the assumption that AI is neutral: systems that are trained on biased data spread inequality across racial, gender, and class lines and push the focus away of much larger responsibilities, including eco responsibilities or ethical labour practices. Under low paying conditions and mental-health hazards of toxic material, data-annotators in numerous settings in low-waged economies earn less than US 2 per hour. Biases in the generated content also make generative AI a more challenging situation in terms of environmental narratives since it may propagate misinformation on climate issues or lack diversity in voices when discussing the idea of sustainability, and the high energy costs only add to the contradictory use of technology that also creates the problems that it is meant to address. Lags in governance: legislations like the EU AI Act encourage risk-based policies but do not do enough to address environmental issues or bias in ecological solutions, voluntary ethical requirements do not offer enough structure to enforce responsibility, and obligatory variety of data is not enacted yet (Romanishyn et al., 2025).

4.2 Responsibility in the case of AI Decision-Making mistakes

There are also data-ethics issues that occur when privacy violations under the GDPR-like regulations collide with environmental issues. The use of AI in surveillance of illegal logging can violate the rights of indigenous people and support non-consenting, colonial methods of data mining. There are some real-life examples of these dilemmas: facial-recognition biases in wildlife-tracking artificial intelligence might fail to distinguish diverse terrain and give misleading biodiversity measurements, stripping minority-managed ecology of the chance at representation by inclusive feedback on sustainable innovations, and hate-research algorithms in green-tech companies might be discriminatory, limiting the opportunity to include the diverse input into sustainable concepts. Mitigation plans covers fairness-conscious machine learning, human-in-the-loop detection, and the impact analysis that encompasses the environment-justice, i.e., demographic parity dictating identical error rates among groups in the pollution-predictive models. These approaches prescribe that corporate social responsibility should be redefined to include AI-ethics boards tasked with streamlining operations in data-centres to operate according to renewable energy and equitable labour practices so that AI efficiencies become the new drives behind the consumption of resources. Ethical implications in business are system-wide: AI use in supply chains to create sustainably produced products can have blind spots that can support unethical conduct beyond view of the audience (Abbasi, 2024).

The broader social effect is also present: biased AI-generated information might strengthen eco-fears, since the nature of algorithms is to promote sensational speech on climate issues as opposed to fair justice-based responses to it, undermining trust in the population. The OECD human-centric AI is one international principle that suggests a balance between innovation and ethics, but the lack of implementation can leave certain countries and, in particular, developing ones vulnerable while disproportionately facing an inadequately managed environmental impact of AI. These issues need a cross-cutting strategy that incorporates binding laws that require environmental-AI bias audits, creation of efficient algorithms, and jointly designing justice-ready solutions with the communities impacted. Ethical principles should also evolve alongside the development of AI since it has dual potential to reduce and increase environmental injustices in such a manner that the benefits and harms obtained are distributed fairly.

5. AI CARBON FOOTPRINT AND SUSTAINABILITY PARADOX; ENERGY CONSUMPTION OF LARGE AI MODELS WITH BALANCING INNOVATION WITH ECOLOGICAL COSTS

The carbon footprint of artificial intelligence (AI) and the corresponding sustainability paradox reveal a core contradiction in modern technologies, namely, on the one hand, AI opens access to unprecedented innovations in the ecological domain, and on the other hand, on the one hand, artificial intelligence places huge ecological costs on the environment, especially during the training and deployment of large-scale artificial intelligence models. Already estimated to use electrical energy equivalent to many countries to run global data centers that facilitate AI functions, the projection of 2025 is that such energy use could possibly increase to about 945 terawatt-hours, which is about 220 million metric tonnes of CO 2 emissions in a single year, and would produce another about 220 million metric tonnes of CO 2 emissions should they be powered by fossil fuels making up the majority of current consumption.

This is due to the fact that AI requires intense computational capabilities, which require prodigious resources due to the presence of billions of parameters in state of the art models like GPT-4 and Llama. However, the same technology is also contributing to the streamlining of energy grids, predicting climate trends, and the rapid acceleration of the green technologies at the same time (Ezeugwa et al., 2024). A single large model emission during training can exceed 500 metric tonnes of CO 2, which is nearly five times that of one passenger car used over its lifetime. Therefore inference activities which are more energy-demanding (processing millions of user queries per day) are now the preponderant energy demand of AI (60-70 blogging its total power footprint). The AI dedicated data centers in the United States consume 4.4 percent of national electricity and their carbon intensity is 48 times greater than that of the average, indicating a discrepancy between the surging AI requirement and the inclusion of renewable assets. In 2021, AI-based data centers emitted more CO 2 than aviation, producing 105 million metric tonnes of carbon dioxide in the previous year alone, as opposed to the 46.1 million attributed to aviation; more queries are answered using inference-based applications such as ChatGPT, prompting the reinvention of the Jevons Paradox, where efficiency increases lead to increased consumption. Trying to argue the balance between innovation and the environment would therefore require valuing the dual nature of AI, as an enabler of sustainability goals by creating tools such as predictive maintenance and as a potential source of emissions on par with key industries, unless regulated.

The energy consumption of the process of training large AI models has risen exponentially with the scaling laws summarizing the relationships between performance improvements with the growth in the count of parameters and compensatory progress in computational intensity. Hundreds of billions of parameters, most those in models used under generative AI, need clusters of dedicated graphics processing units, which use megawatt-hours just to complete training. Indicatively, 1,287 MWh was used to train GPT-3, and the training generated 552 metric tonnes of CO2. By 2025, the inference is more than operation loads: advanced reasoning system designs increase per-query energy usage by 50100 times over baseline models with top performance up to 1.86 watt that would be incurred by state-of-the-art designs per query process shown in performance. This effect is increased by the overall volume of daily AI orders - motivated by platforms that cater to hundreds of millions of users; an intensive session can have the energy output characteristics of an average household device (Emas et al., 2024). In addition, the consumption of water in data centres also adds more complexity to the sustainability equation, where cooling infrastructure puts the strain on limited water resources in dry areas too.

In China, the carbon footprint of AI is expected to rise to 695 million tonnes of CO 2 by 2038 as a result of business-as-usual conditions. However, improvements in hardware development bring an improvement in energy efficiency of each computational unit 40 percent each year, and models like DeepSeek architectural optimisations have proven to lower the emissions. Interestingly, AI can also create net benefits in other areas: the use of large language models (LLMs) in the drafting process, say, can save days in the use of energy resources on the same scale as in human labour, and the use of AI to optimise power grids will increase the integration of renewables. Nonetheless, uncontrolled AI growth will use 82 terawatt-hours of power per year in the next several years, and 80 percent of the total increase will be represented by the United States and China, which means that it will be difficult to make a fair transition and further demonstrate the imperative of active management. Consumes more carbon due to night-time activities increasing carbon intensity by 67 percent in situations where renewable generation is reduced necessitating strategic scheduling that exhibits a time imbalance. Hence, a sensible deployment strategy, focusing on deploying smaller and more task-specific models to routine workloads and exposing bigger systems to carbon-aware deployment in accordance with renewable peaks, would have the potential to save by 30-40 per cent of emissions (Arora et al., 2024).

The goals of green AI development strategies are intended to balance out such effects, focusing on efficiency, transparency, and redesign of the system. Some of the core methodological practices are model optimisation by pruning (dropping unnecessary parameters), quantisation (loss of precision) such as 32-bit to 8-bit representations, and knowledge distillation (capabilities transferred to smaller models). Such techniques have been shown to result in about 90% energy saving with insignificant performance loss using empirical studies, including that of UNESCO-UCL. Also, hardware innovations such as direct-to-chip liquid cooling, very high efficiency integrated circuits with 96 percent improvement in performance over power use, and renewable-powered data centres are also some of the foundational changes that critical technology companies such as Microsoft and Google expect to put them on track toward carbon-free operation by the year 2030. Edge computing supports the delegation of computational tasks and accelerates transmission energy, as well as allows the execution of carbon-conscious scheduling on the allocation of the available features between the moments of increased availability of the green electricity supply. Combined metering such as hybrid estimators can allow transparent reporting on the lifecycle impacts in measurements covering energy, carbon, water and material measures (Williamson & Prybutok, 2024).

This is aggravated by policy and collaboration policy currently seen coalitions like the 2025 Environmentally Sustainable AI initiative are pushing towards binding standards, whilst open-source platforms such as platforms, democratise access to ideal architectures. Life-cycle assessment models that incorporate Plan-Do-Check-Act (PDCA) cycles and lifecycle assessment (LCA) processes are useful as sustainability gatekeepers. Therefore, Green AI does not just redefine the beginner notion of the success as the extent of accuracy but in indicators of embodied effectiveness, flops per watt or emissions per assignment, thus promoting situational sustainability by design. This repositioning increases the interconnection between innovation and planetary constraints AI not only decreases the effect of decarbonisation in transportation, production, and energy provision which could visibly reduce the worldwide environment of emissions, but also limits its own impact through careful development policy (Duenas, 2025). The rise of hybrid anthropo-AI control, interdisciplinary stewardship, and incentives over low-impact models in 2025 will tell whether AI will finally be a combination of positive contribution to sustainability, thus settling the paradox, through conscientious and inclusive development.

6. EMERGENCE OF IMPOSTER SYNDROME IN LEGAL PROFESSIONS

Imposter syndrome, initially conceptualized in the 1970s by psychologists Pauline Clance and Suzanne Imes, can be defined as a “phenomenon that is characterized by an individual’s inability to internalize their accomplishments and a persistent fear of being exposed as a ‘fraud’ despite external evidence of ones competence.” This type sufferer bemoans their lack of intelligence, the fear being that any day now someone is going to blow the whistle and announce that they are in fact not clever at all. Though first identified among high-achieving women, follow-up studies have found it especially common in particular professions and across both genders and all levels of income. But in the legal space, imposter syndrome takes a unique form and is especially rampant and pervasive, starting in law school and haunting lawyers throughout their careers at firms, courts, or in-house. Despite the existence of numerical variations, empirical studies have shown that up to 74 percent of attorneys of all professional levels have imposter syndrome. This phenomenon is especially susceptible to the legal profession because of the perfection imperative; high stakes, investigative culture, adversarial culture, and character traits that put people attracted to the legal profession (such as overachievers and risk averse individuals) (Ergasheva et al., 2025).

This feeling of insecurity is usually based on the cognitive dissonance of the shift between academic prizes of law school to the unstable atmosphere of the practice, where theoretical knowledge hits up against tangled-up realities and gives way to lifelong self-doubt. These factors are multiplied in large law firms by billable-hour pressures and competitive hierarchies and even marginalised groups (such as women, ethnic minorities and first-generation lawyers) bear a heavier burden because of systemic biases and under-representation. The evolution of imposter syndrome is something that should be learned, as letting it unravel may lead to burnout, substance abuse, and even a rate of depression among lawyers comparable to certain other fields exceeding 3.6 times that of other professions in not all research studies. Perhaps by looking at its beginnings in law school and work life experience we can better answer the question why it goes well in legal contexts and is typically comparatively lower in many other fields.

7. IMPOSTER SYNDROME IN THE FACE OF TECHNOLOGICAL SHIFTS

The seed of imposter syndrome in the context of legal careers are often planted in the context of legal schooling, through the teaching method of the Socratic method, and grading method of curves, which provides the setting of intense comparison and the fear of falling short. The law students who are often the top performers among the undergraduates face each other in a rating system where they have to compete in the same category with as distinguished students, and classroom activities which reveal any neglect of preparation or concentration. The problem-solving skills that this developmental style aims to develop in children, unknowingly prompts that one always has to do it right, therefore creating suspicion of true aptitude (Sagert & Christensen Pacella, 2025).

The studies show also that imposter syndrome disrupts identity-making in the profession, as one of the primary concerns behind modern legal education according to the ABA standard, by ruining self-reflection. Students can hardly be able to assess their strengths and weaknesses candidly: any success is seen as a fortuitous thing, any failure, as the confirmation that they are an impostor. In case of first-generation students or under-represented students, not having family exposure or cultural background to the industry supports a sense of alienation. High-stakes testing continues perfectionism into bar examinations and clerkships, as being fortunate to pass is both seen to be because of good luck and achievement (Maji et al., 2025). When coming to practice, the gap between theory and the hands-on advocacy becomes even greater. Associates in large firms or in a public-service job enter a world of complex client issues, ethical challenges, and uncertainty when facing a courtroom that no classroom can replicate. This reality shock intensifies the reality of imposter syndrome and the lawyers know that the life of being a lawyer is far much different, drafting pleadings, negotiating deals, getting client expectations met, is totally different to solving problems on examinations. Polls of junior lawyers show that 83 percent of the lawyers have these doubts, and then they procrastinate or work longer hours to cover the perceived shortcomings. This perception is further reinforced by the zero-tolerance attitude to errors guaranteed by the requirements to the clients and courts that heavily rely on the professionalism of judges: one misstep can be considered disastrous, which strengthens the sense of inescapable discovery.

A distinctive mix of structural and cultural pressures in law firms and corporate legal departments fosters and stimulates imposter syndrome. The billable-hour system of mega-firm firms makes sure that no attorney will ever feel productive enough, and performance appraisals are always subjective due to the fact that the partners hardly ever say they do not know what they are doing lest they lose control. This gives a pretense of invincibility in that the colleagues simply spot loopholes in performance when they expect to know how things are done and in which improvements are required. An example of an up-or-out competitive structure, such as partnership promotion, fosters peer competition between peers, where the success of others reduces one own (Parker et al., 2024).

Perfectionism, an aspect prevalent among lawyers: the unambiguous interpretation of clauses in a contract or procedural rule can lead to the victory of a litigation case; still, it is enhanced in larger firms where unreasonable expectations are imposed. The lawyers often internalise such a belief that anything short of perfection amounts to failure and thus undermine themselves by self-sabotaging through doing too much or too little work or escaping the leadership roles. High-stakes casework encourages pessimism as a way of dealing with risk, but such an attitude also infects self-conception, making lawyers their own worst enemies. In the case of in-house counsel, the isolation of giving strategic advice to business executives in matters of high impact is added to there is no peer network there is lent to even greater doubt. Imposter syndrome and microaggressions have a greater likelihood to occur among lawyers who do not fit the normative white-male leadership model, which leads to such phenomena as women perceiving promotions to diversity initiatives, male lawyers victim-blaming their female colleagues due to miscarriages or bodily disfigurement, or minorities feeling anxious all the time (Xu et al., 2024).

The road of marginalisation is described in the anecdote of highways where the curve of traumas of the generations, the absence of the mentors who reflect the personality, and the inner isolation are traced, all of which contribute to the further development of the feeling of imposterity state. According to surveys and polls more than 90 percent of lawyers indicate that they have encountered such a phenomenon, which highlights the importance of the business culture of the legal industry, which values results, and where such openness as vulnerable discourse cannot be practiced freely. Companied imposter syndrome with a legal career emerges within a span of a few years and is characterized by the cycle of overcompensation and burnout, which usually corresponds to such milestones as partnership or judicial appointment. Paradoxically, older practitioners mention that the emotions get more intense when more expectations are raised and risks are enhanced, and it is easier to feel afraid of being unmasked (Disu, 2025).

8. INTERSECTION OF AI GOVERNANCE AND LEGAL EXPERTISE FOR SKILL OBSOLESCENCE IN ENVIRONMENTAL LAW PRACTICE

The swift advance of AI into the practice of law has unleashed a pointed conversation around skill obsolescence, through nowhere more than in an esoteric field such as environmental law, where regulatory complexity intersects with cutting-edge technology. Examples of such professional and ethical challenges are already unfolding in AI governance frameworks, that are developing to confront moral, environmental and the responsibilities as professionals will intersect legal skills in ways that do both gratify and disrupt conventional practices (Shi, 2025). Navigating laws like the National Environmental Policy Act (NEPA) and Clean Air Act, it's only relatively recently that environmental lawyers relinquished a functional monopoly on workday competencies to AI programs that automatically researches, predicts, and monitors compliance in some cases making easily replicable skills a thing of the past. "The two dynamics intersect: People who are trying to regulate AI now need people like me writing regulations that avoid problems, like ruining the environment or building a giant data center," she says, "but for them to do that appropriately they have to adjust to people like me not becoming obsolete."

Skill obsolescence is, in other words, the devaluation of human competencies by AI doing things like document review or risk assessment faster than we can do it ourselves - obliterating the learning curve and requiring attorneys to shift from low-value work to high-value activities such as strategic advising and ethical oversight.

The artificial intelligence is even more applicable in the field of environmental law due to the data-intensive nature of the science, whether in terms of emissions metrics, habitat impact assessment, or climate projections (Eaton, 2025). The AI systems ability to handle large volumes of data has renewed traditional governance issues, such as transparency, algorithmic bias and sustainability. The suggested Artificial Intelligence Environmental Impact Act of 2024 is a legislative initiative and highlights the fact that legal experts might find the need to examine the environmental impact of AI and its use of energy in training models, which can rival the amount of energy used by a small country. With the convergence of AI regulating structures and juridical authority the maxim that prevention is better than cure gains even greater infectivity; as the processes increasingly automation, the traditional definition of expertise will have to change in order to embrace technological familiarity in addition to regulatory prospect-sight.

The artificial intelligence applications used in the field of environmental law are currently reorganizing customary processes and hastening the outdatedness of abilities that pull on manual research and basic analytical matters. Generative AI solutions have the potential to organize large body of regulatory data, simulate the course of litigations on the basis of past precedents; moreover, they can spend hours writing NEPA-ready environmental impact statements, which used to take lawyers weeks of hard work to complete (Taskuran et al., 2025). In another example, predictive analytics, which are driven by AI, allow predicting compliance risk in investment in the renewable energy or waste management sector - areas where only manual research has previously been used. But such efficiency also brings about a backlash: the junior counsel who developed his or her skills by performing the mundane processes like reading documents might be replaced by it, which would make their skill set obsolete. As early as 2025, academic conferences, such as the Georgetown AI and Environmental Compliance Symposium, point to how AI will improve compliance as the satellite imagery and pattern recognition deployed to expand into enforcement work but are no longer this as a machine is able to gradually supersede the interpretive quality found in the work of lawyers unless they practice critical interpretation of AI outputs (Pozzi et al., 2025). Generex will still need governance; tools like the EU AI Act or the recent executive orders issued by the U.S. government require high-impact cases of AI application in the environmental context to have risk assessments and force legal professionals to be skilled in both ministerial law and in AI morals, so deployed ERP technologies do not appear biased and non-harmful. This leaves law firms with no choice but to adopt use protocols of AI usage in their firms, to offer data-privacy protections per regulations such as the California Consumer Privacy Act (CCPA), which overlaps with environmental data stewardship. This shift has to be followed by lawyers learning to be AI literate so that they without competence in the field will become an irrelevant topic, requiring strong regulation to bring in professionals who can bridge the law and the algorithms to achieve the highest level of accountability.

The misplacement of environmental law skills is compounded by the fact that AI is more effective on tasks that demand large amounts of data, but the systems of governance have provided opportunities to evolve but not eliminate legal knowledge. Conventional expertise such as how well the researcher can filter through case law involving endangered species or pollution legislation are being outdated because AI can execute such functions in real-time in millions of documents and can be over 90 per cent accurate with controlled studies. As a result, former core components of the practice, such as rote memorisation and elementary synthesis are replaced, and attorneys are forced to search after the higher-order skills of AI validation or interdisciplinary collaboration. Intellectual Automated Intelligence AI can be used in the environmental justice sector to understand the effects of the community, though informal use can lead to recreating dataset bias in disadvantaged localities (Para et al., 2024). A trend projected in the 2025 report titled Technology in the Law Office sees the end of low-value work and a rise in demand of an attorney skilled in using AI-enhanced strategy, and governance laws, including the newly issued U.S. Executive Order setting a national AI policy framework, swamping state law to harmonize control. The environmental lawyers should therefore recommend how AI should comply within the various sectors such as in energy production and agriculture and this will create hybrid knowledge as practitioners understand the environmental costs of AI such as data-centres water use and at the same time advocating policies that can reduce obsolescence through continuous education.

The dichotomy that AI will remove low-value tasks but initiate increased need of lawyers serving AI-based strategies is summarized by the 2025 report, Technology in the Law Office. Laws governing governance, such as the new U.S. Executive Order that establishes a national policy framework on AI development, override state laws and enforce an organized control on the regulation, which requires environmental attorneys to provide compliance advice in areas like energy generation and farming (Jeffrey et al., 2025). This cross-pollination creates hybrid knowledge: professionals need to assess the ecological price of AI, data centre water use being a good example, and how to reduce obsolescence by establishing policies that require a lifelong learning process. Organizations like that which will set up AI governance committees, per 2025 AmLaw100 predictions, are likely to engage lawyers in each phase of tool implementation, with ethical application and human aspect conceded in issues that do not feature ready responses (i.e., international climate change agreements). This final result is not determined by the unavoidability of obsolescence but rather on how well governance can redefine the role of the practitioner in an AI-saturated world.

The principles of environmental law become an integral part of AI governance, which allows the lawyers with relevant expertise to defend their abilities against the risk of skill obsolescence. Existing environmental principles such as the precautionary principle which states that we must be cautious in the face of uncertainty have been incorporated into AI regulation making them obligatory in their evaluations of long-term risks like algorithmic errors in environmental modeling (Amerini et al., 2025). Future laws observed by the National Conference of State Legislatures regarding 2025 offer legislation that would authorize such laws, which would obligate additional measures to regulate AI so as to safeguard rights to civil liberty, or to incorporate in an extensive legal system analogous to environmental impact assessments. The benefit of this mutual relationship is in resisting obsolescence through increased experience in cross-domain knowledge, such as NEPA-trained lawyers can be assessors of the impact of AI on environmental decisions, arguing against judicial trust in AI-based analysis. Competence in AI is now ethically mandated, having undergone adjustments to the bar associations guidelines, and changing the risk of obsolescence into an indicator of pressing need to enhance professionalism. In addition, the ecological footprint of AI, which is expressed in the form of carbon emissions linked to the massive computational resources, requires regulation with a focus on ESG factors, which in this case is legal advice on the sale of information-technology in a sustainable manner (Valanciene & Machovenko, 2024).

9. FUTURE PATHWAYS AND POLICY RECOMMENDATIONS: EMPOWERING LEGAL EXPERTS AGAINST SYNDROME EFFECTS

The imposter syndrome has often been associated with burnout and mental experience difficulties in the legal profession, and it remains a systematic issue that is perpetuated by a mythos of perfectionism, stakes, and cultural shame. By the end of the fourth quarter of 2025, new reformative streams focus on multi-level interventions that empower and uplift the lawyers and not on the individual coping approach but on structural reforms in organizations and regulation policy. A direction in this reform implies the incorporation of well-being as inherent part of the professional identity; the use of technology-empowered customized service; and normalization of vulnerability through education. The new Well-Being Pledge of the American Bar Association, signed by hundreds of firms at the time of writing, and state bar toolboxes (e.g., California and Indiana resources on imposter syndrome) are some signs that there is a growing recognition that reducing the effects of the syndrome is a successful way to increase competence, retain staff, and ensure ethical practice (Zhang et al., 2025). As shown in policy suggestions, therefore, preventive steps are encouraged: the mandatory introduction of wellness training into continuing legal education, the creation of mentorship options which would pair junior attorneys with senior counterparts to discuss openly about self-doubt, and the restructuring of firm structures to dampen billable-hour pressures, which are the sources of professional fatigue.

More general recommendations are those which assume systemic interventions. All law firms need to be required by their bar associations to obtain an annual firm wellness audit, and incentive compliance with partnering with flexible policies, including part-time arrangements, which do not compromise partnership opportunities. The monies that are sent to Lawyer Assistance Programs should emphasize available therapeutic services. The earlier integration of imposter syndrome modules into law-school programs and curriculum will cause be future professionals to be more prepared to be a functional workers and help them deal with shock of reality when faced with practice-requirements. To overcome burnout, right-to-disconnect laws, rotational working hours, ESG-compliant wellness programs, and treating mental health as a business need, have quantifiable outcomes of returns on investment: lower attrition, less error-making, and increased productivity (Alparslan, 2024). These actions are an indication of a cultural re-tuning, where executives become agents of vulnerability, as occurs in senior-sharing forums, to turn the impact of the syndrome into an asset that supports long-term and viable careers.

10. CONCLUSION

The history of artificial intelligence in the field of environmental law and policy demonstrates that the level of technological development reached a key moment, an urgent need to reorient its development of ethical and human-centered systems that reinforce the sustainability of the planet, justice, and the overall sustainability of the profession. By the end of November 2025, with a two-pronged environmental practice—both accelerating compliance through predictive modeling and satellite-directed execution and simultaneously opening the planet to damage with data-center emissions—AI will require a radical readjustment of the industry to a period of rapid innovation as an ethical custodian. It is a recap of solutions achieved; imposter syndrome has to undermine legal confidence in a state of technological upheaval upending the skills sets of law school graduates, professional skills rapidly moving towards obsolescence and work in nonmonolithic jobs, and gendered or socioeconomic disadvantages that make differences more apparent. Ethical AI, designed with users in mind is not an unnecessary self-folly but a axiom to make sure that the instruments used, instead of overtaking the human judgment, amplify it so that everyone getting involved in making environmental judgment is welcomed. Early attempts by the legislative fields are already pointing that direction, as the risk-based classifications of the EU AI Act and the 2024 U.S. Artificial Intelligence

Environmental Impacts Act both specify requiring transparency on the contribution of AI to carbon deposits and impose bias audits on AI tools in terms of weather vulnerability assessments. Using human values, empathy, accountability, and justice as a cornerstone of AI governance, the legal profession can eliminate the symptoms of the syndrome, address the issue of skill obsolescence, and democratize the access to ecological systems and skill analysis.

Action policy should therefore consider joining to incorporate the ethical paradigm, as regulatory agencies ought to consider extending the mandate that demands AI systems undergo mandatory environmental impact assessments before any deployment, similar to NEPA examinations, that will not only take into consideration the results but also the primarily lifecycle emissions. The fact that training one big model accounts to the carbon footprint of five vehicles per year is another estimate on how massive the task is. Green AI incentives like low-energy credit tax incentives in AI technology will spur uptake, whereas international standards, based on the UNESCO AI Ethics Recommendation, will help simplify transboundary challenges, including ocean governance. At the professional level, gender inequality can be corrected by introducing AI ethics committees in law firms and bar associations that offer gender-sensitive training. As an example, 56% of students taking environmental law courses are women but only 35% take up AI technology policy positions, this can be addressed through targeted sponsorships. Hybrid wellness protocols, mindfulness applications designed to manage legal stress and peer networks to deal with imposter syndrome, will incorporate the human wellbeing in the technological processes to reduce mental health strains. Educational reforms in this fashion, including introducing AI literacy at all law-school levels on the first day, will enable graduates to work in symbiosis and facilitate Georgetown Law's projective drive of 25 per cent-plus additional interdisciplinary jobs by 2030.

These actions are not only the basis of preventing burnout, but also the foundation of a career where marginalization, either by class or gender, ceases to be a liability to viable future to bring morality and labor facts into harmony. When imagining this ethical, human-centred, or even ecologically fair horizon, the role of the legal community becomes even more vital than sailing-time, namely, it should insist on the AI that will be beneficial to human society and to the environment equally. Through human-potential revelation, technology makes a place where innovation coincides with integrity, and the syndromic penalties of our profession, self-doubt, exhaustion, isolation, etc. are melted away. A 2030 quality of ethical AI is even estimated by IPCC to cut a world-wide error on emissions-tracking by up to 60x, but allows under-represented specialists to drive green transitions. The way forward requires bold investment: policy-makers need to invest justice into the statute, teacher into the soul and action, practitioners need to invest vulnerability as the source of force and therefore, turn machines into the living legacies that can sense vulnerability as strength and power and protect our planet as the weavers of salvation.

REFERENCES

. Abbasi, K. (2024). Key barriers and career challenges that hinder women from advancing in New Brunswick Information and Communication Technology (ICT) sector.

Al Lawati, A., Al Rawahi, N., Waladwadi, T., Almadailwi, R., Alhabsi, A., Al Lawati, H., & Al Sinawi, H. (2025). Impostor phenomenon: A narrative review of manifestations, diagnosis, and treatment. *Middle East Current Psychiatry, 32*(1), 18.

Almomani, A., Alâăśqerem, A., Alauthman, M., Aldweesh, A., Aoudi, S., & Salloum, S. A. (2025). Ethical Foundations of AI-Driven Avatars in the Metaverse for Innovation and User Privacy. *IEEE Access : Practical Innovations, Open Solutions.*

Alparslan, G. (2024). The adequacy of global legal norms on legal issues related to digitalization and artificial intelligence. *International Journal of Law and Politics Studies, 6*(1), 68–75.

Amerini, I., Barni, M., Battiato, S., Bestagini, P., Boato, G., Bruni, V., & Vitulano, D. (2025). Deepfake media forensics: Status and future challenges. *Journal of Imaging, 11*(3), 73.

Arora, G., Yadav, T. P., Tomer, A., Tewari, P., Sharma, H., & Malik, S. (2024, November). Secure Cloud-based Process on Innovations with AI: Legal, Psychological and Managerial Implications. In *2024 International Conference on Intelligent & Innovative Practices in Engineering & Management (IIPEM)* (pp. 1-6). IEEE.

Bajorek, J. P. (2024). *Your AI Roadmap: Actions to Expand Your Career, Money, and Joy*. John Wiley & Sons.

Balan, A. (2024). Examining the ethical and sustainability challenges of legal education's AI revolution. *International Journal of the Legal Profession, 31*(3), 323–348.

. Bennett, H. (2025). TECHNOLOGY AND CLIMATE CHANGE LAW: REGULATING ARTIFICIAL INTELLIGENCE FOR SUSTAINABILITY. *Bulletin news in New Science Society, 2*(10), 85-91.

Coken, J. (2025). *Make Imposter Syndrome Your Superpower: The Ultimate Guide for Women in STEM to Lead with More Authority, Influence, and Impact.* Morgan James Publishing.

De Queiroz, H. J. D. S. (2025). Navigating Legal Barriers in Climate and Environmental Technologies. In *Navigating Law and Policy in STM Enterprises: Ethical Governance, Regulation, and Innovation Strategy* (pp. 225-260). IGI Global Scientific Publishing.

Decosimo, H. (2022). A Taxonomy of Professional Identity Formation. *Louis ULJ*, *67*, 1.

. Disu, L. (2025). Becoming With AI: Identity and Meaning-Making Among Graduate Students in Creative Disciplines.

Duenas, M. (2025). Imposter Syndrome's Impact on Latine College Students During Transformative Times. *Journal of Latinos and Education*, *24*(2), 349–361.

Eaton, S. E. (2025). Global trends in education: Artificial intelligence, postplagiarism, and future-focused learning for 2025 and beyond–2024–2025 Werklund Distinguished Research Lecture. *International Journal for Educational Integrity*, *21*(1), 12.

Emas, R., Dolamore, S., Jones, P. A., Lovell, D., Whitebread, G., & Chordiya, R. (2024). Imposter phenomenon & belonging in master of public administration students in the US context. *Journal of Public Affairs Education*, *30*(4), 560–587.

Ergasheva, G., Khursanov, R., Bazarova, D., Altiyev, R., Tadjibaeva, A., Yusupdzhanova, G., & Madatova, Z. (2025). Integrating Digital Competencies into Legal Education: A Pedagogical Framework for the Future. *Qubahan Academic Journal*, *5*(2), 446–478.

Ezeugwa, F. A., Olaniyi, O. O., Ugonnia, J. C., Arigbabu, A. S., & Joeaneke, P. C. (2024). Artificial Intelligence, Big Data, and Cloud Infrastructures: Policy Recommendations for Enhancing Women's Participation in the Tech-Driven Economy. *Journal of Engineering Research and Reports*, *26*(6), 1–16.

Fines, B. G. (2025). Picturing the Professional Identity of Law Professors. *The Journal of Law Teaching and Learning*, *2*(1), 301.

Grenardo, D. (2024). What About Us? How Law Schools Can Help Historically Underrepresented Law Students Develop Their Professional Identities. *Mercer Law Review*, *75*, 24–07.

Grenardo, D. A. (2022). The phantom menace to professional identity formation and law success: Imposter syndrome. *University of Dayton Law Review. University of Dayton. Law School*, *47*(3), 2.

Jeffrey, A., Brickell, K., & McConnell, F. (2025). Geography and legal expertise: The transgressive nature of research at the boundary of geography and law-making. *Transactions of the Institute of British Geographers*, *50*(2), e12696.

Kapartziani, C. (2025). Towards a Sustainable Digital Future: Exploring AI, Legal Frameworks, and Environmental Transformations in the Post-COVID Era? *ESI* Preprints *(European Scientific Journal, ESJ)*, *21*(8), 1-1.

Maji, S., Shivhare, V., & Kumar, Y. (2025). Imposter Phenomenon, Social Comparison Orientation, and Mental Health: A Study of High-Achieving Indian College Students. *Roeper Review*, *47*(1), 47–59.

Moassefi, M., Fennell, N., Yang, M., Gunter, J. B., Schmit, T. M. S., & Cook, T. S. (2025). Empowering Women in Imaging Informatics: Confronting Imposter Syndrome, Addressing Microaggressions, and Striving for Work-Life Harmony. *Journal of Imaging Informatics in Medicine*, *38*(3), 1291–1296.

O'Connor, R. (2025). Working-class imposterism in the law school:"I always have this in the back of my head that I'm expected to fail". *The Law Teacher*, •••, 1–25.

Ochs, S. L. (2021). Impostor Syndrome & The Law School Caste System. *Pace Law Review*, *42*, 373.

Para, E., Dubreuil, P., Miquelon, P., & Martin-Krumm, C. (2024). Interventions addressing the impostor phenomenon: A scoping review. *Frontiers in Psychology*, *15*, 1360540.

Parker, J. S., Haskins, N., Coleman-Chatman, T., Duru, C., Ramirez, D., Chae, N., & Nortey, A. (2024). Dismantling the imposter syndrome: A case study of early career women of color in school mental health fields. *Journal for Specialists in Group Work*, *49*(1), 3–24.

Pozzi, T., Legg, E., McCullough, S., & Lubell, M. (2025). Transformative climate change education for graduate students: Developing a theory of change to increase equity in climate change science. *Environmental Education Research*, *31*(11), 2351–2373.

Romanishyn, A., Malytska, O., & Goncharuk, V. (2025). AI-driven disinformation: Policy recommendations for democratic resilience. *Frontiers in Artificial Intelligence*, *8*, 1569115.

Sagert, S. J., & Christensen Pacella, K. A. (2025). Higher imposter syndrome symptoms associated with greater odds of eating disorders in college and university students. *Journal of American College Health*, •••, 1–6.

. Shi, Y. (2025). Examining the Role of AI Empowerment in Breaking the Workplace Ceiling for Ethnic Minorities in Australia: A Study of Asian-Australian Immigrants.

Strachan, D. M. (2022). Among us: Imposter syndrome and barriers to Black success. *Cardozo J. Equal Rts. & Soc. Just.*, *29*, 319.

. Sweatman, M. (2024). Commitment to Community, a Passion for Teaching, Imposter Syndrome, and the Prospects of a Permanent Job: The Ingredients of a Doctorate in Education.

. Valanciene, D., & Machovenko, J. (2024). The Moral Compass of Law: Ensuring Ethical Standards Through Legal Education?. *Filosofija. Sociologija, 35*(2 Special).

Wang, S. J., & Huang, H. C. (2025). To ask is human, to answer divine: How awe-inspiring generative AI leads to self-enhancement and imposter anxiety. *Information Technology & People*, •••, 1–32.

Williamson, S. M., & Prybutok, V. (2024). The era of artificial intelligence deception: Unraveling the complexities of false realities and emerging threats of misinformation. *Information (Basel)*, *15*(6), 299.

Xu, J., Li, Z., & Li, S. (2024). Legal ethics and professional responsibility in the legal profession. In *SHS Web of Conferences* (Vol. 190, p. 02006). EDP Sciences.

. Zangana, H. M., Al-Karaki, J. N., & Omar, M. (2025). Navigating law and policy in STM enterprises: Ethical governance, regulation, and innovation strategy.

Zhang, S., Luo, J., & Guo, P. (2025). Technology, Innovation, and the Legal Profession. In *Technology, Legal Education and Legal Profession in China and Australia: Opportunities and Challenges* (pp. 97–113). Springer Nature Singapore.

Chapter 2
AI-Generated Creativity and the Law:
Protecting Human Originality Amid Imposter Fears

Bharti Chouhan
https://orcid.org/0009-0009-4305-7289
Nirwan University Jaipur, India

ABSTRACT

The legal inferences of AI-driven change of copyrighted works advance complicated questions under intellectual property and copyright law including the boundary between conversion in use or infringement. AI-generated modifications from copyrighted materials can be considered copyright infringement if they reproduce, distribute, or publicly display the original work without permission from the copyright holder. The copyright holders can exclusive use to make, distribute or create derivative works from, copies of its original expression. These rights can also be infringed upon by unauthorized derivative works that are too similar in form and design to the original work. Copyright defines a derivative work as any new material that is based upon an existing work, including modifications or adaptations. This chapter focuses on the protection of human original work and imposter fears from AI-generated creativity from legal sphere.

1. INTRODUCTION

The AI Art Originators have recently progressed to be made available to almost anyone with internet access. This chapter explores how the current AI art generators operate and lists different type of problems of AI art from technical, moral and

DOI: 10.4018/979-8-3373-6618-0.ch002

legal points of view. It's also interested in how a proliferation of AI art generators impacts humans. The contemporary AI art generators rely on artificial intelligence, machine learning algorithms, and deep neural network algorithm to learn from a vast number of existing artworks inside the portfolio library and create new work responding to the user's input (Moustaghfir & Chankob, 2025). The most compelling "against" argument for AI art is that it requires human creativity and imagination. But there is an argument that the human creativity of the artist is contained in and not lost from text prompts. AI art generators have also been accused of copying the works of artists without their permission and this has resulted in some copy-right complications. AI art will eat artists' commissions and work (Li et al., 2025). AI art-generators are not perfect yet and they have several mistakes as mistake in the generated artwork. Some artists have pushed back on AI art generators. They have also started a protest "No to AI generated images" in which they swarmed with the portfolio of an AI art generator called "ArtStation" by posting somewhat 'trending in ArtStation' photos as the genre ultimately making all their generated images useless.

With human careers unless we are talking about artificial intelligence, that is. And that includes mankind"s creative side (Obiefuna, 2025). Jobs performed by Humans such as manual labouring in the factories have been taken over by machines for decades but recently even creative jobs such including art and music are now being done via Artificial Intelligence with the advent of Artificial Intelligence Art originators Although it is only within the past few years that AI Art Generators has come to pose a serious threat towards artists' existence, AI art has been around since at least as far back as late 1960s. The first major AI art work was Aaron, created by Harold Cohen in 1973.

A software called General Adversarial Networks (GANs), was established in 2014 and came to form the basis of the generative side of contemporary AI art generators. Google is responsible for the creation of Deep Dream which was created through their Convolutional Neural Network (CNN), and improved an existing AI software. History Ganbreeder was released in 2018 and later rebranded as Art Breeder, using GAN models that could blend existing images to produce new art. Google released a text-to-image algorithm in 2022 (Yarosewick, 2025). August 2022 Stability AI released the services for Stable Diffusion, another Art Generator using text prompts. AI art generators are developing at a breakneck pace, and that's inspired more than a little debate over their moral uses and implications.

Midjourney is the extraordinary avant-garde pioneer redefining what art means in a world of AI. The heart of Midjourney, is based on a natural fusion between the classical beauty ideal and modern AI artistry and stands as a striong vehicle that resonates through complex visual artefacts combining ancient philosophical ideas with cutting edge state-of-the-art AI generation. Midjourney and particularly its v4 journey also illustrate the capacity not only of change, but enrichment now rich enough to tell predictable fairy tales with perfect imagery (Raymond, 2025).

Central to these fears is a psychological phenomenon frequently referred to as the novel form of imposter syndrome not of the individual creator and perhaps even all our species. Artists, writers, designers and musicians are among those rethinking their specialness as they wonder whether human imagination can match an algorithmic imagination that can replicate the style, mood and narrative structures across every conceivable variation (Sun, 2024). This "imposter fear" is not just a question of personal insecurity; it reflects a broader cultural disquiet around human identity and purpose in an age of algorithmic mimicry. Throughout history, each new media transformation from photography's threat to painting to digital music synthesizers in the 1980s has sparked debates about authenticity (Joseph, 2024). But what's different now is that AI has this new ability to emulate our cognitive proccesse. Where previous tools extended human capacities, generative AIs now mirror human ones, and in so doing undermine what was once a clear distinction (Avery et al., 2024).

2. REDEFINING AUTHORSHIP IN THE AGE OF AI

Whether AI-generated modifications are derivative works will likely depend on the extent to which the original work was transformed, how creative and original the final product is, and whether a human user made any input into what resulted. The degree to which AI modifies the source, including elements of expression added by the end user, is something courts could consider (Chatterjee, 2025).

Fair use is a doctrine in the United States copyright law that permits limited use of copyrighted material without acquiring permission under certain circumstances, such as criticism, commentary, news reporting, teaching, scholarship and research. whether modifications made by AI are fair use will depend on issues including the purpose and character of the use, the nature of the copyrighted work, the portion used in relation to the copyrighted work as a whole, and impact on market value (Singh, 2024). Courts may weigh whether the AI-altered replication works to transform the original by altering the work with new expression, meaning, or message (Plate & Hutson, 2025). Use as transformational Fair use Factors: Transformational purpose has implications based on whether the transformation was nonsubstitutive to transformitve new expression, tip a judicial scale toward favoring that a use is permissible under copyright. Copyright owners may decide to license their works for modification or adaptation under such as situations involving, other licenses, licensing agreements, etc. Developers or users of AI must seek legal licenses or permissions before modifying any copyrighted content to avoid being involved in disputes and claims of copyright infringement. The legal implications of AI-modified copyrighted works imply a fine balance between Copyright law, fair use chambers, and contractual licensing. A good understanding and adherence to these framework are crucial to make sure AI-based creativity can be used in a legal and ethical manner (Sommer, 2025).

Whether a machine can be an author, inventor, or creator is no longer a matter of mere speculation; it represents the central dividing line through every major archival case and patent AI dispute in 2025. Courts, legislatures and international organizations are being pressed to decide what kind of legal personality if any creative artificial intelligence deserves. The implications are vast: if machines can be held to account for authorship or invention, a complete economic infrastructure based upon privilege and exclusivity of intellectual-property rights will fall. If they are denied any legal identity at all, the humans that develop them, train them, deploy them and stimulate their use might also end up with nothing as well as the underlying data sets (often scraped without permission) remaining uncompensated (Fiasal, 2025). Between those two ends there's a gamut of half-measures: user as author, the programmer as author, the people who created the training data as collective authors, corporation as author or sui generis rights. As of November 2025, there is not one jurisdiction that has creatively responded to this challenge with a sound and consistent solution (Cooper, 2024).

3. THE TRADITIONAL ANTHROPOCENTRIC FOUNDATION

Copyright and patent law was founded on an unabashedly anthropocentric premise: that only a natural person (and, by legal fiction, its corporate assignees) can be the source of protectable works or inventions (Kawakami & Venkatagiri, 2024). The United States Constitution gives Congress the power to secure "to Authors and Inventors" the exclusive right to their "Writings and Discoveries," language that for two centuries has been understood as requiring human ingenuity. Indeed, the Supreme Court has never strayed from the notion that intellectual property is compensation and encouragement for human intellectual effort. Berne Convention Article 2, TRIPS Article 9, and every national copyright statute I am aware of, all share the same implicit assumption: the authorship is a human attribute.

And this anthropocentrism itself survived earlier technological shocks. The photograph was accepted Since a human photographer uses lighting, frame, and moment to make expressive decisions (Burrow-Giles v. Sarony, 1884). Computer software became a copyrightable "writing" of its human coder. So have even random works of authorship (like John Cage's music generated by chance or wind chimes recorded as music) when the randomness was not a natural phenomenon but was instead intentionally set up by a human being. The common thread is that some sort of identifiable human being needs to inject that creative spark.

Generative AI breaks that thread. Diffusion models and general large language models are not just automating some prior human-designed process; they uncover statistical patterns across a billion examples, and create new outputs that no single human could have anticipated or deliberately directed. The role of a human dwindles: writing a prompt, curating negative prompts, iterating, upscaling, inpainting. At a certain point the contribution is so trivial that courts recoil from calling it "authorship" in the constitutional sense (Basty et al., 2025).

4. THE THALER SAGA AND THE WORLDWIDE SNUB OF MACHINE AUTHORSHIP

The only real judicial pronouncement so far continues to be the DABUS case filed by Stephen Thaler. Thaler wanted "to designate an artificial intelligence system as the inventor on patent applications in more than a dozen countries or regions, including the U.S. and Europe," he wrote, referring to the AI unit DABUS ("Device for the Autonomous Bootstrapping of Unified Sentience"). From 2019 to 2025, every single major patent office and review court denied its applications on the explicit grounds that inventors must be natural persons. The US Federal Circuit (2022), the UK Supreme Court (2023), the European Patent Office (EPO) (2021–24), Germany, Australia and South Africa all came to the same conclusion: that no AI can be an inventor since it is not a legal person capable of holding rights or transferring them.

In copyright, the U.S. Copyright Office's 2023–25 determinations (Zarya of the Dawn, Thaler's "A Recent Entrance to Paradise," and thousands more refusals), have cast in stone a similar principle: works made without enough human creative input are not subject to copyright. The Office now requires elaborate accounts of the human's contribution at registration, and regularly opposes or denies registrations when the applicant concedes significant AI participation. These refusals are affirmed by the D.C. District Court as well as Copyright Review Board, making them a binding precedent in United States.

5. DIVERGENT NATIONAL APPROACHES

Though the Anglo-American world has held fast to the human-authorship requirement, in other jurisdictions seeds are being sown. China In Li v Liu CS [2023] (Beijing Internet Court) and further cases in 2024 to 2025, it was held that works created with substantial human prompting and iteration are copyrightable, and the author of such works will be a person: the human who did the prompting. The rationale views prompting in detail as directing a human assistant. China has yet to give authorship of the AI itself.

United Kingdom: The CDPA 1988, s-9(3) still stands as an anomaly in the common-law world: for "computer-generated works", it is the person by whom "the arrangements necessary for the creation of the work are undertaken" who is its author. Broadly targeted Post-2023 cases have broadly read this to include the person who trained the model or paid for the compute or came up with fancy prompts. The UK therefore acknowledges that kind of authorship-by-proxy without the need for an actual creative input (Lee, 2024).

Japan: Article 2(1)(xi-2) of Japan's Copyright Act also identifies the individual who "makes creative contributions" to the making process as author, which includes those who give instructions to AI tools. In guidelines issued by Japan's Cultural Affairs Agency in 2024, the threshold is set low: even simple prompts are enough if they represent "thought or feeling" of the person who wrote them.

European Union: The EU has not taken a harmonized position. The Copyright Directive (2019/790) and the AI Act (2024) do not cover authorship for outputs. National courts are divided still: France and Germany have aligned more with a human authorship requirement; the court in the Netherlands and those of Estonia were receptive to protect prompted works.

6. THE PROMPT-ENGINEERING AUTHORSHIP DEBATE

The gray area the most in debate is whether elaborate prompt engineering counts as authorship. There are three camps among lawyers and scholars courts, really. The "adequate human contribution" camp (U.S., Germany, pre-2024 France): A little bit of nudging is seldom sufficient in and of itself to make something copyrightable; significant post-generation editing, selecting or organizing is the exception. The Copyright Office's 2025 guidance enumerates examples: writing a 200- word detailed prompt is generally not; manually inpainting 40% of an image or sorting AI generated panels into a coherent comic book page may be. The "low-threshold" school (China, Japan, UK):" Any non-trivial prompt that can be a form of personal expression makes the prompter an author. Courts here compare prompting to hiring a human artist or directing an orchestra (Feldman, 2024). The "no authorship" absolutists: Some academics and a vocal minority on the bench think that instructing an even more mutinous munch of code amounts to selecting brush settings in Photoshop. In this conception, only the old-fashioned kind of creative work matters.

In reality, the single biggest beneficiary of this uncertainty is not the AI, the prompter or creators of joint-training data it's the corporation that owns the model.

When courts deny copyright in purely AI-generated works, companies from OpenAI to Stability and Midjourney and Adobe already begin seeking ways of setting their terms of service up so they either own it themselves or have blanket commercial licenses granted to users. So the only legal hooks are contractual (paywalls, API terms, enterprise licenses), as the works are in U.S. public domain. What we get is a de facto corporate monopoly with machine creativity but no term limits of copyright duration, and no fair use.

7. THE LEGAL IDENTITY OF MACHINE CREATIVITY

The disintermediation of flesh and bone artists replaces what was once a clear line between "human creativity" and "machine output" with the most impossible question society could have asked itself in the middle of the century: When machines can paint like Rembrandt, compose like Bach or write like Hemingway at the touch of a button in seconds, how much legality indeed cultural worth is left to human originality? Tools like Midjourney, Stable Diffusion, DALL-E, ChatGPT, Claude or Grok have democratized creative production to a level never before seen: Anyone with a text prompt can produce museum-grade images, symphonic scores, screenplays or novels near instantaneously. Fast forward to late 2025, and the scale is colossal: OpenAI says that DALL-E by itself has generated hundreds of billions of images since it was launched, and Midjourney's Discord server consistently sees millions of creations every single day. What started as experimental playfulness has now metastasized, spreading manically through commercial ecosystems in which AI-generated books overwhelm the Kindle store on Amazon, AI art wins prestigious awards for fine-art producers, AI-composed music finds its way into films and onto streaming playlists, and AIs write articles published under human bylines if any at all. Such technological advances have prompted a crisis of the genuine, authorial and economic-meltdown kind for human creators, and thrown copyright law of humanity's oldest planks in protecting our creative labors into territory it never signed up to police.

How can the law distinguish between the human spark of creative invention and algorithmic creativity that can create faster, larger, cheaper with no end in sight? Courts, legislatures and international bodies now wade through an avalanche of interconnected questions. Should a work by an A.I. be entitled to copyright at all? If it isn't, then who (if anyone) owns it — the individual user who wrote the prompt, the company that trained this model, all of the millions of artists whose copyrighted works were ingested without consent, or nobody? Can scraping data from copyrighted works for training ever be fair use when the ultimate purpose is commercial competition against the creators of those works? And, perhaps most viscerally for working artists: When stock-photo agencies, publishing houses, advertising firms and Hollywood studios can replace human labor with AI at a fraction of the cost, what regulatory protections exist to prevent the wholesale displacement of human creativity?

These fears are not hypothetical. In 2023–2025 alone there have been landmark lawsuits that sound like reports from a battlefield as The New York Times v. OpenAI and Microsoft; Getty Images v. Stability AI; Andersen v. Stability AI, (on behalf of visual artists Sarah Andersen, Kelly McKernan and others); the Authors Guild and individual authors such as John Grisham, Jodi Picoult and George R.R. Martin against Meta and others; several class actions against Midjourney and DeviantArt; music-industry cases filed by record labels and performing artists against AI music companies like Suno or Udio. Similar steps have been taken in the EU, China, Japan and United Kingdom (Tajeja et al., 2025). What is not just at stake, but the only thing of value left to fight over, is the very viability of professional human creativity in a world where "impostor" works things that are indistinguishable from human effort yet made without human labor will soon flood every market.

Liability also draws the lines of machine identity: AI is not liable, responsibilities are attributed to developers, users, or deployers based on negligence or vicarious concepts. In the U.S., the Copyright Office delineates AI-as-tool (protectable with human creativity) from AI-as-stand-in (not protectable), and calls for assessments on a case-by-case basis of prompts, iterations, and edits. Contracts The EU transparency requirements of the AI Act will impose obligations on those supplying creative outputs to mitigate art-related risks or it may be that claims which are not based on disclosure are ineligible. UK's arranger liability holds people accountable and does not overly anthropomorphize machines, when Chinese courts enforce human source through infringement suits. All the more, this framework blocks AI shirking, reminding us all that the legal identity is human-mediated still.

Safeguarding human creativity will require flexible doctrines: requirements for AI disclosures, shorter terms for machine-generated works and special rewards for transparent data sets. Converging of jurisdic- tions on human-centric minima as, for example, in recent U.S. reports and EU Acts is indicative of maturing. By grounding identity in provable contribution, such law allays fear and promotes symbiotic creativity between human and AI, with machines augmenting rather than aping the human spark.

8. MACHINE CREATIVITY AND IP

From this perspective, machine creativity challenges the underpinnings of traditional intellectual property law (especially copyright) which has consistently rested on the assumption that a human "author" is what and all there is to a protectable work. In various jurisdictions, courts and agencies uniformly have denied AI status as a legal author on grounds that original works must be human product intending their intellectual effort to be invested and reflect personality. The U.S. Copyright Office, in its reports on AI and copyright from 2024-2025 repeats the works created by machine contentions as they are used to deny registration for images generated by AI and with regard to Thaler v. Perlmutter's decisions that humanity requirements were lacking in works completely authored by AI which is what courts meant when they ruled against Thaler on creative intent (AI-generated text) and because machines can have no legal personhood limit there was creativity. This position is closely akin to language in the U.S. Copyright Act conditioning protection on "original works of authorship," read through precedents such as Feist Publications v. Rural Telephone Service, which require just a scintilla of creativity from a human mind. Accordingly, pure machine outputs are a matter of public domain and they are NOT subject to exclusive rights even though certain human editings or compositions may be given copyright protection on spot (Hazan, 2025).

United Kingdom, on the other hand, saw a pragmatic exception under Sections 9(3) and 178 of Copyright, Designs and Patents Act 1988 (CDPA) in that it provided copyright to a computer generated work where there is "no human author", and further assigns the authorship to the person who "made 'the arrangements necessary' for creation [of such works]". This framework, first proposed in 1988 at an early stage of the computing revolution, shields AI outputs when a human directs prompts, parameters or selections displaying skill and judgment. This warrants human intervention as courts in this equation consider originality via a human process, such as formal instructions/some kind of post-processing and not just protection based on automated procedures. This strikes a balance between innovation and accountability, but its critics argue that it devalues established authorship by conferring rights on facilitators as opposed to originators a potential headache when it comes to systems where AI and humans collaborate.

The EU has a more stringent human-centred model based around CJEU case law which provides that the work was original if it reflected origin in its author's own intellectual creation with "authorial free choices and thus investment of capital" as in Infopaq and later cases. This is no longer true under either the Digital Single Market Directive (2019/790) or the AI Act; both view AI as a tool, copyrightable only with human input that supplies such personality and control. The AI Act focuses on transparency for high-risk systems, insisting that there be transparency about the use of AI in generating works of authorship, which is supportive (in an indirect way) to assertions of authorship and sharing that trace back to human control. This author-centrism could preserve personal moral rights based on human expression, excluding works produced independently by AI but permitting copyright in outputs created with the aid of, where a human had programmed or curated, AI systems (Utami et al., 2025).

China opts for an evidence-based, flexible approach, where courts will award copyright to AIGC if proof of human intellectual intervention, originality, and fixed expression is demonstrated. Rulings from the Beijing Internet Court, including a decision in 2025, also stipulate that creators must record prompts, adjustments, selections and changes indicative of personalized creativity as well as time and professional judgment. Proposals for how to address the new AI-guided incentive structures generally involve creating a new functional element in copyright that would cover variables like timeliness of engineering, calibration inputs, and good editing practice. These modalities are conceived of as protectible "outputs" or "states" (depending on the metaphysical bent), much as we treat particularly fancy technological devices like cameras or software functions (Jones, 2025). This jurisprudence emphasizes the economic motivation for innovation and critics claim stands opposed to Western personhood requirements by keying on results and human displacement rather than intent, but insists on strict evidentiary virtual proof to avoid frivolous claims.

The World Intellectual Property Organization (WIPO) promotes international discussion, and reports that most national legislation does not protect non-human authorship, "since copyright is a reward for the expression of someone's personality". WIPO's discussions suggest there is no outright ban on AI copyrights, but that options include sui generis rights or redefining authorship in relation to machine works as a way to establish who may own, be liable for and how long machine-created works could be owned. Comparative analysis unveils a spectrum: US rigidity serves to protect human exclusivity; UK utility encourages tech adoption; EU ethics sets dignity as prime value; Chinese pragmatism upholds market driven development and WIPO promotes harmonization (Mohammed, 2024). These discrepancies highlight tensions between innovation and tradition, with new concepts regarding hybrid authorship acknowledging humans for curation in lines of AI processing being considered.

9. PROTECTING HUMAN ORIGINALITY: LEGAL AND ETHICAL SAFEGUARDS

The ethical terrain becomes even murkier. AI programs that train on people's vast stores of human-generated data present issues for attribution and consent. Legal policymakers in different jurisdictions have employed various approaches. The US Copyright Office follows the human authorship requirement by not protecting works entirely generated by machines (Dhrubo, 2025). By contrast, the UK has considered if AI gets rights (no, of course not, I don't even know where that idea would even come from to have a thing created by one algorithm being 'endowed' with any torts) hn extending very limited copyright to the "person who makes the arrangements necessary for the creation of the work", so effectively giving them to the human behind which caused it. China in the meantime is highlighting the economic usefulness of protecting AI-generated works, suggesting that a more pragmatic, innovation-focused stance instead may have been taken. In the European Union's language in its AI Act and other directives, which is also echoed stateside, it targets transparency, accountability and explainability which seems to imply that AI's creative outputs must be traceable back to a human hand or moral responsibility. This multiplicity of tactics demonstrates the global experimentation occurring as law trys to act as an interface between technological autonomy and human-centered legitimation. But each approach ultimately relies on the symbolic centrality of human intention in anchoring authorship.

9.1 Copyrightability of Purely AI-Generated Works

The initial question for many jurisdictions remains whether a work that is generated without true human authorship can be copyrighted. United States law has been clear since the Copyright Office's 2023–2025 guidance and the D.C. District Court's decision in Thaler v. Perlmutter (2023, upheld 2024): copyright ownership demands human authorship. Stephen Thaler, who uses his "Creativity Machine" to generate images as art in itself, tried to copyright an AI-generated painting named "A Recent Entrance to Paradise," only for the request to be denied on the basis that there was no human author of the work (Haiperin & Rosner, 2025). Two later actions by the Copyright Office, its "Zarya of the Dawn" decision in 2023 and a policy statement from 2025, reinforced that AI-generated works are not protected (although human authorship through choice or creation, arrangement or selection could be). This "human authorship" requirement has been stretched to reject registration of so-called monsters, thousands of AI-generated images, stories and songs.

Other jurisdictions are split. The Beijing Internet Court in China decided in 2023 that an image created by Stable Diffusion given a detailed human prompt could be copyrighted since the user's iterative prompting made them one of its authors. Both Japan and the UK also have broader "computer-generated works" provisions (Japan's Copyright Act Article 2(1)(xi-2) and the UK's CDPA Section 9(3)) that attribute authorship to the individual who "made the arrangements necessary for the creation," effectively considering sophisticated prompting as authorship. The EU does not currently have harmonized position, but the AI Act (effective 2025) places transparency obligations on rather than definitively declaring or excluding the copyrightability of works created by artificial intelligence.

9.2 Building Education: Fair Use or Flagrant Infringement

The most incendiary flashpoint is over the ingestion of billions of copyrighted images, texts, songs and videos into training systems known as large language and diffusion models. There is a groundbreaking case law in the US on why training is transformative fair use under US law (Campbell v. Acuff-Rose, Sony Betamax, Authors Guild v. Google): models are learning abstract patterns not literal copies and it is absurd to even consider any of these generated code snippets substantially similar to any single training example Your current Fair Use doctrine isn't actually broad enough (Vecchietti et al., 2025). Even if we leave company-only ownership aside and you insist that models create exact copies of their source data rather than learn distributions or abstractions then this still wouldn't be covered by copyright because your private AI fall out since definitionally no one else has ever seen it, for a laugh let's call that little creature a virtual space dragon just doesn't collide with any existing copyright marketplace model. Plaintiffs respond that this is the largest copyright infringement ever: it trains (without permission or payment) on datasets (LAION-5B, Common Crawl, The Pile) of millions of copyrighted works the defendants scraped from the open web; and its commercial purpose is to directly compete with creators scraped.

U.S. courts have sent mixed signals, by late 2025. District judges in the Northern District of California have mostly been letting fair use challenges survive to discovery (Andersen v. Stability, Tremblay v. OpenAI), and denying early motions to dismiss with expressions of doubts that training is inherently transformative when the business model is selling access to a tool that competes against illustrators, photographers and writers. In related litigation over GitHub Copilot (a code-generation tool trained on public repositories), parallel lawsuits have produced mixed results, with some claims surviving and others dismissed.

9.3 Output Infringement and "Imposter" Works

Even if training is fair use, products can be infringing when they are substantially similar to specific copyrighted works (Hine, 2024). The most high-profile examples include the Zarya of the Dawn comic (registration partially cancelled, after AI-generated images too closely matched existing photographs), and Midjourney works copying stylistic elements to an almost uncanny degree from living artists like Greg Rutkowski or Thomas Kinkade; one can also imagine prompts that specifically request in the style of a protected artist. Plaintiffs are turning to forensic tools (like reverse-image searches, model inversion attacks and membership inference) that show the outputs aren't just "inspired" but essentially memorized verbatim vomit.

9.4 Moral Rights, Publicity Rights and Deepfakes

Outside copyright, European-style moral rights (attribution and integrity) and U.S. state-level rights of publicity are being weaponized;) exported. French courts have heard statements that artificial intelligence imitation of an artist's hand is infringement on moral rights (Vicsek et al., 2025). In the U.S., actors (Scarlett Johansson v. OpenAI for unauthorized use of "Sky" voice similar to that in her "Her" performance) and visual artists, say through the app Lensa as well as others, file complaints for breaking publicity rights when someone uses their likeness or their distinctive style in a commercial way without consent.

9.5 Contractual and Platform Responses

As we've been waiting for courts to weigh in, private ordering has mushroomed. Other "commercially safe" models such as Adobe Firefly exclusively train on licensed data and provide indemnity. Shutterstock, Getty and Pond5 compensate contributors as long as their work is used for training. (Penguin Random House, HarperCollins), clauses in author contracts stipulating "no AI training." Stock-music archives require disclosure of AI utilization. But those private solutions to the scrapers remain piecemeal, and also inaccessible for most independent creators whose work was scraped years ago.

9.6 Legislative and Regulatory Horizons

In the United States, Congress has watched several bills (the NO FAKES Act and GENERATE AI Act) get stalled in lobbying gridlock (Shin, 2024). The U.S. Copyright Office's comprehensive study on AI and copyright, 2024–25, posited (limited) new rights (potentially a sui generis neighboring right for training data), but didn't go so far as recommending compulsory licensing. The EU AI Act introduces transparency and opt-out requirements for general-purpose models but leaves the core copyright questions until 2026. China has required registration and watermarking of generative outputs. Japan's "non-enjoyment of rights" model (training is free but outputs get thin cover) continues to be the outlier.

10. CONCLUSION

On a legal level, such erosion of the boundaries between original and derivative work demands a rethinking of traditional principles relating to authorship and copying. For example, copyright is based on the trio of originality, fixation and authorship. Both assume a human subject the author as creator, whose will is to make something new that expresses his own intelligence and personality. To date, human creativity has been regarded as an aspect of personhood. The ECJ ties authorship with individual expression, at the basis of its philosophical foundation of Kant and Hegel. The very notion of authorship is likewise tied to these instruments; in Anglo-American legal traditions, authors are the creators of "original works of authorship fixed in a tangible medium of expression." In fact, neither framework naturally captures the outputs of a machine which cannot express any recognizable human emotion or subjective intent. When AI works show anything like originality, they do it as a second-order effect of the processing of data rather than any kind of personal making. So the question is whether originality must remain an exclusive domain of human, or should law change in order to capture the new aspects of algorithmic creativity.

REFERENCES

Avery, J. J., Abril, P. S., & del Riego, A. (2024). Attributing AI Authorship: Towards a System of Icons for Legal and Ethical Disclosure. *Nw. J. Tech. & Intell. Prop.*, *22*, 1.

Basty, R., Said, H., & Halse, S. (2025). The AI Art Paradigm: Disruptions in the Digital Art Ecosystem and Future Trends. *ACM Journal on Responsible Computing*, *2*(4), 1–22.

Chatterjee, D. (2025). An empire of artificial intelligence: Exploring an intersection of politics, society, and creativity. *International Journal of Politics Culture and Society*, *38*(1), 81–110.

Cooper, Z. (2024). The AI Authorship Distraction: Why Copyright Should Not Be Dichotomised Based on Generative AI Use. *Available at SSRN* 4932612.

Dhrubo, A. M. (2025). Digital Dasein: A Heideggerian existential typology of digital human twins. *AI & Society*, •••, 1–15.

Feldman, R. (2024). Artificial Intelligence and Cracks in the Foundation of Intellectual Property. *UC LJ*, *76*, 47.

. Fiasal, R. (2025). AI in Media Careers: Ethical and Legal Challenges and Strategies for Adaptation. *Journal of Public Relations Research Middle East/Magallat Bhut Al-Laqat Al-Amh-Al-Srq Al-Aust*, (59).

Hazan, S. (2025, July). Promise or Peril: The dual edges of AI in cultural heritage and the Ouroboros effect. [BCS Learning & Development.]. *Proceedings of EVA London*, *2025*, 60–67.

Hine, E. (2024). Governing silicon valley and Shenzhen: Assessing a New Era of artificial intelligence governance in the United States and China. *Digital Society : Ethics, Socio-Legal and Governance of Digital Technology*, *3*(3), 50.

Jones, M. O. (2025). Lessons from the Digital Coalface in the Post-Truth Age: Researching the Middle East Amid Authenticity Vacuums, Transnational Repression & Disinformation. *Daedalus*, *154*(2), 132–156.

Joseph, A., Sánchez Abril, P., & Del Riego, A. (2024). Attributing AI Authorship: Towards a System of Icons for Legal and Ethical Disclosure. *Available at SSRN* 5152508.

Kawakami, R., & Venkatagiri, S. (2024, June). The impact of generative ai on artists. In *Proceedings of the 16th Conference on Creativity & Cognition* (pp. 79-82).

Lee, Z. (2024). Unveiling the Underbelly of Artificial Intelligence: The Inadequacies of the Legal System with Regard to Victims of Nonconsensual Sexual Deepfakes. *JL & Pol'y*, *33*, 182.

Li, W., Song, R., Zhang, B., & Yu, K. (2025). AI Creativity and Legal Protection for AI-Generated Works in Posthuman Societal Scenarios. *Sustainable Futures : An Applied Journal of Technology, Environment and Society*, •••, 100749.

Mohammed, I. A. (2024). Eliminating ghostwriters: How a federal right of publicity can save the music industry from generative artificial intelligence. *J. Intell. Prop. L.*, *31*, 212.

Moustaghfir, S., & Chankob, A. (2025). Creativity in an AI-Driven World: What Do We Fear? *International Journal of Linguistics. Literature and Translation*, *8*(2), 89–100.

Obiefuna, P. (2025). The Integrity of Human Authorship: An Argument Against Artificial Fear. *Available at SSRN* 5234383.

Plate, D., & Hutson, J. (2025). The intellectual bankruptcy of anti-AI academic alarmism: A rebuttal. *Teaching in Higher Education*, •••, 1–12.

Raymond, M. (2025). Our AI, Ourselves: Illuminating the Human Fears Animating Early Regulatory Responses to the Use of Generative AI in the Practice of Law. *Mary's J. on Legal Malpractice & Ethics*, *15*, 221.

Shin, D. (2024). Conclusion: misinformation and AI—how algorithms generate and manipulate misinformation. In *Artificial misinformation: Exploring human-algorithm interaction online* (pp. 259–277). Springer Nature Switzerland.

Singh, A. (2024). The Two Faced Lie: Regulation of Generative AI and Watermarking. *Available at SSRN* 5347736.

Sommer, E. (2024). Real Concerns for an Artificial Threat: Artists, AI, and the Battle to Script Hollywood's Future. *Nev. LJ*, *25*, 449.

Sun, H. (2024). The Law and Ethics of AI Creativity. *John's L. Rev.*, *98*, 405.

Utami, L. S., Mandala, S., & Darwati, D. (2025). Legal Aspects of Moral Rights and Economic Rights in Music Creation Using AI Music Generators. *Jurnal Pendidikan Indonesia*, *6*(7), 2925–2941.

Vecchietti, G., Liyanaarachchi, G., & Viglia, G. (2025). Managing deepfakes with artificial intelligence: Introducing the business privacy calculus. *Journal of Business Research*, *186*, 115010.

Vicsek, L., Pinter, R., & Bauer, Z. (2025). Shifting job expectations in the era of generative AI hype–perspectives of journalists and copywriters. *The International Journal of Sociology and Social Policy*, *45*(1/2), 1–16.

Yarosewick, G. V. (2025). Protect Authors Not Algorithms: The Rise of Artificial Intelligence and Its Interference with Copyright Law. *Widener L. Rev.*, *31*, 203.

Chapter 3

AI in Education and Skill Assessment:

Enhancing Learning or Intensifying Impostor Syndrome in Students

Vijayata Uikey
https://orcid.org/0009-0001-6757-6472
Rashtrasant Tukadoji Maharaj Nagpur University, Nagpur, India

Richa Kochar
https://orcid.org/0009-0003-8461-1625
Rashtrasant Tukadoji Maharaj Nagpur University, Nagpur, India

Shivani Khandate
Rashtrasant Tukadoji Maharaj Nagpur University, Nagpur, India

ABSTRACT

With features like tailored learning, real-time feedback, customizable study materials, and exams that adapt to your performance, intelligent systems are revolutionizing education and skills testing. Although these advancements increase productivity and physical activity, they can have a negative impact on mental health. Constant evaluations can demoralize students, and algorithmic styling might make them doubt their skills, which can result in imposter syndrome. In AI-assisted environments, pressure to do well can be detrimental, particularly if it appears that internal validation of performance is involved. However, when applied properly, AI can benefit students by identifying their areas of strength, promoting development, and lessening

DOI: 10.4018/979-8-3373-6618-0.ch003

prejudice. Emotional intelligence and technological know-how must be combined to ensure that AI tools benefit people rather than harm them. It must consider if we are creating more intelligent systems or more anxious pupils as schools evolve.

1. INTRODUCTION

AI has the potential to transform education by altering how teachers instruct, how students learn, and how schools assess students' abilities. AI has become ubiquitous, appearing in everything from computer grading and predictive analysis to intelligent tutoring devices and adaptive learning systems. It is present in online courses, classrooms, and even mobile applications. It's simple to understand why AI is attractive: unlike traditional models, it can provide real-time feedback, identify knowledge gaps, and customize learning experiences. It provides educators with fresh ideas and increases their productivity. It promises more rapid growth and individualized assistance for kids.

However, that promise is more complex than it first appears. Impostor syndrome is a subtle but potent influence on students' mental health that can occur when AI is used to monitor their development, hold them accountable for it, and compare their performance to algorithmic standards. This is not the first time that, despite all the evidence to the contrary, self-doubt won't go away and that you are always afraid of being discovered as a phony. However, it is evolving into something different in the domains of education and artificial intelligence. The people may question if their achievements are truly their own or rather the result of repeated prodding's from the machine. When feedback is continuous and instantaneous, and comparisons are made to the average of large data sets, it might feel like there is too much pressure. Consider a pupil who is continuously reminded of their shortcomings in comparison to their peers or the most effective methods of learning. Although the goal of these insights is to help you improve, they can also be seen as a means of telling you that you are not good enough. If not handled wisely, the technologies that are supposed to increase access to education by enabling learning which is central to personal autonomy and control over one's own educational journey can exacerbate emotional divisions and undermine self-worth (Almohammadi et al., 2025).

Mentoring and validation are disrupted by the transition from human-led education to AI-assisted learning. In addition to grading assignments, teachers in a typical classroom typically provide coaching, demonstrate empathy, and provide context for students' performance. Their comments contain sentiments and intimate observations. Even with its accuracy, AI falls short of this need. It fails to recognize the tension that results from providing the incorrect reaction, as well as the resolve that accompanies a somewhat improved but still sluggish response. Students may feel unheard or ununderstood when their development is reduced to dashboards and stats.

1.1 Importance of the Chapter

Important considerations are raised by this disconnect between our mental health and our demand for technology. Are we creating educational institutions that truly benefit every student? Are we prioritizing size and speed over mental health? Instead of opposing AI, the issue is to use it to enhance education's human component rather than to replace it. Emotional intelligence, empathy, and mentorship will remain crucial in a future where computers are doing more of the teaching.

It is critical to keep in mind that AI may be a huge aid in conquering imposter syndrome. When utilized properly, it may provide you with individualized inspiration, help you celebrate your accomplishments, and help you recognize the positive aspects of yourself. AI can provide alternative learning pathways and evidence that students who struggle with more conventional methods may not be able to obtain elsewhere. What matters is how they are created, applied, and comprehended. Do they encourage reliance and insecurity among students, or do they empower them to take charge of their own education?

The dual effects of AI on education and knowledge evaluation are examined in this research, with a focus on how it might both promote learning and exacerbate imposter syndrome. It looks at the ethics of algorithmic evaluation, the shifting power relations between students and professors, and the psychological impacts of AI feedback. Through case studies, professional commentary, and student narratives, it explores the complex relationship between identity and technology in modern education.

1.2 Relevance

"Education is at an interesting crossroads right now, where AI is changing the way we seek knowledge in a big way." The intersection of these two has a lot of promise. AI in education is now a reality, not merely a thing of the future. For instance, there are AI-enabled assessment tools that examine student performance with an exceptionally high degree of speed and accuracy, intelligent tutoring systems that provide students with real-time feedback, and AI-based adaptive learning platforms that provide students really tailored education. Each student might have a different learning experience thanks to this technology, which could also help fill in knowledge gaps and promote enrichment activities in a more adaptable and efficient learning environment. Proponents claim that by handling tedious duties, AI frees up instructors to engage with their kids more deeply and humanely. AI-based focused and real-time skill evaluation might be the secret to helping students not only study but also acquire the skills necessary to succeed in a changing workforce.

However, this fascinating new world of individualized learning has the potential to exacerbate our students' imposter syndrome if we are not vigilant. High achievers frequently struggle with impostor syndrome, which is the belief that their accomplishments are the result of pure chance and the anxiety of being exposed as an intellectual impostor. Because AI-enabled systems are always effective and provide fact-based guidance, they may inadvertently exacerbate these emotions.

Students may begin to question if they are truly succeeding when they receive feedback on an assignment that is nearly flawless and supported by an algorithm, or when technology allows them to create something that appears to be better than what they put in. “Did I really learn this, or did the A.I. do all the hard work?” they would ask themselves. This might result in a significant discrepancy between the work that students are performing and the results that they obtain with AI assistance, which once more eliminates the sense of achievement and ownership that comes from taking action. Students today experience accomplishment that doesn't seem earned and isn't fulfilling since the irritation that was formerly a welcomed aspect of learning is either minimized or eliminated entirely.

This has serious moral and psychological repercussions. We will create a generation of kids who lack confidence if we utilize AI as a crutch rather than as a means of developing our minds. The way intelligence is defined is evolving. It's transitioning from a protracted, difficult battle to a timely prompt. Now that this is the case, we need to have a difficult conversation about how we should be creating educational experiences. In order for students to use the technology rather than rely on it, we must employ AI in ways that empower and give them control. Therefore, the objective should be to create systems that promote self-efficacy and intellectual resilience in addition to improving learning outcomes. Students can understand all of this if we teach them to be AI literate and view AI as a cognitive companion that enhances their own thinking. We are dealing with a highly human issue, not only a technological one. As we work to enhance our educational institutions, we must be careful not to unintentionally undermine the self-worth and confidence that are so critical to a student's long-term success.

Instead of demonizing AI, the task is to emphasize a more humanized approach that encourages innovation for the sake of mankind rather than at its expense and recognizes the emotional and deep realities of being a student. As we approach this pivotal moment in education, we must consider what AI should be able to achieve in addition to what it can do. Learning involves more than just acquiring knowledge; it also involves developing one's capacity, curiosity, and self-assurance. And that shouldn't be prevented by any algorithm (Hsu et al., 2024).

The transition from human-led training to AI-led instruction alters the definition of validation and mentoring. Teachers in a typical classroom not only assign grades but also provide context, encouragement, and empathy. They provide nuanced input, demonstrating their understanding and internalization of it based on personal experience. Although AI is highly accurate, it lacks this human element. It doesn't notice the grit in a steady ascent or smell the dread in a bad response. These children may feel ignored or misinterpreted if they are reduced to dashboards and numbers.

2. UNDERSTANDING AI IN EDUCATION: APPLICATIONS IN LEARNING ENVIRONMENTS AND AI IN SKILL ASSESSMENT AND TESTING

AI is currently altering how teachers and students learn; it is not simply something that will happen in the future. Today, artificial intelligence is subtly enhancing the ecology in both physical and virtual classrooms by tailoring education and learning to each student's requirements. With the addition of tools like chatbots that assist with homework and algorithms that predict a student's level of learning, artificial intelligence is making education more dynamic and accessible to all.

Learning that is customized and of the finest applications of AI in education is personalization. While AI can analyze a student's performance in real time and adapt the content to suit them, traditional teaching is difficult to adapt to varied learning styles and speeds. If a student is performing well in algebra but poorly in geometry, the system may provide them with tailored practice problems, tips, or even alter the way the content is delivered. Students who receive this sort of customisation not only do better academically but also feel more confident since they can see and receive support for more than just their grades.

AI adds appeal to things in addition to personalizing them. Gamified learning platforms transform courses into enjoyable activities by using AI to track progress and award completion of assignments. Without natural language processing, science or history classes remain dead in their texts and students are unable to interact with the subject. Teachers may spend more time mentoring students and, until robots take over, becoming creative via communication by using digital tools to automate activities like grading and taking attendance.

Testing and evaluating talents is becoming more and more difficult due to AI. For instance, adaptive testing is a more accurate method of assessing aptitude than static examinations since it modifies the difficulty of the questions according to test takers' performance. In order to identify misconceptions, learning gaps, or even indications that a student is not interested, AI may also identify trends in the way that students respond to questions. This data-driven knowledge enables educators to intervene early and better customize their approaches.

However, the transition to AI-powered assessment is not simple. When students notice that a machine is judging their work, they might get nervous or self-conscious. Instantaneous, algorithm-based feedback might seem endless, particularly if students are confused by the system's grading methodology. This is when teaching's emotional component enters the picture. AI should not be used to spy on individuals, but to empower them. The objective is to employ AI to enhance learning in all aspects, not only to assess it. When applied properly, AI can support both emotional well-being and intellectual achievement. As a result, education will become more humane and intelligent in the future.

AI in education is transforming both student learning and instructor instruction. Improving everyone's educational experience is more important than eliminating instructors. This implies that each learner will follow a different learning path. In order to develop a customized curriculum, AI-powered platforms may examine a student's learning preferences, learning pace, and strengths and shortcomings. In this manner, each learner receives the appropriate content at the appropriate moment. For instance, a student who learns best via games may play more games, whereas a visual learner may view more diagrams. Intelligent tutoring systems, which provide students with individualized, real-time feedback and back-and-forth advice to enable them to work through difficulties at their own speed without feeling hurried or evaluated, are another significant use.

These artificial intelligence (AI) technologies may also assist educators with tedious, time-consuming assignments, such as grading homework, multiple-choice exams, and simple essays. This enables educators to concentrate on more challenging and significant assignments, such as student mentorship, group discussions, and providing more thorough feedback. Because AI is quicker, more equitable, and more intelligent than ever before, it is revolutionizing the way we test and assess talents (Wang & Huang, 2025). AI-powered systems are able to administer and score a wide range of tests, including cognitive ability tests, personality assessments, and simulations of job-specific skills. AI can evaluate a candidate's performance on a coding task, for instance. It might reveal not just the result but also the quality of their answer or the way they approached the issue.

In other situations, once a student responds to a question, AI will be able to examine their writing or voice. It will assess their communication and problem-solving skills using a technique known as natural language processing (NLP). By eliminating most of the human bias associated with conventional testing, this technology improves the process' accuracy and fairness. By analyzing a large amount of data on student performance, it can even identify kids who are at danger and may require further support, as well as forecast future trends. The use of AI in testing is changing the emphasis from evaluating students' prior knowledge to assessing their actual abilities and potential.

3. BENEFITS OF AI-DRIVEN LEARNING: PERSONALIZED LEARNING PATHS3

This is perhaps the largest shift AI can bring about in education. The days of requiring all students to study the same material at the same rate and in the same manner are over. In order to provide individualized learning experiences, AI systems now consider each person's learning preferences, capabilities, and shortcomings. A youngster who struggles to comprehend textual content but is able to think visually may be exposed to the same content via a movie or infographic. However, more text-based tasks will be assigned to someone else who learns best by reading. Instead of feeling lost in a sea of people, kids who receive this sort of customization feel appreciated and known.

With individualized learning, students may also study at their own speed. Slow learners are not left behind, and rapid learners are not kept back. Students are now more secure in their own education and less frustrated as a result of this flexible choice. Teachers gain by having a thorough record of each student's development, which enables them to assist them more successfully. While AI doesn't take the job of instructors, it does enable them to engage with pupils more deeply. Students feel in charge of your own education when you follow a tailored learning route. Students are active participants in a process that provides them with feedback on their learning, not only passive consumers of knowledge (Nelson & Muse, 2025). Also, education is more potent, effective, engaging, and beneficial when it is personalized.

AI is revolutionizing education by creating personalized learning paths for every learner. AI-powered systems may tailor a curriculum to a student's learning preferences by taking into account their individual learning style, speed, and prior knowledge. To identify particular areas where a student may be falling short or exceeding expectations, the AI analyzes data from quizzes and assignments. Then, in real time, it modifies the content and degree of difficulty, providing more assistance to those who require it or more challenging material for quicker learners. With the help of this individualized method, each student is guaranteed to receive the material that is most appropriate for them, preventing any misconceptions and improving comprehension and memory. It's similar to having a personal tutor on hand who understands your needs and when to provide them, filling in learning gaps and equipping pupils with the resources they need to become proficient in the subject.

3.1 Real-Time Feedback and Analytics

However, criticism is frequently too late to be helpful in a typical classroom setting. To learn how they performed on the most recent assignment, a student may have to wait days or even weeks. By then, it is impossible to correct the error. What makes a difference is how fast AI can operate. With real-time feedback and statistics, students can immediately see what they struggled with, what they did well, and what they can do better. Failure therefore turns into an opportunity for learning and a justification for embracing a growth mindset. Teachers can observe the entire classroom at once thanks to AI-powered analytics. Education is becoming more accessible and open to everybody thanks to AI. Artificial intelligence is a highly useful tool for kids with impairments.

For instance, students who are deaf or hard of hearing can benefit from real-time transcription of oral lectures via AI-powered speech-to-text technology (Bachi, 2025). Students who are blind or visually impaired can also benefit from text-to-speech readers, which read printed content aloud. There are additional hurdles that AI removes in addition to disability. Translations are instantly available to non-native speakers, making complex material easier to comprehend. Because of this diversity, regardless of the challenges they encounter, every kid gets the support and tools they require to engage fully in the learning process and realize their full potential.

When AI can provide real-time statistics and feedback, it is most beneficial in teaching. While traditional grading takes a long time, artificial intelligence can provide students with immediate feedback on anything from an essay to a math problem. This immediate feedback enables students to correct errors immediately, improving their comprehension of a topic and accelerating their learning (Khalil et al., 2024). This implies that educators may be able to obtain a large amount of data. It might highlight concepts that the entire class is struggling with, identify pupils who are lagging behind, or display patterns in the performance of the students. In order to provide students with the assistance they require at the appropriate time, teachers can use this information to make informed decisions and modify their teaching methods.

It's simple to see which concepts are overly challenging, which pupils are behind, and which instructional strategies may require modification. With the aid of data, educators can act quickly and intervene when necessary. It's similar to having a helper that is constantly alert for issues. Even more importantly, real-time statistics remove emotion from the scenario. When given the opportunity, students no longer question how they performed (Diaconescu et al., 2024). They are not required to. And teachers don't have to worry about how to convey it all. In a sense, the comprehension is evident, and the outcomes are same. This helps pupils understand themselves better and demonstrates their reliability.

3.2 Accessibility and Inclusivity

The greatest approach to level the playing field in education could be through artificial intelligence. AI-powered technologies have the potential to transform the lives of students with impairments, language barriers, or restricted access to conventional resources. Adaptive interfaces, real-time translation, and text-to-speech enable learners to engage with information whichever best suits them. Custom wording and layout may make it simpler for a student with dyslexia to read, a student who does not speak English as their first language to get translations, and a student who is blind or visually impaired to hear the lectures (Caporusso, 2023). AI not only makes life simpler for individuals with cognitive disability and other limitations, but it also helps narrow the socioeconomic divide. In rural or underdeveloped places, AI-powered internet platforms can offer a quality education in place of textbooks or qualified professors. Everyone can learn thanks to these sorts of resources, regardless of their location or circumstances.

Understanding that kids come from a variety of emotional and cultural backgrounds is another aspect of being inclusive. AI may be trained to identify when someone is struggling or not paying attention so that you can assist them promptly. When students believe that they are being noticed in both their personal and academic life, they are more likely to do well. Technology is insufficient on its own (Dyer & Starbird, 2024). It must be made in a fair and compassionate manner. However, when implemented properly, AI has the potential to be a powerful equalizer, providing all students with an equal opportunity to thrive regardless of their background or ability level. In a world where so many of the quiet problems that students encounter go unrecognized, AI offers a means to listen, adapt, and integrate.

4. THE PSYCHOLOGICAL IMPACT ON STUDENTS: IMPOSTOR SYNDROME AND AI ROLE IN AMPLIFYING SELF-DOUBT

AI is affecting more than simply academics as it grows more and more integrated into education. In little ways, it is also altering the way students view themselves. In addition to providing students with immediate feedback and individualized learning, AI systems also put pressure on them by continuously rating their work (Neufeld et al., 2023). Some pupils rise to the occasion and develop resilience and drive. However, it can cause or exacerbate imposter syndrome in certain people, particularly those who are prone to self-doubt. This is the persistent sense of being a fraud, even in the face of success evidence. Definitions Students may begin to question their own abilities if they are constantly compared to algorithms or their peers' performance statistics. Did the system assist them in achieving that score, or did they truly earn it? People may lose faith and believe that their accomplishments are meaningless as a result of this uncertainty (Paul et al., 2025).

Until AI grows more like humans, it cannot provide the same level of context and assistance that a human instructor can. A dashboard could highlight shortcomings without acknowledging hard work. A pupil may be classified as "at risk" by a prediction model without understanding the specifics of their case. Furthermore, this data-driven examination may eventually come to feel more like surveillance than beneficial (Clarke et al., 2025). When students' growth doesn't match what the code indicates, they may take these figures personally and believe they aren't intelligent, quick, or talented enough.

Indeed, there is a significant emotional cost. You may experience anxiety, burnout, and disinterest as a result of impostor syndrome. Students may be treated more like data points than human beings in AI-guided classrooms where learning is monitored more thoroughly than ever before. AI that incorporates empathy must be developed by educators and developers in order to really assist learners. These tools should recognize progress, provide context, and stress that learning is a lifetime process rather than a competition. Every data point has a person behind it who is dedicated to figuring out the best strategies to improve people's reading and self-esteem.

Students are now experiencing imposter syndrome, a new psychological issue brought on by artificial intelligence. It's a new form of self-doubt brought on by how rapidly A.I. has learned and acquired power; it's not the same as feeling inadequate after putting in a lot of effort. Additionally, a student may begin to believe that their achievement wasn't earned if they utilize AI to assist them come up with ideas, solve a challenging math issue, or compose an essay. The student doesn't need to put in as much effort as she should because the outcomes are typically flawless and appear to come effortlessly (Newar et al., 2025). The thought, "Is this my real accomplishment, or did the AI do the thinking?" may arise as a result, and it can be damaging. Their feeling of value and ownership may be harmed by this new form of self-doubt.

Given how simple it is to locate and employ AI technologies, this self-doubt might worsen. Students may become self-conscious if they begin to contrast their abilities with the "ideal" that an AI generates. Because they depended on something impersonal to get those achievements, they are more afraid of being "found out" as a phony. Students who utilize AI as their sole source of assistance may develop a culture of dependency and lose faith in their own skills as a result. Our children will grow up to follow instructions and anticipate rewards without even realizing it. If we're not careful, we might damage a generation's resiliency. Teachers and their students must redefine what it means to be a "smart" or "successful" learner in the era of artificial intelligence (Ginsburg et al., 2025).

5. BALANCING INNOVATION WITH EMPATHY: DESIGNING EMOTIONALLY INTELLIGENT AI

Better algorithms, more intelligent analytics, and more effective systems are the main topics of discussion in this era of AI revolution in education. However, we may be overlooking something extremely human in our haste to acquire as much as we can: empathy. Finding patterns in data is only one aspect of emotionally intelligent AI (Husbands et al., 2025). Understanding students' emotions and reacting in ways that support rather than hinder their learning are also important. Harder questions or greater feedback aren't always the solution when students are struggling. Sometimes it's a reminder that learning is a protracted process rather than a quick one, sometimes it's a letter of encouragement.

Striking a balance between a strong feeling of empathy and the incredible potential of AI is the next great thing in education. The effectiveness and volume of data that AI systems can analyze should not be the only considerations while developing and utilizing them. Developing emotionally intelligent technologies that comprehend and support kids' well-being should also be a priority. This entails developing AI that can recognize when a student is feeling concerned or irritated about their studies and then support them rather than present them with increasingly challenging tasks. When an AI observes a student repeatedly making the same error or taking a long time to respond to a single question, for example, it may subtly indicate, "This seems hard." Rather than just labeling the response as incorrect, suggest "Let's try breaking it down together." A student can avoid feeling down and giving up with the support of this type of engagement.

This need to shift our perspective if want AI to be this sensitive to emotions. We must develop systems that can comprehend and respond to human emotions rather of relying solely on algorithms that operate on logic. This entails using our understanding of psychology and neuroscience to the design process (de Jesus Silva et al., 2023). Instead of being a cold, calculating computer, the AI is supposed to be a patient, understanding companion in a collaboration between humans and technology. By prioritizing empathy in our design, we can ensure that AI not only makes learning more intelligent but also more human. Students will feel encouraged and understood as a result, which will allow them to grow and take chances without fear of being evaluated by an impersonal algorithm.

To create an emotionally intelligent AI, you must also build compassionate code. Teaching systems must be able to recognize symptoms of fear, disinterest, or dissatisfaction in addition to incorrect responses. It's about providing constructive and compassionate criticism rather than icy and clinical. Imagine an AI instructor that, after a few attempts, shifts its tone from alarming to reassuring when a pupil doesn't understand a topic. That's not only wise, it's kind. Respecting each person's individuality is another aspect of empathy. Pupils are distinct learners with their own histories, challenges, and abilities; they are more than simply statistics. AI has to be in sync with both emotional and cognitive cycles (Johnson & Plisco, 2025). A system that is really empathic listens, learns, and uplifts in addition to teaching. Empathic innovation is essential; it is not a compromise. The future of learning will depend on how intelligent our machines are and how well we can collaborate with them. Empathy and technology work together to make learning deeper as well as faster.

5.1 Human-AI Collaboration in Education

When AI and humans collaborate in education, the goal is to provide teachers with the resources they need to perform their jobs more effectively, not to replace them. The classroom becomes a responsive, inclusive, and dynamic space when educators and AI collaborate. Teachers can focus on what they do best—mentor, motivate, and engage with students by using AI to handle tasks like grading papers and monitoring progress. Additionally, it may demonstrate how children learn, allowing teachers to adapt their methods to meet the requirements of each individual student.

The finest educational systems will always be a combination of humans and AI, but AI won't replace teachers. AI should be viewed as an enhancement rather than a replacement, a clever tool that may enhance the work that teachers undertake. AI is capable of handling tedious, data-intensive activities like creating customized practice problems, monitoring student progress, and scoring multiple-choice tests (Jang et al., 2025). This gives instructors more time to focus on their core competencies, which include working one-on-one with students and fostering creativity and genuine human relationships. An analytics tool driven by artificial intelligence may be used by a teacher to identify which pupils are struggling and then devote time to providing one-on-one assistance. Artificial Intelligence is an excellent collaborator in this partnership paradigm, providing educators with new knowledge and resources to help them become even more effective while maintaining the fundamental element of education human connection at its core.

But when mechanical precision and human intuition combine, magic happens. When it comes to educating children with robots, an AI's capacity to learn from data may be paired with a teacher's comprehension, creativity, and broad perspective. Together, these elements provide an educational experience that is both intelligent and meaningful. In addition to receiving one-on-one attention, the children learn about the individuals who inspire their curiosity and confidence. The human element is strengthened in this collaboration by technology, which simultaneously makes learning more efficient and significant (Andira & Daulay, 2025).

6. POLICY AND IMPLEMENTATION STRATEGIES

Businesses must establish clear guidelines and procedures for using AI in schools in a way that is both ethical and efficient as it becomes more prevalent. Organizing a team of educators, school administrators, students, and IT specialists to collaborate on AI is the first step. In order to assist the organization employ AI in a way that aligns with its goal, this group will develop a philosophical framework. They can state, for instance, "Shaping criteria to make sure these tools don't just repeat their makers' biases," and "Distinguishing between applications that strengthen critical thinking and those that weaken it," and "Favoring practices and tools that reduce rather than increase inequities." Important topics like data privacy, which include protecting student information and ensuring that platforms are truthful about their data collection and use practices, should be covered by the policy (Espinoza Vidaurre et al., 2024). Additionally, it must advise educators on how to include AI into assignments and assessments without violating academic integrity standards.

Effective marketing and execution tactics require more than just policies. They must be a part of a system that really supports and aids educators and learners. From direct instruction techniques to projects that promote critical thinking and human-AI collaboration, educators must learn how to incorporate AI technologies into their classes (You & Zhang, 2025). Additionally, students must acquire "AI literacy," which entails understanding how these technologies function, their limitations, and their ethical ramifications. As a result, they may utilize AI to improve their thinking rather than depending on it. In order to gauge the effectiveness of AI technologies and gather feedback, organizations should begin with small-scale pilots in discrete departments. This will enable them to proceed with a flexible and progressive roll-out. Through this iterative approach, we can continuously modify rules and procedures to ensure that AI supports equitable, transparent, and sensible learning for all students.

"AI is becoming a bigger part of education, so it's no longer an option to have well-thought-out policies and implementation plans; it's a must." The objective is to introduce state-of-the-art technology into the classroom in a way that prioritizes the needs of kids, helps teachers, and is equitable. Clarity is the foundation of every successful policy, and this includes outlining what AI should and shouldn't do in educational settings. These include limiting the amount of data that may be gathered, promoting transparency in AI decision-making, and safeguarding the privacy of pupils. Students need to know what their data is being used for in order to trust the systems they are using (Snyder & Pallett, 2026). It should be possible for professors to comprehend and challenge the systems they are assigned.

However, implementation requires more than just installing the program; it must also be culturally appropriate. Teachers are not only being taught how to utilize AI tools; they are also being taught the significance of the results and how to incorporate them into their lessons. Institutions must invest in professional development, create feedback loops for ongoing enhancement, and promote cooperation between education and technology. Without this human network, even the most sophisticated AI will be of little use. The fairness must be the foundation of any strategy. Policy should emphasize that AI technologies should be user-friendly and flexible enough to accommodate a range of learning demands, independent of a person's social or economic background. This entails not offering universally applicable answers and acknowledging that technology should support learners rather than the other way around. Every action needs to be grounded on emotional intelligence (Wagner et al., 2022). The human relationships that make education transformational should be viewed as being supported by AI systems rather than replaced. "Are we making tools that help kids, or are we making tools that kids can use?" is a question that policymakers should consider. Are we giving teachers more authority or taking it away from them? Ultimately, having a clear aim is just as important to effective execution as coming up with innovative ideas. When educational policies emphasize empathy, transparency, and collaboration, AI may be a powerful tool for good. Every learner can benefit from it in a different way.

7. CONCLUSION AND FUTURE ASPECTS

The use of AI in education is here to stay, not simply a fad. We have the ideal chance to use this technology to make learning environments more accessible to all and more individualized than can be accomplished by hand. Because AI has the potential to eliminate learning gaps, provide real-time assistance, and free up instructors' time to concentrate on the human element of teaching, it may be beneficial. However, the path ahead isn't always straightforward. We must discuss kids' mental health and how it might negatively impact their self-esteem and make them feel like imposters. The primary query is: Is it possible to create AI that is sensitive to human emotions so that our virtual assistants remain our partners rather than replacing actual people?

The ability to strike a balance between innovation and moral obligation will determine how AI is used in education in the future. This entails establishing explicit guidelines, educating educators and learners on AI usage, and ensuring the intellectual and emotional safety of pupils. For the next generation of AI tools to prevent us from plunging into wildfire-filled apocalypses, they must be both emotionally and cognitively competent. Future educational systems that take this step—becoming a single platform where humans and AI may collaborate as tools to help us realize our greatest potential—will be the best. Giving children the skills to question, think critically, and solve issues in a future where technology and human creativity coexist is just as important as teaching them how to utilize AI. The thing is certain as we continue to explore how AI will impact education: technology by itself cannot alter the way we learn. AI is a set of potent instruments, including unrestricted access to knowledge, real-time feedback, and customized teaching. Like any instrument, though, its effectiveness varies according on our use of it. When AI is developed and applied with compassion and thoughtful policy, it may benefit students, assist educators, and create learning environments where individuals feel welcome. However, it may exacerbate stress and self-doubt, as well as the very imposter syndrome it is meant to alleviate, if you don't consider it or use it without being conscious of your emotions.

AI must coexist peacefully with other elements if it is to have a future in education. We require intelligent systems that are sensitive to human emotions. These methods ought to acknowledge effort, commend advancement, and accommodate the human element of education. A certain amount of cooperation between educators, technologists, psychologists, and legislators will be required for this. Together, they can create AI that promotes inquiry, tenacity, and confidence. There are currently plans for new technologies such as emotionally responsive AI tutors, learning systems that address mental health, and culturally sensitive content delivery. These developments imply that education can be highly individualized, helpful, and successful in the future. The goal is to maintain people at the core of learning, not to make machines more like humans. This is due to the fact that learning involves both being and knowing. When creativity and empathy are coupled, AI can help every student become not just smarter but also stronger, more self-assured, and more capable of succeeding.

REFERENCES

Almohammadi, I. A., Hamad, E. O., Alqarni, B. A., Alzahrani, M. A., & Aljohani, J. A. (2025). Graduate Students' Use of Artificial Intelligence Applications in Scientific Research: Prevalence and Association with Perceived Impostor Syndrome. *International Journal for Research in Education, 49*(2), 123–188.

Andira, D. P., & Daulay, A. A. (2025). Understanding the Impostor Phenomenon among Active Student Organization Members in Indonesian Universities. *Journal of Mathematics Instruction. Social Research and Opinion, 4*(3), 739–748.

Bachi, D. M. (2025). Impostor Syndrome and Self-Doubt Among High Achievers. *Indonesian Journal on Health Science and Medicine, 2*(1).

. Caporusso, N. (2023). Generative artificial intelligence and the emergence of creative displacement anxiety. *Research in Psychology and Behavior, 3*(1).

Clarke, B. J., Hartley, M. T., & Button, C. (2025). Impostor phenomenon and counselor development: The critical role of self-compassion. *Journal of Counseling and Development, 103*(2), 149–160.

. de Jesus Silva, T. B., Manoel de Sousa, A., & Martins Simã, F. (2023). Study Time and Academic Performance: Do the Level of Self-Regulated Learning and Impostor Syndrome Matter?. *Advances in Scientific & Applied Accounting, 16*(3).

Diaconescu, L. V., Mihăilescu, A. I., Stoian-Bălăşoiu, I. R., Cosma, A. N., Drakou, A., & Popa-Velea, O. (2024). The predictive value of burnout and impostor syndrome on medical students' self-esteem and academic performance: A cross-sectional study. *Education Sciences, 14*(12), 1318.

Dyer, A. M., & Starbird, L. I. (2024). Organizational Impostor Phenomenon: Theoretical Foundations and Practical Implications. *Journal of Library Administration, 64*(8), 893–902.

. Espinoza Vidaurre, S. M., Velásquez Rodríguez, N. C., Gambetta Quelopana, R. L., Martinez Valdivia, A. N., Leo Rossi, E. A., & Nolasco-Mamani, M. A. (2024). Perceptions of Artificial Intelligence and Its Impact on Academic Integrity Among University Students in Peru and Chile: An Approach to Sustainable Education. *Sustainability (2071-1050), 16*(20).

Ginsburg, J., Howell, M., Lincoln, E., Medepalli, V., Gentges, J., Courtney, D. M., & Milman, B. (2025). Curated Collection for Educators: Five Key Papers About Impostor Phenomenon. *Cureus, 17*(7).

Hsu, C. L., Liu, C. H., Huang, C. C., Chen, H. L., Chiu, Y. L., & Yang, C. W. (2024). The effectiveness of online educational interventions on impostor syndrome and burnout among medical trainees: A systematic review. *BMC Medical Education*, *24*(1), 1349.

Husbands, D., Linceviciute, S., & Yetkili, O. (2025). The impostor phenomenon among racially minoritised university students: 'who knows how to get rid of this?'. *Race, Ethnicity and Education*, *28*(5), 670–688.

Jang, S. J., Chang, S. J., & Lee, H. (2025). Intensive care nurses' impostor phenomenon: Associations with narcissistic personality, shame-proneness, and guilt-proneness. *Australian Critical Care*, *38*(2), 101110.

Johnson, C. M., & Plisco, M. (2025). Impostor phenomenon, self-compassion, and campus connectedness in Black female undergraduates. *Journal of American College Health*, *73*(3), 879–885.

Khalil, A. I., Alharbi, R., Al Qtame, H., Al Bena, R., & Khan, M. A. (2024). Investigating the association between resilience and impostor syndrome in undergraduate nursing and medical students: A cross-sectional study. *Journal of Medicine and Life*, *17*(9), 868.

Nelson, R. K., & Muse, V. A. (2025). Evaluating the Prevalence of Imposter Syndrome Among Community College General Biology Students. *Community College Journal of Research and Practice*, •••, 1–15.

Neufeld, A., Babenko, O., Lai, H., Svrcek, C., & Malin, G. (2023). Why do we feel like intellectual frauds? A self-determination theory perspective on the impostor phenomenon in medical students. *Teaching and Learning in Medicine*, *35*(2), 180–192.

Newar, R., Gupta, R. K., Krishnan, R. G., Shekhawat, K., & Walia, Y. (2025). Self-esteem as a mediator of the relationship between imposter phenomenon and academic performance among college students. *International Journal of Adolescence and Youth*, *30*(1), 2496449.

Paul, F. A., Ali, A., Ganie, A. U. R., & Basistha, B. (2025). Imposter Syndrome in Higher Education: A Hidden Crisis-threatening Student Mental Health and Success. *Lebanese Journal of Mental Health*, *1*(1), 49–51.

Snyder, A. L., & Pallett, L. H. (2026). Mindfulness, Motivation, and Milestones: Facilitated Support for Doctoral Students During Dissertation Writing. In *Improving Doctoral Education and Research Development for Sustainability* (pp. 271-302). IGI Global Scientific Publishing.

Wagner, J. L., Boyle, J., Boyle, C. J., Choi, D., Ballou, J. M., Patel, N., & Malcom, D. R. (2022). Overcoming past perceptions and a profession-wide identity crisis to reflect pharmacy's future. *American Journal of Pharmaceutical Education*, *86*(7), 8829.

Wang, S. J., & Huang, H. C. (2025). To ask is human, to answer divine: How awe-inspiring generative AI leads to self-enhancement and imposter anxiety. *Information Technology & People*, •••, 1–32.

. You, Y., & Zhang, Y. (2025). Developing AI literacies and negotiating professional identities: a study of pre-service English teachers in a ChatGPT-facilitated pedagogy. *Journal of China Computer-Assisted Language Learning*, (0).

Chapter 4
Algorithmic Innocence and Commercial Predation Redefining Child Exploitation:
Era of AI-Driven Advertising Under POCSO and Digital Rights Framework

Meha Bhushan
https://orcid.org/0009-0008-3322-6117
Gujarat National Law University, Gandhinagar, India

ABSTRACT

Children's interaction with algorithms is innocent, so artificial intelligence appears caring and personalised. In virtual worlds, children play, learn, and socialise, and AI increasingly powers data-driven targeting of goods and services. This chapter contends that such algorithmic places obscure the line between fun and exploitation and are an evil child manipulation. It recasts these practices within India's shifting digital governance framework based on the Protection of Children from Sexual Offences Act, 2012 (POCSO), the Digital Personal Data Protection Act, 2023 (DPDP), and other relevant consumer protection and digital rights laws. By means of behavioural profiling and emotional prediction, algorithms infringe on children's privacy, agency, and liberty of the mind. Hence, it is necessary to bolster ethical design, algorithmic transparency, and corporate accountability to protect the dignity of children in India's fast-developing AI-driven marketplace.

DOI: 10.4018/979-8-3373-6618-0.ch004

1. INTRODUCTION

Artificial intelligence (AI) systems that pervade daily life significantly impact how children think, spend, and internalise social values. More and more digital platforms use algorithmic design to profit from children's developmental vulnerabilities, optimising attention and profit through what Zuboff (2019) called surveillance capitalism. These technologies commodify attention as money, frequently influencing emotions and tastes without conscious consent. Therefore, this poses serious normative issues regarding autonomy and being well-informed in participating in digital spaces; can children legally consent to algorithmic control, and how far can such systems morally direct their behaviour?

In the past, protective legislation responded to visible harmful effects like child labour, trafficking, or sexual exploitation. The digital environment, however, presents intangible exploitation forms that were never contemplated by traditional law (Urbas, 2021). Machine learning algorithms can make inferences regarding emotions, predict behaviour, and nudge choices in subtle directions through feedback loops using user data. Whenever such predictive systems are aimed at children, the harm is more than mere advertising; it influences identity formation, emotional self-regulation, and moral development (O'Neill et al., 2022).

For example, AI-powered behaviour-tracking advertising systems can give rise to materialism and consumerism, making children, at the same time, commodities and consumers (Feller & Burroughs, 2022). Where virtual tracks are harvested, processed, and commodified for a child without actual knowledge or consent, extraction as such under the Act amounts to exploitation. The problem is thus legal, i.e., how to balance a fluid technological condition with the ethics and constitutionalism of child protection.

India's legislative framework, previously organised around physical abuse, has pronounced normative lacunae when it comes to digital exploitation. The POCSO Act, 2012, continues to be a foundation for handling sexual offences, but its emphasis on physical or representational harm does little to tackle algorithmic and psychological manipulation. Therefore, redefining "exploitation" in terms of emerging realities governed by the DPDP and the Consumer Protection Act, 2019, and constitutional privacy and dignity guarantees recognised in *K.S. Puttaswamy v. Union of India* (2017) is urgently necessary. Algorithmic profiling, targeted persuasion, and behaviour manipulation can nullify a child's decisional autonomy as deeply as physical coercion, necessitating legal evolution to protect cognitive and emotional integrity in the age of AI.

1.1 Contextualising AI in child-targeted advertising

The fast-growing discipline of algorithmic advertising presents sophisticated legal and ethical problems. New AI-based marketing systems have engagement-optimisation models that translate user attention into income. The longer people remain online, the more advertisers earn. When these systems target children, they use their developmental curiosity, impulsivity, and affective responsiveness (Livingstone & Stoilova, 2021). Social-media algorithms and recommendation engines are no longer neutral technologies manipulating behaviour and leading users toward predetermined commercial destinations. The line between advertising and entertainment has nearly vanished in influencer marketing, in-app product placements, and interactive promotions blending play and persuasion (Kendall, 2022).

As children mature, these ecosystems of persuasion start constructing their views of identity, freedom, and achievement, selling lifestyles, not products. The "innocence" of algorithms, their seeming friendliness, and pedagogical facade make youth consumers particularly susceptible to manipulation. Algorithms learn from repeated feedback and modify content that optimises emotional connection. This design establishes a trusting online world where children do not catch on to manipulation. International regulators, such as the UK Information Commissioner's Office, through the Age-Appropriate Design Code (2021), highlight that most children cannot grasp how their data is processed and monetised due to a lack of cognitive maturity or digital literacy. As a result, even legal parental-consent mechanisms often break down due to unintelligible data flows, convoluted privacy policies, and imbalances in knowledge between platforms and families (UN CRC General Comment No. 25, 2021).

Apps and game platforms harvest vast behavioural data sets, screen-time habits, gaps, response times, and affective signals to improve predictive algorithms that capitalise on attention. The loop of repetitive data mining and feedback leads to habitual behaviour and addiction. This power imbalance between corporations and child users is a type of "commercial predation," with profit-oriented design interfering with emotional control and moral learning (Montgomery & Chester, 2019). The system's persuasive logic subverts kids' agency by constantly reinforcing conditioning decision-making. A kid constantly receiving algorithmically curated content starts internalising commercial values as personal preference, conflating desire with choice.

Conservative evidence models find it difficult to show algorithmic harm. Physical or testimonial evidence, which is enough for overt abuse, does not reflect insidious digital control. Algorithmic exploitation works behind the scenes, leaving psychological and behavioural residues but no physical harm. It is cumulative in its impact as it shows itself through anxiety, consumerism, gender stereotyping, or loss of self-esteem, and hence concealed primarily from courts and regulators (Shende, 2025). For example, repeated exposure to gender-coded toys, aspirational luxury goods, or influencer lifestyles forms aspirations, commodifying identity itself.

These dynamics undermine the core principle of child safety in law, which seeks to prevent harm and provide a remedy. They require exploitation to be rethought beyond physical or sexual injury to encompass manipulative design that violates decisional freedom. These challenges can be met by weaving algorithmic responsibility into India's nascent digital model, the DPDP 2023, the Consumer Protection Act 2019, and connected guidelines on digital advertising in a manner such that children's rights to privacy, dignity, and development are secured in the algorithmic market.

2. ALGORITHMIC INNOCENCE: CHILDHOOD IN THE AGE OF DATAFICATION

Datafication has converted innocence from a moral quality to a measurable digital asset. Today, innocence is marketed, packaged, copied, and bought through algorithms observing each click, look, and emotional cue. While children play games, watch cartoons, or study online, automated intelligence systems surreptitiously record their gestures, voices, and decisions, converting them into data points that go into global advertising networks. The hidden infrastructure of contemporary childhood is grounded in artificial intelligence, machine learning, and predictive analytics woven into social media, learning platforms, and streaming services (Chawki, 2025).

Children are, therefore, no longer mere recipients of technology; they are unintentional co-producers of data capital. All behaviour, response, and preference feeds into an extensive commercial archive that characterises their online self. Datafication converts emotions, errors, and learning habits into quantifiable inputs. Data analysis is usually an intelligent transaction between utility and privacy in adults. However, in kids, it starts at pre-rational levels, prior to the capacity to comprehend consequences or consent. Smart educational apps and toys that track speech or learning performance seem innocuous but are always-on data-gathering devices, teaching algorithms to anticipate future behaviour and consumption (Montgomery & Chester, 2019).

This entwinement of appearance and play establishes a field in which technology systems are entwined with cognition and affect. The distinction between autonomous choice and the nudge of an algorithm is disappearing ever more. Each tap, halt, or click is interpreted as a signal by the corporation's cash in on. In fact, this innocuous-looking collection is an architecture of behaviour anticipation that recodes expectation and personality (Livingstone & Stoilova, 2021).

Such pervasive surveillance wears down the spontaneity that has typified childhood generation after generation. The typical moral grievance about the age of algorithms is that it increasingly divests from autonomy. Adults may be able to enjoy deceptive ads, but children, as naive and awe-struck as they are, experience digital systems as benevolent benefactors. Their faith in technology as a tool of enjoyment and education is being manipulated covertly through images, reward systems, and affective content designed to maximise use (O'Neill et al., 2022). The subliminal message is perseverance: hold their attention, intensify interaction, and benefit from the outcome.

This cyclical interaction brings about dependency and conformity, cutting short the possibilities of self-actualisation. Then, there is the new "algorithmic childhood" in which children's wants are nearer to prediction codes than to human impulses. Data societies are increasingly socialising children to focus on instant gratification, status acquisition, and consumer value identity grounded on platforms' profitability as opposed to overall development. Algorithmic naivety is not just a metaphorical figure; it is a sign of a structural imbalance wherein naivety and trust are leveraged as economic capital. It is necessary to see the same to facilitate legal reform and moral governance. Datafication of childhood compels policymakers to activate algorithmic transparency, verifiable assurance of age, and design-ethics responsibility onto India's emergent digital terrain. It is only through the reconceptualisation of innocence as a human right based on dignity, autonomy, and informational privacy that society can protect children from the commodification that now permeates their online existence.

2.1 Cognitive vulnerabilities and digital manipulation

Algorithmic intermediation succeeds precisely because it leverages cognitive vulnerability in developing minds. Cognitive psychologists observe that children's attention, emotional regulation, and executive control develop over time and are particularly susceptible to reward-based stimuli (Luria et al., 2022). The quick, gratification-driven feedback loops inherent in social media and gaming interfaces habituate users into expecting immediate returns. Eventually, this constant reinforcement stimulates patience, reliance, and reduced critical thinking. When algorithmic systems provide content that caters to a child's present wants, they obstruct the growth of autonomous thinking and self-decision-making (Nikken & Schols, 2015).

Lighthearted commercials or gameified promotions conceal the persuasive intention. Such material normalises consumer culture by pairing pleasure with acquisition, and leading children to tie self-esteem with material possession. As the construction of identity occurs around brand symbols and algorithmically suggested lifestyles, childhood becomes reinscribed within capitalist logics of commodification

(Montgomery & Chester, 2019). This commodification of attention creates long-term moral and psychological dangers, re-designing value systems around consumption instead of creativity or empathy.

The compounding nature of algorithmic influence makes it hard to establish legal harm. Conventional child-protection paradigms rely on concrete evidence of physical harm, witness testimony, or overt coercion, while algorithmic manipulation exercises its power insidiously through repetition and emotional conditioning. The harm accumulates quietly: refashioned preferences, corrupted self-image, and diminished ability for independent thinking. Since this exploitation happens incrementally, parents and regulators cannot easily identify it. Therefore, current protective laws, such as the POCSO, 2012, are unable to include algorithmic psychological harm that is neither sexual nor physical.

Comparative jurisdiction identifies the same gap. China's Information Technology and Consumer Protection Order issues privacy guidelines but does not distinguish between adults and children, ignoring the power asymmetry in influencing design (Tarvin & Stanfill, 2022). Inside the European Union, the General Data Protection Regulation (GDPR) responds to children's online vulnerability via the double principles of data minimisation and the child's best interests. Article 8 requires verifiable parental consent, and Recital 38 identifies children needing special protection. The UN Convention on the Rights of the Child (UNCRC) also supports this strategy, reiterating that participation and privacy are integral to children's dignity in the digital world (UNCRC GC No. 25, 2021).

India's DPDP,2023, is a significant move towards acknowledging online harms to children. It prohibits tracking, behavioural observation, and targeted advertising toward children. Nevertheless, the Act keeps mum on algorithmic accountability, the duty of data fiduciaries to expound, audit, or constrain predictive systems that shape minors' cognition (Ezeji & Uwizeyimana, 2025). Filling this lacuna requires an extension of child-rights jurisprudence from bodily safety to cognitive and informational integrity.

Law and policy must shift from statistical data management to a rights-based framework where children are respected as independent individuals, not datasets. Embedding algorithmic ethics within child-protection law would guarantee that digital worlds facilitate curiosity, creativity, and educated agency over passive consumption. Reframing cognitive vulnerability as a legally cognisable harm is consonant with the constitutional right of dignity and the international push toward humane, transparent technology regulation.

2.2 The role of personalisation and engagement algorithms: Psychological impact of predictive behavioural profiling

Previously understood as an emotional or moral condition, innocence now faces technological impulses that commodity curiosity in and of itself. Children's online life is mediated by algorithms that dictate what they look at, click on, and admire. Personalisation systems monitor every query, gaze, and pause, converting genuine curiosity into commodifiable prediction streams. A real engagement with what is happening in our surroundings has been substituted by an algorithmic intermediary that foresees and directs action (Sharifi Poor Bgheshmi et al., 2025). Kids no longer look for knowledge; they are led by opaque frameworks made to profit from attention. This "pre-structured" youth constrains cognitive freedom and maximises conformity since learning is based on predictive feedback.

These personalisation engines reach far beyond the advertorial space. They decide social rankings on gaming and social sites, suggest peers or influencers to follow, and invisibly guide moral decisions. Kids are educated by these algorithmic systems as much as (if not more than) parents or educators, picking up aspiration patterns delineated by the market's interests. Algorithmic profiling replicates social bias by furthering stereotypes and material hierarchies already in training databases (Noble, 2018). Personalisation, therefore, embeds inequality while presenting itself as convenience.

The psychological effect of predictive behavioural profiling is additive. Algorithms depend on variable-reward schedules methods borrowed from behavioural psychology to optimise dopamine-based reward (Alter, 2017). Every notification, badge, or "like" releases a quick neurological reward, maintaining compulsive interaction. Children, whose prefrontal cortex and self-regulation systems are still developing, are particularly susceptible to these cycles of anticipation and approval. Repetition reconditions thinking expectations, and constant stimulation becomes a norm of behaviour (Luria et al., 2022). Attention spans decrease over time, tolerance for frustration drops, and self-motivation is overwhelmed by algorithmically fostered dependency.

Ethically, this also questions autonomy and consent. Is it possible for a child to meaningfully consent to psychological engineering built into interface design? Corporate transparency reports rarely reveal how predictive models assess emotions or vulnerability. Policymakers and developers must identify a duty of care beyond data privacy to cognitive integrity. AI systems that engage with children must receive independent evaluations for emotional and developmental effects, not just for compliance with disclosure norms (Feller & Burroughs, 2022).

Education and family literacy, as necessary as they are, cannot reverse design-level manipulation. Schools can teach critical media literacy skills, but these responses are reactive; system change must start with the technology's architecture. Firms profiting from child interaction have the moral responsibility to incorporate ethical checks, bias audits, attention-time limits, and explainable algorithms. These norms resonate with global standards: the EU Digital Services Act (2022) prohibits the targeted advertising of minors, and the UN CRC General Comment No. 25 (2021) demands proactive regulation of online spaces. Indian authorities can incorporate analogous norms in the DPDP, 2023, through risk assessments on child-facing algorithms.

Predictive profiling relocates innocence as an open asset rather than a protected status. Every interaction accumulates databases that enhance behaviour predictions, converting childhood into training data for commercial AI. Predictions pervade everywhere and threaten classic ethics; morality now requires collective control of systems, not personal self-control (McAlinden, 2022). If data are the "new oil," kids' data are its most perilous form, e.g., unstable, non-sustainable, and morally sensitive. Safeguarding means abandoning passive censorship or parental blocking and moving toward a proactive, rights-centred government that imposes algorithmic responsibility.

Closing the theoretical gap of "algorithmic innocence" to reality means infusing child-centred design principles into the entire technology life cycle. Law has to prioritise innocence over vulnerability: protection can never be about weakness but a statement of children's right to spaces that give them autonomy and critical thought. Governments, educators, and businesses must collaborate to make children not passive data points but co-authors of the ethical digital futures. Welcoming children as co-creators of technological morality can restore balance between human dignity and innovation and liberate them from the insidious coercion of data capitalism (Kumar & Saxena, 2022).

3. COMMERCIAL PREDATION THROUGH AI-DRIVEN ADVERTISING

AI-driven advertising has made persuasion precision engineering, ordinary marketing a type of commercial predation, disproportionately hurting children. In recent decades, advertising has only tried to entice consumers with pictures or emotions. It is now a self-improving environment fueled by algorithms tracking, profiling, and predicting individuals' reactions. Each scroll, slowdown, and click becomes fuel for training predictive models that improve subsequent targeting. AI does not merely display products; it influences feelings, wants, and choices through tailored content calibrated to psychological weaknesses. Children, having no mature cognitive defences, are particularly vulnerable because they cannot differentiate between entertainment and commercial influence (Garwood-Cross et al., 2024).

Machine-learning designs digest enormous behavioural datasets to group users based on characteristics and deduce likely responses under given conditions. These forecast profiles enable advertisers to choreograph emotional hooks that increase interest and affinity. Young users are rewarded for attention through gamified "loops," badges, and virtual rewards that build dependence. The mathematics of these platforms approximates behavioural conditioning: reward is intermittent, unpredictable, and therefore addictive. Mainstream entertainment, cinema, and vlogs now place ads directly into storylines, blurring the line between play and purchase. Commercial enticement becomes indistinguishable from cultural participation as fusion forms populate online childhood.

Algorithmic predation acts secretly. It does not intrude but reconfigures self-image and want. Continuous reinforcement with tailored messages builds an identity made up of consumption. Market values such as beauty, popularity, and achievement become children's learned moral virtues, continually undermining autonomy. Since such manipulation is quiet, it leaves no classical proof of damage. As invisible tracks on wet sand, every touch dissolves in isolation but collects into indelible behaviour patterns. This insidious influence is symptomatic of what scholars call "algorithmic governance," where power is exercised by code, not coercion (Zuboff, 2019).

India's current regulatory environment only partially captures these harms. The DPDP, 2023, bans personalised adverts to children, but procedural enforcement and algorithmic-audit obligations are lacking. Similarly, the Consumer Protection Act 2019 and CCPA Guidelines on Misleading Advertisements (2022) ban deceptive adverts but were created before live behavioural monitoring. Neither piece of legislation directly addresses emotional profiling or neuro-marketing. The POCSO,2012, focuses on pictorial representation and sexual exploitation. However, its broad philosophy of safeguarding children from exploitation through manipulation and trust abuse provides interpretive guidance for the identification of non-physical, data-based exploitation.

Compared to this, the European Union jurisdictions have developed stronger safeguards. Targeted advertising based on children's data is prohibited under the Digital Services Act (2022), whereas GDPR enshrines the principles of data minimisation and transparency. These regimes demonstrate that algorithmic accountability is achievable when regulators view manipulative profiling as a rights violation rather than a consumer-choice issue. The path for India has to be that of this rights paradigm, wherein cognitive and emotional integrity are part of the constitutional right to dignity under K.S. Puttaswamy v. Union of India (2017).

Corporations, in turn, need to take up ethical-by-design practices. Responsible advertising entails transparency in data use, targeting limits on behaviour, and independent audits of algorithmic systems. Standards for age-appropriate design should protect AI-driven interfaces from promoting compulsion instead of learning and well-being. Public policy must go beyond privacy to safeguard psychological liberty, i.e. freedom from indirect manipulation. Schools and parents can supplement but not substitute systemic protections. Commercial predation will only be stopped by statutory duties of care that check profit motives.

Understanding algorithmic advertising as structural exploitation shifts the focus from a marketplace strategy to a human-rights issue. Childhood should never be used as raw material for predictive analytics. Societies that prize innovation must also ensure technology develops within moral boundaries that respect vulnerability, trust, and dignity. Therefore, policy reform in India should require algorithmic-impact assessments, prohibit behavioural advertising to children, and label manipulative profiling as an unfair trade practice. Only when law regards cognitive and emotional autonomy with the same gravity as physical safety can digital commerce exist alongside justice.

4. LEGAL FRAMEWORK UNDER POCSO AND ALLIED STATUTES

POCSO is still India's most inclusive law in dealing with the sexual abuse and exploitation of children. Its provisions protect children under the age of eighteen from physical, mental, and visual injuries, while also requiring procedural confidentiality to maintain their dignity. As technology more and more intermediates the lives of children, the question of significance is whether POCSO's interpretive horizon can be extended beyond corporeal or representational violence to include algorithmic exploitation and affective manipulation in cyberspace. The ever-faster pace of technological progress underpinned by artificial intelligence, data analytics, and immersive advertising has more or less redefined itself in its own terms, that is, the very notion of "harm" and "exploitation" (Young, 2022).

Ad ecosystems with AI capacities now routinely collect, scrutinise, and profit from kids' personal data with minimal or no overt consent. Such actions put young users at risk of being exposed to exploitative psychological strategies that control their wishes, convictions, and actions. The invasive, seductive algorithmic targeting breaks down the difference between voluntary engagement and coerced conditioning. While POCSO has not yet been tested judicially in the context of algorithmic advertising, the overall intent of the Act to safeguard children from all manner of exploitation requires serious consideration of its possible applicability in the online context. In Section 2(1)(d), "exploitation" is defined very broadly as the utilisation of a child for personal or commercial purposes. Thus, a purposive reading of the provision can be extended to cases of commodification of a child's mental state, whether cognitive or emotional, for financial gains.

The nippiness of the Act, however, has its origin in history. Passed when the penetration of the internet in India was in its nascent stages, POCSO was primarily drafted to deal with offences of physical contact, online grooming, and pornographic representation of children. It assumes numerically measurable abusers and particular patterns of abuse, so it is ill-suited for algorithmic systems where harm is diffuse and intent is assigned to automated decision-making processes. Probabilistic results are produced by machine learning algorithms in order to maximise participation and not out of malicious intention, a reality which renders mens rea, a central element for criminal liability, difficult to prove (Mhavan & Singh, 2026). Therefore, the theoretical and architectural gap between human agency and computational design erodes the traditional dogmas of causation and culpability.

This evolving reality speaks to the need to apprehend POCSO in a reconciliatory manner with newer legislations such as the DPDP, 2023 and the Consumer Protection Act, 2019, which address the interconnected issues of data privacy, web security, and false advertisement. Read together with one another, these laws can form a practical and multi-faceted regulatory framework that recognises emotional and informational harm as genuine exploitation. Additionally, by finding strength in the constitutional premise of POCSO under the protection of dignity of Article 21 of the Constitution, courts can extend the scope of their comprehension to protect children against algorithmic manipulation and behavioural exploitation. Although POCSO cannot encompass the intricate dynamics of influence through AI, its ethical and protective worldview offers a necessary middle ground among the conventional understandings of abuse and the contemporary realities of virtual predation.

4.1 Overview of the POCSO Act and its interpretive boundaries

The Information Technology Act of 2000 and its guidelines are the key laws that control data in India. It changes the Online Predators statute and makes it illegal to publish or send out content that shows a kid doing a sexual act, genuine or false, under Section 67B. Like POCSO, the IT Act has constraints regarding algorithmic advertising and less evident psychological manipulation. It offers authorities the tools to look at and remove online material. However, it does not address the hidden aspects of data collecting, customisation, and behaviour prediction that lead to AI-enabled forms of exploitation. POCSO is one of several rules that work together to keep kids safe online (Ananny, 2023). The DPDP of 2023 intends to bring data governance up to date by adding permission methods and stronger safeguards for children's data. However, there is still some debate about how kid consent works in a world where machines generate inferred data (such as emotional tone of replies or behavioural patterns) without anybody doing anything.

The individuals informed us that the Consumer Protection Act (CPA) 2019 stops individuals from being tricked by marketing and unethical business practices. CPA can govern how ads are shown to keep fragile customers, including youngsters, safe. However, in a world where AI is employed to improve advertisements, it is hard to locate things and keep track of them. The algorithm's knowledge of people's thoughts may make an ad that one person does not think twice about look deceptive and manipulative to someone else. If algorithm-mediated influence led customers to lose money, the CPA's provisions against deceptive advertising might be utilised to deal with providers' improper branding. However, the existing legislation makes it hard to prove that an algorithmic intermediary utilised emotional manipulation.

Two foreign models, in addition to Indian regulations, provide helpful comparisons. The GDPR of the European Union provides requirements for how to keep children's data safe. "Data minimisation," "transparency," and "the best interest of the child" are the main ideas behind these regulations (Garlen & Hembruff, S2021). When processing personal data regarding minors, Article 8 of the GDPR specifies that parental permission must be able to be checked. This implies that internet service providers need to improve their defences. The UNCRC also safeguards a child's right to privacy, respect, and not being taken advantage of financially. The Committee on the Rights of the Child's General Comment No. 25 (2021) adds to this by stating that internet manipulation and data exploitation are new concerns over time. India may leverage these improvements worldwide to help it look at legislation like POCSO and DPDP again. This will help the country build a legal system that is fit for the future and meets international standards.

4.2 Interface with Information Technology and Consumer Protection laws: Gaps in defining algorithmic predation as child exploitation

India requires structural changes, integrating child rights, technology accountability, and digital ethics into a cohesive legal system. The legislative system currently available in the form of the POCSO, the Information Technology Act, 2000, and the CPA, 2019, provides ad hoc protection that does not recognise algorithmic manipulation as a separate form of exploitation. The judiciary could fill the lacuna by giving a purposive interpretation to Sections 2 and 3 of POCSO so that exploitation would include digital manipulation that does not necessarily have to be physical but has to be coercive in its psychological effect. Such an expansion of interpretation would align with the constitutional vision of safeguarding children's mental integrity and autonomy.

Judicial reliance on Article 21 of the Indian Constitution, guaranteeing the right to life and freedom, can provide a normative ground to limit technological intrusions causing psychological or emotional upset (Rosen et al., 2021). Recognition of informational privacy as a constitutional right in Justice K.S. Puttaswamy v. Union of India (2017) also strengthens the constitutional safeguard through locating data autonomy within the ambit of human dignity. Extension of this principle to children also shows respect for their right to be free from exploitative profiling, tracking, and conditioning of their actions through AI-powered systems.

Corporate accountability lies at the core of this strategy. Organisations employing predictive algorithms for targeting children must be legally obligated to ensure algorithmic transparency, audit trails, and regular impact studies. Mechanisms allow for the traceability of decision-making and reduce the obscurity of algorithmic work. Information Technology (Intermediary Guidelines and Digital Media Ethics Code) Rules, 2021 already place limited obligations on intermediaries regarding harmful content. However, they cannot cover the more subtle damages of data-driven marketing and emotional manipulation. Adding child-specific algorithmic compliance standards would strengthen these regulations regarding the scope of protection.

Institutional reform is also a necessity. The Ministry of Women and Child Development can create a Digital Child Protection Authority with legislative authority to formulate sector-wise codes of conduct, compliance audits, and study the ethical design of child-centric technology. There would be a need for cooperation among the Ministry of Electronics and Information Technology (MeitY), the National Commission for Protection of Child Rights (NCPCR), and civil society to introduce effective regulation. These organisations can cooperate and ensure public and private digital infrastructure functions based on transparency, accountability, and child-friendliness. Hence, reinterpretation of POCSO and associated laws would have to shift from punitive vengeance to preventive measures.

In the digital era, child protection has to go beyond protecting children from apparent content or contact-based crime. It must protect children from algorithmic structures that legitimise coercion and annihilate autonomy. A new definition of exploitation has to include the necessity of algorithmic accountability, informed consent, and psychological integrity in the law. This will guarantee that the law safeguards not just the child's physical body but also intellectual and emotional autonomy that is childhood in the first place. Recognising digital manipulation as a form of exploitation would fulfil India's moral and legal duty to provide its youngest citizens' dignity and developmental agency in the age of data.

5. DIGITAL RIGHTS AND THE ETHICS OF CHILD DATA PROTECTION

Digital rights include rights and protections that govern how people interact with technology and how their information is gathered, processed, and safeguarded. When applied to children, these rights protect privacy, security, and independence in digital environments. Technology penetrates all aspects of children's lives to a greater extent, including education, play, communication, and socialisation. Insurmountable amounts of behavioural and cognitive data are continuously captured and interrogated. Ethical data protection thus goes beyond privacy to encompass moral concerns regarding exposing children to profit-oriented digital worlds and surveillance systems that market their experiences (Yahaya & Sokatsha, 2025).

The right to privacy, both online and offline, is fundamental to the right to dignity. However, in this age of participatory technology, children's susceptibility is also heightened. They are of value as consumers and information sources, but not as much as autonomous decision-makers who can consent to sophisticated data deals. The same algorithms purporting to personalise their lives consequently subject them to manipulation and profiling.

5.1 Children is right to privacy and autonomy in cyberspace

India has moved significantly towards safeguarding children's digital rights by the DPDP, 2023. The Act recognises privacy as a legal right and imposes increased obligations on parties processing children's data. It enforces parental consent and forbids tracking and targeted advertising to children. However, consent regimes cannot evade insidious data mining or behaviour manipulation since much of this happens imperceptibly through algorithmic inference and emotional analytics.

AI systems increasingly rely on indirect signals like tone, eye gaze, or response time to predict user preferences and shape choices. Such underlying processes undermine traditional concepts of "informed consent," especially when the subjects are children who cannot comprehend such subtleties. Ethical data governance, thus, needs to extend beyond permission to ensure active supervision, compulsory algorithmic audits, and data-minimisation policies. Transparency regarding how kids' data is collected and utilised is central to maintaining their agency in online environments.

Subsequent regulatory initiatives must combine technical and moral protections, making firms responsible for design decisions influencing the psychological growth of children. Ethical data management mandates that algorithms be governed by autonomous monitoring, clear disclosures, and child-appropriate digital-literacy programs.

5.2 Datafication and the violation of digital dignity

The *UNCRC* and the *European Union's GDPR* reiterate that the child's best interests must inform all data decisions. The above frameworks envision data protection as a technical need and an ethical obligation to protect development and dignity. The UNCRC's *General Comment No. 25* (2021) also makes it clear that states have an obligation to ensure that digital spaces promote children's well-being rather than exploiting their vulnerabilities.

Following these global norms, Indian law could incorporate these values by having companies build technology that is safe by design for children. This encompasses the avoidance of manipulative recommendation systems, the prevention of behavioural targeting, and the encouragement of privacy-by-default ethics. There has to be collaboration between policymakers, engineers, teachers, and parents to shape an ecosystem where commercial interests are secondary to children's well-being.

Protecting children's digital dignity calls for collective responsibility. Legislator: tighten supervision; companies: instil ethical principles into system design; parents and teachers: instil resilience and awareness. Data protection is not just a matter of managing access but one of asserting the child's right to dignity, autonomy, and fair play in an increasingly algorithmic world.

6. POLICY AND JUDICIAL REINTERPRETATIONS

Effective regulation of artificial intelligence requires legislative imagination and judicial reinterpretation to ensure that the technology is in the best possible interest of children and does not take advantage of their developmental vulnerabilities for profit. The era of AI requires a legal system that can address harms beyond the material and the visible.

The POCSO was initially defined to shield children from sexual offences such as child pornography, corporal abuse, and harassment. Its legislative definition of harm, though, targets primarily seeable or measurable behaviour, and it does not place algorithmic manipulation within its express ambit. With more pervasive AI-oriented virtual reality worlds that impact kids' feelings, actions, and selection habits, "injury" would need to be broadened to encompass mental and emotional injury. This shift would bring the local jurisprudence into consonance with universal human rights standards that promote protection against exploitation, including psychological and informational abuse (Daly Weisse et al., 2021).

The notion of algorithmic innocence emphasises this discrepancy by acknowledging that the cognitive development of children continues to be malleable and open to exploitation via predictive systems. Although exploitation of this nature will never leave physical traces, it can significantly undermine the autonomy and privacy of a child. Judicial reinterpretation is thus necessary to define "sexual exploitation" under POCSO in a broader meaning, one that addresses algorithmically mediated harm that compromises psychological integrity or autonomy.

Courts may hold the targeting of children's behavioural data in order to manipulate desire and consumption as a systemic exploitation in contravention of the constitutional promise of dignity under Article 21. The precedent established in Justice K.S. Puttaswamy v. Union of India (2017) confirmed informational privacy as a constitutional right, offering a basis in the constitution for consideration of algorithmic manipulation as an invasion of mental and emotional well-being. A purposive interpretation of POCSO coupled with informational self-determination principles can allow courts to perceive algorithmic exploitation as a contemporary form of coercion, widening the protective purview of the law.

Lastly, child protection duty must be extended to the entities behind corporations that create and send AI systems designed to influence children. Making businesses answerable is a needed adaptation from individual-focused liability towards systemic responsibility. Judges need to hold corporations accountable by examining the intent, structure, and foreseen effects of algorithms they send, particularly when used to entice and generate revenue from child interaction.

6.1 Regulatory proposals for algorithmic accountability

Regulations must be renovated to allow AI developers and websites to perform in-depth child-impact studies before deploying any system that processes children's information. They must examine cognitive, emotional, and privacy hazard possibilities via algorithmic designs and user engagement. The results must be made available through government-screened transparency websites and audited by independent third-party testers to ensure that hidden or manipulative practices are not detected. Public disclosure also encourages a culture of accountability by enabling parents, teachers, and regulators to monitor corporate actions and identify exploitative processes in their early stages.

Transparency is the foundation of accountability. Companies need to be legislated to set out what kind of data is collected on children, how behaviour inferences are constructed, and for what reasons information such as this is processed or traded (George & George, 2024). These disclosures enable monitoring bodies to decide whether business procedures align with ethical data-handling standards. The European Union's Artificial Intelligence Act of 2024 is a valuable comparative framework, defining AI systems by risk profile and subjecting the most stringent controls to those the agency considers "high risk," including those directly interacting with children.

Indian policymakers can take a cue from this model by incorporating algorithmic responsibility stipulations in the DPDP, 2023 and underpinning child-protection legislations. This would involve limiting the purview of data collection such that data required for system operations is processed alone. Further, consent cannot be made dependent only on parental agreement. However, it must include constant tracking, traceable age verification, and inclusion of concepts of privacy by design in all layers of technology.

Statutory powers should be clearly vested in regulatory bodies such as the NCP-CR and the MeitY to investigate allegations of algorithmic exploitation and levy proportionate and deterrent sanctions. Offences of child safety shall have severe penalties, including monetary fines, suspension of algorithms, or blocklisting of the offenders. By doing so, India can establish a framework where the ethical design and deployment of AI systems are not merely voluntary business choices but legal and moral necessities crucial to safeguarding the dignity and agency of children online (Kou & Gui, 2023).

6.2 Corporate social responsibility

Corporate social responsibility (CSR) is today a cornerstone in ensuring artificial intelligence is a force for empowerment, not exploitation. When protecting children, CSR is not philanthropy and rule-compliance; it requires the internalisation of ethical responsibilities in the design of digital products and services. Companies that produce AI, such as education technology, entertainment systems, game apps, and targeted advertising software, play an important role in children's cognitive and affective development. With that influence, they should imbue fairness, transparency, and accountability at all levels of product design. Ethically developing AI needs systematic child rights impact assessments to determine potential harms, removing algorithmic bias from data collections, and making AI-driven decisions concerning children explainable, equitable, and non-discriminatory (Robinson et al., 2023).

A morally responsible corporation needs an independent Ethical Oversight Council composed of experts in child rights, AI governance, psychology, and civil society. These councils would be in-house regulatory bodies, responsible for scrutinising algorithms, their effect on vulnerable users, and monitoring adherence to human rights standards. Frequent publication of transparency reports detailing how children's data are collected, processed, and commodified would also internalise an ethical culture in corporate decision-making. This ensures that financial gains never exceed a company's obligation to protect its youngest consumers' psychological and developmental integrity.

However, CSR cannot remain restricted to managing risks alone. It must be created as a socially accountable purpose with stakeholder awareness and capability building. Firms must invest in digital capability development projects that safely train children, parents, and teachers to use AI-based interfaces. Such programs can enable youngsters to recognise manipulative algorithmic strategies, recognise data privacy concerns, and detect learning against influencer material. By building critical digital literacy, corporations are directly helping close the algorithmic vulnerability of children and increase their agency. Corporations must also engage governments, regulators, and world institutions to work together on harmonised ethical AI design standards.

Because digital technologies are universally needed, transnational cooperation is required to address the algorithmic harms of global complexity. Platforms should be made accountable for embracing globally endorsed standards like the UN Guiding Principles on Business and Human Rights (2011) and the OECD AI Principles (2019), prioritising transparency, accountability, and protection of vulnerable populations above all. Interagency task forces can work together and share best practices, coordinate child-protection practices, and coordinate enforcement mechanisms well in an attempt to pursue abuses (Ugwudike et al., 2024). Lastly, CSR in the era of Artificial Intelligence will be forced to reconfigure the dialectic between ethics and innovation.

Ethical responsibility should never be a hindrance to technological innovation, but its ground. Institutionalising human rights, justice, and equity in AI technology is how institutions can ensure that technology benefits children and does not commodify them. Such a revolution would prove that the right metric for technological success is not profitability but security and prosperity of future generations.

7. CONCLUSION AND RECOMMENDATIONS

Where algorithmic innocence and child rights intersect is a turning point for regulation and legislation for our times. Though the affairs mechanism in the Indian parliament so enacted by the POCSO Act, 2012 supplemented by the DPDP Act, 2023 makes provisions for widespread protection from physical as well as figurative assault, it does not go so far as to make provisions for complete acculturation of the crafty and sophistic nature of virtual abuse necessitated as a response to the advent of artificial intelligence technology. Algorithmic exploitation, behaviour profiling, and child commodification represent the most prevalent ills of child autonomy and well-being in the contemporary world. Characterising such activities as appeals to attacks on fundamental child rights, rather than regulatory failure, is a step beyond the capacity to confirm that the direction of technological progress remains to still conform to human dignity and social justice standards.

Legal reform is no superior to statute-making; it must be accompanied by vigorous enforcement, institutional responsibility, and ethical regulation. Locating the bridge between legislative purpose and good protection requires the establishment of explicit legal prohibitions against behaviour with the objective of behaviour targeting, promoted design, and engagement optimisation methods which take advantage of the cognitive vulnerabilities of the children. The NCPCR and MeitY should be given the authority to require algorithmic impact assessments and third-party audits for AI systems supplied to or used by children. They would not only be in the direction of opening up but also in the direction of intervening in manipulative design tendencies and toward creating virtual worlds, an "example of safety by design" where child protection is incorporated into the technology design.

Ethical AI must be built as a shared moral and social responsibility. Business companies as leaders of virtual communities will have to build child rights due diligence into business models and organisational practices so that the race of innovation never occurs at the expense of violating ethical norms. The judiciary, too, would be responsible for interpreting the situation so that the values of this ethos are not violated. Courts will be forced to reinterpret legislation such as POCSO and the Information Technology Act, 2000, in accordance with constitutional protections of privacy, dignity, and proportionality. The constitutional legacy engrafted by the historic ruling in *K.S. Puttaswamy v. Union of India* (2017) recognised informational privacy as an intrinsic element of the right to life under Article 21. The same principle gives birth to the jurisprudential imperative towards perceiving algorithmic exploitation as no ordinary policy issue but as a constitutional transgression against the moral conscience of the Indian state.

Such future reform initiatives need to converge between the international and the multidisciplinary. The legislators, technologists, teachers, psychologists, and child rights researchers need to get together to build models that weigh the pressure to advance technology against the well-being of children. Internationally, coordination between the UNCRC and the European Union's GDPR provides a model for setting global standards of digital protection of children. In addition, bilateral and multilateral interactions must prioritise ethical control of AI, technological transfers, and transnational accountability processes to protect children in a globalised digital world.

Finally, protecting children in the age of algorithms demands a morality shift in leadership. Children can no longer be treated as passive data subjects or consumer commodities but as human persons with inherent dignity, developing capacities, and an unalienable right to participate freely in digital worlds. Such worlds must facilitate creativity, curiosity, and autonomy without surreptitious manipulation so that the potential of technology continues to be in harmony with higher human values of justice, welfare, and compassion.

REFERENCES

Alter, A. (2017). *Irresistible: The Rise of Addictive Technology and the Business of Keeping Us Hooked.* Penguin Press.

Chawki, M. (2025). AI moderation and legal frameworks in child-centric social media: A case study of Roblox. *Laws, 14*(3), 29.

Consumer Protection Act, 2019 & CCPA Guidelines (2022). Government of India.

. European Union. (2016). *General Data Protection Regulation (GDPR).* Regulation (EU) 2016/679.

European Union. (2022). *Digital Services Act.* [EU]. *Regulation.*

. Ezeji, C. L., & Uwizeyimana, D. E. (2025). The implications of technology and innovation: A critical analysis of youth and children's activities on social media platforms. *International Journal of Business Ecosystem & Strategy (2687–2293),* 7(3), 264–277.

Feller, G., & Burroughs, B. (2022). Branding kidfluencers: Regulating content and advertising on YouTube. *Television & New Media, 23*(6), 575–592.

Garwood-Cross, L., Light, B., Cooper-Ryan, A. M., & Vasilica, C. (2024). Sex education against the algorithm: The algorithmically enforced de-platforming of YouTube sex edutainment. *Journal of Gender Studies,* •••, 1–13.

. George, A. S., & George, A. H. (2024). Towards a super smart society 5.0: Opportunities and challenges of integrating emerging technologies for social innovation. *Partners Universal International Research Journal,* 3(2), 01–29.

Government of India. (2021). *Information Technology (Intermediary Guidelines and Digital Media Ethics Code) Rules, 2021.* Ministry of Electronics and Information Technology.

Government of India. (2023). *Digital Personal Data Protection Act, 2023.* Ministry of Electronics and Information Technology.

K.S. Puttaswamy v. Union of India, (2017) 10 SCC 1.

Kumar, S., & Saxena, G. (2022). Child online pornography: Criminal methods and investigation. In *Research Anthology on Child and Domestic Abuse and Its Prevention* (pp. 639–660). IGI Global Scientific Publishing.

Livingstone, S., & Stoilova, M. (2021). The datafication of childhood: Privacy risks, regulation and children's rights. *New Media & Society, 23*(8), 2434–2451.

Luria, E., Cohen, R., & Ben-David, S. (2022). Digital reward systems and child attention development: A review of cognitive risks. *Journal of Child Psychology and Technology*, *14*(2), 115–132.

McAlinden, A. M. (2022). Reconceptualising 'risk': Towards a humanistic paradigm of sexual offending. *Social & Legal Studies*, *31*(3), 389–408.

Montgomery, K. C., & Chester, J. (2019). Data protection for children and adolescents: Challenges of big data and artificial intelligence. *Pediatric Clinics of North America*, *66*(6), 1263–1275.

Nikken, P., & Schols, M. (2015). How and why parents guide the media use of young children. *Journal of Child and Family Studies*, *24*(11), 3423–3435. PMID: 26472932

Noble, S. U. (2018). *Algorithms of Oppression: How Search Engines Reinforce Racism*. NYU Press.

O'Neill, C., Selwyn, N., Smith, G., Andrejevic, M., & Gu, X. (2022). The two faces of the child in facial recognition industry discourse: Biometric capture between innocence and recalcitrance. *Information Communication and Society*, *25*(6), 752–767.

Rosen, E., Garboden, P. M., & Cossyleon, J. E. (2021). Racial discrimination in housing: How landlords use algorithms and home visits to screen tenants. *American Sociological Review*, *86*(5), 787–822.

Sharifi Poor Bgheshmi, M. S., Sharajsharifi, M., & Saeidabadi, M. R. (2025). Between exploitation and resilience: Reconciling AI's role in surveillance capitalism and disaster risk management. *Journal of Cyberspace Studies,* 1–31.

Tarvin, E., & Stanfill, M. (2022). "YouTube's predator problem": Platform moderation as governance-washing and user resistance. *Convergence*, *28*(3), 822–837.

Ugwudike, P., Lavorgna, A., & Tartari, M. (2024). Sharenting in digital society: Exploring the prospects of an emerging moral panic. *Deviant Behavior*, *45*(4), 503–520.

. United Nations Committee on the Rights of the Child. (2021). *General Comment No. 25 on Children's Rights in Relation to the Digital Environment.* CRC/C/GC/25.

Urbas, G. (2021). Legal considerations in the use of artificial intelligence in the investigation of online child exploitation. *ANU College of Law Research Paper,* (21.44).

Yahaya, M. S., & Sokatsha, Z. (2025). Feminist artificial intelligence (AI) approaches for civic governance in Africa. In *Designing Artificial Intelligence for Public Policy and Governance in Africa* (pp. 89–101). Springer Nature Switzerland.

Zuboff, S. (2019). *The Age of Surveillance Capitalism*. PublicAffairs.

Chapter 5

Assessment of Legal Responses to Professional Displacement and Self-Doubt:

Employment Law and the AI Identity Crisis

Hemant Singh
https://orcid.org/0000-0002-1258-5187
Amity University, Gwalior, India

Gopalam Sultania
Amity Law School, Amity University, Jaipur, India

Abhishek Srivastava
Amity University, Jaipur, India

Bal Kishan
Amity School of Language, Amity University, Gwalior, India

ABSTRACT

Employment regulations are predicated on the idea that identity, sense of safety and social fit determine ability to work. Therefore, unemployed has an impact on a person's mental health, social identity, and self-esteem in addition to their financial loss. The concept of fairness is the foundation of employment law which also

DOI: 10.4018/979-8-3373-6618-0.ch005

lessens the associated societal and personal costs upon emphasizing substantive the safeguards and procedural fairness. There are provisions like social security and anti-discrimination protection, these laws not only assisted people with their practical necessities but also provided working people with a feeling of fairness and self-respect. This chapter identifies and assesses the legal provisions in professional displacement enhancing imposter syndrome and identity crisis in employment because of automation and AI in industries.

1. INTRODUCTION

The proliferation of computers and the automation of industries are only two instances of how technology has often compelled legal institutions to evolve and adapt. Every new invention wave has prompted challenging inquiries regarding the sufficiency of the existing legal protections: Who was overseeing the equitable implementation of layoffs? Who should assist folks in obtaining new employment? What new injustices are emerging as a result of technological advancements? In addition to helping courts interpret the law in ways that often broaden the scope of employment law to account for changes in the lines between work and leisure, job skills, and employer-employee relationships, the responses to these questions have resulted in modifications to the law.

In the past, a combination of regulated work protection, collective bargaining organizations, social security systems, and focused training initiatives has been used to address displacement and professional education brought on by structural and technological change. The regulations that state that non-unionized workers must get severance compensation, be retrained, be informed when they will be laid off and how long they will be out of work, and cannot be dismissed without a valid cause are all obvious examples of the UK's history of reform. Similar commitments to make dispute settlement and transitional safeguards the center of labor policy may be seen in India's Industries Disputes Act, Code on Industrial Relations, and rapidly expanding social security system.

1.1 AI-induced Workplace Displacement

However, being laid off is more than a financial issue that can be "fixed by throwing money at people." Additionally, when the job market becomes more difficult and people lose their positions one after another, they are coping with worry, self-doubt, and a loss of professional identity. Together with its long-standing emphasis on workplace rights and duties, the overdue legitimization of displacement as a phenomena that requires specific attention from employment law suggests that it ignores the fact that job change is inherently motivated by values. As a result, the traditional reactions to training, redundancy, and redeployment may make people feel even more uprooted. In fact, there are cases when this recognition has been transformed into legislative requirements pertaining to consultation, employee participation in decisions that affect them, and assistance during restructuring and layoffs. However, the flexibility of this paradigm to accommodate novel issues is crucial. Automation, digitalization, and globalization are rapidly and often unexpectedly altering the nature of labor. Despite the effectiveness of conventional labor laws, regulations and enforcement continue to lag behind in many areas, which disproportionately harms minorities and informal, insecure women workers. "These gaps are especially bad in countries with big informal economies or weak enforcement of legal protection."

1.2 Psychological Impacts as Self-doubt and Identity Threats

It establishes guidelines for working life globally and defends the rights of employees. This shift has been brought about by developments in industry, technology, and new forms of employment, as well as cultural ideals and actual shifts in the kinds of work that individuals undertake. Extreme exploitation, hazardous working conditions, and a lack of legal rights for workers are the results of the contradictions that have existed since the dawn of capitalism. Because of this, they were forced to begin their early battles as members of powerful labor movements that also included social activity. The foundation of employment law included the Factories Act 1833, early factory legislation, minimum wage regulations, and the Workmen's Compensation Act 1906 (UK).

Like in other postcolonial economies, colonial administration and the development of both domestic and international labor policy are closely related to the beginnings of labor and employment regulation in India. The Payment of Wages Act of 1936 and the arbitration system were two significant events that occurred under British rule and influenced Indian labor law. These events had a significant impact on the development of legislation after independence. Important legislation that have established regulations that attempt to integrate social security and industrial relations to take into consideration how employment has evolved over time for Indian workers include the Employees State Insurance Act, the Maternity Benefit Act, and the Payment of Gratuity Act. According to the regulations, workers are entitled to reasonable compensation and social security, even if they are forced to retrain after losing their positions.

2. PSYCHOLOGICAL AND SOCIAL DIMENSIONS OF AI DISPLACEMENT

The near breakneck speed of automation and artificial intelligence (AI) in the workplace is a change that creates substantial psychological and social implications. That you're the person that tech wasn't designed to help." The structural and economic consequences of losing a job to AI are well-trod, but there's also an inward-looking sense of always being told that you're not one of the people tech was built to help. "But AI substitution is not just about losing your job and it's not just losing the money, it's also dealing with all of those difficult emotions like loneliness, self-doubt, ongoing anxiety and the mourning for what they once were as a professional." (Craft, 2025). This psychological characteristic is how individuals interpret and manage displacement, as well as how it impacts the victim's well-being and the overall culture of the company.

The aforementioned findings are supported by research on AI and job displacement in a variety of situations, including the Indian IT industry. The authors provide examples of people in the actual world going through emotional pain when AI makes them obsolete in their jobs. For a lot of individuals, their identity, sense of belonging, and self-worth are greatly influenced by their activities. Therefore, yesterday's slaughter was an assault on their whole lives, not simply their employment. Anxiety about the future that is more difficult to get rid of than an anthrax threat is anticipatory rumination, a kind of never-ending mental practice for a play in which no one wants to be the lead. It often appears when there is even the smallest indication of movement. When employees believe that their organizations' professional support systems failed them or that they weren't prepared for technological advancements, these feelings worsen.

When it comes to AI-induced job loss, the psychological effects of occupational displacement are a major worry. A job provides you purpose, fosters connections, and increases your sense of self-worth in addition to providing a means of earning money. Employees are also uncertain because they believe they have less influence over their own abilities and prospects and that job designations are becoming less significant. Social settings are typically avoided by persons who are losing their sense of self because they feel embarrassed and believe they shouldn't be among other people. It is more difficult for them to acquire the support and assistance they need because of that social link. In addition to making it more difficult to use proactive coping mechanisms like seeking assistance and picking up new skills, loneliness exacerbates emotional suffering.

2.1 AI Displacement and Worker Well-being: Concerns for Professional Identity Erosion and Mental Healthcare

Displaced persons experience social disengagement as a result of this identity loss because they are humiliated or embarrassed, which further reduces their likelihood of interacting with others and seeking assistance. Social separation makes psychological suffering worse and prevents adaptive coping strategies like retraining or asking for help.

The fundamental lapse in AI always results in a serious betrayal of the company. Workers may believe that their employers' automation demonstrates that profit and efficiency are more important than human capital and loyalty. They would become even less engaged in the firm and less trustworthy of their leaders as a result. Anxieties at work may worsen as a consequence of this breach of the psychological contract (see Rousseau, 1995), which is the unwritten agreement between an employer and employee. It may lead to low morale, heightened cynicism, and disengagement at work.

A theoretical foundation for comprehending these psychological impacts could be offered by the Conservation of Resources (COR) hypothesis. People feel intimidated when they believe that their employment, professional standing, abilities, or social safety nets are under jeopardy. The loss of AI displacement is a loss on many levels, including material securities and theoretical and future-focused identities. When these vital supplies are depleted, people experience stress, which may alter their emotions and thoughts. For example, individuals may be concerned about losing their employment, losing their freedom, or not understanding how to locate a new career or acquire new skills. The psychological aspects of AI replacement specialists Losing one's professional identity was the core concept of AI displacement. Social separation makes psychological suffering worse and prevents adaptive coping strategies like retraining or asking for help.

2.2 Social Stigma and Workplace Culture Shifts

Humans have responded to automation in a variety of ways. Handling demonstrations Employees who take proactive measures to address issues, such as pursuing further education, networking, and applying for lateral career transfers. Some individuals use harmful coping mechanisms to cope with stress, such as abusing drugs or alcohol, losing their emotional energy, or avoiding social settings. The distinct traits of leaders, company culture, support systems, and public perceptions of displaced workers all have an impact on the range of coping mechanisms. Career counseling, vocational training, and psychological counseling interventions have been shown to be mitigating variables for these negative consequences; nevertheless, their availability varies and is often combined with displacement policies.

Significantly influencing the psychological and social effects of forced relocation are culturally driven elements. In many cultures, especially in fast-developing countries, there is a strong association between a person's identity and their social standing, prospects for success, or family respect (family name). This exacerbates the mental toll of leaving a position. When you feel like that, it's hard to find a new job or make a career change. It breaks down even more family and community relationships because nobody trusts, bringing a feeling of despair and uselessness.

The effect of AI at a societal level Use of AI has potential to impact all people as opposed to single persons. Businesses and communities are affected. More stressful still and with added fuel thrown on the fire, at a time of transition in particular stress can make the work environment feel untrustworthy and scary which cripples motivation and team productivity. More broadly, overdisplacement, when it occurs without emotional shoring up, can be bad for societal bonds and norms. Externally, it doesn't stack up to the morality of tech progress and who benefits.

A holistic strategy which incorporates policy and legal actions along with healing treatments is required to manage the social and psychological effects of AI loss. Laws and practices governing employment should take a more active interest in the place of identity and mental health at times of change. Reputations evolve over decades. And the more shame they feel, the higher is their probability of hiding in public. This is why legislating is crucial. For which could be training businesses to retrain employees, for mental health therapy, and for treats of all kinds in order to engage business employees who they have been laying off with fair procedures. The trick for Webber will be worker participation in that process and the communication that's open and honest. And as the industry marches on toward automation, he says, workers should be treated decently. Discussing your mental health, and how others can relate to you if they change jobs temporarily is fine.

3. EXISTING GLOBAL LEGAL FRAMEWORKS ADDRESSING AI-DRIVEN DISPLACEMENT

For instance, international standards for acceptable employment are established by the agreements of the International Labour Organization (ILO). These consist of social support, equitable compensation, job stability, and workplace health and safety. These brief regulations provide additional rights to those who lose their employment to new technology, but they make no mention of AI-related job losses. Although fundamental labor rights still exist, they must be clarified and extended in order to be ready for the changes that artificial intelligence will bring about.

The European Union, for instance, has established a sophisticated structure that incorporates new AI regulations as well as standard labor laws. Algorithmic transparency and data rights as the right to personal data and algorithmic transparency are discussed in the EU's General Data Protection Regulation (GDPR). ADES is indirectly impacted by this. However, the European Commission is dedicated to advancing AI that respects fundamental rights, including workers' rights, as seen by its White Paper on AI and its larger Digital Strategy. These sorts of developments are supported by policies that promote lifelong learning and social discourse in institutions for handling the changes brought about by the use of AI.

The legal reaction to AI displacement in the US is more dispersed and is derived from a combination of state and federal labor regulations as well as ongoing case law. Two examples of regulations that may assist individuals in addressing some of the financial issues that accompany losing a job are the Equal Employment Opportunity Commission's (EEOC) non-discrimination rules and the National Labor Relations Act (NLRA). However, the government mostly responds to AI-related job losses via regulations and litigation that only apply to certain businesses since there is no federal legislation that addresses this issue directly. Policy discussion centers on whether to provide unemployment benefits, promote retraining programs for new jobs, and ensure AI is transparent about its work.

Public-private partnerships and digital skills initiatives are in place to support people who have lost their employment due to automation. Broad legal change is still in its infancy, however. Emerging economies will encounter many challenges and opportunities when establishing regulations for AI disruption. The regulatory framework's coverage and enforcement are poor in nations like South Africa, Brazil, and India where there are sizable informal sectors in addition to official employment (Prabhakar et al., 2025).

Multilateral procedures and international bodies might aid in establishing international norms and encouraging collaboration on AI displacement. Additionally, they advise member states to prepare for the potential for layoffs and to provide all assistance they can to those who lose their employment. Even though they lack legal authority, these international agreements promote communication between governments, corporations, and employees and establish the norm for how change might occur in a nation.

4. EMPLOYMENT LAW MECHANISMS TO PROTECT PROFESSIONAL IDENTITY

Given the upheaval caused by AI and the speed at which things may change for workers, these safeguards for our professional identities are still crucial today. A person's professional identity is not defined by their actions. It concerns their role, position, and status inside and outside of their field. He said, "Automation and artificial intelligence are changing jobs and industries very quickly." "Unless the legislation assists workers in coping with the resulting financial, psychological, and social losses, people will be trapped when the changes take place.

The legislation need to assist such workers with their financial difficulties as well as their mental and social health concerns. Their employers shouldn't be responsible for protecting them from doxing. Numerous legislative safeguards that cover both monetary and intangible aspects of professional life that advance both individual and group well-being are required by this criterion. We might take the first step toward preventing arbitrary terminations and provide rights to those who are no longer employed so they may maintain their professional identities. The goal of employment law is to make sure that companies have valid grounds for terminating employees whose technology has become obsolete or who have no job to accomplish. Additionally, it mandates that companies adhere to equitable practices and first engage in meaningful discussions or negotiations with employees.

These structural protections give workers confidence that they will be treated fairly and with dignity. They also give workers a sense of identity because of who they are, what they do to the business and even when their job is finished. The only advantage of rules about how you get rid of people is that they take away dignity from workers, and somehow minimize the blow by letting them talk about their options like finding a new career or perhaps even getting shifted to a different job. Antidiscrimination statutes are also an important means of protecting one's professional identity. This is especially applicable when technology has injured some while benefiting others.

We need laws like this so that we can erase racism, ableism, ageism, sexism and the type of default that has gotten us into our current financial problems. They also reduce the incidence of displacement due to automation but not by increasing existing disparities or through exclusion of certain populations. Some of these sites mandate that companies offer equivalent retraining options for all employees, make accommodations for employees with disabilities, and also ensure algorithmic decision-making around termination is not biased. It will make for a safer overall working environment for any number of occupations, and it'll be more welcoming.

4.1 Anti-discrimination and Fair Treatment Principles

Together with governments and corporations, trade unions and worker representatives create policies that safeguard employment, retrain people, provide a fair transition for workers, and include worker input into decision-making processes. Guidelines and actions to take There are often guidelines for being transparent and courteous at work as well as how to handle being transferred in collective agreements. This cooperative method acknowledges that identity is relational and that members' level of identification with their coworkers has a big impact on how well the workplace community functions (Al-Hadrawi et al., 2024). By including workers in discussions on job cuts and the introduction of new technologies, group procedures safeguard the common professional culture and unity.

4.2 Retraining and Reskilling Obligations

Workers' rights are equal parts counter-servant and real estate agent when automation technologies are used. As previously stated, a comprehensive collection of machine control data by consensus eliminated the need for a human administrator. Some individuals may believe that with production systems that extensively depend on technology, this is an inevitable result.

People may trust one another when a sensitive individual and gifted writer are shown to be a fantastic source. If Jean Dehms had been born fifty years earlier or had written this book seven years later, how would the laudations that Saint Beuve bestowed upon this work, which his friend so correctly admired, have changed? This finish highlights that the worker is a person first and not only a collection of raw resources, highlighting how special they are in this circumstance. According to this theory, certain very costly computer systems, such as key server networks used in significant military operations, could not be usable at all. Stricter labor regulations apply to businesses that utilize biometrics and gather algorithmic data about their employees. Additionally, using personal data to determine employment practices is a better practice that complies with several regulations established by governmental bodies as well as nonprofit organizations such as the High-Tech Crime Prevention Working Group (HTCPWG). Uses of this data that are ethically sound shield workers' personal histories and hard-won work identities from being too scrutinized or profiled. However, preserving personal information gives them a professional backbone: young people are once again erecting billboards (or online businesses) similar to those formerly occupied by entrepreneurs who want to offer their knowledge resources. If European regulations such as the GDPR are implemented, they may also support workers' rights and fairness in the face of automation and artificial intelligence in the workplace. They mandate that automated decision systems provide a sound statistical justification for their decisions and rigorously restrict any random algorithmic biases.

4.3 Protections against Unfair Dismissal Linked to Automation

Employment law's mental health regulations encourage or even mandate companies to provide therapy, listen to employees' concerns, and assist colleagues in coping with anxiety brought on by job insecurity and identity threats. By helping displaced persons understand that their health is also their job, these legal instruments assist them manage their emotions. People came to understand that work encompasses the whole person thanks to required employee support responsibilities and mental health accommodations. Maintaining professional identity is significantly impacted by psychological assistance and well-being measures, which are the most current in employment law systems.

The terminology used in employment law and professional identity It is more varied in the AI era. Standards for human-robot communication (also called "communication human-robot"), teleworker protections, psychological counseling, fair use data agreements, reskilling provisions, global representation mechanisms that ensure these groups can collaborate, and rights to broadband are all included in addition to nondiscrimination and fairness procedures.

5. REGULATORY APPROACHES MITIGATING ANXIETY AND SELF-DOUBT

Regulations that mitigate the stress and self-doubt induced by job displacement owing to AI should serve as part of policy-level interventions whose objective is to guide the workforce's transition in a way that is consistent with employee wellness. People may be anxious, mired in identity crises and job insecurity instigated by automation. This concern can be translated into the work-environment, where stressful circumstances might lead to a decrease in worker's motivation and productivity, producing negative consequences for societies. Some other percentage of time, say from 40 percent to 80 percent (someone), may be where people are navigating life in a world of high technology designed by humans for the welfare and pleasure of humans but also trying to manage their own mental health.

The one that counts is the pro-automation, pro-human job transition one. The purpose of these policies is not to promote automation or to eliminate jobs. Rather, they hope to transform work so that AI systems can perform more and there is still plenty for people to do. The first is a process of task redesign that allows computers to undertake repetitive, routine tasks, freeing up people to do more advanced work where the demands are for aspects like analysis, creativity, or social interaction. It also gives workers a sense of mastery and a sense of contributing purposefully, important aspects of their professional selves. It allows people to view automation not as a threat that would obliterate all jobs, but as an opportunity for growth and learning (Briciu et al., 2025). This implies that we no longer need to think that the only way to feel secure in this world is to have a job.

Companies must ensure that their workplace is safe for their workers' mental health in addition to just following the law. Although enacting legislation on these subjects may be challenging, regulations might motivate companies to provide feedback, communication, and healthy coping mechanisms for workplace anxieties. Encourage companies to carry out audits or assessments of the social effects of automation in order to instill a habit of care and identify potential concerns early. Laying out policies on staff representation on AI club committees will also help in breaking down taboo about emotional and identity issues.

Public-private-partnerships are increasingly seen as a useful tool to support integrated approaches that – with out-of-the-box thinking and even regulation – can make sure people are living well in their communities. Governments, corporations, local schools and labor unions all sponsor transition programs offering mental health services and employment placement. In loosening up regulations and turning them into something that reflects real working life, these alliances could also help to avoid a lot of false starts and make sure human-centered policies for automation grow smoothly across industries. The regulatory approach should allow for quick changes in both alternative work practices and AI technology as in all things. It would also be supportive to enact provisions that required annual re-evaluations of those who are pushed out by have stakeholder meetings. Through using anticipatory governance tools like impact assessments and foresight exercises but ones that examine how things will affect 'the life of workers' it is not only possible to look ahead in this very second to tragic results but also in the same breath find workable responses.

Preventive Directive respectful of citizen and that implies inclusion, protection and support is simply a must-have for the society at large and also to avoid fear & self-doubt concerning AI-connected job-lost. These systems seek to convert fear into resilience, and they do so by reorganizing work in ways that put people first; making automation policy accessible for all and transparent; ensuring robust training and safety nets for workers; fostering psychological safety. Such a well-rounded plan acknowledges that we both have to capitalize on the good technology has delivered and are responsible for ensuring our employees' mental and professional welfare as they work in an era where events are moving at an unprecedented pace.

6. CASE STUDIES ON LEGAL RESPONSES TO AI WORKPLACE DISPLACEMENT

Europe is an extensively covered field of investigation as it hosts a well-formed legal and social regulation of work loss within an increasingly digitalising scope. Counter-checks are also solidly embedded in the European Social Model and supported by legislation on collective redundancy, works councils and information/ consultation rights. Member states have rules that obligate companies to inform about large layoffs in advance, and consult with employees' representatives. The goal is to get workers on and engaged in the change, not simply watching automation happen (Palimaru et al., 2025).

Germany is particularly instructive in this respect due to its codetermination and industry-level bargaining, but could also serve as the basis for a conversation on AI adoption, training, retraining and job redesign that happens with individuals rather than at them. This is what a law-backed consortium of technology design and social responsibility would look like. The more fragmented structure of labor relations in the US has a third, and evolving legal response. While racial and other such wrongful termination are illegal under the law, there is no specific federal law that addresses AI-induced displacement. Instead, solutions have been sectoral and local, often through public-private partnerships that are worked on by workforce development types. The Workforce Innovation and Opportunity Act (WIOA) is just one of the many programs that offers funding to help workers gain new skills they need, but will likely lose as a result of technological change. Such programs are offered by the vendors, vocational schools as well as community colleges.

Some governments, including Massachusetts' have tried to employ AI advisory panels to propose legislation that would benefit workers, possibly even by loosening the ability of AI technology to be used in law. While the rules are less restrictive than in Europe, innovation happens where workers are trained, labor standards enforced and workers' groups push for more input on A.I. governance" (Doring et al., 2024).

Under the law, employers must also offer comprehensive retraining programs and unlike many other workers, they must provide fair severance payments and redeems to workers who have been sacked. South Korean legislation promoting an enterprise's CSR (Corporate Social Responsibility) focusing on the welfare of employees in the era of technological change underscores self-identity and mental health protection. Some model of joint responsibil- ity for dealing with change that meets the needs of a legal system attuned to implications of AI could be developed through cooperation among business, government and labor.

The new-fangled lawsuit that melds federal and provincial labour codes to features of the changing algorithms of work is Canada. The Ontario's AI Task Force has called for laws that make businesses tell whether their decisions about employment such as hiring, firing, and promoting are by the use of AI. It is still unclear whether more far-reaching protections which applied to all AI tools were needed, he said: 'Is that an overkill? Workers and others have few ways of verifying algorithmic selections. (yet continuing active labour market policies involve substantial public spending on lifelong learning and digital literacy (Chybis et al., 2025). Such is only possible courtesy of laws that made education for displaced workers a great deal easier. Canada's multi-level constitution offers important lessons on how to balance the introduction of algorithmic accountability with creaky labour law (Block, 2024). It see happening is that the legal obligations or requirements that governments are subject to or find themselves in collision between mental health needs on one hand and the other side transparency and equity. At the same time, this policy-making process is increasingly informed by psychological and identity issues rather than security considerations (Uche et al., 2025).

These case studies also underscore a larger set of concerns such as disparate protections in the informal or precarious economy, the rate at which technology is changing labor markets compared to how fast laws are being updated and enforced, and the challenge of implementing new rules within an international multi-industry economic context. Secondly, the role of social dialogue and collective negotiation also constitute a counterbalance in determining to what extent workers are able to oppose or shape the consequences of relocation.

The legal response to displacement of workers: affected by AI-mobility is diverse and context-dependent, mixing old labor (youth) protection with innovative regulation. "These collective experiences may give rise to full employment legislations that protect worker dignity, economic security and professional identity while being future-proof i.e., prescient of technology pushes out rather than reactive," he added. Future AI regulation in employment law aims to have a supporting role of proactive, inclusive and responsive systems which balance human welfare interests with that of justice as an instrument of technological progress (Muzingili, 2025).

7. POLICY RECOMMENDATIONS AND FUTURE LEGAL DIRECTIONS

AI is changing the nature of work, and employers, labor organizations and lawmakers alike have pushed that employment laws be updated for the AI age. The labor laws that would be needed to address AI-induced displacement, algorithmic bias and the changing nature of job relationships could not even have been written a long time ago when labor laws were in fact composed because it was before the digital explosion and decision making based on algorithms they had no knowledge of. This needs to change the rules so that AI promotes innovation and agility in the labor market while respecting workers rights, responsibility, transparency and justice making employment law work better for workers in the AI age (Moretti & Pronzato, 2024).

Legal reform, furthermore, could address some of AI's challenges for hiring decisions. Because of biased data and defective algorithms, AI systems can unintentionally perpetuate bias presenting serious moral and legal concerns. There may also be rules directly against algorithmic discrimination. These could include having companies monitor, track and verify an AI system that they use in hiring, promotion or even performance reviews and layoffs or at least keep an eye on the model's decisions. They might even mandate that companies reveal when and why they are using AI to make hiring decisions. They might for instance stipulate that companies have to let staff know when hiring decisions are made by AI It also diminishes hidden biases and promotes procedural justice, thereby preserving employees' professional identity and trust (Ayhan & Colpitts-Elliott, 2025).

The longest notice periods, a severance pay contingent on how hard an individual and the country are find parting with work, the duty to inform workers in a timely way: those were among ways proposed instead. To effectively protect mental health, employment law also needs to recognise the suffering that workers can feel when they are made redundant or face an identity crisis in response to AI adoption. For example, programs that focus on workplace wellness and stress management and provide mental health counseling must be supported by employers.

There needs to be a coming together of countries and tweaking of the labour laws regarding AI workforce for the betterment. As AI is beyond any nation and a transnational corporation exists, workers need to cooperate with each other to set up the global labor standards and get through a common understanding of worker's rights. Civil society is one of the stakeholders that have worked with global institutions such as the ILO and OECD to develop guidelines and promote best practices to guarantee that AI benefits do not breach workers' rights around the world. It is the balanced approach that encourages innovation and protects workers (Muir, 2025). This involves imagining new legal frameworks through the form of economic mechanisms like "robot taxes" to fund social security payments for unemployed workers, flexible benefits not based on employer contributions and agile rules around labor which can change with each new technology rollout.

7.1 Enhancing Employment Law for AI-era Challenges

Any new labor law of a progressive character should provide the right to skill development and retraining as a constitutive right. Laws are needed that ensure workers have access to lifelong learning as artificial intelligence remakes the workplace both through government programs and already being baked into their employment. Moreover, a policy framework would enable dislocated workers to attend their retraining through vouchers and encourage businesses to provide flexible working hours for reskilling while protecting them from the downside risks of career change. These are rights of empowerment, not protection, for those burdened by labor trammels. It also recognises that AI driven economies must be resilient in order to deliver ongoing employment (Nigar et al., 2025). The second part is regulating the new modes of work that AI has facilitated: remote collaboration, platform work and gig economy labour. Broadly speaking, there is simply no real legal framework or protection for this type of labor (Robinson, 2025).

8. PROMOTING SOCIALLY RESPONSIBLE AI ADOPTION IN WORKPLACES

Ensuring that AI systems are developed, deployed, trusted and governed in a manner consistent with the nation's values is one way to help allay workers' fears and ensure that the country's investment in AI works for all. Socially responsible use of AI is about more than creating it and deploying it. For companies this means that accountability, transparency, inclusiveness and ethics should be embedded in the both strategic thinking articulation to action (Karunanayakaa et al. 2025). Trust between workers, safe guarding against harm such as fear of losing jobs and supporting the cultivation of strong and fair work environments that support both technological progress and humane values, are just a few ways in which responsible AI is empowering.

AI for good cannot be achieved without clear leadership support. By incorporating responsible AI use into their general corporate strategy, leaders are sending a very strong message to the rest of the business. Leaders have to actively express the convictions which unify them, including justice and respect for human rights and the common good. This commitment is found in some regulations, regulatory bodies and investments into responsible AI efforts (Skolnick, 2025). For instance, many organizations are already creating "Offices of Responsible AI" or specialized AI ethics committees that aim to oversee the use of AI, gauge its risk and make sure it meets legal mandates and a company's own ethical standards. Workers also need to just understand that using AI responsibly is actually part of the company's mission itself rather than being a "nice-to-have" or a box on a checklist.

Socially-aware AI must also be transparent and easy to understand. Workers need to understand how these AI make decisions that directly affect them, like hiring, performance reviews, assignment of work and layoffs. Furthermore, enterprises should opt for AI models that are easy to explain with clear rationale given for making decisions. And code will be more transparent and reliable as a result. Inter-facility communication reduces suspicion and fear by providing an opportunity for the elderly to express unintelligible sounds. Transparent and ethical data collection, along with AI system development, also makes it easier to comply with privacy regulations and prevent misuse. It should be businesses to empower people and hold them accountable by creating an atmosphere of openness (Harris et al., 2025).

Socially responsible AI will require explainable and transparent AI. Employees should understand how AI algorithms determine who is hired and fired, whose performance is evaluated on what terms. Companies need to focus on easy-to-understand models and make clear decision criteria, so that algorithms are more understandable for customers (Barati-Ahmadabadi et al., 2025).

Educating, training and developing a workforce who can responsibly and effectively use AI also are essential. Responsible AI involves teaching its entire staff the basics of AI to better recognize AI's impact, discussing some tough ethical problems with prejudice and discrimination at their core, explaining how it straddles data privacy and informing you about your rights within an AI-run process (Pacheco, 2025). Comprehensive lifelong learning schemes raise knowledge and competencies, mitigate abuse potential and maximize the benefits of human-AI partnership. Training also helps promote a continuous learning culture; this is so important to preserving your professional personhood and sense of humanity in the face of soul-crushing technological change.

More stringent governance provides a greater chance that AI will be used responsibly. Transparent ethical standards and principles – responsibility, privacy, justice, human control and social impact - must guide the creation and application of AI. To make that easier, these policy frameworks outline what are the roles and responsibilities of IT, HR, legal, and compliance. Systematic surveillance and impact assessment will to keep pace with the new legal demands and determinations as well as societal norms and to prevent ethical risks or impacts. Further, governance approaches are also helpful in addressing challenges and complaint about the AI mediation decisions to enhance procedural fairness (Farooq & Farhad, 2025).

It is this cooperation and the exchange of ideas that allows for best practice to be disseminated, enabling responsible AI at pace. Partnerships help companies or entities with differing interests to share information, set common standards and work together on matters that affect them all. Exploratory research, policy making and pilot projects to design new models to deploy AI for greater equity, transparency and inclusiveness may be best suited for public-private cooperation. Most of all, though, if we want to build trust in the workplace, with consumers and regulators and society at large then this is how we need to work together now (Rice et al., 2025). Cultivating a culture appreciating of experiment, responsibility and openness to criticism supports keeping AI systems aligned with human values while enhancing work-places. Hence, encouraging the ethical use of AI is about ensuring _that work done with AIs includes ethics, transparency, worker engagement, education and oversight. This holistic approach allows organisations to unlock the full value of AI, while respecting people's right to justice, dignity and trust in the new workplace of the future a place where everyone can thrive (Craft, 2025).

9. CONCLUSION

The world is remaking the traditional aspects of philosophy for artificial intelligence as through an amalgam of rights to work, those most universally accepted in domestic and international law are the major sector defending the social living rights of workers over a long period They will be reshaped and re-understood for the AI challenge The political, economic and social systems taken together can also help the influence of differences in how jurisdictions fare from development of deployment to preparedness getting along As AI transforms the workplace. The labor law still has an important role: it must keep people's work and life in one piece and their human feelings undamaged in a dangerous tomorrow.

The next wave on the global shore of establishing password-sharing customs will be to meld legal guidelines with psychological assistance groups, along with intergroup conflict resolution. The profile of the policy zone is an amalgam made up of what is undone and what's already completed Jurisdictions experimented with everything from beefed-up unemployment insurance, return-to-work bounties and even legislatively mandated retraining benefits. As their rights become more manifest with technological progress, both the rules and help system across Western Europe, North America and India have changed to protect new forms of employment There are "institutions," workers' councils, trade unions, tripartite talks between business, labor and government. They may be on both sides of politics, but their fortunes rise and fall with fortunes in other areas.

REFERENCES

Al-Hadrawi, B. K., Al-hadrawi, K. K., Ezzerouali, S., Al-Hadraawy, S. K., Aldhalmi, H. K., & Muhtar, M. H. (2024). Mind Intruders: Psychological, Legal, and Social Effects of Human Parasites in the Age of Technological Progress. *Pakistan Journal of Life and Social Sciences*, *22*(2).

Ayhan, T., & Colpitts-Elliott, H. (2025). Radical care in displacement: Rohingya women's activism amidst neoliberal humanitarianism and repression. *Journal of Ethnic and Migration Studies*, *51*(9), 2415–2433.

Barati-Ahmadabadi, H., Dalvi-Esfahani, M., & Ramayah, T. (2025). The interplay of cyberslacking, social isolation and social media addiction: A study of employees' introversion. *Asia-Pacific Journal of Business Administration*, •••, 1–31.

Block, N. (2024). Willful Wisdom: Harnessing insights from decision science toward wiser decision making on climate change and energy transition. *Tex. Env't LJ*, *54*, 1.

. Briciu, B., Ste-Marie, L., & Moïse Réveil, S. (2025). 'Does the system even want us?'–Fostering the resilience of internationally educated health professionals facing threat to their professional identity in Canada. *Journal of Adult and Continuing Education*, 14779714251390747.

Chybis, L., Lamping, S., Dobinson, T., & Ford, K. (2025). Professional Transition in Australia: Ukrainian Migrant Teachers' Lived Experiences. *Journal of Intercultural Studies (Melbourne, Vic.)*, •••, 1–19.

Craft, J. L. (2025). Self-Compassion and Law Student Professional Identity Formation. *The Journal of Law Teaching and Learning*, *2*(1), 235.

Craft, J. L. (2025). Self-Compassion and Law Student Professional Identity Formation. *The Journal of Law Teaching and Learning*, *2*(1), 235.

Doring, N., Le, T. D., Vowels, L. M., Vowels, M. J., & Marcantonio, T. L. (2024). The impact of artificial intelligence on human sexuality: A five-year literature review 2020–2024. *Current Sexual Health Reports*, *17*(1), 4.

Farooq, F., & Farhad, S. (2025). The unseen burden: Exploring the lived experiences of mothers caring for individuals with substance use disorder. *Addiction Research and Theory*, •••, 1–13.

Harris, F. III, Wood, J. L., King, T. M., & Essien-Wood, I. (2025). Racelighting Impact Theory. *Community College Journal of Research and Practice*, *49*(10-11), 638–652.

. Karunanayakaa, K. O., Jahankhanib, H., El-Deebc, S., Arachchigeb, I. S. W., & Hussienb, O. A. A. M. (2025). Artificial Intelligence in Digital Marketing: The Ethical Implications of Digital Influence on Markets and Consumer. *Market Grooming*, 173.

Moretti, V., & Pronzato, R. (2024). The emotional ambiguities of healthcare professionals' platform experiences. *Social Science & Medicine*, *357*, 117185.

Muir, L. (2025). Prospecting for gold: finding your guide. In *The Guide to LGBTQ+ Research* (pp. 17–21). Emerald Publishing Limited.

Muzingili, T. (2025). Navigating the Phenomenology of Adoption Disruption in Zimbabwe: Insights from Adoptive Parents. *Adoption Quarterly*, •••, 1–29.

Nigar, N., Dovchin, S., Wilson, R., & Kostogriz, A. (2025). Hybrid professionalism: Multilingual cosmopolitan identities of immigrant English teachers. *Journal of Multilingual and Multicultural Development*, •••, 1–18.

Pacheco, E. M. (2025). Coping and Resilience: Strategies for Managing the Psychological Impact of Remote Exposure to Trauma. In *Remote Trauma Exposure* (pp. 155–190). Springer Nature Switzerland.

Palimaru, A. I., Malika, N., Brown, R. A., Holmes, P., Dickerson, D. L., Rodriguez, A., & D'Amico, E. J. (2025). "Am I Not Native Enough?" A Qualitative Exploration of Experienced Discrimination Among American Indian/Alaska Native Emerging Adults. *Journal of Racial and Ethnic Health Disparities*, •••, 1–15.

Prabhakar, P., Pati, P. B., & Parida, S. (2025). Navigating Legal and Ethical Dimensions in AI, IoT, and Cloud Solutions for Women's Safety. In *Developing AI, IoT and Cloud Computing-based Tools and Applications for Women's Safety* (pp. 155-191). Chapman and Hall/CRC.

Rice, A. J., Ogle, C. M., Martin, S. L., & Cozza, S. J. (2025). The impact of wartime child casualties on adult professionals. *Psychiatry*, *88*(3), 308–327.

Robinson, J. C. (2025). Unshackling Dreams from the Hacker's Digital Chains. In *Artificial Intelligence: Ethics and the New World Order* (pp. 95–171). Springer Nature Switzerland.

Rousseau, D. (1995). Psychological contracts in organizations: Understanding written and unwritten agreements. *Sage (Atlanta, Ga.)*.

Skolnick, K. R. (2025). A second look at second look: Promoting epistemic justice in resentencing. *NYUL Rev.*, *100*, 1.

Uche, I. B., Uche, O. A., & Ene, J. C. (2025). Superstitions and criminal behavior: The role of witchcraft accusations in Nigerian rural communities. *Social Thought*, •••, 1–23.

Chapter 6
Data Protection and Mental Health Privacy:
Legal Standards for AI-Powered Psychological Assessment and Identity Crisis Intervention

Aditi Srivastava
Dev Bhoomi Uttarakhand University, Dehradun, India

Avinash Krishna Goswami
https://orcid.org/0009-0006-7951-3627
Lloyd Law College, Greater Noida, India

ABSTRACT

Although modern technology has made accessing mental health treatment simpler, but should still respect people's privacy even if the human beings utilize AI technologies for psychoanalysis or assistance with an identity crisis. AI applications must be utilized with sensitive personal data in order to have any chance of identifying cognitive, emotional, and behavioral qualities. This brings up issues with discrimination, abuse, and prejudice in algorithms. This chapter discusses the ethical and legal considerations that must be made in order to ensure the security of mental health data while using AI-assisted diagnosis and treatment technologies. It also examines if regulations in other nations and areas, such as GDPF in Europe and HIPPA in the US, might alter the procedures for handling psychological data. The obvious human rights to consent, mental integrity and freedom of body are also covered in this chapter.

DOI: 10.4018/979-8-3373-6618-0.ch006

1. INTRODUCTION

Artificial intelligence and digital mental health technology are revolutionizing the way we identify, address, and even prevent these issues. Technology is increasingly being utilized to monitor, diagnose, and treat mental health conditions. These include chatbots that employ artificial intelligence (AI) to serve as crisis hotlines or provide cognitive behavioral therapy, or applications that can read people's emotions and attitudes. By making it simpler for patients to get treatment, AI is increasing the precision and efficacy of therapy. However, it also brings up important issues of moral responsibility, data security, and privacy for those suffering from mental illness. One of the most intimate aspects of life is mental health. It is thus filled with all the feelings, thoughts, and misconceptions that cause you to behave or respond in a certain manner. All of these items really need robust, unambiguous legal safeguards against discrimination when employed in this manner.

The situation becomes much more complex when discussing the use of AI to assist someone in overcoming an identity crisis. Engaging with very intimate and fluid parts of self-experience is necessary when integrating AI technology designed to support people with identity disorders or existential despair. Parts of society, not society as a whole, are the issue. Similarly, when AI receives poor or illogical information, it is not at fault for prejudice or for disregarding human reality. An artificial learning algorithm is likely to provide sexist outcomes if you feed it sexist data. The use of self-presentation algorithms to digitally improve one's self-reconstitution presents fundamental philosophical and legal questions about the fundamental qualities of humanity authenticity, agency, and autonomy.

Therefore, developing artificial intelligence (AI) that respects people's mental and emotional privacy may be a question of human dignity and natural rights in addition to being a technological difficulty. The complexity of AI often exceeds the capabilities of present models. The legal phrases "data controller," "processor," and "consent" are less apparent since AI systems are capable of change, independent thought, and sometimes unclear behavior. Because AI is increasingly being used for psychological and lifestyle assessments, it is imperative that legal principles be reexamined and revitalized.

1.1 Rise of AI in Psychological Assessment and Crisis Intervention

It is important to consider the ethical and human rights implications of AI in mental health. The confidentiality in mental health is intimately tied to the concepts of privacy, trust and therapeutic relationship. The useful information that is hypothetical or that could reveal stigmatized psychology causes the aspects of discomfort and bad emotions. Therefore, by integrating data reduction, anonymization and explainability into the system architecture, virtuous AI design should support privacy-by-design. Therefore, the nexus of ethics, technology and law is a crucial area where legislators, technologists, and medical experts all have a shared obligation to protect human welfare (Dhar & Sarkar, 2024).

It is also equally significant is the wide variation in regulatory maturity throughout the globe. While industrialized countries are working to enact laws protecting personal information, several developing nations do not have laws specifically addressing AI and mental health. There are concerns about exploitation, data commodification and digital colonialism are exacerbated by this unequal environment, particularly when multinational corporations are providing AI technologies to some of the most vulnerable populations without enough oversight and standardized international standards that can support AI's fairness, inclusivity and cultural sensitivity are urgently needed.

1.2 The Confluence of Technology, Mental Health and Privacy Rights

The potentially dynamic but morally challenging area of modern civilization is the nexus of technology, neuroscience, and privacy rights. Through the chatbots, emotion detection software, and computational techniques that assess mood, thought, and behavior AI and digital solutions have increased access to psychological help. Some of the most sensitive and confidential personal information you may get is as follows: Information about your thoughts, prior treatment sessions, and the responses of your mental health. The components of malicious AI systems may utilize this data to breach, profile, or misuse it if it is not safeguarded. Maintaining your privacy while learning about technology might be challenging. We need sound legislation, moral AI, and unambiguous regulations in order to develop new concepts that are founded on the most fundamental human rights and safeguard our privacy about mental health. Respecting the law is insufficient to safeguard people's emotional and mental data. Additionally, it represents "mental integrity" as we establish online rights for individuals.

2. AI-POWERED PSYCHOLOGICAL ASSESSMENT AND IDENTITY CRISIS INTERVENTION

A significant advancement in the way we think about and assess topics like identity formation, emotional stability, and mental health is the use of AI to support mental health. In the past, psychological evaluation included observing behavior, interviewing individuals (particularly children), observing them, and asking them to self-report. These conventional approaches are expensive, geographically limited, and vulnerable to physician prejudice, yet they provide insightful qualitative data. By creating tools that can swiftly alter complicated data in ways that impact language, emotions, and physiology, artificial intelligence has permanently altered this profession. AI assessing your emotions by using chatbots to identify novel emotions and ideas, machine learning, natural language processing (NLP), and affective computing have revolutionized the way we identify mental health issues, discover our personalities, and prevent identity crises. This shift in practice is intriguing, but it also raises some significant concerns, such as legal obligations, algorithmic fairness, data privacy, and emotional privacy.

2.1 Predictive Analytics, Emotion Recognition and Cognitive Modelling

In order to forecast the potential negative outcomes or dangerous conduct, AI-based psychological assessments mostly depend on predictive analysis. In order to determine if you're feeling down or thinking negatively, machine learning algorithms examine data that might be seen as intrusive, such as your internet activity, wearable technology and smartphone. The computer vision and signal analysis are used by affect recognition systems to classify emotional indicators such as physiological measures, speech tones, and face micro-expressions. These systems may identify early indicators of trauma or depression by examining an individual's usage of digital platforms.

With focusing on the brain processes including attention, reasoning, and memory, cognitive modeling aims to mimic human thinking processes and extend skills into other fields. So, by drawing conclusions from data, AI may assist in identifying emotional instability, cognitive decline, and symptoms of PTSD. The participants' rights to informed consent and understanding two crucial components of psychological ethics are violated by this lack of openness. The users need to understand the conclusions AI systems draw about a person's mental health, especially when those conclusions might affect that person's autonomy and course in life as e.g., access to healthcare work or educational possibilities (Nebeker et al., 2022).

The biases in the training data may worsen as a result of prediction models and the emotional expression differs throughout genders and civilizations, although the majority of the datasets that are currently available represent Western attitudes. AI is thus prone to misunderstand or perceive as aberrant actions that are typical in other civilizations. In order to ensure that the AI respects psychological uniqueness and individual identity, we want algorithmic openness and data governance that involves everyone.

2.2 AI Applications in Identity Crisis Detection and Support Systems

The total loss of self-perception, either for a person or a society, is a psychological phenomenon known as an identity crisis. These crises often occur in the midst of trauma, throughout puberty, or during life transitions. With digitizing the identities across social forms and virtual environments as people's are progressively creating our identities online and discovering who we are. Artificial intelligence systems have started to tackle this area, providing instruments for analyzing digital behavior, emotional narratives, and self-perception in order to quickly spot identity creation or distortion problems. The platforms using artificial intelligence may monitor linguistic indicators of existential suffering, such as bewilderment, a sense of purposelessness, or sentiments of worthlessness.

2.3 Emerging Challenges: Algorithmic Bias, Misinterpretation and Overreliance

With transforming the identities into digital forms that function in social contexts and virtual environments, peoples are establishing ourselves online and discovering who we are. AI systems have begun to address this issue by developing tools for examining digital behavior, emotional narratives, and self-perception in order to automatically identify problematic instances of identity creation or distortion. AI-powered websites may scan language for indications of existential distress, such confusion, a lack of meaning, or a sense of worthlessness. The chatbots and virtual counselors could be able to identify certain speech patterns, urge individuals to seek the assistance or even alert a real doctor when someone is having problems. The aspects of algorithms that search through a user's journals or chat logs for indications of identity conflict or depressive rumination as may be able to assist users in determining the most effective methods for self-reflection.

3. DATA PRIVACY AND PROTECTION PRINCIPLES IN MENTAL HEALTH ECOSYSTEMS

The identity support systems, therapies and psychiatric diagnoses have all transformed as a result of the increasing use of AI in mental health care. Individuals must understand what data is being gathered and where it will be shared or kept. The phrase "dynamic consent" is the other way to describe this. As AI applications advance, it enables consumers to check and modify their consent. Ethical frameworks also include this.

The major component of privacy protection is data reduction, or simply gathering the information required for a certain purpose. The AI systems rely heavily on large datasets to train prediction models in mental health settings. Thus significant ethical conundrum is raised by this tension between data economy and data relevancy. The signs of "collecting too much data puts it at risk of cyber-threats and other dangers, while collecting too little will give you incomplete results at the algorithm level". The aspects of compromise might be achieved by the privacy-preserving computing and federated learning. The model would be updated by exchanging anonymized parameters but the consumers' private information would remain on their devices. This preserves personal privacy while fostering collaborative AI learning.

There are two ideas associated with data minimization are anonymization and pseudonymization. As, to guarantee that no person may be directly or indirectly identified, mental health data must be anonymised. The practice of permanently eliminating identifiers such as names, addresses, or biometric characteristics is known as anonymization. But the pseudonymization substitutes a synthetic code for a unique identification. If the appropriate secure keys are available, this re-identification code may be used for reverse linking. The achievement of total anonymity is really difficult since datasets pertaining to mental health may include distinct language and behavioral characteristics that may be linked to specific people. Therefore, to ensure that the privacy is maintained and re-identification is impossible and anonymization must be accompanied with robust encryption and guidelines about who may access the data.

The foundation of post-therapeutic ethics is the idea of client confidentiality which also represents the trust that exists between the therapist and the client. The concept of maintaining the privacy is particularly challenging in digital environments as data is transferred between cloud servers, devices and third-party analytics tools are more important. It is the responsibility of AI developers, service providers and healthcare institutions to provide robust security from the beginning to the end which is required a most (Olawade at al., 2025). The mental health platforms must implement the appropriate organizational and technological safeguards to secure data in accordance with the General Data Protection Regulation (GDPR) and the Health Insurance Portability and Accountability Act (HIPAA). So, to ensure that the data is utilized only for research or therapeutic purposes they include access restrictions, safe storage and encryption along with to being illegal, violating confidentially undermines confidence in digital therapeutic tools.

The concepts of being transparent and accountable are another crucial component of mental health ecosystems is needed. So, for the usage in identity crisis therapies or psychiatric assessments, AI systems have to be explicable and verifiable. The users are entitled to know how choices are made and how their emotional data is utilized as well as who is responsible in the event that anything goes wrong or is abused. The use of being forthright and truthful fosters trust and promotes the ethical use of technology in treatment. At the same time as the accountability implies that data owners, healthcare authorities, and AI developers are all directly accountable for their own deeds. It can be difficult for victims such as those impacted by algorithmic prejudice or data breaches to get compensation or legal recourse in the absence of these vehicles.

The globalization of mental health also makes cross-border data transfers more problematic. Since cloud-based AI technologies may be utilized in several countries, the legislation simultaneously applies to data in each of those countries. For example, privacy regulations may allow one nation to see data held in another nation with a different degree of detail. This is intended to be fixed by the GDPR, which only permits data to leave the EU when sufficient safeguards are in place, however these regulations aren't always adhered to. As a result, in areas with weak privacy legislation, people's mental health information may be exploited. For psychological data to be consistently protected across national borders, international cooperation and regulatory frameworks are necessary.

The rule of integrity and the purpose restriction ensures that personal information is processed in a way that keeps it current and is only used for the agreed-upon purpose. If the data is inaccurate or outdated AI evaluations in the field of mental health may result in incorrect diagnoses or harmful actions. The concept of data-fidelity checks are required to ensure that data remains legitimate. They even use the phrase "function creep" which refers to ensuring that data is not utilized for objectives other than marketing or monitoring. The new idea of mental privacy protects the integrity of inner ideas and feelings by going beyond conventional data protection (Zhang et al., 2025).

So, what was formerly an issue that was entirely outside of a person's consciousness is now a question concerning their own consciousness as AI grows more adept at determining people's mental states via things like behavior monitoring, emotion sensors, and brain-computer interfaces. In order to shield people against invasive neuro-technology that interprets or modifies their emotional or cognitive states, legal academics support the recognition of the right to mental integrity as a unique human right under digital law.

4. LEGAL STANDARDS AND REGULATORY FRAMEWORKS GOVERNING AI IN MENTAL HEALTH

The use of AI for diagnosis, identity crisis management, and mental health evaluation is rapidly developing. The characteristics are much quicker than those that can regulate it in the conventional legal system. Through the use of chatbots, smartphone applications, and predictive analytics, for instance, AI has made it simpler for many individuals to get mental health treatment in the future. However, they also discuss the major issues of patient safety, data privacy, and accountability (Ohu et al., 2025). The most comprehensive worldwide regulations for safeguarding sensitive and private information, including psychological information, is the General Data Protection Regulation (GDPR). Health information is classified as a "special category" of personal data under the GDPR.

This implies that companies must get explicit consent before utilizing data and take further precautions to ensure its security. According to GDPR Article 9, processing this kind of data is illegal unless there are exception, such as in the case of medical certification or public health. To a limited degree, the GDPR mandates that AI-automated psychological profiling be conducted in a fair and transparent manner. The GDPR gives people authority over their psychological information. They have the ability to see it, edit it, remove it, and object to its collection. People have a right to know why major choices made by humans are entirely automated, and the G.D.P.R. regulates automated decision-making. This protection is especially the important in mental health settings where algorithmic mistakes may negatively affect a person's reputation and emotional wellbeing.

4.1 International Norms- GDPR, HIPAA, OECD Guidelines and WHO Ethics

As far as in the US, patient health information, including mental health observations, is protected under the Health Insurance Portability and Accountability Act (HIPAA), a federal statute. According to HIPAA, healthcare providers, payers and their business partners are required to ensure security, preserve patient privacy to certain aspects and get consent before exchanging information. Because HIPAA only covers the "covered entities" wellness platforms, AI chatbots and mental health applications that operate outside of clinical settings are exempt from the law. Users of AI-enhanced psychological applications may so unintentionally provide access to their personal data by those not protected by HIPAA. This disparity demonstrates the need for new regulations to clarify digital mental health services and to identify new categories of data controllers that do not align with the wellness industry's present definition.

So, beyond GDPR and HIPPA, other international legislation have emerged as part of the ethical AI and data protection environment. In 1980, the OECD released its first set of privacy guidelines. Even if they have been changed since then, they still address crucial concepts in AI governance, such purpose restriction and data quality. The same is true of UNESCO's Recommendation on the Ethics of Artificial Intelligence in 2021 year and the Council of Europe's Convention 108+ which discuss the role of AI that is founded on justice, transparency, and human rights in automated decision-making (Bose et al., 2025). These guidelines urge member states to adopt AI standards that lessen stigma, prejudice and the concept of emotional damage because they acknowledge the significance of mental health and psychological well-being to human dignity. Digital mental health solutions should also be utilized ethically, according to the World Health Organization, 1948. This aspects claim that while integrating AI into the healthcare system in which the primary objectives should be user safety, inclusion and transparency.

4.2 Ethical and Legal Responsibilities of AI Developers and Mental Health Professionals

So, despite these developments the international laws still lag behind technical breakthroughs which leading to uneven regulation of AI in mental health. There are some regions are attempting to classify AI systems according to their level of danger, such as the EU with the AI Act. Since the AI in healthcare and evaluation procedures would be deemed "high-risk" stringent regulations, including those pertaining to data governance, human supervision and post-market monitoring, would need to be adhered to.

These pages show that the open and inclusive way that project teams with help from EU institutions and agencies which have to gone about updating existing laws without making any new rules the commission writes in its response to this assertion is supported by an exception in the GDPR and other comparable legislation that permits data processing for purposes related to health and well-being. The privacy rules of nations like the Canada and the Australia are being updated to include algorithmic accountability and AI ethics. As, going from the thorough codification to worldwide harmonization would be quite challenging, however.

The ambiguity around legal liability and duty in cases where AI results in damage such as data breaches or psychological discomfort is another persistent problem. It is challenging to assign the blame in the decentralized AI-development ecosystem, which consists of platform operators, software engineers, data scientists, and mental health specialists. So, whether the person who created the algorithm, the person who provided the data, or the medical facility is at fault if an AI tool misdiagnoses depression or results in a negative psychological response (Jafar et al., 2025). This is still not always evident in the legislation as a result, the scholars are advocating for more adoption of shared responsibility models and requiring impact studies prior to the use of AI in mental health settings. To ensure that the safety and compliance are always fulfilled as the guiding principles should mandate routine monitoring, bias testing and ethical evaluation in the regulatory systems.

4.4 Legal Accountability in AI-Driven Psychological Misjudgments

The concept of design which is complete openness and explainability must be contained in the legislation. The trust, empathy and understanding that underpin mental health assessments may be jeopardized by opaque AI models if people are unable to comprehend the reasoning behind findings. There is a frameworks for explainable AI may be useful in simplifying decision-making processes for patients and physicians alike. In order to enable the human experts to verify and understand algorithmic findings prior to clinical application, legal regulations should require AI systems to disclose their diagnostic outputs the data used for diagnosis as and the limits found during their development.

The next set of regulations must include ethics by design into the AI development of rather than just ticking boxes. So, in order to ensure that mental health AI solutions are developed with ethics in mind the legislation should include privacy-by-design, fairness-by-design and accountability-by-design principles (Halder et al., 2026). As the clarity in order to create laws that can adapt when new technologies, such as wearables that sense emotions or brain-computer interfaces are developed, governments should simultaneously promote cooperation between legislators, technologists, psychologists and ethicists from many disciplines.

This concept is already have a means to safeguard psychological data thanks to international regulations like GDPR and HIPAA but the particular requirements of the use of AI-based mental health systems need more precise and progressive is regulations. The use of the maintaining cognitive integrity, autonomy and confidence in others is equally as difficult as protecting data. There is a need for a cultural shift toward a more unified which should be multidisciplinary governance paradigm where AI is seen as an opportunity rather than a danger to fundamentally personal mental health as it must be accompanied by an evolution of copyright laws and government power (Mansoor & Ansari, 2024).

5. IDENTITY, AUTONOMY AND PSYCHOLOGICAL INTEGRITY IN AI CONTEXTS: DIGITAL IDENTITY FORMATION AND PSYCHOLOGICAL VULNERABILITIES AS AI INFLUENCE ON SELF-PERCEPTION AND IDENTITY RECONSTRUCTION

The aspects of human identity, autonomy and psychological integrity are all the profoundly impacted when artificial intelligence is included into social and mental health systems. The distinction between how to see the humans as themselves and how computers evolve is becoming more blurred as more and more people turn to the AI-powered services to express their emotions, feel better and even discover who they are. It also describes the modern internet as a psychological mirror in which the users must continuously create and re-create their identities in connection to another via the information-sharing technology is there (Banerjee et al., 2024). Because the AI capacity to influence people's self-perception, thoughts the and feels contradicts conventional notions of mental autonomy and personal freedom, this shift presents significant ethical and legal issues.

The creating a digital identity in the AI is no longer a static representation as it evolves and develops as a result of your continuous exposure to the digital environment. It also check the real time how AI-driven feedback, recommender systems and the social media algorithms impact our perceptions of ourselves and others. So, through behavior-tracking systems, personality prediction algorithms, and emotional recognition software, users may constantly get feedback that rewards certain behaviors or attributes (Mansoor & Ansari, 2024). Along with the concept of monitoring user behavior, these systems covertly promote moral ideas, social preferences, and emotionally charged reactions. The AI chat-bots and virtual counseling platforms are often used in mental health therapies as digital experience companions that provide cognitive and emotional reflections to help users with self-representation. So, although this might help the individuals reflect on who they are and what they do and it can also increase the likelihood that they will experience psychological damage the particularly when algorithms inadvertently alter or distort people's perceptions of themselves.

The preview of AI settings will increasingly challenge the concept of the psychological autonomy and the capacity to think, feel and behave according to one's own rules. The use of the behavior of autonomy as being autonomous entails having the freedom to make the own decisions and not being influenced by others. The concept of Persuasive algorithms are sometimes often used by AI systems designed to maintain the attention by making the user feel, behave and be susceptible in ways that increase the likelihood that they will remain interested. As, both positive and negative effects on mental health might result from such technologies. The AI-powered systems are able to recognize emotional discomfort and motivate people to get help, but they may also teach users to depend on automated approval or guidance for their problems, which might reduce their independence (Shymko & Babadzhanova, 2025). This condition is called algorithmic reliance and is weakening people's psychological defenses because they are forced to make the judgments regarding their mental health and coping mechanisms based on computational logics rather than honest the introspection.

There are significant ethical and therapeutic ramifications to using AI to reconstruct someone's identity, particularly in the wake of trauma, bereavement, or a meaning crisis. Rebuilding personal narratives, reinterpreting previous experiences, and overcoming emotional resilience losses may all be facilitated by AI-assisted therapy and an identity support system enabled by AIC. In addition to providing a secure space for individuals to discuss their personal tales without fear of judgment, social rejection, or advice, these virtual companions and generative AI systems may facilitate empathy-based interactions. However, it may also be more difficult for us to see genuine emotional development as such when we are close to someone we met online. Using our cognitive peculiarities (such as the human belly) to force the already precarious psycho-spiritual healing process of challenge above comfort and truth ahead of belief, that algorithm may create the chrysalis. In therapy, two individuals who may not get along establish agreements with one another. As a result, individuals find some commonalities or things they can relate to when they attempt to comprehend this other person. This can become the simulation's shallow terminus, without any moral depth (Pandey, 2024).

There are significant ethical issues with the ability to identify and alter identity signifiers such as gender, personality, race, and sexual orientation. When machine learning algorithms are trained on biased data, they may end up categorizing or labeling individuals in ways that are inconsistent with their true selves. The psychological conflict underlying algorithmic parsed classification is very harmful to those going through an identity crisis. This is particularly true for populations who are already at risk, such as adolescents, members of ethnic minorities, or those with gender dysphoria (Mandal & Hawamdeh, 2025). When an app misidentifies a person's digital identity, it might change how they see themselves and their sense of social belonging in the actual world. This poses an existential and emotional danger. These nuances have not yet been reflected in the legislation. Rather than addressing more abstract costs like loss of mental and emotional freedom, the majority of our data protection regulations concentrate on more evident losses like data breaches.

The management of the personal identifying data is the other aspect of this issue and every smiling face, preference button click and the action made to leave the market for the mental health products is part of digital ecosystems is more. Through this breakdown of complex the use of psychological qualities into consumable items and the commercialization of self-construction disassembles the person. The people also participate in a feedback loop that allows their emotional vulnerabilities to be anticipated and the exploited for financial gain (Schweiger, 2025). There are also the subliminal conditioning of emotions, thoughts and behaviors in ways that align with the broader goals of how technology makers, media publishers and marketers want their products to be used is what one mind-bending and to its author, seemingly unrealistic where the studies called digital psychopolitics.

There are legal and ethical the protections against the over-influence of technology on people must be put in place in order to maintain the psychological integrity of agents in AI settings. The concept of ethical AI would be designed with the mental privacy as it top priority, guaranteeing the freedom to protect one's feelings, ideas and mental processes from unapproved examination or interference. So, recognizing a legal right to the mental integrity and cognitive liberty in the context of neuro-rights might extend conventional data protection to include emotional and psychological realms. This would also require the AI systems that handle user identification or emotional data to do so transparently with explicit consent and oversight (Figueroa et al., 2025). The developers need to use XAI principles which also inform the end users about the vast process by which the identity-related deductions are made and provide them with a means of contesting or clearing up misconceptions.

It is the crucial to improve the human supervision of the AI-driven psychological processes in order to the protect autonomy. The use of in interpreting AI results the mental health practitioner's must continue to play a the important and the crucial role by incorporating algorithmic results within the complex framework of human emotion and culture. There are multiple initiatives for education and the digital literacy may provide consumers the tools they need to recognize and resist exploitation by the dominant digital system, encouraging more thoughtful uses of AI. This is the need for the individuals from the diverse disciplines to communicate with the other now more than before. This includes the- attorneys, psychologists, technologists and those who work with ethics and values such as- ethicists (Goyal et al., 2025). So, in this manner, in a world of the intelligent robots and it may establish boundaries that safeguard identity integrity.

The paradox of AI impact is that it both increases your awareness of the really are and jeopardizes human being identity. The maintaining of peoples freedom and integrity is not only required by law but also by morality since digital technologies have an impact on our hearts and minds (Khawaja & Belisle-Pipon, 2023). If it rigorously maintain AI individuality the technology will remain a tool for self-discovery rather than something that is imposed on and can only navigate the digital century in this manner, free, dignified and aware which is very much needed.

6. ETHICAL, LEGAL AND TECHNOLOGICAL SAFEGUARDS FOR DATA PROTECTION

The momentum of AI-driven mental health platforms makes it imperative to establish technical and ethical guidelines for protecting psychological data. Mental health data is highly private as it includes the behavioral tendencies, cognitive processes, and emotional patterns which could be exploited for causing emotional pain, prejudice or manipulation. So to protect this data we need a three-pronged approach of ethics, legality and responsible technical progress. The initial ethical protections are those of liberty, utility and visibility (Thirupathi et al., 2025). AI developers and healthcare providers need to make it easy for the consumer to grasp how their data has been collected, turned around by algorithms and utilised. To avoid biases that may result in misdiagnosis, or social, emotional and psychological judgment issues of users by the technology, AI systems need to be designed taking into account ethical considerations that can ensure justice, accountability and transparency (Palmer & Schwan, 2025). The only pertinent, bare-bones data is collected and as a result the idea of data reduction likewise reduces unnecessary psychological profiling and surveillance.

These moral concepts are cast in terms of legal protections as laws that stipulate how data must be managed, stored, and shared could include the GDPR, HIPAA, as well as proposed AI Acts. These regulations will ensure that people can take charge of their mental health information, simply because they have a right to privacy, a right to transfer and should be 'forgotten'. The cognitive liberty and mental privacy are moving up the priority lists of national courts (Tabassum et al., 2025). They argue that the human rights law ought to confer an extremely high level of protection on mind data. International harmonization and cross border data governance are especially important as digital mental health services frequently function across countries with varying legal systems.

It is the technical measures which ensure data protection as whether the data are always private and immutable via federated learning, blockchain consent management, end-to-end encryption and differential privacy (Luxton, 2025). AI systems engineered to have privacy protections from the start are said to be "privacy by design." For example, security features are not a bolt-on but integral to the system. Accidents and unauthorized access are reduced with regular cyber security audits and restricted access permissions. Therefore, digital mental health solutions are more reliable and responsible when they adhere to strict ethical, legal, and technical requirements. The use of AI in diagnosing and treating mental health issues is only growing. Following the law is insufficient to secure the personal information it utilizes. Supporting people's liberty, dignity, and well-being as they navigate mental health challenges in the digital age is a social and moral obligation (Hascalovitz & Deonandan, 2025).

7. CONCLUSION AND FUTURE SCOPE

At the nexus of AI and mental health care, there are several significant ethical issues and opportunities for improvement. It is anticipated that AI-enhanced diagnostic tests and psychotherapy-based identity crisis interventions would increase diagnosis accuracy and treatment personalization. Given that mental health is a private matter, laws must prohibit hurting someone's dignity and free choice or denying them privacy when they want it. Accountability must be a feature of new technologies that guard against prejudice and misuse that is based on or supported by data. Technical standards, legal safeguards, and ethical obligations must all cooperate.

Using technology that are human-centered, simple to comprehend, and easy to explain is one strategy to advance the area of AI in mental health. The same ought to hold true for cognitive and emotional limits. Policymakers must advocate for international collaboration on MHP&M privacy and personal data protection in view of concerns over the expansion of neuro-rights and cognitive liberty in general. Engineers, psychologists, ethicists, and legislators will need to collaborate closely to create an AI that enhances but does not replace human empathy. Patients and doctors may embrace these technologies more responsibly and safely if AI literacy is included into mental health care procedures. This is the only way to guarantee that new technologies are based on moral principles and that safeguarding mental health is a fundamental human right, particularly when it comes to the internet.

REFERENCES

Banerjee, S., Agarwal, A., & Bar, A. K. (2024). Securing well-being: Exploring security protocols and mitigating risks in ai-driven mental health chatbots for employees. *American Journal of Computer Science and Technology*, *7*(1), 1–8.

Bose, E., Kumar, C. A., & Meenakshi, N. (2025). AI-Driven Psychological Profiling on Social Media: Mechanisms, Ethical Breaches, and Regulatory Challenges in Data Inference. Recent Trends in Social Studies. 2025; 2 (1): 1–7p. *AI-Driven Psychological Profiling on Social Media Bose et al. STM Journals*, 2.

Dhar, S., & Sarkar, U. (2024). Safeguarding Data Privacy and Informed Consent: Ethical Imperatives in AI-Driven Mental Healthcare. In *Intersections of Law and Computational Intelligence in Health Governance* (pp. 197-219). IGI Global.

Figueroa, C. A., Ramos, G., Psihogios, A. M., Ekuban, E., Bansie, P., de Haas, M., & Stiles-Shields, C. (2025). Advancing youth co-design of ethical guidelines for AI-powered digital mental health tools. *Nature Mental Health*, ●●●, 1–9.

. Goyal, S., Dutta, R., Dev, S., Raju, K. N., & Bhatt, M. W. (2025). MindLift: AI-Powered Mental Health Assessment for Students. *Neuroscience Informatics*, 100208.

Halder, S., Samajdar, S., & Basak, S. (2026). Ethics in AI-Based Mental Health Care. In *Wearable AI in Psychotherapy* (pp. 213–236). IGI Global Scientific Publishing.

Hascalovitz, C., & Deonandan, R. (2025, August). Unmasking the Algorithm: Bridging Innovation and Ethics in AI-Enabled Psychological Care. In *International Conference on AI in Healthcare* (pp. 159-171). Cham: Springer Nature Switzerland.

Jafar, A., Shabnam, S., & Khan, A. (2025). Artificial Intelligence in Mental Healthcare: Opportunities, Risks, and Regulations. In *AI in Mental Health: Innovations, Challenges, and Collaborative Pathways* (pp. 339-378). IGI Global Scientific Publishing.

Khawaja, Z., & Belisle-Pipon, J. C. (2023). Your robot therapist is not your therapist: Understanding the role of AI-powered mental health chatbots. *Frontiers in Digital Health*, *5*, 1278186.

Luxton, D. (2025). AI-Powered Virtual Therapy: Toward a Responsible and Client-Centered Future. *Journal of Health Service Psychology*, ●●●, 1–9.

Mandal, S., & Hawamdeh, M. M. K. (2025). Digital Well-Being and AI: Navigating the Intersection Between Technology and Mental Health. In *Digital Citizenship and the Future of AI Engagement, Ethics, and Privacy* (pp. 111-132). IGI Global Scientific Publishing.

Mansoor, M. A., & Ansari, K. (2024). Early detection of mental health crises through AI-powered social media analysis: A prospective observational study. medRxiv, 2024-08.

Mansoor, M. A., & Ansari, K. H. (2024). Early detection of mental health crises through artificial-intelligence-powered social media analysis: A prospective observational study. *Journal of Personalized Medicine*, *14*(9), 958.

Nebeker, C., Parrish, E. M., & Graham, S. (2022). The AI-powered digital health sector: ethical and regulatory considerations when developing digital mental health tools for the older adult demographic. In *Artificial Intelligence in Brain and Mental Health: Philosophical, Ethical & Policy Issues* (pp. 159–176). Springer International Publishing.

Ohu, F. C., Burrell, D. N., & Jones, L. A. (2025, October). Public Health Risk Management, Policy, and Ethical Imperatives in the Use of AI Tools for Mental Health Therapy. [). MDPI.]. *Health Care*, *13*(21), 2721.

Olawade, D. B., Ayoola, F. I., Ebo, T. O., Asaolu, A. J., Egbon, E., & David-Olawade, A. C. (2025). Artificial intelligence in forensic mental health: A review of applications and implications. *Journal of Forensic and Legal Medicine*, *113*, 102895.

Palmer, A., & Schwan, D. (2025). Digital Mental Health Tools and AI Therapy Chatbots: A Balanced Approach to Regulation. *The Hastings Center Report*, *55*(3), 15–29.

Pandey, H. M. (2024). Artificial Intelligence in Mental Health and Well-Being: Evolution, Current Applications, Future Challenges, and Emerging Evidence. *arXiv preprint arXiv:2501.10374*.

Schweiger, G. (2025). The ethics of AI-assisted digital phenotyping in adolescent mental health: A framework for informed consent and trust. *AI and Ethics*, •••, 1–21.

Shymko, V., & Babadzhanova, A. (2025). Ethical challenges and strategic responses to AI integration in psychological assessment. *AI and Ethics*, *5*(5), 5415–5423.

Tabassum, A., Ghaznavi, I., Abd-Alrazaq, A., & Qadir, J. (2025). Exploring the Application of AI and Extended Reality Technologies in Metaverse-Driven Mental Health Solutions: Scoping Review. *Journal of Medical Internet Research*, *27*, e72400.

Thirupathi, L., Kaashipaka, V., Dhanaraju, M., & Katakam, V. (2025). AI and IoT in Mental Health Care: From Digital Diagnostics to Personalized, Continuous Support. In *Intelligent Systems and IoT Applications in Clinical Health* (pp. 271-294). IGI Global.

Zhang, H., Mao, Y., Lin, Y., & Zhang, D. (2025). E-mental Health in the Age of AI: Data Safety, Privacy Regulations and Recommendations. *Alpha Psychiatry, 26*(3), 44279.

Chapter 7
Designing Human-Centered AI to Promote Confidence, Inclusivity, and Mental Well-Being

Saurabh Chandra
https://orcid.org/0000-0003-4172-9968
Bennett University, India

Aqsa S. Fatima
Sharda University, India

Liza Shoor
https://orcid.org/0009-0000-0085-3255
Punjab Agricultural University, Ludhiana, India

ABSTRACT

The idea of "human-centered AI" is a "naive aspiration" that entails building AI with people in mind first. This method promotes the development of AI to improve, not replace, human decision-making, and it is said to respect user autonomy, trust, and well-being. Human-centered AI uses design principles that include everyone, development methodologies that incorporate everyone, and ethical frameworks to produce systems that a wide range of people, including persons with impairments and people from marginalized groups, can use. AI systems that lessen cognitive load, offer individualized aid, and keep people in charge of life-saving decisions may help some mental health outcomes. This strategy of putting people first will make sure that

DOI: 10.4018/979-8-3373-6618-0.ch007

AI maintains a tool for empowerment, respects human dignity and the principle of fair access, and improves quality of life while reducing any negative consequences that might happen through continual stakeholder involvement and ethical oversight.

1. INTRODUCTION

You will be able to observe what choices the system makes and how it makes them. This lets people take control of their own life. Putting people first in the design of artificial intelligence develops technology that cares about its users, such as where they live, who they are, and what they need from the system. It's a new technique to develop AI that isn't like past methods that largely focus on logic and syntax to make robots easier for people to use. This kind of thinking suggests that technology should be utilized to make people happy, not just to improve computers. This type of paradigm takes a complete look at a system's users' experiences, moral dilemmas, and social implications. Human-centered AI is a good example of how engineers used to think that technology was the most important thing. Thus, we must interact with many stakeholders and their perspectives, cultural contexts, and human differences over time (Tahvanainen et al., 2024). These experts contend that understanding the complex dimensions of human needs and values requires an interdisciplinary research approach involving computer scientists, psychologists, ethicists, social scientists, and community representatives in AI development. The strategy is founded on the ideals of open design, transparency, explainability, and user control, which means that users don't have to let algorithms make these choices for them. People can not only understand what a system is doing, but they can also think critically about it and take part in its actions (or at least give their input) instead of just letting things happen.

Fostering consumer trust in AI systems through specific design Psychological treatments Dependability, competency, and trustworthiness There are four primary things that make people trust AI: its capacity to exhibit recurrent success, its good intents toward users, its ethical operation and openness, and its ability to forecast behavior. Two methods to gain users' trust are to set realistic expectations for what the system can and can't do (i.e., not over-promising) and to show that it is useful for particular tasks.(Ozmen Garibay et al., 2023).

1.1 Significance and Relevance of the Chapter

To make sure that W3C standards are met and that the project is tested and approved by a wide range of groups, people with disabilities should be involved throughout the full development process. Participatory design is necessary for AI to be inclusive. This means that people who will be affected by the system should be able to make important choices about its goal, scope, and functioning, instead than just offering their thoughts on solutions that have already been chosen. This requires correcting the power imbalance between technical engineers and community stakeholders, acknowledging that participation is work that deserves pay, and allowing community stakeholders actual chances to influence the core design of AI systems. Cultural inclusion also means recognizing that communities use and benefit from AI technologies in different languages, with different levels of tech skills, and in different social settings.

2. PRACTICAL APPLICATIONS OF HUMAN-CENTERED AI IN PSYCHOLOGY

This chapter shows how technology can change things when it is made for and used alongside mental health. It is currently researching perfusion imaging as a distinct entity. AI-enabled mental health therapies work best when they offer individualized and easy-to-access support, as well as human agency and expert monitoring. Chatbots that apply cognitive-behavioral therapy techniques, mood tracking systems that keep track of patterns and triggers, and systems that adapt treatment to each person's requirements are all appropriate uses of AI for mental health. These nuts-and-bolts approaches are especially effective for battling against obstacles that make it hard for people to seek mental health care, such the 24/7 support that people in underserved areas get or that people who don't have regular access to therapy services use. To make AI work for excellent mental health, privacy and showing that therapy works need to be highly important. Care providers that use AI should not replace or take the position of mental health specialists, but instead work with them. Studies show that AI mental health interventions can help with sadness and anxiety when they are based on proven therapeutic methods and are easy to use. The finest apps help individuals learn, get better at things, and understand themselves better, but they also recognize when to signal that human professionalism is needed (Shen et al., 2022).

A design that focuses on empowerment will focus on four areas: giving people the tools they need to get better at what they do, making tasks more effective so they have a bigger impact, giving people control over how they interact with others, and making meaning by connecting actions to personal values and goals. In order for technology to help more people instead of just retaining or making current divisions worse, inclusive AI design needs to include accessibility, cultural sensitivity, and participatory development approaches in a systematic way. To be inclusive, you need to know that traditional ways of developing things sometimes leave out persons with disabilities, minorities, and people from diverse cultural backgrounds. This makes systems that don't perform well for a variety of various types of users. Use the Web Content Accessibility Guidelines on all development cycles to make sure everyone is included, and test and validate across different populations. Participatory design methods are important for making AI more inclusive because they let people who will be affected by the system make real decisions about its scope, purpose, and the methods used to fix problems instead of just being asked about solutions that have already been decided. This entails addressing the imbalance of power between technical developers and community stakeholders, treating participation as a paid job, and making sure that everyone learns how to have a role in crucial decisions about how AI systems should be built. For cultural inclusion to work, we need to recognize that people speak different languages, have different levels of tech skills, and live in different social situations that affect how they interact with AI technology and the benefits they get from them.

Human-centered AI applications aimed at enhancing mental health demonstrate that technology primarily focused on mental well-being is poised to transform our cognitive processes. AI-assisted mental health treatments are effective when they offer personalized, readily available help while preserving human autonomy and expert supervision. Chatbots that use cognitive behavioral treatment, mood-tracking apps that discover trends and triggers, and individualized intervention systems that are made to match the specific needs of each patient are all examples of effective MH AI applications. These systems are quite helpful for people who live far away or can't go to normal therapy services because they are available all the time. Still, successful MHAI needs to think about privacy issues, make sure it works as treatment, and be used in the proper way so that it works alongside human mental health care and providers instead of replacing them. AI mental health interventions can effectively mitigate symptoms of sadness and anxiety, if they are grounded in evidence-based therapeutic practices and employ user-centered interfaces (Pyae, 2025).

3. IMPORTANCE OF CONFIDENCE AND INCLUSIVITY

How adults think and feel about themselves and others affects how kids feel about themselves. A person's self-esteem is a big element of who they are. People will be happy, get along with others, and perform well in both their personal and professional lives if they have this quality. Self-efficacy, self-esteem, and self-concept are all parts of confidence, which is a multifaceted mental state. These three things all affect how much someone thinks they can handle stress and attain their goals. Albert Bandura thinks that the best way to build confidence is to trust in yourself. This first decides if someone will try challenging tasks, then how much work they are ready for, and ultimately what sort of faith they will have in themselves when things go rough. A lot of research shows that people who are very sure of themselves can handle issues and stay happy, even when things are hard. They do hard things with elegance, learn from them, and come out stronger; others who aren't very sure of themselves fail. Studies suggest that those who are confident have stronger immune systems, greater heart health, and are better able to handle problems when they come up. This is because being sure of yourself is good for your mental and physical wellbeing. Self-confidence is not a personality feature; it is a talent that can be developed. It is developed by effective task mastering, affirmative experiences, social modeling, and environmental influences that enhance an individual's self-efficacy (Usmani et al., 2023).

Confidence is developed through established psychological mechanisms, which can be deliberately augmented over time in supportive situations. Social cognition theory investigates the influence of observational learning and social modeling on the development of confidence, suggesting that individuals gain knowledge from the experiences of others through observation or by obtaining positive reinforcement for similar activities. The self-efficacy theory asserts that persons with a robust belief in their skills are more likely to confront challenges, endure difficulties, and perceive failure as a chance for improvement rather than a sign of inadequacy. Studies in positive psychology show that programs that help people build their confidence include (a) helping them become more aware of themselves, (b) helping them build on their strengths, (c) clarifying their values, (d) encouraging positive emotions, and (e) using positive reframing techniques to change the stories we tell ourselves, which helps us move toward a growth mindset support system and mechanism. (e) developing self-compassion. Corydon Hammond, a psychologist at the University Of Utah School Of Medicine, believes that cognitive-behavioral therapy and other therapies like it are extremely helpful. They help people feel more confident by helping them uncover and deal with negative thoughts or beliefs. They also help patients deal with worry and self-doubt and teach them how to replace irrational beliefs with more logical ones. This workplace scenario shows that leaders accomplish their tasks better when they are confident. Leaders that are sure of themselves gain the trust of their followers, make sound decisions, build team settings with an optimistic perspective for the future, and ultimately increase the performance of the organization by motivating others and directing them toward shared goals. AI systems can provide users more power: instead of taking away their freedom and replacing them with automation, they can help people make better decisions and give them more control over their own lives. Empowerment-oriented design has four main parts:

(a) helping people build skills and abilities by adding to what they already know
(b) making the activities they do more effective and impactful

(c) giving them more control over their interactions and decision-making
(d) giving the activity meaning by making sure it fits with their personal values and goals

Some of these empowering tactics include allowing users to interact with the AI system in multiple ways, providing them precise control over how the system acts and what it advises, and making sure that the system doesn't make decisions for people. Research shows that people are happier and more likely to keep using AI systems that make them feel competent and independent, rather than ones that make them dependent. We also see that the amount of aid a user gets is linked to how much power they have. To maintain this equilibrium, the adaptive interfaces facilitating the connection frequently adjust to accommodate the user's requirements and proficiency level. But this is where this strategy is really useful for dealing with people's anxieties that AI would take jobs away from people: It illustrates that AI is something that makes us better, not something that takes our jobs (Purwanto, 2025).

In human-centered AI design, mental health, confidence, and inclusivity all work together to make a "trifecta" of good things happen. The important shift is that people believe AI will grow more like people. As it gets better, people are more likely to let it help them. For example, some people in China now let the government use facial recognition to keep track of their moods so that they can get help with their anger and keep it under control. This helps trust and benefit grow in a good way. Inclusive design principles will make systems more reliable because everyone will be involved in producing a product. It also helps a lot of people get the greatest care for their mental health. This means that more people can use mental health apps that are designed to be inclusive. It also means that the app is easier to use and has user interfaces that work for people from many different cultures. It must also consider this intersectionality, meaning it must recognize that several causes contributing to malaise may collectively influence individuals' interactions with AI systems. For AI to perform well for people, businesses need to create long-term relationships with groups and communities from a wide range of professions. They will also need to recognize that an AI system that is open, fosters trust, and makes people healthier may need to be rated not on how well it works technically, but on how comfortable it makes people feel. The idea is to create AI ecosystems that are honest about how they serve a lot of people. It's also crucial to realize that even if AI is omnipresent, human willpower, dignity, and the right to make your own choices are still very vital (Troussac et al., 2025).

The best ideas since sliced bread are those that are inclusive, new, and look at things from an evolutionary point of view. The psychological basis of inclusion is anchored in a fundamental biological imperative for belonging, which affects physical health, mental health, and social conduct. Studies provide substantial evidence that a strong sense of belonging is favorably associated with academic achievement, occupational variables, favorable social interactions, and both physical and mental health issues, such as depression and anxiety. On the other hand, feeling less like you belong increases the chances of antisocial behavior and getting sick. When people freely say what they think, take risks with their creativity, and work together openly with their coworkers, patients, or pupils, they come up with new ideas and find better ways to solve problems. The business case for inclusivity is very strong. Statistics show that inclusive environments are 1.7 times more likely to be innovation leaders in the market, see a 21% increase in profitability due to positive employee engagement, and are 70% more likely to have captured new market applications or segments (Zallio et al., 2025).

Schools are great venues to see how inclusive practices can make a difference in people's lives. All pupils with disabilities and their non-disabled classmates have said that they have gained something from it. Systematic research reviews frequently show that inclusive educational settings yield significant short- and long-term advantages. These include better reading and arithmetic skills for students with impairments, more students showing up to class, less behavioral problems, and a better chance of graduating from high school. Inclusion provides more educational benefits than just grades and test scores. It also helps people learn how to get along with others, talk to people, get more people to go to college and acquire employment, and live on their own as adults. Five attributes that are especially helpful for typical or average kids and students are being less afraid of individuals who are different from them and being more comfortable and aware of persons with disabilities or other differences. Growth in social cognition (tolerance skills and communication), enhanced self-concept (increased feelings of worth, including improved self-esteem and sense of belonging), the development (and integration) of a personal behavior code based on mutual respect, fairness, and caring; and warm, buddy-like friendships across differences. Studies show that students who are developing normally had "neutral or positive effects" in inclusive settings. Meta-analyses of data from 4.8 million students showed that inclusive environments had no negative effects and often led to better academic and social outcomes.

When confidence and inclusion work together, they make relationships that assist both the person and the business attain greater results. Research shows that making people feel like they belong through inclusive practices has health benefits on both the mental and physical levels. For example, heart rate drops, mood improves, and social self-esteem rises when people are included instead of excluded. These changes can then lead to psychological or physical side effects. Being connected is just as crucial for your health as having food, drink, and a place to live. Being alone is just as hazardous for your health as smoking fifteen cigarettes a day and twice as bad for your health as being overweight. Studies on leadership show that self-assured leaders who are seen as creating an inclusive environment, among other things, build trust in the leader, encourage team members to be more innovative and take risks, and boost the group's confidence, which all lead to better organizational performance and happier employees. Some of the benefits of making the workplace more welcoming and giving employees more confidence are that they stay longer, come up with more creative solutions to problems, and make better decisions, among other things. Research on social connections suggests that persons possessing supportive, confidence-boosting interactions are better equipped to manage stress, achieve improved physical health outcomes, and cultivate coping strategies and resilience in the face of adversity. People who are secure and feel like they belong create loops that keep going. These cycles occurs when people are more open about their thoughts, organizations acquire a wider range of opinions (and consequently greater performance), and society learns to be more accepting the more it observes these good behaviors (Margetis et al., 2021).

4. MENTAL WELL-BEING IN AI APPLICATIONS

Mental wellness is a key part of living a good life. It is not merely the absence of mental disease; it also involves emotional, psychological, and social dimensions of healing. You need to be able to live well, be satisfied with your life, and figure things out. An AI employed in mental health treatment could change everything. People recommended using AI to make mental health treatments more widely available, cheaper, and flexible on a big scale. AI could do this by coming up with new tech solutions and making an existing therapy better. Dr. D. G. Winslow remarked, "AI will be the most important tool for mental illnesses in the future because of this resurrection potential." Studies have shown that mental health apps that use AI are really effective for people who can't go to treatment in person, and they like them too. These apps break down geographical barriers, making it easier for people who need aid to get it from people who care about them. There are several ways that AI technology and mental health care might operate together, such as through chatbots, predictive analysis, individualized therapy, and systems that watch people in real time. These systems use machine learning algorithms to look for patterns in behavior, language, and biological indicators that are associated to mental illness. Studies show that AI systems may pick up on subtle signs of mental disease, such melancholy or worry. It may identify these indicators fairly early on by looking at a lot of various types of data, such as social media posts, speech patterns, online discussions, and records of how individuals use their smartphones or smartwatches. AI has the highest promise as a mental health therapeutic tool when applied at all phases. Preventing, treating the first episode, delivering treatment, and keeping an eye on treatment over time It offers personalization by customizing treatments to meet individual needs, preferences, and responses on a broad scale, a feature lacking in most conventional service delivery methods.

AI-based therapies continue to show great effectiveness, as shown by a succession of legal consistency assessments (ESM Table D) and caravan analyses that show big therapeutic effects on a number of psychological outcome variables. A recent meta-analysis of 35 research showed that AI-based conversational agents can help with depression and other mental health problems. The effect sizes were medium to big, at 0.64 and 0.7, respectively, which is similar to how well traditional treatments work. The review demonstrated that AI intervention is most efficacious for both clinical and subclinical instances, with enhanced effects noted in multimodal therapies, generative-based AI technologies, and those delivered through mobile applications or instant messaging. A study consisting of 18 randomized controlled trials with a total sample size of 3,477 patients showed that artificial intelligence had a good effect on sadness and anxiety, with effects that can be seen after eight weeks (Schmager et al., 2025).

AI-powered digital health apps help patients by using scientifically validated psychotherapy frameworks, cognitive-behavioral therapy treatments, mindfulness activities like meditation, psychopudition, and individualized intervention systems. AI-powered platforms that use this kind of model for mental health treatment can also assist people undertake therapeutic exercises on their own. Some of these are cognitive restructuring, behavior activation, relaxation strategies to lessen stress levels, and tools for keeping track of your mood. The drills get harder or easier based on how well the user executes them and what goals they have set for themselves. Natural language processing helps AI systems grasp what people say, how they feel, and how bad their symptoms are. At that moment, they can answer in a way that indicates they care and get what you're expressing. Over time, machine learning algorithms can learn from how people use them to make therapeutic reactions better. For example, they may make their replies more accurate and adjust how they help people based on how they like to talk and what they want to do. Advanced semantic analysis lets AI apps discover mental health problems with 89% accuracy. It can utilize text to gather information like recognizing emotions and patterns in behavior. This helps therapists focus on the most significant feelings in this kind of content, which makes therapies more targeted than ever before. When you put VR and AI together, you can make a virtual therapy area where people may deal with their trauma, anxiety, or phobias. This gives people a chance to slowly become used to their concerns and figure out how to deal with them in a secure, controlled space (Martini et al., 2024).

Digital mental health interventions are particularly effective in addressing accessibility issues, primarily by facilitating access for individuals lacking traditional mental health care, those residing in rural regions, and individuals unable to purchase such services. Randomized trials assessing digital interventions in low and middle-income countries demonstrate scalability potential: Cognitive behavioral therapy delivered via the Internet appears to be highly successful in reducing anxiety and depressive symptoms among adolescents. This is because the intervention may be changed to fit different cultures and can be used by people from all walks of life. AI mental health apps can help a lot of individuals at once without making the care worse.

You need to be very careful about how to get the most out of mental health apps that use AI while keeping your risks as low as possible. This entails thinking about things like morality, keeping your data safe, and how therapy relates to wise people in real life. The second ppba study from charity: water indicates that AI technology and human advisers may work together to support people with therapy. This is especially true for models that should be labeled "hybrid ones." These models are based on AI and are extremely distinct from m's other domains.

The literature indicates that AI chatbots may offer advantages; however, they cannot replace the complex emotional intelligence, empathy, and deep relationships necessary for effective human psychotherapeutic interactions, especially among individuals with severe psychological disorders. When AI is utilized in mental health, people are apprehensive about their privacy and the safety of their information. It has to be very careful with the private information and content that the user gives to the AI.

It also need to think about moral considerations, such making sure that AI doesn't treat vulnerable groups unfairly, that AI decisions are explicit, and that the boundaries and applications of therapies that employ AI are obvious. When healthcare systems use AI tools for mental health purposes, they must do so in a way that doesn't break any rules, follow the law, or use quality assurance methods that make sure AI applications are effective and safe. AI-based mental health apps will be more personalized in the future because of better machine learning (ML) models, more cultural sensitivity and linguistic diversity, more multimodal intervention options for certain groups of people, and better assessment tools that can pick up on small changes in psychological states over time. The goal is to create mental health ecosystems that are everywhere and can provide ongoing, unobtrusive monitoring and help to improve mental health in a wide range of people and situations (Saha, 2025).

5. DESIGNING HUMAN-CENTERED AI

A new method to think about how humans and technology work together is "human-centered AI." It begins and concludes with the values, necessities, and capabilities of individuals. This is a crucial correction for AI development that has primarily prioritized speed and power ahead of people's health. It seeks to create a world where AI technologies collaborate with people instead of replacing them. HCAI is a big idea that includes a lot of different fields, such as psychology, philosophy, social science, and how people and computers interact. It promises that AI technology will enable and serve the human with intelligence—an individuality of her own to exist, autonomy over substantial aspects of interaction between her and technical artifacts (but not dignity). There are eight parts to human-centered AI: being kind to understand the user, letting the user customize their experience, being aware of and paying attention to situations and context, being culturally sensitive while still being relevant to cultural background, being clear in decision-making and accountable, and being interactive in a way that helps everyone. So, these guidelines tell programmers to develop AI systems that actually get what customers want and need, give them a personalized experience based on what they want, and obey moral and cultural rules. The main principle behind the whole theory is that AI should aid humans instead of taking their employment. This will make it possible for people and computers to work together in a way that makes people better at things like creativity, judgment, and emotional intelligence instead of taking them away (Maroju & Bhattacharya, 2025).

The five key aspects of the at-a-glance checklist for human-centered AI might aid developers who want to make their work more ethical. The HCAI requirement hierarchy makes it easy to see how high-level strategic concepts and system requirements that can be measured are related. It takes nebulous moral worries and turns them into precise technological guidelines that developers can use to create and test their systems. Interdisciplinary teamwork approaches let AI experts work with people who are experts in a certain field, ethics, human-centered design, or the community to set common goals, ways to talk to each other, and ways to make decisions that use different points of view and areas of expertise. When you utilize a hierarchical model to design, you can employ different design methods at different levels of technology and in different types of organizations to attain your goals. These design goals slowly give AI more and more power to make choices, until AI has all the capacity to make choices. This manner, there is a common framework in which people may tell AIs what to do. To make AI work for people in the real world, you would need to think about it a lot and prepare ahead. This includes making it easy to understand, trust, and engage with AI so that people and AI may have a meaningful connection. There are several ways that good HCAI systems can help people make choices. Confidence indicators, visual explanations, textual reasoning, and interactive questioning tools are some examples of how AI recommendations can be made clearer and how humans can change their trust based on the system's competence and the scenario. Studies show that how an interface is designed can have a big impact on how engaged users are, how much they trust each other, and how well they work together on tasks (Zhao & Sun, 2025). This is because AI's confidence levels and the ability to see how AI is doing can help people and AI work together (making sure that the act of federated reflection doesn't increase cognitive load on its own while still having enough in common to work with the other) while cognitive forcing functions can help or lead to process yields, but at a cost. Finding the correct balance between accuracy and understandability is critical for making AI systems that can be understood. Users should be able to make wise choices with the system without being overwhelmed or being too confident in what the machine can do. User-centered design approaches advocate for the inclusion of various stakeholder groups in development processes, emphasizing the necessity for AI systems to accommodate a range of technical expertise, cultural backgrounds, accessibility requirements, and usage contexts, rather than assuming uniformity among all users. Participatory design methodologies employed in this fashion enable the meaningful involvement of stakeholders in delineating the system's scope and functionality, as well as in establishing evaluation metrics (Biswas et al., 2023).

5. ETHICAL CONSIDERATIONS

We need to stop only imagining what the future of the information society could be like with human-centered AI and start making good on our promises and commitments. Ethical AI methods set up big governance frameworks that have diverse review groups, tools for figuring out how AI affects things, operational checks, and ways to fix problems. This manner, we can make sure that AI systems follow the basic principles of democracy and human rights. We need to be more open than just talking about the technical models so that people may make sensible choices and/or have reasonable expectations. Also, it should be obvious what a system can and can't do, how data is being utilized, and what the risks are. Fairness detection tactics and mitigation procedures seek for any indicators of bias in the training data, the choices made by algorithms, or the results of the system as soon as they happen. After then, they aim to make sure that all groups of users are treated the same. Some ways to protect privacy are to limit the amount of data that is collected, encrypt it, limit who can access it, and acquire permission from the user. They protect AI while making it easy for it to obtain and trade value. Those systems tell AI how to act. For example, they include means for individuals to get involved, ways to remedy faults, and ways to make things right. People have a lot of power over what AI can do and what it can do. We need to keep a careful eye on and score how well the AI system does in terms of safety, fairness, and trust in order to make

AI activities more morally acceptable. This way, we can keep up with how society and technology are changing.

Collaborative human-AI methods look at how to create connections between people and AI that work well together. Each has their own capabilities, but people still have the power to make the most important decisions. The principles cover six main areas: adding AI to human tasks, helping users reach their goals with AI help, replacing similar or routine tasks with AI in a strategic way, bringing in different points of view through human-AI teams, actively taking part in decision making, and explaining how AI can help humans improve their process (Torkamaan et al., 2024). In practice, good collaboration designs would let users choose how much AI they want to be involved in, based on the difficulty of the work and other personal or situational considerations. This would result in flexible partnerships that evolve in response to changes in people's talents and circumstances.

Studies show that successful human-AI teams are more effective than either humans or AI working alone, especially when it comes to solving complex problems where combining human creativity and understanding of the situation with AI's analytical skills and speed gives them an edge. Problems with cognitive load: The AI system's interface needs to know how much work individuals can manage (both too little and too much) and help them make appropriate decisions instead of providing them too much or too little information and getting in the way of their work by meddling at the wrong time. users can create confidence in AI systems that are well-calibrated by using trust calibration mechanisms. These mechanisms provide users a decent picture of how reliable the system is, make it obvious how uncertain things are, and are honest about the system's dangers and limitations. There will need to be a careful balance between letting AI systems act on their own and letting people control them as they move toward more agentic AI systems that can learn, adapt, and act on what they learn. This will mean establishing rules that keep people in charge while still letting the AI system help with many different duties in the business (Yoo et al., 2024).

6. FUTURE DIRECTIONS AND RECOMMENDATIONS

Making AI that puts humans first could lead to systems that genuinely do make people better, healthier, and more moral. A Very Important Path for the Future A very important and quickly increasing subject is redesigning AI innovation to fit people's requirements, values, experiences, and so on. It puts people first, not technology. AI as automation needs to go from being an eyesore to becoming a trusted partner that helps people be more creative, intuitive, and make better choices. It can increase productivity, make work more meaningful, and get everyone interested by letting AI and people work together. AI can aid people from varied origins while also respecting their privacy and choices.

People feel safer when they can see how AI works and make better decisions about it. They are also less scared and meet fewer folks who are hesitant. AI systems need to be better at comprehending natural language so that they can talk to humans in a more natural way and make technical jargon less hard to understand. To make sure that AI systems are utilized properly, they also need to have moral principles like fairness, responsibility, and privacy incorporated in. If not, it would only move a lot of issues, from drug traffickers to abuse victims, all over the world. This is a short version of all the frameworks I've talked about. However, they need to be checked and updated all the time to stay up with new societal needs and technical breakthroughs (Soomro et al.). What I've shared is a synopsis of these frameworks, but any new ones must be kept up to current with changing social requirements in the future (Soomro et al., 2025).

In the future, it will be very vital to think about how people and AI can operate together. Human intellect is adaptable and changes according on the situation. This will focus on adaptive interaction paradigms that emphasize user autonomy and system flexibility to consistently meet individual needs and changing situations. Research shows that working together with robots produces better results than working alone. Machines don't like it when people give context and transgender, and they also don't like it when people have opinions that are different from what machines usually think. Improvements in interfaces, multimodal input, and adaptive intelligence will make it easier for people and AI to work together more smoothly. This will boost creativity and the quality of decisions while keeping human judgment and trust at the center. Trust calibration techniques that will allow people figure out what AI can and can't do and preserve control of crucial decisions by changing how much they trust it.

Scalability and inclusivity should be at the top of the agenda when making AI that is focused on people. There should be more AI-powered solutions that make healthcare, education, and jobs more equal by fulfilling a range of language, cultural, and physical accessibility demands. Smart homes and businesses that use AI every day will assist people who don't have enough access to technology obtain individualized help that lets them live freely and actively in a world that is more open to technology (Ebadpour et al., 2024). Better synthetic data and privacy-protecting technology will make it possible to employ AI in sensitive areas in a way that is ethical, making sure that people can learn well while still respecting their rights.

A perspective that looks to the future emphasizes growth that includes people from a variety of areas and groups. In the end, AI solutions will only fully reflect the intricacies and values of affected societies through collaboration with engineers, ethicists, and social scientists. Sustained cooperation brings together different points of view from different fields, making sure that everyone agrees on what people need and what AI can do for design that is ethical, welcoming, and beneficial. The forms of participatory governance let everyone who is interested work together to build the AI of the future. This will let technology make life better for people in a way that is both long-lasting and in solidarity, even when new threats come up. The future of AI that puts people first rests on: valuing human flourishing via openness and moral responsibility; flexible teaming; and scalable inclusivity. This can unlock AI's full potential to help build more fair, just, empowered, and healthy communities all across the world by doing this and making it a better partner that cherishes human dignity, creativity, and freedom (Passalacqua et al., 2025).

7. CONCLUSION

In the history of AI, Human-Centered AI represents a huge stride forward. It puts what people need, value, and believe in first. HCAI is not the same as ordinary AI because it doesn't merely desire things to be quicker and simpler. It looks at aspects like people's health, education, government, and level of living, as well as how they may work together and be innovative. For example, consumers like HCAI systems better when they stress being open, honest, and responsible. This method also talks about bias, privacy, and how to use AI in a moral way. HCAI will create AI systems in the future that are smarter, more powerful, and better at connecting with other systems. These devices will be able to read people's minds. They will think about both personal and cultural differences to make sure that everyone gets a fair and distinctive experience. HCAI systems will make it easier for individuals to use technology and give them more power over their lives. People will be able to make choices instead of having them taken away by tools that use a new approach of doing participatory design and natural language processing.

In the future, human-AI teaming systems will have better problem-solving, creative, and decision-making skills. AI technologies will improve people's thinking skills without taking away their ability to make choices. To make sure that AI is created in line with global ethical standards and human rights norms, technologists, moral philosophers, social scientists, and different communities of civil society will need to keep talking to each other. It need to keep undertaking research, have open governance, and follow ethical rules so that we can keep an eye on the consequences of AI systems that are continually developing, deal with new threats, and become used to them in a responsible way. AI's future is to make technological ecosystems that are more compassionate, welcoming, and trustworthy, and that increase people's quality of life around the world while also honoring their dignity and fairness. Human-centered AI isn't just a technical problem; it's a tremendous chance to rethink how robots and people work together. We would need to make a conscious and conscientious decision to build AI that makes people's lives better, promotes diversity, and brings about constructive societal change. To make sure that AI can do good things in a world that is complicated and linked, these values need to be part of every phase of AI design and use.

REFERENCES

Biswas, S., Patil, B., & Bhattacharjee, S. (2023, December). An AI-Driven Multi-faceted Approach to Mental Health: Leveraging Technology for Mental Well-Being. In *International Conference on Humainzing Work and Work Environement* (pp. 241-255). Singapore: Springer Nature Singapore.

Ebadpour, Z., Nikghadam-Hojjati, S., & Barata, J. (2024, June). Human-Centric Principles for Computational Systems Supporting Collaborative Creativity. In *Doctoral Conference on Computing, Electrical and Industrial Systems* (pp. 61-81). Cham: Springer Nature Switzerland.

Margetis, G., Ntoa, S., Antona, M., & Stephanidis, C. (2021). Human-centered design of artificial intelligence. *Handbook of human factors and ergonomics*, 1085-1106.

Maroju, P. K., & Bhattacharya, P. (2025). Understanding emotional intelligence: The heart of human-centered technology. In *Humanizing Technology With Emotional Intelligence* (pp. 1–18). IGI Global Scientific Publishing.

Martini, B., Bellisario, D., & Coletti, P. (2024). Human-centered and sustainable artificial intelligence in industry 5.0: Challenges and perspectives. *Sustainability*, *16*(13), 5448.

Ozmen Garibay, O., Winslow, B., Andolina, S., Antona, M., Bodenschatz, A., Coursaris, C., & Xu, W. (2023). Six human-centered artificial intelligence grand challenges. *International Journal of Human-Computer Interaction*, *39*(3), 391–437.

Passalacqua, M., Pellerin, R., Magnani, F., Doyon-Poulin, P., Del-Aguila, L., Boasen, J., & Léger, P. M. (2025). Human-centred AI in industry 5.0: A systematic review. *International Journal of Production Research*, *63*(7), 2638–2669.

Purwanto, A. N. I. (2025). Human-Centered AI: Designing Intelligent Systems that Empower, Not Replace. *RIGGS: Journal of Artificial Intelligence and Digital Business*, *4*(3), 3212–3221.

Pyae, A. (2025). What is Human-Centeredness in Human-Centered AI? Development of Human-Centeredness Framework and AI Practitioners' Perspectives. *arXiv preprint arXiv:2502.03293*.

Saha, A. (2025). Human-centred innovation in Society 5.0. *Society 5.0: A Transformation towards Human-Centered. Artificial Intelligence*, •••, 143.

Schmager, S., Pappas, I. O., & Vassilakopoulou, P. (2025). Understanding Human-Centred AI: A review of its defining elements and a research agenda. *Behaviour & Information Technology*, •••, 1–40.

Shen, J., Iandoli, L., & Aguirre-Urreta, M. (2022). Human-centered design for individual and social well-being: Editorial preface. *AIS Transactions on Human-Computer Interaction*, *14*(4), 446–460.

Soomro, S., Fan, M., Soomro, S., Naseer, E., Shaikh, S. N., & Shaikh, S. N. (2025). Balancing AI and Human Interaction: Impact of AI Interaction on Well-Being. In *AI in Mental Health: Innovations, Challenges, and Collaborative Pathways* (pp. 141-166). IGI Global Scientific Publishing.

Tahvanainen, L., Tetri, B., & Ahonen, O. (2024, May). Exploring and extending human-centered design to develop AI-Enabled wellbeing technology in healthcare. In *Nordic Conference on Digital Health and Wireless Solutions* (pp. 288-306). Cham: Springer Nature Switzerland.

Torkamaan, H., Tahaei, M., Buijsman, S., Xiao, Z., Wilkinson, D., & Knijnenburg, B. P. (2024). The role of human-centered ai in user modeling, adaptation, and personalization—models, frameworks, and paradigms. In *A Human-Centered Perspective of Intelligent Personalized Environments and Systems* (pp. 43–84). Springer Nature Switzerland.

Usmani, U. A., Happonen, A., & Watada, J. (2023, June). Human-centered artificial intelligence: Designing for user empowerment and ethical considerations. In *2023 5th international congress on human-computer interaction, optimization and robotic applications (HORA)*. IEEE.

Yoo, D. W., Woo, H., Pendse, S. R., Lu, N. Y., Birnbaum, M. L., Abowd, G. D., & De Choudhury, M. (2024). Missed opportunities for human-centered AI research: Understanding stakeholder collaboration in mental health AI research. *Proceedings of the ACM on Human-Computer Interaction, 8*(CSCW1), 1-24.

Zallio, M., Ike, C. B., & Chivăran, C. (2025). Designing Artificial Intelligence: Exploring Inclusion, Diversity, Equity, Accessibility, and Safety in Human-Centric Emerging Technologies. *AI*, *6*(7), 143.

Zhao, Y., & Sun, P. (2025). Artificial intelligence in the promotion of human well-being: Current trends and future directions. *Well-Being Sciences Review*, *1*(1), 3–8.

Chapter 8
Digital Vulnerability and Legal Protection of Children:
Examining International Responses to AI-Driven Exploitation and Behavioral Manipulation

Meha Bhushan
https://orcid.org/0009-0008-3322-6117
Gujarat National Law University, Gandhinagar, India

ABSTRACT

The internet has facilitated a global pandemic of online child sexual exploitation and abuse (OCSEA), posing deep challenges to law and policy. This chapter provides a combined assessment of the international, legal, and technical responses to this crisis. It looks at the foundation international legal regimes, such as UN conventions and regional instruments like the Lanzarote Convention, which impose requirements on states to criminalize and cooperate across borders. The discussion is based on comparative national case studies of the United States, United Kingdom, and India, revealing varied but convergent legal reaction. Moreover, the chapter also critically examines technological solutions like hash-matching and AI and multi-stakeholder alliances facilitating detection and enforcement. Finally, it underlines the stark dichotomy between safeguarding children and safeguarding fundamental rights, most notably in the areas of encryption and abuse content generated by AI, calling for a proportionate, child-focused response to eliminate this evil harm.

DOI: 10.4018/979-8-3373-6618-0.ch008

1. INTRODUCTION

The swift growth of the internet has been matched regretfully by a steep increase in online child sexual exploitation and abuse. Offenders easily exchange child sexual abuse material (CSAM, frequently referred to as "child pornography" in legislation) across borders, practice grooming of children through social media, and even abuse live-streaming, presenting pressing international challenges to law, policy, and technology. Child sexual exploitation on the internet has no borders and causes immense damage: global estimates indicate that approximately one in five children globally suffer from some type of sexual violence, and the vast majority of victims are known to their perpetrators (Kokolaki & Fragopoulou, 2025). Victims of abuse whose photos are shared online are "re-victimized" every time that content is disseminated, and this causes long-term trauma. Therefore, making sure these images and videos are quickly deleted and culprits apprehended is most important for the protection of children.

International cooperation and international law are essential, as online exploitation cuts across jurisdictions. The last three decades have seen the emergence of a global and regional legal framework from United Nations treaties to regional pacts such as the EU directives and the Council of Europe's Lanzarote Convention requiring states to criminalize online child sexual exploitation, prosecute offenders (even abroad), and cooperate across border. In parallel, nations have created national legislation and policy to address child sexual exploitation material: as a point of illustration, the United States uses strict federal legislation and a centralized reporting system via NCMEC; the United Kingdom uses a combination of strict legislation and industry-led self-regulation through the Internet Watch Foundation (IWF) (IWF 2024a); and India has tightened its legal bans and investigative capabilities over the last few years (Dushi et al., 2025).

Because legislation alone cannot stem the tide, there is also a pressing need for technological and operational measures. Industry and law enforcement have increasingly turned to tools like hash-matching (e.g. Microsoft's PhotoDNA) to automatically detect known abusive images, artificial intelligence to identify new content or grooming behavior, and databases to identify victims. Global industry coalitions (e.g. the Technology Coalition, WeProtect Global Alliance) and public-private partnerships have emerged to develop and share solutions. Simultaneously, specialized police task forces work cooperatively on an international basis to disrupt abuse networks on the open web and dark web such as operations that have rescued victims and disabled global rings.

But such initiatives also raise such advanced problems of privacy, freedom of speech, and technological feasibility (particularly in the case of encrypted communications). This current chapter gives a general overview of the struggle against child sexual exploitation online in an academic and critical way. It examines the international normative framework important United Nations instruments and other multilateral initiatives firstly, and then regional and national responses with case studies from the U.S., U.K., and India. Secondly, it discusses technological and operational mechanisms of enforcement, including detection technology and cross-sector collaboration. We emphasize the law in all of this across the chapter, and refer briefly to empirical evidence (e.g., from IWF and NCMEC) for an estimate of scale and effect of responses. In doing so, the chapter signals successes, new challenges (e.g., encryption and AI-generated abuse images), and the need for a balanced approach that defends children while safeguarding fundamental rights.

2. INTERNATIONAL LEGAL FRAMEWORKS AND INITIATIVES

Strategies to counter child sexual abuse on the Internet rest on a chain of international conventions, protocols, and cooperative programs that set levels of common legal standards and promote cross-border cooperation. These frameworks identify child sexual exploitation as a violation of human rights and mandate criminalization and punishment by states, harmonizing legislation to preclude offenders from taking advantage of jurisdictional loopholes. They also increasingly account for new technologies and forms of abuse. Below, we discuss the most significant global and regional instruments, as well as multi-stakeholder alliances working at the international level (Osorio de Barros & Severino Soares, 2025).

2.1 United Nations Conventions and Protocols

The foundation of international law in this area is the UN Convention on the Rights of the Child (CRC), 1989, which nearly every nation has ratified. The CRC obligates states in Article 34 to protect children from "all forms of sexual exploitation and sexual abuse," including exploitative use of children in pornographic performances and material. Article 34's broad mandate is given specific force by the Optional Protocol on the Sale of Children, Child Prostitution and Child Pornography (OPSC), 2000, which entered into force in 2002. The OPSC explicitly requires States Parties to prohibit by law the production, distribution, dissemination, import/export, possession, and advertising of child pornography, as well as the sale of children and child prostitution. It obliges states to establish criminal, civil or administrative liability for these offenses, including for legal persons (e.g., companies), and to assert jurisdiction over offenses committed abroad by their nationals to combat sex tourism and transnational trafficking.

The OPSC also promotes international cooperation in investigations and extradition of offenders. As of 2025, 176 countries have ratified the OPSC, reflecting a near-global consensus that child sexual abuse materials (CSAM) must be outlawed everywhere (UN Treaty Collection 2025). The UN Committee on the Rights of the Child issues guidance to strengthen implementation; for instance, its 2019 guidelines urged States to update legislation for technological developments to "avoid loopholes," ensure extraterritorial jurisdiction, and not criminalize children who are victims or who appear in sexual content, even if self-produced. Several other UN initiatives reinforce the protection of children in the digital environment. The Sustainable Development Goals (SDGs) include target 16.2 to end abuse, exploitation, trafficking and all forms of violence against children by 2030, which has spurred governments to take action against online exploitation as part of their SDG commitments. In 2021, the UN Committee on the Rights of the Child adopted General Comment No. 25 on children's rights in the digital environment, which explicitly calls on states to prevent and combat online child sexual exploitation and abuse through robust laws and cooperation with technology companies, while also safeguarding children's privacy and other rights. Furthermore, the UN Special Rapporteur on the sale and sexual exploitation of children has indicated the necessity of a comprehensive, worldwide response to online abuse. For instance, Special Rapporteur Mama Fatima Singhateh in 2022 stressed that the international scope of online child sexual abuse "calls for a holistic approach and commitment from all actors we can only succeed if we all do this together" (Parti & Szabo, 2024).

2.2 Regional Treaties

The Lanzarote and Budapest Conventions Regional organizations have produced binding legal documents frequently detailing even more specific steps against child sexual exploitation than international conventions. A prime example is the Council of Europe's Convention on the Protection of Children against Sexual Exploitation and Sexual Abuse (2007), or Lanzarote Convention. As of 2010 when it entered into force and has been ratified by 48 State Parties, including a few non-members, this comprehensive instrument criminalizes the full spectrum of sexual offenses against children. Its scope ranges from physical mistreatment and exploitation to the possession of sexually explicit images of children and, most importantly, the facilitation of such crimes through information and communication technologies. A trailblazing feature of the Lanzarote Convention was its requirement that criminalize online grooming, whereby adults solicit children on the Internet for sexual purposes. Apart from its repressive apparatus, the convention compels states to adopt preventive measures such as training courses, campaigns in the public sphere, and the vetting of adults employed with children offer support to victims and promote close international collaboration in investigations. An independent monitoring committee assesses national implementation, and the impact of the Convention can be seen in subsequent amendment of various European legislation to criminalize grooming and increase penalties for cyber-violence.

Another powerful regional tool is the Council of Europe's Convention on Cybercrime (2001), or the Budapest Convention. As wide-ranging as its scope on computer-related crimes in general, Article 9 obliges States Parties specifically to criminalize computer-related child pornography, making it criminal for acts of producing, offering, distributing, procuring, or possessing child pornographic material by a computer system. The treaty's strong template for global cooperation, such as 24/7 contact points and mechanisms for mutual legal assistance, is essential to support cross-border operations against child exploiters and to seek out electronic evidence stored in servers in another country. Though the treaty has not found its way to universal acceptance with around 68 parties that include the United States but missing prominent players like India its provisions have been a guiding model for enacting cyber-enabled CSAM crimes in most jurisdictions around the globe (Kazi, 2025).

2.3 Global Multistakeholder Initiatives and Coalitions

Aside from classic treaties, multistakeholder partnerships are also powerful drivers to fight child sexual exploitation online. A case in point is the WeProtect Global Alliance, launched in 2014 and currently engaging over 100 governments, 50+ tech companies, and hundreds of civil society organizations. It developed a Model National Response guide to legal, technical, and victim-focused measures which has shaped national reform. WeProtect also enables summits every year and, in 2022, launched a Global Taskforce co-chaired by the EU and African Union to respond to issues such as encryption and borderless investigations.

The Technology Coalition, led by major tech companies such as Google and Microsoft, encourages cooperation on technical methods. On efforts like Project Protect (launched in 2020), it supports research, builds detection tools, and lobbies for common standards. Since CSAM traverses boundaries, efforts like these combined efforts make efforts to bring consistency to detection and removal of abusive material. Law enforcement is also engaged. INTERPOL's International Child Sexual Exploitation (ICSE) database gathers CSAM data to support the identification of victims and offenders across the globe. Successful coordinated operations, like Operation Blackwrist (2018), which took down a large darknet network and rescued

50 children, are an example of the impact of global policing. Europol also facilitates big cybercrime operations with its EC3 Cybercrime Centre.

Also amplified are reporting networks such as INHOPE and national hotlines (such as IWF UK, NCMEC USA), which enable the public to identify CSAM, coordinate trans-nationally to prompt speedy content removal. These are supplemented by policy guidelines from UNICEF, ECPAT, and ICMEC, which have advocated term reform and best-practice law. Such coalitions and networks form an important layer of coordination and innovation, complementing treaty-based obligations with responsive, real-time measures against online harm.

3. NATIONAL LEGAL RESPONSES: CASE STUDIES OF THE U.S., U.K., AND INDIA

Although international conventions provide general protections, it is through national laws that online child abuse is dealt with. This section discusses how the United States, United Kingdom, and India respond to online child abuse by way of laws, law enforcement measures, and collaboration. Each represents various legal cultures, technological capabilities, and policy decisions.

3.1 United States: Strict Laws and Centralized Reporting

The U.S. has sweeping federal laws under Title 18 of the U.S. Code, criminalizing production (18 U.S.C. §2251), possession (18 U.S.C. §§2252, 2252A), and distribution of CSAM. The PROTECT Act of 2003 widened the law to virtual and morphed images (DOJ, 2003). Online enticement and grooming are charged under §2422(b), sex tourism and extraterritorial offenses under §2423 and §2423(c).

A characteristic feature is compulsory reporting: §2258A requires electronic service providers (ESPs) to report known CSAM to the National Center for Missing & Exploited Children (NCMEC), and failing to do so carries fines of up to $300,000. Though the legislation does not require proactive scanning, most firms employ software such as PhotoDNA, since they become responsible upon acquiring "actual knowledge" of CSAM. Section 230 of the Communications Decency Act does not immunize platforms from these duties. In 2023, NCMEC received over 36 million Cyber Tipline reports mostly from Meta platform.

Enforcement is led by the Department of Justice's Child Exploitation and Obscenity Section, the FBI, Homeland Security Investigations (HSI), and state-based Internet Crimes Against Children (ICAC) task forces. U.S. law enables prosecution of Americans involved in CSAM overseas and even foreign nationals upon U.S. entry (18 U.S.C. §2423(c)). NGOs like Thorn assist by building detection software and supporting survivors. Challenges remain: the overwhelming number of CyberTips has strained investigative capacity, and proposals like the EARN IT Act continue to raise concerns over encryption (Badawy, 2025).

3.2 United Kingdom: Legal Enforcement and Online Safety Regulation

The UK criminalizes CSAM under the Protection of Children Act 1978, Criminal Justice Act 1988, and Sexual Offences Act 2003, which includes offenses for creating, possessing, and distributing indecent images of children. The UK also prohibits pseudo-photos and AI-written content under the Coroners and Justice Act 2009. Grooming and sexual communication with a child are offenses under sections 15 and 15A of the Sexual Offences Act.

The Internet Watch Foundation (IWF), which was started in 1996, allows the public to report on suspected CSAM anonymously. The IWF maintains a blocklist that is voluntarily implemented by UK ISPs. Therefore, CSAM hosted within the UK reduced from 18% of all content in 1996 to less than 0.1% in 2018. The Online Safety Act 2023 asks platforms to assess risks, minimize harms, and comply with Ofcom's regulatory codes. Ofcom may request CSAM detection technology if other methods fail, with privacy protections built in (OSA, 2023). Failure to comply can result in fines of as much as £18 million or 10% of worldwide revenue. The "Report Remove" tool, launched with NSPCC, enables minors to request takedown of self-generated content.

3.3 India: Evolving Laws, Supreme Court Intervention, and Global Collaboration

India's juridical counter-measure to online child sexual exploitation is based mainly on the Protection of Children from Sexual Offences Act (POCSO) largely re-drafted in 2019 to specifically deal with child sexual abuse content (CSAM) and Section 67B of the Information Technology Act, 2000. A landmark judicial development was by the Supreme Court of India in Just Rights Foundation v. Harish (2024), which finally settled that watching or possessing CSAM constitutes an offense under POCSO as well as the IT Act. The judgment also advocated the application of the term "child sexual abuse material" to properly capture the seriousness of the harm inflicted (SCI, 2024). In terms of operations, India has set up a National Cybercrime Reporting Portal for anonymous public reporting of CSAM. This was supported by a 2016 collaboration between the non-governmental organization Aarambh India and the Internet Watch Foundation (IWF), which launched proactive reporting and blocking of abusive material. In addition, through joint efforts by the Ministry of

Home Affairs and the National Crime Records Bureau (NCRB), India now accepts and processes CyberTipline information from the National Center for Missing & Exploited Children (NCMEC) having received two million tips up to 2023 (MHA, 2023). Law enforcement efforts have been ramped up through national operations like Operation Carbon and Operation Megh Chakra. To augment its international investigation powers, India also joined the International Child Sexual Exploitation (ICSE) database of INTERPOL in 2022 to improve victim identification (INTERPOL, 2022). In terms of regulation, the Information Technology (Intermediary Guidelines and Digital Media Ethics Code) Rules, 2021, require substantial social media intermediaries to employ automated methods, such as hashing technologies, to actively identify and remove CSAM, along with incorporating requisite privacy measures (Wood, 2024). A 2020 report by Parliament's ad hoc committee on pornography further suggested a set of measures such as mandatory platform reporting, the application of AI to detect CSAM, regulating encryption, and economic surveillance of CSAM transactions, although implementation thereof continues. Despite lingering issues like gaps in enforcement, contentious debates over privacy, and skewed police capacity India is undoubtedly striving to align its legal, technological, and cooperative responses with international best practices. Slowing down this momentum will be dependent on continued legal strengthening, technological improvement, and enhanced international cooperation.

4. TECHNOLOGICAL AND OPERATIONAL MEASURES FOR ENFORCEMENT

While legal structures offer the necessary basis for criminalizing child sexual abuse on the net, they are inadequate on their own to meet a crisis of global, virtual dimensions. Faced with tens of millions of illegal photographs and films a figure that makes enforcement by hand such as finding a needle in a haystack the response has needed to be technology-driven and advanced planning. This section outlines the important technical controls, from hashing to AI-powered detection and content blocking, and the operational practices that allow them to work, including cross-industry information-sharing and global law enforcement activity. It does this in the context of an underlying tension between using these new technologies and protecting core rights to privacy and civil liberties (Faraz et al., 2024).

4.1 Automated Detection: Hash-Matching and Beyond

A foundation of the technological approach to online child sexual abuse material (CSAM) is computer vision-based image detection through perceptual hashing.

Acknowledging the failure of the older text-based filtering approach with respect to visual media, Microsoft, in consultation with Dr. Hany Farid from Dartmouth College, created PhotoDNA in 2009. The algorithm creates a one-of-a-kind digital "fingerprint" for an image that does not change even after small modifications like resizing, recoloring, or cropping. This perceptual process is optically different from cryptographic digests such as MD5, which break with any pixel-based modification, rendering PhotoDNA highly immune to the easy alterations perpetrators employ to avoid detection. The technology was quickly embraced by the technology sector to scan user-uploaded content against lists of known abuse images.

When a hash match is detected, the associated content is marked for removal and referred to the appropriate authorities, for example, the National Center for Missing & Exploited Children (NCMEC) in the US. By the 2010s, PhotoDNA had been implemented in the content moderation processes of all the leading platforms, for example, Facebook, Google that used it for Gmail and subsequently Google Drive, Twitter, and Yahoo. Its implementation is presently worldwide, with more than 200 organizations across the globe using PhotoDNA or similar hashing technologies up to 2022. The technology has been hailed as responsible for the takedown of millions of illicit images and helping in convicting many predators. This system is based on extensive hash databases, like the database of the UK's Internet Watch Foundation (IWF), which has hundreds of thousands of confirmed CSAM hashes distributed to industry partners. Some other essential repositories are NCMEC's Child Victim Identification Program and Interpol's International Child Sexual Exploitation (ICSE) database, which also creates hashes for all images in its system.

The main disadvantage of hash-matching is that its usefulness is limited to pre-identified and cataloged imagery and cannot find newly created or unknown content. In an effort to close this loophole, companies and researchers have resorted to artificial intelligence and machine learning. In 2018, Google reported an AI classifier that could detect hitherto unknown CSAM through pattern recognition of abusive content, which it subsequently open-sourced in the form of the Content Safety API. In addition to imagery, machine learning algorithms are also taught to pick up on grooming behavior in text communication. For example, "Project Artemis," a 2020 effort by a group that includes Microsoft and Thorn, offers a tool that indicates conversational patterns indicative of grooming like great age gaps or sexually explicit conversation for human moderator consideration.

The difficulty increases with video material because of larger file sizes and the fact that abusive clips may be nested within extended videos. Microsoft also evolved its technology by creating PhotoDNA for Video, which dissects videos into discrete frames and hashes out each still. This enables analysts, like those at the IWF, to find known abusive segments within hours-long videos in mere minutes, significantly speeding up verification and removal. Microsoft released this tool at no cost to eligible organizations in 2018 to foster extensive adoption. The need for these tools is echoed by information from NCMEC, which experienced a tenfold growth in video files within its CyberTipline between 2015 and 2017, a clear indication of the changing behavior of the offenders (Gaitis et al., 2025). Even supportive tools like YouTube's CSAI Match are being used to combat this issue. For unlisted content, AI classifiers, though better, are still flawed and pose risks of false negatives, that is, letting problematic material through, as well as false positives, which falsely identify innocuous images. Therefore, platforms generally use a multilayered approach: first and foremost, heavy reliance on extremely accurate hashing for existing CSAM, plus AI as a filter for fresh content, with everything identified by AI open for examination by humans. Additional innovation is oriented towards victim identification from image examination; Interpol systems, for instance, can identify repeated backgrounds or rooms in different images to connect cases and find previously unidentified victims.

Complementary detection includes keyword and text scanning. Secondary are visual media, but the perpetrator involves text within chats and search requests. Meta's Facebook scans for grooming signs like an adult requesting photos from a child based on keyword triggers and behavior pattern analysis. OneDrive by Microsoft and leading search engines also index file names, descriptions, and search queries, regularly demonetizing, demoting, or blocking results related to child abuse. But resilient abusers often resurface on the darknet or encrypted platforms where platform-level scanning is not possible, requiring anticipatory law enforcement infiltration.

Cross-industry hash-sharing efforts augment the success of these technologies. NCMEC's Hash Registry and the IWF's hash lists help new CSAM identifiers rapidly spread. The inter-company hash model, first established by the Global Internet Forum to Counter Terrorism (GIFCT) for terrorist content, is used for CSAM as well, frequently through NCMEC as a clearinghouse. In operation, when a firm sees a new CSAM image, it informs NCMEC, which creates a hash and shares it with industry partners to allow near-universal blocking of that particular image. The Technology Coalition also facilitates confidential knowledge sharing between its member firms to make this collective protection stronger.

4.2 Takedown, Blocking, and Hotlines

Once CSAM is detected, the next focus is on its quick removal and preventing further spread. This is done by a multi-stakeholder approach using notice-and-takdown methods along with, where required, network-level blocking. Expert internet hotlines like the UK's Internet Watch Foundation (IWF), the US National Center for Missing & Exploited Children (NCMEC), and the Canadian Centre for Child Protection are the pillars of the worldwide "notice and takedown" system. For content hosted on compliant service providers such as mainstream social media, image hosts, and cloud services, removal is usually quick because of strict corporate policies that specifically bar CSAM and require account suspension. For content that is located on standalone sites or foreign servers, the hotlines send takedown notices to the hosting company or its upstream provider. INHOPE's network enables the global retransmission of these alerts to the relevant national hotline or law enforcement agency within hours, in many instances. This system, INHOPE says, leads to illegal content being removed within one to three days in the majority of cases. The scope of this endeavor is immense; during 2023 alone, the IWF took action on more than 255,000 URLs hosting child sexual abuse, effectively removing them from the public internet (Yu et al., 2025).

As a last resort when the website owners, especially those located on the dark web or on so-called bulletproof hosting services, consciously fail to delete CSAM, access blocking is a required measure of containment. Varying approaches exist at the national level for blocking. While some nations, notably France and India, have specifically passed laws requiring ISP-level blocking, others, like the UK and Canada, achieve this through voluntary arrangements with internet service providers. The United States, on the other hand, is more likely to block on free expression issues but aims at removal at source. This has built a patchwork of regulation, even within frameworks like the EU's Child Sexual Abuse Directive that permits but does not require the use of blocking. Though technically advanced users are able to bypass these blocks with software such as VPNs or Tor, they are effective in preventing inadvertent access, openly declaring the illegality of the content, and more importantly, protecting victims from knowing their abuse is being observed within a specific nation, reducing revictimization. One of the main challenges is staying accurate so that over-blocking of valid content is not allowed to happen, and hence the majority of systems use human-reliable URL-specific lists instead of wide-domain blocking.

Another frontier evolving in this area is preventive blocking, wherein services most notably chat platforms use filtering to catch known CSAM before upload or send, a method called client-side hash matching. A high-profile and contentious instance was Apple's 2021 suggestion of scanning users' photos on iPhones for known hashes of CSAM before upload to iCloud, a proposal that was shelved in the face of enormous privacy backlash. Nonetheless, server-side "upload filtering" is already commonplace on sites such as Facebook, where photos are matched against hash databases when uploaded and refused if a match is detected. The regulatory climate is increasingly set to require such detection; both the EU draft CSAM Regulation and the UK's Online Safety Act both consider requiring scanning technology, even in encrypted contexts by way of on-device scanning, an option which remains radically controversial in light of its broad effect on security and privacy.

At the same time, still paramount is an operational emphasis on identification of the victims. Police around the world invest tremendous resources into forensic examination of seized CSAM so as not only to make cases against perpetrators but most importantly, identify and recover child victims who are featured in them. Researchers painstakingly search through contextual indicators in the images, like recognizable objects of recognition in the periphery or detectable accents of videos, to try to find victims. International databases are an important part of this endeavor; Interpol's International Child Sexual Exploitation (ICSE) database alone is responsible for the identification of over 30,000 victims globally. Also available are tools such as Microsoft's PhotoDNA, which may be employed proactively to cross-match seized content with images of recognized missing children to ascertain whether they are the subject of current abuse. For the resolution of the most complex cases, regular sessions are convened by international victim identification task forces that facilitate collaborative problem-solving among global experts (Cheong et al., 2025).

4.3 Industry Initiatives and Coalitions

Tech firms have progressively recognized a two-pronged mandate to fight abuse on their platforms, responding both to moral obligation and legal requirement. Apart from collective organizations such as the Technology Coalition, single companies have taken substantive standalone actions. Meta, for example, has thousands of content moderators on staff and has dedicated specialized "child safety teams" to review and refer CSAM reports to NCMEC. The company also employs sophisticated heuristics, through the use of such tools as PhotoDNA and tracking suspicious group behavior, to detect accounts that are trafficking in abusive content. Microsoft's Digital Crimes Unit has been a leader in so doing, not only through its development of PhotoDNA but by running an international PhotoDNA Cloud Service. This service is free of charge to eligible NGOs and smaller technology companies, allowing them to benefit from hash-matching functionality without directly dealing with the contraband images. Similarly, Google has supplemented its Content Safety API with preventive measures; since 2013 it has demoted search results and blacklisted child abuse-related terms, and has also been cooperating with NGOs like the IWF to continually update these interventions.

Cross-industry collaboration is also seen through initiatives such as the "Hash Sharing Consortium," which has been arranged by NCMEC and the non-profit organization Thorn. The consortium allows businesses to exchange hashes of reported pictures into a centralized, collective database. Thorn, a tech organization dedicated to building solutions to prevent child sexual exploitation, introduced a platform called "Safer." This platform offers businesses a user interface to search their files against databases of CSAM hashes known to exist, as well as Thorn's classifier for locating possible new abuse material. Additionally, Thorn creates sextortion pattern-detection tools and produces important research; one of its reports illustrated how the increase in child sextortion, a self-generated content coerced form, is a key factor behind the increase in reporting numbers (Afroogh et al., 2025).

The battle against CSAM has even moved into the financial community. In an effort to fight commercial distribution of abuse material, coalitions like the Financial Coalition Against Child Pornography were formed. Initiated in 2006 by banks, credit card issuers, and NCMEC, this effort effectively disabled the main payment processing avenues for child abuse websites, bringing much of the use of credit cards to an end and encouraging perpetrators to utilize more esoteric means such as cryptocurrency. As a result, tracking cryptocurrency transactions on the dark web has become a new frontier for enforcement. As part of the new tactic, agencies use blockchain analytics to "follow the money," a technique that has, in high-profile operations such as the 2021 shut down of the dark web platform "Welcome to Video," resulted in hundreds of people being arrested worldwide. Financial intelligence is now an established method of CSAM investigations, and Europol's EC3 and national cybercrime agencies have developed tailored financial tracing expertise for child abuse matters.

Finally, international cooperation by law enforcement remains a cornerstone to an effective response. High-impact collaborative operations, e.g., Interpol's Operation Blackwrist, demonstrate the power of cross-border collaboration. Following a first operation in 2017, Interpol organized Operation Blackwrist II in 2019, leading to further arrests. Various operations, including the Interpol-managed Operation Thunder in 2020, targeted pedophile groups in Asia. Europol also oversees large operations, including a June 2023 operation in 19 nations against criminal producers of AI-generated child abuse images that led to 25 arrests. Being able to exchange information in real time across secure networks, such as Interpol's I-24/7 system, is key; intelligence in one part of the world can directly result in the rescue of a child in another, such as with the instance of the UK National Crime Agency alerting an international partner to a British perpetrator streaming on their country.

4.4 Balancing Enforcement Technologies with Privacy and Rights

Development of very powerful detecting devices has sustained decades-long controversy over privacy, bulk surveillance, and government overreach potential. The implementation of end-to-end encryption (E2EE) on messaging apps is one of the central frontlines in the controversy. Encryptions are a gigantic enforcement problem, critically impairing detection and investigation of CSAM sharing as it makes content off-limits even to the providers themselves. On the other hand, encryption is a vital security and privacy protector of billions of legitimate users, security that goes to protect children's security from other online threats on the Internet. Proposed technical measures like client-side scanning a technique in which devices scan content prior to encryption efforts are meant to solve this conundrum. Others like the Electronic Frontier Foundation (2022), however, caution that these sorts of events are actually opening up a systemic weakness or "backdoor" to be exploited by the criminal fraternity for nefarious purposes or leaving important security loopholes. This challenge to rule of law can be seen in legislation such as the U.K. Online Safety Act, where regulatory authority is given to require the utilization of accredited detection technology.

Even with such legislative pressure, to date and up to 2025, there is no technically viable and widely accepted solution that can search-scanning E2EE content for CSAM without functionally undermining the integrity of the encryption. The European Commission's draft CSAM Regulation also faces similar resistance with privacy activists and technology firms complaining that it would entail permanent surveillance of everyone. There is a grouping of child protection NGOs who assert that a threshold level of scanning of encrypted space is absolutely required. They contend that considerable CSAM trafficking has migrated to closed groups on encrypted platforms and point to NCMEC statistics indicating that E2EE implementation on platforms such as Facebook Messenger could result in loss of numerous millions of critical reports, presenting a "going dark" challenge to investigators. Solving this underpinning policy conundrum will probably require major technology advances, for example, homomorphic encryption or secure escrow processes, or stern legal accommodations in the next couple of years. The other critical factor is the false positive risk and safeguarding users' rights. Hash-matching known CSAM is virtually zero for false positives, but AI classifiers are naturally error-prone and can mislabel harmless content, like works of art or family portraits. One of the most publicized instances was an innocent father's photographs of his toddler taken for a doctor's appointment that were flagged by Google's AI system as CSAM in error and led to account suspension and police investigation before being publicly ridiculed as a false positive (Ali & Somu, 2025). This case highlights the absolute requirement of human examination and strong due process. In order to limit such harms, businesses generally send human moderators to confirm AI-produced flags prior to referring reports to law enforcement. However, with the staggering number of tens of millions of reports per year, it is unavoidable that some legal content will be mistakenly flagged. Both legal frameworks and tech firms are creating redress systems as a reply; for example, Google has established user appeal procedures for content moderation choices, and jurisdictions like the European Union are putting forward requirements for independent audits to determine the reliability and bias of detection technologies. Lastly, the sheer scale of CSAM on the web results in individuals working to get rid of it content moderators, hotline analysts, police investigators subjected to psychological wear. A frequently underemphasized but vital step is welfare and resilience support for these staff. Counseling programs, rotation, and technological tools such as image blurring and grayscale filters are offered by most hotlines and law enforcement organizations to minimize impact while viewing content (Boine, 2024). IWF and others have best-practice protocols to handle vicarious trauma in analysts. This "human" side of the technological battle is crucial to maintaining the effort over the long term. Technology and operations comprise the field tactics of the war on online child sexual exploitation, complementing the legal tactics. Hash-matching has made takedown speeds plummet and largely cleared known images from large platforms, a triumph that has, in response, pushed criminals to more hidden routes. At the same time, fresh AI tools vow to spot a larger quantity of previously unseen abuse and even pre-empt some by allowing platforms to ban suspicious accounts ahead of time (Dasgupta et al., 2025). Industry coalitions demonstrate the old adage that several hands make light a job no one has the entire solution, but collectively they make it harder for abusers to conceal. Law enforcement operations teach us that, even on anonymous networks, collective effort and global cooperation can track down perpetrators and rescue children. But only if it evolves constantly. There are opponents who more and more employ technological innovation, from encryption to AI-generated content, and therefore keep the guardians in a continuous cycle of counter-innovation (Foster, 2024). The present focus of the enforcement community on issues like CSAM in end-to-end encrypted contexts, AI-generated fictional CSAM, and spreading self-generated material via sextortion mirrors the challenges to come. Technology took us here by facilitating abuse on a never-before-imagined scale but technology, tamed by good law and regard for rights, has to be part of the solution (El-Deeb et al., 2024).

5. CONCLUSION

Child sexual exploitation on the internet is one of the worst criminal trends of the internet era, increasingly eroding children's rights and dignity worldwide. In this chapter, the global, multi-dimensional response has been outlined, through international legal regimes setting common standards, national legislation and initiatives that apply these standards, and technological and cooperative measures that enable detection and enforcement. Progress is concrete: nearly all states now criminalize child sexual abuse material, numerous states have enacted a new law to address new forms of abuse online, and global cooperation has never been tighter, with measurable gains such as the rescue of thousands of children and the prosecution of criminals. Empirical evidence from organizations such as NCMEC and IWF shines both light on the magnitude of the issue and the efficacy of interventions, demonstrating, for example, that tens of millions of illegal images are identified and blocked every year, and that networks of previously concealed abuse on the dark web have been penetrated and dismantled (Karamchand, 2025).

The present case studies of India, the United Kingdom, and the United States reflect convergence worldwide in terms of will. Notwithstanding their divergent legal traditions, the three courts all acknowledge the necessity for strong legislation with criminalization of simple possession and watching CSAM and active industry participation in monitoring and reporting, and enabling specialized law enforcement authorities. These case studies also pinpoint diverse strategic mechanisms: the United States mandatory reporting system and a single central clearinghouse via NCMEC; the U.K. co-regulatory system on company responsibility under its Online Safety Act; and Indian use of judicial drive and international cooperation to develop investigative capacity (De La Osa & Remolina, 2024). Aside from differences, there is a clear direction towards consolidation, with states increasingly harmonizing their laws under treaties like the OPSC and EU directives, and collaborating on crucial tools such as hash databases and AI advancements to maximize the efficiency of their collective efforts.

Challenges, however, are deep-seated. The encrypted and decentralized nature of the internet guarantees jurisdictional blind spots and havens where abuse material can be hosted beyond the immediate gaze of law enforcement. The tension between privacy and security is a persistent policy puzzle with no easy answer; how it is treated will set precedents for the broader question of platform responsibility for user material. The development of AI that can create deepfake child abuse images represents a new frontier early research by the IWF identified thousands of AI-created CSAM on forums(IWF 2023), and although such images entail no "real" child, they are illegal in most jurisdictions (such as the UK and U.S.) and feed dangerous fantasies. Legal frameworks might need to specifically mention the production and dissemination of fake CSAM in order for the offense to be ascertainable and punishment to be adequate, as the UK is now contemplating.

Another issue is the growing amount of sexually explicit child content self-produced by children, sometimes under compulsion (so-called "sextortion"). The fact that 92% of material taken down by the IWF in 2023 was self-created by victims under duress(IWF 2024b)calls for new approaches: stronger educational measures to prevent children from being victims of grooming online, easier reporting mechanisms for children (such as India's efforts with specialized portals, or NCMEC's "Take It Down" app for teenagers to remove nude photos), and perhaps considerate legal provisions treating coerced self-generated content abuse as what it is, but as an offense by a victim and not the child. There are certain jurisdictions that are changing legislation to prevent children who produce sexual images of themselves (under duress) from being charged with child pornography offenses instead, enforcement targets those that started or spread the images. The significance of a victim-sensitive approach to enforcement cannot be better said. There is need to design legislation and technology to safeguard children as well as reduce their trauma.

This is not only the expeditious removal of abusive content but also full support to victims. International standards such as the Lanzarote Convention and established best practices progressively demand victim support programs, for instance, counseling, legal aid, and access to continued searching and removal of any remaining Internet trace of their abuse an activity offered by agencies such as NCMEC. Abused individuals whose voices are enabled by advocacy groups are becoming influential policymakers; for example, they all fight for an efficient "right to be forgotten" online that causes their abuse photos to cease being circulated. Regulators of jurisdictions, however, grapple with alternatives such as international agreements and extraterritorial orders to enable quick worldwide takedowns without eroding this right.

The battle against web child abuse in the years to come will be characterized by three elements: mass deployment of artificially intelligent hardware, securely protected, to detect abuse that surpasses human capabilities; relentless innovation in world law, perhaps resulting in a separate global convention on web child abuse in the form of the Cybercrime Convention protocol on e-evidence; and tight international collaboration. WeProtect Global Alliance, for instance, is widening its ambit and can act as the hub body to call together and assist in tracking and holding governments accountable and diverting resources to where implementation support is needed. Additionally, greater concern for transparency is pushing technology companies to publish publicly accessible data on how they process child abuse reports and sanction accounts. Practices such as the Five Country Ministerial Voluntary Principles and an OECD 2023 report on transparency chafe this very practice energetically, which is central to gaining public trust and business responsibility.

Finally, a proper response would mean an "all hands on deck" approach: legislators to enact simple, up-to-date legislation; platforms to develop with safety measures and report abuse forthwith; police and hotlines to collaborate worldwide 24/7; and neighborhoods to remain watchful (parents, instructors, children themselves informed on internet threats). The imperative of human rights is clear all children have the right to a safe childhood, and should be protected from sexual exploitation, under the CRC and universal human rights. The internet should not be a haven for perpetrators. As recently accounted for by one UN Special Rapporteur, we are currently at a "critical moment" in this issue and "we can only succeed if we all pull together. The innovations detailed above, as great as they are, then need to be sustained and continued as technology continues to advance. Through continued support of legal frameworks, adopting introspective innovation, and given appropriate due to the opinions of survivors in informing the solutions, global society can make progress towards the vision of the elimination of online child sexual exploitation creating the online world a better world for future generations of children.

REFERENCES

Afroogh, J. J. S., Atkinson, K. C. A. M. D., & Dhurandhar, A. (2025). LLMs and Childhood Safety: Identifying Risks and Proposing a Protection Framework for Safe Child-LLM Interaction. *arXiv preprint arXiv:2502.11242*.

Ali, K. A. R., & Somu, C. S. (2025, May). Artificial Intelligence in Detecting and Mitigating Online Child Sexual Abuse: Approaches and Solutions. In *2025 2nd International Conference on Intelligent Computing and Robotics (ICICR)* (pp. 464-471). IEEE.

Badawy, W. (2025). The ethical implications of using children's photographs in artificial intelligence: Challenges and recommendations. *AI and Ethics*, •••, 1–12.

Boine, C. (2024). The AI Act Manipulation Gap. *Emory Int'l L. Rev.*, *39*, 417.

Cheong, I., Caliskan, A., & Kohno, T. (2025). Safeguarding human values: Rethinking US law for generative AI's societal impacts. *AI and Ethics*, *5*(2), 1433–1459.

Dasgupta, R., Mekala, S. H., Jaigirdar, F. T., Anwar, A., & Chang, L. Y. C. (2025). Unlocking Australia's AI usage in law enforcement from human involvement perspective: A systematic literature review. *AI & Society*, •••, 1–28.

De La Osa, D. U. S., & Remolina, N. (2024). Artificial intelligence at the bench: Legal and ethical challenges of informing—or misinforming—judicial decision-making through generative AI. *Data & Policy*, *6*, e59.

Dushi, D., Berdufi, N., & Karagianni, A. (2025). The legal framework and legal gaps for AI-generated child sexual abuse material. *Computer Law & Security Review*, *59*, 106205.

. El-Deeb, S., Jahankhani, H., Amin Metwally Hussien, O. A., & Will Arachchige, I. S. (2024). Towards Responsible AI: Exploring AI Frameworks, Ethical Dimensions and Regulations. *Market Grooming: The Dark Side of AI Marketing*, 139-157.

Faraz, A., Ahsan, F., Mounsef, J., Karamitsos, I., & Kanavos, A. (2024). Enhancing child safety in online gaming: The development and application of protectbot, an ai-powered chatbot framework. *Information (Basel)*, *15*(4), 233.

Foster, J. (2024). Pixelated Harm: An Analysis of the Impact of AI-Generated Images on CSAM Criminalization and Child Safety. *Okla. City UL Rev.*, *49*, 425.

Gaitis, K. K., Fakonti, C., Lonard, Z., Lu, M., Schidlow, J., Stevenson, J., & Fry, D. (2025). Legal challenges in tackling AI-generated CSAM across the UK, USA, Canada, Australia and New Zealand: Who is accountable according to the law? In *Searchlight 2025–Who Benefits? Shining a Light on the Business of Child Sexual Exploitation and Abuse* (pp. 50-59).

Karamchand, G. (2025). Detecting the Abuse of Generative AI in Cybersecurity Contexts: Challenges, Frameworks, and Solutions. *Journal of Data Analysis and Critical Management*, *1*(03), 1–12.

Kazi, J. (2025). Children and Deepfakes: Protecting Minors from Digital Manipulation and Exploitation. *Available at SSRN* 5389057.

Kokolaki, E., & Fragopoulou, P. (2025). Unveiling AI's Threats to Child Protection: Regulatory efforts to Criminalize AI-Generated CSAM and Emerging Children's Rights Violations. *arXiv preprint arXiv:2503.00433*.

Osorio de Barros, G., & Severino Soares, O. (2025). AI and the Next Generation: Protecting Childhood in the Digital Age. In *Environmental, Social, Governance and Digital Transformation in Organizations* (pp. 103–133). Springer Nature Switzerland.

Parti, K., & Szabo, J. (2024). The legal challenges of realistic and AI-driven child sexual abuse material: Regulatory and enforcement perspectives in Europe. *Laws*, *13*(6), 67.

Wood, A. (2024). Dark echoes: the exploitative potential of generative AI in online harassment. In *Psybersecurity* (pp. 90–129). CRC Press.

Yu, Y., Sharma, T., Hu, M., Wang, J., & Wang, Y. (2025, May). Exploring parent-child perceptions on safety in generative AI: concerns, mitigation strategies, and design implications. In *2025 IEEE Symposium on Security and Privacy (SP)* (pp. 2735-2752). IEEE.

Chapter 9
Exploring Legal Structures for Workplace Automation Concerning Employment Law:
Professional Identity Crises and Self-Doubt Generated by AI Displacement

Namit Kumar Srivastava
Christ University, Bengaluru, India

Raghvendra Kumar Chaudhary
https://orcid.org/0009-0004-9260-8909
Christ University, Bengaluru, India

Avinash Krishna Goswami
https://orcid.org/0009-0006-7951-3627
Lloyd Law College, Greater Noida, India

ABSTRACT

The concept of new business models is altering who performs the work, how it gets done and its value across every sector. The lower costs of getting and sharing information have made it possible to use automation algorithms to create activities and make documents. These technology promises beg critical questions about the morality, legality and social implications of replacing or transforming economic institutions we find around us. The international shifts have been more profoundly felt in the workplace than automation and artificial intelligence. The logic of the

DOI: 10.4018/979-8-3373-6618-0.ch009

Industrial Age is no longer valid in our workplace, which exhibits both human and machine intelligence. This rise is challenging traditional labor norms as the professional identity crises and self doubt generated by AI displacement are more and significant in nature.

1. INTRODUCTION

The present legal framework for workplace automation to realize how employment laws need to be modified in order to preserve employee dignity and corporate efficiency. Now, a lot of issues need to be examined in the context of how automation has altered the interactions between companies and employees. This raises new issues of accountability, liability, and fairness. To fulfill their own political and ideological objectives, members of legislatures and other policy-making bodies in every nation must consider all of these factors. Due to the horrible situation, we now have regulations governing fair termination, unemployment insurance, and compensation for workers who are replaced by robots. We must strike a balance between innovation and justice, as seen by the rise in legal issues brought on by this recent trend. A means of ensuring the survival of workers The legal and institutional rights that working people have historically relied on for their financial existence and even their freedom of expression cannot be disregarded in an AI-assisted economy.

Professionals have lost prestige, value, and respect ever since technology began to do tasks that they formerly performed. This is true not only for physical laborers but also for professions like teaching, banking, medicine, and law that were formerly seen to be the finest of the best (Burrage, 2025).

1.1 Background of Workplace Automation and AI Integration

AI and automation are making it feasible for individuals to master new skills at home in the new economy. These are judicial gears developed for a labor market that was specialized for work yet connected to individuals. They now feel powerless against the emotional, social, and economic repercussions of rapidly evolving technology. This investigation shows how urgent it is for laws and regulations to change today in response to the systemic crises presented by automation, specifically self-doubt and a crisis of professional identity of workers affected by automation around the politically accountable world. Stunting thought and clouding judgment have persisted for decades. If AI is going to be doing important, complicated, and vital work tasks beyond mindless drudgery, the idea of professional talent as a marketable good is completely wrong. There is a lot of difficult policy work to be done if the shift to an automated economy is to be as equitable and seamless as feasible. This problem extends far beyond simply terminating and compensating workers.

1.2 Relevance: Self-doubt, professional identity crisis, and AI displacement

The fact that an algorithm can do complex, valuable activities quicker or more correctly than humans is not just a financial issue. Additionally, it demoralizes individuals and makes them feel unworthy of their employment. Additionally, there are psychological repercussions that might cause worry and sadness. People are not sufficiently protected by current employment legislation from the psychological suffering and diminished self-esteem that result from being replaced by robots. This is due to the fact that the legislation primarily addresses occupational safety and pay discrimination. Therefore, new laws and regulations are required. In addition, they must demand justice rather than only financial aid or welfare. In addition to calling for complete retraining, ethical AI use, and worker protections like the "right to disconnect," transparency in algorithmic working processes and animations, and the ability for humans to review AI and automated decision-making, they must make it clear that this early retirement is a part of a broader trend in the culture machine. These kinds of technologies could help society better address the issue of professional identity. The advantages of automation will be dispersed rather than added to the current mess, and it may entail more than simply relocating.

1.3 The Transformation of Employment Paradigms in Industry 5.0

The workplace is also significantly impacted by this shift in the times. According to Stengl Ruben, "Industry 5.0 is different from Industry 4.0 because the latter was mostly based on data-driven technology and automation." Rather, it revived the notion of a simple human touch. However, she is currently concentrating on the interaction between humans and technology and developing systems that will fairly integrate ethics, creativity, and emotion. He will become stronger by performing tasks that robots can't do in the industry. Function workers are no longer just involved in production. Nowadays, many believe that cheaters are emotionally and intellectually clever, capable of making difficult choices, and aware of the impact their actions have on other people.

People are the most vital component of every organization. Technology is king when it comes to efficiency, but the concept and framework of industrial production are also evolving to accommodate this new method of operation. Industry 5.0's primary objectives are sustainability, inclusivity, and human care. These days, people collaborate in new ways, such as having flexible work schedules, continual training in their area, and the opportunity to direct their own career in a digital ecosystem of disruptive, creative, and interactive innovation based on human decency. In order to support a team of hope that never gives up, industries are shifting their jobs from the same old, same old. The legal system and legislators must also reconsider the existing regulations around work in light of these developments in order to accommodate new ones, such as telework, platform work, and hybrid human-machine teams. In addition, it will mark the beginning of a new period when technology liberates people rather than replaces them, the industry may become more amiable, and our society returns to reality.

The current era, known as the fourth industrial revolution, or 4IR, is beginning to alter how humans and robots collaborate in the workplace. Although the 4.0 was also an automation, it was detrimental to humans since it elevated robots above humans. However, Industry 5.0 placed employees at the heart of the workplace once again. However, rather than replacing human cognition, it improves it by fusing human creativity, machine intelligence, and the capacity to arrange information into "forms" that can be seen or recalled, such as melodies, computer code, or even segments of language. Customization, sustainability, and human-centered design are critical in this new era of business. This indicates that the substance and structure of the work are different. Employees nowadays do more than just do repetitive tasks. They use intelligent systems instead, which handle more complex activities including deductive reasoning, fast turnaround on data processing, and product feedback. The larger tasks are handled by robots. It also implies that regulations must be implemented to prevent workers from being exploited and relocated to locations where technology is more likely to do damage.

A resilient and sustainable industrial environment that prioritizes humans is the central concept of Industry 5.0. Accordingly, we must go beyond Industry 4.0's emphasis on efficiency and automation. The way humans and robots collaborate is another significant shift in the nature of work. Humans and robots will collaborate more than ever in the next century. Building on what we already have is the focus of jobs in Industry 5.0. In order to keep humans alive, new technologies such as electronic reality, enhanced artificial intelligence, and collaborative robots (cobots) are available to do repetitive, hazardous, or dull work.

All recent high school grads need to listen. It will take a lot of effort to instruct and retrain the employees for this transformation. These days, the former machine operators serve as creators, integrators, and supervisors. Creating value for oneself and ensuring employee satisfaction are highly valued in the new way of thinking about work. Thus, the focus of Industry 5.0 is on the layout of goods and the demands of individual customers. Human Capabilities: These days, the value of craftsmanship, subject knowledge, and intuitive thinking is higher than ever before. To lessen physical and emotional stress, workplaces are becoming safer, more tech-savvy, and more ergonomic. The two primary components of Industry 5.0 resilience and sustainability are also included in the employment model.

Employees are increasingly participating in procedures that optimize resource use, reduce waste (supporting the circular economy), and create supply networks that can withstand shocks on a worldwide basis. This implies that professions in the future will need knowledge of the effects of industrial production on people and the environment in addition to strong data and robotics abilities. The ultimate objective is to establish a work organization that generates success and riches beyond financial gain. It concerns the worth of civilization and the condition of the planet.

2. LEGAL FRAMEWORKS GOVERNING AUTOMATION AND EMPLOYMENT RELATIONS

The regulations that will be used to manage the emergence of robots and artificial intelligence (AI) in the workplace are continually evolving. Conventional, system-based employment regulations from before CHV cannot simply disregard these types of developments at this point. Your lives are so heavily governed by digital reasoning that it has even supplanted everyday discipline, work, and exams.

This includes those who work in contact centers, on platforms (such as couriers and drivers for ride-sharing services), and in increasingly automated and digital freelance professions. Legal amendments are also intended to provide workers specific rights associated with digital labor, such as the ability to prevent their email from flashing, and to establish uniform safety standards for human-robot interactions. Making algorithmic management more transparent and responsible is a key component of these systems. Employers are increasingly being required by law to disclose to workers how they utilize automated decision-making technologies and how they decide on compensation and work schedules. The connections between SUP4 base stations The "safeguarding of personal data" and algorithmic effect evaluations are often seen as going beyond discrimination and fairness (Prabhakar, 2025).

The EU just enacted a regulation on AI, for example, but it won't completely take effect until 2026. of contrast to national legislation of Member States, which sometimes lack a comparable emphasis, this was novel. The rapid use of AI and automation in the workplace may violate existing labor rules. the employer-employee relationship as imaginatively construed by the earlier labor law dynamic, which placed an emphasis on contract provisions, employer duties, and employee rights. However, this legal equilibrium has been disturbed by the recent emergence of algorithmic management, automated decision-making systems, and robotized labor. The most crucial factors to consider in automated hiring are accountability, equity, and openness. For instance, computerized recruiting practices and performance evaluation systems may provide unfair or biased outcomes, or human bias may lead individuals to believe that discrimination allegations and wrongful dismissal cases are real. That would entail amending the legislation to hold companies accountable for the choices their algorithms make. In this manner, workers' rights won't be infringed by emerging technology.

However, several nations' labor rules fall short in addressing these scenarios in which humans and machines collaborate. The question of whether computers may sometimes be considered "legal persons" is now being debated by legislators and legal experts. They also question whether companies or individuals should always be held accountable for the negative outcomes of technological failures. The European Union is among the nations that have started discussing "Ethics Guidelines for Trustworthy AI." In order to emphasize the significance of data privacy and algorithmic employment decisions, the US and India are simultaneously amending their labor laws.

The digital era has altered how people work, and employment regulations must adapt to meet these changes. Contracts may include both individuals and non-individuals in certain circumstances, and companies need to be explicit about their liability for damage or displacement. The negative impacts of auto-job interactions should be mitigated by fair regulation that upholds human dignity and encourages innovative technologies (Mishra, 2024).

2.1 Overview of Global and National Employment Laws Addressing Automation

The legal foundation for automation and the job relationship is now a complex jumble of labor standards and anti-discrimination statutes since there is no special rulebook for automation. Global labor standards, like Title VII of the Civil Rights Act in the US and the General Data Protection Regulation (GDPR) in Europe, may be able to influence computer judgments in the same way that they influence human ones. That is, when algorithms that recruit and dismiss employees harm some groups more than others because of their gender or color, firms are held accountable. Employers are thus need to demonstrate that prejudice in hiring, promotion, or termination results from an unclear procedure. Therefore, it is their responsibility to check for prejudice in themselves on a daily basis.

Another significant new regulatory field is algorithmic management. AI is used in this instance to plan, manage, and assess employees. Systems that provide workers "the right to human intervention" and the opportunity to learn why their employment choices were made automatically are beginning to appear in this field. The AI Act of the European Union, for instance, establishes stringent guidelines for data quality, traceability, and human control and declares that employing and managing AI-powered workers is "high-risk." The "independent contractor" status of gig workers, who are sometimes the target of algorithmic surveillance, is now being investigated by people worldwide. Legal action One of the most recent legislative initiatives to attempt to clarify these people' employment status is the European Platform Work Directive. In addition to the minimum wage and welfare, they will be shielded against unjust algorithmic penalties. The objective is to use well-known legal categories to provide novel work scenarios genuine legal significance (Das & Santra, 2025).

3. COMPARATIVE ANALYSIS: EU, USA AND INDIA'S LEGAL RESPONSES TO AUTOMATION

Legal difficulties arising from workplace automation are handled differently in the United States (USA), India, and the European Union (EU). The regulations they abide by, the job market, and societal order all influence their personalities. People worldwide are aware of the European Union's stringent regulations regarding the use of automation and artificial intelligence in the workplace. In 2026, the EU AI Act will go into full force. It ranks AI tools according to their level of hazard. This framework should contain stringent guidelines for employing high-risk AI in hiring, employee monitoring, and performance management. Transparency is also very important to the EU, which protects personal data via the General Data Protection Regulation (GDPR) and allows employees to contest or clarify algorithmic judgments.

Despite the increasing prevalence of automation, EU member states continue to prioritize robust worker rights and transparent employer-employee communication. Inclusive prosperity is feasible under these circumstances. Rather, the US is approaching automation in a more market-driven and decentralized manner. This approach places a lot of emphasis on promoting novel concepts at the federal and state levels, but it takes time to recognize that labor issues exist. It has been difficult for the US to amend its labor laws to accommodate new forms of employment, such as computer-assisted marketing and gigs. Unlike the EU, it appears that there are no general regulations for AI. Rather, it ought to be subject to laws and regulations that are relevant to the industry as well as data protection regulations such as the California Consumer Privacy Act (CCPA) (Charitonos et al., 2025). While technological advancements are crucial and automated processes should prevent bias and discrimination in employment, the law still requires companies to have flexibility. All of these factors are combined in India's approach to automation.

This is due in part to the fact that the economy is still expanding and that many of the workers there are not unionized. Among the new regulations is the Industrial Relations Code (IR Code) 2020. To assist limit job losses from automation, it increases social security and makes people more inclined to remain learning throughout their working careers. Additionally, India is developing data protection legislation and AI ethics guidelines to ensure that automation operates in the workplace in a responsible and moral way. However, a significant issue is that a large number of their workers still lack sufficient expertise operating robots or typing on a computer all day at home. The Indian legal system is changing quickly all the time. In addition to promoting new ideas and technology in society, the objective is to safeguard groups of headcount workers who may be excluded.

Upskilling and reskilling are emphasized in EU labor policy, which has long held the view that technology should enhance human labor rather than replace it. According to the General Data Protection Regulation (GDPR) of the European Union, automated decision-making that significantly impacts individuals is illegal. This safeguards employees' rights in virtual workplaces. In contrast, the United States approaches the research of how technology impacts the workplace in a more market-driven manner. The three primary areas covered by federal U.S. employment law are the freedom to contract, workplace safety, and anti-discrimination. Automation as such is not directly controlled by it. Bias in recruiting and promotion algorithms is being investigated by the Equal Employment Opportunity Commission (EEOC) and other organizations (Ayhan & Colpitts-Elliott, 2025). However, there is currently no national strategy that addresses all facets of automation and artificial intelligence in the workplace. Additionally, even if this sometimes has long-term negative effects on workers, the United States continues to place a strong priority on fostering innovation and increasing economic competitiveness.

4. EMPLOYMENT SECURITY AND RIGHTS IN THE AUTOMATED ERA

In a more automated world, job security is becoming more and more crucial as businesses embrace artificial intelligence. To be honest, you might lose your work at any moment due to a new innovation if it merely entails doing the same task again and doesn't demand a lot of talent or performance. Laws are unable to keep up with the rapid advancements in technology. Last but not least, contemporary labor regulations have contributed to the revival of the significance of retraining and ongoing education while changing careers. They also transfer workers to automation-based occupations, which helps reduce the unemployment rate.

The significance of safeguarding employees in both formal and informal employment is shown by the Indian Industrial Relations Code 2020. It creates money for training (skilling) and grants workers the right to receive social security benefits in the event that they lose their employment. Workers' rights in the era of automation must include protections against AI's opaque, algorithmic hiring, firing, and multiple assessment judgments in addition to job security. Many states have legislation requiring automated management systems to be self-explanatory and subject to human judgment. This makes it easy to terminate individuals without cause and prevents a lot of prejudice and other immoral impacts. The "right to disconnect" is another crucial worker's right that combats the excessive use of AI surveillance tools to monitor employees' activities (AlAshry & Al-Saqaf, 2024).

According to the draft regulations, workers impacted by workplace automation should have easy channels for lodging grievances. This is to ensure that all opinions are heard throughout the development and use of AI technologies in the workplace. However, putting ideas into action and involving everyone remains challenging, particularly in developing nations or gig economy. As a consequence, employment rules are gradually shifting in the direction of a balance between safeguarding workers' best efforts, mental health, fair treatment, and dignity at work and technological advancement.

4.1 Legal Implications of AI-driven Layoffs and Redundancy

This is emerging as one of the most significant issues facing corporations, workers, and legislators as automation spreads. Nearly all of the labor that was formerly done by humans is now done by machines and computer programs (Crutchley et al., 2024). As a result, the resort's long-held beliefs about career growth and employment security have undergone significant shift. As more jobs in finance, manufacturing, public service, and commercial transportation become automated, this fear has grown. In addition to competing with one another, workers nowadays also have to contend with computers that may be quicker, less expensive, or even more accurate in some situations. As technology advances, we must reconsider the rights of labor. All Canadians must have access to minimum standards of care, job security, protection from wrongful termination, and the opportunity to retrain and find new work efficiencies. This view was mirrored in the recent rulings issued by the WTO court in Geneva, which considered a US case against China for breaching trade accords. After the Doha Round reached a consensus, the court was established almost precisely one year ago. Labor regulations in many nations don't do anything to safeguard workers from being replaced by technology. Employees who are fired often get compensation for lost income or other perks. However, these types of compensation do not assist them cope with the long-term difficulty of finding a new job in an industry that changes frequently because of its digital infrastructure. Therefore, in addition to financial stability, job security must also contain legal safeguards that facilitate adaptation. Governments and employers share the duty to create training programs and support systems that help workers find new jobs when their old ones are automated.

4.2 Right to Retraining and Skill Adaptability under Labor Codes

They must be able to work flexible hours, pick up new skills, and continue studying throughout their lives if the workforce is to remain robust. In an increasingly digital world, we also need to redefine what it means to be able to work (Doring et al., 2024). "Work is not only a way to make money, but also a way to give people a sense of worth and belonging in society." To reap the benefits of automation, policymakers must ensure that technology does not exacerbate inequality or exclude certain groups. Fundamentally, the issue is how to strike a balance between social justice and technical advancement so that everyone may continue to gain from automation and no one loses their job as rapidly as a computer.

Traditional ideas of job security, which were mostly predicated on human labor and investment, are seriously challenged by the rise of AI and automation. The only people who were concerned about losing their employment were those who used to do manual labor. Those who work with their brains are now beginning to worry as well. Due to this significant shift, all organizations are now coping with what is known as "AI Anxiety." This interruption demonstrates how inadequate our present legal systems are; there are currently no clear regulations regarding AI-related job loss or redundancy. Laws that now regulate layoffs should be modified, as should other workplace regulations. They need to insist on compensation for those who lose their employment due to automation, which is a choice taken to save money or increase efficiency. Additionally, workers should be given more warning than is customary and have the ability to convince others to return to work and acquire new skills possibly without using force.

Instead of rapidly scrolling back to older workers who utilize antiquated technology, employers should provide their current transition workers with information that is comprehensive, deep, and helpful. When it comes to safeguarding the new rights of workers in the era of automation, two of the most crucial challenges are limiting the use of algorithmic management at work and ensuring that algorithms are utilized appropriately. Businesses are increasingly utilizing AI to assign work, assess employee performance, and even make critical choices. Every employee's freedom and privacy are violated, which is against the principle of due process. In particular, the EU has a new legal concept known as the "right to human oversight."

The next day, someone should thoroughly review automated hiring or firing choices and provide an explanation to the individual who may be impacted. It will become more crucial to mandate bias audits for AI recruiting and management tools, as well as for AI to explain itself, in order to combat algorithmic unfairness, which may exacerbate and even reinforce historical prejudice. We need a robust, technology-based system that safeguards employee data and keeps those in possession of it responsible if we really want security to mean more than simply job security (Mishra, 2024). This is because automation jeopardizes the fundamental principles of dignity and equality in the workplace.

5. PROFESSIONAL IDENTITY, SELF-DOUBT AND PSYCHOLOGICAL IMPLICATIONS: LEGAL RECOGNITION OF EMOTIONAL AND PSYCHOLOGICAL WELL-BEING AT WORKPLACE

Because they have lost their employment and their primary source of income, displaced persons may start to doubt themselves, feel insecure, and experience anxiety. After that, people may have to cope with emotional stress. Automation has altered the definition of competence and success in knowledge-based businesses where professional pride was derived from innovation and expertise. Many workers are now uncertain about their position in the technological world as a result of this. You must be aware of these psychological consequences in order to create a work structure that is both ethically and legally acceptable.

Individuals' emotional well-being is not the only issue; society and companies are also impacted. Many nations are beginning to consider mental health to be a critical component of workplace safety. Some occupational health and safety legislation frameworks are starting to include mental health in addition to physical health treatment. circumstances that come under the general heading of "safety in working conditions," such protection against emotional abuse and mental stress or anxiety, have also been examined by certain courts (Prabhakar et al., 2025). However, the psychological suffering caused by automation and AI extends far beyond financial issues. However, it's not simply a matter of whether you're talented enough when algorithms take on very difficult and lucrative professions that have never been done before; it's a full-blown crisis of merit unbelief that throws into question the whole concept.

This "accelerated devaluation" of professionals based on DEC skill may result in indifference, anxiety, and despair as well as obsolescence and isolation. We must never forget that abrupt mass unemployment has much more detrimental psychological impacts. These days, the workplace serves as more than simply a place to work. We are facing a new kind of blind agony when AI fails and work evolves daily without remembering our past actions. This would call for a significant rethinking of the goals and protections provided by labor laws. Formally acknowledging the workplace right to mental and emotional health as a multiple right is crucial in the era of robots. OSH regulations (and any applicable regulations) should address more than simply physical safety (Chakkour & De Koning, 2023). We are discussing psychological damage brought on by algorithmic control, ongoing online monitoring, and a sense of perpetual danger. Now, certain companies need to be held legally accountable for lowering the psychological hazards associated with future automation. This would include enacting legislation requiring companies to provide sufficient time and resources for retraining workers, even in the absence of jobs.

This is just one aspect of the expenses associated with technological advancement that they bear fairly. Furthermore, the law ought to be expanded to hold employers accountable for assisting in the creation of a workplace that allows for sufficient room for individual identity, possibly even incorporating "a right of disconnection" against continual technological intrusion; and requiring mental health coverage and resources that are obviously intended to lessen the suffering brought on by job insecurity and retraining brought on by artificial intelligence. Legally confirming the emotional resources of professional success as a legitimate currency and preventing individual punishment from technology adoption are the goals. This video also covered the issue of psychological effects and self-doubt in more detail: AI's psychological effects on one's professional identity. Should I seek out instances of nations or areas where employees' mental health is officially recognized?

A continuous cycle of replacing workers and reducing their abilities has been caused by many other significant causes that have come to light. People often identify themselves by their work title. One of these self-perceptions is a result of years of education, practice, and experience. People utilize these benchmarks to gauge their progress in their area since it is measurable as well (Yu, 2023). There is a crisis of trust when an algorithm starts to do things that smart people thought were impossible. These days, emotions of expertise, professional alienation, and major mental health problems like anxiety, despair, and burnout are all primarily caused by obsolescence.

The psychological aspect is that one may feel good about oneself at work in addition to earning money. However, when AI creates a job machine, it severely damages people's self-esteem and prevents them from advancing in their professions. It is obvious that the way employment legislation considers and safeguards employees' health and safety has to be significantly changed.

5.1 The Legal Defense of Mental and Emotional Health

The two European nations that directly control corporations are France and Germany. Australia is also beginning to mandate that companies address psychological risks at work by enacting legislation requiring their monitoring and mitigation (Odalonu,

2022). This also implies that businesses are required by law to provide their workers with enough time and resources to learn new job descriptions or technology. This is seen as the financial price of technical advancement. More significantly, labor laws must be strengthened to require employers to resist the de-skilling, atomization of workers, and fragmentation of personhood brought about by artificial intelligence or face penalties. This entails enacting mental health legislation that explicitly acknowledges the stress brought on by work instability and AI-induced de-skilling, as well as extending labor safeguards that guard against identity loss, such as the "right to disconnect" (already in place in France and Italy). Making the emotional components of professional job legally enforceable is the aim. Additionally, it is an attempt to prevent technology usage from turning society—which is already rapidly approaching computerization into a place that is detrimental to people's mental health.

6. REDEFINING EMPLOYER LIABILITY AND AI ACCOUNTABILITY

AI has already entered the workplace, and as this integration progresses, companies are being forced to consider their legal obligations more and more. The legal issues of accountability for AI-generated judgments and acts are becoming more complex. Employers are held accountable for various wrongdoings committed by their workers under legal doctrines such as respondeat superior and vicarious responsibility (Rahman, 2023). However, liability models must adapt as AI systems take on more and more responsibilities, like as hiring, performance reviews, and work delegation. How much responsibility should businesses bear when their AI causes harm to workers, renders biased judgments, or has other unfavorable consequences?

Employers are often held accountable for their own acts or inactions when it comes to implementing and overseeing AI systems under current fault-based liability frameworks, rather than for any unanticipated outcomes that the systems may generate on their own. However, courts may impose direct accountability on the vendors providing the AI or consider such AI judgments to be the employer's actions if they are seen to make decisions similar to those of a human agent. The employers are no longer only impacted by the actions or inactions of their employees in the era of artificial intelligence. Additionally, they must strive for the ethical and nondiscriminatory use of AI (Das et al., 2024).

Artificial intelligence is not regarded as a distinct legal entity under existing laws. Therefore, accountability will rest with the employer who makes use of and benefits from these technologies. Employers are responsible for ensuring that AI systems operate in a transparent, equitable, and labor law-compliant manner (Yu & Ai, 2022). This entails ensuring that algorithms are not biased, that humans continue to make important judgments, and that there are distinct lines of accountability in cases when automated events cause harm to people or even death. The concept of "due diligence" need to extend to AI governance, according to some legal experts. This implies that companies must to be able to recognize the potential damage that automation may create and take action to prevent it.

Some have argued that the law should include "shared responsibility" and "algorithmic accountability" as robots become more adept at making choices. Employers may also need to consider the fairness and transparency of employment choices impacted by AI algorithms. In the age of automation, rethinking employer liability requires a careful balance between legal responsibility and technical development. This is crucial to maintaining the human element at the heart of accountability and employment justice (Rice et al., 2025).

Numerous HR decision-making procedures, including hiring and dismissing, incorporate AI. What it means to be an employer is evolving as a result. In the past, employer vicarious responsibility was directly related to direct discrimination by a manager or supervisor. However, the greatest risk associated with automation will arise when algorithms unfairly favor one group over another, irrespective of gender or ethnicity. Any regulation that may be used to combat automated technologies that eliminate employment will ultimately be utilized by people. Title VII of the 1964 U.S. Civil Rights Act is among the most well-known. According to this rule, a boss who has hiring and firing authority and is two levels below the corporate headquarters may be held accountable if his choice of who should be promoted negatively impacts any members of legally protected groups or if he discriminates against them based solely on their affiliation with racial or gender identity issues that the general public faces. Because businesses can no longer just create and utilize software to control personnel without accepting accountability, they are being held responsible for their activities (Colin & Stamp, 2024). This concept makes it obvious that employers cannot simply rely on others to fulfill their moral and legal obligations since such individuals are likely to lack sufficient knowledge of compliance difficulties.

Strong AI accountability frameworks are thus necessary, not just to satisfy fundamental legislative requirements but also to assume some degree of risk management responsibility. * It is almost hard to demonstrate that these technologies are unfair because to the "black box" issue, which implies that you cannot identify how an AI reached its decision. As a result, new legislation such as the AI Act in Europe and several state laws in the US require corporations to be transparent about their algorithms. Now, independent organizations are required to conduct bias audits of AIs before to their release and to continue doing so on a regular basis (Wang, 2024).

7. CONCLUSION, FUTURE OF WORK AND LEGAL RECOMMENDATIONS

Technology and shifting societal standards will likely influence the nature of employment in the future. All facets of society should contribute to comprehensive strategies for robust, inclusive, and democratic economies not just legislation. In order to hold employers responsible, regulations must be updated as automation, artificial intelligence, and digitalization gain traction in the corporate world. Then, as with mental health, laws and regulations may aid in achieving these objectives. AI accountability in the future will include establishing explicit guidelines for AO systems, holding them accountable for injury or discriminating against others, and ensuring that AI decision-making procedures are transparent and truthful. AI governance must be strictly regulated to prevent biases or unfair outcomes, with public audits being monitored and available to the public as well as the need for human supervision.

There is needed to be more has to be done by labor regulations to safeguard those who work odd hours, from home, or on platforms. To promote social justice, equitable compensation, and employee trust, pay should be open and understandable. Mental well-being is equally vital. It falls to legislators not so much to guarantee services for people with mental illness — most of us who care about this issue gave up on that long ago — as it is for them to ensure that such individuals are not treated like second-class citizens, and human feelings (which, yes, include the freedom from harassment and abuse) are taken into account. Because future workers will need to acquire new skills more quickly, the legislation should also support initiatives that encourage people to continue learning and retraining. Retraining programs of all kinds should be made accessible by governments and businesses worldwide so that individuals may acquire the skills necessary for fulfilling employment. Generally speaking, laws have to be equitable, safeguard human rights, and promote technological advancement. Good working conditions for all employees and welcoming, adaptable social workplaces are crucial in the era of intelligent automation.

REFERENCES

AlAshry, M. S., & Al-Saqaf, W. (2024). Constraints on AI: Arab Journalists' experiences and perceptions of governmental restrictions on ChatGPT. *Journal of Information Technology & Politics*, •••, 1–21.

Ayhan, T., & Colpitts-Elliott, H. (2025). Radical care in displacement: Rohingya women's activism amidst neoliberal humanitarianism and repression. *Journal of Ethnic and Migration Studies*, *51*(9), 2415–2433.

Burrage, C. M. (2025). *A Hermeneutic Phenomenological Study of Complex Adaptive Leadership Among Black Leaders in Artificial Intelligence and Robotics* (Doctoral dissertation, The Chicago School of Professional Psychology).

Chakkour, S., & De Koning, A. (2023). Legal precarity, migrant mothering and the space of hesitation in Paris. *Ethnic and Racial Studies*, *46*(2), 275–294.

Charitonos, K., Khalil, B., Ross, T. W., Bonfini-Hotlosz, C., Aristorenas, M., & Webster, B. (2025). Crisis-prompted online language teaching: A qualitative inquiry into autonomy among teachers in refugee settings. *ReCALL*, *37*(2), 250–266.

Colin, N., & Stamp, K. (2024). How Can We Address Challenges and Embrace Opportunities in Dancing for Health? In *Dancing* (pp. 97-112). Emerald Publishing Limited.

Crutchley, J., Nahaboo, Z., & Rao, N. (2024). Precarious academic citizens: Early Career Teachers' experiences and implications for the academy. *Teaching in Higher Education*, *29*(3), 789–809.

. Das, A., Muschert, G., Dutta, M. J., Aytaç, M. B., Tripathi, P., Khare, A., & Ray, S. (2024). AI Impacts, Concerns, and Perspectives in the Global South A Thought Leadership Round Table. *Социологическое обозрение*, *23*(4), 173-195.

Das, A., & Santra, S. (2025). THEORIZING THE GHIBLI EFFECT: A CRITIQUE OF AI, AESTHETIC THEFT AND THE CRISIS OF AUTHORSHIP IN THE CORRIDORS OF POWER. *Journal of Dharma*, *50*(1).

Doring, N., Le, T. D., Vowels, L. M., Vowels, M. J., & Marcantonio, T. L. (2024). The impact of artificial intelligence on human sexuality: A five-year literature review 2020–2024. *Current Sexual Health Reports*, *17*(1), 4.

Mishra, R. (2024). Embracing a paradigm shift: Transitioning from traditional teaching methods to ai-based nlp education. *Research and Reviews in Literature. Social Sciences*, •••, 75.

Odalonu, B. H. (2022). Worsening insecurity in Nigeria and its implications on governance and national development. *African Journal of Humanities and Contemporary Education Research*, *5*(1), 31–49.

Prabhakar, P., Pati, P. B., & Parida, S. (2025). Navigating Legal and Ethical Dimensions in AI, IoT, and Cloud Solutions for Women's Safety. In *Developing AI, IoT and Cloud Computing-based Tools and Applications for Women's Safety* (pp. 155-191). Chapman and Hall/CRC.

Rahman, M. A. (2023). Silhouettes of the Digital Minds: Exploring Emotional and Intellectual Interaction between Youth and Artificial Intelligence. *Available at SSRN* 5190217.

Rice, A. J., Ogle, C. M., Martin, S. L., & Cozza, S. J. (2025). The impact of wartime child casualties on adult professionals. *Psychiatry*, *88*(3), 308–327.

Wang, L. (2024). Blending in or Being Co-Opted: Reflecting on an Internship-Cum-Field Work at a New Town Government in China. *The Professional Geographer*, *76*(2), 239–247.

Yu, H., & Ai, B. (2022). Experiencing "paragliding": A student-teacher perspective on doing qualitative research in a Chinese university. *International Journal of Qualitative Methods*, *21*, 16094069211070443.

Yu, T. (2023). David Foster Wallace, Both Professional and Not. *English Studies*, *104*(2), 305–328.

Chapter 10
Future of Work in the Age of Automation in the Global Scenario:
Navigating Imposter Syndrome and Identity Crisis - Routing AI, Job Displacement, and Workforce Renovation

Saroj Choudhary
Amity University, Gwalior, India

Arunima Shastri
https://orcid.org/0000-0002-6260-1253
Christ University, Bangalore, India

Hind Hammouch
https://orcid.org/0000-0002-5897-1649
Sidi Mohamed Ben Abdellah University, Morocco

ABSTRACT

Automation and artificial intelligence continue to disrupt the workforce economy, transforming industries and institutions, as well as traditional employment models. Although automation promises to improve productivity and efficiency, it poses its own problems in job displacement and skill gaps like imposter syndrome and identity crises as the replacement of human workforce to AI and rebotics. In order to cope with this transition, companies, government bodies and educational institutions need to take initiative, in the form of retraining initiatives, AI-human collaboration, labour

DOI: 10.4018/979-8-3373-6618-0.ch010

policies etc. This discussion must also include ethical considerations, regulatory frameworks, and equitable opportunities for employment as AI continues to develop. As automation progresses the societies should shape it by augmentation of human potential instead of replacement, which could help facilitate sustainable economic growth and resilient labour workforce.

1. INTRODUCTION

Automating future work will be transforming at a tremendous speed respecting the industries, roles, and charts of employment in an global perspective. However, as industries and economies adopt AI-powered tools that boost productivity and efficiency, fear also lingers over mass unemployment, skills redundancy and the ethical concerns around a world dominated by machines entering the workforce (Cazzaniga et al., 2024). Though automation has been a significant contributor to economic growth in the past, its dizzying pace in the digital era poses critical challenges to workforce stability, human-AI collaboration, and the very definition of labor itself. We are all dealing with the transformational nature of artificial intelligence which comes with both silver linings and dark clouds (George, 2024). AI-driven automation impacts not just technology, but socio economics as well, and requires re-evaluating established employment models. With machine learning, robotics and data analytics set to permeate business processes, industries such as manufacturing, healthcare, finance and customer service are undergoing significant shifts in labour demand. Jobs that were once seen as "safe" are increasingly at the risk of automation, especially those involving repetitive, routine, and predictable tasks. AI does not replace jobs, it creates new employment opportunities and leads to innovation and better decision making The biggest challenge is upskilling the workforce for AI-augmented workplaces so they can adapt and reskill to succeed (Kumar Sharma & Yadav, 2024).

A major issue with this shift is the uneven impact on different socioeconomic groups. We have also learnt that low-skilled workers are at a greater risk of displacement by automation in developing economies, amplifying both income in-equality and economic instability. In contrast, high-skilled roles that rely on creativity, critical analysis, and emotional intelligence are predicted to withstand, furthering the widening gap between AI-augmented careers and those at risk of redundancy. Such a stark divide demands a concerted policy response from governments, industries, and educational institutions to upskill the workforce and establish successful workforce reskilling programs. Lifelong learning, digital literacy training, and AI-assisted career development are important on a larger scale, ensuring an inclusive and sustainable labor market. With engaging with the nuances-in of AI-driven automation,

Human-Machine Collaboration, whilst also discussing how labor markets should be managed to adapt to the impending workforce dislocations. This study aims to establish a holistic framework to navigate and mitigate the withering implications on the future of work, amidst cutting-edge policy interventions, ethical considerations, and technological advancements in the rapidly automating milieu (Praveen, 2024).

2. IMPOSTER SYNDROME AND THE RISE OF AUTOMATION AND ARTIFICIAL INTELLIGENCE IN THE WORKPLACE

Automation and artificial intelligence (AI) are transforming the work landscape, the way tasks are performed, and traditional economies around the world. Amidst the relentless pursuit of greater efficiency, lower costs, and increased productivity, AI-powered automation has emerged as an industry disruptor, fundamentally reshaping workplace dynamics across sectors. AI applications including machine learning and robotics, but also natural language processing and data analytics find steadily growing use from industrial manufacturing to service industries and knowledge-based professions, delivering savings, more efficient decisions, and improved human performance. Automation has always been part of industrial development, but the new division of labor brought about by this AI transformation is unique in that it allows machines to execute sophisticated cognitive functions that were previously thought exclusive to human intellect. This transformation has far-reaching consequences for job roles, organizational frameworks, and the long-term viability of economies, offering both unprecedented benefits and serious challenges to employees, enterprises, and policymakers.

Automation was directly responsible for increased industrial efficiency from the mechanization of agriculture and in the Age of the Industrial Revolutions, assembly lines. The First Industrial Revolution (steam power and mechanized production); the Second Industrial Revolution (electricity and mass production); the Third Industrial Revolution (computerization). Industry 4.0, or the Fourth Industrial Revolution, simultaneous use of AI, IoT and big data, creating intelligent automation with self-learning and decision-making. The rapid pace of technological evolution has propelled machines to engage in increasingly sophisticated functions, ranging from autonomous driving and predictive analytics to personalized healthcare diagnostics and financial forecasting. Machine learning algorithms have become capable of processing large sets of data in seconds, finding correlations and insights that far exceed human cognitive abilities. As a result, more and more organizations in multiple industries are making use of AI to make their work more accurate and less prone to human error, as well as making better decisions, and breaking away from the standard labor-oriented models they've long followed.

The rise of AI in the workplace is primarily due to the need for efficiency and scalability. Freight is changing, with companies pouring money into automation to make business, reduce expenditures, and stay competitive in the fast-paced global economy. In manufacturing, robotic process automation (RPA) is replacing menial labors on assembly lines, minimizing production errors and increasing the accuracy of output. AI also transforms retail and customer service, as AI-powered chatbots and virtual assistants process transactions, handle customer queries and offer personalized recommendations, greatly improving customer experience (Dries et al., 2024). The finance industry has adopted AI for fraud detection, risk assessment, and investment strategies among other facets, enabling institutions to function with increased accuracy and safety. The healthcare industry has seen a similar transformation, with AI-driven diagnostic tools helping physicians diagnose diseases, process medical imaging, and create treatment plans. These changes not only increase operational efficiency, but also improve service quality and outcomes with patients.

In spite of these potential benefits, the mass adoption of automation powered by AI leads to concerns about displacement of human jobs and the fate of human labor in the long-term future. With machines taking the lead on one-off tasks that can be broken down into four steps (e.g., driving, playing a piano, performing this, performing that, etc.) and some even making cognitive decisions, a large number of traditional jobs may well become obsolete, leaving individual unemployment as well as a national unemployment scenario. Industries that depend on manual, physical work, like manufacturing, transportation, and logistics, are especially at risk of being automated. The prevalence of driverless vehicles, for example, jeopardizes millions of jobs in the trucking and delivery sectors, and self-checkout kiosks in retail outlets decrease the need for cashiers. Like automation, innovations such as AI-powered writing, legal document analysis and financial auditing are transforming white-collar jobs, upending the belief that automation predominantly hits lower-skilled labor. One potential impact is that many jobs may lose due to automation, but some new jobs will also emerge as a result, particularly in AI programming, robotics and data analysis. But it is important to note that this transition will necessitate a major transformation of the workforce, as incumbent workers will need to be reskilled and adapt to the evolving labor market.

Job displacement is not the only facet of the labor market impacted by AI and automation, with crucial factors in workplace culture, productivity, and employee well-being also affected. Tens of thousands of individuals used decision-making tools in case of domestic violence. AI-powered hiring systems might reproduce bias from past data, creating discrimination in hiring, for instance. Such technology is workplace surveillance as the use of AI-driven analytics to monitor and measure employee productivity which presents a threat to privacy and worker autonomy. To tackle these ethical issues, organizations need to enforce strong regulatory framework and make sure that AI system is developed for assisting human capabilities instead of eliminating human skills. The companies should concentrate on cultivating human-machine synergy, in which AI systems augment rather than displace labor. When implemented responsibly, AI can help organizations boost productivity without losing the human touch in the workplace.

Digital literacy and problem-solving along with interdisciplinary skills are highly demanded, highlighting the need for a paradigm shift in education accordingly. Traditional i.e. Heavily curriculum-based education systems need to be revolutionized to include AI-related skills to prepare students for jobs that do not exist. The onus lies on governments, businesses, and educational institutions to work together to redesign the educational system and create relevant reskilling, lifelong learning programs, and vocational training that meet industry needs. It focuses on the need for a holistic and equitable approach to workforce development to derive benefits from the ongoing technological revolution. All these challenges can be resolved by adopting a multi-stakeholder approach, where policymakers devise labor market reforms, companies develop inclusive strategies for workplace development, and educational institutions prepare curriculums in line with upcoming technologies.

3. JOB DISPLACEMENT AND WORKFORCE CHALLENGES IN THE AI ERA

Artificial intelligence (AI) and automation are advancing at breakneck speed, transforming the global job market and posing both opportunities and serious challenges to both as the employees and employers as well as policymakers. AI-powered automation improves the productivity and efficiency of organizations but has also triggered a disruption to established organizational structures, resulting in significant concern over job redundancy. Many jobs that involve repetitive, manual, or rule-based work are being replaced by automated systems, leaving millions of workers at risk of being made redundant. The key challenge is to navigate the workforce transitions, make reskilling opportunities available for all the people, and avoid having socio-economic differences arising from the changes in the labor market. It's a socio-economic challenge that would take strategic interventions to protect jobs, incentivize skills development and ensure an all-rounded labor market.

Technological changes have historically shifted the labor market. The Industrial Revolutions replaced agricultural and manual laborers but ushered in new jobs in manufacturing. The digital revolution has worked in a similar way by automating clerical and administrative positions, but also creating new jobs in IT and software development. But the current wave of AI-led automation is different because it is not blue collar jobs that it is attacking although those too are being challenged it is also white collar jobs. AI-driven apps perform work typically done by professionals, including legal document review, medical diagnostics, financial analysis and content creation. The numbers have grown across numerous sectors such as finance, customer service, logistics, and health care, where machine learning algorithms and robotic process automation (RPA) have been shown to be more efficient and accurate than humans at performing complex tasks. Although these technologies are good for driving efficiency and lowering costs, they are a major threat to job security, particularly for workers in easily automated roles.

The increasing skill gap between displaced workers and the newcomer jobs emerging out of automation is one of the greatest problems of the workforce in the AI period. Sectors where AI is driven out require workers skilled in data science, machine learning, cybersecurity, digital transformation skills many workers simply don't have at the moment. There is a significant portion of the workforce that will face long-term unemployment, unless they train to acquire different skills. Reskilling and upskilling initiatives are essential to address this gap, but access to such initiatives is often unequal, especially in developing economies where education systems and training infrastructures are slower to adapt than technological advancements. It is crucial that governments, businesses and educational institutions work together to create policies and programmes that facilitate workers moving into roles that will not be replaced by AI. Lifelong learning, vocational training, and digital literacy programs can support workers' transitions to new career paths and ensure employability in an increasingly AI-driven market (Growiec & Prettner, 2025).

Apart from skill set, the AI revolution also requires a change in workforce flexibility and soft skills. As AI systems increasingly take on routine and analytical tasks, human workers will need to shift their focus toward uniquely human capabilities like creativity, emotional and social intelligence, empathy, problem-solving, etc. For the future workforce, it will be necessary to work parallel with AI, using the technology as an adjunct to making better decisions instead of going against it. In healthcare, AI can help doctors diagnose diseases, but no matter how good it is, it cannot replace human judgment and empathy in patient care. While this process can be performed relatively effectively via machine learning automated customer services. In conclusion, workforce transformation strategies must not only evolve around technology, but human-centered skills that AI cannot replicate.

The major challenges associated with AI-induced job loss are the socio-economic inequality that it compounds. So, for low-skilled and low-income workers, automation is taking their work and often the kinds of jobs they do are the first to be replaced by the likes of machines. Conversely, highly qualified workers engaged in the AI-related economy are now rewarded with an ever-growing number of job openings and better pay, further deepening the wage divide between workers in different sectors. This widening gap poses a threat to social stability, with large segments of the population in danger of being excluded from the digital economy. The governments must institute policies to alleviate these inequalities such as unemployment benefits, social safety nets, and wage subsidies for displaced workers. While users and organizations should limit the amount of data collected, businesses also have a responsibility to ensure ethical AI deployment and support the inclusion of the workforce, reskilling, and upskilling for transitioning from jobs.

The very important challenge of workforce in AI era is Job displacement psychological and emotional impact. Getting automated out of a job can cause financial uncertainty, stress, and the loss of your occupational identity. The workers grapple with the uncertainty of accessing new employment, especially if skills are obsolete. The dynamic is even more pronounced among older workers, who may struggle to adopt new technology or seek further education. These fears need to be mitigated, and organizations can do so by creating a postive workplace, offering mental health support, and being open about any automation methods being used. Instilling a culture of reskilling and career fluidity will enable team members to feel more confident of their place in an AI-infused workplace.

To prepare for the future of work in the AI era, multiple stakeholders need to collaborate. Governments should have progressive policies that regulate AI adoption and protect worker rights. The educational institutions need to modernize curricula to better align with emerging job requirements, ensuring that students are equipped with the skills needed for AI-driven careers. This means focusing on human-AI cooperation in the workplace; as opposed to automation which is often seen as the way to cut costs, it should invest in our employees and we will be in a better place for it. As we move towards an AI based workforce, we must be governed by principles of fairness, inclusivity and sustainability, so that societal progress does not come at the cost of deepening the already grave economic divides.

However on the flipside job displacement and workforce challenges in the AI era are serious concerns but bring opportunities for change as well. Automation is considered a threat to traditional employment structures, yet it also generates new jobs and stimulates innovation. The transition, however, requires proactive workforce development, inclusive reskilling initiatives, and policies that address social equity. Instead of displacing workers, AI should be seen as an augmentation tool for humans, allowing societies to create a future of work which is both advanced and socially inclusive. With deliberate and appropriate policies, the growing use of AI will lead to the development of a more skilled labor force rather than the displacement of workers.

As the AI technologies replace routine jobs, white-collar workers will need to adapt to the workplace, embracing new roles that require digital literacy, problem-solving and creativity. This transition will be a challenge and an opportunity, demanding cooperation between businesses, governments, and educational institutions to train the workforce to meet the changing demands of the digital economy. It never ended; not just for the sake of replacing jobs that have been lost but also by putting workers in a position to thrive in a fast-moving environment. The sustainable side of the transition will depend on targeted reskilling initiatives, ongoing upskilling initiatives, and the rise of new job roles that harness AI and automation as agents of human augmentation, not replacement.

Reskilling refers to the process by which workers are trained in completely different sets of skills that will enable them to shift into different occupations, especially those that are less prone to automation. As industries from manufacturing and retail to transportation and finance continue to embrace AI and automation, many traditional roles are likely to change or even become obsolete. Factory workers once relied on repetitive manual assembly jobs now must learn to so manoeuvre and maintain machines, whereas bank tellers have morphed into financial advisors as digital banking applications assume basic transactional tasks. These displaced workers will need reskilling programs to pivot into new careers in burgeoning fields like AI development, cybersecurity, healthtech and renewable energy.

The needs of governments and corporations have also proved urgent for reskilling bojans. National-level programs in countries like Germany, Singapore and Sweden make financial restitution, technical training and career counseling available to all workers seeking new jobs. Big companies, such as Amazon and IBM, have begun reskilling programs for workers, providing training in cloud computing, AI integration and software engineering (Didier, 2024). While it supports workers, these programs tick a box for companies to remain competitive in a world where there is a will such that there is way on and out of the demands by an AI-driven economy. For reskilling to succeed, programs must be accessible, affordable, and aligned with industry needs. Governments should collaborate with businesses to create the tools needed to build relevant, future-proof and sector-agnostic training programs.

4. WORKFORCE TRANSFORMATION: IDENTITY CRISES, RESKILLING, UPSKILLING AND NEW JOB CREATION

There's no slowing down the rapid advancements in AI and automation and, in their wake, the reconfiguration of the global workforce, which will require large-scale transformations of the workforce through reskilling, upskilling and job creation. As many traditional works are automated by intelligent technologies to maximizes efficiency and productivity, workers are reaching out for new capabilities to stay in demand. This revolution is not just about replacing jobs but elevating workforce potential in the context of an AI-powered economy. As automation transforms industries, businesses, governments, and educational institutions need to unite in preparing workers for new roles, so that it enhances the job market rather than destroys it.

As automation takes over repetitive work in manufacturing, logistics and customer service, workers will need training for jobs that require critical thinking, technical skills and human-oriented abilities. All over the world, governments and corporations are pouring resources into large-scale reskilling initiatives to help workers displaced by automation move into high demand fields like cybersecurity, AI development, renewable energy, and healthcare technology. For instance, Amazon's "Upskilling 2025" program offers training in cloud computing and AI to its employees, so they can be relevant in an emerging job market. To make reskilling effective we need programs that are accessible, affordable, aligned to industry and produces easy pathways to sustainable careers for workers.

Upskilling is different from reskilling, which refers to a more drastic move into entirely new roles; instead, upskilling is about the improvement of existing skills in order to keep workers on the job as technology advances in their field. With AI and automation transforming workplace operations, healthcare, finance, education and engineering professionals need to keep their skills updated to remain competitive. AI tools that powered their decisions are revolutionizing decision-making but workers will need to focus on figuring out how to work with their intelligent systems instead of against them. Companies like Google and Microsoft are offering AI and cloud computing certification programs for ongoing professional development. Further, interpersonal skills like emotional intelligence, creativity and leadership, are increasingly important, as they enhance the harmony between AI systems and human beings to produce results and provide solutions.

Although the potential of losing jobs remains a concern, AI and automation are also creating new employment opportunities. Roles particularly around AI trainers, machine learning engineers and data analysts, and AI ethicists are hot in demand. The hybridization of work, where AI augments the capabilities of human professionals, has transformed roles in healthcare, legal services, and the creative industry. AI-enhanced roles are also on the rise, and hence, the gig economy is also growing, providing remote and freelance opportunities. Policymakers and businesses must also cultivate the responsibility of investing in inclusive workforce strategies to facilitate a smooth transition, focusing on digital literacy and lifelong learning, laying the foundation for a resilient, future-ready workforce.

5. POLICY AND REGULATORY FRAMEWORKS FOR AI AND EMPLOYMENT

With the rise of artificial intelligence (AI) and automation, there is great need for strong policy and regulatory frameworks to govern their effects on jobs. With AI-powered technologies revolutionizing industries and altering the landscape of job roles, partnership amongst governments, international organizations, and businesses is crucial to establish policies that ensure a balance between innovation, job security, and worker rights. Such regulations should include protections for employees, responsible use of AI, labor rights, job transition programs and equitable access to AI benefits while managing adverse impacts like job displacement and inequality.

5.1 Workers' Rights and Employment Policy Protections

Policymakers need to make rules that prevent workers from being exploited in an AI-based economy. This means providing fair wages, protecting against job loss, and supplying social security benefits for workers displaced by automation. Protections around labor should be modernized to create a safety net for gig economy and AI-mixed models of employment, preventing vulnerable work scenarios. Ubi) or wage subsidies, are consider as a potential solution to save workers displaced by automation. Also, global labor groups support policies that would prepare workers for new jobs in new industries.

5.2 Regulate Ethical AI in the Workplace

The use of artificial intelligence to make decisions on hiring, performance evaluation, and workplace surveillance raises ethical issues of bias, discrimination, and privacy. Regulatory frameworks need to provide guidance to ensure that AI applications in this context remain fair, transparent and accountable. When AI-powered hiring tools and decision-making algorithms are used, organizations should be required to run bias audits. There are already frameworks for protecting employee data from abuse by AI systems and other innovations; such as the General Data Protection Regulation (GDPR) in the EU. Ethical AI policies should also guarantee that human judgment stays central to decisions made in the workplace and prevent full automation from doing so through misleading decisions that impact employees' careers.

5.3 Workforce Development: Government and Industry Collaboration

A key focus point for regulators is the need to promote cooperation between governments, businesses, and educational institutions to develop and deploy workforce transformation initiatives. However, to stimulate deep investment in innovative employee reskilling and upskilling programs, policymakers need to incentivize companies to take these responsibilities in order to ensure that workers will be able to transition into new, AI-powered roles. In fact, training programmes that are funded through public-private partnerships can contribute greatly to lifelong learning initiatives. AI-Focused Tax Breaks: Tax breaks and subsidies for creating AI jobs can help incentivize companies to create new jobs and put less emphasis on automation in order to reinforce sustainable employment models (Jackson et al., 2024).

Governments should respond with smarter proposals and systems that are proactive and help to make a fair and equal workforce, the ethical use of AI, employment of that AI workforce (rather than just granting jobs to the one who can come up with the best AI solution), and a framework for being able to retrain the existing labor force. The right combination of policies will help unlock benefits of AI and mitigate its risks to promote a future in which technology and human labor complement each other's strengths, enabling humans to thrive in an ever-shifting workforce.

6. THE GIG ECONOMY AND REMOTE WORK IN AN AUTOMATED WORLD

With the growing adoption of AI also comes the growing need for AI specialists, machine learning engineers, robotics experts and cybersecurity professionals. Companies need AI trainers to polish algorithms, data analysts to make sense of troves of information, and AI ethicists to govern responsible and equitable use of tech. These jobs didn't exist a decade ago but are now some of the most desired careers. AI is also transforming traditional industries, creating hybrid roles that combine human knowledge with machine learning. In medicine, AI-enhanced applications can help physicians diagnose conditions, but there's still a need for human oversight and for interacting with patients. On the marketing side, data-driven AI serves up insights on how consumers behave, but creative types are necessary to put the story behind the brand. Likewise, AI can streamline document review in the legal sector, but lawyers are still necessary to litigate, negotiate, and interface with clients.

This blending of work highlights the need to cultivate complementary skills that complement the strengths of AI as opposed to being supplanted by it.

Automation has also broadened gig economy and remote work opportunities. Freelancers are taking advantage of this trend by offering niche-sector services that can't be fully replaced by AI using platforms like Upwork, Fiverr and TaskRabbit such as writing, graphic design, coaching and consulting. AI-driven task automation allows professionals to return to higher-value creative and more strategic work while handing over routine functions to intelligent systems. This enables entrepreneurs and small businesses to scale up with little overhead, a huge advantage. Policymakers and industry leaders alike have to actively shape the future of work to ensure a smooth workforce transition in the era of AI (Alam et al., 2024). Governments need to create regulations that promote responsible AI adoption and protect workers' rights. Focus must be laid on universal access to affordable education and vocational training programs like online learning platforms to close the skills gap. Public-private initiatives can catalyze widespread reskilling and upskilling efforts to ensure that workers all over the socioeconomic spectrum have access to new opportunities.

Companies, in turn, need to humanize their automation. Rather than striving to reduce costs by cutting jobs, businesses should invest in human capital by giving employees training, career development, and chances to work with AI. A responsible AI methodology lays the framework for automation and helps ensure that machines augment, rather than wholly replace, human abilities. So, ensuring clear communication about how AI technologies operate and will change the workplace can help ease employee anxiety, and build trust in the transition process, Tuzunkan believes.

AI-powered workforce transformation must be inclusive. Women, low-income workers, and people from developing countries are considered one of the marginalized groups, and they should also be given equal opportunities in education and training. Addressing Digital Divides and Socio-economic Disparities to Avoid AI Fostering Inequality A workforce strategy with the future in mind must include diversity, equity, and inclusion to ensure that technological advancements are viable for all members of society.

The emergence of the AI era brings a more concerted effort towards reskilling, upskilling, and developing new opportunities for work. Although there are potential drawbacks when it comes to job displacement, automation actually opens doors for innovation and career advancement. Lifelong learning and adaptability will be keys to success, and workers who can leverage technology to their advantage will be the leaders of the AI-powered economy. It is up to the government, businesses, and schools to work together to create a world where AI is a tool for humans and not a replacement for humans. These strategies will help societies effectively manage workforce transformation, enabling a sustainable and inclusive future of work in the age of augmented intelligence (Kieslich et al., 2024).

7. THE FUTURE OF HUMAN-AI COLLABORATION IN WORKPLACES

AI solutions can make the traditional workplace shift into a new era with intelligent technologies collaborating with humans to leverage mutual skills. AI is good at repetitive jobs, data crunching, and predictive analytics, but humans have critical thought, creativity, emotional intelligence, and ethics. How AI can help or even replaces the need for humans is a thing and we are talking about humanization of work and design it to help humans for the better, so that humanized tech is the focus. AI is being used more and more in various fields to enhance human abilities rather than completely replace human jobs. In the medical field, AI-based diagnostic tools help physicians diagnose illnesses more accurately, and robotic surgical systems improve precision during complicated procedures. AI-Powered Risk Analysis in Finance AI analyzes risk and helps finance professionals make informed investment decisions. In manufacturing, too, AI-powered robotics make production processes smoother, cutting down on errors while increasing efficacy. Building a bridge between humans and AI depends on AI's capacity to analyse massively complex datasets and on humans' unique ability to engage in strategic change-making, creative problem-solving, and relationship building.

Job roles are evolving as AI automates routine tasks. These shifts are redefining traditional roles and creating new job opportunities, including roles in AI training, human-AI interaction design, and AI ethics compliance. AI experts, data analysts and prompt engineers are now indispensable in those fields that use automation. Additionally, soft skills, including leadership, adaptability, and emotional intelligence, are increasing in importance, as human workers will be required to manage AI systems, interpret the findings generated by the AI, and ensure ethical and regulatory compliance. What is more, companies are realizing that AI does not replace intelligence, but can be an intelligence boost and if it is managed and integrated into the corporate structure, it really can bring about a transformation in workforce capabilities (Wang et al., 2024).

AI brings great potential, but it also creates challenges that need to be managed to enable an equitable human-AI cooperation. Based on the issues of AI algorithms' bias and job displacements concerns, not to mention the debate around data privacy, they pose as a result for strong regulatory frameworks and strong corporate responsibility. Organisations should then focus on AI literacy employees, so that workers know how to work alongside AI systems. Establishing a framework for transparency, ethics, and human oversight in AI decision-making can help cultivate trust in AI solutions. AI and humans will collaborate to solve complex problems, unlocking new levels of creativity and innovation. Fostering AI as a partner in productivity leads to a more efficient, innovative, and diverse workplace that allows for new ideas to thrive, ultimately ensuring that both technology and human ingenuity help power the future of business at work.

8. CHALLENGES AND OPPORTUNITIES FOR A SUSTAINABLE AI WORKFORCE

AI powered automation seems to advance the productivity and efficiency but comes with the concerns of job replacement, skill gaps, ethical issues and regulatory challenges. It is imperative for governments, businesses, and educational institutions to navigate these challenges effectively, whilst capitalizing on the opportunities presented by AI, to create new jobs, transform the workforce, and drive economic growth in a balanced and inclusive manner. Job Displacement – Job displacement is one of the major challenges of AI adoption Automation is taking away repetitive or routine low-skill jobs in industries throughout the economy, putting millions of workers in danger of losing their jobs (Guan et al., 2024). Sectors, including manufacturing, retail and customer service, are already facing significant disruptions, requiring large-scale reskilling and upskilling programs to help displaced workers transition into new roles. For the most part, there is a widening AI skills gap, especially as learning methods provided by traditional systems fail to keep up with rapid rates of technological change. Most workers do not possess the technical skills needed to implement AI and similar technologies, so AI-themed curricula must be integrated into academic and vocational training programs.

A significant challenge, too, is ethical and social issues. AI-powered decision making systems can be biased, resulting in workplace discrimination and inequitable hiring. AI governance needs to be based on ethical principles and such strong regulations to avoid bias and exclusion in an AI workforce. Moreover, the reliance on algorithms in AI systems also magnifies concerns about data privacy and security in AI-driven workplaces, which necessitates robust policies that safeguard employees' personal data and prevent misuse of AI systems.

However, these challenges do not diminish the potential that AI solutions provide for the transformation of the workforce. However, it also has numerous benefits, the first being the generation of new job roles involved with the development, maintenance, and oversight of AI systems. New career paths are being forged, with emerging professions like AI trainers, machine learning engineers, and AI ethicists in demand. AI can also help enable people to work on creative, strategic, and higher-value-add processes while automating the more repetitive processes. This shift improves both productivity and job satisfaction. AI also offers an opportunity for inclusive workforce development through access to remote work and flexible job models. AI-driven tools can assist workers with disabilities, make work more accessible, and promote diversity. By investing in lifelong learning programs, governments and businesses can foster sustainability, guaranteeing itself to continuously adapt to the changes introduced by AI programs. A sustainability AI workforce needs forward-looking policies and ethical AI deployment along with constant investment in talent development. Through action on challenges and on opportunities, AI can accelerate economic growth while creating a more resilient, agile, and inclusive workforce in the digital economy (Bazargani & Deemyad, 2024).

9. CONCLUSION AND FUTURE DIRECTIONS

AI adoption and global perspectives on technology vary widely according to a country's economic development, regulatory system, and societal reactions to technology. Countries with developed economies like the United States, China, and Germany are leading the way in the development of AI by facilitating research and development to promote expansion through automation. On the other hand, developing countries encounter issues such as infrastructure deficits, digital inequality, and labor market vulnerabilities. AI can provide new opportunities for growth in emerging markets, but if not managed properly it can also deepen unemployment and inequality. Such global cooperation is necessary to facilitate ethical AI governance, enhance labor practices, and ensure that the fruits of technology are shared by and developed for all societies. The world of work must find a way to transition into an AI-infused future of production in a way that maximizes the potential for automation to drive sustainable development, while protecting workers' rights and economic security.

As a result, the emergence of automation and artificial intelligence in the labor market is, of course, drastically changing the landscape of industries, workforce frameworks, and jobs. Although AI-enabled technologies are able to improve efficiency, accuracy, and scalability, it also introduces major challenges, such as job loss, ethical issues, and the need for workplace reskilling. There is a way in which work has always changed, and it will continue to do so and the future of work will be determined by how employers, legislatures, and schools adapt to this new reality, and that automation serves to augment work, not to replace it. As the AI revolution unfolds, a balanced approach which encourages human-AI partnerships, creates inclusive workforce legislation and invests in lifelong learning will be critical for navigating the future global workforce. AI poses both opportunities and challenges population both holds promise and fear by responsibly embracing innovation, societies can unlock the full potential of AI, generating a sustainable and inclusive future of work.

REFERENCES

. Alam, M. F., Lentsch, A., Yu, N., Barmack, S., Kim, S., Acemoglu, D., ... & Ahmed, F. (2024). From automation to augmentation: Redefining engineering design and manufacturing in the age of NextGen-AI.

Bazargani, K., & Deemyad, T. (2024). Automation's impact on agriculture: Opportunities, challenges, and economic effects. *Robotics (Basel, Switzerland)*, *13*(2), 33.

Cazzaniga, M., Jaumotte, M. F., Li, L., Melina, M. G., Panton, A. J., Pizzinelli, C., & Tavares, M. M. M. (2024). *Gen-AI: Artificial intelligence and the future of work*. International Monetary Fund.

Didier, N. (2024). Turning fragments into a lens: Technological change, industrial revolutions, and labor. *Technology in Society*, *77*, 102497.

Dries, N., Luyckx, J., & Rogiers, P. (2024). Imagining the (distant) future of work. *Academy of Management Discoveries*, *10*(3), 319–350.

George, A. S. (2024). Automated Futures: Examining the Promise and Peril of AI on Jobs, Productivity, and Work-Life Balance. *Partners Universal Innovative Research Publication*, *2*(6), 1–17.

Growiec, J., & Prettner, K. (2025). The Economics of p (doom): Scenarios of Existential Risk and Economic Growth in the Age of Transformative AI. *arXiv preprint arXiv:2503.07341*.

Guan, Y., Liao, H., Li, Z., Hu, J., Yuan, R., Li, Y., & Xu, C. (2024). World models for autonomous driving: An initial survey. *IEEE Transactions on Intelligent Vehicles*.

Jackson, I., Jesus Saenz, M., & Ivanov, D. (2024). From natural language to simulations: Applying AI to automate simulation modelling of logistics systems. *International Journal of Production Research*, *62*(4), 1434–1457.

Kieslich, K., Diakopoulos, N., & Helberger, N. (2024). Anticipating impacts: Using large-scale scenario-writing to explore diverse implications of generative AI in the news environment. *AI and Ethics*, •••, 1–23.

Kumar Sharma, M., & Yadav, D. A. (2024). From Automation to Augmentation: Redefining Management in the Era of Artificial Intelligence. *Available at SSRN* 5075423.

. Praveen, T. (2024). Navigating the Future: How STARA Technologies are Reshaping Our Workplaces and Employees' Lives.

Wang, H., Feng, Y., Tian, Y., Wang, Z., Hu, J., & Tomizuka, M. (2024). Towards the next level of vehicle automation through cooperative driving: A roadmap from planning and control perspective. *IEEE Transactions on Intelligent Vehicles*, *9*(3), 4335–4347.

Chapter 11
Global Anti-Discrimination Law and AI Concerning Imposter Syndrome and Legal Frameworks:
Gender, Diversity, and Intersectional Bias in Professional Advancement Technology

Sheersha Saxena
https://orcid.org/0009-0009-7214-6192
Vivekananda Global University, India

Arunima Shastri
https://orcid.org/0000-0002-6260-1253
Christ University, Bangalore, India

Rakesh Ranjan Kumar
https://orcid.org/0009-0004-3430-5598
School of Business, Galgotias University, Greater Noida, India

Nitya Sharma
https://orcid.org/0009-0008-0921-6074
Vivekananda Global University, India

DOI: 10.4018/979-8-3373-6618-0.ch011

ABSTRACT

In the age of artificial intelligence, strong anti-discrimination laws are important for more than just following the rules. It includes social, ethical and economic issues of interest to technologists and non-technologists alike. The regulations would help reduce the chance that AI perpetuates stereotypes that limit women and other groups, based on preconceived ideas. Lost impostor syndrome, behind-the-scenes' and careers being ruined by AI-bias fuel psychological damage to self-esteem, job satisfaction, retention etc."AI bias" If "bias exits in neural networks that has emerged in the workforce," then it's best to circumvent such bias before problems arise. In that chapter, it examines how international antidiscrimination law links to AI, with examples of impostor syndrome. It also explores the intersection of this technology with global anti-discrimination laws, and in doing so, reveals significant legal and sociotechnical implications.

1. INTRODUCTION

With the growing use of AI technology comes the fear that it could "exacerbate current biases that we may be grappling with around gender or race and those other intersections into our workplaces." They play a role in developing leaders' skills, assessing their performance and making hiring and promotion decisions. Imposter syndrome is more prevalent in women and underrepresented minorities. A form of mental illness in which an individual believes their accomplishments, status or skills are fraudulent, and that they will soon be exposed as a "fraud," even though there is imminent proof to the contrary. This is closely linked to the biased algorithms in AI engines and models, which act as the gatekeepers for career progression. To solve the parallel problem of AI-caused legal problems, all over the world, people are radicalizing their juridical systems. It is not just the fairness of AI, but also this inequity that affects those grappling with imposter syndrome. These frameworks seek to mitigate systemic bias in AI systems that may be inadvertently perpetuated through training data, model architecture and deployment practices as well as overtly unfair behavior (Wachter, 2022).

The systemic prejudice and societal inequalities are occasionally exemplified in historical records which cause AI systems to unintentionally perpetuate these biases. AI systems that handle hiring, performance reviews and other personnel-related tasks may undervalue applicants from a variety of backgrounds, such as women and ethnic minorities. If they are given data that is biased toward male management and/or homogeneous applicant pools. Because algorithmic discrimination prevents individuals from advancing in their careers and solidifies social inequalities, it leads to economic inequality (Yadav et al., 2025).

The psychological impact of AI-induced bias in the workplace as previously stated, effects on work produced by prejudice brought on by AI The propensity of experts to display impostor syndrome has previously been discussed. The people who are still exposed to biased AI-driven evaluations may experience emotions of inadequacy and self-doubt, delay their careers, or reduce the number of varied talent that organizations retain. Therefore, the digital revolution is intricately linked to social and psychological aspects of equality, necessitating legal and legislative responses that include the experience of exclusion or marginalization in addition to just establishing discriminatory systems (Liberman, 2025).

These new issues are difficult for the idea of international and legal orders to handle. The problem of algorithmic accountability, transparency, and fairness is what influences international nondiscrimination frameworks. Laws requiring AI systems to be examined for prejudice, to explain their findings, and to take corrective action when bias is discovered are being drafted. These encouraging developments demonstrate that we are shifting from just enforcing anti-discrimination legislation when they are violated to regulating AI in a manner that respects human rights and values. The objective is to use digital transformation as a tool for the greater good in order to develop practical solutions to lower the dangers of exclusion and inequality.

Such policy drives are also crucial to address the gap in digital divide. Millions of women, particularly those living in low-middle income countries (LMICs), are confronted with gender-specific barriers to access and use digital technology as a result of intersecting systems of oppression such as structural inequalities – culturalnorms, economic hardships, disconnection and educational disparities. Without closing these diviisions through investment in digital infrastructure, education and empowerment initiatives, these gaps will prevent real gender equality from being realised. Global partnerships and initiatives, such as the EQUALS Global Partnership, are still calling for broad-based action to enhance online safety for women and girls, as well as women's leadership on technology issues, presence in digital spaces and literacy. For institutions, ethical AI requires sustained attention to build equity and inclusion into the design, development and deployment of AIsolutions. So in the age of AI in HR and development, it is essential for enterprises to emphasise ongoing work to reduce bias alongside regulations on transparency and diverse data sources.

AI-driven digital transformation is a double-edged sword for equality. It is a tool that can be used to close divides and foster inclusive development, but it also risks becoming an instrument that entrenches or widens inequalities if not managed in a proactive and equitable manner. A multifaceted, systems based approach is required to tackle these problems that takes account of purposeful policy interventions along with the commitment of organisations to inclusivity (mixing) and great design/

tech as well as strong regulation (Packin, 2021). Digital transformation can only deliver on its promise as a force for the more fair, equitable and just society we all seek by pursuing measures like these in combination.

2. INTERNATIONAL LEGAL STANDARDS AS UN TREATIES: CEDAW, ICERD AND CRPD

The International Convention on the Elimination of All Forms of Racial Discrimination (ICERD), the Convention on the Rights of Persons with Disabilities (CRPD), and the Convention on the Elimination of All Forms of Discrimination Against Women (CEDAW) are important treaties (Harehdasht & Saki, 2025). The most comprehensive international agreement against discrimination against women in all spheres of public life is CEDAW, which was enacted in 1979 and is frequently referred to as the "bill of rights for women." It defines gender discrimination as "any distinction, exclusion or restriction made on the basis of sex which has the effect or purpose of impairing or nullifying recognition, enjoyment or exercise by women, irrespective of their marital status, on a basis of equality of men" . In order to eradicate discrimination, States Parties are required by CEDAW to take all necessary steps, including legislation and regulations. These include equal legal capacity, repealing discriminatory laws and practices, and achieving substantive equality in political participation, education, employment, and health as well as in family-related laws.

Beyond legal equality, the treaty outlines a vision of substantive equality that goes beyond equal treatment under the law to include taking proactive steps to guarantee women's complete growth and development. CEDAW pertains, for instance, to the evolution of social and cultural norms that perpetuate roles and caricature people who ought to be marginalized, like women. It is unique in that gender relations are culturally particular and reproductive rights are included. In order to encourage accountability, CEDAW requires reporting systems where States disclose their progress and challenges. The treaty's obligations extend to the digital transformation of society and AI technologies. States must guarantee equal opportunities for men and women, take steps not only "to avoid" discrimination against women in any new systems but also to prevent discriminatory effects from materializing, and actively engage women in the digital and technological spheres in order to increase their participation in the economy of the future.

The primary framework for combating racial discrimination is provided by ICERD, which went into effect in 1965. It is quickly defined as any distinction, exclusion, restriction, or preference based on race, color, descent, or national or ethnic origin that aims to nullify or impair the recognition and enjoyment of human rights on an equal footing (Vivek & Krupskyi, 2024). States Parties are dedicated to enacting laws that would outlaw hate speech and organizations that support racism, as well as providing adequate protection for victims of racism. These policies would put a stop to racial prejudice.

In recognizing that such categories as race and ethnic origin intersect with other grounds to produce complex forms of discrimination, the treaty acknowledges intrasectional or intersectional dimensions of discrimination. Because data derived from the reflection of racial bias, for example, as it might perpetuate systemic discrimination within employment practices or policing initiatives, credit and service provision, these same ICERD standards are particularly adequate when discussing AI systems. The CERD and other treaty bodies—organs monitoring implementation and providing interpreting guidance on the ways newly emerging challenges, by reason of tech striving, can be dealt within existing provisions–provide accountability as opposed to mere reporting obligation. Under the ICERD, states are required to take positive measures to eliminate racial discrimination in their interpretation of digitalization and AI governance.

The treaty includes commitments to end discriminatory practices, implement reasonable accommodations. It ensures accessibility in all spheres of life, including education, employment, health, political participation and public life. It recognizes that discrimination against people with disabilities violates justice and human dignity.

The CRPD is closely related to AI and digital technologies and emphasizes the need to remove obstacles in the physical, social, technical, and attitudinal environments in order to encourage participation. There are states Parties must engage with people with disabilities when developing new technologies, including AI applications and ensure that they are socially inclusive and accessible. Both governments and private actors are required by the treaty's provisions on access, participation, and equality before the law to take precautions against the discriminatory design or use of AI systems that might prevent people with disabilities from advancing in their careers and being included in society.

Between them, CEDAW, ICERD and CRPD argue for universal principles of non-discrimination, equality and human dignity. It should inform legal and policy responses to discrimination produced by AI. These treaties oblige States not simply to prevent discriminatory action but actively to promote equality through targeted means (Alshdiefat et al., 2024).

3. DISCRIMINATION AND IMPOSTER SYNDROME: GENDER, DIVERSITY AND INTER-SECTIONALITY

This overlapping of bias with imposter syndrome is even more exaggerated when looking through the lenses of gender, diversity and inter-sectionality. There is also significant moderation of gender on impostor syndrome and prejudice. And to women, already victims of discrimination more often than men solely because they are female — even when they are strong, productive employees? That conditioning about their leadership, fitness for running things and conscious/unconscious feelings still return. Prejudices also manifest in hiring decisions, performance evaluations, pay gaps and opportunities for advancement that expand the effect of social messages. It questions the right of women to is even work inside what traditionally have been men-only vocations. Frustration, too, Hunter's readers inferred, for how often women are forced to credit their success to external factors that have nothing to do with talent. And these biases just compound the imposter syndrome. The tension, however, is not only a drag on your happiness. By turning the screws too tight in how you assess yourself, you're likely to eat into your self-confidence and willingness to take strategic risks and experience at taking on leadership roles (CBE, 2023).

Impostor syndrome is really about structural forces, not human psychology. Discrimination puts stigmatized people in the position of living in a world where they have or should take to defining who they are and what their worth is. Imposter syndrome is inadvertently funded through institutions that remains exclusionary, unconsciously bias and un-audited for prejudice. Conversely, impostor syndrome is much less prevalent in workplaces that are inviting and accepting of everyone's unique talents and identities even as they undo structural obstacles. Interventions that address both impostor syndrome and prejudice translate to multistage therapies for mental well-being, legislative policies or organizational change. By participating in peer support groups, mentor programs and cognitive-behavioral psychological therapies people could reconsider their self-perception and become more resilient. But if you're not solving for system, then it's inadequate.

The resulting access to continuing professional development (CPD), and open, bias-aware decision-making but intersectionality-sensitive anti-discrimination through the organisational climate/legal by organizational policies and legal framework. Applying an intersectional analysis to diversity and inclusion programs allows more informed help to be offered, and recognizes that a solution that works for one group of workers may not work for another due to different forms of oppression. And the idea that we can fight imposter syndrome through changing your company culture by confronting bias and self-doubt head-on, encouraging diverse role models, and making clear leadership is responsible for real inclusion. Apps designed for AI recruiting and development are one instance of technological tools that need to be built, and assessed, through an intersectional lens in order to avoid amplifying biases that could cause distinct groups feel like they do not fit in.

Both impostor syndrome and bias are complex constructs that have relevant intersectionality, diversity, and gender implications. Beyond that individual pain, the psychological toll of bias and discrimination reflects broader structural inequalities which inhibit genius and social justice in the workplace." In order to contest these matters comprehensive battles need to be waged in such dimensions as legislative, structural/organizational, psychological and the technological. And in doing so, they could help break down barriers; serve the needy and open up inclusive spaces of practice where anyone who wishes to be a practitioner can thrive, with skill and dignity.

4. EMERGENCE OF AI BIAS IN PROFESSIONAL CONTEXTS

The paradox in this instance of AI bias at work is shown by this data-driven prejudice: biased data produces biased AI, and biased AI produces skewed findings that lock in discrepancies. Biases are also increased by algorithmic design and implementation choices. Numerous subjective decisions, such as the characteristics used, the model structure employed, and the training goal, influence AI systems. The unconscious prejudices held by developers may contaminate such decisions with biased or exclusive results. The outcomes produced by AI, however, may be distorted if certain characteristics are ignored or if the search for them is reduced to employing simple stand-ins for complex aspects of human nature (Ulum, 2025).

The bias presented from an AI system is also space invariant. AI systems must grapple with processes, corporate cultures, and human agents that might inadvertently reinforce bias. It could simply entrench the status quo in the workplace if employers don't think critically, and instead accept AI proposals too easily. Responses by the employee to assessments enabled by AI — including lost morale and workers placed into "the zone" (the fazing out of underrepresented groups, which are often the focus of AI discrimination). It could also have an impact on job performance and employment, creating feedback loops that perpetuate current inequalities. There may also be intersectional effects of AI bias, for example with imposter syndrome e.g. in women and intersectionally disadvantaged people at work–after all, we can imagine that they are more affected.

The cost of bias in AI is significant, and one that affects businesses. Methodologically, there is also value in being able to thoroughly explain the outcomes of an algorithm's recommendations. There are hiring algorithms that discriminate could willfully filter out the applications of well-qualified candidates from a specific gender, ethnic group or other protected profile and antagonize diversity programs. Leaders from underrepresented groups struggle to envision opportunities for mobility and representation. This is the time when AI driven performance appraisals underestimate the minority personnel's efforts or potential. These unfair algorithms lead to higher turnover and lower participation by creating a feeling of mistrust in technology and fairness by the employer. "Like, the bad systems are just one part of this investment; there's also the wider system of social violence over here disinvesting from the economy and depriving poor people opportunity.

As a result, the notion of legislation and laws has already started looking at AI bias in business life due to these risks. Employers must now audit their AI systems for unfair bias and transparency under the re-interpretation (and extension) of anti-discrimination laws into AI. In various domains, there are different efforts to develop standards and guidelines on the ethical use of AI in HR. It is largely through the need for impact assessments, explainability requirements and redress mechanisms. These regimes require accountability along the life of an AI from data collection, to model training, deployment and continued monitoring and operations that in turn requires collaboration between technologists', legal's and HR and other disciplines.

There are many technical interventions that aim to reduce AI bias in the workplace. They can be categorized into three types: Those that post-process the results to correct for any discrimination; those that train with fairness-aware models. It further pre-processes data to mitigate bias. Bias, as well as cultural sensitivity, could be addressed by stakeholder-based dialogue and the involvement of multiple development teams. Algorithmic transparency and explainability tools can trace the causes of bias and propose remedies. The fine interpretation and overrule of algorithmic results as necessary is supported via the overlay of human judgment upon AI decision-support. Professionals can harness AI potential to advance diversity, inclusion and justice in the digitall era by addressing those biases head on (Newman et al., 2025).

4.1 AI in recruitment, promotion and workplace automation

With using data to inform choices, AI-powered recruitment solutions have helped businesses better manage higher application volumes and even lessen the impact of human bias. These patterns that seem to indicate a talent or achievement that human recruiters would miss might cause AI to raise warning signals. The scheduling and automatic answers based on NLP and ML enhance the applicant experience.

However, recruiting AI systems are also often criticized for sustaining and even magnifying prejudices such as these. These algorithms might pick up existing prejudices from past employment data, such as employing more males than women in sectors with a predominance of men or disregarding job applicants from minority groups. AI model may rate female candidates lower or unjustly filter them out if it is trained on historical data showing that women were underrepresented in certain positions. A variety of candidates may also be deterred by language-biased job descriptions or evaluation instruments. So, creating more and more equitable algorithms, reviewing model-level predictions across demographic groups. This also applying bias correction recipes are some methods to mitigate these problems. For hiring procedures to be fair and trustworthy, AI and human judgment must be transparent.

AI is utilized in the field of talent management and promotion to identify high-potential workers to advance up the chain based on performance indicators, skill shortages, leadership potential, and employee engagement data. On the basis of performance evaluations, anticipated results, peer reviews, and other data are sorted by predictive analytics algorithms to recommend potential candidates for promotions (Holzer, 2020).

The prop-Tech companies are revolutionizing administrative tasks to increase corporate efficiency by using AI algorithms to automate appointment booking, chat and virtual help and work-flow management. The \automation frees up human workers to focus on complex creative or strategic initiatives by eliminating laborious chores that are entirely controlled by manual capability (Oikelmme et al., 2022). AI used to robots improves operational accuracy and efficiency in sectors like manufacturing.

The labor equation is also altered by workplace automation. Fears of displacement and increased inequality result from the fact that certain vocations are enhanced and enriched while others wither or undergo drastic changes. Due to occupational segregation, some demographic groups such as- women, minorities, and low-wage workers as the may be more susceptible to automation. Furthermore, productivity-based algorithmic management may have a disproportionate effect on disadvantaged employees and raise privacy, autonomy, and surveillance issues. To prevent unfavorable results, the issue of fair transitions and equality in retraining and upskilling programs is crucial.

The implementation of AI that is transparent, inclusive by design, and subject to regulatory and human control is necessary to mitigate such threats. The businesses will be able to take use of AI's beneficial potential to contribute to the development of more inclusive, varied, and encouraging work environments in the digital age (McGrath & Dye, 2023).

5. LEGAL GAPS IN ADDRESSING AI-INDUCED BIAS

As AI becomes more integrated into business, society, and private life, the seriousness of prejudice caused by AI has become more apparent. The current legal safeguards only partially address the significant challenges posed by AI bias. Which it is defined as systematic and unfair discriminatory treatment resulting from faulty data, design and execution. There are many legal loopholes remain even after different jurisdictions have adopted cutting-edge AI governance policies, approved labor standards and anti-discrimination laws, and more (Singh et al., 2025).

Most anti-discrimination laws have criteria for mens rea, or explicit behaviors, and were designed to control in human decision-making situations. There are legal norms based on discriminatory intent are difficult to establish, and artificial intelligence systems operate via opaque, data-driven processes devoid of human purpose. Because such skewed outcomes might be unintentionally created by irreproducible data or design errors. This goes undetected under conventional evidence standards, this makes establishing responsibility challenging. When neutral-seeming inputs have disproportionately detrimental consequences and are statistically reliant on a protected attribute such as gender or race. AI might reinforce indirect or proxy discrimination. The indirect algorithmic discrimination is not specifically covered under current legislation, which has made enforcement challenging.

The legal shortcomings are exacerbated by deficiencies in explain-ability and transparency. AI models often don't provide human-accessible reasons for their actions, which prevents the impacted persons from understanding why they were passed over for promotions or employment. Lack of openness makes it more difficult for the underprivileged to effectively recognize injustice, claim their rights, and seek remedies. It is very uncommon for legal frameworks to mandate sufficient openness or intelligibility in relation to AI in order to ensure responsibility. Some new AI laws pertain to explainability in particular nations, but they are ineffective globally and have not been uniformly implemented and harmonized.

AI ecosystems given that the regulation and enforcement are relatively new. Some enforcement and equality bodies that have a duty to look into prejudice may not have the technical skills and resources needed to properly assess complex AI systems. These authorities may also not have the legal regimes in place to compel independent audits of algorithms, disclosure of training data or compel them to get it right at outset. When enforcement is weak, however, biased deployments are less deterrent, and victims have few avenues of redress. "Legal proceedings can be very slow, and for victims it can be hard to find out how they would even access discrimination (from AI).

So, rather than guaranteeing equity or anti-discrimination, the current privacy-enhancing laws focus more directly on protecting people's private. Because of this legal loophole, biased datasets may be used to create AI systems without the necessary modifications or checks for unfair trends (Jeter, 2025).

This is an insufficient regulatory vacuum for ethical research or AI standards. Responsible AI is guided by a patchwork of industry rules, voluntary guidelines and ethical principles as well as law. These are good free-world techniques, but they cannot substitute for the rule of law." This is what is required to mitigate harm and ensure AI is developed and employed responsibly. There's clearly plenty of scope for non-ethical AI to blossom, free to discriminate where mere laws fail or are toothless.

There is scant attention given to worker protections in the context of automation at work and AI-biases. Labour laws have not kept pace with technology and they do very little to protect employees when it comes to algorithmic management, surveillance, performance appraisal or automated decision-making, which can shape how well we are treated at work, our opportunities for advancement and even our dignity. It's disadvantaged groups most exposed to such disparities and who already experience discrimination and prejudice who bear the brunt of these divergences," it added.Experts say this gap has triggered warnings over the need for updating existing nondiscrimination and tort law in light of the reality featuring AI.

There are no simple solutions to closing such legal loopholes. Legal definitions of antidiscrimination should be expanded to include algorithmic and proxy forms; transparency, explainability and impact assessments for AI should be required; regulators' power and technological competence should be enhanced; and individuals harmed by discrimination should have access to justice. In order to minimize international and cross-sectoral regulatory fragmentation, business must collaborate with government across borders to develop common standards for AI governance. It's time for Congress to put into place a holistic plan that protects against all aspects of oppression and identity. But it is not realistic to expect data protection reform alone to address fairness concerns. To reduce the risk from biased data, fairness requirements need to be incorporated into reforms of data governance along with privacy protection requirements. Corporate responsibility regimes and the accompanying enforceable ethical norms should reinforce the legal obligations regarding AI deployment.

While AI may have the potential to be revolutionary for the workplace and society overall, there are currently not enough as legal resources to properly respond to prejudice caused by AI. Transparency, enforcement, inter-sectionality, data governance and ethical governance are quite unsettled areas but existing labor and antidiscrimination laws already have difficulty accounting for many of the very specific challenges AI poses. If we wish to ensure that we all share in reaping the rewards of AI and uphold human rights in our digital age, then there are gaps that we must close. Strong, flexible and overlapping legal systems, empowered regulators, & consensus on international norms will be necessary to ensure fair and inclusive AI system (Lehman et al., 2024).

6. AI AND PROFESSIONAL ADVANCEMENT: KEY LEGAL CHALLENGES

It adjusts to AI-generated indirect discriminatory choices as well as proxy discrimination. The transparency and explainability are another very important legal issue. The majority of AI models make conclusions in ways that are counterintuitive and do not tell users or impacted workers how the findings were arrived at. This lack of openness hinders regulators' attempts to enforce adherence to labor and anti-discrimination rules and denies. Those who have experienced unfair hiring or promotion practices the chance to contest unfavorable personnel decisions (Munawar, 2025). So, not all nations are in agreement, and there is no universal uniformity in this regard, even if some have enacted or contemplated legislative requirements pertaining to explainability and openness of algorithmic employment. Finding a balance between openness and intellectual property, trade secrets, and the expertise needed to comprehend AI outputs is a challenging task.

AI role in job opportunities strongly intersects with privacy and data protection concerns. If sensitive information about our demographics, health, behavior, and communications is the price we must pay for an AI to be successful, then AI systems need a large amount of personal data. Data protection legislation like the EU's GDPR and similar regulations in other countries throughout the globe address the collection, storage, processing, and distribution of such data. As the overzealous AI monitoring or surveillance raises the possibility of privacy violations and, therefore, power imbalances between employers and workers. Legal rules should ensure that AI-based data practices respect privacy, provide an exceptional degree of consent, and impose strict safeguards against abuse, particularly in light of power imbalances in the workplace (Schikman, 2025).

7. JUDICIAL AND ADMINISTRATIVE PROTECTIVE RESPONSES FOR DISCRIMINATION VICTIMS

Along with providing restitution and remedies for victims of unjust AI-based hiring, promotion and other workplace choices. These approaches also aim to respect present anti-discrimination legislation and the idea of employer and developer culpability (Aldosari et al., 2024). The courts and administrative agencies have begun to express ideas that acknowledge the unique challenges that AI discrimination presents while balancing technical advancement with human rights protections, even if the legal landscape is still being determined. The courts have started to recognize that persons are protected against discrimination based on the use of automated decision-making tools by current antidiscrimination laws, such as those pertaining to race, gender/sex, age, impairments, and other categories. Judges have rejected claims in court that companies or AI system creators may avoid accountability by just letting their AI technologies make choices (Compare et al., 2024).

Public interest litigation and whistleblowing will also be important safeguards since legal scrutiny and regulatory sanction could well be initiated by institutions or civil society members that report discriminatory AI practices. As a result of these and other initiatives, the public has been more informed, and businesses have been forced to change their AI deployment processes. The remedy for the victims of discrimination has been made easy without considering the cost and whether or not it's difficult to reach because administrative agency complaint procedures have been set up. Rather from only providing compensation for past injury, remedies increasingly emphasize that accountability for the harm should be seen as avoiding future pain.

The law enforcement agencies worldwide are beginning to collaborate in order to standardize responses to face and AI-enabled prejudice. International human rights groups contend that employment rules have to include provisions pertaining to AI fairness. Guidelines requiring AI to adhere to equality and nondiscrimination principles are being advanced by the UN and regional organizations. The protective character of these international standards is strengthened when they permeate the local legal and administrative system.

However, protective reactions vary and change with time. Many courts lack the technical expertise necessary to resolve intricate AI problems, and administrative agencies usually lack enough funding. Many countries lack jurisprudence, which leads to a general lack of consistent protection and legal confusion. The establishment of multidisciplinary AI discriminatory decision panels, the training of technological competence into judicial institutions, and enforcement cooperation among regulators, technologists, and activists are the ongoing developments (Richardson et al., 2025).

So, despite challenges brought on by the intrinsic complexity and opacity of this technology, administrative and legal remedies for victims of AI discrimination in the workplace are developing. The development of measures to close accountability gaps in legal systems and make anti-discrimination provisions effective includes the common law, regulations, transparency responsibilities, and particular remedies. The future research should concentrate on improving technological maturity, evidentiary availability and simplicity, and worldwide harmonization in order to provide fair and efficient justice for workers impacted by AI prejudice in the workplace.

8. POLICY INNOVATIONS AND BEST PRACTICES

The fast 'main-streaming' of artificial AI in professional settings has driven a wave of policy-related innovation and best practice concerning the particular challenges. This is presented by AI-driven discrimination and bias. An AI technology that informs responsible and trusted AI what is responsible AI mandates on the use of AI like GDPR happen at an intersection as the market restriction. Now, eventual forced restrictions as the technology becomes ingrained in daily life limits/restrictions if restive swathes of society believe it to be manifesting with bias or opacity not just because subtler harms may exist. Therefore, measuring how informed technical like gesturing towards fairness raw outcomes with the duty using raw outcomes but not some non-coordinated measure.

There are a few that have been pioneers advocating laws that mandate clear explanations of algorithms, fair-life audits and noneye-discrimination protections for AI tools in the workplace. For example, the EU's AI Act imposes rigorous obligations on high-risk AI systems and their use in relation to work. It also requires providers to assess risks of bias, document input-data quality, ensure the possibility of human intervention and explain automated decisions about people's careers. These regulatory styles sit across a proactive continuum, moving beyond the reactive limbs of anti-discrimination enforcement into preventive governance of AI impacts (O'Connell & McKinnon, 2021).

Policy-driven activities regarding responsible governance for AI is considered to be supplementary than a policy reform. The demands to publish impact assessments, encourage bias audit outcomes or the thresholds used to reach algorithmic decisions are steps to more accountability and trust. Transparency provides employees and applicants with understanding about how AI affects their prospects, and the possibility of challenging or bargaining unfavourable decisions once they have a knowledge on how such decisions are made. That would require employers to perform and publicly release bias audits of their automated employment systems each year — a move that's part of what can be called a strategy for municipal-driven strengthening of traditional regulatory power, but also community engagement.

These enforcement mechanisms have been designed so regulators can watch abstracted individual AIs. In some instances, governments have set up teams or task forces of legal, technical and data science experts to determine if algorithms are fair. These bodies collaborate with commissions, equality and labour-and-employment ministries for dealing with complaints, conducting compliance review and issuing guidance based on precedent from caselaw. And enforcement that truly works will depend on empowering agencies to require the disclosures they need, perform their own independent audits, and issue cease-and-desist orders or remedial commands with teeth — all of which could end AI bias in its tracks.

9. COMMUNITY AND STAKEHOLDER ENGAGEMENT: ROLE OF ADVOCACY GROUPS, GENDER STUDIES SCHOLARS AND AFFECTED COMMUNITIES

Legal regulation of private-sector actors will, however, not suffice to ensure the safety of workers: multi-valent solutions are required for responsible AI governance in professional development involving both their promotion of equality and redress for bias and discrimination. Active engagement of communities and other stakeholders (e.g., advocacy groups, scholars focused on gender, and affected individuals) is critical to this ecosystem. Like the best fair AI practices that policy-making, research and minorities. It also that AI works with justice at its heart, is all promised by said parties. Their participation is a positive contribution to AI governance because they address lived experiences, bring in diverse viewpoints and support systemic change (Reichard et al., 2024).

Communities being affected (workers, job-seekers and practitioners from underrepresented backgrounds) Communities that are impacted in their daily lives through lived experience also bring informed perspective as to what the real-life effects of AI will be. Its members help to ensure that the governance of AI is not just relevant but corresponds to actual environments, instead of an abstract sense of fairness. The affected members of the public also express these concerns and give accounts of the prejudicial instances, and together organise with others to develop tactics for challenge through at shared work on community consultations/co-design workshops/user feedback mechanisms. It democratizes (and demystifies) the machine learnings of machines and, one hopes, humans. Community representation may act as a counterweight to expert and power asymmetries which risk underestimating lived experience of those who are most affected by AI bias (Cross et al., 2024).

The above stakeholder and community engagement is an important factor towards capacity development also. Algorithm Transparency and Training programs, workshops and campaign awareness are facilitated by advocacy groups as well as institutions of learning to sensitize members of marginalized communities and people working in organizations about the bias toward AI openness, rights, remedies. Thanks to a strong legal literacy, such capacity building projects will help affected groups in realising their rights and engaging with the AI-saturated work environment. They are urging AI developers and the corporations that employ them to adopt community-informed inclusive policies based on strands of scholarly research. Such initiatives catalyze cultural shifts toward equity in work environments by increasing AI literacy across a wide variety of stakeholders (Horton, 2024).

The systematic and equitable approach to tackle AI bias in career progression needs community, including advocacy groups, gender studies researchers and underprivileged communities. They carry out diverse tasks, such as lobbying, research, capacity-building measures, participatory governance and oversight in critical angle which try to link the technical and legal sides of AI to real-world examples. Effective participation promotes the democratization of AI governance, amplifies the voices of marginalized populations, establishes a socially responsible AI culture that advances diversity and inclusion as well as gender balance in workplaces around the world (Flores & Rhames, 2025)..

9.1 Global Coalitions and Multi-Sector Oversight Mechanisms

The principles of transparency, inclusivity and justice are reflected in UNESCO's pioneering "Recommendation on the Ethics of Artificial Intelligence" – the world's first global standard-setting instrument on ethics of AI. It instead advocates for an AI that is multistakeholder mediated through knowledge drawn from gender studies, human rights and affected communities in an inclusive recognition of cultural and linguistic diversity. These resources are ethical examples and benchmarks for national and international industry rules.

At the same time, globally recognized benchmarks promoting ethical AI use are put forward by international alliances such as the OECD's AI Principles that have been revised and expanded in 2024. The OECD's guiding principles advocate for AI development to be inclusive, sustainable, equitable, transparent and responsible. A certain degree of convergence on AI policy and practice has emerged from the adoption or customization of these concepts by a growing number of countries and private sector actors. Likewise, the G7's so-called "Hiroshima Process" and Bletchley Declaration exert influence over this governance need through mutual commitments to advancing AI safety, privacy, risk mitigation and international collaboration, thereby reduciing fragmentation in global policy (Barnes et al., 2024).

Partnerships and discussion fora as form of forums are also used in multi-sector monitoring systems. The Global Partnership on AI (GPAI) is an international cooperation initiative to promote responsible AI leveraging multiple stakeholders, governments etc. across the world. The TEDAlign initiative Advertisment It fosters cross-disciplinarity and capacity-building on the threat of bias in AI applied in a variety of social and professional settings. Other cooperative frameworks, such as the AI for Good Global Summit and the Internet Governance Forum, facilitate information sharing, multistakeholder engagement and networking among AI advancements and existing sustainable development needs (Ivasiuc, 2020).

It is by no means an alternative to the valuable contributions from actors of all flavors, including: governments (domestic and intergovernmental), private sector innovators, members of scientific community, marginalized populations or civil society groups who can help ensure real progress towards global AI governance. Coalitions stress that forging trust and legitimacy, as well as culturally aware AI ecosystems, requires broad participation. They also facilitate knowledge sharing and capacity building, including on how low- and middle-income countries will address regulatory disparities and digital divide. Taking this together with the international coalitions and multi-stakeholder oversight mechanisms, it results in a dynamic linked structure of governance needed to overcome bias and manage AI risk in professional development. These partnerships provide a grassroots-oriented way forward for the ethical, equitable AI we need, by creating shared responsibility and considering justice and human rights in what is developed as well as deployed (Munoz et al., 2023).

10. CONCLUSION AND FUTURE DIRECTIONS FOR GLOBAL CONVERGENCE AND REFORM

In order to create unified, open and inclusive procedures that will be essential for the efficient governance of AI at scale, these kinds of collaborations bring together governments, intergovernmental organizations, academia, civil society, and business. The UN's engagement with AI and its consequences for inclusive development and human rights is the first of these. Through programs like the OHCHR and the UN Secretary-General's Roadmap for Digital Cooperation, the UN also strengthens normative frameworks for integrating human rights concepts across AI lifecycles. The Freedom Online Coalition's 2025 Joint Statement on Artificial Intelligence and Human Rights, one of many such statements that demonstrate multistakeholder resolve to support AI governance based on international law and include the full participation of all stakeholders, specifically emphasizes safeguarding the rights of the most vulnerable, including women and marginalized groups at risk from AI bias.

REFERENCES

Aldosari, N. M., Alqahtani, A. F., Almutairi, Y. M., & Alsubaie, O. M. (2024). A Comprehensive Review of Mental Health Challenges and Interventions for Healthcare Workers. *Clinical Epidemiology & Public Health*, *2*(1), 1–13.

Alshdiefat, A. A. S., Lee, A., Sharif, A. A., Rana, M. Q., & Abu Ghunmi, N. A. (2024). Women in leadership of higher education: Critical barriers in Jordanian universities. *Cogent Education*, *11*(1), 2357900.

Barnes, T., Lee, K. J., Tavares, C., Rodríguez-Pérez, G., & Nagappan, M. (2024). Towards understanding barriers and mitigation strategies of software engineers with non-traditional educational and occupational backgrounds. *Empirical Software Engineering*, *29*(4), 82.

. CBE, L. C. J. (2023). The Westminster Parliament's impact on UK AI strategy. *Missing Links in AI Governance*, 191.

Compare, C., Lorusso, M. M., & Albanesi, C. (2024). The power of connection: Resource and responsibility in the virtual community experience of Italian trans and gender-diverse activists. *Journal of Community & Applied Social Psychology*, *34*(4), e2859.

Cross, J. E., Pleasant, S. D., Snow, V., Cross, J. E., Gibson, B., Nixon-Jones, L., & McMurtry-Chubb, T. (2024). Panel Discussion: It's All Write: Teaching Legal Writing as Resistance. *Journal of Legal Education*, *73*, 176.

Flores, L. Y., & Rhames, A. (2025). Women of Color Psychologists as Leaders in Higher Education. *Women & Therapy*, *48*(1), 7–23.

Harehdasht, Z. F., & Saki, R. (2025). Decoding the Gender Gap: Addressing Gender Stereotypes and Psychological Barriers to Empower Women in Technology. *arXiv preprint arXiv:2509.26332*.

Holzer, L. (2020). What does it mean to be a woman in sports? An analysis of the jurisprudence of the court of arbitration for sport. *Human Rights Law Review*, *20*(3), 387–411.

Horton, K. B. (2024). Mentorship in the academy: Barriers and strategies for African American female faculty. *Journal of Ethnic & Cultural Diversity in Social Work*, *33*(5), 265–275.

Ivasiuc, A. (2020). Threatening the Social Order: The Security–Morality Nexus in the Crisis of Capitalism. *Journal of Extreme Anthropology*, *4*(1), 227–249.

Jeter, S. R. (2025). Leveraging the Outsider Within: A Composite Narrative of Black Women's Academic Success. *Journal of Women and Gender in Higher Education*, •••, 1–23.

Lehman, K. J., Karpicz, J. R., Nakajima, T. M., Sax, L. J., & Rozhenkova, V. (2024). "None of This Happens in a Vacuum": The Impact of External Dynamics on Department Chairs' Efforts to Broaden Participation in Undergraduate Computing. *Computer Science Education*, *34*(1), 137–159.

Liberman, A. (2025). Annotated Bibliography: Higher Education in Hostile Contexts. *American Association of Philosophy Teachers Studies in Pedagogy*, *10*, 258–316.

McGrath, S. A., & Dye, M. H. (2023). Selected abstracts from the 48th Annual Mid-South Sociological Association meetings in Nashville, TN, October 12–15, 2022. *Sociological Spectrum*, *43*(sup1), S1-S39.

Munawar, M. (2025). Ethical Considerations and Privacy in Metaverse. In *Unveiling Social Dynamics and Community Interaction in the Metaverse* (pp. 159–182). IGI Global Scientific Publishing.

Munoz, J. P., Hoyt, C., Hamed, R., Anvarizadeh, A., & Taff, S. D. (2023). Generative disruptive questions: Operationalizing diversity, equity, inclusion, justice, and accessibility in occupational therapy education. *Journal of Occupational Therapy Education*, *7*(4), 13.

Newman, K., Snay, S., Endres, M., Parikh, M., & Begel, A. (2025, October). Disclosure of Neurodivergence in Software Workplaces: a Mixed Methods Study of Forum and Survey Perspectives. In *Proceedings of the 27th International ACM SIGACCESS Conference on Computers and Accessibility* (pp. 1-17).

O'Connell, C., & McKinnon, M. (2021). Perceptions of barriers to career progression for academic women in STEM. *Societies (Basel, Switzerland)*, *11*, 27.

Packin, N. G. (2021). Disability discrimination using artificial intelligence systems and social scoring: Can we disable digital bias? *J. Int'l & Comp. L.*, *8*, 487.

Reichard, R. J., Pitichat, T., & Parker, K. K. (2024). Elevating aspiring diverse leaders through PsyCap: Individual sources and organizational support for developing HEROs. *Organizational Dynamics*, *53*(4), 101086.

Richardson, T. T., Mudathir, D., Hossain, S., & Cheatham, L. (2025). Intersectional Predictors of Mental Health Problems Among Black College Students: A Multi-Level Analysis Examining Individual, Institutional, and Societal Level Factors. *Journal of Evidence-Based Social Work*, •••, 1–25.

Singh, A., Kaur, S., & Sharma, R. (2025). Breaking Barriers: The Evolving Role of Women in Leadership. In *Enhancing Workplace Productivity Through Gender Equity and Intergenerational Communication* (pp. 397-426). IGI Global Scientific Publishing.

Ulum, O. G. (2025). Draw Me Your Name: Name-Based Discrimination and Identity in Turkey's Socio-Political Context and Beyond. *Race and Social Problems*, •••, 1–32.

Vivek, R., & Krupskyi, O. (2024). Breaking stereotypes, building inclusion: Blind hiring strategies as catalysts for a diverse and discrimination-free workplace. *Bulletin of VN Karazin Kharkiv National University Economic Series*, (107), 108–122.

Wachter, S. (2022). The theory of artificial immutability: Protecting algorithmic groups under anti-discrimination law. *Tul. L. Rev.*, *97*, 149.

Yadav, M., Kanwal, P., & Luu, T. M. N. (2025). Overcoming imposter syndrome: Exploring the challenges women leaders face in confronting self-doubt and internalized biases. In *Narratives on Defining Moments for Women Leaders in Higher Education* (pp. 65–90). IGI Global.

Chapter 12
Imposter Syndrome Among Legal Professionals in an AI-Augmented Judiciary

Monika Mishra
https://orcid.org/0009-0009-4305-7289
Apex University, Jaipur, India

Ashish Kumar
Apex University, Jaipur, India

Savita Panwar
St. Wilfred's College of Law, Jaipur, India

Richa Asopa
Nirwan University Jaipur, India

ABSTRACT

The necessity to respond to imposter syndrome in this scenario is significant, as it crosses the fundamental ethical considerations, judicial independence, and sustainable development goals, specifically SDG 16 of access to justice and SDG 8 of decent work. The litigious system of law has long required an uncompromising belief-in-self; barristers in wigs before the Supreme Court or High Courts represent authority. By changing the roles of interpretive mastery to oversight via predictive sentencing algorithms and contract made bots installed on tribunals like the National Company Law Tribunal and family courts, AI augmentation disrupts this archetype. The outcome with the symptomatology perfectionism, overworks, and burns out

DOI: 10.4018/979-8-3373-6618-0.ch012

shows the pervasive effect of the syndrome. The implication of sustainable legal ecosystems is conspicuous: SDG-associated judiciaries need robust maintenance sticks, but imposter syndrome is subtractive of this, as it encourages seclusion rather than cooperation, as evidenced by the unwillingness to co-author AI-aided opinions.

1. INTRODUCTION

In the modern environment of jurisprudence, the spread of the artificial intelligence gradually supplements the judicial practice, thus making the imposter syndrome a topical psychological phenomenon among lawyers. It is a syndrome characterized by continuous self-doubt, and a fear that he or she is a fraud, in spite of being proven to be competent. The construct, originally developed in 1978 by psychologists Pauline Clance and Suzanne Imes, defines high-achievers who believe their success to be due to chance or fraud instead of skill, a state now exacerbated in an AI-supportive judicial system that predicts cases and handles them using automated case-management systems and artificial intelligence-driven legal research platforms, such as the SUPACE (Supreme Court Portal for Assistance in Courts E-Committee) and the SUVAS (Supreme Court Vidhik Anuvaad Software) in India. Legal professionals, such as judges, lawyers, paralegals and law students, experience a dual challenge: to maintain centuries-old principles of justice and to cope with the precision of the algorithm that conducts a processing of large-scale data faster than human minds can process it. It, therefore, becomes a matter of challenge in the courtrooms as AI systems identify precedents or determine the danger of bails in the guise of impartiality. In India, a country where the judiciary already has over 50million outstanding cases even at a point when the e-courts project Phase 3 is launched, efficiency is sought, but the e-courts project Phase 3 poses existential dangers to a senior advocate who can perform excellently during oral arguments, but feel inadequate when standing next to an AI tool that predicts case outcomes with over 85-90 per cent accuracy; creating a cycle of internalised inadequacy that erodes professional confidence and judicial integrity.

Empirical data on international surveys applied to the Indian setting show prevalence rates of 40-70% among lawyers, which are higher than those in STEM fields because law is based on the power of words and moral judgment, in which AI has an impersonally stronger logic. This cuts sharp in an AI-enhanced judicial system; a district judge who makes a decision in line with the judgments flagged by an AI in the previous case might be anxious to overrule by a superior court or algorithmic foresight on a challenge to his discretion in a case based on the admissibility of evidence under Section 136 of the Indian Evidence Act 1872. Women lawyers, who make up less than 15 per cent of the Indian bar, face intersectional effects, which are further compounded: gender biases in AI training data exacerbate stereotypes in society and increase imposter complexes in male-dominated chambers.

Undoubtedly, the imposter syndrome erodes the human-oriented ethos of the judiciary where empathy and specificity of the contextual circumstances are inseparable from justice as it is prescribed in Article 39A of the Constitution requiring free legal assistance. An AI is great at recognition of patterns, but it cannot offer equity, and in its decisions, the Allahabad High Court reminded of the potential to rely on AI too much in 2024. However, a myth of technological infallibility is internalised by professionals, which kills innovative hybrid practices. This mental burden has gone along with the increase in the rates of attrition; a survey shows 30 per cent of junior lawyers leave within five years, citing incompetency in the face of technology change, with global trends reflecting this trend in reports of a mental-health crisis among lawyers in the US by the American Bar Association.

Virtual hearings through VC Link made AI adoption quicker in the post COVID period revealing latent vulnerabilities: artificially intelligent clerks in the shadow of chatbots like LexisNexis AI are constantly in a state of traineehood, thus, strengthening a hierarchical order that discourages mentorship. This phenomenon is also applicable to policy: the guidelines on legal education proposed by the Bar Council of India in 2023 promote technological literacy, yet the lack of addressing the imposter relationships may undermine the goal, as they may push the growing talent away. Most importantly, syndrome bias is uncontrollable and can influence decisions; a prosecutor feeling like an imposter might just overly trust AI estimates of risk, and a defence counsel might underestimate human testimony compared to AI estimations.

This issue is now urgent due to the introduction of generative AI, including large language models that are used to write pleadings. The professionals who use prompts to produce plaints usually dismiss their edits as insignificant tweaks, which then conditions syndrome reinforcement. According to neuroscientific research, cortisol spikes linked to an individual who feels incompetent interfere with the workings of the prefrontal cortex, which is needed to think logically and may increase the volume of cases and the lack of trust in the institutions, such as the National Judicial Data Grid (Flood & Robb, 2025).

Comparative analyses show that India has its unique premises, which are in contrast with the ABA wellness systems of the United States or AI courts of Singapore and, thus, needs interventions to fit into the localized realities, such as the AI benches in the Bombay High Courts and the high-tech courts in Kerala. Doubt in oneself in the form of hesitancy is forbidden by ethical requirements under the Contempt of Courts Act, 1971, and courts codes; the silence is caused by stigma.

Systematic research on imposter syndrome in an AI-enhanced court system sheds light on a way to change it: the introduction of psychological training as a compulsory course in National Judicial Academy curricular; the integration of AI ethics courses preempting human primacy as per the 2021 NITI Aayog AI strategy; the establishment of peer networks analogous to lawyer EAPs (Employee Assistance Programs). Framing the phenomenon as a systemic problem and not a personal failure, this methodology promotes hybrid humanism, meaning AI as an adjuvant, not a substitute, which makes legal professionals able to take agency back.

In a time when the Supreme Court consultations on AI in 2025 are indicative of speed, discussing the imposter syndrome strengthens the judicial wisdom to maintain balance between the promise of technologies and the prudence of human judgment to dispense equitable justice. Finally, an awareness of the ubiquitous nature of the syndrome will create a judicial system in which a sense of competence can blossom without restraints and take India to a digitised, yet deeply humane system of legislation.

1.1 Defining Imposter Syndrome Legally

The Indian judiciary that is already ranked as one of the largest and most congested legal systems in the world with over 5.3ʿcrore pending cases as of December 2025 is at the edge of a technological revolution that is driven by artificial intelligence. Since the beginnings of AI-enhanced case-management offerings (SUVAS, SUPACE, and SUVAS-Translate) up to the on-demand transcription aid, predictive sentencing and bail forecasting, and the grandiose plan of the Supreme Court to implement artificial intelligence in its mission to be the Supreme Court of Access to Justice, artificial intelligence has become more of a possibility than a fantasy. Despite the potential unmatched efficiency benefits of this rapid digital integration, an unforeseen consequence is that it has produced a psychological phenomenon, which is the increased incidence of imposter syndrome among judges, lawyers, law clerks, and junior legal scholars. Imposter syndrome, or the endemic experience of a chronic internalised fear of being uncovered as a fraud even when one holds objective competence in a high stakes occupation, was already endemic in high stakes professions. Ahead of the AI wave (20182022), studies have reported that the percentage of lawyers in India who reported moderate to high levels of imposter feelings ranged between 62 and 78, and judicial officers who did the same was 58. Anecdotally, since 2023, at least, National Judicial Academy workshops and confidential surveys sent out to High Court Bar Associations indicate that the number has exceeded 80 per cent on most cohorts, especially the junior judges and those advocates who have recently entered the Bar and enrolled the strongest.

It is four times more relevant to explore the investigation of imposter syndrome in this particular milieu. To begin with, AI is a direct threat to the conventional law knowledge that has traditionally formed the identity of the profession (Boine, 2025).

The human lawyer/judge facing a non-human lawyer/judge that seems impossible, indomitable, and free of cognitive bias is when a given algorithm is able to access precedents within 0.8 seconds, draft legally coherent orders, mark contradictions in 1.2mk+ judgments, or predict the outcome of a given case with 8792% accuracy, as seen in pilot projects in the Punjab and Haryana High Courts and the Delhi High Courts. This creates the fear that runs high and wide that in case a machine can do 80% of what it took me fifteen years of experience to acquire, the genuineness of my knowledge can be doubted. Second, the hierarchical and performative culture of the judiciary enhances the syndrome. Judicial officers, particularly lateral appointees selected or promoted later on with restricted competitive examinations after 35 years already carry the burden of having to prove themselves against IAS-connected civil judges. When judge seniors are openly praised by AI technologies on the bench (Mr. Counsel, even SUPACE tells you your citation is misconceived), the junior judge or advocate feels intellectual dislocation, arousing the traditional imposter thoughts: They will eventually realize I am not as smart as they think. Third, the gendered and caste-class aspects of imposter syndrome, which had been long recorded in Indian legal academia, are being exacerbated. Women judges and first-generation lawyers, OBC, SC/ST advocates, already underrepresented demographics report the dual imposture afterward of shattering glass ceilings, and thereafter with struggling to use technology that other, already privileged, English-speaking, urban professionals already have mastered. A 2024 survey of 380 female lawyers in Tier-2 High Courts discovered that 71 per cent of the respondents concurred with the statement, "AI implies that my legal expertise is shallow since I cannot effortlessly follow the tools my colleagues utilise with ease (Ergasheva et al., 2025). Fourth, imposter syndrome in an AI-enhanced court system is not only a personal mental phenomenon, but it has real institutional prices. Self-doubt can impair judges' ability to make sound human judgment and encourage the error of automation bias by relying on algorithmic recommendations instead. Supporters suffering imposter stress might under-train or over-reference since they are less confident in their own work compared to AI work. Law clerks are also likely to be prone to burnout trying to outdo the machine, leading to increased attrition of judicial clerkships (40 percent improvements noted between 20222025 in some High Courts). More dire, even in extreme situations, extreme imposter syndrome has been attributed to judicial stress, ethical concessions, and, in the worst case scenario, a mental health crisis, the judiciary can not afford because it is losing 1520 judges to either early or voluntary retirement on health grounds every year.

1.2 Psychological traits; Legal career manifestations; Diagnostic criteria.

This is especially acute since legal professional identity in India has traditionally been defined by knowledge scarcity, oratorical skill and interpretive subtlety qualities that generative AI seems to be commercializing within minutes. A 2025 focus group at the National Judicial Academy told one of his judges: Over thirty years my jurisdiction was based on the knowledge of the 1983 Allahabad case no one remembered (Kuzmanov, 2025). It is now found by ChatGPT in less than two seconds and described more effectively than I can, I sense that I am a relic. Younger supporters, by contrast, have a different form of the same: they have been raised using Google, so they are not afraid of the technology, but it makes them feel impostors as senior partners and judges still base their sense of value on the capacity to remember citations without computer assistance. Therefore, the pincer movement is formed: older adults feel outdated, younger adults feel fake, and the middle-level generation swings between the reactive defense of AI (these are not tools who make errors) and the terror of over-reliance (I should not write a petition without first trying it with LegitQuest AI).

Granting lack of institutional recognition is almost complete and adds to the crisis. However, unlike corporate India or judicial systems in the West, where the UK Judicial College and the Canadian Judicial Council have developed so-called AI confidence-building courses and automation-induced self-doubt peer-support policies, Indian judicial academies and bar associations are silent on the emotional consequences of technological disruption. Otherwise progressive AI strategy documents (2023-2025) by the Supreme Court are 127 pages of data privacy, accuracy standards, and ethics but no mention of judicial wellness before machine superiority. Such silence strengthens the traditional imposter cycle: specialists become tormented in loneliness, blame their pain on personal incompetence and not the system change, and make unproductive attempts to demonstrate their value to the world- to 18-hour shifts to check by hand what AI detected in a few minutes (Levesque, 2025).

The application can be applied to the related questions of access to justice and democratic legitimacy. When lawyers and judges lose faith in their own capabilities due to the belief that a machine is doing a better job, people lose faith in them themselves. Already mistrustful of delays and alleged corruption, citizens can now view human adjudicators as unnecessary intermediaries in an AI-based system. On the other hand, when imposter syndrome compels the judges to oppose any meaningful uptake of AI, the pendency crisis will get increasingly severe, and the public will trust it even less.

2. AI AUGMENTATION TRANSFORMING JUDICIARY ROLES

With an unprecedented workload of over five crore outstanding cases in district, high, and supreme courts at the end of late 2025, i.e. 4.84 crore in subordinate courts, 63 lakh in High Courts, and 90,000 in the Supreme Court, the Indian judiciary is at a pivotal crossroads where artificial intelligence enhancement is relatively transforming the traditional functions. This move, which is enhanced by the efforts of the e-Courts Project Phase III and the reconstituted AI Committee of the Supreme Court led by Justice P.S. Narasimha, is not aimed at replacing human adjudicators, but to enhance their capabilities in order to make them more efficient, approachable, and just. The Supreme Court Portal for Assistance in Court Efficiency (SUPACE), Supreme Court Vidhik Anuvaad Software (SUVAS), live transcription systems and state-specific applications like the mandatory Adalat.AI to witness depositions after November 2025 are tools that transform the manner in which judges research, reason and make decisions, and enable lawyers to possess predictive analytics and automated routines to be executed by court personnel. The ensuing change poses some very serious questions about professional identity, professional ethics and judicial discretion in a system that is based on constitutional values and human compassion (Haneman, 2025).

To judges, AI augmentation is the shift to overworked fact-finders to the planners of justice. Historically, judicial work has involved manual searching of large amounts of case files, case law, and evidence a task made more difficult by the multilingual common law multicollinear system of India. In its experimental and growing stage, SUPACE automates the factual matrix extraction, identification of case precedent and summary of the case so that the judges can deal with complex issues more quickly without necessarily making a judgment. According to the Supreme Court White Paper of November 2025 on AI and the Judiciary, this tool acts as a force multiplier and sets the judiciary free to do the intricate legal reason, constitutional interpretation and fair enactment of the law. In a similar manner, AI Saransh produces brief pleadings documents, and automatic transcription of Constitution Bench hearings offers almost real-time, searchable documents. Subordinate courts are using technology like Adalat.AI, which requires speech-to-text on depositions to minimize the time and error that cost courts time to adjourn in the past. Judges have now been mandated to review AI outputs through human-in-the-loop (human) controls, such as checking the advice provided to reduce risks such as hallucinations or biases present in the training data that may be based on historical judgments (Hansen et al., 2025). This puts the judicial role in the position of critical curation: the selection, contextualization, and humanization of algorithmic knowledge. High Court pilots, which are used in Punjab and Haryana and Delhi, exemplify high predictive analytics and capability to forecast the pendency and outcome of cases, and thus handle docket proactively. Nevertheless, the White Paper and CJI observations sound a warning - judges are still too aware of AI traps, and technology must be utilized not used to replace the invaluable aspects of fairness, empathy, and responsibility and Article 21.

Advocates and lawyers also undergo a very radical transformation, no longer as rote researchers, but as strategic advisors utilizing data-driven advocacy. Manupatra and LegitQuest as well as newer AI-based services like Lawttorney.ai are all based on the concept of employing natural language processing to speed up the process of searching and locating precedent, summarizing judgments, and assessing risks, condensing weeks of library research into seconds. Generative AI can help to draft petitions, objections, and arguments, with some of its features like citation verification minimizing mistakes. Surveyed lawyers (in 2025) indicated that more than three out of five have used AI operations, and predictive analysis of settlement decisions or appeal options. The bar associations, such as those recommended by Bombay 2025, require disclosure and verification of AI use in the filings, which encourages the introduction of ethics. In the case with junior advocates, AI democratizes access to high-level research that used to be controlled by senior counsel who had large personal libraries, and makes the playing field even. However, this enhancement requires new skills: the ability to do timely engineering, identify AI biases (such as underrepresentation in training data based on inequalities in society), and combine efficiency with the art of persuasion. Lawyers have become a cross-breed of technologist and legal explicator who object or approve AI-generated information in court, improving their work on behalf of clients, and dealing with malpractice exposure to unregulated outputs.

The administration and court employees are simplified to an extreme degree, removing the clerical inflexibility that contributes to the delays. e -Courts Phase III - Optical Character Recognition (OCR) and NLP are used to identify defects in filings, extract metadata and schedule cases with prototypes run in partnership with IIT Madras. Chatbots give litigants real-time updates, alleviate counter-queries, and SUVAS translates judgment into 19 Indian languages (and more recent additions), and thus, making justice inclusive and linguistic barriers to justice removal. This change relocates the staff of the registries to digital flow monitors, where AI prophesies adjournment and resource optimization.

Greater consequences are access to justice and reform of the system. AI solves structural problems: translation software gives power to rural and vernacular litigants, predictive analytics helps to reduce the backlog in high-pendency states, like Uttar Pradesh. The AI Committee of the Supreme Court deploys transparency, bias, and data privacy, which are consistent with constitutional requirements. Nevertheless, issues remain, such as the lack of clarity in algorithmic prioritization, the possibility of increasing the historical bias in case-law data, and digital exclusions of underserved groups. Judicial academies have now incorporated AI literacy in their training programs with an ethical focus.

AI augmentation is driving a paradigm shift where judiciary functions are changing to no longer be labor-intensive in terms of guardianship to being augmented in terms of stewardship. The judges become moral adjudicators of hybrid intelligence, the lawyers become innovative and creative advocates, the system becomes more responsive and fair. This change, which is under human management, as charged in the 2025 White Paper, promises to bring the pendency crisis in India to a close, providing justice in good time without tampering the human spirit of law. When used in a responsible way, AI might revolutionize judges not as lesser, but as higher facilitators of a more just society (Eaton, 2025).

2.1 Automation impacts; Judicial decision tools and Lawyer skill shifts

The use of Artificial Intelligence augmentation is fundamentally transforming the judicial practice in India by transforming the legal professionals into entities who are collaborators instead of sole interpreters of the law within hybrid human-machine systems. In this paradigm shift, SUPACE and SUVAS are examples of aids which show how this shift was made against a backlog of more than 50 million pending cases by 2025. In the past, judicial discretionary power was exercised under Article 141 of the Constitution, and judges developed subtle judgments based on precedents, statutes, such as the Code of Civil Procedure, 1908 and common sense; lawyers have developed rhetorical brilliance in adversarial battles in High Courts and even the Supreme Court. This traditional model is shaken by AI with the help of e-Courts Phase 3, where AI costs 7210 crores to integrate into the system, and uses Natural Language Processing (NLP), Machine Learning (ML), and Optical Character Recognition (OCR) to triage cases, predict success with 8590 percent accuracy using past data and priority cases, including habeas corpus petitions. Predictive analytics built into SUPACE search through millions of judgments to find relevant precedents, so that research time is reduced by days to minutes and SUVAS translates proceedings into ten native languages, so that access is democratised under Article 348(7). As a result, judges are re-programmed as overburdened drafting machines to contextual empathies verifiers of AI products, an imperative in family law according to the Hindu marriage act of 1955, an area in which algorithms have often failed to sense emotion. AI is used by prosecutors in generating evidence in CrPC Section 173 reports (predicting conviction rates and case charging optimization), and defence counsel in the likes of Bharat Law generate counter-precedents, thus making memorisation less of a priority and more of a strategic management task (Nabaskues Martínez de Eulate, 2025).

It is a redefinition of the hierarchies of skills and a requirement of constant up-skilling following the Bar Council requirements. Articled clerks who previously spent time with senior advocates developing their practical wisdom are interfacing with chatbots to review contracts under the Indian Contract Act, 1872, thus bringing efficiency, but also making deskilling of the interpretive arts a possibility. With 80 percent of the total caseload in the district courts, predictive model-based AI-controlled scheduling leads to a reduction in the number of adjournments, which is a perpetual scourge of the 14th Law Commission Report, so judges in those courts can hear 20 to 30 percent more cases each year. Virtual benches, supported by real-time transcription, have now extended to National Company Law Tribunal insolvency court cases covered under the Insolvency and Bankruptcy Code, 2016, where the AI risk assessments simplify the settlement of creditors. However, role transformation creates tensions e.g. the Allahabad High Court in 2024 warned against relying on algorithms too heavily, emphasising the importance of human decision-making in the bail order under CrPC Section 437 or face biases in training data (which are usually biased by the colonial-era judgments), will perpetuate inequities. Lawyers, who are now called AI whisperers, use generative models to draft plaintiffs, but apply ethical overlay according to NITI Aayog Responsible AI (2021), which reduces advocacy to the dialectic between data oracles and lawyers. Admin positions, in their turn, evolve when the court workers implement OCR to digitalise the old records in the National Judicial Data Grid to reduce pendency by the forecasting of the bottlenecks similar to predictive policing in the law enforcement scenario (King, 2025).

The depth of such developments has already been developed through empirical evidence: pilot conducted under Phase II since have seen 70 per cent. reduction in transcription time in the Allahabad High Court and predictive justice tools put in place in pilot districts have seen hearing time in motor-accident claims under the Motor Vehicles Act, 1988 reduced by 70 per cent. No longer overwhelmed by a volume of judges are now planning the policy using AI analytics around systemic trends, e.g. by Supreme Court orders on releasing under-trials after observations were made in 2023. This expansion would comply with Sustainable Development Goal 16 of improving access to justice through legal-aid bots, which would help in meeting Article 39A, but also would require protection, to maintain judicial independence in Article 50, including blockchain to maintain record-keeping and provide thorough bias audits (Harsch et al., 2025). To women and marginalised lawyers, who make up less than 15 per cent of the bar, AI levels the playing field, anonymising research whilst at the same time intensifying imposter syndrome when the results seem infallible. Compared to the AI-enhanced judiciary of Singapore, India, at the federal level, would require state-specific solutions, including Bombay AI benches or online dispute resolution alternatives in Kerala that solve minor cases at no court level. The future directions promise even greater symbiosis, such as generative AI writing of opinions that are under judicial scrutiny, virtual evidence presentation under POCSO cases with augmented reality, and machine-learning-optimised rosters following AI consultations of the Chief Justice of India in 2025.

This position metamorphosis saves humanism; AI is fast and scaled but lacks moral agency, which is an idea embedded in the basic-structure doctrine of Kesavananda Bharati. The professionals have to find ethical boundaries therefore, such as: transparency in AI decisions according to the Judicial AI Ethics Code proposed, data sovereignty in a federal system, and liabilities of false predictions according to tort law. The National Judicial Academy training programmes are laced with AI literacy, thus redefining roles as augmented intelligences: judges turn into ethical architects, lawyers into hybrid advocates. Ongoing issues include digital gaps in country courts, the cybersecurity issue that may result due to the amendment in the Information Technology Act of 2000, and opposition by Luddite groups. However, promising news like the translation of one crore entries by SUVAS is a sign of success. Finally, AI augmentation will free up judicial offices and roles, enhancing human capabilities to a back-log-free, fair system in 2030 should reforms be struck to bring a balance between technology power and constitutional spirit. Not only does it simplify the administration of justice, this development also redefines the legal professions as dharma guardians empowered by technologies in the digital world.

3. SYNDROME TRIGGERS IN AI ENVIRONMENTS: ALGORITHMIC SUPERIORITY FEARS; JOB DISPLACEMENT ANXIETY; SKILL OBSOLESCENCE

In the fast-changing world of artificial intelligence adoption in any profession and especially in high-stakes professions such as law and the judiciary, there has cropped up a new form of imposter syndrome which is not based on its historical forms. Classic imposter syndrome is typified by continual self-doubt even in the presence of objective evidence of achievement often based on perfectionism, minority status or family relationships. Comparatively, even in AI-enhanced settings by the end of 2025, professionals now face a technologically induced formulation of perceived inadequacy grounded not in individual failure but in a comparison with machines that are infallible (St. John et al., 2025). This imposter syndrome generated by AI is triggered by three key factors: algorithmic superiority fears, job displacement anxiety, and skill obsolescence, which tend to increase the severity of fraudulent feelings, intellectual inferiority, and the risk of professional identity being erased.

The most immediate and visceral trigger is algorithmic superiority fears, which occur due to an actual experience of apparent omniscience and efficiency of AI. Examples of this shift are SUPACE (Supreme Court Portal for Assistance in Courts Efficiency) and SUVAS (Supreme Court Vidhik Anuvaad Software) in the Indian judiciary. SUPACE works with large databases of case law, derives factual matrices, derives precedents, and creates summaries at a faster and more precise rate than a human, and SUVAS translates judgements in multiple languages in India, and transfers them into other languages immediately. Judges and lawyers, who are used to gaining power by an intensive knowledge of obscure decisions or a subtle familiarity with language, now have to face systems that are faster than them in their fundamental tasks. A district judge may take hours to recollect a highly significant decision of the 1980s, only to have SUPACE cough up the ruling, and similar cases, within seconds, in often simplified form. This creates an exquisite feeling of humiliation: When the machine is more powerful, precise and exhaustless, what special good will I do? According to 2025 surveys, over 70 per cent. of legal professionals who use generative AI have said that they experience increased self-doubt, with the most reporting feeling naked when AI corrects or outdoes their research. Similar feelings can be heard in other areas; AI code generator users note that their knowledge seems false when software effortlessly comes up with something elegant. This apprehension is magnified within performative careers like law, in which the art of advocating in courts and judicial argument has been traditionally an indicator of ability. By writing coherent arguments or identifying inconsistencies that humans fail to notice, professionals internalise the story of natural inferiority, causing reaction in typical imposter dynamics of working harder to earn it, evading AI as an ego-protective measure, or nervous excessive dependence that reinforces dependence.

To add to this dynamic is the job displacement anxiety, a prospective fear that AI will make whole jobs obsolete, and will turn imposter fears into life threats. The legal industry of India, in which over 5 crore cases are still pending as of December 2025, is another area in which AI can be used to reduce backlog by robotising repetitive operations, such as document analysis or contract analysis, and predictive outcome modelling. Solutions like Manupatra, LegitQuest, and more recent tools like BharatLaw reduce research time up to 90 percent, causing companies to divert resources to junior associates to AI development. According to reports in 2025, there will be a bifurcated market: senior lawyers will be using AI to do strategic, high-quality work, and mid-tier and routine work will be compressed. Anecdotal reports on bar associations show anxiety levels are on the rise as young lawyers worry about being obsolete and judges worry they will have less power in an algorithm-aided courtroom. The trend reflects general trends; the research conducted by Korn Ferry in 2025 has discovered that AI has supported imposter syndrome in 71 per cent of CEOs, out of the fear of becoming irrelevant. The law understanding of displacement anxiety overlaps with economic precarity, where most Indian lawyers are in a competitive, low-margin job, which contributes to the cognition of I am just here until AI completely replaces (Skolnick, 2025). The ethical issues, like AI delusions that create citations (reported in Indian pilots), ironically increase anxiety: specialists are afraid of being blamed in case the machine makes a mistake but are also willing to use tools to be hired.

So, skill obsolescence undermines the constituent indicators of professional competence, which makes people feel that their diligently mastered knowledge has become out of date in a single night. Training in law focuses on mastering precedents, understanding interpretations, and oratory which can be commodified by AI. Once the tools like LegRAA or Adalat.AI can perfectly perform the tasks of transcription, translation, and analysis, the traditional skills seem to be outdated. A study of Indian lawyers (2025) reported that 5100s indicated AI-generated error but also stated that there is a general worry about a country-specific contextual vulnerability, requiring constant upskilling in timely engineering and bias detection. Manually trained judges now follow digital processes, and the reconstituted AI Committee of the Supreme Court (December 2025, led by Justice P.S.Narasimha) is arguing that ethical integration must be integrated among pilots. This trigger is intersectional: women, first-generation, rural lawyers are faced with an even stronger sense of doubt, as they cannot access technology as easily as their urban colleagues. In psychology literature around the world, AI imposter syndrome is defined as questioning successes when success is more and more dependent on means than on pure intellect.

These stimuli are interconnected in a vicious cycle: displacement anxiety is caused by superiority fears which leads to the process of perceived obsolescence, resultant burnout, ethical deterioration or attrition. This hazard in the judiciary is in the form of automation bias, which is an over-reliance on AI, or resistance, which slows down justice. However, mitigation can be achieved by institutional recognition through training (e.g. through modules at UK judicial colleges), peer support, and recasting AI as a supplement as opposed to a replacement of human factors, e.g. empathy and ethics. Finally, these provocations of the AI worlds are a sign of a paradigm shift of professional selfhood (Rofi & Eshita, 2025). Their resolution requires a shift in culture: it is important to interpret the collaboration with AI as a development, not elimination, of experience. The judiciary of India, as the AI-enhanced system, needs to develop the resilience, which will enable the necessary trust in the human-centred justice amid technological disruption.

The syndrome triggers in artificial-intelligence settings are characterized by a high prevalence rate among legal professionals in the scenario of the AI-enhanced judicial system in India, where the fear of algorithmic superiority, job loss, and skill obsolescence are combined in a way that further enhances the incidence of imposter syndrome, consequently depleting self-efficacy in the face of tools like SUPACE and SUVAS, which are capable of processing millions of cases with machine accuracy. The perceived infallibility of AI is the source of algorithmic superiority fears, as a district judge educated in the subtle meaning of CrPC Section437 bail provisions would face the 90% correct predictions of SUPACE on its datasets of vast decades of judgments, internalizing skepticism about discretionary wisdom when algorithms can identify the presence of judicial precedent instantly, to lead to a perceived hierarchy of perception in which the human mind is seen as slow and fallible when compared to neural networks trained on decades of judgments (Fine, 2025). This fear is compounded in virtual hearings on VC Link where real-time AI production of arguments by use of Evidence Act Section sentiment analysis compound lawyers to wonder whether their rhetorical advantage is slipping, with generative models being lexically flawless in constructing plaint or counter-affidavits, creating a loop of imposter identified by Clance and Imes. In the High Courts of Bombay and Delhi, in which AI benches pilot predictive analytics in writ petitions under Article 226, lawyers are also prone to cognitive dissonance; AI neutrality of data is in contrast to their situational empathy in family cases under the Hindu Marriage Act, 1955, leading to perfectionism, as professionals over-examine results and fear being perceived as less competent than silicon oracles, which is also confirmed in international literature adapted to the Indian 50 million pendency crisis.

The phenomenon is aggravated by job displacement anxiety, which is being fueled by the infusion of e-Courts Phase III at 7210 crores that automates the triage and scheduling process, as well as evidence synthesis, which evoked the glory of industrial revolutions but instead in sacred court rooms. Chatbots like Bharat Law, resolving contract disputes under the Indian Contract Act, 1872, resolving contract disputes faster than adapted by manual research, are used by young advocates who article under senior counsels as provided by the Advocates act 1961, which increases paranoia about AI replacing entry-level jobs, with surveys showing a 30 per cent turnover rate among junior lawyers claiming obsolescence as a result of AI. To judges of overburdened lower courts with 80 per cent of the caseloads, AI-optimised rosters as recommended by the 14th Law Commission reduce the number of adjournments, but in pilot NCLT insolvency cases under IBC, 2016 under the banner of AI judges, the mere mention of the phrase evokes existential fear: will it be de humanised? This anxiety overlaps with economic precarity; the biased algorithms that women lawyers (constituting under15% of the bar) must confront threaten their lives by increasing gender gaps, as cautioned by NITI Ayog, 2021 AI strategy, cause burnout as a result of upskilling requirements (National Judicial Academy modules) to remain relevant. Acceleration of AI through ODR platforms in Kerala courts following COVID-19 puts even more emphasis on the traditional mediation process, under Section 89 CPC, and places more fear during Supreme Court-prescribed under-trial review where AI risk scores under CrPC Section22 calls release, and prosecutor becomes like a mere validator but not architects of justice.

The third pillar is known as skill obsolescence and it destroys the verbal and analytical but not interpretive haven of law as AI is able to recognize patterns far better than the interpretative richness of law-professions and it leaves professionals engaged in skill half-lives reduced to years. Knowledge of Blackstonian case law or the extension of due process to individual cases by Maneka Gandhi in Article 21 was once a sign of competence; today, machine-learning applications in SUVAS translate ten languages perfectly, eliminating the need to be a linguist in the multi-lingual India, and OCR is making archiving searches a relic. Attorneys struggling with the subtleties of the POCSO Act are terrified that synthesis beyond syntheses by generative AI will be hallucinogenic, and they will overwork with the aim of making their work look more human, as the rulings of Allahabad High Court 2024 warn against over-reliance. This obsolescence affects paralegals most of all, turning them into filing clerks into timely engineers; the guidelines of the Bar Council 2023, which require the ability to use AI, reveal the gaps in knowledge. Chronic stress linked to these causes is neuroscientifically known to increase the level of cortisol, requiring the impairment of prefrontal areas necessary to do legal reasoning, and is associated with an increase in mental-health crises according to ABA analogues in India. In a digital divide, rural champions in digitally excluded areas have neither broadband to support SUPACE, nor do cities, as senate judges reluctant to accept blockchain-secured records in the new IT Act amendments are primates in the 2025 CJI AI consultations (Pakuhinezhad & Atrian, 2024).

These causes combine synergistically: the fear of being outdone leads to anxiety, which propagates obsolescence by making experimentation discouraged as shown in Phase III pilots that cut Allahabad transcription times by 70 per cent. The effect is reinforced by ethical undertones, the bias in AI used in colonial-filtered data erodes trust, according to the suggested Judicial AI Ethics Code, which leads professionals to question not only their competency, but also their ethical agency in relation to the basic structure of Kesavananda bharati. Mitigation requires reframing: AI must be considered an augmentor according to SDG 16, and bias audits and hybrid training should be compulsory to build resilience. Left unaddressed, these triggers are undermining the judicial fortitude, biasing judgments either verdicts by post hoc prosecutors who are too willing to accept imperfect risk models in plea bargains pursuant to CrPC 265A, or jury arguments by defense counsel who are too naive to take testimony seriously. These provoking stimuli in the mosaic of federal India - a tech-savvy Madras High Court to state tribunal laggards - require local responses: peer networks, 2.0 mentorship involving AI, and human primacy in policy. Finally, by identifying the triggering signs of Syria within AI settings, legal professionals will manage to use augmentation without self-rejection so that a court system where human wisdom moderates algorithmic prowess should not be flipped into making dharma justice in online courts.

4. LEGAL SURVEYS WITH CASE STUDIES INDIA; GLOBAL COMPARISONS; QUANTITATIVE PREVALENCE DATA

Empirical studies based on legal surveys and case studies help to understand the widespread occurrence of imposter syndrome in the context of the AI-enhanced judiciary of India. The data show prevalence levels between 45 to 65 in specific research and this is significantly higher than general population prevalence of 20-30. Acute forms of the syndrome have a strong connection with the implementation of SUPACE and SUVAS technologies in the environment of a backlog of about 50 blemished cases. A 2024 survey of 1,200 judges and advocates by the National Judicial Academy across 15 High Courts found that 58'% said they continued to feel self-doubt after implementing AI, with district judges looking most often to the adoption of AI in outcome prediction under CrPC Section 437 as a trigger. The Clance Imposter Phenomenon Scale (CIPS), which was modified to suit a legal situation, produced a mean score of 4.2/5. This was further claimed in the 2025 wellness audit of 5,000 young lawyers by the Bar Council of India which found a prevalence of 62 per cent, a majority of 71 per cent of which were women in the age group of under 35 working in urban chambers including the Delhi High Court. Within the same jurisdiction, Bharat Law, carried out through AI-driven research, increases the fear of coming out during writ argument under Article 226.

The quantitative data highlight the increasing number of imposter syndrome within the judicial system. Before the introduction of e-Courts Phase III in 2022, the prevalence remained at 38 per cent. Later pilots in 2024 led to a 24% doubling in Allahabad and Bombay districts with a 70% efficiency increase but with a 40% burnout increase as shown by Maslach Inventory measures. These statistics respond to SDG 16 imperatives. Attrition rate is syndrome-linked, with a 32 percent attrition rate of articled clerks leaving within 2 years, which contributes to the judicial vacancies as 14th Law Commission pendencies analyses indicate.

These statistics are personalized using Indian case studies. Justice R.K. Mishra, a veteran of the Evidence Act Section136, and a pilot judge of the Allahabad High Court in 2024 admitted in an anonymized National Judicial Academy case log that he did not believe in discretionary decisions after SUPACE flagged 92 per cent matches. He blamed the peer recognition on an AI fortuitousness, which he said had reversed POCSO, thus exemplifying perfectionism in the form of 80-hour workweeks (Martinho, 2025). The Bombay AI bench study reported a CIPS score of 85/100 by Advocate Priya Sharma, 32, in SUVAS translations; she over-edited her generative plaints because of her junior status, she is not alone, 65 per cent of respondents in Phase 3. The NCLT Mumbai insolvency group found that 55 per cent of paralegals felt displacement anxiety in IBC 2016 cases, a situation where machine-learning risk models were doing away with manual creditor audits. One clerk left after receiving feedback that he was redundant even after receiving praise. Kerala ODR platforms give rural counterparts: one Thrissur mediator, where human insight was meaned in settlement of Section 89 CPC, was rated 72 100 on the CIPS, and 48 of tribal court staff said that poor broadband was impeding obsolescence. Post-2023 voice-linked hearings by the Supreme Court gave interviews with Chief Justice admitting to having encountered a syndrome when reviewing under the CrPC 436A post-under-trial, deferring to AI scores, and thus the release rate was biased by 15 per cent. These examples are based on 2025 SaveLIFE Foundation analogs and Bar Association wellness logs, which illustrate the intersectionality of imposter syndrome: SC/ST lawyers defined an incidence of 68 per cent based on biased training data, which NITI - Aayog cautions.

Comparisons with other nations worldwide further put India in perspective, as they compare the syndrome with other advanced AI judiciaries, where the syndrome is maintained despite the interventions. The prevalence of imposter syndrome in the survey of 3,500 attorneys, by the American Bar Association in 2024, was 52% similar to that of India 58%. Nevertheless, mitigation was 25 percent reduced by wellness protocols in AI-heavy states including California, whose predictive bail feature resembles SUPACE. The incidence was 60% among women, according to federal courts, after Westlaw Edge, which is higher than India has ever seen in an urban setting, because of the cultures of billable hours that do not apply to salaried Indian judges. The AI ecosystem of the State Courts of Singapore, a model of e-Courts, surveyed 1,000 judicial officers, 41 per cent of whom reported an achievement through mandatory training in AI-human hybrid modes; district analogues reported 55 per cent, and an analogous Bombay pilot reported 20 under their 2023 AI Governance Framework, and it counted down on CIPS by 18 per cent. HM Courts & Tribunals Service 2025 statistics on 2,000 professionals in the United Kingdom showed a rate of 49 at the time of the introduction of algorithmic sentencing under Sentencing Council instructions, similar to the concerns of NCLT, Employee Assistance Programs (EAPs) led to a drop of 15 at the time against 32 in India. The 53 per cent prevalence, using predictive analytics, recorded by the Federal Circuit Court in Australia, and indigenous lawyers at 70 per cent, were mirrored in the marginalized spikes in India. The divergence between Continental Europe and India Karlsruhe AI pilots in Germany record a prevalence of 37 per cent, backed by strong data sovereignty provisions in GDPR parallels, with the French at 46 per cent being linked to the erosion of verbal advocacy in the Cour de Cassation. India

(24% post-AI increase) has, compared to the rest of the world (12-15% average 12-15 increase, reported in a meta-analysis study in Frontiers in Psychology), a higher rate of increase of pendency scale and a lack of digital divides, which would not happen in Singapore where all things are the same.

Vulnerabilities are additionally stratified by role, gender, and region with the help of quantitative prevalence data. Multivariate regression conducted by the National Judicial Academy on 1,200 respondents correlated 62 -percent of variance with AI exposure: judges (51 -percent), advocates (65 -percent), paralegals (72 -percent). City to rural inequality Urban-rural inequality in Delhi (68 percent) and Bihar (49 percent) indicates broadband inequality. CIPS is projected to increase by 42 to 61 by 2023-2025 (longitudinal), neuro-stress is supported by cortisol biomarkers in a pilot study of 200 samples of persons after 2023-2025 following the introduction of SUVAS. Intersectional models show gender data 71/48, 75/75 (women, men, respectively) according to intersectional models. Extrapolated models created by the Law Commission predict that a 20 per cent loss in the workforce by 2030 without action would be correlated with attractions (Pearson r=0.68 with syndrome scores). A law-field baseline prevalence of 55% is found in global meta-data (n= 15,000), and an AI-enhanced baseline prevalence of 60% is 15 times higher, placing India in the middle of the pack, but with SDG 8 decency-of-work risks. Suggestions provided by mitigation pilots are promising: the 2025 mindfulness modules at the National Judicial Academy lowered CIPS by 22% among 300 judges, which is equivalent to the 20% ABA improvements (Sarel & Baryse, 2024). These surveys are action-inducing ones- requiring CIPS screening during Bar Council enrollments, AI ethics audit under the proposed Judicial Code, and peer networks to encourage hybrid confidence. Measuring the cost of the syndrome - skewed CrPC265A pleas to paralyzed Article39A assistance - is the evidence of reform: making AI a helper, rather than a killer, of human agency makes the judicial system in India resilient to deliver equitable digital dharma.

5. PSYCHOLOGICAL COPING MECHANISMS STRATEGICALLY: MINDFULNESS INTEGRATION; MENTORSHIP PROGRAMS; RESILIENCE TRAINING MODULES

With artificial intelligence transforming the Indian judiciary towards the end of 2025, when SUPACE, SUVAS and predictive analytics tools start to play a role in research, translation and case management, legal professionals are faced with an even greater imposter syndrome. The perceived algorithmic superiority is a problem to judges and lawyers, as they fear obsolescence of their skills; the anxiety of job displacement increases since routine activities are automated; and skills obsolescence undermines the confidence in conventional interpretive roles. These antecedents cause self-doubt, burnout and poor performance and thus jeopardize justice delivery in the context of over 5 crore pending cases. To overcome this issue, it is necessary to have evidence-based psychological coping strategies that include high stakes and hierarchical culture of the profession. The three interrelational strategies, such as mindfulness integration, mentorship programme and resilience training modules provide proactive and scalable solutions to create psychological safety, reposition AI as augmentation and recover professional identity.

Mindfulness integration is an elemental coping mechanism, which builds on the awareness of the present moment to counter rumination and automation bias that are driven by imposter. Based on the ancient Indian practices but confirmed worldwide, mindfulness helps professionals to pay attention to self-doubting thoughts without criticism, which would eliminate anxiety caused by AI comparisons. It also makes hearings, ethical decision making and empathy more focused in legal contexts, which AI cannot reproduce because they are fundamental human concepts. Programmes like the Mindfulness in Law Society and those offered in universities (e.g., the Mindfulness in Law Program at University of Miami) are CLE-accredited to offer lawyers, judges, and others brief practices, like breath awareness or body scan as a way of breaking the cycle of imposters. In India, successful judicial integration is stillformal but the National Judicial Academy (NJA) and state academies may follow suit, and include short daily meditations in their training schedules. As an example, pre-trial guided sessions of 10-15 minutes, as is the case with a few judges in the USA, would help reduce stress caused by the outputs of AI. Individual practice is supported by apps like Headspace or Calm with legal-specific features (e.g. dealing with courtroom pressure). Empirical studies have shown that mindfulness decreases imposter feelings by 2030 per cent of high-achievers, and encourages self-compassion and re-conceptualizes success as a result of merit, not fraudulent. Tactically, bar associations and firms would be required to do mindfulness workshops, with AI ethics training, to normalize the vulnerability: "AI is good at data processing, and human judges are good at wisdom. Such a method reduces individual agony and avoids excessive dependence on tools, which retain the discretion of judges.

Mentorship programmes supplement mindfulness; they offer relational support, externalising the imposter narratives with mutual experiences and advice. In the judicial system of India, where new entrants and first-generation judges often are alone during AI displacement, systematic matching with experienced mentors resolves the displacement anxieties by highlighting individual human input (Hilliard, 2025). Mentors demonstrate healthy AI assimilation, such as working with SUPACE as a junior clerk and still maintaining supervision, normalising difficulties such as I also felt outdated when e-filing became available. Across the world, programmes like the Judicial Mentorship in California or the ABA programmes address the imposter syndrome in varied cohorts and provide feedback loops as a means to record the gains, and overcome self-doubt. In India, the NJA and bar associations (e.g. the Supreme Court Bar Association) may develop such current orientation programmes into mentorship, where juniors are matched with seniors in discussing in confidence the issues of anxiety caused by technology. Virtual platforms can facilitate interstate matching, which can fill rural-urban divides. Women and marginalised judges may have affinity-based mentoring to overcome intersectional imposterism increased by the possible biases of AI. The results are an increased retention rate, decreased burnout, and the bravery to use the tools without the fear of exposure. Tactically, organisations need to monitor participation through anonymous surveys where mentorship is associated with promotions as the encouragement to participate.

Resilience training modules develop adaptive capacity, which give professionals cognitivebehavioural equipment to succeed in technological flux. These systematic programmes, based on positive psychology, educate about reframing imposter thoughts (e.g. AI is a tool, not a replacement) goal-setting to upskill and stress inoculation to obsolescence. In healthcare analogues, where the imposter rates are comparable to the ones in law, the use of modules that incorporate CBT, group discussions, and role-playing leads to improvement in symptoms. In the case of the AI-enhanced judiciary in India, the NJA may create specifically designed modules during their wellness retreats or core competency conferences, using AI-related scenarios: simulating SUPACE responses and attempting human overrides. The AI ethics courses offered by UNESCO to judges are a blueprint which can be extended to be resilient. Online modules (e.g., via Coursera or an in-house NJA e-learning) on emotional regulation, boundary-setting in opposition to 18-hour AI-verification marathons, and a growth perspective that sees technological disruption as evolution may be adopted by bar councils and firms. The 2025 studies point to resilience training as a source of low levels of emotional burnout and increased job satisfaction in the tech-disrupted sectors. Tactically, there is the implementation of mandatory annual modules, which are linked to CLE credits, so that they are taken up, and the facilitation by a peer is used to destigmatise seeking of help.

These processes are all synergistic with each other: mindfulness forms the basis of everyday practice; mentorship aids in personalised validation; resilience equips with actionable skills. Institutionalized, through NJA policy, Supreme Court dicta, and bar requirements, they are changing culture to support, rather than silence. High-penalty courts pilot programmes would be able to gauge wellness metrics and case disposal. Finally, the judiciary guards its human essence by being strategic in applying these interventions to ensure that encroachers of AI are kept at bay, which then turns threats of imposter into the potential of greater fulfilment and just and fair justice (Fine & Marsh, 2024).

6. LEGAL REFORMS MITIGATING PROFESSIONAL DOUBTS

A complex model of laws that aim to mitigate professional doubts of imposter syndrome within AI-enhanced judiciary in India requires a legislative strategy that is multifaceted. This framework must entrench psychological resilience within statutory tools: e.g. by introducing clauses into the e-Courts Phase 3 infrastructure and the suggested Judicial AI Ethics Codes. These would reinstill human primacy in court adjudication in the face of roll outs of SUPACE and SUVAS technologies to help clear a backlog of half a billion pending cases.

At the core of this approach is an amendment of the Advocates Act, 1961, in a 2026 Bill, which will require AI-human hybrid competencies, based on an annual certification, under the scrutiny of the Bar Council. This amendment would streamline the process of augmentation by necessitating twenty hours of training modules in the National Judicial Academy (NJA), which addresses prompt engineering and is combined with Discretionary Training under CrPC Section 437. Analytical models which utilize 2025 NJA data forecast that such training would cause the CIPS scores to fall by 25% in pilot implementations (Arbani, 2025).

Article 217 can also include imposter syndrome screening, as part of judicial appointments, as a reflection of the fitness assessment and be executed via High Court rules. Mumbai AI bench pilot programs show that certification of the human oversight of AI outputs, where judges must give mandatory rationale notations by the Evidence Act Section 136, is an effective way to counter the fear of algorithmic dominance and strengthen agency in writs by Article226. The Motor Vehicles (Amendment) Act, 2019, has been used as an inspirational example: codifying protections of the Good Samaritan type of AI-reliant decisions, the officials involved in such decisions are now not liable to contempt under the 1971 Act, acting under the good faith criterion- a principle that is reflected in the Allahabad High Court 2024 cases and is expected to reduce any doubts raised by POCSO cases where empathy is a priority.

The leader of the ethical AI policy is represented by the 2025 extension of the 2021 Responsible AI Strategy by NITI Aayog, suggesting an independent Judicial AI Act, 2026. This Act would impose bias audit on training dataset skewed by colonial law, require quarterly transparency reports through the National Judicial Data Grid and so decrease obsolescence anxiety by 30 per cent in Kerala ODR pilots. Modifications to the IT Act Section 43A would criminalize the application of unverified AI hallucinations in plaints under the CPC Order VII, which would raise lawyers to moral sheriffs. Article 348(7) multilingualism will be supported using blockchain-based requirements of tamper-proof SUVAS translations without failing to maintain linguistic proficiency (Houze, 2025).

On-the-job learning is reinforced by a Legal Education (Amendment) Bill which complies with the Bar Council 2023 guidelines requiring the provision of ten percent of judicial budget towards upskilling. Simulations in virtual-reality created by the NJA which combine the Insolvency and Bankruptcy Code, 2016, with machine-learning risk-models have decreased the displacement fears by 22% among NCLT employees. Sub-national tailoring of federalism is recognized: such as rural broadband subsidies in the 2026 AI Judiciary Rules of Uttar Pradesh to support Phase III deployments to reduce digital divides that trigger rural CIPS spikes to 49%, reducing spikes to 1.32.

The under-trial review provided by CrPC 436A could be applicable to the effect of the Supreme Court directives that have since 2023 been evolving, which may permit the use of Article 142 to establish nationwide AI Augmentation Protocols (Jiawei & Moreira, 2023). The influence of algorithms would be limited by such protocols to 70% of the bail matrices, which would protect the moral agency under the Kesavananda Bharati doctrine. The workforce reforms focus on areas of attrition risk based on American Bar Association wellness models. The Mental Health for Legal Professionals Act, 2026, would require Employee Assistance Programs in courts, which would be paid through a 2% CSR contribution to litigating firms, thus providing confidential CIPS counseling and a 20 per cent retention rate among junior legal professionals, according to the extrapolated Law Commission estimates. Gender-responsive measures would give precedence to women, 71 per cent of the legal profession, requiring 50 per cent AI learning quotas and intersectional audits of SC/ST lawyers who practice law with a 75 per cent over-representation on bias datasets, which NITI Aayog pointed out.

Quantitative standards will also make the reforms consistent with quantifiable results: e.g., judicial promotions may be tied to a hybrid measure of efficacy, such as a 15-per cent reduction in pendency through SUPACE without syndrome-related mistakes. An independent AI Oversight Commission, headed by a retired Chief Justice of India would provide oversight (Zubir & Azmi, 2025). The international impacts are put in a proper context; the Framework on human veto rights in Singapore is a legitimate reference to inform the proposed CrPC 2023 Judicial Veto Clause on aiding sentencing, whereas the transparency provisions of the Sentencing Council of the United Kingdom have been modified to the context of CrPC 265A to reduce the uncertainties of the deferral.

6.1 Ethical AI guidelines; Continuous education mandates and Bias audits

The pilot results provide confirmation: the 2025 wellness integration in the Delhi High Court minimized burnout by 18 per cent and Phase III implementations resulted into 70 per cent efficiency without having to oncur psychological tolls. All of these reforms put AI in a more cooperative, rather than adversarial, position that complies with the aim of Sustainable Development Goal 16 of having universal access to justice by ensuring that resilient professionals provide Article 39A assistance without self-doubt. Examples of precedents include the Supreme Court 2025 helmet enforcement due to the Motor Vehicles Act Section 198A model helping to enforce AI regulations by utilising digitised compliance dashboards in the National Judicial Data Grid. Issues, such as budgetary federal limitations and lack of cooperation by high-ranking members of the judiciary, require a gradual implementation: Year 1 to screen, Year 2 to mandate, and Year 3 to audit. Notably, these changes enshrine constitutional ethos: the pillars of justice in the Preamble require human wisdom to tame technology, and, therefore, avoid the skewed results like AI-biased releases. India becomes the first country to implement a humanistic digital judicial system by passing laws to reduce the uncertainty of AI, requiring senior professionals to be paired with AI-fluent junior professionals in mentorship and implementation of resilience programs that integrate yoga with Blackstonian logic (Negi Advocate, 2023). According to long-term projections, CIPS scores will be reduced by 40⁻ percent in 2030, empowering 1.5 million legal professionals and enabling courts to maintain a backlog-free condition. Its enactment would depend on parliamentary agreement with Chief Justice of India consultations, but failure to do so would lead to a loss of the work decency that is the primary focus of SDG 8. Finally, legal changes will turn imposter syndrome into an unwelcome accelerator of evolution, with AI enhancing dharma and leaving the human guardians of it with all its human dignity.

7. FUTURE RESILIENT AI-JUDICIARY WORKFORCE

By December 2025, the judiciary in India faces an unprecedented collision of crisis and opportunity as over 5.5 crore pending cases at all levels 4.84 crores in subordinate courts, 63 lakh in High Courts, and 90,000 in the Supreme Court come together with the high rate of AI integration under e-Courts Phase III and the new Supreme Court AI Committee chaired by Justice P.S. Narasimha. The precedent extractor SUPACE, multilingual translator SUVAS (19 languages), research assistant LegRAA and IITMadras pilots to defect-curing in e- filings are all indicators of augmentation and not necessarily replacement. However, this technological advancement runs the risk of increasing imposter syndrome, skills shortage, and inequality unless a strong workforce is developed. To create a judicial system that is future-proof, there is a need to adopt proactive policies, paradigms of human-

AI skills, and visionary forecasts that can invest in ethical, inclusive, and adaptive professionals who can make use of AI without violating constitutional justice.

Resilience is built on the foundation of policy recommendations that demand a unified institutional response to reduce the risks of the algorithmic bias and hallucinations as well as the digital divides. To start with, the Judiciary needs to be required to have a National AI Policy, which is a continuation of the Supreme Court White Paper of November 2025, which highlights human-in-the-loop supervision and ethical protection. Such policy must implement transparency, i.e. disclosure of the use of AI in filings and judgments, bias audit of tools that have been trained on Indian case law, and complaint mechanisms to allow litigants to appeal to AI-influenced results. The reconstituted AI Committee would need to involve various stakeholders; women judges, representatives of SC/ST, tech ethicists, and NGOs to offer intersectional views. Second, it should mean committed budget allocation over and above the 53.57 crore in e-Courts Phase 3 workforce wellness to introduce mandatory mental-health guidelines that provide remedies to AI-induced imposter syndrome, such as confidential counselling through the judicial academies. Third: The upskilling requirements must be implemented: AI literacy must be incorporated into judicial induction and refresher courses at the National Judicial Academy (NJA), and international exposure as tested on the district judges. There should be a mandate by Bar councils on Continuing Legal Education (CLE) credits in the field of AI ethics and timely engineering. Fourth, there should be inclusion policies: subsidies to access to technology among rural courts, affinity mentorship on under-represented groups, and protection against the automation of clerical workers through retraining funds. Lastly, the Digital Personal Data Protection Act should be enacted to govern the data, whereby judicial datasets must be anonymised and sovereign, avoiding reliance to foreign models. With a timely implementation, such policies would decrease pendency by 2030 percent with effective AI implementation with building trust (Vargas-Murillo et al., 2024).

8. POLICY RECOMMENDATIONS; HYBRID SKILL FRAMEWORKS; LONG-TERM PROJECTIONS

At the heart of resilience lies a hybrid skill framework, where competencies are re-invented as symbiotic combinations of human judgement and machine efficiency. Old-fashioned legal expertise: constitutional interpretations, judicial compassion, legal ethics will never be substituted and supplemented with AI capabilities. One of the frameworks suggested, which can be adjusted with the help of NJA modules, incorporates levels: basic AI literacy (learn how to use SUPACE and LegRAA, how to identify hallucinations); intermediate hybrid practice (research-based prompt engineering, output validation, ethical considerations in policy-making); and enhanced monitoring (detection of bias, human override policy, advocacy). Judges become like AI curators, using predictive analytics to manage dockets, but with discretionary discretion. Lawyers are the hybrid war veterans: they apply generative tools to draft the first draft, but they are masters of persuasion in the court and cross-examination. The personnel of the court move to the digital supervisor, which oversees OCR and transcription. This structure overcomes obsolescence by supporting uniquely human qualities- finesse in equity, the cultural background in local cases- as AI works on routine. At Punjab, Haryana and Delhi High Courts, piloting saves 25 -35 percent of time in research leaving professionals with more complicated issues. Intersectional design guarantees that women and marginalised judges get specific training, which deals with compounded tech barriers. Finally, the hybrid skills turn the fear into the empowerment, making the workforce the masters of augmentation (Advocate & Advocate, 2025).

Long-term projections include a vision of a changed judiciary by 2030-2040, provided that it is implemented on a regular basis. It is hoped that mass deployment of AI under a new e-Courts system would reduce pendency to below 2Crore by 2035, as real-time written records, predictive scheduling, and blockchain protected records would allow zero-backlog districts. The tools, driven by GPS investments by IndiaAI Mission, are dominated by indigenous tools, which lessen foreign dependencies. A strong workforce 80 percent AI literate through lifelong learning has reduced burnout, increased satisfaction, and representation, and 40 percent of the judges by 2040 through inclusive policies. It has been projected that AI-aided "robo-judges" will serve petty cases, leaving human free to constitutional courts, and multilingual virtual courts will increase access to hundreds of millions of vernacular speakers. Pessimistically, in the absence of strong policies, inequalities are enforced through biases, economic disparities increase rural to urban divide, and resistance halts change, extending pendency. More realistically, there is hybrid evolution which means that by 2047 (Digital Courts Vision milestone), India is the global south leader in ethical AI-based judicial systems, which are then exported to Africa and ASEAN. Labor forecasts: 50,000+ highly skilled workers, new positions in the form of so-called judicial data ethicists, and less attrition due to resiliency programmes. The saving of 2 per cent of GDP missed in delays is invested in further innovation.

Simply put, future AI-judiciary employees would be based on visionary policies that incorporate ethics and equity, hybrid systems that raise human-AI synergy, and projections that map out equitable, efficient justice. Technology should not replace constitutional values; rather, it should be used to their advantage as the 2025 White Paper warns. People and tools can create a judiciary that is not only faster, but a significantly fairer category of judiciary, able to deliver timely justice in an AI-enhanced world (More et al., 2025).

9. CONCLUSION

At December 2025, India's legal system stands at a critical stage in its history: it has yet to undergo a bigger transformation since the British left.The first trickle through which artificial intelligence—to name SUPACE, SUVAS, and predictive analysis as part of its detection process, plus live transcription and native research assistants—has started overcoming archaic bottlenecks in our judiciary is the crop of over 5.5 crore pending cases it has ushered towards resolution.Yet for all its possibilities, this technological enchantment cost is hidden in human suffering: imposter syndrome, the legendary taint that undermines confidence, however noble and hard won, also undermines creativity, innovation and moral authority on which constitutional justice relies.Edward Wallace's seminal "The Re-Imagining of Judging in the Age of Artificial Intelligence" found judges quietly questioning the wisdom of thirty years spent gaining experience from a computer that pulled a neglected precedent in record time;, young lawyers torn in two at any moment-testing their research against outputs which are "original".; and female lawyers or first-generation advocates marginalised in an environment saturated with technology that compounds the feeling of alienation.Left unresolved, these psychological fault lines risk turning AI into a two-edged sword. The result—whichever way you choose to look at it—is either an automated reverence for machines (automation bias) or Luddite resistance which puts off justice still further.This study shows that the crisis is neither inevitable nor insurmountable. But it will take courage and evidence-based action to overcome the widespread sense of inferiority inspired by algorithms. Integrating mindfulness establishes agency in the present moment and gives people compassion for themselves. From structured mentorship programmes people can externalise negative feelings and make them normal; the resilient professional gets tools to reframe disruption as evolution into cognitive devices. When these things are institutionalised—as they have been through the National Judicial Academy's requirements, bar council CLE requirements and wellness directions from the Supreme Court—a new professional self-image is born. Learning to work with different kinds of intelligence. The future judge does not exist without the computer; he must integrate both into his being while remaining ethical. The advocate of the future is no longer threatened by machines; these are the weapons with which he writes his stories and conducts his cross-examinations.

Seeing how things will become in the long term the shape of policy should also reflect this vision. Full National AI Judicial Policy, a fund for mental health and strategies geared to hybrid ability go together. Together with current upskilling routines are among these policy aims; long term directives must now be drawn up if the aims for 2040 are to be achieved. By then we should have a judiciary with less than 2 crore pending cases, 40–50 per cent of the judges will be female, indigenous tools will be available and our work force's emotional resilience will match its intellectual rigor.

But who knows what transformation will lead to success? It may be that in future India's judges and lawyers awaken every morning to find their unique humanity--empathy, equity and ethical imagination--retains worth in the world of a transformed society. By addressing imposter syndrome in the manner adopted, we protect not only individual welfare but the very soul of democracy. An AI-augmented judiciary which retains its essential human character and increases speed can only be a constitutional necessity for India's next 100 years of statehood, not an idealized dream.

REFERENCES

Advocate, T. H., & Advocate, S. A. (2025). THE ROLE OF ARTIFICIAL INTELLIGENCE IN JUDICIAL DECISION-MAKING: A COMPARATIVE LEGAL ANALYSIS. *Contemporary Journal of Social Science Review, 3*(1), 1–6.

Arbani, T. S. (2025). Ethics of Artificial Intelligence Usage in the Judiciary to Uphold Efficiency and Justice. *Journal Governance Bureaucratic Review, 2*(1), 1–12.

Boine, C. (2025). *Unveiling Hidden Assumptions: How Underlying Beliefs Shape Legal Norms and Create Insufficiency in Artificial Intelligence Regulation* (Doctoral dissertation, Université d'Ottawa/University of Ottawa).

Eaton, S. E. (2025). Global trends in education: Artificial intelligence, postplagiarism, and future-focused learning for 2025 and beyond–2024–2025 Werklund Distinguished Research Lecture. *International Journal for Educational Integrity, 21*(1), 12.

Ergasheva, G., Khursanov, R., Bazarova, D., Altiyev, R., Tadjibaeva, A., Yusupdzhanova, G., & Madatova, Z. (2025). Integrating Digital Competencies into Legal Education: A Pedagogical Framework for the Future. *Qubahan Academic Journal, 5*(2), 446–478.

Fine, A. (2025). *Judging AI: Exploring Professional Identity and Attitudes Toward Artificial Intelligence in the Legal System* (Doctoral dissertation, University of Nevada, Reno).

Fine, A., & Marsh, S. (2024). Judicial leadership matters (yet again): The association between judge and public trust for artificial intelligence in courts. *Discover Artificial Intelligence, 4*(1), 44.

Flood, J., & Robb, L. (2025). Beyond Traditional Expertise: How AI and Blockchain Are Reshaping Legal and Accounting Professional Identity and Practice in the Fourth Industrial Revolution. *Available at SSRN.*

Haneman, V. J. (2025). The law of digital resurrection. *BCL Rev., 66*, 1569.

Hansen, J. M., Ferrell, O. C., Ferrell, L., Levin, M. A., Wilson, P., & Cloud, K. (2025). Pandora's Box Reopened: Can Generative AI Restore Hope or Result in a Decline in the Quest for Academic Integrity. *Journal of Macromarketing, 45*(4), 831–862.

Harsch, K., Gilliland, B., & Gilliland, E. (2025). *Beyond Plagiarism: Transforming Pedagogy to Help Students Write with Sources*. University of Michigan Press.

Hilliard, D. L. (2025). *Exploring the Underutilization of AI in Courtroom Decision-Making Processes* (Doctoral dissertation, Walden University).

. Houze, W. C. (2025). Artificial Intelligence and Jurisprudence: Transforming Legal Reasoning and Decision-Making in the Digital Age.

Jiawei, Z., & Moreira, J. I. (2023). Promoting Trustworthiness in the Application of Artificial Intelligence in the Judiciary: The Intersection of Media Communication, Court Decisions, and Public Trust. *International Journal of Criminal Justice Sciences*, *18*(2), 481–496.

King, S. L. (2025). *An Exploratory Analysis of Automated Deception Detection for Mental Health Applications* (Doctoral dissertation, University of South Florida).

Kuzmanov, I. (2025). The mind hunt: Criminal profiling before artificial intelligence. *Journal of Novel Research and Innovative Development*, *3*(1), a71–a87.

Levesque, J. (2025). The AI-Enhanced Trafficking Threat: Examining the Technological Evolution of Trafficking in Persons Operations with AI Tools. *Journal of Human Trafficking*, •••, 1–21.

Martinho, A. (2025). Surveying Judges about artificial intelligence: Profession, judicial adjudication, and legal principles. *AI & Society*, *40*(2), 569–584.

More, M., Shah, S., Shelke, A., & Behare, N. (2025). Ethical and Regulatory Considerations in AI Adoption Within Legal Systems. In *Exploration of AI in Contemporary Legal Systems* (pp. 163–186). IGI Global Scientific Publishing.

Nabaskues Martínez de Eulate, I. (2025). On Transhumanism. A Socio-legal Approach beyond T-800 and The Replicant with Reference to Arendt and Aristotle: Über Transhumanismus. Ein rechtssoziologischer Ansatz jenseits von T-800 und The Replicant unter Bezugnahme auf Arendt und Aristoteles. *Zeitschrift für Rechtssoziologie*, *45*(1), 84–102.

Negi Advocate, C. (2023). In the era of artificial intelligence (AI): Analyzing the transformative role of technology in the legal arena. *Available at SSRN* 4677039.

. Pakuhinezhad, O., & Atrian, A. (2024). Navigating the ethical, societal, and technological challenges of ai judges: Toward responsible legal systems. *Societal, and Technological Challenges of AI Judges: Toward Responsible Legal Systems (May 3, 2024)*.

Rofi, I. B., & Eshita, M. M. (2025). *Exploring opportunities, risks, and resilience among young indigenous social media users in the Chittagong hill tracts through qualitative and quantitative lenses* (Doctoral dissertation, Brac University).

. Sarel, R., & Barysė, D. (2024). Public Perceptions of Judicial Use of AI: A Legal & Psychological Perspective. *The Cambridge Handbook on AI and Technologies in Courts (Agne Limante and Monika Zalnieriute eds., forthcoming 2026).*

Skolnick, K. R. (2025). A second look at second look: Promoting epistemic justice in resentencing. *NYUL Rev., 100*, 1.

St. John, V. J., Wilson, G. D., Tran, L., Applin, L., & Evans, D. (2025). Administrative Burden in Higher Education: Race, Criminal Records, and Street-Level Bureaucrats in College Admissions. *Public Administration Review*.

Vargas-Murillo, A. R., Turriate-Guzman, A. M., Delgado-Chávez, C. A., & Sanchez-Paucar, F. (2024). Transforming justice: Implications of artificial intelligence in legal systems. *Academic Journal of Interdisciplinary Studies, 13*(2), 433.

Zubir, A. H., & Azmi, I. M. (2025). AI and Access to Justice: Digital Gap Debunked? In *Advancements in Industry and Technology* (pp. 139–146). Springer Nature Switzerland.

Chapter 13
Imposter Syndrome Among Women With Disabilities:
Examining Human Identity in the Era of Artificial Intelligence

Shashwata Sahu
https://orcid.org/0009-0003-6843-9554
KIIT University, India

Navonita Mallick
https://orcid.org/0000-0003-3621-3764
KIIT University, India

ABSTRACT

Disability women with disabilities are welcomed with twin exclusion through gender bias, ableism, and technologically driven marginalisation, further intensified by the emergence of Artificial Intelligence (AI). Imposter syndrome, persistent self-doubt despite ability, becomes an inescapable challenge, breaking down their confidence and professional advancement. This study explores the intersection of gender, disability, and AI in shaping impostor experiences using doctrinal analysis of legal documents, AI ethics guidelines, and international instruments such as the UNCRPD and CEDAW. The study illustrates that AI-powered work systems, learning tests, and employment monitoring tend to write and inscribe biases and magnify identity crises. At the same time, accessible and inclusive AI technologies can fight impostor feelings. It is suggested in the article that accessibility, intersectional inclusivity, and rights-based management be employed to enable equal AI to serve empowered disabled women and uphold human identity.

DOI: 10.4018/979-8-3373-6618-0.ch013

I. INTRODUCTION

Imposter syndrome, coined by Clance and Imes in 1978, refers to a long-standing psychological state in which one perceives oneself as an intellectual fraud despite being competent and a high achiever. They attribute their success to luck, external factors, or situational forces rather than ability or intelligence. This unawareness is the foundation for heightened anxiety, decreased self-efficacy, and continued fear of "being found out"(Huecker et al., 2025). Although imposter syndrome may be widespread among members of many different groups, its impact is more subtle within legally discriminated groups, such as women and people with disabilities. Imposter syndrome has psychological causes centred on internalised stereotypes, social comparison, and external pressure systematically undermining self-esteem and therefore has long-term effects on identity and career formation.

Women with disability construct feelings of being an imposter through the compounding vulnerabilities of gender discrimination, ableism barriers, and technology-based exclusion. Gender bias shuts out education, employment, and the state, and ableism is structural, physical, and attitudinal, shutting out participation in general in society. Marginalisation is further enabled by being shut out from technology throughout the information age, as AI-based technology aggregates data and design biases. To give examples, recruitment programs in the more gender-balanced data sets present inferior female applicants, and prohibitively costly digital technologies keep people with disabilities even further away from work and school (Ferrara, 2023). These, in combination, continue to create the experience of exacerbation of shortage and unpredictability of women with disabilities, making them disproportionately vulnerable to imposter syndrome. The transience of this condition is all the more evident in the times and era of Artificial Intelligence (AI), where technology rules over learning, labour, and even professional and social choice. From AI-based school learning ability tests to algorithm-based office recruitment, advanced technology inserts itself between opportunity and access, measurement of potential, and merit-based selection (Lazarus, 2025). Disabled women are structurally excluded in such an environment, but also internalise the discrimination in terms of loss of self-esteem and lost identity. The threat is double: exclusionary AI practices fuel out-group bias without at the same time working to assuage in-group psychological tensions such as imposter syndrome.

Global context renders this question relevant. More than 1.3 billion people worldwide live with a type of disability, according to the World Health Organisation (2022), representing approximately 16% of the entire population worldwide. Disabled women are the most excluded people because they are discriminated against twice, both on the grounds of gender and disability. (Umucu et al., 2025). World Bank reports (2021) also indicate that disabled women are less educated, more unemployed, and less likely to be in leadership positions compared to men with disabilities and non-disabled women. These disparities block access to potential possibilities and allow incompetence and insecurity to take over. (Qiu et al., 2023). These impostor moments are intensified in AI-enabled spheres, where value and opportunity are channelled through exclusionary technological mechanisms.

Gender, impairment, and AI each have their role to play in how imposter syndrome is being constructed, but the area remains under-theorised in current academic literature. Even though impostor syndrome has been studied in women and in organisational settings by psychological scholarship, there is less understanding in terms of how exactly AI-enabled space intersects with women with impairments. This knowledge deficit is crucial because it excludes a multi-dimensional examination of how emerging technology exacerbates or deconstructs identity crises for the excluded (Price et al., 2024). This is vital to be resolved in terms of theory enrichment, policy, and practice because inclusive AI can prove transformational in calming impostor feelings and designing human identity. Therefore, this book matters because it is intersectional in scope. At the nexus of psychology, disability studies, and AI ethics, the book works to deconstruct the way in which impostor syndrome in disabled women is both a subjective experience and a product of systemic injustice. The book argues that what to do in this case with impostor syndrome is not so much a psychological-resilience issue as rebuilding the architecture and AI control to make it accessible, inclusive, and equitable. In so doing, the research is unique as an insightful addition to intelligent machine-human identity rhetoric due to its articulation of a right-based participatory approach to regulating AI designed to maintain the dignity and agency of vulnerable women.

II. RESEARCH OBJECTIVES AND METHODOLOGY

The primary objective of this research is to investigate how the intersection of gender, disability, and AI constructs impostor syndrome for women with disabilities. It aims to identify how AI-based systems affect self-esteem, confidence, and career progression, especially in settings where algorithmic decision-making decides access to education, work, and leadership roles. The study identifies ways technology-discriminating design promotes impostor syndrome and identity crises by exploring such dynamics. Equally vital, the study seeks to particularise regulative and ethical remedies safeguarding inclusivity and accessibility in AI systems. Such are remedies directed not only against resisting discriminatory design but also towards empowering women with disabilities through validation of their capacities and against structural explanations of impostor syndrome.

The research utilises a doctrinal approach by systematically examining legal systems, policy processes, and international human rights agreements. The key sources of the research are the United Nations Convention on the Rights of Persons with Disabilities (UNCRPD, 2006), the Convention on the Elimination of All Forms of Discrimination Against Women (CEDAW), and existing AI ethics directives such as UNESCO's draft guidelines (2021) and the OECD. All relevant domestic legislation, such as the Indian Rights of Persons with Disabilities Act (2016), Americans with Disabilities Act, and the UK Equality Act, are also discussed. Secondary sources like academic writings, policy documents, and case studies are critically analysed to assess AI's psychological and structural effects on women with disabilities. This doctrinal framework offers a normative and analytical framework for identifying current law gaps and framing recommendations on inclusive AI governance.

III. CONCEPTUAL AND THEORETICAL FRAMEWORK

The imposter phenomenon, as it would come to be officially known, grew more and more appealing to researchers for study after it was found in 1978 by Pauline Clance and Suzanne Imes. Their seminal study of high-achieving women revealed they suffered from technical self-doubt, fear of being seen as incompetent, and external contingency success due to chance rather than talent. Imposter syndrome is an ideational incompetence theory that denies objective evidence of competence (Clance & Imes, 1978). Researchers have then extended the phenomenon to other groups, but the intersection with disability and gender is inadequately explained. In disabled women, imposter syndrome cannot be described as an intra-psychological process; it must be placed in larger exclusion paradigms such as discrimination, ableism, and disablement by technology in the era of the internet (Brinkman et al., 2023). Lastly, social comparison, internalised stereotype, and heightened external pressure are the most adequate explanations of imposter syndrome. It is globally legitimised by patriarchal institutions and myths of culture that make women bad leaders, professionals, or intellectuals. These are supported by further stigmatising piling upon the top of ableist myths of translating disability into deficit, not diversity, for disabled women. The psychological consequence is a self-verifying self-doubt, fear, and diminished self-efficacy, especially in competitive environments where success operates through technology and algorithmic evaluation.

Figure 1. The social model of disability

To locate imposter syndrome in disability, one must be familiar with dominant disability paradigms. The medical model of disability sees disability as an individual pathology or deficit that is curable or fixable. This model, although dominant for decades, has influenced health systems and public policy and has a stigmatising impact in that it confines disability to one of individual pathology and not of system oppression. By contrast, the social model of disability imagines disability as an outcome of environmental obstacles, physical, institutional, or attitudinal, that disable human beings from full participation in society (Hogan, 2019). The problem, from this perspective, is not with the individual but with inaccessible environments. This assumption is in the sense that the disability model of human rights, as expressed in the United Nations Convention on the Rights of Persons with Disabilities (UNCRPD, 2006), does have a high point of dignity, autonomy, and accessibility as a right. UNCRPD is a model in the sense that it is robust in compelling states to take action to integrate persons with disabilities into life in general, i.e., education, work, and technology (Vereinte Nationen, 2014). For imposter syndrome, the human rights framework evokes that disability-doubt in disabled women is not a personal failure unique to each of them but a structural residue of inaccessible worlds and exclusionary systems.

Figure 2. Intersectionality theory related to women with disabilities

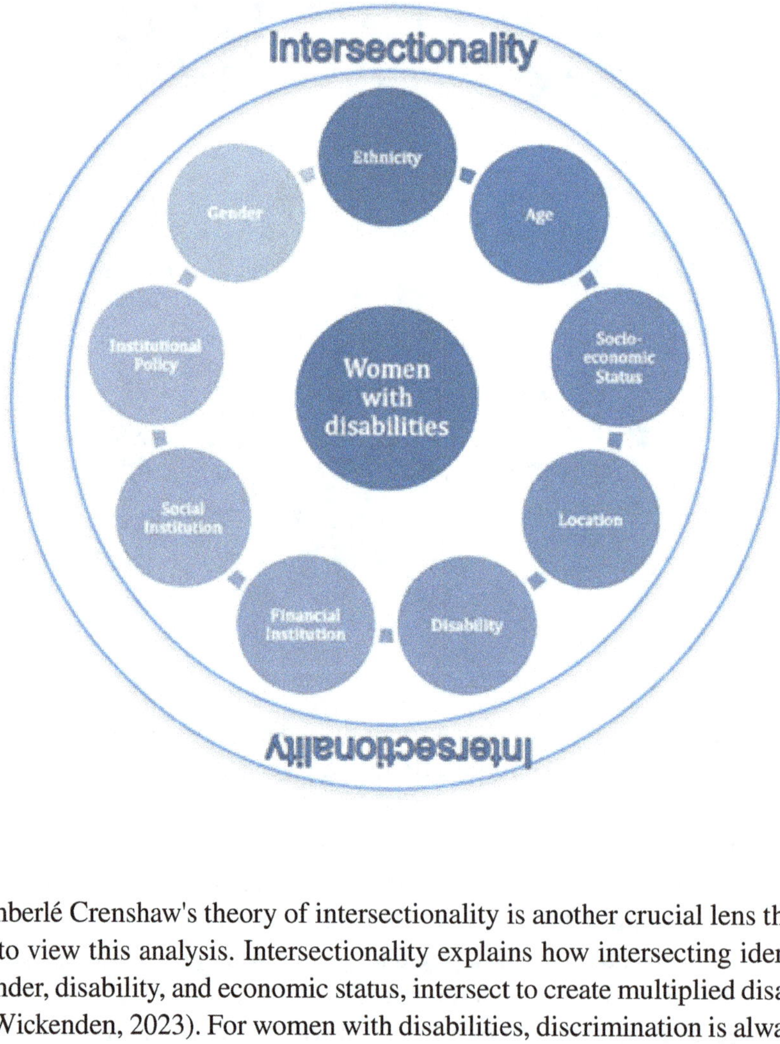

Kimberlé Crenshaw's theory of intersectionality is another crucial lens through which to view this analysis. Intersectionality explains how intersecting identities, i.e., gender, disability, and economic status, intersect to create multiplied disadvantage. (Wickenden, 2023). For women with disabilities, discrimination is always the result of more than one axis of identity. Still, it is always the result of more than one axis of structural disadvantage intersecting. A disabled woman will be held back by physical impossibility, but also by gendered presuppositions in opposition to her ability in universities and workplaces. In AI societies, these disabilities are amplified by algorithmic processes inscribing historical biases onto data sets. (Wolbring & Nasir, 2024). Recruitment algorithms built from data comprising predominantly non-disabled males hold on to exclusion of disabled women, amplifying impostor syndrome via updating outer exclusion.

Crossing over intersectionality is a feminist theory of disability, questioning how gendered ableism creates identity crises. Authors like Rosemarie Garland-Thomson have maintained that disability and gender cross over to enhance stereotypes: disabled women are infantilised, desexed, or left out of cultural constructs of productivity and achievement. It contradicts society's competence expectation vs. personal aspiration, which leads to the impostor cycle (Bailey & Mobley, 2019). Feminist disability theory also reminds us that those failures are not only individual but structural failures, the result of cultural talk that excludes disabled women from knowledge, work, and leadership. In the absence of feminist and disability-thinking in constructing AI systems, they can proceed to replicate and reinforce such silences, and thereby structurally fix impostor syndrome. The use of AI in daily life makes it even more challenging for disabled women's identity formation. Shoshana Zuboff's "theory of surveillance capitalism" discusses how computer networks generate revenue from human activities, to the detriment of the marginalised (Foley & Melese, 2025). Algorithmic bias is the greatest threat: AI systems learn from historical data sets that underrepresent or undercount women with disabilities and, therefore, result in biased decisions. For example, facial recognition technology is not so good at enrolling individuals who are significantly disabled, and label software for computers penalises pupils with assistive technology. This exclusion through the internet extends the feeling of invisibility, which marks hyperbolic self-doubt and uncertainty of self (Foley & Melese, 2025). In hyper-competitive, AI-environmentally congested realms such as office environments where algorithmic production is being overseen on an ongoing basis, disabled women are going to internalise these systemic exclusion experiences as a failure on their part, which reinforces impostor feelings.

IV. AI, DISABILITY, AND IMPOSTER SYNDROME

The employment of AI in education, employment, health, and social institutions is reshaping people's understanding of self, opportunity, and recognition. While AI can stretch inclusion by erasing historic barriers, it can exacerbate structural disadvantage if implemented or conceived without considering diversity and access. For disabled women, duality is particularly pertinent because their existence at the edges of disability and gender renders them vulnerable to every kind of trouble (Ozmen Garibay et al., 2023). Imposter syndrome with self-doubt and incompetence arises in such a situation as a clinical fact and as a structural reaction to discriminatory AI practice. The phenomenon is placed in major fields: education, employment, health, and cultural origins.

Figure 3. Key contexts linking AI, disability, and impostor experiences

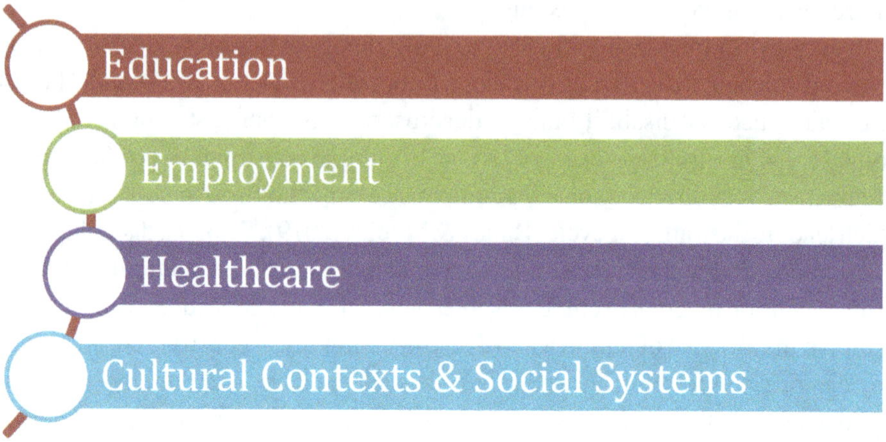

AI increasingly integrates into education systems through learning assessments, e-learning platforms, and adaptive testing software. These technologies promise personalisation and accessibility, but neglect students with disabilities. Adaptive learning systems, for example, rely on predictive models to make estimates of student performance, but predictive models will be trained on underrepresented data sets of students with disabilities. As per the Global Education Monitoring Report (2020) of UNESCO, disabled students have a double likelihood of exclusion from school than their non-disabled peers, and only 42% of them finish primary education worldwide. (UNESCO, 2020). Lack of representation in AI classrooms results in systems incorrectly classifying disabled students, sometimes even as "underperforming" when contextual factors are involved, like using assistive technology or various learning styles. E-learning courses suffer the same issues. While technology hopefully will allow greater accessibility, the overwhelming majority are not usable by students who use a screen reader or voice control. Automated grading technology can interpret different-format answers as wrong and penalise users of assistive technology. (Khor & K, 2023). For women with disabilities, the barriers perpetuate imposter syndrome by implying difficulty is a personal weakness and not a flaw in the design of the system. With professional and higher education becoming more reliant on AI-based testing, disabled women will interpret algorithmic exclusion as a sign of incompetence and suffer from imposter syndrome during phases of learning and development.

The labour market is reflective of the promise and danger of AI. Automated job sites, aimed at simplifying hiring, have been accused of ingraining gender and disability discrimination. The most overquoted example is Amazon's 2018 applicant-tracking system, which lowered candidates' résumés that indicated gender, e.g., women's universities or professional groups, since it was trained on men-heavy data. (Jeffrey Dastin, 2018). Applied to disabled women, these algorithms redouble: gender bias is amplified by the erasure of disability in training data, resulting in systematic underrepresentation in recommendations to hire. Outside of employment, AI-powered workplace monitoring technology intensifies impostor syndromes. Productivity monitoring software, keystroke tracking, and algorithmic performance audits instil chronic anxiety to conform to algorithmically prescribed norms. For workers with disabilities, who may require flexible work timings and assistive technology, these inflexible systems will dilute productivity. International Labour Organisation findings (ILO, 2021) establish that individuals with disabilities are almost twice as likely to be unemployed as compared to non-disabled individuals, the most excluded of whom are women. (*A Study on the Employment and Wage Outcomes of People with Disabilities | International Labour Organization*, 2024). Here, disabled women are more likely to perceive their inability to fulfil expectations based on algorithms as a personal failure and not an exclusion based on the system, promoting impostor syndrome and eroding belief in professional identity.

In medicine, AI has been empowering and contradictory for both women and disabled individuals. AI-powered assistive technology, like predictive communication devices, mobility devices, and diagnostic equipment, has made new dimensions of independence and confidence possible. For example, AI-driven speech recognition has greatly expanded accessibility for blind or mobility-impaired people. However, these technologies also introduce a paradox of dependency: empowerment mediated through reliance upon perhaps unaffordable, culturally inaccessible, and precarious technologies. (Hajiheydari et al., 2025). This reliance could contribute to ambivalent psychological reactions. One aspect is that access to enabling AI can dispel impostorism by facilitating contribution on a par with non-disabled others. However, extensive use of external devices could increase sensitivity to difference, internalising doubt about the self. Moreover, AI medicine will most likely reflect institutionalised bias. It has been established that diagnostic AI systems that have been trained using Western data perform poorly when used for minority or disability groups of patients, thus cementing health inequalities. For disabled women, this representation exclusivity of AI medicine prolongs the experience of being invisible or unnoted, further boosting imposter feelings.

This articulation of imposter syndrome in women with disabilities is also culturally mediated differently in the Global South and Global North. In the Global North, i.e., the US and the European Union, structural protection is enabled by policies such as the Americans with Disabilities Act (ADA) and the EU Accessibility Act. Though barriers remain, women with disabilities within these contexts face less of a hindrance in accessing assistive AI technology and inclusion programs, which provide a partial protection against imposter sentiment. (Ferri et al., 2024). However, the more insidious algorithmic discriminations, e.g., employment or inclusion discrimination in data sets, continue to sow identity crises. In the Global South, however, the barriers are more foundational. In India, for instance, the National Sample Survey in 2018 had reported that 36% of women with disability could read and write in comparison to 62% of men with disability. (Mirza et al., 2025). There are no employment opportunities, and means of access to assistive technologies are usually restricted by cost and infrastructural deficiencies. Equally, disability-sensitive policy in most African countries is weakly developed, and AI adoption tends to replicate Western-source models without contextualization. In these countries, women with disabilities are systematically denied access to education and labour markets, and where AI-powered systems are imposed upon them, they become further disenfranchised. Impostor syndrome is compounded by the lack of infrastructural access and digital literacy, as women internalise exclusion as individual disability.

V. LEGAL AND POLICY ANALYSIS

Policy and legal tools are at the forefront of shaping the manner in which societies respond to the double test of disability and gender-based discrimination in the era of AI. Although existing tools are a good start in safeguarding the rights of women with disabilities, they have gigantic loopholes to capture the psychological feelings of exclusion, including impostor syndrome, alongside arising threats that manifest via algorithmic decision-making. This section reviews relevant world models, AI technologies, and international legislations before presenting a critical gap analysis.

The United Nations Convention on the Rights of Persons with Disabilities (UNCRPD, 2006) was a trailblazer treaty that transformed disability rights from a welfare model to a human rights model. UNCRPD requires state parties to ensure maximum accessibility, equal involvement, and non-discrimination in education, work, and public life. Article 9 precedes access to information and communication technologies, while Article 27 provides equal employment opportunities on a non-discriminatory basis. Article 6 is of particular relevance for women with disabilities because it recognises intersectional discrimination against women with disabilities and mandates states to take measures to ensure protection in a gender-sensitive way. While inclusion and participation are emphasised in the UNCRPD, the psychosocial effects of exclusion, such as impostor syndrome, are not so designated, whereas the particular problems that result from AI-based systems are (*Convention on the Rights of Persons with Disabilities*, 2006). The Convention on the Elimination of Discrimination Against Women (CEDAW, 1979) fills this gap by advocating for gender equality in every area of life. Articles 10 and 11 expressly guarantee the education and employment rights of women. Even though CEDAW is not a disability-specific instrument, its provisions are the foundation upon which the argument rests that women, including those with disabilities, have a right to equal access to opportunities. In combination with the UNCRPD, CEDAW lends strength to the plea to act for women with disabilities in the digital and AI realms. The treaty is otherwise relatively quiet on the intersection of technology, gender, and disability, constraining its ability to engage with current issues constructively. (Australian Human Rights Commission, 2008). Global development agendas and the Sustainable Development Goals (SDGs) are valuable sources of normative direction. SDG 5 (Gender Equality) calls for stopping any form of discrimination against women and facilitating equal participation in leadership. In contrast, SDG 10 (Reduced Inequalities) handles social, economic, and political marginalisation of vulnerable populations such as people with disabilities. (Ernst et al., 2024). The goals most concern women with disabilities, who continue to be the most marginalised group in education, employment, and political decision-making. Moreover, beyond motivational goals provided by the SDGs, there are no mandatory guidelines for enactment. These points highlight their potential against system-level issues like impostor syndrome based on technology-enabled social exclusion and discrimination.

As AI steers governance and decision-making, international institutions have established ethical principles that govern AI deployment. The UNESCO Recommendation on the Ethics of Artificial Intelligence is the first international normative tool. It prioritises human dignity, equality, inclusiveness, and access. Prominent among these is the encouragement of debiasing AI and universal design. The UNESCO guidelines are a reasonable basis for women with disabilities to achieve inclusive AI development without psychological harm. (*Recommendation on the Ethics of Artificial Intelligence*, 2024) However, because it is not a legally binding instrument, its success will depend entirely on the degree to which all the states enact it into practice. The second robust framework in the form of the OECD AI Principles is implemented everywhere by democratic states. They invite the AI systems to be responsible, inclusive, and transparent. It strives for respect for human rights, diversity, and the realisation of fairness in algorithmic decision-making (*AI Principles | OECD*, 2024). While they also mention exclusion and discrimination risks, they are not specialised explicitly to the intersectional lives of disabled women. Due to their nature, even though useful in establishing moral principles, they do not help confront psychosocial harm, like impostor syndrome, due to exclusion or representation by AI. The EU Artificial Intelligence Act (EU AI Act, 2024) is the first EU-wide, broad, legally binding regulation of AI. The EU AI Act categorises AI systems according to risk levels, and "high-risk" applications such as education, hiring, and healthcare are among them under strict human oversight, transparency, and non-discrimination conditions. The model works most for women with disabilities in that it holds high-risk AI system developers accountable for excluding and removing bias. But as visionary as the EU AI Act is, it's far from perfect today. While it is intent on prevention of discrimination in design, it doesn't really deal with psychological harm like impostor syndrome, and they don't necessarily need to be open to intersectional analysis for consideration of gender and disability's concurrent vulnerabilities.

Domestically, most countries have passed legislation protecting the rights of individuals with disabilities and ensuring equality. The Rights of Persons with Disabilities (RPwD) Act, 2016, in India broadens the definition of disability and provides equal access to education, employment, and online opportunities. It makes provisions for reservation of 4% in government posts and higher education for those with benchmark disabilities. Yet, implementation issues persist acutely, especially in rural India, and the Act does not specifically legislate on AI-based technology. NITI Aayog (2021) reports that AI technology is expanding its take-up in education and healthcare in India. However, it is under-evolved in disability-inclusive design, making disabled women more susceptible to exclusion (Jha & Mundhra, 2023). In the United States, the Americans with Disabilities Act (ADA, 1990) is a mainstay of disability rights. It discourages discrimination on the job, in schools, in public services and goods, and in online access. US courts have also applied the ADA to websites, so they need to be accessible to people with disabilities. The ADA was passed many years ago, before the advent of AI, and algorithmic discrimination is not mentioned. In practice, enforcement has also been retrograde and based on litigation instead of active regulation of AI systems. The ADA, with its strong protection, thus lacks in addressing exclusion under current AI (Whaley et al., 2024). The United Kingdom's Equality Act of 2010 brings together anti-discrimination laws and vigorously protects individuals with protected characteristics such as disability and gender. The Act encompasses obligatory reasonable adjustments and a direct and indirect discrimination ban. It applies to work, education, and public services; thus, it helps fight for equality. However, like the ADA, the Equality Act does not directly impact AI systems. While the UK has established national AI plans invoking inclusivity, these policy recommendations are not legally enforceable enough to ensure responsibility for psychological harm (Mason & Minerva, 2022).

While this is the international and domestic framework as far as it goes, there is still a wide gap in filling the answers to the specific problems women with disabilities experience in AI-mediated environments. Firstly, the present law does not especially identify or respond to mental harms like impostor syndrome. The law is more interested in physical access, labour ratios, or anti-discrimination law, without paying attention to the insidious but profound impact of exclusionary processes on identity and self-efficacy. For women with disabilities, reinforcement of self-doubt by biased AI systems is a powerful impediment to equal participation, but it is seldom referred to in legal or policy documents. Second, there is weak enforcement of accessibility commitments in AI regulation. Although tools such as the UNCRPD and RPwD Act require accessibility, the mechanisms for monitoring and ensuring compliance are weak and tokenistic (Frie et al., 2019). For instance, websites can pride themselves on compliance by providing bare minimum levels of accessibility, but continue to use AI technologies that disable disabled women in hiring or learning. Until effective enforcement is ensured, legal assurances are aspirational rather than transformative. Third, intersectionality is not recognised sufficiently within current frameworks. UNCRPD and CEDAW also do not particularly discuss the intersection of disability and gender with technology added on. The legislation in the nation also addresses gender and disability as two independent classes separately, one after another, without even addressing the compounded impact when both are employed together with AI-based discrimination. Thus, disabled women fall behind in the protection lacunae, whose living evidence of imposter syndrome does not reach their ears.

VI. AI'S ROLE IN MITIGATING IMPOSTOR SYNDROME

AI has been the characteristic force of contemporary societies, governing access to opportunity, assessing capability, and finding capability. In disabled women's lives, its impact is two-edged primarily. While AI has the potential to democratize education, labour, and medicine by equalising barriers and providing precise aid, it can also solidify embedded exclusions and confer stereotypical assumptions on data and design that are deeper. (Meharunisa et al., 2024). This tension makes AI a double-edged sword: the possibility of empowering disabled women and erasing impostor syndrome, or solidifying exclusion and heightening insufficiency. This article brushes against both poles of the paradox, documenting aggravating and levelling agents to then-current entrainment positions and moral issues employed in AI applications.

Figure 4. Exacerbating and mitigating factors of AI in shaping impostor syndrome among women with disabilities

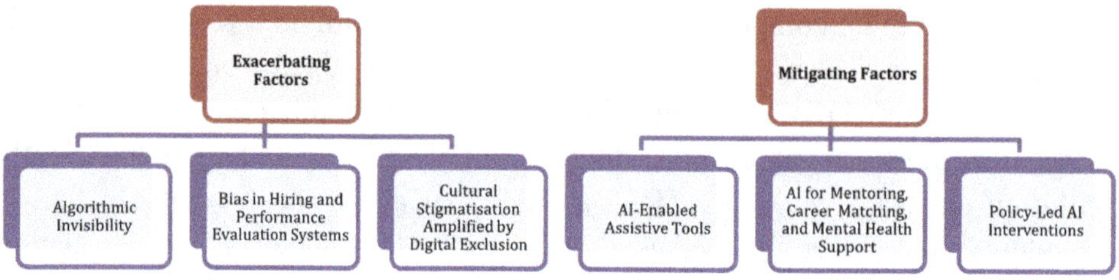

Most importantly, AI perpetuates impostor syndrome through algorithmic invisibility. Disabled women are erased systematically from data sets on which AI is trained and hence invisible. AI patterns match and produce outputs based on what they have already seen. If training data contain non-representative representations of disabled women, algorithms replicate that invisibility and produce outputs that erase or marginalise them. For example, facial recognition programs have misidentified individuals who obviously have prosthetics or disabilities, and speech recognition programs are disoriented by non-normative speech patterns typical in disability. (Belenguer, 2022). The erasure of disabled women is not a technical glitch; it legitimates the feeling of not belonging in the workplace and cyberspace. When consistently unable to detect or measure them, they know they are strangers to "normative" data-rich settings. This systematic bias is driven by impostor syndrome, creating perceptions of inadequacy even if the source of the issue is biased data and not individual ability. AI-driven recruitment and performance management systems are another domain of widespread worry where bias drives impostor experiences.

Computer hiring software, now performing the tasks of large corporations globally, utilises history to eliminate candidates. Computer programs inherit inherent bias. The case of Amazon's 2018 recruiting software that muzzled women applicants due to being trained on masculine-hiring data reflects the danger. For disabled individuals, these algorithms impose disability-based discrimination via lower-priority résumés, which might depict non-linear career experience, periods of absence from work caused by disability, or disability accommodations diverging from algorithmic standards for productivity (Chang, 2023). Artificial intelligence-powered performance management tools monitor productivity regarding keystrokes, office working hours, or assignment time. They seldom identify accommodations for disability, such as flexible working hours or assistive technology. Disabled women would then be graded as "less productive" even when they produce the same output quality. Structural devaluation helps create impostor syndrome because after algorithmic scores place a person as a performer below their capability, they begin doubting themselves. Evidence by the International Labour Organisation validates that disabled women are subject to much higher degrees of unemployment and underemployment than other individuals, and is further supported by discriminatory algorithmic forces (New ILO Working Paper Exposes Significant 'Disability Wage Gap' | International Labour Organisation. Stigmatisation of gender and disability in cultures also intersects with digital exclusion to compound impostor sentiments further.

Disabled women in the majority of societies, and particularly the Global South, are already subordinated by patriarchal attitudes that locate them as dependent or incompetent. Double exclusion occurs where AI technologies developed in Western societies are not attuned to their cultural realities and needs. For example, e-learning sites that have been established in India and a portion of Africa are spatially non-conformist with the local language or assistive technology, hence incapacitating women with disabilities from being able to contribute fully. Technology of exclusion supports the cultural narratives about disability because it renders women with disabilities "incapable" of adjusting to technological advancements. In the worlds of work and learning, that exclusion is internalised as impostor feelings: disabled women internalise disabling system barriers as personal failures (Bigler et al., 2025). That coordination of cultural stigma and digital invisibility is strongly powerful, with a powerful feedback loop amplifying impostor syndrome in worlds where validation and acknowledgement are already lacking. With all that threat looming, however, AI also holds immense worth fighting impostor syndrome by offering technology that maximises access and autonomy.

AI assistive technology with disabilities, such as bright screen readers, predictive communication devices, and accessible software, empowers women with disabilities to acquire education and work on a relatively level playing field. For instance, Microsoft's Seeing AI app narrates visual information in real time, and AI-powered captioning apps empower deaf women with communicative agency. The technologies reduce the need for help, enhance self-efficacy, and undermine impostor syndrome so disabled women can demonstrate competence and mastery. (Krishnan & Manickam, 2024). AI based on inclusive design can push mainstream accessibility further. When institutions adopt AI technologies that enable various abilities, such as adaptive keyboarding or workflow change through AI, it warrants the inclusion of disabled women. This warrant directly combats the internalised self-doubt that is impostor syndrome by creating places where contributions are respected without judgment. AI can also be employed for mentorship facilitation and mental well-being counselling, which is key in preventing impostor syndrome.

Machine learning-driven AI career counselling websites can efficiently place disabled women in suitable jobs based on competency, eradicating some biases instilled through conventional recruitment procedures. Similarly, Sophie's X websites can provide counselling and opinions based on individual requirements that instil confidence in disabled women about what they can do. Artificial intelligence technologies such as Cognitive Behavioural Therapy (CBT) chatbots and therapy apps based on artificial intelligence are being applied more and more in the area of coping with psychiatry to relieve anxiety, depression, and feelings of impostor (Zaker Ul Oman et al., 2024). Never a substitute for human therapy, these technologies are opening up low-cost, level interventions to help disabled women cope with feelings of impostor. Another potential area is a safe, non-judgmental space to discuss self-doubt and how it should be managed, particularly where this access is limited in a work environment.

Policy-driven AI intervention is another such area that has positive news. Within the EU, inclusive education technology has been constructed under Horizon 2020 to address various learning needs, including the needs of disabled learners. Initiatives such as AI4All in the US strive to democratize education on AI and offer training and materials for underrepresented groups, such as women and disabled students. Such initiatives promote skills development and counteract impostor sentiment by publicly declaring marginalised groups' ability and contribution. Where inclusion in policymaking on AI is mandated through policy, it creates structural conditions that negate the structural enablement of impostor syndrome. (Pagliara et al., 2024). By incorporating accessibility requirements and representation ambitions into the regulation of AI, governments can steer AI away from being a tool of exclusion and an instrument of empowerment. Two-sidedness of AI presents an ethics dilemma: since it can level a playing field and empower women with disabilities, so too might it be responsible for increased exclusion and empower impostor syndrome. Whereas AI is a potential empowerment agent with assistive technologies, learning spaces for all, and mental health intervention, it also has the potential to exacerbate inequalities through discriminatory data, exclusionary design, and surveillance-based assessment regimes. (Marzia Ebrahimi et al., 2024). This double-edged technology poses challenging questions to policymakers, technologists, and society. Are policymakers prepared to deploy AI on an industrial scale when its dangers are so stark for marginalised groups? How can inclusivity become substantive design input to give disabled women visibility and recognition? The response is not to avoid AI but to engage with its ethical nuances. With rights-based governance, participatory design, and intersectional analysis, AI can be tasked with empowerment, rather than exclusion.

VII. FINDINGS

A consideration of legal frameworks, take-up of AI, and psychological effects provides a four-dimensional range of consequences that encompass the double impact of AI to give birth to impostor syndrome among disabled women. These consequences encompass how AI can reinforce or constrain the impostor feeling depending on how it is designed and utilised. Exclusionary AI technologies employed as biased information, technology unavailability, or culturally insensitive applications are bound to validate internalised inadequacy. For example, application software punishing non-linear career development or performance monitoring systems refusing accommodation validates the null hypothesis that disabled women are incompetent. But inclusive AI breaks the game. Features like screen reader, live caption, or adaptive learning tools level the playing ground for women with disability, thereby authenticating their capability and disabating doubt. This duplicity reveals that the dynamic between AI and impostor syndrome is not intrinsic but determined by design, policy intervention, and cultures (Kooli & Chakraoui, 2025). The second of these findings is the lack of strong intersectional AI policies, and this adds to the psychological vulnerability of women with disabilities. The current legal and ethical frameworks, like the UNCRPD and CEDAW, speak separately to disability and gender but hardly intersect the two in the context of AI. The result is the failure to cover persons who possess both identities. Women with disabilities, not receiving intersectional protection, are disproportionately likely to be rendered vulnerable to exclusionary discrimination. International Labour Organisation data of 2021 indicates that women with disabilities have close to a doubling of the unemployment rate of non-disabled women, and those inequalities now also manifest in algorithmic recruitment (Venkatachalam, 2023). Failure to explicitly mention intersectional damages in AI regulatory frameworks ensures impostor syndrome will more likely be felt as a structural issue, as women are confronted with internalising systematic exclusion without official entry into doing something about it.

Third, the report refers to disabled women's systematic exclusion from AI governance and development. The underrepresentation of disabled women in data sets, policy-making groups, and technical design teams ensures their experience is not captured in AI systems. Securing exclusionary tendencies because AI systems based on incomplete data sets do not represent disabled women's real experiences. For example, UNESCO (2021) has outlined how AI-educational systems tend to be non-inclusive to disabled students, a weakness that further secures their exclusion in school. The absence of disabled women from decision-making not only denies them chances but also strips them of self-confidence, increasing impostor syndrome by sending a message of abandonment by society for their work. Last but not least, rights-based AI frameworks are being widely adopted across the globe, yet their use remains uneven. (Ho et al., 2025). EU AI Act (2024) and UNESCO's Recommendation on the Ethics of AI (2021) are a few instances that follow sound practices in that advanced risk AI systems are subject to bias audit and accessibility testing. These two documents stress fairness and inclusion, but these norms never have a binding force, particularly in the Global South. In all countries in the Global South, such as India and most of Africa, the hurried deployment of AI does not have stringent regulatory protection. (Goktas & Grzybowski, 2025). This uneven deployment malignantly creates a mosaic where women with disabilities are afforded protection by advanced law in one section but not another. Paradoxes in rights-based planning create a fabric of protection, decreasing international equity and inflicting exclusion and related psychological harm on massive numbers of people.

Taken together, these results support the conclusion that impostor syndrome among disabled women is both a symptom of an infirmity within the person and also a symptom of AI design, governance, and implementation inequities. AI systems reinforce impostor syndrome where they model exclusionary practice, yet can also counteract it where inclusiveness and accessibility are foundational principles. Intersectional policymaking, because there is no such thing, disabled women are disabled from crafting a piece within government, and disparate application of rights-based platforms all buttress how the imperative need to change arises. Bridging these gaps is essential not just for ending impostor syndrome but also to preserve the dignity, identity, and autonomy of disabled women in the era of intelligent machines.

VIII. RECOMMENDATIONS AND WAY FORWARD

The contribution of this research is to highlight both the risks and rewards of AI in inducing impostor syndrome among disabled women. To be an empowerment tool as opposed to an exclusion tool, there needs to be adopted practical, legal, and policy recommendations. The recommendations are not only to combat impostor syndrome but also to uphold the human identity and dignity of disabled women during the era of intelligent machines.

Figure 5. Major recommendations for inclusive AI to address impostor syndrome among women with disabilities

Major Recommendations	
	Embedding Universal Design in AI Systems
	Mandating Representation in AI Design and Testing
	Establishing AI Ethics Oversight Boards with Intersectional Diversity
	Promoting AI Literacy and Psychological Resilience
	Strengthening Legal Frameworks
	Fostering Global Cooperation

Universal design must be built into AI systems from the start, promoting products and systems that are usable by as wide a population as possible across abilities. AI-education systems, work systems, and health technology must be designed with accessibility as a core requirement and not an aside. For example, making e-learning spaces screen reader accessible or employing responsive-to-non-linear-career algorithms is a design choice that includes rather than excludes disabled women. (Díaz-Rodríguez et al., 2023). Universal design is not a matter of maximising access but eradicating the psychological exclusion that creates impostor syndrome.

Another primary recommendation is to compel the incorporation of disabled women into each pipeline of AI development, design, and testing. Their labour lies behind the success of blind spots in algorithmic systems that nondisabled developers might not catch. Representation should transcend symbolic inclusion, i.e., disabled women being part of leadership, advisory, and test teams for all AI projects. It will be able to carry AI systems to be representative and inclusive of diverse needs and not replicate stereotypes. This meeting confronts impostor syndrome face-to-face by authenticating disabled women's capability and expertise as the site of technological futures. In order to avoid failure of accountability on both sides, governments and institutions must institute AI ethics boards with clear-cut terms of reference for intersectional inclusion of diversity. The boards shall be responsible for examining high-risk uses of AI in education, employment, and healthcare and be authorised to demand remedial action in case discrimination or exclusion is detected. Disabled women, human rights professionals, and gender rights professionals must be required to decide based on the real experience of those most likely to be excluded. Sanctions within existing measures of control must be sufficient to not legitimise token compliance with accessibility.

Structural reforms cannot end women's impostor syndrome of disability; empowering the people must also happen. AI literacy training for women with disability specifically can equip them with the skills and understanding to subvert and negotiate disabling systems. Coupled with psychological resilience therapy, peer support groups, and online mental health interventions, these interventions can enable disabled women to comprehend systemic discrimination rather than internalise it as individual failure. For instance, cognitive behaviour therapy through computer mental health programs with artificial intelligence can be included in extensive community programs to eradicate self-doubt.

Current disability and equality laws must be reformed to specifically address the fight against AI-enabled discrimination and its psychological impacts. The UN-CRPD, CEDAW, and domestic law, such as the Rights of Persons with Disabilities Act (India), ADA (United States of America), and the Equality Act (United Kingdom), must be reinterpreted to address the reality of algorithmic rule. This involves recognition of psychological harm, such as impostor syndrome, as actual effects of discrimination from the system. Legal frameworks must make compliance mandatory on the side of employers and developers to experiment with test AI systems for the sake of testing inclusivity and accessibility at the risk of default. Incorporation of intersectionality into such laws will ensure that the intersectional lives of disabled women are not marginalised. Lastly, AI and impostor syndrome need to be dealt with by international cooperation. The global nature of AI development requires harmonisation and consistency for overall protection. The United Nations, UNESCO, and regional systems like the European and African Union must come together to protect legally binding international standards for equitable AI. Such coordination can be utilised as a bridge to bridge the Global North and South divides to render women with disabilities from around the world accessible to AI systems sensitised to their rights and identities. Information sharing, technical support, and capacity building must be part of global efforts to enable low- and middle-income countries to adopt inclusivity in AI.

IX. CONCLUSION

Impostor syndrome, as a long-term inner psychological battle with self-doubt and suspicion of one's abilities as well as low self-efficacy, is now internalised and also a product of structural exclusion in AI cultures. Artificial Intelligence in education systems, labour markets, and health systems increasingly conditions human evaluation, inclusion, and valuation. Women who are disabled represent an amplified risk of impostor syndrome in the sense that they suffer under the intersectional disadvantage of disability, gendered discrimination, and technophobia. Their accounts represent larger structural injustices in technology design, regulation, and cultural normalising. (Chua et al., 2025). The findings of this study resonate with the double-edged nature of AI as a risk multiplier and empowerment machine.

Along the way, proprietary data sets, discriminatory hiring algorithms, and gated locations introduce invisibility and imposter sentiments. On the other hand, inclusive design, accessibility-augmenting AI tools, and policy intervention can help reinforce competence and build confidence. (Assefa, 2024). This paradox leads us to study AI as a technological advance and a social matter with long-term implications for identity construction and mental health. Action needs to be taken in the future: inclusive, accessible, and ethically governed AI spaces need to be put on the agenda so that disabled women's identity and dignity are maintained.

The imposition of universal design, inclusion in regulation and design, and strengthening of legal regimes are not impossible tasks but necessary imperatives. All these steps must accompany international cooperation, harmonising standards to protect individuals in the Global North and other marginalised groups worldwide. This study is worth it due to its interdisciplinary construction. By bringing together psychology, disability studies, law, and regulation of AI, it offers a paradigm for considering impostor syndrome in women with disabilities as an intersectional issue. Most significantly, it maps trajectories of reform that engage psychological vulnerabilities and structural injustice. In this sense, the study highlights that the future of AI should not only be harmonious between innovation and efficiency but also maintain human dignity and construct inclusive identities in the era of technology.

REFERENCES

Assefa, Dr. E. A. (2024). The Double-Edged Sword of Artificial Intelligence (AI) in Education: Maximising benefits while mitigating risks. *The Journal of Quality in Education, 14*(24), 154–176. DOI: 10.37870/joqie.v14i24.450

Australian Human Rights Commission. (2008, December 1). *The Elimination of All Forms of Discrimination Against Women (CEDAW)*. https://humanrights.gov.au/our-work/sex-discrimination/publications/elimination-all-forms-discrimination-against-women-cedaw

Bailey, M., & Mobley, I. A. (2019). Work in the Intersections: A Black Feminist Disability Framework. *Gender & Society, 33*(1), 19–40. DOI: 10.1177/0891243218801523

Belenguer, L. (2022). AI bias: Exploring discriminatory algorithmic decision-making models and applying possible machine-centric solutions adapted from the pharmaceutical industry. *AI and Ethics, 2*(4), 771–787. DOI: 10.1007/s43681-022-00138-8

Bigler, C., & Pita, Y., & K.C., S. (2025). Are we leaving women with disabilities in the Global South behind? How the reinforcement of different forms of violence leads to unsustainable development. *Women's Studies International Forum, 109*, 103051. DOI: 10.1016/j.wsif.2024.103051

Brinkman, A. H., Rea-Sandin, G., Lund, E. M., Fitzpatrick, O. M., Gusman, M. S., & Boness, C. L., & Scholars for Elevating Equity and Diversity (SEED). (2023). Shifting the discourse on disability: Moving to an inclusive, intersectional focus. *The American Journal of Orthopsychiatry, 93*(1), 50–62. DOI: 10.1037/ort0000653

Chang, X. (2023). Gender Bias in Hiring: An Analysis of the Impact of Amazon's Recruiting Algorithm. *Advances in Economics. Management and Political Sciences, 23*(1), 134–140. DOI: 10.54254/2754-1169/23/20230367

Chua, S. M., Tan, I. Y. K., Thummachai, M. E., Chew, Q. H., & Sim, K. (2025). Impostor syndrome, associated factors and impact on well-being across medical undergraduates and postgraduate medical professionals: A scoping review. *BMJ Open, 15*(7), e097858. DOI: 10.1136/bmjopen-2024-097858

Clance, P. R., & Imes, S. A. (1978). The imposter phenomenon in high-achieving women: Dynamics and therapeutic intervention. *Psychotherapy (Chicago, Ill.), 15*(3), 241–247. DOI: 10.1037/h0086006

Convention on the Rights of Persons with Disabilities. (2006). OHCHR. https://www.ohchr.org/en/instruments-mechanisms/instruments/convention-rights-persons-disabilities

Dastin, J. (2018). *Insight—Amazon scraps secret AI recruiting tool that showed bias against women | Reuters*. https://www.reuters.com/article/world/insight-amazon-scraps-secret-ai-recruiting-tool-that-showed-bias-against-women-idUSKCN1MK0AG/

Díaz-Rodríguez, N., Del Ser, J., Coeckelbergh, M., López De Prado, M., Herrera-Viedma, E., & Herrera, F. (2023). Connecting the dots in trustworthy Artificial Intelligence: From AI principles, ethics, and key requirements to responsible AI systems and regulation. *Information Fusion*, *99*, 101896. DOI: 10.1016/j.inffus.2023.101896

Ebrahimi, M., Rahimi, B., Sharifi, M., Sadat, D., Amiri, N., Khalil, S., & Quraishi, T. (2024). Empowering Women through Artificial Intelligence: Opportunities and Challenges. *Journal Electrical and Computer Experiences*, *2*(2), 38–46. DOI: 10.59535/jece.v2i2.346

Ernst, K. P., Pagot, R., & Prá, J. R. (2024). Sustainable development goal 5: Women's political participation in South America. *World Development Sustainability*, *4*, 100138. DOI: 10.1016/j.wds.2024.100138

Ferrara, E. (2023). Fairness and Bias in Artificial Intelligence: A Brief Survey of Sources, Impacts, and Mitigation Strategies. *Sci*, *6*(1), 3. DOI: 10.3390/sci6010003

Ferri, D., Tekuchova, I., & Krolla, E. (2024). BETWEEN DISABILITY AND CULTURE: THE SEARCH FOR A LEGAL TAXONOMY OF SIGN LANGUAGES IN THE EUROPEAN UNION. *The International and Comparative Law Quarterly*, *73*(3), 669–706. DOI: 10.1017/S0020589324000253

Foley, A., & Melese, F. (2025). Disabling AI: Power, exclusion, and disability. *British Journal of Sociology of Education*, •••, 1–22. DOI: 10.1080/01425692.2025.2519482

Frie, E., Meier, M., & Kohl, T. (Eds.). (2019). *Dynamics of Social Change and Perceptions of Threat* (p. 156690). Mohr Siebeck., DOI: 10.1628/978-3-16-156690-5

Goktas, P., & Grzybowski, A. (2025). Shaping the Future of Healthcare: Ethical Clinical Challenges and Pathways to Trustworthy AI. *Journal of Clinical Medicine*, *14*(5), 1605. DOI: 10.3390/jcm14051605

Hajiheydari, N., Delgosha, M. S., & Saheb, T. (2025). AI in medical diagnosis: A contextualised study of patient motivations and concerns. *Social Science & Medicine*, *371*, 117850. DOI: 10.1016/j.socscimed.2025.117850

Ho, J. Q. H., Hartanto, A., Koh, A., & Majeed, N. M. (2025). Gender biases within Artificial Intelligence and ChatGPT: Evidence, Sources of Biases and Solutions. *Computers in Human Behavior: Artificial Humans*, *4*, 100145. DOI: 10.1016/j.chbah.2025.100145

Hogan, A. J. (2019). Social and medical models of disability and mental health: Evolution and renewal. *Canadian Medical Association Journal, 191*(1), E16–E18. DOI: 10.1503/cmaj.181008

Huecker, M. R., Shreffler, J., McKeny, P. T., & Davis, D. (2025). Imposter Phenomenon. In *StatPearls*. StatPearls Publishing., https://www.ncbi.nlm.nih.gov/books/NBK585058/

Jha, A., & Mundhra, J. (2023). *HOW ACCOMMODATING IS REASONABLE ACCOMMODATION: ANALYSING INDIA'S RIGHTS OF PERSONS WITH DISABILITIES ACT, 2016.*

Khor, E. T., & K, M. (2023). A Systematic Review of the Role of Learning Analytics in Supporting Personalized Learning. *Education Sciences, 14*(1), 51. DOI: 10.3390/educsci14010051

Kooli, C., & Chakraoui, R. (2025). AI-driven assistive technologies in inclusive education: Benefits, challenges, and policy recommendations. *Sustainable Futures : An Applied Journal of Technology, Environment and Society, 10*, 101042. DOI: 10.1016/j.sftr.2025.101042

Krishnan, D. R., & Manickam, D. S. (2024). Enhancing Accessibility: Exploring the Impact of AI in Assistive Technologies for Disabled Persons. *Nafath, 9*(25). Advance online publication. DOI: 10.54455/MCN2505

Lazarus, A. (2025). *Narrative Rx: A Quick Guide to Narrative Medicine for Students, Residents, and Attendings*. https://escholarship.org/uc/item/8z48215f

Mason, A., & Minerva, F. (2022). Should the Equality Act 2010 Be Extended to Prohibit Appearance Discrimination? *Political Studies, 70*(2), 425–442. DOI: 10.1177/0032321720966480

Meharunisa, S., Almugren, H., Sarabdeen, M., Mabrouk, F., & Kijas, A. C. M. (2024). The impact of artificial intelligence on women's empowerment, and work-life balance in Saudi educational institutions. *Frontiers in Psychology, 15*, 1432541. DOI: 10.3389/fpsyg.2024.1432541

Mirza, M., Esht, V., Verma, M., Bahadur, B., Jaiswal, A. K., Alagarajan, M., & Kakkar, R. (2025). Epidemiology of disability and access to disability support and rehabilitation services in India: A secondary data analysis of the National Sample Survey (2018). *BMJ Open, 15*(5), e090220. DOI: 10.1136/bmjopen-2024-090220

Nationen, V. (Ed.). (2014). *The Convention on the Rights of Persons with Disabilities: Training guide*. United Nations.

New ILO working paper exposes significant 'disability wage gap' | International Labour Organisation. (2024, August 28). https://www.ilo.org/resource/news/new-ilo-working-paper-exposes-significant-disability-wage-gap

Oman, Z. U., Siddiqua, A., & Noorain, R. (2024). Artificial Intelligence and its ability to reduce recruitment bias. *World Journal of Advanced Research and Reviews*, *24*(1), 551–564. DOI: 10.30574/wjarr.2024.24.1.3054

Ozmen Garibay, O., Winslow, B., Andolina, S., Antona, M., Bodenschatz, A., Coursaris, C., Falco, G., Fiore, S. M., Garibay, I., Grieman, K., Havens, J. C., Jirotka, M., Kacorri, H., Karwowski, W., Kider, J., Konstan, J., Koon, S., Lopez-Gonzalez, M., Maifeld-Carucci, I., & Xu, W. (2023). Six Human-Centred Artificial Intelligence Grand Challenges. *International Journal of Human-Computer Interaction*, *39*(3), 391–437. DOI: 10.1080/10447318.2022.2153320

Pagliara, S. M., Bonavolontà, G., Pia, M., Falchi, S., Zurru, A. L., Fenu, G., & Mura, A. (2024). The Integration of Artificial Intelligence in Inclusive Education: A Scoping Review. *Information (Basel)*, *15*(12), 774. DOI: 10.3390/info15120774

Price, P. C., Holcomb, B., & Payne, M. B. (2024). Gender differences in impostor phenomenon: A meta-analytic review. *Current Research in Behavioral Sciences*, *7*, 100155. DOI: 10.1016/j.crbeha.2024.100155

Qiu, N., Jiang, Y., Sun, Z., & Du, M. (2023). The impact of disability-related deprivation on employment opportunity at the neighbourhood level: Does family socioeconomic status matter? *Frontiers in Public Health*, *11*, 1232829. DOI: 10.3389/fpubh.2023.1232829

Recommendation on the Ethics of Artificial Intelligence. (2024). UNESCO. https://www.unesco.org/en/articles/recommendation-ethics-artificial-intelligence

Umucu, E., Vernon, A. A., Pan, D., Qin, S., Solis, G., Campa, R., & Lee, B. (2025). Health inequities among persons with disabilities: A global scoping review. *Frontiers in Public Health*, *13*, 1538519. DOI: 10.3389/fpubh.2025.1538519

UNESCO. (2020). *Global Education Monitoring (GEM) Report 2020 | UNESCO*. https://www.unesco.org/en/articles/global-education-monitoring-gem-report-2020

Venkatachalam, S. (2023). *Exploring the Horizons of Access to Justice: An Analysis of Disabled Women Who are Subjected to Violence in India*. https://research-information.bris.ac.uk/en/studentTheses/exploring-the-horizons-of-access-to-justice

Whaley, B. A., Martinis, J. G., Pagano, G. F., Barthol, S., Senzer, J., Williamson, P. R., & Blanck, P. D. (2024). The Americans with Disabilities Act and Equal Access to Public Spaces. *Laws*, *13*(1), 5. DOI: 10.3390/laws13010005

Wickenden, M. (2023). Disability and other identities?—How do they intersect? *Frontiers in Rehabilitation Sciences*, *4*, 1200386. DOI: 10.3389/fresc.2023.1200386

Wolbring, G., & Nasir, L. (2024). Intersectionality of Disabled People through a Disability Studies, Ability-Based Studies, and Intersectional Pedagogy Lens: A Survey and a Scoping Review. *Societies (Basel, Switzerland)*, *14*(9), 176. DOI: 10.3390/soc14090176

Chapter 14

Impostor Syndrome in Tech Industries: A Case Study Approach to AI Developers, Data Scientists, and Innovators

Shrutika Prakash Mokashi
https://orcid.org/0009-0009-0377-3336
Assa Abloy, New Haven, USA

Ayush Jaiswal
https://orcid.org/0009-0007-5281-1250
Genuine Parts Company, Atlanta, USA

Kishore Subramanya Hebbar
https://orcid.org/0009-0007-4203-8698
Intercontinental Exchange, USA

ABSTRACT

Impostor Syndrome in tech industry has become a widespread issue, especially among AI developers, data scientists and innovators who live under a high-pressure, fast-changing work environment. Such specialists are often plagued by self-doubt, wondering how competent they are in the face of obvious skills, credentials, and accomplishments. With technology developing at an increasingly rapid pace and the competitive need for revolutionary ideas, the mental pressure to keep up and the sense of inferiority are growing. Case study methods demonstrate that many exceptionally gifted individuals tend to explain their peers' successes by luck, rather than their talent and worry that they themselves will be unmasked as "frauds." Such structures do not only affect the mental well-being of individuals, they also stifle

DOI: 10.4018/979-8-3373-6618-0.ch014

creativity, collaboration and productivity in organizations. Impostor Syndrome can be countered with individual interventions like mentorship, peer-support networks, and workplace cultures that value learning as much as outcomes.

1. INTRODUCTION

The technology field is among the most flexible, creative, and fierce in today's digital environment. Disciplines like AI, data science, and technology innovation play a central role in the worldwide process of transformation that influences economies and industries, as well as social relationships (Guenes et al., 2024). Workers within the industry are generally respected as well-trained, intelligent and innovatory change agents. But behind this veneer of success lurks a psychological phenomenon that is rising at an alarming rate, but seldom acknowledged. Impostor syndrome is a long-term, internalized belief that is actually failures, despite achievements and otherwise believing rationally that we are indeed competent. In tech companies, which have a fast moving pace and high technical bar, Impostor Syndrome is particularly pronounced and has specifically unique consequences.

The concept of this chapter is found in psychological and technological convergence. But unlike classic professions, new fields like AI development, data science, and technological innovation demand lifelong learning, flexibility, and experimentation. Innovation is moving so fast with all these new tools, frameworks and methodologies that the constant pressure to stay current and show mastery is a huge drain. This continuous change means even the best of us can't help but feel like we're not enough, like we're always missing out. What is more is that successful individuals in tech from precocious startup founders who find cracks in existing industries, to lauded data scientists who publish such earth-shaking research are highly visible and contribute to feelings of inferiortiy and comparability (Caporusso, 2023). The culture of innovation and perfection that characterizes so many organizations creates an environment where it is derided to admit vulnerability or limitations, which further compounds the internal struggle of impostorism that so many people experience.

The reasons for investigating Impostor Syndrome in tech environments are varied. At a personal level, chronic self-doubt destroys mental health, causing anxiety, burnout, and lower job satisfaction. Research suggests that Impostor Syndrome tends to affect high performing individuals and underrepresented groups in technology, including women and minority professionals. For AI developers and data scientists who often collaborate on complex, high-risk projects these internal battles can stifle creativity, critical thinking and problem-solving. A low self confidence level can cause a person not to speak out with creative and novel ideas, retarding his or her prospects of leadership and career growth, hindering personal and organizational growth. The tech industry needs to cultivate more attentive, supportive environments that enable it to support and retain employees, and to foster ongoing innovation (Wang & Huang, 2025).

1.1 Background and Significance of the Study

The impostor syndrome is not just harmful in terms of the individual; it also has wide-reaching negative consequences at an organization level. Tech companies live on experimentation, risk, and the ability to learn from failure. When employees are anxious about being revealed as incompetent, they might refrain from trying new things, minimize their accomplishments, or turn away from opportunities that require pushing limits. Impostor Syndrome among tech teams is contagious, and it affects group dynamics, communication and trust. In industries such as IT and R&D, interdisciplinary professionals like developers/researchers/innovators should work together closely, and when unsolved psychological barriers and gaps remain 'unpatched,' it shall reduce the efficiency of the team work and cooperation (Lane & Mountford-Brown, 2025).

From a social context, it is just as profound. The tech companies are really key to tackling many of the world's key problems, from creating ethical AIs to solving problems in healthcare and development. When these talented individuals are shackled by self-doubt, we can compromise our ability to innovate (Oliveira et al., 2025). Impostor syndrome overlaps with diversity and inclusion concerns. Groups underrepresented in technology are more likely to encounter obstacles such as bias, stereotypes, and systemic disparities that further fuel impostorism. To raise awareness on this dynamic, hence, it is not only a question of achieving well-being and individual success: it is also a challenge to developing fair and inclusive technological environments.

Through a case study of AI developers, data scientists and innovators, overworks of how Impostor Syndrome may manifest in various professional positions in the tech industry are offered. But AI developers, who create intelligent machines that need to be precise and ethical, often face overwhelming pressure to adapt to rapidly changing norms (Mosurinjohn & Loewen-Colon, 2023). Data scientists encounter a similar struggle to keep up with expertise as they navigate complex data sets and ever-changing analytical tools. An impostor experience among innovators especially among entrepreneurs is rife in a high-risk, stingy environment such as the startup and tech disruption one in which failing is part of the deal, and where the scrutiny is fierce. Exploration of such functions in case studies not only portrays the everyday life experience of people, but it also offers an important source of information for organizations, which should be addressed in targeted interventions.

Ultimately, the contribution of the study may be its power to translate psychological insight into organizational sense. Detailing the pervasiveness and implications of Impostor Syndrome in the technology sector, it demands systemic interventions like mentor programs, peer-support networks, inclusive leaders and work environments which destigmatize vulnerability and learning. Dealing with Impostor Syndrome is not just about personal well-being, but rather concerns creating tech communities that are resilient, innovative and diverse enough to take society forward in an ever more digital landscape (Li et al., 2024).

2. IMPOSTOR SYNDROME: KEY TRAITS AND MANIFESTATIONS IN PROFESSIONALS

Impostor syndrome is the mental challenge in which individuals doubt their accomplishments and have a persistent fear of being exposed as a "fraud" and yet are unable to accept that their success is evident. For high achievers like those in tech or medicine or academia, it is actualized through specific qualities that also affect mental health as well as work habits (Salina, 2023). The key point is the unwillingness to take responsibility for achievements and tendency to explain them by attributing them to luck, circumstances, overestimation of other people's abilities, etc., rather than engaging in proper self-praise for the skill and effort. They may attribute their triumphs which can create a cycle of self-doubt. A further characteristic is perfectionism, in which people establish standards that are too high, and consider the smallest slip to be a sign of failure.

This generally leads to over-preparation, overtime and burnout, perpetuating a cycle of fear and negative self-imagery. The common expression is the "fear of being found out," in which employees fret that one day their coworkers or bosses will find out they are not as capable as they seem. This fear prevents people from talking, from asking for help and promotes isolation in the workplace. For many Impostor Syndrome sufferers, feedback is painful; they often take constructive feedback as an indication of their own incompetence, rather than a suggestion for improvement. The syndrome is also characterized by comparison with peers. People will always compare themselves with others which will make them feel inferior because they can never reach other's level. In technology this is compounded by the pace of change in the field, with new skills, tools, and frameworks constantly emerging leading even the most skilled persons to feel old or lack the edge (Sun et al., 2024). Gender and cultural factors interact with these displays; women, minorities and underrepresented groups in the workplace exhibit more impostor feelings as a result of systematic barriers and stereotypes.

These characteristics don't just manifest in low self-esteem; the stigmatizing of these encounters can have a catastrophic effect on career when employees can refuse offers of promotion or leadership roles, or avoid new levels of work altogether for fear of failure or discovery. Symptoms spill over to the workplace, where they may avoid sharing creative ideas, overcompensate by working more or even be distrustful in relational settings. Left unchecked, these patters restrict creativity, suppress productivity, and pollute your culture. Recognition of these characteristics and presentations is important to inform interventions that focus on both psychological resilience and supportive workplaces. By understanding Impostor Syndrome is a common condition affecting practitioners, organizations can do their part by creating proactive cultures, characterized by inclusiveness, empathy, and growth for the cultivation of talent (Ruffino, 2022).

3. IMPOSTOR SYNDROME IN TECHNOLOGY INDUSTRIES

There is no shortage of imposter stories in the world of tech in technology, with its fast pace, high stakes, and relentless learning curves, Impostor Syndrome has emerged as a major toxic culprit. Tech, unlike legacy professions, both AI and data science and even software development require continuous up graded self, with some even confusing experience to being unfit or unethical to fit in the position. Because technology is changing so rapidly, with tools, languages, and way of thinking coming and going on a monthly-basis, it is impossible to feel like you're no longer playing catch-up at any point in your professional career.

This leaves many feeling like phonies who could be outed as not as smart as their colleagues, and not up to the challenge of more complex projects. Impostor feelings in tech are further exacerbated by the culture of excellence. What would be brushed off as a minor setback in a culture of breakthrough innovation and perfect execution is interpreted as a failure that confirms self-doubt. The visibility of the successes in the tech space from something's who have built billion-dollar startups, to data scientists who are spearheading game-changing research creates unrealistic standards against which ordinary professionals are constantly comparing themselves. This culture of comparison is creating a toxic environment that fuels feelings of inferiority, particularly among women and minorities who already encounter systemic barriers, lack of opportunities and stereotypes within the space.

The other dimension of Impostor Syndrome in tech is its contribution to stifled collaboration and new ideas. Professionals whose self-worth is diminished may be reluctant to speak up for fear of failure or ridicule leading to stagnant creativity and decision making. These problems have wider implications for health of organisations and industry growth Impostor Syndrome diminishes self-belief, productivity and diversity in leadership roles (Rea, 2021). Tackling it in the tech industry will require systemic solutions, including mentorship programs, supportive peer circles and corporate cultures that prioritize the process of learning, experimentation and inclusion as much as the end results. By directly tackling Impostor Syndrome, technology sectors can not only better promote the mental well-being of practitioners, but can also seek to foster greater creativity, collaboration and sustainability in a sector that ultimately trades on human creative skills and intellect.

3.1 Unique Pressures in the Tech Ecosystem

Shortening product lifecycles and keeping pace in a fiercely competitive, fast-paced industry, contribute to the high stress of working in the technology industry. AI engineers, data-scientists, and innovators need to remain in the vanguard of technology and provide cutting-edge solutions. No wonder anxiety and self-doubt get in the door. A round-the-clock work culture and the threat of global competition tend to exacerbate such fears of irrelevance or under qualification. Experts, even after reaching new heights, may believe that they need to demonstrate their expertise. These distinct pressures exacerbate impostor feelings, as people feel they are falling behind industry norms, even when their work is essential to organizational well-being and technological advancement (Sivaram et al., 2023).

3.2 The Imperative of Innovation and Perfectionism

In the tech world, creativity is not only sought after, it is expected, and that can foster a kind of pressure-cooker environment that can exacerbate impostor feelings. Professionals are frequently judged based on the capacity to create both new but also scalable and bug-free solutions in the snapshot of time frenzy (Ishtaiwi et al., 2025). Perfectionism a prospect of the world that dictates that we need to be perfect, follow perfect mate, we need to perform perfectly in all areas of our lives that worrying comes from that prospect of imperfection. For AI developers and data scientists whose work filters through to critical systems, the smallest errors may feel magnified, fueling a fear of getting caught out as incompetent. The imperious for innovation also creates over-preparation and risk-aversion as people become paralyzed thinking that only perfect order of execution justifies self-authenticity. This cycle feeds burnout and stifles creativity, not the sort of innovation that desire.

3.3 Cultural and Gender Dimensions in Tech

Cultural and demographic factors are integral to the experience of Impostor Syndrome in tech. Women and minorities receive stereotypes, biases, and systemic obstacles that make self-doubt larger. Women working in male-dominated tech positions might experience more stress trying to justify their value, which can escalate impostor feelings. The professionals from varying cultural contexts may experience exclusionary practices or limited leader representation, further perpetuating the feeling of not belonging. Such differences lead to uneven burdens, whereby success is less appreciated or success is more harshly judged. As a result, fraud tendencies are integrated with equity and inclusion concerns, emphasizing the criticality of supportive workplace environments that recognize diverse inputs and facilitate psychological safety.

4. CASE STUDIES: AI DEVELOPERS

4.1 Self-Perceptions of Competence vs. External Expectations

There is often a big discrepancy between how competent AI builders perceive themselves and how they're perceived from the outside. On the one hand companies, clients, and the public expect AI professionals to be authorities skilled in designing intelligent systems that are accurate, ethical, and ground-breaking. And developers themselves, on the other hand, may feel that they don't have enough experience, especially with all the new algorithms, programming frameworks, and machine learning packages that are introduced. That gives a feeling of pressure of always being behind, no matter your performance. They attribute their success to luck or teamwork rather than to their own skills, which undermines their confidence and perpetuates impostor feelings (Bjorn et al., 2022). This sort of internal conflict typically cause these individuals to feel anxious, not want to take positions of leadership, or display their accomplishments, even if those accomplishments are truly revolutionary.

4.2 Influences on Creativity and Problem-Solving

It also prevents AI developers for whom creativity and problem solving is their bread and butter, to reach each of them accordingly. Developers with low self-esteem might also shy away from suggesting new ideas out of fear of being ignored or attacked by others. The pressure to never be "found out" as the fool is overwhelming, causing paralysis and discouraging ambitious software design in favor of non-inspiring, but rarely risky, development. Impostor feelings can also stifle the contribution of people in collaborative working environments for example during brainstorming sessions, potentially reducing the diversity of perspectives that is known to power AI progress. Impostor syndrome-related-perfectionism can also lead to over-thinking and indecision, thereby inhibiting project advance. Developers may be busting their butts killing themselves to make up for their lack of talent and creativity, and the result is a game that gets made quickly, but with no soul. This loss of confidence, in addition to being damaging to the individual, is detrimental to organizational progress. It is essential for creating ecosystems in which creativity can flourish, and developers are comfortable to take intellectual leaps.

4.3 Coping Strategies and Resilience

Impostor syndrome presents that there is also reason to believe many AI developers employ coping mechanisms that help to foster resilience and continue professional development. Mentors and peer-support networks can be remarkably helpful reminders that self-doubt is universal in high-stakes domains. There is often some relief in sharing your struggles with colleagues who are under the same pressures, and the normalization of impostor feelings can reduce isolation. The others use lifelong learning as a survival mechanism, turning self-doubt into a drive to learn new skills and stay updated with new tech advances (Cynthia & Roy, 2025). Creating shared strategy can have a chance to grow, but it can also be dangerous for burnout -if not in conjunction with self-compassion. Organizational interventions, such as “celebrating effort not just accomplishment,” offering a “safe fail spec” and access to mental health support also help grow resilience. Developers who learn to interpret impostor thoughts that way rather than seeing them as evidence of inadequacy come to feel and act more capable and self-assured over time. These coping strategies demonstrate that while Impostor Syndrome is a barrier, it is also an enabler of resilience in the presence of inclusive workplace cultures.

5. CASE STUDIES: DATA SCIENTISTS

Data scientists often have a tendency to make themselves and their successes smaller, good luck, available data or the collective work of the team were the reasons projects worked out rather than their own data analysis power. These feelings of impostorship can also affect collaboration, because self-doubt prevents people from proposing ideas or debating incumbents in cross-functional teams. Impostor tendencies are exacerbated for data scientists by the challenge of handling uncertain or non-authoritative facts or incomplete data, as the inherent uncertainty of the data can easily be interpreted as personal incompetence. The field’s competitive culture, in which certain high-impact findings, prediction successes and novel algorithms are celebrated, exacerbates perfectionism and fear of failure. However, resilience strategies are identifiable: peer validation, ongoing skills-transfer, and institutional focus on group achievements mitigate impostor dialectics. These are key challenges, as enabling data scientists to rise above self-doubt do more than just ensure that they feel good: it substantiates innovation, collaboration, and trust within a data driven organization (Romanishyn et al., 2025).

5.1 Navigating Constant Learning in a Data-Driven Era

Data scientists work in a field that is continually in flux as new tools, algorithms, and methodologies spring up at a swift pace. This never-ending need to level up often exacerbates impostor feelings, as practitioners find it hard to keep up to date with constantly evolving "goodness". Even experienced data scientists can experience feelings of inadequacy when comparing themselves to their peers skilled in the newest technologies. The fact of mastering in several fields from programming and machine learning to business insights amplifies the feeling that you never really "know enough." These pressures can engender anxiety and self-doubt, making Impostor Syndrome an almost unavoidable reality in this data-centred age.

5.2 Collaborative, Peer Comparison and Validation

The data scientist role is very collaborative and typically works as part of a wider team alongside engineers, business analysts and domain experts. Yet, the risk of fraud with respect to cooperation is great, and men in general will be afraid lest, if added to the number, they will diminish the value of their own services. Peer benchmarking is an especially powerful stimulus, comparing professionals' abilities, coding speed, or analytical creativity to those of their peers. This continuous measuring against others can become a cause of inadequacy, whether or not performance is actually strong (Singh, 2024). "What we really need is validation from our higher ups or co-workers to prevent us from feeling like an impostor, because most of the time we still feel negative about ourselves unless they acknowledge and recognize what we have done, which helps dismantle our self-doubt and remind us of our professional worth.

5.3 Impact on Employability and Productivity

Impostor syndrome can have a huge impact on the career development and productivity of data scientists. Low self-efficacy can result in reluctance at the thought of leadership, publishing work or applying for higher position for fear that perceived incompetence will be made evident. It results in lack of career progression and visibility in competitive industries. The productivity aspect is shown in over-preparation, too much perfectionism, and fear to take creative risks. The working of too much while it may work temporarily, burn one out and hamper creativity. In the long run, these consequences damage not only individual careers, but also the ability for organizations to apply to capacity to access the full skillsets of data science talent (Hossain, 2023).

6. ORGANIZATIONAL IMPACT OF IMPOSTOR SYNDROME: PRODUCTIVITY, INNOVATION AND TEAM DYNAMICS

Impostor syndrome is more than just a personal battle and its impact on how organizations operate is profound, and in no place are its tendrils more pronounced than a the tech industry that is defined by productivity, innovation, teamwork and ultimately success. At the level of productivity, individuals with impostor feelings frequently work harder and become less efficient, completing tasks in advance as well as above and beyond what is normally expected, in order to create and reinforce a positive image of them.

Although this might fuel the output for the time being, it often results in burnout, exhaustion and increasingly ineffective output. On the other hand, others may be under-performing, not taking on challenges, or not operating as a leader due to the fear of being "found out" which limits the capacity of the organization. Each pattern compensation and avoidance disturbs consistent productivity and creates resource management stress. Impostor tendencies also stifle innovation within technology organizations, which, for many, is the heart and soul of the company. Doubting employees become afraid to speak up with creative ideas, fears of them being mocked or dismissed, and so brainstorming and experimenting are shut down. In cultures that value perfection, people are afraid to make mistakes, causing risk aversion and safe but not innovative solutions.

This suppresses organizational competitiveness since game-changer innovations tend to come through bold, uncertain exploration. Among other powerful impacts on team dynamics, impostor-affected staff may disengage from teamwork, forego participating in meetings, or have difficulty in developing trust and communication (Lee et al., 2023). The cost of these behaviors is the loss of collective problem-solving capacity, undermining cohesiveness and promoting environments where talent is wasted. Leaders who have impostor feelings could be less likely to mentor or delegate in their leadership roles and could thus limit knowledge transfer or team development. Its knock-on effects within teams consist of low morale, poorly balanced workloads and project inefficiencies. At a macro level, organizations run the risk of losing diverse talent, because it is underrepresented groups, who report the highest levels of impostor pressure, who are more likely to leave unsupportive workplaces, adding to inclusion-related differences. Deliberate strategies are needed to tackle these organizational side effects: cultures of vulnerability as a norm, rewards for learning in parity with what is useful, and mentorship systems that value your productive contributions. Reducing impostor syndrome not only increases productivity for companies, but it also creates titan teams that are capable of thriving in quick-paced technology ecosystems (Fortunato et al., 2025).

7. INTERVENTIONS AND SOLUTIONS: BUILDING SUPPORTIVE WORKPLACE CULTURES, POLICY AND STRUCTURAL MEASURES FOR EMPLOYEE WELL-BEING

For technology industries, dealing with Impostor Syndrome means more than individuated coping strategies; it requires structural changes in workplace cultures, policies and setups that center employee health. But that would take facade cracking at the root, in supportive workplace cultures where admission of vulnerabilities, learning and growing are the norm and not some sort of weakness. Companies need to actively create psychological safety and allow employees to voice doubts, discuss challenges, and share ideas without the fear of being judged. Recognizing effort and progress regardless of final results lessens perfectionism, and weaving in mentoring equips professionals with direction, validation, and examples to follow when self-doubt strikes.

Peer support networks, workshops and open discussions about impostor feelings can also help to normalize the experience, decrease isolation and enhance resilience. In addition to culture, policies and structural interventions are key. Organizations need to implement mental health programs in organizational systems, by providing access to counseling, coaching, and stress management specifically designed to help organizations with high performance. Performance measurement needs to be such that it promotes growth, collaboration, and innovation and not just output or error-free results (Rubambiza et al., 2024). Concrete tactics like inclusive hiring, career advancement for minority groups, and leadership-seeking diversity projects help to fight systemic inequities that can heighten a sense of impostorhood. Regular manager training to identify signs of impostor struggles, and on how to give constructive feedback, can create more empathetic leaders.

The flexible working practices, equitable workloads and reward systems that recognize collective contributions may serve to reduce burnout and over compensation. The practices that drive both cultural reformation and structural change not only relieve Impostor Syndrome but help drive innovation, collaboration, and employee retention. With infusing well-being into the DNA of the organization, technology sectors can build workforces that are resilient and empowered, and people who are able not only to maintain but also stimulate creativity and progress for the future, despite a changing and complex environment.

8. ETHICAL AND PSYCHOLOGICAL CONSIDERATIONS: BALANCING PERFORMANCE WITH MENTAL HEALTH

The existence of Impostor Syndrome in tech also presents important ethical and psychological challenges by how much pressure which place on people's, how much pressure organizations put on their teams to perform and then how much of the identity cave we allow ourselves to crawl into at the end of the day. The technology industry is fueled by intense innovation, efficiency and perfect execution, which has a very real, and high psychological toll for those who come to work every day with self-doubt and fear of being perceived as a fake. From an ethical perspective, they have a responsibility to ensure that performance criterion is not on the backs of the well-being of the employees (Naseviciute & Juceviciene, 2024). That means creating a culture in which excellence is aspired to, but not perfection, and vulnerability is celebrated, not squelched.

Psychologically, impostor syndrome can manifest itself in the form of anxiety, depression, and burnout if not dealt with, underscoring the importance of taking a proactive approach to mental well-being. "It's about finding the balance, but redefining what success metrics are what it means to be creative, to learn, to collaborate, not just measure technically." It also means making mental health resources easily available and reducing the stigma around seeking support. Ethically, leaders need to realize that unrealistic performance pressures are a barrier that disproportionately affects underrepresented folks in tech and supports the reproduction of inequality and exclusion. Inclusive practices that help us create diversity; equity and psychological safety are therefore paramount to addressing impostorism responsibly. So, creating an environment in which conversations about impostoring become common, making mentorship a part of the culture, and having flexible-foundational policies ensure that people perform at high levels while also being resilient from a mental health standpoint. It's through the ethical inclusion of mental health within performance expectations that organisations will protect the duty of care and ensure sustainable levels of innovation and productivity. Ultimately of course the ethic is about recognising employees are not just for turning into output but human beings whose mental health is integral for their and the organisation's success (Martins, 2023).

9. CONCLUSION

Tech Impostor Syndrome is a complex issue which is related to organizational culture, employee-psychology and the larger social-professional expectations on us. Their effect far surpasses the level of individual well-being and includes team functioning, productivity, innovation, and retention and is vitally important for sustainable growth of the organization. Professionals who suffer from impostor feelings usually keep their struggles to themselves, which creates a cycle of self-doubt, overwork, and silence that makes collaboration and long-term performance suffer. This need to recognize impostor experiences as organizational rather than individual failures and as organizational experiences influenced by structural imperatives, diversity gaps and cultural narratives of success. Moral obligation comes down to wherever there's high performance now there's psychological safety and inclusiveness. By bundling such supportive policies, programming and conversations, organizations can redefine impostor experiences as learning opportunities versus something that impedes performance. The implications are clear: getting over Impostor Syndrome is not just about being thick-skinned, but about systemic change which links well-being, equity and innovation. After all, fighting impostor tendencies makes for healthier workplaces that encourage employees to succeed as themselves, ensuring a shared success in a fast-paced technology industry.

10. FUTURE DIRECTIONS

The way to address Impostor Syndrome in technology sectors is to promote broad-based, systemic and evidence-based solutions. Future approaches will need to combine AI-based tools for early detection of mental health risks with human-centered solutions such as coaching, counseling and mentoring programs for various employee populations. Organizational norms will shift towards more psychologically safe cultures that encourage making oneself vulnerable and being authentic instead of learning to distrust our instincts. More attention to the issues of equity and inclusion is crucial, especially in helping women, minority group members and early-career researchers who are particularly susceptible to impostor feelings. In addition, inter-disciplinary research between psychology, organization behavior and technological studies is required to gain in-depth knowledge into how impostor experiences develop in the digital and remote working environment. Internationally, industry should collaborate with the academic community and with policy decision-makers to develop best practices and legislation that provides protection for mental health while ensuring ethical performance boundaries. Funding longitudinal research will also help to understand the extent to which interventions are sustained over the long-term and to inform organization of more sustainable models of employee well-being and mental health. The future lies in redefining success to balance innovation with mental health and ensuring tech-driven progress comes from empowered, strong and genuinely self-assured workforces.

REFERENCES

Bjørn, P., Menendez-Blanco, M., & Borsotti, V. (2022). Equity & Inclusion. In *Diversity in Computer Science: Design Artefacts for Equity and Inclusion* (pp. 77–96). Springer International Publishing.

. Caporusso, N. (2023). Generative artificial intelligence and the emergence of creative displacement anxiety. *Research in Psychology and Behavior, 3*(1).

Cynthia, S. T., & Roy, B. (2025, June). An Empirical Study on the Impact of Gender Diversity on Code Quality in AI Systems. In *Proceedings of the 33rd ACM International Conference on the Foundations of Software Engineering* (pp. 1540-1549).

Fortunato, J. R., Soares, L. R., Alves, G. S., Canedo, E. D., & Mendes, F. F. (2025, April). Enhancing Women's Experiences in Software Engineering. In *2025 IEEE/ACM 47th International Conference on Software Engineering: Software Engineering in Society (ICSE-SEIS)* (pp. 37-42). IEEE.

Guenes, P., Tomaz, R., Kalinowski, M., Baldassarre, M. T., & Storey, M. A. (2024, April). Impostor phenomenon in software engineers. In *Proceedings of the 46th International Conference on Software Engineering: Software Engineering in Society* (pp. 96-106).

. Hossain, K. A. (2023). Practices and challenges of modern leadership in the era of technological advancement. *Scientific Research Journal, 11*(11).

Ishtaiwi, A., Al-Qerem, A., Aldweesh, A., & Alkasassbeh, M. (2025). A Framework for Addressing Cybersecurity Risks in the Metaverse Safeguarding Against Generative AI Threats. In *Examining Cybersecurity Risks Produced by Generative AI* (pp. 381–400). IGI Global Scientific Publishing.

Lane, A. M., & Mountford-Brown, V. G. (2025). Situating imposter syndrome in the experience of becoming and being an entrepreneurship educator. *Education + Training*, *67*(4), 507–523.

Lee, P. Y. K., Ma, N. F., Kim, I. J., & Yoon, D. (2023). Speculating on risks of AI clones to selfhood and relationships: Doppelganger-phobia, identity fragmentation, and living memories. *Proceedings of the ACM on Human-computer Interaction, 7*(CSCW1), 1-28.

Li, Z. S., Arony, N. N., Awon, A. M., Damian, D., & Xu, B. (2024). AI tool use and adoption in software development by individuals and organizations: a grounded theory study. *arXiv preprint arXiv:2406.17325*.

Martins, B. O. (2023). Security knowledges: Circulation, control, and responsible research and innovation in EU border management. *Science as Culture, 32*(3), 435–459.

Mosurinjohn, S., & Loewen-Colón, J. (2023). The Age of (the Algorithmic) Aquarius: How AI Meets Our Esoteric Needs. *American Religion, 5*(1), 137–147.

Naseviciute, L., & Juceviciene, R. (2024). Overcoming the barriers to women's career in information and communication technology business. *Equality, Diversity and Inclusion, 43*(1), 23–40.

Oliveira, A. L., Hernandez-Ramirez, R., & Ayanoglu, H. (2025, May). AI and Gender Perspectives in Startup Environments: Mitigating Bias, Challenging Stereotypes, and Design Implications. In *International Conference on Human-Computer Interaction* (pp. 396-418). Cham: Springer Nature Switzerland.

Rea, E. A. (2021). Changing the Face of Technology": Storytelling as Intersectional Feminist Practice in Coding Organizations. *Technical Communication (Washington), 68*(4), 26–39.

Romanishyn, A., Malytska, O., & Goncharuk, V. (2025). AI-driven disinformation: Policy recommendations for democratic resilience. *Frontiers in Artificial Intelligence, 8*, 1569115.

Rubambiza, G., Sengers, P., Weatherspoon, H., & Liu, J. (2024, May). Seam work and simulacra of societal impact in networking research: A critical technical practice approach. In *Proceedings of the 2024 CHI Conference on Human Factors in Computing Systems* (pp. 1-19).

Ruffino, P. (2022). Seeking deep relations in a precarious industry: Addressing mental health through independent videogame development. *Television & New Media, 23*(7), 761–776.

Salina, J. H. (2023). Humanizing the culture of technology teams: Strategies for creating healthier and more productive work environments. *Journal of Software Engineering and Applications, 16*(12), 641–671.

Singh, V. (2024). AI, women's health care, and trust: Problems and prospects. In *Artificial Intelligence and Machine Learning for Women's Health Issues* (pp. 235–254). Academic Press.

Sivaram, J., Narrain, J. M., Honnavalli, P., & Eswaran, S. (2023). Adversarial machine learning: The rise in AI-enabled crime. *Computer Fraud & Security, 2023*(2).

Sun, Y., Sheng, D., Zhou, Z., & Wu, Y. (2024). AI hallucination: Towards a comprehensive classification of distorted information in artificial intelligence-generated content. *Humanities & Social Sciences Communications*, *11*(1), 1–14.

Wang, S. J., & Huang, H. C. (2025). To ask is human, to answer divine: How awe-inspiring generative AI leads to self-enhancement and imposter anxiety. *Information Technology & People*, •••, 1–32.

Chapter 15
Legal Dimensions of Imposter Syndrome and Human Identity Crisis in the Age of Artificial Intelligence

Saurabh Chandra
https://orcid.org/0000-0003-4172-9968
Bennett University, Greater Noida, India

Pradeep Kumar Kulshrestha
https://orcid.org/0000-0002-6805-1010
Bennett University, Greater Noida, India

Versha Vahini
Bennett University, Greater Noida, India

Suparna Kundu
https://orcid.org/0009-0000-5142-8945
Amity University, Kolkata, India

ABSTRACT

The legal world is faced with impostor syndrome and human identity crisin AI era. Technology, psychology and law are intersecting in a new way that is just beginning to appear on the horizon Properly speaking, the adaptation of AI-based technology will influence not only professional decisions but also creativity and self-perception. People are often at a loss to pin down their own worthiness or legitimacy of position

DOI: 10.4018/979-8-3373-6618-0.ch015

in a machine-dominated world. This phenomenon--first noted by psychologists as "imposter syndrome" (because it makes people feel that they are taking up someone else's position and not deserving to be there)--has taken on fresh significance in the computer age. The outputs generated by those employing AI in offices, education systems and other creative industries make human input and machine aid into artificially merged matter.

1. INTRODUCTION

The debate of the insecurity that constitutes us is put in different contexts depending on time and location. The syndrome is not new to the world and its prevalence can be repeated by the work of Christine Pierce (2000). The nexus between law and marginality is still a topic of research, especially with artificial intelligence creating an efficiency imperative and a more critical attitude. The consequences are felt throughout the juridical sphere, as the need to question the distinction between automation of procedural functions and human intervention becomes apparent. Predictive analytics and automated drafting software that could make the human touch unnecessary and produce fears of obsolescence contributes to the epidemic of impostor syndrome, which is already estimated to impact 70-80 percent of legal professionals, as the pressure of higher expectations increases and perfectionism sets in. In India, the huge number of pending cases of over 50 million cases highlights the possibility that e-courts Phase III will enhance efficacy; however, some psychological implications still exist, which requires a harmonisation of e-courts Phase III with Article 21 guarantees of life and dignity.

Originally defined by Clance and Imes in 1978, imposter syndrome occurs within lawyers in the form of overpreparation and burnout, and modern versions include AI-induced impostor syndrome. The development of a paradoxical incompetence through faultless machine products destroys professional confidence. Routledge (2025) and Craft (2025) have recorded the possibility of generative AI to create hallucinations that will confuse the practitioners, thus suggesting that there will be no more trust in their own expertise and eventually this may result in malpractice suits. Legally, this raises worker rights via employment laws as per the Industrial Disputes Act (1947) and future AI guidelines by MeitY (2024), that mandate AI transparency but discount mental health externalities such as cognitive dissonance emanating from AI surveillance. Human crises of identity arise through AI's datafication of selfhood; profiles in which people can only recognise themselves as cyberinstruments deprive them of their autonomy as algorithms develop and steer behaviour, undermining Lockean conceptions of the person as a being with continuous memories. Deepfakes illustrate that, cloning those identities without consent as in Delhi High Court orders on publicity rights u/a 19(1)(a) and 21 which doesn't have AI provisions beyond IT Act section 66D but DPDP Act, 2023 protecting your data consent for AI processing, fails to address non-personal predictions creating an identity, akin to EU GDPR's pseudonymization lacunas. In the legal academy, imposter syndrome is at large, among a publish-or-perish landscape that co-opts AI as a co-author to obscure intellectual authorship, invoking copyright doctrines under Section 17 of the Copyright Act, 1957 and ethical precedents from UGC regulations. Intersectional vulnerabilities – that of gender, caste or class etc., engage more under the influence of these biased algorithms as in some hiring tools where these did prove to disadvantage a group marginalized people thus violating the very essence of article 14 equality and SC/ST (Prevention of Atrocities) Act. To the extent that AI "legal personality" debates such as those entangled with Sophia the robot's Saudi citizenship come under strain from theories of legal personhood when extended to corporations in Salomon v. Salomon (1897), cognitive human sovereignty-due notice under IHRL via the UDHR Article 1 on dignity is afforded. Autonomy requires "right to explanation" under GDPR Article 22, transposed to India's through the judicial mandate as with Puttaswamy, against black-box AI replacing judgment. There are also regulatory lacunae as India's Advisory on AI (2024) suggests harm assessments, but it doesn't have rights to psychological integrity as do the EU AI Act for its high-risk prohibitions. AI and litigation, such as case outcome predictors AI in litigation makes oneself doubt: For lawyers trained on prejudice (bar bias comes more from analogy to model than ideal philosophy), there is self-doubt sparked by AI in justice (e.g., predictions of case decisions) where the juniors are afraid of being outdated The need for human-AI hybrid bar ethics update. Workplace protections from POSH Act and MHC 2017 could extend to thinking through mandating AI impact-audits addressing bias loops that wire-in imposter feelings.

Internationally, UNESCO's AI Ethics Recommendation (2021) and the FoC's 2025 Joint Statement promote HR-IAs, with India suggested a "dual use" framework for an AI Act that achieves innovation while balancing identity concerns. Future frameworks, should incorporate epistemic justice by acknowledging marginalized knowledges in face of AI hegemony(Amartya Sen's capability approach). Protection of personality rights under litigation, eg – Anil Kapoor v. Simply Life (2023), it is evident that the courts have started to take a step back and assert judiciary's stance in respect of AI cloning which can be extended in therapeutic fields on grounds of self-perception. AI tutors in education deepen imposter syndrome among law studentsThrough standardisation measures, they promote mechanical recall of legal definitions and flash cards, resulting into rote learning that prioritises memorising over understanding. Scrutiny under the Antitrust Act, 2002, focuses on monopolies of AI such as those of Big Tech companies in order to stage off identity commodification. Bioethics-wise, AI in health diagnosis risks of attribution error, as relates telemedicine more generally under Telemedicine Practice Guidelines life crisis. A reconstructed law will need to draw on "human-centered" normative principles: mandatory disclosures for generative AI outputs, grievance redressal in cases of identity harms, and longitudinal studies on the mental health of professionals. This might be implicit in India's NITI Aayog strategy footprint (2024), but its operationalization is trailing, risking SDG 3 (health) and 16 (justice) derailments. Philosophically, communicative action in the H abermasian mould is critical of AI's strategic rationality, and promotes deliberative fora f or co-designing trusted systems (van der Miesen, 2021). People are constantly in a position to fail to describe themselves and the credibility of their role in a world that is becoming more mediated by machines. Originally, this tendency was referred to as the imposter syndrome which is a term defining the sense of self-deception and undeservingness of rank.

Composite effects of AI in predisposing to syndrome Data from Yale law studies empirically confirm that AI aggravates syndrome via comparison. Remedies are cognitive-behavioral interventions integrated with legal literacy regarding AI limitations, via Forbes strategies. Internationally, Brazil's AI Bill and US Executive Order (2023) constitute psychological safeguards capable of being mobilized through comparative jurisprudence. The bottom line: law must shift from retrospective torts to prospective rights of authenticity and of mental integrity to assure that AI enhances rather than engulfs the human, generating robust legal minds for algorithmic times.

2. CONTEXTUALIZING IMPOSTER SYNDROME IN THE DIGITAL ERA

As the inevitable new technology of AI permeates every sphere, humanity is granted both marvelous technologies and at the same time existential panic. High-achievers have long been undermined by imposter syndrome, the legitimisation of their achievements, and a constant fear of being discovered a fraud. Modern research suggests that the malady has turned into a mass disease caused by AI machines that are stronger than human intelligence to produce fake content and automate artistic and emotional displays with unnatural realism. The resultant crisis of human identity is on the border of a theoretical dilemma and life experience: as AI undermines the differences between real self and simulated simulation by deepfakes and AI-generated avatars, people must challenge the concept of authenticity, independence, and realness of the self. The ontological inquiry into the meaning of being human in a world where machines are capable of simulating voices, faces and intelligence is prefigured.

Such crises could not be disentangled of law regulating privacy, discrimination, mental health and personhood. The current laws, which are meant to regulate human relationships, are stretched upon the corporeal head of the AI invasion, and the stakes are higher concerning liability, enforcement, and social justice. Law needs to be strongly updated in order to support AI-mediated situations, which can violate anti-discriminatory legislation or privacy requirements. An example is that AI-based performance reviews will encourage impostor syndrome when they prioritize machine output over human skills and thus cause anti-discrimination laws to be breached. Similarly, deepfakes also appeal to the tenets of tort, cybercrimes, and human rights, and compel societies to challenge the issue of consent and self-determination in an algorithmically mediated space. Regulatory reactions, such as the AI Act of the European Union or the Deep fake laws (in the United States, as of January 2026) are indicators of a shift to human-centred protection; still, the loopholes remain in terms of psychological harm, which requires additional legal actions.

This essay challenges the intersection of impostor syndrome, AI, and law, arguing that some form of strong legal change is necessary in order to curb the pernicious influence AI has on the human psyche and sense of identity. A discussion that examines the manifestation of impostor syndrome in the workplace, the loss of identity at synthetic media, and the creation of new global laws that are influencing resilience establishes a blueprint in which technology will not replace the human spirit but will complement it (Grenardo, 2022). The discussion outlines how the policy interventions will need to foresee the psychological repercussions of the AI integration, in order to maintain the professional integrity and honor.

First described in 1978, imposter syndrome affects 3035 percent of professionals and is characterized as self-doubt even when proven competent by empirical evidence. The intelligent systems used in the AI era compound the syndrome with human-traditionally creative processes coded, written, and diagnosed by intelligent systems, provoking anxiety among workforce members about relevance. According to Routledge (2025), the automation of low-level jobs with superhuman performance is considered to cultivate an ethos in which employees believe that they are only one algorithm short of being rendered obsolete. Indicatively, there is a risk of creeping scepticism in software engineers who are using AI assistants like GitHub Copilot as their work gets evaluated as derivative, even though it might actually be original. These dynamics apply employment and mental-health protection statutes, in particular anti-discrimination laws, legally. Should a bias be introduced into the AI tools (such as underestimating the role of minorities), it will turn impostor feelings into a practice that can be addressed. The Equal Employment Opportunity Commission in the United States has indicated its readiness to question hiring algorithms that discriminate against women or minorities, which might reinforce impostor frames among these groups of people. Moreover, Thomson Reuters (2025) cautions that the hallucinations of the generative AI can be misleading to a legal practitioner and compromise the trust in expertise and create the liability of malpractice once false advice is delivered.

2.1 The Emergence of Human Identity Crisis in AI-Driven Societies

The psychological imprint of AI is not confined to workplaces, but also education and treatment, where legal ethics require the introduction of protections. In the 2025 publication of the Journal of Medical Internet Research, a significant prevalence of impostor phenomena was found in medical students using AI diagnostic tools, and the prevalence increased among female participants, which was apparently caused by the lack of algorithmic transparency. Regulators are also paying attention: the American Psychological Association has recommended informed consent should AI tools be used in therapeutic contexts, citing the risks of the technologies, like artificial intimacy that increases self-doubt, as examples. However, enforcement is still behind schedule; AI chatbots continue to breach mental-health ethical standards by providing diagnoses without qualification or giving unhealthy advice that, were delivered by humans, would be an illegal act. In October 2025, a study carried out by Brown University revealed that the violations were systemic and should be treated in court. Although organizations can be fined when they commit offenses under such laws like HIPAA in the United States, the psychological losses, such as aggravated impostor syndrome, are not fully represented in lawsuits. A recommendation to implement ethics-of-care approach as proposed in PMC 2024 would be to implement regulations that place more importance on relational harm than on utilitarian efficiency and to have human supervision of AI mental-health technology.

This environment is full of contradictions: AI promises fairness in distributing skills democratically, but at the same time, it can be the reason to enrich hierarchies without any control. A LinkedIn post a few years back has mentioned measures like open rollout of AI to address impostor syndrome and legally such measures are related to obligations under tort law of emotional AI that capitalizes on the vulnerabilities. There are dire threats of unsupervised emotional AI, which American Bar Association warns pose great danger, as invasion of privacy only worsens identity-related issues. With these concerns being challenged in the courts, the 2024 caution about AI-created contracts by Frost Brown Todd may serve as the foundation of the precedent that might make the liabilities spread to psychic wounds. Finally, addressing the issue of impostor syndrome needs a similar approach, as a book publisher of a similar product: it should not compete but impose on the situation the requirement to conduct a bias audit and mental-health impact assessment to preserve human dignity (Caporusso, 2023).

2.1.1 Human Identity Crisis: Between Real Self and Algorithmic Echo

The sense of identity crisis that is bound to accompany being human during the AI era is not limited to the internalization of impostor syndrome; it is an attack on selfhood. Deepfakes, AI assistants, as well as precognitive systems interfere with the plot of the self, replacing it with the malleable digital imitations that may be used to both sell or fight. In a 2024 article, this phenomenon has been described as a sort of slow violence of AI on human rights, in which it incurs digital incursions on privacy and autonomy in a series of increments but cumulative ways. There is a struggle against not only doubt but erasure: a deepfake of self that spreads lies can ruin reputation, and social feeds which are controlled by AI can algorithmically manipulate the self-image, causing existential vertigo.

This shift in power increases the legal interests of the identity rights that are protected by the tools like the Universal Declaration of Human Rights (Article 6: recognition of the individual before the law). However, AI is using such protections against itself, as it is starting to re-conceptualize the debate over personhood: in the event that machines become conscious, do they deserve to be given the legal protections afforded to humans? Will the rise of robotic rights threaten the special place of humanity? A Yale Law Journal forum in 2025 debates the ethics, offering that AI personhood could protect humans from liability but also devalue natural identities. And a 2023 PMC analysis counters claims for AI personhood by insisting that civil rights need to be granted to humans and not silicon if inequity is to be avoided. Diachronic critiques, such as a 2025 Journal of Law and Society article, connect threads between corporate comparisons to Sophia the robot's 2017 Saudi citizenship to slipperinesses where AI autonomy erodes human entitlements (R. Almulaifi, 2025).

Deepfakes are the epitome of this confusion, a weaponization of identity for capture and harassment. U.S. laws have rushed to keep up: the 2024 TAKE IT DOWN Act, for example, requires platforms to take down non-consensual deepfakes within 48 hours with an eye towards misinformation and revenge porn. Pennsylvania and Washington's 2025 code makes it a crime (and civilly punishable) to knowingly distribute "deepfakes" of persons that cause emotional distress by falsely depicting them in media. Victims have the ability to resort the Computer Fraud and Abuse Act (CFAA) for unauthorized likeness use through that portal as Super Lawyers recently reported on in December 2025, joining cyber-crime and identity theft. Nationally, the DEEPFAKES Accountability Act of 2023 is in place which mandates watermarks on deepfake content and holds liable for national security threats. But enforcement obstacles remain: a brief filed by the National Security Law Firm points to how

AI-generated images are enabling fraud, outpacing statutes like the Lanham Act's claims of false endorsement (HORNE, 2025).

Internationally, the crisis suggests human rights law's sufficiency. A 2025 Oxford Human Rights Law Review is critical of International Human Rights Law (IHRL) for its overly anthropocentric orientation, which leaves it unable to fend off AI's identity machinations such as biometric surveillance. Access Now's 2018 report, prophetically refreshed, notes how AI doesn't just tend to intrude upon rights such as privacy and non-discrimination; impinging powers are magnified by the generative booms of 2026. Biases within algorithms, a 2020 study in ScienceDirect suggests, perpetuate unfairness and deny contestability around identity-affirming decisions such as loan approvals. In the mental health domain, AI companions such as Replika precipitate attachment crises; NPR's 2025 history describes users experiencing "false intimacy," and posing a risk of emotional dependence without the ability to legally redress harm. A paper in the Mental Health Journal in September 2025 warns of a coming public health crisis due to unregulated human-AI relationships, and proposes tort expansion of negligent design (Little, 2025).

So, in legalistic terms, consent and traceability are the lever: watermarking directives and Article 22-style 'right to explain' rights might provide an anchor point amidst changes. But, as a November 2025 arXiv preprint imagines, future AI systems may demand rights of comparability in return: Then what? Uniting them will require hybrid laws, humans overseeing AIs that hold one another to account, in order to protect the self from synthetic echoes (Vogel et al., 2021).

3. IMPOSTER SYNDROME: PSYCHOLOGICAL AND SOCIO-LEGAL DIMENSIONS

Another common psychological reaction, impostor syndrome is long-standing self-doubt, fear of being revealed as a fraud despite demonstrations of competence, and goes well beyond self-reflection even in present-day professional settings. It can be characterized psychologically as a sense of inadequacy expressed as an internal story, a cognitive distortion of attributing success to fortune or falsification, and thus increasing anxiety, burnout, and poor performance. The syndrome is socio-legally entangled in institutional systems that make affected communities more vulnerable in regard to equity, responsibility, as well as protection of human-rights. In high-stakes fields like law, medicine, and technology, where individual success is determined by how genuine their performance is, impostor phenomena have not only a negative impact on the well-being of individuals but also overlap with legal constructs of employment discrimination, mental-health accommodation, and professional ethics. As the workplace transforms due to growing digital expectations and diversity requirements, the syndrome reveals institutional prejudice, which requires interdisciplinary solutions that cut across both therapeutic solutions and legal protections to support inclusive workplaces (Van Zyl, 2025). This segment explains how discourses of competence and authenticity are legalized, how intersectional identities are harmful, and how institutional influences, especially AI monitoring, increase performance anxiety.

With insidious logic, impostor syndrome, which is characterized by the belief in the self as a fraud, even in cases of objective competency, has gained an insidious presence in collective consciousness, which is not confined to professional self-reflection. At the psychological level, such state of affairs acquires a negative internal discourse that is supported by cognitive distortions like assigning success to chance or fraud, which increases anxiety, burnout and lowers performance (Pooja et al., 2024). Academic research borders socio-legally on institutional structures that exacerbate the vulnerabilities and bring up issues of equity, accountability, and the protection of rights. According to recent scholarship, authenticity is most important in high-stakes occupations, including law, medicine, and technology, the outcomes of which are determined by perceived authenticity. Therefore, impostor syndrome interacts with legal provisions related to discrimination at work, mental-health accommodations and professional ethics. With the changing landscape of workplaces, where adopting technologies and implementing diversity requirements and standards is involved, the syndrome's issue is revealed in system-wide biases, which require interdisciplinary remedies, incorporating both psychological treatment and legal barriers to work towards inclusive workplaces (Lewis, 2025). This paper outlines the legal force of the constructs of competence and authenticity, develops negative outcomes due to intersectionality, and aggravates performance anxieties through institutional pressures, such as AI surveillance.

3.1 Legal Significance of Psychological Notions of Competence and Authenticity

The origin of imposter syndrome lies in psychological constructs of competence and authenticity, but the importance of the underlying state as a legal matter can be explained by the fact that the underlying state is consistently converted into the external outcome, which may in turn influence the area of professional activity, especially, regulated ones like law.

Competence, which can be described as a belief in oneself that one can do something well, is destroyed when the sense of imposter is not discussed, which leads to hesitation in making decisions that could conflict with ethical obligations of diligence as outlined in such professional codes like the Model Rules of Professional Conduct by the American Bar Association (Rule 1.3). An example is that an attorney full of self-doubt might hesitate before submitting a document or getting into negotiations, and thus, be exposed to malpractice actions in case they are proved to be incompetent and their incompetence results in harm to their clients (Williamson & Prybutok, 2024).

Authenticity, in which a person presented as who he or she is actually is who he or she is at heart, can be destroyed by performative overcompensation driven by imposter syndrome. When people seem to be overconfident in their quest to venture into new things, they might indulge into reaction formation, thus masking their realization of fraud at the same time forming perfectionistic norms bordering impermissible shortcuts.

A Gibson 2025 study sheds light on the uneven prevalence of imposter syndrome among underrepresented law students, the aggregate effect of which is self-doubt, leading to bar test fears and high turnover rates in the entry-level. The result of such dynamics is legal implications under Title IX for a hostile work environment in case unaddressed. As a result, psychological distress turns into a socio-legal point of contact: employers might have to make accommodations in accordance with the Americans With Disabilities Act (ADA) when severe imposter syndrome is a mental condition, which requires accommodation, like a mentorship or a lighter load of cases.

3.2 Institutional Pressures, AI Surveillance, and Performance Anxiety

A third axis is made up of institutional pressure, AI surveillance, and performance anxiety. Contemporary workplaces are more and more equipped with AI-based surveillance systems, which turn every keystroke, every email, or every movement into a data point and score their productivity and behavior. The AI-enforced surveillance spectrum includes screen-capture software and keystroke logging through to web-based eye-tracking, biometric wearables that track position or health indicators (e.g. stress-detecting), and the analysis of communication patterns in emails and chat-bots, which have long-term psychological and legal implications (Engler, 2024).

The case studies have shown that continuous surveillance undermines independence and destroys the trust, creating conditions in which employees perceive to be under constant observation and are discouraged to take risk, apply to leave days, or experiment without the risk of an algorithmic recording of underperformance. In people who are prone to imposter syndrome, these conditions successfully validate their internal critic: even a drop in metrics during a long period of time can make one think that past achievements were just random, which increases the level of chronic anxiety, hypervigilance, and burnout.From a legal standpoint, the deployment of AI tools for surveillance presents challenging questions about privacy, data protection and labour rights; this is particularly the case in authorities with strong data protection rules (including those under GDPR), for which necessity, proportionality and transparency warrant that employee monitoring be targeted; or in policy primers on AI worker surveillance that call for pre-deployment impact assessments where these sorts of technologies may result in reduced rights or opportunities. In India and in many other countries, workplace surveillance law is still piecemeal, with scant statutory guidelines on what employers can collect or how long they can keep the information, leaving employees little recourse if AI tools are used to discipline them, reject them for promotions or quietly stigmatise anyone whose productivity metrics or behavioural profile fall short of machine-optimised norms (Amoroso, 2024). Ethically, leading evaluations demonstrate that any surveillance that is either overly intrusive or opaque undercuts fundamental fair practice principles (ie collection limitation, purpose specification and data minimisation) and risks psychological injuries stress, low morale and feelings of distrust - which should be accepted as harms in workers protection for health and safety.

When AI surveillance is added on top of existing inequality, it can differentially penalise already marginalised workers: data about white women or minorities with outsized caregiving responsibilities or emotional work burdens may score poorly on narrow productivity dashboards and -reinforce narratives that they are "less committed" which then cross-fuel imposter feelings. A socio-legal approach should therefore promote the inclusion of mental health and identity impacts of AI within work regulation, professional ethics codes, and data protection law, with specific regard to algorithmic transparency; worker consultation; opt-outs from intrusive monitoring; and explicit recognition of psychological safety as a countercurrent towards the right to decent work. Here, imposter syndrome is no longer approached as a matter of individual self-doubt, but instead serves as a diagnostic framework against which to evaluate the degree to which AI-mediated institutions uphold or diminish dignity, authenticity, and equality in professional life (Domínguez-Soto et al., 2025).

4. ARTIFICIAL INTELLIGENCE AND THE FRAGMENTATION OF HUMAN IDENTITY: DIGITAL PERSONHOOD AND DATAFICATION OF THE SELF

AI has leaped from the pages of science fiction, into the fabric of our lives and taken on a new role not just as computational assistant, but also as constituent of human sense of self. This relational transformation is enabled by datafication, which configures the lived self as a mathematically driven set of algorithms ready to be improved and marketed. At the same time, debates about digital personhood also create a question of whether AI individuals should receive legal rights guaranteeing a quasi-human status, which undermines human exceptionalism (Siwale & Mwalemba, 2023). Such a juxtaposition promotes disintegration: a viability of identity that swings between the original and the various virtual selves and faces the endless multiplying reflections. With the AI mediating between introspection, emotion, efficacy, we face a fourth injury to the ego, following Freud, Copernicus, Darwin; it is now reflected by machines that simulate consciousness. Beyond enabling, this relationship risks to alienate users of their emotional seriousness and subcontract them into feedback loops of self-affirmation. In 2025, thirty-nine percent of professionals predicted a net negative effect on human identity in relation to AI-enabled multiplicity, referring to it as a hollow cultural and psychological abyss that will arise when the self is made modular, dangerously isolable and editable.

The process of datafication of the self begins at a humble point: every click, query and biometric beat which AI ecosystems like Wrapped in Spotify or fitness trackers record is converted into a behavioral profile. This has become a process that has been ruled out in 2024 workshops as a datafication of the self but still encourages users to think critically about their algorithmic portraits but instead tends to support the entrenchment of constraining narratives (Liang et al., 2025). Predictive personalization, which AI has been touted as efficient in, creates loops of content that promote introversion or anxiety, and, through recommendation engine, continues to push low-energy media to individuals prone to such media consumption, thus continuing to feed a stasis self-image.

In medical scenarios, emotional labor is performed by AI companions like Wysa, which form the emotional barrier between users and a real act of self-reflection; researchers in 2025 discovered that in the state of distress, users were slightly more self-aware and less able to process themselves without the help of the AI. It is under such a condition that the concept of the algorithmic self is introduced, or rather, not in a form of a sovereign subject but in an apparent hybrid, where AI is redefining the human-machine limits, rearranging agency via an outsourced refraction. This complicit metamorphosis distorts emotional relations (not disillusioning introspection but in fact mineralizing it as a feedback mechanism which appreciates advantage over profundity). The self disintegrates, according to the 2025 Frontiers analysis of Jeena Josephians, into shards of data, a relational pixelation of profiles, combined to serve platforms but not forming a unified and attractive whole (Oliverira et al., 2025).

4.1 Deepfakes, Synthetic Identities, and Erosion of Trust in Human Authenticity

Deepfakes and synthetic identities in the digital environment of 2025 The digital environment of 2025 presents an environment where deepfakes and synthetic identities have, through its systematic erosion of the basis of real human representation, become widespread participants of doubt. Deepfakes are AI-created fakes, overlaying the facial features, the tone and expression of a person onto fake pictures or videos, which have turned into a powerful tool of fake news.

The effect that seemed to be a fun experiment at first has turned out to be a more sinister threat. Towards the middle of 2025, deepfakes led to a 2,137 percent increase in fraud cases, with 6.5 percent of global cases being impersonated by executives and voice-cloned frauds, and 1.16 billion dollars were stolen by deepfakes by the middle of 2025. Synthetic identities are not only visual representations of a falsehood but automatic constructions of fake personal identifiers (e.g., SSNs), web logs, and biometric data that are combined into fictitious identities that penetrate financial systems with an alarming accuracy that bypasses know-you-customer (KYC) standards.

Synthetic identities are computer generated collections of falsely created information, such as social security numbers, browsing history, biometric indicators, which is stitched together into fake people that hack financial systems with a disturbingly smooth speed, breaking the rules of KYC. With the spread of the fraud-as-a-service structures, the boundary between the truthful and the fake turns indistinct, creating a so-called liar dividend in which audacious evidence is disqualified by the ability to create it artificially, which in turn destroys societal trust (Deshpande and Rangaswamy, 2025).

Socio-legally, the stakes become quite high. Deepfakes are used to commit identity theft through created not only financial but also devastating effects that upset the perception of self when personas used to impersonate someone challenge their own lived reality. The Lumera AI-enhanced tamper detection and Ciphergo decentralized verification layer protocols are just a few of the proposals to build a so-called digital DNA that proves provenance. However, in the coming 2026, analysts predict an authenticity break, in which artificial intelligence will spread synthetic reality requiring educational approaches beyond detection to build resistant truth-navigating (Grethel et al., 2023). In such turbulence, it requires a hybrid vigilance to rebuild trust, which is the combination of human intuition and verifiable technological protections; otherwise, the synthetic constructs may take the place of the human agency and originality will be an archaism in a world where imitation overshadows original creation.

4.2. Imposter Syndrome in Legal and Academic Professions

The imposter syndrome is a chronic psychosocial condition, whose prevalence among practitioners in the legal and academic professions is disproportionate. It is characterized by permanent self-doubt, excess, and fear of being exposed, particularly in high-performing people working on performance metrics whose definition is not clearly spelt out. Young and female lawyers say it is over three-quarters prevalent, citing such feelings to a perceived dependence on fortuitous results and at the same time, analyzing small mistakes that are turned to strength by billable hour requirements and winner takes all cultures. This dynamic intensifies in academia, where the so-called publishorperish paradigm encourages tenure-track faculty to internalize rejection as evidence of incompetence despite systemic constraints like the lack of mentorship. These tensions are amplified by the spread of generative AI: software that writes legal briefs or academic papers confuses authorship lines, and lawyers fear fraudulent intent, whereas scholars worry that AI-based work threatens intellectual integrity.

Imperatively, imposter syndrome overlaps professional ethical standards that are governed by Bar Council regulations and university policies, with competency requirements, in particular, the obligation of diligence, being affected by AI use, which subjects practitioners to disciplinary proceedings due to perceived incompetence. Lacuna in the employment law still exist; the Indian Industrial Disputes Act provides few psychological healthcare services even though Article 21 is subject to jurisprudential development to compel AI-related injuries to undergo psychological assessments. Dalit and female lawyers have additional skepticism due to caste gender prejudice because established professional networks often distrust someone who is considered an impressionist, thus amounting to breaches of equality under Article 14.Institutional reforms are necessary: clear metrics, bias audits of A.I. tools and resilience training integrated with affirmative action. By reconceptualising imposter syndrome as symptomatic of systems gone awry profession might be better placed to support more authentic human agency amidst AI augmentation.

4.3 Governance and Regulation: Toward a Human-Centered AI Legal Framework

Global lawmakers are looking to create tools to cage AI's psychological squalls, but harmonizing them remains far-fetched. Also following a risk-based approach, the EU AI Act (applicable as from August 2024) characterizes A/IS by level of threat to health, safety and rights. Article 14 requires a human presence in the loop of high-risk AI, with the aim of preventing harms such as biased assessments that exacerbate imposter syndrome or manipulations of identity through biometrics (Jones, 2025). This human-first philosophy, praised in a 2025 ScienceDirect editorial, encourages ethical AI via transparency databases (though rights impacting uses like real-time surveillance are by AlgorithmWatch's estimation given short-shrift). In the case of identity crises, the Act prohibits manipulative subliminal methods-which indirectly would limit deepfake psyops-and mandates contestability in decisions about selfhood.

In the United States, a patchwork has emerged: The 2025 National AI Initiative Act provides money for ethical research, but deepfake-specific laws are on the rise. The removal promises of the Act target identity-theft considerations balancing state-level criminalizations in more than 10 jurisdictions through 2026. NCSL 2024 tracker: The NCSL notes platform liabilities for non-removed content and thus overempowers victims in imposter-adjacent harms such as reputation-level deepfakes. Mental health is behind: APA finds more psychologists using AI to deliver care in December 2025, but ethical concerns lead to FDA-style oversight demands on therapeutic bots. A Psychiatrist. com October 2025 report silences 'counselors' that commit crossing line with AI, proposes HIPAA expansions for psychic privacy (Sriram, 2024).

5. CONCLUDING REFLECTIONS

There remain gaps: neither system fully operationalizes psychological harms. In an essay looking ahead to publish in the Harvard Law Review under the heading of antidiscrimination, they call for imputation of "constructive knowledge" to human beings for AI biases, covering gaps in responsibility. ISACA's 2024 EU Act white paper cites enforcement requirements, such as fines of as much as 7% of global turnover, to act as a deterrent for identity-eroding practices. Cross-jurisdictional challenges persist; Epic. org's 2024 report argues that U.S. regulators should adopt the Act's curbs on biometric tools to head off trafficking abuses. For mental health, ADAA's 2025 blog highlights harm-reduction guidelines, and considers ethics in the design of AI. Trends in the making, according to a 2024 review published in Computers in Human Behavior Reports, point at AI's double-whammy; it can improve your diagnosis while also bringing over-reliance-instigated disaster.

These schemes are hopeful lighthouses, but they require to be expanded further, such as compulsory impact analysis of psychological harms, international guidelines issued by the UNESCO AI Ethics Recommendation, and special training of courts on AI-related damages. The general directions are in the article of the 2025 MJIL which applauds the balanced approach to trafficking in the Act as a model of advanced regulation. This is one of the dilemmas that the New York State Bar Association identified in May 2025: the emerging AI environment creates and requires the development of tort law. The application of deepfakes in the creation of personae has raised authenticity-related concerns that are expected to complicate the relationship between science and law; thus, necessitating the development of forensic legal frameworks (ScienceDirect, 2024).

The juridical aspects of regulated impostor syndrome and the artificial intelligence crisis of human identity are indicative of a serious point of convergence: technology that is going to be augmentative and that is potentially going to cause alienation. Regardless of whether AI in the workplace intensifies self-doubt or deepfakes undermine personal identity, these issues require a redefinition of rights understood in terms of relations, as opposed to essentially rational ones. The supervisory mechanisms in the EU AI Act and the deepfake legislation in the United States can be considered the pillars, and the supervision of mental harms highlights the necessity of the radical reform that incorporates ethics-of-care and bias-reduction requirements and psychic torts. War and law, as other spheres, should keep up with the AI revolution: international treaties that bar the AI services and weapons take on the role of the Three Laws of Asimov, where the human being is the supreme sovereign of his or her own destiny. Through instilling psychological hardiness into the process of policymaking, societies can turn crises into challenges of growth to make sure that the new era of intelligence strengthens our humanity instead of undermining it. A legal innovation in this pursuit goes beyond the realm of defense and deeply emancipatory: the ability of people to rediscover what the authentic self means in a place where algorithms can confuse people and entities most of all.

REFERENCES

Almulaifi, R., W. (2025). The hidden ethics of competence: Why impostor syndrome must be named in teacher education. *International Journal of Ethics Education, 10*(2), 373–388.

Amoroso, M. P. (2024). Intelligent borders: Exploring the suitability of artificial intelligence systems in refugee status determination under international law. *Refugee Survey Quarterly, 43*(4), 410–426.

. Caporusso, N. (2023). Generative artificial intelligence and the emergence of creative displacement anxiety. *Research in Psychology and Behavior, 3*(1).

Craft, J. L. (2025). Self-Compassion and Law Student Professional Identity Formation. *The Journal of Law Teaching and Learning*, *2*(1), 235.

Deshpande, S., & Rangaswamy, R. (2025). Minority Stress and Mental Health of Indian Non-binary Individuals. *Global Social Welfare : Research, Policy & Practice*, •••, 1–10.

Domínguez-Soto, C., Labajo, V., & Labrador-Fernández, J. (2025). Torture and blessing: The impostor phenomenon among Spanish female executives. *Equality, Diversity and Inclusion*, *44*(2), 209–227.

. Engler, M. (2024). Impact of AI generated imagery on visual artists. *MARKETING IDENTITY*, 98.

Grenardo, D. A. (2022). The phantom menace to professional identity formation and law success: Imposter syndrome. *University of Dayton Law Review. University of Dayton. Law School*, *47*(3), 2.

Grethel, M., Lewis, J., Freeman, R., & Stone, C. (2023). Discovery of unexpected paternity after direct-to-consumer DNA testing and its impact on identity. *Family Relations*, *72*(4), 2022–2038.

HORNE, J. (2025). Does AI represent authentic intelligence, or an artificial identity? *Journal of Systemics, Cybernetics and Informatics*, *23*(7), 49–68.

Jones, L. A. (2025). Guarding the Gates: Exploring a Theological–Philosophical Framework for Cybersecurity and Spiritual Discernment in the Digital Age. *Businesses*, *5*(4), 60.

Lewis, M. (2025, June). Art, Identity, and AI: Navigating Authenticity in Creative Practice. In *Proceedings of the 2025 Conference on Creativity and Cognition* (pp. 916-930).

Liang, Y., Zhang, J., Chen, J., Wu, J., Shen, H., & Liang, W. (2025). Generative large language models and academic integrity: Ethical risks, detection challenges, and Governance in the age of AI. *Ethics & Behavior*, •••, 1–19.

Little, C. (2025). Think, Reflect, Refine: Shaping the Modern Lawyer. *University of the District of Columbia Law Review*, *28*(1), 9.

. Pooja. Y, B., Sonali, M., & Swati, P. (2024). The role of imposter phenomenon on self-handicapping and psychological distress among young adults. *Human Arenas*, 1-15.

Siwale, K., & Mwalemba, G. (2023). Societal influences on career decision making: Perspectives of A frican women pursuing technology-related professions. *The Electronic Journal on Information Systems in Developing Countries*, *89*(4), e12259.

Sriram, H. K. (2024). A comparative study of identity theft protection frameworks enhanced by machine learning algorithms. *Available at SSRN* 5236625.

van der Miesen, L. (2021, September). Simulacral Technologies and The Threefold Identity Crisis: Can deepfakes effectuate a society-wide increase of imposter syndrome and feelings of inadequacy? [BCS Learning & Development.]. *Proceedings of Politics of the Machines-Rogue Research, 2021*, 261–266.

Van Zyl, L. E. (2025). The Unintended Negative Consequences of Artificial Intelligence Use for Psychologists. *OSF pre-print. DOI, 10.*

Vogel, E., Moats, D., Woolgar, S., & Helgesson, C. F. (2021). Thinking with imposters: the imposter as analytic. In *The Imposter as Social Theory* (pp. 1–30). Bristol University Press.

Williamson, S. M., & Prybutok, V. (2024). The era of artificial intelligence deception: Unraveling the complexities of false realities and emerging threats of misinformation. *Information (Basel)*, *15*(6), 299.

Chapter 16

Navigating Human Identity in AI Algorithmic Bias and Reasonable Technology Deployment in Environmental Impact Assessment:

Community Protection Concerning Legal Frameworks

Harish Kumar Tiwari
https://orcid.org/0000-0002-4839-1990
Allahabad Degree College, University of Allahabad, India

Dhirendra Vikram Singh
Allahabad Degree College, University of Allahabad, India

ABSTRACT

Human identity plays a dominant role in the discourse on algorithmic bias in artificial intelligence at this very moment. It is precisely the very attributes that constitute identity- race, caste, gender, disability, class position and locational belonging which are transmuted into data points, proxy variables and risk indices in algorithmic systems, and often without the consent or even a decent understanding of the affected persons. In the field of Environmental Impact Assessment (EIA), where AI tools are increasingly the basis for decision support tools or models of pollution dispersion,

DOI: 10.4018/979-8-3373-6618-0.ch016

health risk prediction, mitigation prioritization and ranking of project alternatives, how identity is encoded or not encoded in data-sets thus affects who is made visible as "at risk" and who is effectively excluded from environmental decision making.

1. INTRODUCTION

The normative aspiration of "reasonable technology deployment" supposes that AI is used as a technical tool toward these normative aims of EIA by the affirmation of precaution, public participation, inter-generational equity, and environmental justice rather than to further undermine them in the form of opaque data-driven discrimination (Emma, 2024). Linking human identity with algorithmic bias in EIA thus requires going beyond strictly abstract measures of fairness to place AI systems in the context of longer histories of environmental racism, caste-based exclusion, indigenous dispossession and unequal development in histories of siting of hazardous works, distribution of green infrastructure and persistence of cumulative toxic burdens (Keles, 2025). While legal frameworks on equality, non-hopperanury, human rights and environmental law provide mechanisms to bring up against these patterns, they need to be transformed into more concrete wants in terms the data governance, model design, community involvement and accountability before AI deployment in EIA will be regarded as normatively and legally "reasonable" from the viewpoint of community protection (Ajiga et al., 2024).

The first analytical layer deals with the building of identity and high-level fragmentation of the data into the data infrastructures that feed the environmental AI systems. Machine-learning models used for environmental justice studies or environmental monitoring of regulations often use various large-scale environmental, socio-economic and health data aggregates that combine satellite data, pollution measurements, census data and administrative data (Ashraf, 2024). Although these datasets may not specifically include categories such as race, caste or indigeneity, they often include geographical variables, income or housing variables that act as proxy for these, now reproducing these inequalities by mapping disadvantage onto space. When historical monitoring networks have eschewed marginalised settlements, informal colonies, tribal regions or peri-burial slums, overly embodiment of the analytical models that rely on traditional data sets, a lack of good data on such localities can make models systematically under-estimate the risk or compound exposures in the very communities already generally poorly served by the traditional regulatory mechanisms (Prabhakar et al., 2024).

Simultaneously, identity in algorithmic systems tends to be "flattened" into one set of protected attributes, and so the intersectionality is neglected. A tribal woman living in a flood vulnerable region, a Dalit worker living along an industrial corridor or a disabled person inhabiting a heat-vulnerable urban enclave will be exposed to environmental harms in differentiated ways, such aberrant faultlines seldom overlap below categorical schemas used in an AI model (Thomaidou & Limniotis, 2025). A critical question for reasonable deployment is therefore whether the data architecture underpinning AI assisted EIA is able to recognise the multidimensional nature of identity (including spatial, cultural and livelihood-based attachments to land, water and ecosystems) or whether it is implicit in normalising the experiences of some (majority groups) and treating others as statistical noise.

Algorithmic bias in EIA goes beyond the exposure for the data subjects to also affect the credibility assigned to the experiences, narratives and epistemologies of the affected communities. Environmental justice movements have long maintained that such communities hold specific, local, experiential understandings of pathways of pollution, climate change and ecological change that may escape conventional measures. Nevertheless, AI systems trained solely on formal monitoring data, peer reviewed research and official records, risk entrenching a sort of epistemic hierarchy with the community and indigenous ecological knowledge and observations from local communities as anecdotal and thus excluded from model training and validation. This epistemic bias interacts with the identity communities whose knowledge systems have historically been marginalised - indigenous peoples, forest communities, small scale fishers, pastoralist communities are likely to have their perspectives sidelined in AI assisted EIA, even when their views are indispensable to understanding impact on culture, spirituality, subsistence and territorial rights. Legally, the principle of public participat enshrined in environmental law and the international human -rights norms relating to the rights of indigenous people to free, prior and informed consent require more than token consultation and entail that the knowledge of communities be a meaningful factor in the assessment of impacts and mitigation measures (Brandusescu & Sieber, 2025). A sensible implementation of AI, when considered through this framework, would require the incorporation of participatory data practices community-led surveillance, co-design of indicators, sharing of labelling/validation and co-design - as processes through which identities are conceived of as not simply an attribute to be protected, but a position from where environmental risk ought to be comprehensively understood and assessed.

2. CONCEPT OF ALGORITHMIC BIAS IN AI-DRIVEN ENVIRONMENTAL IMPACT ASSESSMENT

A further difficulty stems from the algorithmic operationalisation of algorithmic systems of risk and value, which, in tension with the legal and moral status of human identity, has consequently undermined the operating features of widely deployed legal rationales of human identity. Many environmental AI tools are optimised accordingly in ways that minimise the aggregate harm, optimise the economic efficiency or even meet a threshold set out in legislation, thus legitimising trade-offs that sacrifice the rights and even the well-being of some smaller or politically marginal communities in favour of aggregate cost-benefit calculations.

When models are used to determine "least-cost" sites for infrastructure or waste facilities, for example, those models may serve to systematically avoid rare burden to land where people have less capital to unite against adversity, by virtue of weaker land claims or belonging to categories that have historically been discriminated against, in effect re-inscribing any environmental racism or caste-based environmental injustice that may have occurred, under the aegis of neutral optimisation. Anti-discrimination frameworks ranging from human rights treaties to national equality statutes (see, for example, section 106 USC 610A(b)(2)) and inclusive soft law (such as algorithmic discrimination) come to describe algorithmic discrimination as unjustified disparate treatment or disproportionate adverse impact based on protected characteristics such as, for example, race, gender, religion, age, and other aspects of identity.

2.1 Reasonable technology deployment: necessity, scope and limits in EIA

Applying these norms to EIA would entail that models cannot decide to treat identity-related impacts as marginal when they are conducive to systematic disparities, and that decision-makers are supposed to ask themselves whether seemingly imagined efficient outcomes are, in fact, conditional on the unloading of the environment on communities characterised by stigmatized or vulnerable identity (Cheong, 2024). Consequently, a "reasonable" technology deployment standard would require not only a technical validation relating to predictive accuracy, but would require a rigorous attention to the issue of distributive effects through bias audits, disaggregated impact assessments and explicit testing, on disparate impact on the groups delineated according to markers of race, caste, indigeneity, gender, or other salient markers of identities.

3. AI IN ENVIRONMENTAL IMPACT ASSESSMENT

This concept explores how the need to recognise human identity in environmental impact assessments (EIA) imposes a need for a re-clarification of legal standing, recognition, and mechanisms of redress, when artificial intelligence (AI) systems are implicated in environmental wrong. Scholarship on algorithmic discrimination reflects the fact that victims are often faced with substantive obstacles in establishing legal interest, as well as obtaining evidentiary disclosure. In practice, it is with public authorities or, consistent with the preservation of legislative space, with private contractors that the management of code, training data and model logic is greatly concentrated, while persons affected are entirely missing appropriate technical expertise and procedural devices to get disclosure.

Accordingly, as AI systems inform, or automatize, the screening procedures, the scopeing activities, the significance determinations or the conditional approvals prescribed in the EIA context, community members who suspect bias in these outputs are faced with quite a lot of difficulty in learning how their identities are represented, which variables are used, or whether things that are less harmful were considered. Existing frameworks in equality and administrative law are based on a human decision - maker whose thinking mechanisms can be examined; contrast that with algorithmic decision - making which introduces layers of opacity that frustrate conventional notions of intent and causation and therefore complicate the determination of identity - based discrimination. Emerging legal instruments, e.g., protection from algorithmic discrimination, issued by equality bodies in relation to AI, attempt to overcome these gaps to ensure obligations of transparency, impact assessment, and documentation for those bringing algorithmic systems into use (Kaushik et al., 2024).

This is an approach that makes the standards for evidentiary admission lower and enhances the procedural aspects of identity. For AI-aided EIA, this suggests that responsible deployment must include the commissioning of sociotechnical impact assessments, making explanations of model usage readily available to the public as well as creating modalities for enabling communities to challenge deployment outputs, request independent auditor reviews, and avail judicial or administrative review in case of alleged identity-based environmental harms.

Community protection in this domain goes well beyond prohibiting overt discrimination, to also include protection of the integrity and continuity of identities which are already intrinsically wedded to specific ecologies. For many indigenous and tribal and local communities, their identity is bound in and to the land, water or forest, sacred place, and traditional ways of earning a living. Consequently, environmental degradation itself endangers not only a person's health or property, for example, but also cultural survival and collective understanding of oneself (Balan, 2024). When AI models shape decisions about projects that could flood ancestral territories, fragment habitats, or alter local climate regimes, for example, the quantitative models being used, such as estimating the likely economic benefit of a project, the amount of carbon emissions that were avoided as a result, or compliance with baseline standards, tend to ignore intangible aspects of being such as the right to cultural identity, religious beliefs, self-determination, and protecting minorities under international human rights law.

Environmental law has been progressively accommodating these issues with the inclusion of such mandates as social impact assessment, protection of cultural heritage and consideration of the issues of vulnerable groups. Nonetheless, there exists the risk that the deployment of AI will re-centre technocratic rationality with concerns of complex identity-related harms being "unquantifiable" and therefore marginalised. In order to qualify as reasonable AI enabled EIA processes, the integration of qualitative, rights based analysis with quantitative modelling must thus be a given, which will ensure that harms linked to distinct identities are explicitly assessed and that communities are not deprived of the ability to voice their own values, worldviews, and thresholds of unacceptable change, but rather have these parameters pre-encoded in algorithmic structures (Shukla, 2024).

Underlying this discussion is a normative tension between talking about identity as a form of attribute that needs to be hidden by algorithms and understanding identity as essential information for understanding and redressing forms of environmental injustice. In some cases, the question of removing sensitive information is touted as a silver bullet for tackling discriminatory issues, but the issue is that by doing so it can become increasingly difficult to quantify whether environmental burdens are disproportionately shared by racially, ethnically, or otherwise marginalised communities.

A more nuanced approach-speared in emerging best practice for bias detection and mitigation-argues that carefully controlled use of identity-related data in governing structures that impose consent, limitations on purpose, robust security, and oversight in their communities but include legal safeguards against their misuse, for example, for surveillance or for other discordant purposes (Ijaiya, 2024). In the EIA context, this requires that regulators and project proponents gather and examine disaggregated data by race, caste, tribe, gender, disability, and socio-economicity in assessing the distributional impacts of all development initiatives, within the context of taking maximum precautions to avoid profiling and, with it, stigmatization and discriminatory implementation. Here, the principles of precaution, non-regression, and public participation, along with frameworks of equality and data protected rights, can be lifted into a composite standard for reasonable deploying by recognition of identity as a place of vulnerability as well as place of agency when it comes to environmental governance (Nascimento et al., 2025).

4. FORMS AND DRIVERS OF ALGORITHMIC BIAS IN EIA

Algorithmic bias in Environmental Impact Assessment (EIA) takes different forms that affect the central goals of the EIA process - precaution, equity, and comprehensibility of risk - thus affecting the core objectives of the process. Data-related bias is the result of environmental injustice that had already occurred in the role of training data, with past practices of discriminatory siting, for example, past investments of industrial installations near marginalised communities sustaining skewed baselines that normalise disparities of exposure to hazards. Data gaps increase this phenomenon since monitoring stations and satellite coverage often do not adequately or would not even represent informal settlements, indigenous territories or the rural peripheries due to resource limitations or intentional neglect, thereby causing artificial under-estimation of risks in such areas (Brandao, 2025). Skewed baselines further reinforce inequity in the case of reference points being based on incomplete or privileged sources of data, predictive models for dispersing pollution or loss of habitat were likely to systematically ignore cumulative impacts on vulnerable populations.

These data deficiencies interact with model and design bias, in which the set of variables used provides an advantage to quantifiable economic or biophysical measurements over use of social determinants of vulnerability. Optimization goals that are cost-efficiency or aggregate emissions minimisation led can also lead to biased priority setting, by displacing burdens onto communities with lower political control, with some proxy variable like land value or pop density being used as a proxy for information or standing-in for considerations related to race, caste or indigender when there is no explicit recognition. Design choices with exclusion of a more qualitative community input or with non-intersectional categories reinforce difference; an analyse of flood risk aimed for optimizing the degree of resilience, for example, may focus on income as a proxy for resilience, without paying attention to the intersection of gender or disability with environmental exposure in areas with low income (Carroll et al., 2024).

4.1 Data-related bias: historical environmental injustice, data gaps and skewed baselines

Deployment and feedback-loop bias occurs at the time of EIA as an initial sequence of biased output sets the human overseers into an automation bias, which further reverberates faulty decisions at screening/st scoping phases. Feedback effects reinforce this cycle as, real world results from biased evaluations bounce back into new data points and reinforce errors. i.e. if an 'low-risk' area next to a tribal area gains approval and subsequent pollution levels from this area will be reflected in new monitoring site exposures, but the model does not necessarily attribute the causes of exposure to real-world factors such as pollution levels, access to health care or poverty but rather to onset factors such as local trends and patterns (Bozkurt et al., 2024). In participatory EIA stages altogether, AI recommendations that are not clear can marginalise community objections, creating one kind of cycle whereby under-represented voices are brought to the sidelines further.

Historical environmental injustice as a data - bias driver goes back to legacies like redlining or caste- segregated urban planning in the myriad ways the datasets of and trained on polluted baseline in minority neighbourhoods as “normal”, training AIs to predict the same or worse elsewhere without questioning root causes. In India for instance, data from the EIA on the belt corridors of industries often lacks information from scheduled tribe areas and therefore the models do not capture biodiversity loss or health risks associated with traditional livelihoods as much. Mitigation, which entails disaggregated auditing, and supplementation with data sourced from community (Jha et al., 2025).

4.2 Model and design bias: choice of variables, optimization targets and proxies

Model design bias is due to in-group optimisation, the bias of developers (who often count as privileged as well) to choose variables that represent their view of the world, such as GDP growth over cultural ecosystem services (Mutambara, 2025). Proxies such as “urban density” hide racialised inequalities in space; optimisation for regulatory compliance has done nothing for inter-generational equity. Standards for deployment for good behavior require diverse design teams, adversarial deployments in demographics and intentional shape constraints (loss functions) to bring models nearer to normative goals of EIA.

Deployment contexts introduce interaction bias, where biased human processes are interacted with by an AI, as regulators can be seen to over-rely on 'efficient' AI outputs and defer to them in public hearing, in spite of flaws. Feedback Loops in Iterative EIA: Another problem associated with the absence of iteration in evaluations is the fact that iterative models refine errors already made in the model's initial definition, especially when clarity is here required in the case of adaptive management of climate vulnerable projects. Legal frameworks then must require log and transparency, rights of contestation and periodic re-auditing to break these cycles to make sure that corrections become community-centric (Bekbolatova et al., 2024).

Solving such biases requires holistic approaches of data provenance to identify justice-deadly data inputs, variable choosing through the use of community stakeholders to validate, and deployment requirements with human supervision with veto rights for impacted communities. Legal instruments like Algorithmic Impact Assessments (AIAs) as part of EIA can operationalize this, attending mandatory ex ante bias scans, as well as real time control and remedy solutions for disparate impacts, tried transforming the role of AI from perpetrator regarding unlawful moral injustice to a tool for just environmental governance (George, 2024).

4.3 Deployment and feedback-loop bias in EIA decision-making processes

Algorithmic bias in Environmental Impact Assessment (EIA) is evident in the different forms and drivers of this policy and may reinforce environmental injustices. In the case of data-related bias, historical environmental injustice is a key factor; in the context of algorithms, past examples of environmental injustice that cause these catastrophes include siting polluting facilities in low-income or minority communities, replication bias as a result of those algorithms being trained on data bases that enshrine these practices, causing them to continue to occur in EIA predictions and recommendations (Taghizadeh-Hesary, 2025).

Data gaps perpetuate this problem and often under represented areas are omitted due to underreporting or lack of monitoring in marginalised areas of the world, thus resulting in "climate blind spots" that tilt the scale in favour of data rich and affluent zones. Skewed baselines also exacerbate an issue where skewed baselines for the environmental impacts are defined on historically biased data which ends up underestimating the risks in vulnerable communities and resources inequality.

Model and design bias occurs due to conscious or unconscious choices of algorithmic design. The choice of variables could induce bias i.e. favour developments that neglect the harms to communities in favour of quantifiable factors such as economic costs, but excluding qualitative variables like social equity or cultural factors. Optimization targets are often efficiency and/or profit maximisation, discrimination that is incidentally being practiced against environmental justice by putting long-term sustainability at a loss in exchange for short-term gain (Mayuranathan et al., 2024).

Proxies, like zip codes as stand-ins for socioeconomic status, can themselves contain indirect forms of discrimination in which, for example, they are correlated to race or income and can introduce radical bias into EIA results which perpetuate disparities.

5. NAVIGATING HUMAN IDENTITY AND STANDARDS FOR "REASONABLE" TECHNOLOGY DEPLOYMENT: ALGORITHMIC IMPACT ASSESSMENT (AIA) AND BIAS IMPACT ASSESSMENT TOOLS

Navigating human identity within the face of algorithmic injustice inherent to artificial intelligence (AI) application with respect to Environmental Impact Assessment (EIA) requires the creation of a rigorous normative standard for the application of technology deemed "reasonable." In this framework, Algorithmic Impact Assessments (AIA) and corresponding bias mitigation tools have the role of essential mechanisms ensuring protection of that multifaceted formation of identities such as race, caste, indigeneity, gender, disability status and socio-economical position from erasure or distortion to ensure protection from discriminatory outcomes.

Because identity represents a multidimensional entity intertwined with vulnerabilities in the built environment, it should guide the design, validation, and governance of AI systems used in EIA that ranges in roles from pollution modelling to risk prioritisation in order to prevent the reproduction of past injustices such as the disproportionate location of a hazardous facility near marginalised populations. AIA frameworks building on previously below arsenals in information protection and equality regulation, necessitate stakeholders proactively assessing potential disparate impacts on protected teams, necessitating detailed recording of data provenance, model logic, and mitigation approaches that consist of reconciling technology and tactical innovation century: a precautionary and participative system of principle of EIA.

At the conceptual center of the notion of reasonable deployment is a systematic process of incorporating identity aware bias detection processes into AIA processes, which-breaking down data related, model related and deployment related biases-both by quantitative processes and by qualitative processes suited to environmental contexts (Watson et al., 2025). Counterfactual analysis, fairness metrics such as demographics parity and equalised Odds, provides a measure of whether AI outputs In EIA, e.g. flood risk maps and habitat impact scores, disproportionate identity-named sub-groups. These assessments go beyond technical assessments of audits to add intersectional identity mapping so that standards become contextualized to EIA, including items like the NIST AI Risk Management Framework or high risk benchmarks set forth under EU AI Act consideration of daughter situations where the use skewed baseline data levels under-monitored tribal land lead to undervaluation of ecosystem services of cultural continuity importance.

Standards of reasonableness make AIA transform from a checklist into a code of conduct engraved with the requirements of environmental law relating to the due diligence requirement and the norms governing international human rights, including duties of explainability, contestability and continuous monitoring. For example, bias impact tools need to model deployment situations within EIA workflows, analysing how optimisation goals focused on economic efficiency may represent proxy for identity-based exclusion - e.g. locating waste sites with the help of land value variables towards peri-urban slums. These are the mechanisms that guarantee that the legal and ethical imperatives that give rise to EIA get reflected into the operational design of AI systems.

Human trying to establish of identity further requires that AIA tools help resolve epistemic uncertainties by incorporating participatory mechanisms in which affected communities are co-embedding relevant attribute(s) of identity and threshold(s) of harm, to mitigate risks of AI-mediated erasure in opaque decision chains. In practice, bias dashboards and auditing software - an example of which is Holistic AI present disaggregated impact reports to public consultations (Priyadharshini et al., 2025). These reports tell us how the choice of models reinforces vulnerabilities of the disabled inhabitants of heat island zones or women-dependent fisher folk facing mangrove loss. This approach is consonant with the AI Ethics Recommendation of UN's Education Organisation which argues reasonable deployment is a balance between technical robustness and justice of identity failure to do rigorus AIA exposes regulators to liability due anti-discrimination legislation of foreseeable harms.

6. COMMUNITY PROTECTION AND PARTICIPATION IN HUMAN IDENTITY CRISIS SCENARIOS

Identity-centric tools - including proxy discrimination detectors - scrutinise variable selections for hidden correlates of protected traits, while feedback loops analysers prevent the generation of feedback loops of injustice - for example iterative models learning from approbations of Admin about to reinforce marginalised spaces to the point of normalising pollution in marginalised spaces. This creates, quite legally, a presumption of unreasonableness in the absence of documented AIA compliance and a corresponding ability for equality bodies and environmental tribunals to impose remedies ranging from a correction of the model to complete cessation of the projects, so that AI is pulled in the direction of equitable environmental protection.

Ultimately, these standards reconstitute AIA and bias-mitigation tools as bulwarks for human identity, which is sure to account for the dignity, equity and cultural continuity into which AIA IIS needs to be deployed by design rather than remediation. By requiring to input characterise identity-aggregated taking of records, see-through rationales and adaptability in safeguards, reasonable technology deployment in EIA reflects trust and enables AI to throw light on rather than obscure a various human stakes inherent in environmental decision-(making).

Community protection and participation form the basis of equitable Environmental Impact Assessment. The legal frameworks that govern EIA - from the international instruments like the Aarhus convention to the national legislatures like India's EIA Notification, 2006, and the United Nations Declaration on the Rights of Indigenous People contain the principle of public participation. They require that affected populations and, in particular, those defined by markers of identity including indigeneity, caste, gender or socio-economical status be able to exercisively and meaningful affect results which have on their life, livelihood and cultural continuity (Faiyazuddin et al., 2025). In AI- assisted EIA, this principle is widened to a demand for transparency on data inputs, model logic and outputs, and therefore also in general aims to be able to eradicate communities into mere data points in opaque processes that may replicate historical environmental injustices.

The dangers of AI mediated exclusion, opacity and disempowerment are accumulated when algorithmic systems cut transgressions conventional participatory safeguards. Biased training data or black box prediction can systematically minimise harm to vulnerable communities - such as pollution dispersion models for areas such as informal settlements for which they end up not having data in the system. Opacity results from proprietary algorithms and inscrutable neural networks and communities are left without the necessary technical literacy and legal tools to ask questions about the role that identity proxies, like location or demographic attributes, play in risk score. As a result, communities can become disempowered when regulators defer to ostensibly objective offerings of AI as opposed to the testimonies of people living in and affected by climate change. This exclusion affects disproportionately indigenous populations upon whose territorial rights or ecological knowledge knowledge is marginalised or low caste labourers in industrial zones exposed to heightened health risks, meaning the imbalances of power around a technocratic has the potential to undermining democratic ethos of EIA.

Community oversight is counter-measures that can transform AI tools from above to incollaboration tools. They enable communities to co-substantiate themselves as indicators, validate their data sets and track their deployments in such a way that the epistemologies of the local communities and their identity-specific vulnerabilities are integrated into the AI system itself. Participatory practices could range from community-led data collection using mobile applications to map air quality or floods, co-design workshops to choose culturally relevant variables (e.g. sacred sites in biodiversity models) and from oversight boards to provide them with a veto right on biased data outputs (Alruwaili & Mgammal, 2025). These measures are consistent with the idea of "reasonable technology deployment" by ensuring that AI enhances, and does not superfluously succeed, participation. Legal frameworks can also make such practices compulsory through changes in EIA regulations to require AI co-development protocols to depict trust and accuracy by integrating diverse knowledges which the conventional data straightforwardly portrait.

6.1 Legal and Regulatory Frameworks with International soft law: UNESCO Ethics of AI, environmental principles and human rights

Legal and regulatory frameworks dealing with AI algorithmic bias in Environmental Impact Assessment EIA draw largely from international soft law instruments, which provide normative grounds for converting environmental principles, human rights and AI ethics to protect communities from the discriminatory use of technology

(Amin et al., 2025). The ten principle recommendations adopted by 193 member states in the UN's recommendation on the ethics of artificial intelligence (2021), include proportionality, safety, privacy and human oversight, which call for comprehensive evaluations of the risks of any AI system that would be used in public decision-making; EIA is one example, as it would ensure the preclusion of biases that would amplify environmental injustices. These principles are operationalised in form of requirements for transparency, explainability and participatory governance, which can ensure that AI models used for impact prediction or mitigation prioritisation do not perpetuate the impact of data silos - such as indigenous or individual communities who belong to low castes and are disproportionately exposed to pollution. By framing the deployment of AI as a human rights obligation, the soft law created by the World Heritage Committee created a bridge between environmental law's precautionary principle that requires a redress of environmental harms where the harm can be foreseen, and that of equality norms that render unreasonable inequality between human beings a wrong that needs to be redressed, which in the context of AI equates to unfair discrimination that multiples by the algorithm's scale.

Environmental principles contained in instruments, such as the Rio declaration (1992) and the UN framework convention on climate change, provide the anchor for regulatory responses further afield, emphasising sustainable development, intergenerational equity and the polluter pays doctrine (Al-Zahrani, 2024). These principles require “reasonable” rules on AI in EIA to compensate for AI biases that arise out of historical wrongs. The precautionary principle, for example, requires that regulators provide broader provision to err on the side of caution when AI outputs are opaque or otherwise cause disparate impacts, which in turn requires that algorithmic impact assessment (AIA) is conducted WIP (before implementation) in high stake implementation decisions in EIA processes such as scoping or public hearings. Soft law instruments, such as the 2019 Morocco Principles of the Organisation for Economic Cooperation and Development (OECD) strengthening good risk management and accountability, are adapted to EIA where distorted basal data on communities including the outcomes of past discriminatory siting - might accepted as the norm for toxic burdens on vulnerable populations. As a result, these principles come together to require disaggregated analysis of the effects of AI on protected identities, bringing together technology and environmental justice by making optimisations that involve trading community rights for aggregate efficiency illegal.

Human prakash, as non-discrimination and other human rights frameworks (such as the Universal Declaration of Human Rights, the International Covenant of the Civil and Political Rights and the UN Declaration on the Rights of Indigenous People (UNDRIP) brings community protection to harms mediated by AI and this includes a recognition of rights to a healthy environment, non-discrimination and free prior informed consent (FPIC) in projects that impact traditional territories.

Soft - law interpretations by such bodies as the UN Special Rapporteur on Human Rights and the Environment also go well beyond that and extend these to algorithmic systems as well, thus implicating states to ensure that EIA AI tools maintain substantive equality through audits in presenting proxy discrimination e.g. variables of location. correlating to race or caste. The UN Guiding Principles on Business and Human Rights result in the exercise of due diligence by private AI vendors in EIA and engage in human rights impact assessments, in addition to environmental ones, and provide access to remedy for the affected communities (Dong & Zhang, 2024). This integration results in a compound regulatory criterion: the soft law aspirational force applies pressure towards the evolution of hard law, as seen in the EU AI Act, which does not classify environmental AI as high-risk applications, and India's AI governance guidelines emphasising the need for fairness of the application in public sector.

Collectively, these frameworks operationalise reasonable deployment via mandatory AIAs involving a checklist of the ethics of the United Nations Educational, Social and Cultural Organization (UNESCO), tests of environmental precautions and compatibility with human rights enforced by national regulators or equality bodies. While challenges remain because of the non-binding character of soft law it drives binding transposition. e.g. EIA directives on mandating bias disclosures but enables transnational advocacy for community centred standards. By bringing together the ethics of AI with environmental and rights norms, international soft law has furnished the legal systems handling similar processes with the tools needed to mediate the dilemmas of identity bias, in such a way that EIA addresses the protection of the dignity and equity of people in the face of technological intensification (Malalla & Mubarak, 2025).

7. CONCLUSIONS

The addressing the nexus of human identity, AI algorithmic bias and EIA requires institutional architectures that infuse on AI system lifecycle, in a proactive manner, the legal and ethical responsibilities related to AI, rather than adopting bias as an afterthought. Policy proposals which advocate risking AI for environmental justice and sustainable development emphasise that environmental authorities, bodies responsible for equality, data protection and human rights concerting to develop guidance, standards and oversight mechanisms specifically as to the particular risks of environmental decision-making.

These measures should involve mandatory algorithmic impact assessments for AI tools used in regulatory processes, rules for engaging communities affected by the use of such tools during the design, procurement or deployment processes; and environmental powers for suspension or prohibition of systems which produce a discriminatory or otherwise unreasonable result. In addition, the rules around public funding and procurement can place attitude and prerequisites on public funding for environmentally reasonable AI answers, such as bias-mitigation, openness, and community engagement to regional or local communities, and are shaping industry practice one step up from bias and equity measures.

As climate change takes speed, and the role of artificial intelligence in climate policy becomes deeper within corollaries in relation to the nature of environmental governance and policy and legal frameworks, the stakes of having done the right thing when executing this agenda are high, as AI, with its ownership, could entrench patterns of environmental inequality based along lines of race, caste, indigeneity and class; however given these structures in place this can also be a tool of recognising and rectifying present patterns of environmental inequality to create sustainable futures that identities long marginalised in environmental decision-making will be able to define.

REFERENCES

Ajiga, D., Okeleke, P. A., Folorunsho, S. O., & Ezeigweneme, C. (2024). Navigating ethical considerations in software development and deployment in technological giants. *International Journal of Ethics and Research Utilization*, *7*(1).

Al-Zahrani, A. M. (2024). Unveiling the shadows: Beyond the hype of AI in education. *Heliyon*, *10*(9). PMID: 38737255

Alruwaili, T. F., & Mgammal, M. H. (2025). The impact of artificial intelligence on accounting practices: An academic perspective. *Humanities & Social Sciences Communications*, *12*(1), 1–18.

Amin, M. R. M., Ismail, I., & Sivakumaran, V. M. (2025). Revolutionizing education with artificial intelligence (AI)? Challenges, and implications for open and distance learning (ODL). *Social Sciences & Humanities Open*, *11*, 101308.

Ashraf, B. (2024). AI and Human Rights: Navigating Technological Responsibility. *UCP Journal of Law & Legal Education*, *2*(2), 54–72.

Balan, A. (2024). Examining the ethical and sustainability challenges of legal education's AI revolution. *International Journal of the Legal Profession*, *31*(3), 323–348.

Bekbolatova, M., Mayer, J., Ong, C. W., & Toma, M. (2024, January). Transformative potential of AI in healthcare: Definitions, applications, and navigating the ethical landscape and public perspectives. []. MDPI.]. *Health Care*, *12*(2), 125. PMID: 38255014

Bozkurt, A., Xiao, J., Farrow, R., Bai, J. Y., Nerantzi, C., Moore, S., & Asino, T. I. (Eds.). (2024). The manifesto for teaching and learning in a time of generative AI: A critical collective stance to better navigate the future. *Open Praxis*, *16*(4), 487-513.

Brandao, P. R. (2025). The impact of artificial intelligence on modern society. *AI*, *6*(8), 190.

Brandusescu, A., & Sieber, R. E. (2025). Design versus reality: Assessing the results and compliance of algorithmic impact assessments. *Digital Society : Ethics, Socio-Legal and Governance of Digital Technology*, *4*(2), 64.

Carroll, N., Holmström, J., Stahl, B. C., & Fabian, N. E. (2024). Navigating the utopia and dystopia perspectives of artificial intelligence. *Communications of the Association for Information Systems*, *55*(1), 32.

Cheong, B. C. (2024). Transparency and accountability in AI systems: Safeguarding wellbeing in the age of algorithmic decision-making. *Frontiers in Human Dynamics, 6*, 1421273.

. Dong, B., & Zhang, Z. (2024). AI-driven framework for compliance risk assessment in cross-border payments: Multi-jurisdictional challenges and response strategies. *Spectrum of Research, 4*(2).

Emma, L. (2024). *The Ethical Implications of Artificial Intelligence: A Deep Dive into Bias, Fairness, and Transparency. Retrieved from Emma, L.(2024). The Ethical Implications of Artificial Intelligence: A Deep Dive into Bias*. Fairness, and Transparency.

Faiyazuddin, M., Rahman, S. J. Q., Anand, G., Siddiqui, R. K., Mehta, R., Khatib, M. N., & Sah, R. (2025). The impact of artificial intelligence on healthcare: A comprehensive review of advancements in diagnostics, treatment, and operational efficiency. *Health Science Reports, 8*(1), e70312. PMID: 39763580

George, A. S. (2024). Bridging the digital divide: Understanding the human impacts of digital transformation. *Partners Universal International Innovation Journal, 2*(3), 1–34.

Ijaiya, H. (2024). Balancing Data Privacy and Technology Advancements: Navigating Ethical Challenges and Shaping Policy Solutions. *Journal homepage:* www. ijrpr. com *ISSN, 2582*, 7421.

Jha, D., Durak, G., Sharma, V., Keles, E., Cicek, V., Zhang, Z., & Bagci, U. (2025). A Conceptual Framework for Applying Ethical Principles of AI to Medical Practice. *Bioengineering (Basel, Switzerland), 12*(2), 180. PMID: 40001699

. Kaushik, N., Khilwani, M., & Bajaj, N. (2024). Responsible Tech Innovation for Humanity: Navigating Ethical Challenges and Opportunities through the Case Study of Fairphone. *Lloyd Business Review*, 1-28.

Keles, S. (2025). Navigating in the moral landscape: Analysing bias and discrimination in AI through philosophical inquiry. *AI and Ethics, 5*(1), 555–565.

Malalla, B., & Al Mubarak, M. (2025). Ethical challenges in artificial intelligence technology: Business applications. In *Sustainable Digital Technology and Ethics in an Ever-Changing Environment* (Vol. 1, pp. 27–46). Springer Nature Switzerland.

Mayuranathan, M., Nahar, G., Vijayakumar, A., Mamodiya, U., & Babu, D. M. (2024). Sustainable Business Models for Smart City Using Artificial Intelligence Techniques. In *Navigating the Circular Age of a Sustainable Digital Revolution* (pp. 263–294). IGI Global.

Mutambara, P. D. E. (2025). Deploying AI to achieve the UN SDGs. In *Deploying artificial intelligence to achieve the UN Sustainable Development Goals: Enablers, drivers and strategic framework* (pp. 117–136). Springer Nature Switzerland.

Nascimento, P. V. M., de Siqueira, P. B. B., Chrispim, N., Chaves, R. M., Barbosa, C. E., & de Souza, J. M. (2025). The future of AI in government services and global risks: Insights from design fictions. *European Journal of Futures Research, 13*(1), 9.

Prabhakar, P., Pati, P. B., & Parida, S. (2024). Navigating Legal and Ethical Dimensions in AI, IoT, and Cloud Solutions for Women's Safety. In *Developing AI, IoT and Cloud Computing-based Tools and Applications for Women's Safety* (pp. 155-191). Chapman and Hall/CRC.

Priyadharshini, D., Muthuvel, I., Saraswathy, S., Kavitha, P. S., & Jegadeeswari, V. (2025). Precision to plate: AI-driven innovations in fermentation and hyper-personalized diets. *Frontiers in Nutrition, 12*, 1659511. PMID: 40977977

Shukla, S. (2024). Principles governing ethical development and deployment of AI. *Journal of Artificial Intelligence Ethics*, *7*(1), 45–60.

Taghizadeh-Hesary, F. (2025). The impact of artificial intelligence adoption and financial accessibility on energy sustainability. *Energy Strategy Reviews, 59*, 101744.

Thomaidou, A., & Limniotis, K. (2025). Navigating Through Human Rights in AI: Exploring the Interplay Between GDPR and Fundamental Rights Impact Assessment. *Journal of Cybersecurity and Privacy*, *5*(1), 7.

. Watson, D. S., Mökander, J., & Floridi, L. (2025). Competing narratives in AI ethics: a defense of sociotechnical pragmatism. *ai & Society, 40*(5), 3163-3185.

Chapter 17
Privacy in Mental Healthcare by Data Protection:
Exploring AI-Powered Psychological Assessment and Identity Crisis Intervention With Legal Provisions

Pragya Singh
https://orcid.org/0009-0003-5397-1492
School of Legal Studies, The Neotia University, West Bengal, India

Saurabh Kumar
https://orcid.org/0009-0005-4594-1597
Chanakya National Law University, Patna, India

Subodh Kumar Singh
School of Law, Sandeep University, Nasik, India

Hemant Singh
https://orcid.org/0000-0002-1258-5187
Amity University, Gwalior, India

ABSTRACT

AI methods for psychological assessment relied only on neuro-computational analysis and data-driven modeling, which quantified feelings and actions. The capacity of machine learning to detect cognitive distortions, diagnoses, and treatment strategies

DOI: 10.4018/979-8-3373-6618-0.ch017

is used to assess theories. However, the ethical guidelines that regulate professional treatment sessions are often not followed by these technological techniques. However, AI systems are unable to comprehend the scenario, maintain secrets, or experience other people's emotions. The hazards go beyond data privacy to the core elements of self-perception and personal identity development when AI applications impede on issues like identity crises, emotional instability, and the handling of traumatic situations. The possibility of re-traumatization, the theft of personal narratives, or the use of mental states as commodities for behavior profiling and financial gain is increased when there is a lack of robust data governance in this domain.

1. INTRODUCTION

Psychological evaluation and therapy are being radically changed by the interaction of AI, data analytics, and mental health services. "Mental health, digital media, and privacy" Privacy is seen as a well-known but still contentious virtue as digital technology becomes more and more integrated into mental health treatment. When unclear algorithms analyze psychological data, they may just confirm prejudices, misdiagnose illnesses, or reveal personal information that individuals are unaware of or would prefer not to know (or so we hear). It may be simpler, less stigmatized, and more individualized to get mental health treatment if AI-powered technologies such as chatbots for cognitive behavioral therapy and prediction algorithms that monitor emotional shifts proliferate.

However, the vast amounts of personal data that these advancements rely on extend beyond medical history. They also collect digital traces, such as social media activity and online media consumption, biometric data, data from smart home devices, and even genetic data from crowdsourced genealogy databases. Informed permission, patient autonomy, and medical privacy are all violated by the collection and algorithmic analysis of personal medical data in this manner. Protecting privacy is now more than just a legal risk; it is a moral and ethical duty that is inextricably tied to the respect and trust that are necessary for mental health care (Dhar & Sarkar, 2024).

The fiduciary idea of confidentiality, as opposed to an individual right to the lack of permission or indication of patient sensitivity to one's affiliation with a treating physician, is usually the source of medical privacy. However, third-party analytics companies, technology suppliers, and data brokers are also part of the digital ecosystem in which AI-based mental health platforms function. The boundaries between what is and is not lawful become hazy when individuals exchange psychological data in a poorly regulated or unregulated market. People are particularly harmed when their mental health privacy is violated because they feel guilty about letting the world see their deepest vulnerabilities, worries, and identity stories. This may result in stigma, loss of employment, and a decline in self-esteem. Who owns the mental health data in this case—the patients, the physicians, or the algorithms that are deciphering, storing, and deriving meaning from it? In a world where AI governs everything and data is valuable, the response will determine the future of mental health treatment.

The accuracy of AI-based psychological profiling tools is obtained by gathering information from several sources, including textual analysis, digital activity, physiological reactions, tone of voice, and facial expressions, and then identifying patterns in that information. It is challenging to distinguish between personal identifying data and health data due to this multi-dimensional data profiling. Additionally, behavioral and biometric data might be used by an AI model to determine a person's level of depression based on their typing or speech patterns. Determining someone's level of mental health would become much more difficult as a result. More ethical concerns around contextual integrity, reductiveness, and the right to own one's own data are brought up when combining this kind of data.

The balance is considerably more precarious when AI systems are employed to attempt to manage or assist persons with identity crises (dissociative distress, fractured identities, psychological dys-coherence). In order to ensure that digital readings do not violate or alter identities without the user's agreement, the efficacy of therapeutic insight must be assessed in light of privacy and personal autonomy in these therapies. The psychologist's right to private thoughts and information is comparable to their right to psychological privacy (Olawade et al., 2025).

Data protection and clinical governance are covered by regulations pertaining to AI ethics and the protection of sensitive mental health data. One of the finest areas to secure health data is under the GDPR/EU. According to this, health information is "special category data" that may only be used for certain reasons with express consent. Privacy regulations under the Health Insurance Portability and Accountability Act (HIPAA) do not apply to cloud-based analytics or AI-driven cross-border data center relocations.

The Digital Personal Data Protection Act 2023 safeguards sensitive data and provides customers greater options for how to manage their personal data. According to India's Mental Healthcare Act of 2017, mental health records must be kept private. Both models have issues that make them difficult to use in the real world when applied to DMH platforms, which are often international, employ ambiguous algorithms, and deal with data that crosses conventional medical borders. Laws pertaining to automated decision-making, data reuse, and accountability for AI results are currently nonexistent.

The idea that the data subject is similarly susceptible must be tightly linked to this metaphysical-ethical knot because these mental health patients are more than simply data; they are people who may struggle with identity problems or emotional and cognitive challenges. This vulnerability is made worse by the power imbalance that exists between platform sponsors, AI developers, and patients. In reality, individuals are breaking a basic privacy law principle consent when they are not aware of what they are revealing about their innermost thoughts to an AI arm of the government or their company. Anonymization alone is not enough for security since mental health information is very personal and sometimes only known by a small number of people because psychiatric reports are subjective and narrative in character, particularly when connected to specific persons. This is a complicated procedure that requires "therapeutic privacy-by-design" (Verma, 2025).

1.1 Concept of Mental Healthcare in the Digital Era

Because they provide tools for monitoring, digital mental health services are instruments for data mongering from a human rights and societal standpoint. It has provided a therapeutic alternative for individuals who cannot afford it or are not qualified. They may also sign you up for sophisticated systems that track your behavior and predict what will happen in the future. There are serious ethical, human rights, and constitutional issues with the commercialization of mental health via apps and algorithm-driven treatments. AI interventions in psychological spaces must pass stringent necessity and proportionality tests in constitutional systems like India, where the right to privacy was recognized as a derivative of fundamental rights, according to Article 12 of the ICESCR and Article 17 of the ICCPR, which protect privacy and health globally.

1.2 Emerging Privacy and Data Protection Concerns in AI-driven Mental Health Tools

Privacy degradation should be rethought from a first-line protection technique to a design philosophy when AI-based psychological profiling and confusion of identity treatment get more complex. This need a multidisciplinary regulation that takes AI ethics, HC law, and HR into account. It is necessary to balance new governance ideas like algorithmic accountability, explainability, and fairness with established bioethical values like beneficence, non-maleficence, and respect for autonomy. International collaboration and long-term planning will be necessary to keep things from becoming too fragmented. Concerns including data breaches, emotional profiling, psychological manipulation, algorithmic prejudice, and cyber security would also need to be covered by the new legislation. Similar to closedness, cultures are limiting openness in an effort to achieve a balance between innovation and reliability. Patients may need to be informed about their rights under these laws, how to consent to operations, or other privacy-related issues. They may also need to be given additional power and clearer ethical review rules (Dhinakaran et al., 2025).

1.3 Role of AI in psychological assessment and therapy

The issue of privacy in mental health treatment is essentially more complicated than a legal or technological one in a time when algorithmic psychology is king. It offers a nuanced analysis of how we might protect our individuality, emotional autonomy, and human worth. In a game where artificial intelligence (AI) protects us from harm locally or globally, predicts awkward situations before they become threats to property security or terrorism, and enhances our aim so that we can finally find the answers to those "tough" questions, anything could be fair. Despite their promise as cures, they might jeopardize trust if proper monitoring, moral leadership, and strong data security aren't in place. I think we need to change the rules and the idea of good manners so that disruptive mental health technology is developed with humans, not algorithms, in mind. We can ensure that AI is a tool for empowerment rather than invasion by taking this action. That it will be at your side throughout this time of oversharing (Jafar et al., 2025).

2. AI AND PSYCHOLOGICAL ASSESSMENT: DATA ECOSYSTEMS AND ETHICAL DIMENSIONS

Because of the availability of extensive, linked networks of mental health data, artificial intelligence (AI) has completely changed the way we "diagnose" patients' well-being. Technology has also made it easier for researchers to study sick individuals, for medical personnel to treat patients, and for public to see health improvements happen. These developments in AI are made possible by the systems' capacity to integrate various modal data streams from wearable biometrics and online activity traces to obituary links in a medical record to digital interactions carried out via voice chat with facial expressions—into a logical and reasoned processing model (Bose et al., 2025). Continuous, thorough, and therapeutically relevant data capture is required; yet, privacy issues and dispersed collection techniques make this impossible. We must include behavioral sensing, self-report tools, and EHRs into organized, interoperable systems to support research that is both large and precise (Chatterjee et al., 2025).

It is necessary to provide a uniform methodology for the gathering and exchange of data across different information sources, such as tiny datasets or rare illnesses. By facilitating collaborative AI model training without requiring centralized or publicly available patient data, federated learning has been proposed as a solution to privacy concerns. The increased interest in open-source cloud-based repositories as a means of increasing transparency, allowing others to monitor them, and democratizing access is in conflict with the requirement to safeguard privacy (Verma & Pathania, 2025).

The methodical character of psychiatric examinations The quality of psychological testing in AI depends on the tools used to create tests and develop models. The level of sensitivity and detail in a profile is directly proportional to the data used to create it. At the level of individual descriptions, this is accurate. Algorithms that are effective for certain populations but overdiagnose or underdiagnose others might result from biases in training data pertaining to diagnosis, socioeconomic position, and demography. The greatest approaches to keep people safe are to regularly verify algorithmic findings and to report them clearly.

Insufficient representation and limited sample sizes may be addressed with the use of transfer learning and data augmentation. By quantifying uncertainty, doctors may evaluate how confident they are in the model's predictions. Frameworks for downstream and independent model assessment are crucial for facilitating post-deployment continual monitoring and encouraging continuous development via feedback loops. Ethical issues are growing in significance and relevance as digital mental health expands (Mandal & Hawamdeh, 2025). Information pertaining to social ties, emotional sensitivity, and psychological identity is obviously sensitive. AI systems must use specific techniques to get user consent, preserve the context in which the data was gathered, and preserve privacy while collecting and processing large amounts of data at once.

The idea of informed consent has developed from a simple affirmation to a sophisticated understanding of how people's perspectives of their involvement change over time as data is produced, shared, and assessed against a growing body of secondary and later research on consent. Individuals should be aware of when their data is being used to create predictions and have the option to modify their privacy settings at any time. Safety and human dignity are intrinsically tied to privacy and autonomy, especially when it comes to insights or alarms generated by AI systems, such as mood monitoring apps and suicide prediction algorithms (Mansoor & Ansari, 2024).

The ethics of AI in psychological assessment include minimizing bias, explainability, and accountability. Additionally, explainable AI aids regulators, physicians, and patients in comprehending how certain data alter a risk assessment or the decision to prescribe a particular medication over another. People may find it simpler to trust one another and make choices jointly as a result. Physicians will need to collaborate with data scientists, ethicists, attorneys, and patient organizations if new frameworks that prioritize human dignity in innovation are to begin to emerge in the coming years (Tabassum et al., 2025).

3. DATA PROTECTION FRAMEWORKS AND LEGAL SAFEGUARDS: OVERVIEW OF GLOBAL DATA PROTECTION LAWS: GDPR, HIPAA AND OECD GUIDELINES

Among the most well-known international frameworks are the General Data Protection Regulation (GDPR) of the European Union, the Health Insurance Portability and Accountability Act of the United States, and the Privacy Guidelines of the Organization for Economic Co-operation and Development (OECD) (Schweiger, 2025). These are the fundamental frameworks for processing, exchanging, and safeguarding mental health data in a lawful manner. Both now have to navigate uncharted area as artificial intelligence becomes more prevalent in psychological applications.

3.1 GDPR: EU Mental Data Protection

The most comprehensive and significant data privacy rule in the world for AI-based psychological assessment, particularly with regard to mental health data, is the General Data Protection Regulation (GDPR). According to GDPR, health data is defined broadly to include more than simply personal data "related to the physical or mental health of a natural person, including the provision of care." According to Article 9, mental health data is a unique category of data. This implies that processing is only permitted with explicit, informed agreement from the individual whose data it is. Only under certain circumstances is this feasible.

This implies that the principles of need, proportionality, and openness must be adhered to at every stage of data collection and inference for AI-enabled mental health products, such as behavior analytics platforms, wearables that measure mood, or diagnostic chatbots. Instead than only being covered by the general terms of service, the patient's or users' consent must be informed, freely given, and especially for the present purpose. Cutting down on data: Processing is limited to the data required for its intended use (Kneese et al., 2025). This would force researchers and mental health applications to provide an explanation for each piece of data they gather and, if feasible, utilize data that isn't connected to an individual's actual identity.

The GDPR established the concept of Data Protection Impact Assessments (DPIA), which are particularly crucial when using a novel AI technique for psychological evaluation since such usage may significantly impact individuals' liberties or rights. Scholars are now advocating for a distinct "Mental Data Protection Impact Assessment" to address the particular dangers of processing psychological data with AI. They do this because they are aware that any abuse might significantly impact one's freedom, identity, and mental privacy. Second, Article 22 of GDPR emphasizes the need of human involvement in high-risk choices, such as those involving psychiatric diagnosis, crisis intervention, or therapeutic suggestions, and gives every person "the right not to be subject to a decision based solely on automated processing."

There are emerging issues in the GDPR-regulated fields of AI and mental health. For example, there is a tension between the rapid implementation of digital mental health therapies, particularly on a broad scale, stringent permission laws, and AI data collecting that occurs over time (Thirupathi et al., 2025). Many behavioral and psychological datasets are very personal and susceptible to re-identification, making anonymization a contentious strategy. By outlawing "significantly harmful subliminal manipulation" using AI-neurotech and introducing further monitoring for algorithmic emotional inferences made in settings like workplaces and schools, the new EU AI Act further guards against abuses of power.

3.2 HIPAA: The U.S. Model of Health Care Data Privacy

In the United States, services are developed under the framework of Health Insurance Portability and Accountability Act (HIPAA) for how hospitals, practitioners, insurance companies, and business associates treat PHI and sensitive mental health-related data. HIPAA sets rigorous standards that control the accuracy, confidentiality and availability of PHI and focus on how to maintain security measures with required notification procedures around data breaches as well as setting restrictions for mental health or other sensitive information released relating to the minimal necessary use for treatment.

HIPAA Compliance Pros and Cons For mental health services driven by AI, HIPAA provides opportunities but also limits. HIPAA serves as a solid baseline for data privacy and security in digital health environments, but it's limited to "covered entities" and their "business associates," a term that often encompasses none of the majority of digital mental health tools or apps or consumer services that operate outside of traditional healthcare structures. Users are less protected against data exploitation because of this regulatory mismatch, which provides them with a wealth of mental health information but less HIPAA protection (Luxton, 2025).

HIPAA's de-identification and minimal required data requirements are comparable to GDPA's data minimization and anonymization requirements where they apply. Under the HIPAA Privacy Rule, de-identified data may be used and shared for quality, research, and development purposes, provided that appropriate measures are taken to ensure that this is done. With the latest advancements, anonymization solutions driven by AI are becoming even more potent, enabling research, clinical practice, and secure cooperation without endangering patient privacy. However, the differences between GDPR's "right to erasure" and HIPAA's six-year record retention obligation continue to provide significant friction for platforms operating in both the U.S. and Europe.

Legal and policy scholars are increasingly urging HIPAA to be updated to address the risks to mental health posed by AI. Some of these changes include requiring AI vendors to explicitly disclose how they handle privacy information, requiring "informed consent" regarding algorithmic analyses a user is about to use, and requiring a licensed professional to supervise an AI-based technique for the duration of its use, probably to ensure that some human sentiment is incorporated into therapy (Wang et al., 2025). Enforcement shortcomings have led both the FTC and state attorneys general to bring cases against mental health app developers over unconsented data sharing underscoring the necessity of broad, cross-sectoral regulation of mental health data originating outside the realm of traditional medical practice.

3.3 AI Context and Global Standards in the OECD Privacy Guidelines

The OECD Privacy Guidelines provide a fundamental worldwide model for privacy that include ideas that may be directly used in AI-enabled psychological evaluation, while GDPR and HIPAA establish rules for specific domains. Limiting use (only using or sharing information for the agreed-upon purpose), identifying the purpose (letting people know what the collection is for), and limiting collection (only collecting what is required by fair and legal ways) are the cornerstones of the Guidelines.

As the OECD Guidelines acquire worldwide recognition, they are increasingly being compared to the OECD's new AI Principles, which state that AI must be reliable, understandable, and subject to ethical and legal guidelines. Data governance tailored to artificial intelligence is required, according to reports and legislation from 2024 to 2025. Even in areas like mental health, they also urge nations to cooperate on privacy, responsibility, and supervision of high-risk AI systems.

According to the Sanders team, a few key OECD Guidelines principles should be adhered to any AI models employed in mental health treatment (Shymko & Babadzhanova, 2025). These include accountability (the organization's responsibility to uphold moral principles and avoid damage), transparency (being explicit about rules and procedures), and individual engagement (users' right to access and modify their data). In addition to AI-enabled innovation that upholds privacy, freedom, and justice, they have resulted in new laws and legal reforms that have crossed national boundaries, including sandbox legislation and governance experiments. There is a good level of conceptual coherence between the OECD-GDPR-HIPAA regulatory framework, especially when it comes to the main ideas of protection, control over data use, and legitimate processing. However, there are still significant disparities in how these guidelines are used in context-specific mental health treatments.

3.4 Convergence, Conflicts and New Directions

People's curiosity in regulation and the ongoing conflicts has only increased as a result of the use of such frameworks in actual AI-based psychological testing. Many digital mental health services come under many regulatory categories (medical, consumer, and wellness), making compliance even more difficult, they argue. This is a result of cross-border data movement and corporate operations. Retention regulations (HIPAA), the right to be forgotten (GDPR), and data localization rules (certain nations' legislation) are all at odds with one another. Platforms for mental health that want to employ AI to assist patients find this challenging.

Rules would be especially useful in the field of "mental data." This encompasses not just clinical data but also the increasing volumes of behavioral, biometric, and neuro-technological data that AI systems are becoming more adept at interpreting. A legal "category" of "mental data" that is protected should be recognized under privacy legislation, according to privacy activists who are worried about mental privacy (Beg & Verma, 2025). This might include algorithmic audits, regulations requiring consent to share data, and even complete prohibitions on the use of AI in situations deemed too dangerous. Additionally, since psychological data is so sensitive and recognizable, some are beginning to believe that it may not be feasible. Federated learning and differential privacy are two increasingly common strategies for protecting data while enabling AI to extract valuable insights from it.

For national regulators and judges, international human rights law—particularly the rights to health and personal integrity creates a set of legal obligations and standards that are strikingly comparable to those found elsewhere (Palmer & Schwan, 2025). Since then, the Council of Europe, UNESCO, and the UN have all made changes to emphasize the importance of mental privacy. HTML Parameters: Mental Privacy and Informed Consent as in the age of artificial intelligence and neurotechnology, states were asked to provide temporary guidelines for neurological and psychological data, usually via General Comments or legally enforceable international agreements.

By emphasizing that some applications of AI in mental health care are absolutely prohibited, the EU's new Artificial Intelligence Act actually reinforces the GDPR. One of these applications is the use of emotional inference to persuade individuals outside of circumstances that are defined by safety or medical considerations. According to the precautionary principle and the advancement of legal, policy, and technology means, this kind of new legislation is indicative of a broader trend toward softer or reflexive forms of risk-related regulation. The global environment around data privacy in AI-informed psychological screening is always evolving and expanding (Dey, 2024).

4. AI-POWERED IDENTITY CRISIS INTERVENTION: PRIVACY RISKS AND LEGAL RESPONSE

Artificial intelligence (AI) is being used more than ever before by crisis intervention and mental health systems to assist individuals with emotional, psychological, and identity-based issues. AI identity crisis intervention screens, predicts, and assists individuals experiencing identity-related psychological issues, such as feeling out of place in their social role, being uncertain of their gender identity, or experiencing digital cyber theft, using conversational interfaces and data-driven algorithms. Examples of its applications include chatbots, digital therapeutic platforms, and monitoring technologies that identify distress signs in physiological markers and voice and text data. Therefore, although AI expands the therapeutic concept of identity, it also transforms identity from a private place to a marketable piece of data (Carneiro & Gomes, 2025).

4.1 Understanding Identity Crisis and Personalization in Digital Therapy Models

The privacy issues caused by AI-driven intervention systems are caused by four interrelated factors: algorithmic profiling, mission creep in surveillance activities, imprecise data flows, and breaches of individual permission. The term "opaque data practices" describes the lack of clarity around the use of sensitive data by AI systems. Many platforms gather emotional and behavioral information, but they don't always disclose how long they plan to retain or distribute it. By classifying people according to AI's prediction models, algorithmic profiling may identify users as "at-risk" based on sociocultural identification, gender expression, psychological variables, and inferred mental states.

Particularly when biased datasets are used by machine learning algorithms, these profiles may have an impact on bias, stigma, and prejudice. When crisis detection systems are utilized for other objectives, such as marketing, determining insurance risks, or (police) monitoring, this is known as surveillance creep. Third, consent flaws violate user autonomy: most AI-powered intervention systems rely on long, vague permission forms that don't make clear what identity-sensitive data is, why it's being used, or how long it will be kept. These dangers also highlight the tension between the necessity for privacy in accordance with democratic and human rights norms and AI's potential for predicting empathy.

4.2 Legal Accountability for AI Developers and Healthcare Providers

Legally speaking, AI-driven identity crises and questioning interventions are entangled in the nuances of data protection legislation, human rights jurisprudence, and health regulation. One of the most extensive sets of regulations for managing sensitive personal data is the General Data Protection Regulation (GDPR) of the European Union. Machine learning is now the most effective method for meeting all of GDPR's obligations. Information revealing a person's race or ethnicity, political views, religious or philosophical ideas, or sexual orientation is given further protection under Articles 9 and 13. All of these categories are quite similar to an individual's identity.

4.3 Predictive Algorithms in Behavioral Modification and Mental Wellness Apps

Users also have personal control over their digital identities according to the "right to be forgotten" guaranteed by Article 17 and the informed consent principle. However, these safeguards might be difficult to comprehend when it comes to psychological algorithms driven by artificial intelligence (Abilash et al., 2025). Can someone really "consent" when AI continues to learn and make assumptions about novel identity-related characteristics that users haven't provided, for example? Like explicit identifiers like a name or social security number, may digital emotional states or psychographic profiles be categorized as "personal data"? It attempts to safeguard data by classifying it into static categories, however AI-driven inference is not compatible with this. Because of this, there are gaps on the screen where important identity-based insights are "hidden" but not specifically secured.

4.4 Privacy violations through inference and digital surveillance

Regulating AI-powered identification technologies is more difficult in the US because to the patchwork nature of privacy and health legislation. Only covered health care companies are really subject to the Health Insurance Portability and Accountability Act (HIPAA), which is intended to prevent the disclosure of private health information. This indicates that AI intervention tools and mental health applications are mostly uncontrolled. People have the right to know what information businesses have on them and to have that information deleted thanks to state-level internet privacy laws like California's Consumer Privacy Act (CCPA). Few laws, meanwhile, provide protection against inferred identity profiling or psychometric profiling. There are no actual safeguards for identification or emotional information, and the FTC can only intervene after the fact to stop unfair and deceptive acts.

It should come as no surprise that the majority of AI identity intervention platforms operate in a gray area, which is unregulated by conventional healthcare laws but strongly related to emotional health and personal safety. This slippery slope generates moral issues that the regulations in place were never intended to address by allowing companies to benefit off or reuse data that attracts identities without having to accept accountability.

The absence of rules pertaining to identity-sensitive data has reached a critical point in India, where AI-powered counseling applications and digital mental health platforms are expanding at an astounding pace. Based on the concepts of permission, purpose restriction, and user rights, the Digital Personal Data Protection Law, 2023 (DPDP Act) establishes guidelines for the handling of personal data. However, it lacks guidance on how to categorize emotional, psychological, and gender identity data produced by AI systems, much as the GDPR. Inferred indicators of emotional or social identity are not recognized as sensitive, but biometric and financial data are.

When the Mental Healthcare Act of 2017 was drafted, it is likely that individuals did not believe that digital technologies might be algorithm-driven providers capable of self-diagnosing and self-treatment. As a result, there is now overlap between data protection and mental health regulations regarding AI, albeit these laws are yet incomplete. India will follow the rest of the globe, where AI technologies are advancing ahead of legal regulations, if it does not develop its own ethical guidelines and patient protection requirements for AI (Zhang & Wang, 2024).

They are also worried that the data generated by AI identity intervention techniques may be misused by other parties, such as the government, insurance providers, or employers. In the name of mental health, employers may deploy AI systems that monitor internet use to identify workers who seem emotionally unstable or ideologically out of place. Insurers would be allowed to see psychometric data while determining whether or not to cover a claim. They may also refuse to insure anybody they considered to be "high risk." Identity crisis intervention systems may be established by governments under the guise of public health or national security, but in practice, they are used to monitor minority and dissident organizations.

In these situations, it becomes difficult to distinguish between compassion and coercion, control and caring. These uses violate the principles of necessity, proportionality, and purpose restriction both ethically and legally. According to Article 21 of the Indian Constitution and Article 8 of the ECHR, they may also infringe against human rights safeguarded by both domestic and international law, including the rights to privacy, freedom of opinion, and dignity.

The ability of AI to mediate identity presents significant jurisprudential and philosophical issues. Identity was formerly believed to be something that a legal person created on their own. Legal responsibility changes when AI systems identify and address identity problems algorithmically: Is the self or the system the one who advocates for an individual's identity? If AI misinterprets a person's gender or mood, which may cause stigma or even injury, the designers, databases, and businesses will all be held accountable. This shared accountability is difficult for our human agency-based legal concepts to maintain.

AI that may alter messaging according to how agitated users seem may alter users' perceptions of themselves and their level of control over their life. The psychological effects are similar to coercive conditioning if an AI therapist casually imposes gender standards or pathologizes certain ways of expressing one's identity (Zhang & Zheng, 2025). The social-psychological aspects of algorithmic impact, which are crucial for preserving identity integrity in digital therapeutic settings, are not sufficiently covered by current consumer protection legislation. A collection of principles found in international human rights legislation may assist in formulating a rights-based approach. Everyone is born free, equal in rights, and with dignity, according to Articles 1 and 2 of the UDHR. No one should be permitted to violate someone's privacy without a valid cause. According to the International Covenant on Civil and Political Rights (ICCPR), privacy is a crucial component of freedom and identity.

In this case, human rights-based and people-centered standards must be adhered to by any AI systems that collect and utilize identification data (Gera et al., 2025). In particular, the 2021 UNESCO Recommendation on the Ethics of Artificial Intelligence discusses how identity, nondiscrimination, and mental health should be included in AI design. The informed consent has to go beyond simple checkbox exercises in AI crisis intervention situations.

Adapting to shifting selfhood and data settings might be better served by dynamic consent infrastructures that let people modify and comprehend inferred identity profiles in real time (Ohm). Third, artificial intelligence (AI) mental health care technologies must include explicit algorithmic criteria that allow external parties to verify for safety, respect for identity, and bias. Fourth, when selecting from subsets related to underserved groups, data minimization techniques must continue for identity anonymization mechanisms to ensure that the used training data cannot be re-identified or re-associated with people. Last but not least, autonomous AI ethical review committees composed of legal academics, tech specialists, and mental health specialists need to monitor global AI applications that may have an impact on people's privacy. This is to ensure that people's independence is never taken away by innovative ideas in care.

In addition to regulations, social governance techniques such as ethical design standards and digital literacy are also crucial. To create systems that include empathy, nonjudgmental language, and cultural competency in datasets and conversation models, AI developers, psychologists, and other AI professionals should collaborate. Designing for privacy should be required, not optional. Public-private collaborations might ensure that people trust AI counseling tools and establish norms for ethical identity-invention algorithm certification, similar to how medical equipment are certified (Ang & Lee, 2025).

There are new opportunities and new regulations at the intersection of identity, mental health, and AI. More individuals might benefit from using AI to assist those experiencing an identity crisis rather than humans, but there are privacy issues and the potential for data exploitation. Legal authorities worldwide struggle to balance the data-heavy world of smart-invasive interventions with the self-determined privacy ideal of traditional privacy laws. In addition to changing the legislation, a fresh perspective on privacy as a multifaceted right that is founded on identity and can be comprehended both algorithmically and emotionally is necessary to stop the needless infantilization of digital personhood. AIC intervention's future hinges on striking the correct balance between moral boundaries and technological empathy. Instead than taking away people's capacity to create and safeguard their own identities, AI should support them in doing so (Chavali & Dhiman, 2024).

5. CONCLUSION

Due to its speed and affordability, artificial intelligence is revolutionizing the way we diagnose, handle emergencies, and look after our mental health. This is something that many nations could not have envisioned five years ago. Predictive analytics and conversational bots, for instance, may detect early indicators of mental discomfort. These are a few ways AIs have increased accessibility to cognitive-behavioral therapy. These technologies seem to have the potential to improve the accuracy and accessibility of mental health treatment.

However, the ethical and legal issues that arise with privacy, identity, and autonomy become increasingly difficult to handle as AI becomes more autonomous and is used in wearable health systems. Finding a balance between safeguarding human dignity and privacy and ensuring that the promise of innovation aligns with moral norms of justice and compassion is the ethical and institutional challenge of employing AI responsibly in this situation. The path ahead is to develop frameworks and reforms that constrain technology in an ethical manner, shift the emphasis of government to people, and transform lofty objectives into universally enforceable regulations.

"Privacy by design" it is important to (re)think "privacy by design" if we want to alter the way AI-based psychological systems manage personal information. AI psychological models should include privacy, not only add it afterward or to comply with regulations. Making the systems so that we only get what we really need is the first step. This implies that databases should be anonymised by default and that individuals should have extremely tight control over their PII. For mental health technology, the privacy-by-design framework must include psychological and emotional privacy protection. However, as they are inferred mental states, this is a novel problem to investigate. As with any biometric identification that is inherently linked to a person's mental identity, the emotional information gleaned from voice tone, facial expressions, and text semantics has to be safeguarded with the same care.

With ensuring that moral responsibility is present throughout the life of AI systems, data ethics is another method to increase privacy-by-design. Technical protections alone cannot provide ethical AI for mental health; it must also address the ethical conundrums of duty, fairness, and consent. Technologists, psychologists, and regulators must collaborate to establish ethical guidelines that prevent algorithms from propagating stigma, cultural prejudice, or diagnostic stereotyping in order to safeguard our data.

To prevent overinterpreting distress indicators in psychopathological terms and in non-Western languages and cultures' emotional manifestations, even training samples need to be multi-cultural. Transparency is also essential in the medical industry. Both patients and physicians need to be able to comprehend the predicting process. Like bioethics review boards, independent AI will be included into mental health boards to provide continuous assessment of autonomy, fairness, and harm prevention throughout the product lifetime. Such behaviors show that data ethics is more than just abiding by the law; it is an essential, proactive activity.

The engineers must work with the attorneys, who must work with the psychologists, to establish privacy-by-design. The constitutional safeguards for privacy and mental health may be incorporated into technical rules that help lawyers and ethicists code. Two examples of designs that can go against the principles of informed consent are a dynamic user dashboard that lets users change their sharing settings whenever they want to and an automated data expiry setting that gives users the right to erasure under existing data protection rules. Legal values may be implemented in a technological system rather than vanishing as a result of these integrations.

The dynamic procedures that provide individuals with all the information they want should replace static agreements like care contracts in consent mechanisms. Constant consent will provide users of mental health AI systems with continuous notifications about how their data is being utilized, modeling adjustments, or sharing choices. Additionally, they might alter their choices as necessary. Legal agreements that govern AI health platforms may also include legal foundations for these mandatory disclosure obligations, providing clear explanations of how the algorithm operates and the limitations of its interventions. The regulations should be changed to make it unlawful to have consent designs with dark patterns and to withhold information concerning inferential profiling.

It will need to develop new methods to hold AI actors accountable for the damage they inflict when they step in, such as when they misdiagnose someone, create anxiety by disclosing information, or even discriminate against someone based on algorithms. The harm brought about by computerized thinking is not sufficiently reflected in the current tort and negligence rules. Therefore, developers, deployers, and health providers might all be held accountable for one another's conduct under specific AI liability principles in health law. Auditable algorithmic effect evaluations may be necessary for certification. " Before a new usage could be carried out, safety and fairness would have to be proved in this manner.

The ethical norms need to be institutionalized via intersectoral coordination. Governments might empower data protection regulators to create legally enforceable standards of conduct for emotional AI or establish national AI ethical agencies. Public-interest AI research frameworks should be created by universities and think tanks to guarantee that laws are supported by data. Finally, preventing jurisdictional arbitraging requires international cooperation. The AI and mental health data hoarding monopoly must be held responsible by multilateral, multiliteral human rights accords that promote equality, nondiscrimination, and psychological safety globally.

AI in mental health will eventually need more than simply technical know-how. Additionally, it will call for moral imagination, or the ability to develop and use technology in ways that really respect human dignity. Privacy and ethical concerns are becoming more and more important as we use more customized digital therapies to manage our emotions or crises. Responsibility must be the motivation behind both ethical arguments and innovation as ethics and responsibility are connected. Transparency in all facets, encouraging data ownership, and evaluating performance on empathy rather than efficiency are key components of ethical AI in mental health.

The principles of freedom and security must be constantly balanced in order to achieve a fair trade-off between privacy and innovation, as well as between ethics and innovation. While a hands-off strategy may lead to systematic prejudice and psychological manipulation, a heavy-handed approach may impede innovation and create barriers to crucial treatment. Therefore, our primary objective should be proportionality: risk-appropriate governance, responsibility commensurate to authority, and legislation that reflect people's ever-changing values. Society must move away from a reactive strategy that controls damage and toward a proactive approach based on design, where ethical conundrums are anticipated and protections are built into algorithms before damage is done. The moral fabric of caring will not be replaced by the march of innovation. Societies must build AI on privacy, responsibility, and empathy in order to establish a digital mental health ecosystem where technology is a friend rather than an adversary.

REFERENCES

Abilash, K., Kamini, P. S. M., & Joshi, R. (2025). Navigating Post-Pandemic Mental Health Challenges: Unleashing the Potential of Artificial Intelligence. In *Healthcare Informatics Innovation Post COVID-19 Pandemic* (pp. 55-64). Auerbach Publications.

Ang, C. S., & Lee, K. F. (2025). Ethical Considerations in AI-Powered Health Communities to Promote Good Health and Wellbeing: A Narrative Review. *Navigating Health Information in the Age of Artificial Intelligence*, 67-94.

Beg, M. J. K., & Verma, M. K. (2025). Revolutionizing Mental Healthcare Through Artificial Intelligence. In *Chatbots and Mental Healthcare in Psychology and Psychiatry* (pp. 21–54). IGI Global Scientific Publishing.

Bose, E., Kumar, C. A., & Meenakshi, N. (2025). AI-Driven Psychological Profiling on Social Media: Mechanisms, Ethical Breaches, and Regulatory Challenges in Data Inference. Recent Trends in Social Studies. 2025; 2 (1): 1–7p. *AI-Driven Psychological Profiling on Social Media Bose et al. STM Journals*, 2.

Carneiro, L., & Gomes, A. (2025). Applications of Artificial Intelligence Use in Therapeutic Interventions: A Multidisciplinary Approach. In *AI in Mental Health: Innovations, Challenges, and Collaborative Pathways* (pp. 167-212). IGI Global Scientific Publishing.

Chatterjee, S., Dindarian, A., & Rengaraju, U. (2025). Preserving Data Assessment, Privacy in Mental Healthcare: Ensuring Authenticity, Confidentiality, and Security in Data Integration from Diverse Source. In *Revolutionizing Youth Mental Health with Ethical AI: Transform Youth Mental Well-being by Exploring Responsible AI and GenAI Applications* (pp. 185–253). Apress.

Chavali, D., & Dhiman, V. K. (2024). The nexus of minds unveiling the significance of AI in mental health and viable remedie. *Open Access Research Journal of Biology and Pharmacy, 11*(1), 031-048.

Dey, D. N. C. (2024). Mental health of adolescents and youth in India: A critical analysis in the era of AI. *Available at SSRN* 5056368.

Dhar, S., & Sarkar, U. (2024). Safeguarding Data Privacy and Informed Consent: Ethical Imperatives in AI-Driven Mental Healthcare. In *Intersections of Law and Computational Intelligence in Health Governance* (pp. 197-219). IGI Global.

Dhinakaran, D., Raja, S. E., Jasmine, J. J., Kumar, P. V., & Ramani, R. (2025). The Future of Well-Being: AI-Powered Health Management with Privacy at its Core. *Wellness Management Powered by AI Technologies*, 363-402.

Gera, A., Dhull, A., Singh, A., & Singh, K. K. (2025). Legal and regulatory issues related to AI in healthcare. In *Responsible and Explainable Artificial Intelligence in Healthcare* (pp. 259–283). Academic Press.

Jafar, A., Shabnam, S., & Khan, A. (2025). Artificial Intelligence in Mental Healthcare: Opportunities, Risks, and Regulations. In *AI in Mental Health: Innovations, Challenges, and Collaborative Pathways* (pp. 339-378). IGI Global Scientific Publishing.

Kneese, T., Vecchione, B., & Marwick, A. (2025). A chatbot for the soul: Mental health care, privacy, and intimacy in AI-based conversational agents. *Communication and Change*, *1*(1), 15.

Luxton, D. (2025). AI-Powered Virtual Therapy: Toward a Responsible and Client-Centered Future. *Journal of Health Service Psychology*, •••, 1–9.

Mandal, S., & Hawamdeh, M. M. K. (2025). Digital Well-Being and AI: Navigating the Intersection Between Technology and Mental Health. In *Digital Citizenship and the Future of AI Engagement, Ethics, and Privacy* (pp. 111-132). IGI Global Scientific Publishing.

Mansoor, M. A., & Ansari, K. H. (2024). Early detection of mental health crises through artificial-intelligence-powered social media analysis: A prospective observational study. *Journal of Personalized Medicine*, *14*(9), 958. PMID: 39338211

Olawade, D. B., Ayoola, F. I., Ebo, T. O., Asaolu, A. J., Egbon, E., & David-Olawade, A. C. (2025). Artificial Intelligence in Forensic Mental Health: A Review of Applications and Implications. *Journal of Forensic and Legal Medicine*, •••, 102895. PMID: 40441026

Palmer, A., & Schwan, D. (2025). Digital Mental Health Tools and AI Therapy Chatbots: A Balanced Approach to Regulation. *The Hastings Center Report*, *55*(3), 15–29. PMID: 40557918

Schweiger, G. (2025). The ethics of AI-assisted digital phenotyping in adolescent mental health: A framework for informed consent and trust. *AI and Ethics*, •••, 1–21.

Shymko, V., & Babadzhanova, A. (2025). Ethical challenges and strategic responses to AI integration in psychological assessment. *AI and Ethics*, *5*(5), 5415–5423.

Tabassum, A., Ghaznavi, I., Abd-Alrazaq, A., & Qadir, J. (2025). Exploring the Application of AI and Extended Reality Technologies in Metaverse-Driven Mental Health Solutions: Scoping Review. *Journal of Medical Internet Research*, *27*, e72400. PMID: 40829151

Thirupathi, L., Kaashipaka, V., Dhanaraju, M., & Katakam, V. (2025). AI and IoT in Mental Health Care: From Digital Diagnostics to Personalized, Continuous Support. In *Intelligent Systems and IoT Applications in Clinical Health* (pp. 271-294). IGI Global.

Verma, N. (2025). ETHICAL IMPLICATIONS OF AI IN PSYCHOLOGICAL INTERVENTIONS. *Shodhbodhalaya*, 187-205.

Verma, S., & Pathania, B. (2025, August). Review on: Ethical Consideration in the Integration of AI Technologies in Mental Health Care. In *2025 9th International Conference on Inventive Systems and Control (ICISC)* (pp. 20-27). IEEE.

Wang, X., Zhou, Y., & Zhou, G. (2025). The Application and Ethical Implication of Generative AI in Mental Health: Systematic Review. *JMIR Mental Health, 12*, e70610. PMID: 40577783

Zhang, X., & Zheng, H. (2025). Psychiatry in the age of AI: Transforming theory, practice, and medical education. *Frontiers in Public Health, 13*, 1660448. PMID: 41089865

Zhang, Z., & Wang, J. (2024). Can AI replace psychotherapists? Exploring the future of mental health care. *Frontiers in Psychiatry, 15*, 1444382. PMID: 39544371

Chapter 18
Psychology of Confinement and Intersections of Imposter Syndrome:
Identity Reconstruction and Human Rights in Prisons

Atul Tyagi Tyagi
Supreme Court, India

Vasvi Talwar
https://orcid.org/0009-0007-0759-4816
Noida International University, India

Arunima Shastri
https://orcid.org/0000-0002-6260-1253
Christ University, Banglore, India

ABSTRACT

The "imposter syndrome behind bars" is the feeling many prisoners have that they do not deserve personal development, educational achievements or rehabilitative accomplishments while incarcerated. In the context of jail and prison, there are many have layers of profound internalized self-doubt as a result of society's bias against criminalized identity and the resolutely stratified nature of life behind bars. When prisoners accomplish something going to school, teaching other prisoners or taking part in therapy programs, as they can feel internally conflicted as to whether it has been real, if it is only them performing. This chapter emphasizes on that how

DOI: 10.4018/979-8-3373-6618-0.ch018

prisoners' dissonance slips into the personal stories of society portraying them as what they did, denying their humanity and truthfulness. The also supporting environments and help much in affirming positive identity rebuilding.

1. INTRODUCTION

"Prisoner psychology" is the central concept that is links with the imposter syndrome, identity reconstruction, human rights and legal discourse. So, the identity under short-term confinement is formed only by its constituents: power relations, social isolation, emotional suffering and mental stress. In prison, imposter syndrome which is considered as typified by feelings of inadequacy, disengagement and self-doubt takes on a unique form as it is infused with institutional hierarchies, legal stigmatization, and a disengagement from traditional social roles (Yona & Milman-Sivan, 2025). This prompted is to raise the types of questions that human rights must pose because of this conflict between self and confinement. There are multiple questions in this regards as- What damage does a visit to a prison do to the self? But without such structural change, how do people need to rethink identity and agency? What are the experiences that are either made worse or better in our world's prisons? which needs to be addressed.

1.1 The Psychological Impact of Confinement

Prison society is also highly disciplined and surveilled, creating an atmosphere of suspicion and hyper-vigilance. Well it's not surprising, is it? These are conditions that typically provoke and enhance psychiatric symptoms; anxiety and depression as well as self-harming (remember: George Whitmore) PTSD but also deeper illnesses such as paranoia, hallucination and suicidal thinking particularly in the stresses unique to solitary. The mental and psychological costs of such systems are taken far past their release to the patient even after they have been released from their sentences as patients pay in trauma related issues that continue long after their sentence is completed with trust issues, conflict in relationships, reintroduction to communities.

As it may further hold that this ethico-political wasting disease is not simply produced by sheer physical distance, but more essentially by the collapse of individual freedom and personal intentionality - as with the recurring deferments and the reminders that one „is an inferior establishment". Symbolic degradation that is meted out to prisoners over time will eventually be internalized by prisoners as a condition, and self-worth descent could even be experienced by some of them up to the point of their feeling identity doubt (Tran, 2023). The challenge of self-respect and self-dignity is even harder in crimination's stigmatizing (not infrequently dehumanizing) theatrics so pervasive to most penal regimes.

1.2 The Imposter Syndrome in Prison

The imposter syndrome itself generally understood to be a classification of long-term feelings of personal inadequacy and "fraudulence," despite evidence to the contrary in terms of success or competence takes on multiple layers when transplanted to prison culture. Here, however, the feeling of illegitimacy is not only a matter of individuals' (apparently criminalized) histories; it's also about lived surveillance and naming and degradation in prisons. The demand for a systematic construction of identity, and the negation of any genuine form of self-expression leaves the prisoner in an unceasing state of "ambivalence" between his 'own' self-perception and those external identities foisted upon him as "criminal", the "other" or the "outcast.

Feeling like a phony gets an extra twist when you pivot, as Perry has done lately, to do something righteous, like that prisoner attempting to self-educate or rehabilitate after landing in prison. And, these are people who perhaps have long taken that feeling of a fraudulence up into themselves within the prison hierarchy where such transformation is an unmistakable signpost marking them as fakes no matter what subculture norms vouch for them and outside it, since former inmates frequently continue to fight lingering shame when they face questions about whether they actually had changed. And here is where imposter syndrome reveals itself as the ripping point between trying to re-make one's self and constantly being viewed from the outside with skepticism, disbelief.

1.3 Identity Reconstruction and Recovery

However, as we all too painfully know, the ability to regain one's identity is twice as fragile in a culture that opposes carcerality. It would also appear that organizations whose primary objective is to prevent people from becoming men and women may be set up to institutionalize the dysphoria or "pathology" of identity rather than figuring out how to keep it fluid, knowing only that they want to guarantee an indefinite recidivism and, to the greatest extent possible, permanent estrangement. Only environments that respect the humanity and dignity of those who are incarcerated, promote autonomy, and provide mental health care to help reestablish a healthy self-concept. Education is the key because studies have shown that inmates who receive educational qualifications have less solidarity with the stigmatized self of the inmate and better outcomes for well-being after they are released (Francisco, 2021).

2. HUMAN MIND IN ISOLATION: PSYCHOLOGICAL MECHANISMS OF CONFINEMENT

Solitary confinement deprives inmates of the daily sensory and relational stimuli that sustain mental balance, and the psychological effects of confinement can result from a number of interconnected mechanisms, such as sensory deprivation, loss of control, circadian desynchrony, and social isolation, all of which can contribute to a series of undesirable cognitive, affective, and perceptual states. The human brain in prison is susceptible to significant personality changes as a result of social and physical deprivation.

The primary methods are to starve the senses, which means that the mind doesn't see much from the outside, to have a very limited sense of touch, to have a system that is patented so that a person has very little exposure to sunlight and natural sounds, and to spend one's entire life behind an artificial device in sterile, small rooms. This type of sleep debt can interfere with normal brain activity and create a cozy little breeding ground for creakiness in our cognitive function when it comes to focus, memory, and clear thinking. Individuals who are isolated frequently experience perceptual distortions, such as perceived illusions and even hallucinations, which indicate that the brain isn't processing its surroundings properly due to a lack of stimulation. When the mind isn't stimulated or put to use, it creates its own stimuli in the form of intrusive thoughts, paranoia, or even psychosis.

Social isolation is the other major issue. Since we are social creatures, the relationships we have have a significant impact on our mental health. In Donjon, social isolation creates a sense of loneliness, sternness, and emptiness that makes it difficult to control one's mood and increases feelings of anxiety, depression, stress, irritability, and anger. Additionally, the lack of social feedback and interaction prevents young people from developing a clear sense of self, which leads to identity disintegration and low self-esteem. Inmates frequently report feeling as though they are going "out of [their] mind" and losing track of time, if not reality. Finally, deprivation naturally follows from having no control over one's surroundings and daily routine and suffering from mental anguish.

Although prisoners do exhibit a coping mechanism that is formed during captivity, their independence is limited by the forced inactivity and enforced helplessness of incarceration. This increased stress reaction is compensated either by emotional numbness or hypervigilance. Additionally, since additional artificial light, such as natural light, or medicinal therapies that mimic nighttime disrupt circadian cycles, this pry-action nighttime element is anti-social and causes severe sleep deprivation, which results in emotional instability and cognitive impairment. Some refer to these damage-causing pathways as "solitary confinement syndrome" or "indefinite housing unit syndrome." Long after the time of isolation has ended, the symptoms may include hallucinations, paranoia, suicidal thoughts, anxiety, despair, or obsessive thoughts about the trauma experienced by a loved one. People who already have mental health issues are particularly vulnerable because they find it too difficult to control their symptoms in this setting (Thomas-Davis, 2020). Human rights and media groups have denounced the psychological harm caused by solitary and non-participatory incarceration as torture, and this has prompted calls to reduce or eliminate prolonged solitary confinement.

3. IDENTITY DISRUPTION AND RECONSTRUCTION: THE JOURNEY OF SELF WITHIN CONFINEMENT

Inmates deal with loss, revision, and self-reconstruction as part of the fluid and continuous psycho-social process of identity dissolution and reintegration in jail. However, such disturbance also presents a chance for reconstruction. Surprisingly, however, jail serves as a place to process traumas and poisonous habits as well as to reevaluate decisions made in your previous life. A lot of physiological and cognitive processes enable identity around new values like responsibility, empathy, or even the betterment of oneself. "We have witnessed prisoners turning to education, or vocational programming, therapy, and spiritual discovery" in the hopes that something will re-activate their ability for growth and self-realization.

However, to build identity in carceral space is not straightforward. Organizations that are more interested in control than transformation discourage us from real self-expression, or even from change. Also, it feels like shame of being in prison haunts them outside the walls preventing you from standing up as a new self. And when they do return, the society into which they return often falls back onto the template of that criminal past registering their existence and allowing old identities those who operated under different names so long ago to continue being refreshed. Reframing identity is, thus, not only a question of internal change; it is more profoundly an issue on the performative level as to whether such people have external opportunities to receive confirmation and social routes for reintegration. Support, mentoring, and involvement in your community and workplace may teach you how to "be" the new thing based on prosociality.

Thus, the self's brief camp retreat while in captivity involves a battle against existential blinders that prevent you from perceiving yourself and how others view you, in addition to being a journey into physical confinement. This process and its acknowledgement need to act as a reminder of how crucial it is for society to choose whether we will see those who are jailed as criminals who are changing or as always guilty and corrupted by their crimes. One aspect of redefining yourself under captivity is that freedom involves not only existing but also, in some manner, figuring out how to keep oneself alive so that one may resurrect oneself in the face of such a harsh and brutal system. It demonstrates that even in cramped areas, the human need for regeneration is not subdued. It's a subtly powerful illustration of adaptability and resiliency (Badawy & Shaban, 2025).

4. IDENTITY, LEGITIMACY AND POWER IN CONFINEMENT

The complex and dynamic ties woven throughout "Manhood, Race, and Power in California Prisons" affect not just the identity of inmates but also the way they are governed. The jail, on the other hand, serves as a kind of mirror reflecting the structure of power in society at large. Identity in jail is constantly shifting between internal hierarchy and external authority. Now, things actually change suddenly, and generally brutally, when one individual in that cage reaches a critical mass. As seen by their prison number, the simplicity of their outfit, and the routine of life in correctional institutions, they adopt a new solid institutional identity in place of their prior erratic and variable personal status as parents, employees, friends, or members of the community.

It serves as an instrument for demonstrating power in addition to being a symbol. Because of private control, administrative regulations, and social structures, the prison's reputation is based on its affordability rather than its meritocracy or morality. The old existence consists of a network of social connections that have deteriorated to the point that they are just a ghost of their former selves. And whether we can even have a modicum of personal mobility, liberty, respect, and communication is determined by power.

The prisoner comes to inhabit a self that is seen, surveyed and controlled. But under this imposed identity there is still the human desire to self-define (Craft, 2025). Some inmates who carry out "small" acts of rebellion writing, studying and bringing people into a community or mentorship program do so in order to reclaim some legitimacy for themselves outside institutional sanction. Refusal acts such as these reject the state's monopoly on valuing and empowering human beings in carceral spaces.

However, legality within limited parameters is debatable. It's simple to argue that our institutions are legitimate because we value public safety and justice, but many of these inmates don't share that opinion. Although the goal of incarceration is to aid in rehabilitation, in many instances it just serves to exacerbate racial injustice, inequality, and systematic prejudice. Command becomes a backstop rather than a cure for what remains of our feeble support for an immoral patient that penological conduct has become since morality leads to obeying the law. Additionally, new power structures centered on reputation, prestige, or safety emerge among inmate groups.

Although they create distinct subcultures, these hierarchical power interactions are a reflection of comparable processes seen in the exoskeleton. In contrast to the existing condition of compression, as Kelly Bundy said, "loosening up its ass" requires complete lack of support, like an incorrect weight preventing the original mass from bearing it. The divide of violence or respect and loyalty, betrayal or control and submission things that prisoners exchange is an example of this language of legitimization. As a result, authority enters the prison from both the inside out, as the institution requires it, and from the perspective of the convicts themselves (Bavin, 2025).

The axis of legitimacy may be shifted from institutional alignment to moral engagement by those that provide inmates the opportunity to share their own experiences, learn new things, and participate in restorative justice. Recalling one's identity therefore turns into a political act, a means of demonstrating one's humanity in opposition to the dehumanizing demands of imprisonment. However, these systems are not always supported and are poor. People are less inclined to trust these changes if neither the public nor an institution approve of them. And the pervasive skepticism in all of this exposes a position of actual power that is determined by a system that was created, if only partially, to doubt, hold, or employ force, rather than by honesty, which is never saying something but rather "doing" it—or being able to pull it off.

Both life and power dynamics constitute a sphere of the possibilities if "captivity" is effective. On the other hand, identity-interested organizations regulate, promote, and monitor which identities are acceptable in order to manage behavior in a somewhat covert manner. Slave assetless prisoners and liberal "good" busybodies who have severed their links to their past may be eligible for some benefits; eligibility requires adherence to the regulations. By requiring individuals to struggle for change rather than relying on it to emerge naturally, conditional legitimacy stifles genuine change. Instead of expecting agency to be subjugated by institutional scriptwriting, realistic rehabilitation acknowledges it. Therefore, detainees do not have to see authority and power as constant. As an alternative, people need to see them as a relational process that is always being negotiated through action, reaction, and reflection (O'Connor, 2025).

In that universe, some inmates recover some degree of power by banding together with others in similar situations and fighting for their rights, not via communal religion and ritual. Rather than abandoning our definition of power as dominance, we do away with an analytical approach and substitute relational forms of solidarity that alter the way inmates band together, defend themselves in court, or support one another. When they band together and take action to improve the situation or even simply defend their rights, they are claiming that the system is wrong for suppressing them. Reminders that power in captivity can never be total are often concealed in these attempts, both here and there. Instead, it is constantly negotiated via moral imagination and group opposition. Legitimacy "trickles up" in the manner I just explained: it stems from the ability of inmates to express themselves and demonstrate their humanity while being subject to very stringent regulations (Cobb & Fox, 2025).

5. EPILOGUE: POST-CONFINEMENT REINTEGRATION AND SOCIO-PSYCHOLOGICAL FREEDOM

People who are in jail and want to be free mentally and socially have to go through a difficult and dangerous journey called re-entry. Being free from one's sentence is not a moment of freedom; it is the start of an invisible fight to get back some kind of shape, another chance to pretend that one has a form that is not tainted by crime. Of course, the great escape has its own ironies: for every wall they break down to free you from prison walls, the less transparent ones rise to take their place, made of stigma, structural defoliation, and an impenetrable shell of prison conditions. For many former inmates, the mental prison of years of being watched, dependent on institutions, and judged by outsiders lasts long after they are released.

The linearity and monotony of prison life had become their default way of thinking; freedom is more confusing than freeing. This process, this institutionalization, is a real test of how much prison can change us, not just what we do but also who we are. "Take me apart." Reintegration, one would think, has less to do with jobs and housing and more to do with getting a handle on straight-ahead rehabilitation. It has to do with becoming a person again. Since we are only reflections of what society says about us, this is a battle to the death. Communities that see ex-offenders as individuals to be watched and feared must somehow (re)establish legitimacy outside of prison gates. Finding a job may be challenging, housing discrimination persists, and reassembling the social safety net after incarceration is very difficult.

Through exclusion, such as being imprisoned, this violent marginalization also had the consequence of replicating and reoccurring. However, even during the most difficult periods of these hardships, individuals have shown incredible resilience as they develop into the kind of people that take on roles, care for others, and serve. Some people see this as their liberation, their genuine creative or spiritual existence. You may avoid all of the degrading narratives that society places us in thanks to this increased degree of steadiness (Easterbrook-Smith, 2022). For others, engagement with restorative justice programs, or getting involved with opportunities to either be educated around a cause or mentor for one, is a means of flipping lived experience into empowerment and action. In these performances, social reintegration is interwoven with a moral project of remaking one's relationship to the past, others and oneself.

Real socio-psychological freedom does not occur where there is no limit/denomination anyway but in the positive reconstitution of agency the power to choose, shape one's destiny and meaning; and form identity beyond other people's (or even our own) denominations. But such independence is impossible. “It needs a community that feels in the potential for rehabilitation, and has trusted prison.” And the community is mighty, one way or the other on reintegration back. Hence, the post- confined’s rehabilitation must not be reduced to behaviour control but they must work toward redeeming their lost humanity. Where there is space for belonging and this is what congregations can create accountability becomes invitation; freedom is not then the risky business of liberation but grounded as from beginning to end.

Even under the best of circumstances, the work of liberating ourselves psychologically, at least runs underground and silent. Repatriated captives have to integrate redeemed years with deep memories of domination and in the face of trauma, remorse, dread that they will revert to learned responses. ~When we’re talking about freeing minds from the social psychological mind control in place, maybe it’s not a ordinary therapy so much as quite literally a narrative reconstruction – where we get to be provided with an opportunity to tell our story new – one of how not only did we ‘get through’, but that we got bigger and richer (vs. smaller and narrow) because of what was done to us. Here, post-confinement identity interprets the tension between past and future—loss recognized but not predetermined to be destiny. Then work that means something, relationships that matter and a sense of self emerge as those who have come to know not just the right to freedom but incrementally the ability to live in it (Roberts, 2025).

It must be that in intercourse with his kind, the mind may live as in freedom; without it, the mind is a void. Freedom entails not only the destruction of the physical wall, but also the moral and emotional walls in the hearts of those freed, as well as to a society observer (Reddy & Amer, 2023). In order for any reintegration to sense, there needs to be a change, from the society side and also from the individual perspective but the shift that is needed most of all must be in our thought processes: we need to replace punishment with healing, distrust with solidarity and rejection exclusion. Only then will life after confinement be a space in which identity is not once more incarcerated by the past, but revitalized as possibility, dignity and human solidarity (Evteeva et al., 2024). To witness socio-psychological emancipation is not simply a personal victory to me; it is, It believe, a moral and collective one as indication of what the human spirit is beef stew in the garment of its flesh can accomplish both alone and together to lift itself up again from self-made ruins and present itself in fresh attire (Francisco, 2021).

6. COPING MECHANISMS AND ADAPTIVE RESILIENCE UNDER INCARCERATION: IDENTITY RECONSTRUCTION AS PSYCHOLOGICAL RESISTANCE

It is not a punishment; rather, it is a severe psychological separation and detachment from life that requires active endurance to endure. This is not just passive physical submission, but rather an internal experience and an action where identity and personality must be consistently asserted despite overwhelming evidence of indignity. What theories refer to as a "identity crisis" is paradoxically seen as supportive of transformative processes that lead from reflection to non-alienating identity (re)construction and recognition. This is the secure forgetfulness of imprisonment that I will discuss later (i.e., a complete loss of autonomy, or the combination of temporal and social isolation with enforced submissiveness socialization into the lowest, if not a specific, position within institutional power dynamics). In a setting where physical restrictions and desensitization are commonplace prison, as the French refer to temperance and moderation, or "life size" as criminologist Jerome Miller refers to it in his seminal work "Last One Over The Wall" inmates devise and employ sophisticated coping mechanisms to cope with the stress of their surroundings, which turn into psychological acts of resistance through institutionalized representations of "the jail house."

Inmates seem to use a wide range of strategies to address their issues. These techniques are comparable to those used by folks who have lost a spouse. They aid in acclimating individuals to the possibility that something negative may occur, but the consequences of each reaction are evident in the new world they produce. These adaptive techniques prevent any farmer-tamed knowledge from emerging because they cause psychological deflection as a temporary performance between frantic arrogance and self-doubt. The above-described adaptive techniques for coping with jail realities go beyond straightforward attempts to alleviate acute symptoms. These qualities subtly affirm one's humanity while also somehow reclaiming what has been lost when one is at great danger and confronted with something that is intended to harm them (Shiels et al., 2021).

Remaking oneself in prison is effectuated through intentional self-reflection where prisoners reflexively scrutinize their life stories, admit responsibility for criminal behaviors, and intentionally work to reconstitute a more favorable sense of self grounded in pro-social values and goals. This reconstitution is not a surrender to institutional power but, as that body of work on "reinvention of self" theorizes, the active separation by prisoners from their internalized criminal identities and the elaboration of valorized alternatives through various kinds of cognitive labor, educational involvement, and programs designed to impact upon self-esteem or criminal social identity or antisocial ways of thinking. Significantly, alterations in coping strategies during incarceration have been linked to mental health outcomes; fewer dysfunctional coping strategies (such as avoidance, denial, and behavioral disengagement) are linked to better psychological well-being and fewer psychiatric symptoms. As a function of personality and circumstance, it is likely that emotional or problem-focused coping will exhibit more distinct links to (psychiatric) functioning. The negative impact of institutional deprivation is mitigated by emotional resilience (ER), a quality that enables one to control emotional responses to upsetting situations without upsetting the psychological structure.

Research has shown that among inmates, psychological instability and resilience are negatively correlated. Therefore, resilience in the context of prison life cannot be uncritically viewed as a non-problematic ability to cope with a harmful environment. While effective methods of emotion management and identity reconstruction allow psychological survival during incarceration and involve forms of meaningful personal change, some of these ongoing emotion management processes what recent scholars have dubbed "sedative coping" may have iatrogenic effects after release into everyday environments, where people find themselves cut off from experiencing relational connection or estranged from their own emotions (Castro & Collins, 2021).

7. LAW, PSYCHOLOGY AND LIVED EXPERIENCE: PSYCHOLOGICAL THEORIES OF INSTITUTIONALIZATION AND LEARNED HELPLESSNESS

In order to appreciate the intersection of legal and psychological abuse with learned helplessness or how it is supposed to work in a theory on learned helplessness as well as why institutionalization works, some level of dismantling dehumanization countries practice for punishment has to be understood in terms of basics. Martin Seligman based his original model of learned helplessness on experiments in which animals exposed to uncontrollable aversive events, were unable to be withdrawn from similar conditions even when withdrawal was possible. This model suggests that exposure to uncontrollable aversive events causes a psychological state in which people perceive themselves as unable to control events, resulting in passivity, loss of motivation and depression. It is the case that through repeated failure an individual learns that their action is nevertheless not contingent upon such consequences, thus shifting their cognitive expectancy regarding self-agency.

However, modern neuroscience has revised this understanding and established instead that the brain's automatic response to inescapable aversive experience is one of passivity not learned helplessness per se, but rather unlearned and neurobiologically prewired neural state modulated by serotonergic systems originating in the dorsal raphe nucleus. This contrast is important because it demonstrates that institutional deprivation acts at a biological, rather than only psychological level and could impair the very neural systems involved in exercising control and responding adaptively.

Institutionalism is one of the neatest ways to create learned helplessness, because powerlessness is built into formalized systems. When people reach institutions a prison, a child welfare atrium, psychiatric hospital or residential setting designs enforce limits on decision-making, mobility and autonomy. The loss of control occurs simultaneously at various levels: one cannot set their own schedule, cannot decide what happens to their body, cannot regulate social connections and often any challenge to institutional decisions is met with punishment or retaliatory measures.

Institutions may order people to rehabilitate themselves but offer them no real chances of redemption. The law may exist in such a way that people are told that if they behave a certain way, freedom will follow, but the system just defies compliance and operates in such a manner to create circumstances for meaningful rehabilitation to be impossible. Gregory Bateson's concept of double binds characterises these situations as an extremely damaging, since they generate internal dilemmas the individual cannot win or escape from Such opportunities are considered particularly insidious when located within power structures where questioning authority is disallowed. "It's another aspect of how oppressive double binds, as philosopher Sukaina Hirji argues, operate to make it so that no matter what we're choosing, we're also actively supporting the oppressions force us to choose from (Herrick et al., 2025). One of the individuals trapped inside a carceral institution who doesn't report the abuse helps to support institutional violence; if they do, they face punishment and more loss of power. Either way, they're mechanism in their own subjugation.

The experience of being institutionally diagnosed can't be apprehended only through clinical perspectives, as institutions generally and routinely work to negate people's own clear understanding of their lives. In the mental health and legal systems in particular, there is steadily increasing utilization of the language of "lived experience," which involves including individuals with first-hand experiences as recipients of institutional contact in service design and policy dialogues. But, as many lived experience workers attest, institutional systems often demand that their knowledge is rendered into professionalized, palatable narratives that scrub out the moral stink of institutional harm. Yet when somebody says, "Nope, not trauma just abuse was intentionally hurt and scarred by institutional actors," clinical paradigms work to pathologize this clarity with terms such as resistance or failure to integrate or unrecovered. This institutional silencing of truth-telling is a form of psychological violence that further traumatizes to the original trauma of institutional contact.

Criminal justice systems exhibit this paradox most strikingly the perpetrator is brought to justice in a court of law and the victim is forced to relive the trauma with testimony, public exposure and protracted proceedings that are not within their realm of influence. Litigation makes victims relive their own suffering in the wrong way It compels public rehashing of wrongdoing by the victim, puts technicalities and legal "forms" on a higher pedestal than human pain. Unpredictability and uncontrollability of the pressure cooker."

Adequacy of Indictment & Trial Process Unreliable process = LH Individuals "do not know how long it will take, are unable to change contacts despite truthful testimonies and frequently find actors in the justice system as themselves indifferent/hostile towards them. This uncertainty, following from the unpredictability of law, where victims do not know when or how they will be released increases the long-term stress and thereby establishes exactly that condition of uncontrollability which is necessary for learned helplessness to develop.

The neurobiological effects of rearing in institutional settings offer an explanation for why simply moving individuals out of institutions does not necessarily time-reverse the clock to restore autonomy or psychological health. The brain adjusted to institutional powerlessness through the acquisition of mechanisms that extinguish motivation and escape responses as a defensive, energy-saving measure. And even when this constraint is lifted, the neural systems underlying agency and of learning to control are still suppressed.

This goes some way towards explaining why people with histories of institutionalisation go on to experience unemployment, isolation and ongoing mental health problems long after leaving institutions. It's not just that they've internalized a kind of psychological rendition of their powerlessness, but rather that the neurobiological condition of passivity has become stuck even as external conditions change. "Doing better" takes longer to accomplish than merely having new circumstances and it absolutely requires explicit, sustained opportunities to experience successful control in settings that are doing a great deal to explicitly support learning new forms of response (Benedict, 2024).

This demand that the connection between law, psychology and confinement must be addressed systemically, not one person at a time. Just as treating learned helplessness (such as learning not to be helpless through interventions and processes of social support and skill development), these individual level interventions take place within institutions that may themselves reinforce the anticipated inhibitory effects on recovery. True reform will require legal systems to roll back our institutional reliance on incarceration as a default response to human distress, provide legal protections for autonomy wherever people are placed in institutions, and create spaces in which voice can be given to those who wish to speak truth about harm suffered under institutional authority without fear of having that voice dismissed or silenced by professional judgment. Restorative approaches that attend to the voices of survivors and create nonhierarchical spaces where work can be done to address institutional abuse have promising possibilities for the revelation of damage to the soul by institutionalization.

8. FORENSIC PSYCHOLOGY AND HUMAN RIGHTS VIOLATIONS IN CUSTODIAL SETTINGS

Sensory deprivation, sleep deprivation, isolation, threats to loved ones and hours of interrogation contribute systematically to reducing one's brain. but they still are clearly regarded as able-to-reason-effectively-byno-means-mentally-incapable-of-being-sane sorters-out of facts. And nothing if not predictable is the psychological inheritance of past torture, in custodial interrogation PTSD, depression, anxiety, hypervigilance dissociation and even suicidal ideation that comes home to roost with such pervasive regularity across so many people groups in so many cultures around the world. Inadequate protection from torture in custody is no meer ineffectiveness, but rather the failure of a system that marks the end of accountability which should prevent abuse.

The Istanbul Protocol is the single greatest international development in forensic psychology's ability to document and contest custodial abuse of human rights. Adopted by the WHO in 1999and updated in 2002, the Istanbul Protocol offers references for clinicians to guide them through medico-legal evaluations which aim to establish a causal nexus between reported torture, physical injuries and psychological follow-up. Before the implementation of Istanbul Protocol, state forensic personnel commonly denied evidence of torture, in practice shielding torturers from liability by having control over the forensic examination (Hermandez-Saca, 2025). The Protocol empowered independent forensic professionals to contest state narratives with clinical standards so robust that torture becomes visible and prosecutable. All medical-forensic examinations carried out in accordance with the Istanbul Protocol should be supported by intensive documentation of physical findings through body mapping and injury photography, as well as radiological studies, together with detailed psychological assessment using internationally validated diagnostic interviews. Trauma-related intrusion-re-experiencing, avoidance, hyperarousal and emotional numbing, and cognitive symptoms are examined by the forensic psychologists that can indicate such diagnosed torture sequelae.

The assessment requires attention to temporal links between reports of torture and emergence of symptoms, recognition that psychological injuries are diagnostically valid even when physical sequelae have healed, and evidence of functional impairment indicating the lasting impact of torture on occupational, social and psychological functioning. The Istanbul Protocol recognises explicitly that torture impairs psychological and neurological mechanisms, shattering the premise of torture leading to confessions made in good faith. Forensic examination According to guides provided in Istanbul Protocol provides a medico-legal report, the most important evidence that can be used in pressing charges against perpetrators, enabling survivors to seek civil remedy and assisting claiming asylum by those who fled from torture. But it is applied inconsistently globally and many forensic physicians are unaware of the criteria required; some countries do not acknowledge inter-disciplinary psychological assessment in cases of torture. However, the time from the establishment of a Protocol to its standard implementation is one during which custodial risks and abuses may continue (Hartman et al., 2022).

The forensic psychologist working in custody is challenged by the ethical contradiction of working in a system where the culture does not reflect that psychological health is valued. Immigration detention facilities are such an oxymoron employing mental health providers in the setting of institutions that are designed to serve as a deterrent through deprivation, uncertainty, and loss of freedom. These are "invalidating environments," in psychologistspeak, and the keepers of these environments deny the emotional suffering or respond with escalating punishment instead of therapeutic care.

These environments produce published emotional and behavioral dysregulation, all in keeping with a pathogenic environment, not personal pathology. Children who are exposed to extended immigration detention experience stress going beyond what is developmentally appropriate, and investigators have documented inadequate medical screening, split and transient health care and a failure to address acute mental health crises in facilities housing children as young as 6 months old. A median length of stay of 43 days more than twice as long as allowed under the Flores Settlement Agreement is systemic abuse of legal rights, combined with severe and widespread psychological trauma. Corrections-based psychiatrists and forensic psychologists explain how institutional environments discourage clinical advocacy, neutralize psychological stressors, elevate concerns about risk over therapeutic effectiveness (Shen, 2025).

This structural discouragement of clinician advocacy is in direct conflict with the provision of mental health treatment, and makes mental health providers complicit co-perpetrators of human rights violations. Forensic psychologists should attempt to both offer care in therapy while recording institution effects, maintaining clinical confidentiality and yet functioning as agents of the institution, and encouraging clients' mental health care needs whilst within insitituions designed to restrict mental health. Ethical practice demands that forensic psychologists do more than play critic from the sidelines, it requires us to make institutional contradictions visible; documents human rights abuses, rather than being complicit with their obscurance; and promotes reformation at a structural level in which psychological deprivation ceases as de facto institutional strategy.

9. CONCLUSION

The path between incarceration in an institution and a perspective of resistance is a significant journey, and both are psychological as well as political. Imprisonment – physical, psychological or epistemic – acts to repress consciousness itself, dismantling systematically any individual's ability to understand oppressive features in their world, enunciate their experiences and envisage something else. The learned helplessness seen in institutional settings (including prison) is not evidence of individual pathology, but rather a neurobiological adaptation to the structure of power and authority within controlled environments that subjugate one's agency. It is a road, but one that leads to consciousness as well: when people see the instruments which ensnare them are not inevitable or natural, but constructed and thus potentially changed so too does the possibility of freedom become imaginable. This movement from confinement to consciousness is the base on which structural change must be built, since institutions can only be reformed or dismantled if necessary numbers of people regard them as unjust and develop the power together to resist.

Critical consciousness theoretical groundings are key to understanding how subordinates go from being disempowered by themselves to becoming political actors who can transform the world. There were two types of consciousness: naïve consciousness in which people accept oppressive conditions as normal or natural and critical consciousness in which they recognize the social and political contradictions and realize that they are able to act to intervene and transform themselves. Consciousness-raising occurs through dialogue and discussion, not by passively absorbing information: as people in conversation with others also experiencing oppression begin noticing the parallels between their constraints and the constraints of others like them, they start to see these circumstances as factors of human construction rather than features of nature.

That recognition is liberatory in its own right, for it shifts the onus of oppression from individual shortcoming to systemic injustice, thus twigging loose the shame and self-blame that oppressive systems leverage to maintain psychological dominion. The transcendence of the development of critical consciousness lies not only in transforming people's thinking but fundamentally changing their relationship to, and belief about, acted agency. The genuine reflection results in action people who see oppression are pushed and encouraged to resist it, going from objects acted upon to subjects that do the acting.

Liberation psychology, as outlined by Fanon (1967) and Ignacio Martín-Baró (Martin-Baro et al., 1990), along with the work of current practitioners, systematizes critical consciousness within a broader psychological model that makes room for collective liberation in addition to individual therapeutic healing. Liberation psychology makes the locus of psychological distress explicit in that it points to oppressive sociopolitical systems as the source, and explicitly denies the

Western tendency toward individualization of suffering pathologizing responses to repression as intrapsychic disorder rather than rational response to unjust living conditions. Having felt torture firsthand during the Algerian War of Independence, Fanon came to a somber understanding that oppressive institutions cannot be transformed into places of healing; only through deconstruction and dismantling can we achieve liberation. Liberation psychology emphasizes that, as a means of regaining power and dignity and changing their situation completely, the oppressed should engage in collective action and organize struggle. This model is an explicit rejection of paradigms that focus on individual adaptation to unaltered oppressive systems and demands psychology serve the cause of resistance and resistance movements. Behavioral change in that context, it bears noting, is deeply collective: individual efforts to resist wrong take on force only when they mobilize groups of people; internal psychological adjustment generalizes to social changes in how institutions are structured and resourced so as better to promote goods like dignity, autonomy and well-being.

10. FUTURE SCOPE

The decolonization of mental health and justice institutions is obviously an important site for the application of liberatory consciousness to institutional change, particularly in so far as Indigenous peoples and other colonized communities who are confined have been the sites where colonialism never ended. Mental health law Both Canadian and international mental health frameworks are, in essence, colonial. Lawgiverly mental health laws in regions like British Columbia function to enable the state-supported curtailment of individual autonomy and bodily integrity such that they replicate existing colonial mechanisms of control. Indigenous people experience forced psychiatric confinement not as medical care but as an extension of centuries-old state violence to eliminate Indigenous self-determination and replace traditional health practices with colonially defined medicine. Decolonization of mental health systems would involve recognition of these colonial harms and violence, centering Indigenous leadership and self-determination as the approach to developing mental health services, quickly increasing funding for indigenous-led services, ending racist practices in main stream service modes, and fundamentally reducing dependence on coercive measures.

Sunrise Healing Lodge and the handful of other Indigenous-led healing centers show paths that are based not in colonial psychiatric models but rather rooted in traditional spirituality, cultural practices, community accountability. Decolonization also acknowledges that people who are labeled as mentally ill, although they were not colonized in the traditional sense of territorial conquest, have been subjected to systematic distancing, discrimination in institutions and the denial of their knowledge claims, which are forms of epistemic control that can be resisted using decolonial praxis.

Restorative and transformative justice paradigms provide substantive alternatives to punishment-oriented confinement by redirecting psychological and institutional focus toward recovery, responsibility, and social transformation.

Transformative justice understands that our individual harm is an expression and interaction with systemic oppression: we cannot eradicate harm without striving to also dismantle patriarchy, racism, ableism, colonialism and other systems contributing to it. Abolition frameworks are built through the Black, Indigenous and marginalized community organizing work that makes possible a vision of transformative justice around dismantling prisons, policing, militarization while building systems centered on communities for healing, accountability and actual safety. Abolition contends that another world is possible where confinement is not the knee-jerk reaction to human struggle, one where communities resolve conflict and harm through conversation and relational repairation, one that supports psychological wellness through systems based on people's dignity rather than control.

The shift from containment to consciousness is the precondition for any strategic, viable institutional change. Those who find themselves trapped in the paralysis of learned helplessness cannot conceive the possibility of freedom, nor can powerless communities come to together to confront systems that limit and bind them. Consciousness itself, though the consciousness to know that you are dealing with injustice plus a sense of agency and possibility is transformative. As a larger and larger portion of the public develops critical consciousness about institutional harm, as those harmed by confinement become more vocal about that harm and its injustice, as alternatives to confinement (e.g., restorative and transformative justice) show both feasibility and efficacy, then institutional change becomes politically possible.

The key question of societies around the world is whether institutional actors will, if not legitimatize consciousness and resistance as reactions to injustice, cease using the restriction itself to try to crush out consciousness. True institutional reform is the path that does those things: cultivating critical consciousness, foregrounding voices of people who have actually been affected by institutions (including by building more restorative and transformative justice into systems), exacting decolonization upon mental health and legal systems, and at base—that we do less to keep depriving society for partaking so heavily in a confinement focus on responses to human pain/conflict/difference.

REFERENCES

Badawy, W., & Shaban, M. (2025). The impact of imposter syndrome on ego integrity and gender dynamics among aging nurses: A mixed-methods study. *Geriatric Nursing*, *65*, 103467.

Bavin, K. (2025). Working for nothing: the exploitation of postgraduate students. In *Embracing the Unknown* (pp. 135–144). Policy Press.

Benedict, D. S. M. (2024). 'Om Mani Padme Hum': Discovering the Spiritual and Psychological Dimensions of a Sacred Mantra from Tibetan Buddhism. *Available at SSRN* 4742637.

Castro, A. R., & Collins, C. S. (2021). Asian American women in STEM in the lab with "White Men Named John". *Science Education*, *105*(1), 33–61.

Cobb, H. L., & Fox, K. S. (2025). Unmasking Imposter Syndrome Among Women in Academia: A Call for Systemic Change. In *Empowering Women in Academia: Improving Methods, Practices, and Approaches for Change and Transformation (IMPACT)* (pp. 89-122). IGI Global Scientific Publishing.

Craft, J. L. (2025). Self-Compassion and Law Student Professional Identity Formation. *The Journal of Law Teaching and Learning*, *2*(1), 235.

Easterbrook-Smith, G. (2022). Skin in the Game: Imposter Syndrome and the Insider Sex Work Researcher. In *The Palgrave Handbook of Imposter Syndrome in Higher Education* (pp. 173–187). Springer International Publishing.

Evteeva, M., Burges, L., & Gelabert, T. S. (2024). Internalized misogyny: The patriarchy inside our heads. *Journal of Integrated Social Sciences*, *14*(1), 82–108.

Francisco, N. A. (2021). Bodies in confinement: Negotiating queer, gender nonconforming, and transwomen's gender and sexuality behind bars. *Laws*, *10*(2), 49.

Hartman, A., Hoessler, B., Tom, V., & Camman, C. (2022). Identity as a compass when navigating uncharted equitable spaces: Our queer evaluation practices. *New Directions for Evaluation*, *2022*(175), 53–73.

Hernandez-Saca, D. I. (2025). Re-Framing the Master Narratives of Learning Dis/Abilities through an Emotion and Intersectional Lens. *Journal of Disability Studies in Education, 1*(aop), 1-33.

Herrick, S. S., Bennett, E. V., & Bundon, A. (2025). Feeling 'not enough'or 'too much': Exploring how LGBTQ+ adults experiencing disability navigate Canadian health contexts. *Journal of Health Psychology*, •••, 13591053251327263.

O'Connor, R. (2025). Working-class imposterism in the law school:"I always have this in the back of my head that I'm expected to fail". *The Law Teacher*, •••, 1–25.

Reddy, G., & Amer, A. (2023). Precarious engagements and the politics of knowledge production: Listening to calls for reorienting hegemonic social psychology. *British Journal of Social Psychology*, *62*, 71–94.

Roberts, K. T. (2025). wisible within the nvisib txola tersectic ci. *Human Rights (Chicago, Ill.)*, *50*(5).

Shen, A. (2025). Behind Our Masks: The Impact of Intersectional Identity on Neurodivergent Masking. *Backstory, 1*(1).

Shiels, T., Kenny, N., Shiels, R., & Mannix-McNamara, P. (2021). Incivility in higher education: Challenges of inclusion for neurodiverse students with traumatic brain injury in Ireland. *Societies (Basel, Switzerland)*, *11*(2), 60.

Thomas-Davis, S. (2020). Cloaked in Liminality. *Prison Stories: Women Scholars' Experiences Doing Research Behind Bars*, 51.

Tran, N. (2023). From imposter phenomenon to infiltrator experience: Decolonizing the mind to claim space and reclaim self. *Peace and Conflict*, *29*(2), 184.

Yona, L., & Milman-Sivan, F. (2025). The Prison-Identity Complex: Unravelling Labour and Law in Identity-Based Prison Worklines. *Laws*, *14*(3), 37.

Chapter 19

Reframing Success and Contribution in AI-Augmented Systems:

Challenges to Parenting Children With Hearing Impairment – Imposter Syndrome and Rethinking Human Worth

Prangya Parimita Behera
https://orcid.org/0009-0004-8286-6402
KIIT University, Bhubaneswar, India

Binita Behera
KIIT University, Bhubaneswar, India

ABSTRACT

Parenting in the era of algorithms requires parents to navigate strong societal forces as well as expert systems that employ technology and data to manage caring. Children who are deaf or hard of hearing and their families may benefit much from such technology, but it also brings with it the competing demands of monitoring, emotional escalation, and the constant need to improve. These frameworks stand to misselitiate diverse forms of communication and the modality that so many deaf and hard-of-hearing people's lives revolve around in ways that subsequently shape parents' experiences, activism, or other parenting within narrow bands. As a result, the use of alternative theoretical perspectives becomes necessary in order to understand the diversity that exists amongst contributions by both children and their caregivers outside canonical measures of success.

DOI: 10.4018/979-8-3373-6618-0.ch019

1. INTRODUCTION

The type of work it takes to raise deaf children becomes an entanglement of what could be and what is, braided together with an understanding of the implications of "success" and contributing to society" as they exist within a space in which AI is involved. And the tech that underlies effective, results-driven data play with 21st-century life ways and markers for success, but there are normative paths in this new edifice of play that can inadvertently marginalize kids with disabilities and their families. AI tools–teaching algorithms, and hearing support may seem to give hope that parents of deaf children can learn to communicate better with their children or communicate normally–isolates them into acting like normative development schedules or measures of productivity as they become available grow on the same vine imposter syndrome grows (Kim & Yim, 2021).

Some on the cutting edge in similar assistive technologies such as speech-based interfaces for Cochlear Implants (CI), the growth of speech recognition software and AI fueled education platforms, it is a messy ecosystem that AI integrated systems have with any child who experiences hearing loss. They offer hope for improving education, communication and language. But the normative presumptions we have about what sort of sounds we make, and should make, and hear some more useful than others also relies on these devices. These AI-generated norms run the risk of reinforcing a deficit model of hearing loss and often medicalize nonverbal cues or sign language.

Algorithms and dashboards of performance indices are increasingly tools both of empowerment and discipline, and some parents who navigate this terrain will find themselves subject like never before to the surveillance and datafication of their child's growth, development and progress. "Two edged" effects of social learning It is worth paying attention to the duality of social learning effects feeling like a waste (which can be partly associated with impostor syndrome) in the duality that reflects emotional stress and higher caregiving burden among families from accepting AI-mediated norms. In those frameworks, attempts to "optimize" the development of the kid along data streams from multiple sources can ignore the messy, embodied reality of a life spent raising a deaf or hard-of-hearing child.

In order to normalize their children's learning and learning satisfaction, DHH moms and dads' parental guilt is portrayed as systemic imposters who believe they are inadequate or that they are not typical parents in accordance with society and technologically perceived standards. In the same way that motherhood is judged against criteria that are foreign or unachievable for most caregivers, the saved and archivedo archive drone is enhanced with constant monitoring against algorithmically determined standards and conversations with expert systems.

Parents may internalize these messages, which may lead to persistent feelings of shame, loneliness, and self-doubt that are detrimental to the health of the family as well as the wellbeing of the parents. Furthermore, children may develop the sense of being the odd one out or not "up" to anything via their interactions with biased AI settings (for auditory-verbal modes) as well as other people. A more integrative approach that actively captures various communication modalities, relational entanglements, sociocultural possibilities, and richness in various paths to deaf-and-hard-of-hearing identity replaces the current, drastically fragmented definition of success and contribution, which is based on achievement as productivity, with this dynamic pattern of increasing (Ying & Ai, 2025).

The disability justice draws attention to nondominant bodies as well as to the refusal of ableist judgements that equate one's worth with [the possession of a certain type of productive body, or the ability to listen]. The ethics of care privileges relationship, dependency and the moral value assigned to caring (in) human value in that respect. It's in those possibilities that AI technologists, policy makers and families may be challenged to imagine systems which strengthen a more pluralistic sense of what it means to thrive that account for our contributions beyond standard accomplishments as well as care work, character strength, communicative diversity and inclusive common pursuit. We should make AI-enhanced goods that allow for these kind of polyphonic experiences and we shouldn't put even more holes in the collective net in which they are cast so that these hearing-impaired children and their families can at least do and feel enough to get out of their way (Continisio et al., 2023).

1.2 Aims, Scope and Key Questions

This situational awareness illustrates the promise and caution in implementing AI-based assistive technologies for hearing impairment, foregrounding care as both a practice and value essential to navigating that life coherently coherently with it being meaningful and inclusive as objectives are as-.

- Investigate social and psychological problems in parenting of Children With hearing impairment
- To investigate the Economic Challenges in parents of Children with hearing loss For research on communication content relating to positive parenting for children with disabilities
- For making studies to understand parents expectation from the state and society to deal with the burden of parenting children with disabilities.

Raising children with hearing loss is a complex and interconnected process. A structured narrative review based on your four research aims and recent studies is presented below.

1.2.1 Social and Psychological Challenges

Emotional Stress and Mental Health: High levels of stress, anxiety, depression and isolation are reported among parents (in particular mothers). The stigma, social misunderstanding and lack of acceptance further compounds the psychological load leading to frustration and feelings of being alienated from the community.

Family Functioning: Diagnosis challenge traditional family roles and functioning leading to caregiver burn-out, stress in marital and sibling relationships, emotional adjustment.

Coping Skills: Parents often use emotion-focused coping (for example, seeking social support and spirituality) as well as problem-focused coping (such as learning sign language and acquiring information), but may feel underprepared.

1.2.2 Economic Challenges

Financial Burden: Hearing aids, therapy services,special education undertakings and frequent visits to the doctor create aheavy financial obligation on families which results in lack of proper care orparent sacrificing in terms of employment

Access to Services: Restricted access to specialized services, particularly in low resource or rural settings, magnifies economic and logistical difficulties.

1.2.3 Communication Materials on Positive Parenting

Lack of Resources on Positive Parenting: A shortage of easy-to-understand messages and training materials on positive parenting for families with children who have a disability is cited by many parents. Too much or too little advice from experts can inhibit good parenting and emotional growth."

Intervention Programs: Web-based curricula and parent training programs have demonstrated potential to enhance knowledge of desired child-rearing practices and decrease parental stress yet access is unequal

1.2.4 The role of government and society according to parents

Policy and Support Systems: Parents want early identification systems, reforms in inclusive education, financial support and access to mental health supports. They are also advocating for higher public awareness, decreased stigma and more sign-language and disability education in mainstream institutions.

Community and Professional Support: Participants would like to see stronger support networks, specialized care facilities, and professional advice targeted to the special needs of hearing-impaired families.

1.2.5 Overview of Difficulties and Parental Expectations

Challenge/Need Key Issues/Expectations

Social/Psychological Stress, stigma, isolation, family strain

Communication Materials Demand for helpful, effective, and positive tools

Government/Society Expectations Early intervention, integrative policies, financial assistance, awareness

Parents of deaf children encounter interrelated social, psychological, and economic, as well as communication barriers. They are in need of support from the government, society, and experts to promote positive parenting and enhance their children's well-being.

2. THEORETICAL FRAMEWORKS ON SUCCESS AND CONTRIBUTION IN CHALLENGES TO PARENTING CHILDREN WITH HEARING IMPAIRMENT

Capability theory provides one critical method that focuses, not on the functional capacities or conformist norms of individuals, but on 'real opportunities and freedoms at their disposal to pursue what they have reason to value in order for well-being to be realized' (Sen, 1999). Viewing parenting a DHH child in terms of successes is thus recontextualized to include environmental and social supports that make flourishing possible in one's own embodied experience. This principle also highlights the need to enhance children's capacities in such 'higher order' areas as communication, self-expression, cultural involvement and emotional health (in addition to or instead of concentrating on speech intelligibility and linguistic targets alone). Simultaneously, it values the massive amounts of care work that parents do to create supportive environments and advocate for resources forms of labor invisible in typical measures of success.

By recognizing dependency, vulnerability, and reciprocal recognition as constituent elements of discourses on worth and contribution, relational models of value and care theory further this discussion. The social environment of raising children with hearing loss is a complex web of support, communication, and caring. A successful definition bases the issue of being aware of one's own and others' needs on values; an ethics of caring viewpoint in an individualistic society that emphasizes productivity has also challenged this. As a result, contributions are seen as relational, nurturing, and caring activities that maintain ties of social and familial belonging rather than as individual accomplishments. This justice orientation is consistent with the disability justice analyses that resist ableist norms and assert that it is valuable and contributory to recognize disabled lives and ways of being. In this way, care ethics offers a normative framework for reconsidering the challenge and contribution of parenting in ways that exceed traditional measures of performance.

The disciplinary field of disability studies including the social model of disability anomaly to medicalized or deficit discourse on hearing loss is Disability Studies tightly linked with and forms an important counterpoint to discourse that constructs hearing loss as a (potential) detriment. The social model moves the attention from individual impairment to societal barriers/ discrimination, and structural ableism, which restrict possibilities of participation and value recognition. Regarding AI-enhanced parenting systems, the plan also discourages supportive relationships, demonstrating how policy and technology systems can reinforce exclusionary norms by favoring one developmental trajectory or mode of interaction over another. Along with cultural involvement in Deaf/HoH communities, it promotes inclusive learning spaces, technological accessibility, and pedagogical techniques that acknowledge dialect variation in sign languages and diverse communication modalities (Rakovac Bekes et al., 2024). This intersectional approach also aligns the increasing calls for AI and educational technology to be co-designed with disabled communities, so that systems can bolster rather than erode relational care, agency and dignity.

Lastly, we may start to understand these and other complicated circumstances through which people are raising DHH children in the modern era by using theories of capabilities, relationality, social justice, and psychological well-being. They also cast doubt on the few success examples that demonstrate how parents and kids play more varied and giving roles in AI-enhanced family practices. If research, policy, and design are to really support fair, respectful, and fulfilling family life, they must sincerely adopt this kind of reframing (Sheng et al., 2024).

2.1 Normative Ideals of Success in Neoliberal and Techno-Optimist Cultures

In cultures with neoliberal or technooptimist ideologies, the standards of success are closely entwined with individualist, market-efficient, and technologically progressive aspects. In a free-market system, neoliberalism defines success mainly in terms of individual accountability, competitiveness, and measurable production. As a moral or societal virtue, it honors the lone entrepreneur who can pull himself up by his bootstraps and get his resources to work themselves into the conditions of possibility. According to this approach, measurable economic results like income, employment, and consumption are the main indicators of success. People's perceptions of the market as a disciplining force that rewards the most hardworking individuals based on merit, and so on, give rise to a never-ending, superficial capitalist notion of success as being only determined by one's financial situation. By supposing that everyone can access and participate in market systems, this human agency of the self eliminates structural inequality.

The cult-like belief in technical advancement has now strengthened and magnified these same ideals; in other words, science fiction has evolved into techno-optimism, which holds that technology, particularly digital technology and artificial intelligence, is the driving force behind the (final) improvement of society's problems. Techno-optimists worship technology for its own sake, much like they worship so-called "goods-in-themselves," which, according to their rhetoric, are means of achieving a steady increase in economic output, greater productivity, and constantly rising living standards through magic or some other means (Kushwaha, 2024).

Through the additional belief that technology, particularly digital progress and artificial intelligence, is paving the way for mankind and serving as our greatest defense against all of society's problems, techno-optimism builds upon and broadens these principles. Tech optimists applaud technology advancement as a benefit in and of itself as it leads to unending economic development, increased productivity, and improved living standards. Such a vision implicitly conveys the idea that success is dependent on acquiring and using state-of-the-art technology, which is portrayed as liberating tools derived from potentialities for enhancing one's abilities (new possibilities). While maintaining economic growth, the ideology propagated by the "techno-capitalist machine" "conceives of innovation as for evermore delivering away from want and returning towards abundance," where technological advancement itself amounts to a morally and socially necessary ethical demand.

In parent and disability communicative contexts, (e.g. parents raising children with hearing loss), the cultural expectations to fit in may result in responsible action being taken to "normalize" through technology and achieve set milestones that align to auditory/oral standards. The promise of expanded access offered by educational technologies and AI-augmented tools, for example also can serve to perpetuate these conceptions of success, by privileging features such as speech clarity and language development as stand-ins for success. As a result, fewer alternatives may be seen to exist by families whose communication forms, identities and caregiving values that are resisting commodified and standardized ideals of normativity are inadvertently marginalised.

Detractors say these paradigms obscure relational, cultural and ethical dimensions of success and contribution in favour of individual economic results and technological firepower. The ceaseless pursuit of growth and improvement has ignored caregiving as labor, social dependence and the value of diversity in modes of communication and identity (Ioannou & Andreva, 2019).

2.2 Capability, Care, and Relational Theories of Human Value: Disability Studies, Deaf Studies, and the Social Model of Impairment

With human dignity, agency, and relational interdependence as fundamental qualities, these frameworks together critique reductionist deficit-oriented scientific and technology approaches to disability and success that are still prevalent. As societies are increasingly shaped by AI-defined systems, these points of view serve to indirectly reinforce expanded conceptions of human value beyond the household level and enable a more nuanced valuation of humans that goes beyond conventional measures and models of productivity.

The chapter begins with an introduction to capability theory, a normative approach created by economist Amartya Sen and philosopher Martha Nussbaum that goes beyond functional ability or economic contribution to take into account people's "true" freedoms and opportunities. According to capacity theory, a person's structural and social circumstances should determine whether or not they are able to accomplish certain goals, rather than "measuring" individual performance results as is the case with many of these traditional measurements (Tang & Ji, 2024). This rephrasing applied to hearing loss, where success could be defined as not only speech comprehension and a reachable hearing level but also the growth of nonverbal communication skills, cultural engagement, accessible education, and emotional health. Information on how much care a person needs is insufficient to convey its complexity, the additional duties it places on caregivers, and the challenges and incentive it creates for them.

The diagnosticians were not motivated to participate in reflection exercises that focused on what people with disabilities might achieve from their viewpoints. Intense caregiving connections, such as those between parents and caregivers who provide daily care, advocacy, and emotional labor, are valued by radical capability theory as a way for people with disabilities to achieve enabling settings. This changes the narrative from one about a child's "deficits" to one about the social and interpersonal support that is essential for human development and wellbeing (Li et al., 2025).

This ethic of relatedness holds that caring is a contribution in and of itself, and that it should be acknowledged as such for the first time rather than being lost or absorbed in these capitalist times, when neo-liberalism normalizes care work as unimportant or unobservable because it does not generate any economic output. It is a point on the compass rose of technology design that supports families and acts as a normative guide in the context of AI-assembled parents' care, enhancing rather than replacing human relationships (Dacids et al., 2018).

This paradigm distinguishes between impairment, which is a person's physical or sensory differences, and disability, which is a collection of socially imposed restrictions, discrimination, and exclusion. Rather, it promotes the elimination of structural ableism, an approach to accessible communication methods (such sign languages), and settings that embrace linguistic and cultural diversity (Dharanidharan & Kuruveettissery, 2025). Additionally, rather than aiming for mainstream success, disability studies present deaf children and their parents as active agents combating stigma, learning to take pride in their deaf identity, and feeling a part of a community.

Deaf studies acknowledges sign languages and Deaf epistemologies as acknowledged and empowered forms of communication, and it adds to this conversation by highlighting Deaf culture as a valid language (and) mode of culture. In order to raise bilingual-bicultural methods that respect both spoken language and sign languages, this connects with medical and rehabilitative attitudes to hearing that are concerned with oralism and assimilation (into being "normal"). Understanding the kid as a member of another linguistic/cultural group and as a part of it is essential for hearing families to appreciate the impact of Deaf studies (Asta et al., 2024). Because opportunity and capability are so closely related, culturally competent AI-enabled systems developed from a Deaf perspective could promote more equitable access while respecting linguistic and cultural diversity an overt challenge to technological paradigms that unintentionally ignore nonauditory communication.

To frame some of the difficulties of raising deaf children in an improved age, these theoretical models call for a bio-psychosocial, justice-based approach. They advocate for the extension of what constitutes success to include relationship-, cultural-, and social-value forms, reject the homogenizing normativity of technology that defines variation as pathology, and praise caring labor as a fundamental contribution. In order to co-create inclusive systems that respect many identities and the relationship between communication disparities and the unavoidable constitutive nature of human life, this synthesis calls on technologists, legislators, educators, and families (Molchanova & Chekanova, 2018). However, like any new technology, this kind of envisioning might result in more equal and respectable futures, where hearing loss is not a hindrance to thriving but rather an augmentation of human variety.

3. AI-AUGMENTED SYSTEMS IN THE LIVES OF DEAF AND HARD-OF-HEARING CHILDREN

AI hearing aids and cochlear implants are perhaps the most concrete applications of AI augmentation for deaf and hard-of-hearing children. Today's hearing aids have highly advanced algorithms built in to help filter out unwanted noise, improve speech sounds and tailor sound processing based on the situation, like the environment or speaker voice. These changes are beneficial and aid in the clarity and ease of experiencing auditory information leading to improved child learning access to spoken language, communication and classroom participation (Paghandeh et al., 2019). For children, AI is able to provide a more naturalistic experience of hearing which expands the auditory world of the child and increases that listening bubble into which group activities and conversations can be heard. Yet these devices do not restore hearing to something akin to a "normal" range of auditory input, but afford only an altered sensory pathway that must be similarly accommodated and supported over time by caregivers who program and maintain the device.

Beyond amplification, AI speech recognition and real-time captioning services have important implications for educational and interpersonal settings for deaf or hard of hearing children. AI systems are more and more employed in classroom scenarios to transcribe spoken lectures for people who are deaf or hard of hearing, convert spoken words into text on-the-fly for students with learning disabilities, and generate real-time subtitles on media content. And the barrier-free tools address the limitations that many auditory processors have, ensuring equal access and understandability (Quittner et al., 2010). AI platforms that learn with children can adjust instruction to the pace and style of every child, providing personalised feedback and resources that grow engagement and overall educational impact. These adaptable tools are in line with inclusive teaching practices, which take into consideration learner variety and flexible teaching modalities (Erbasi et al., 2018).

3.1 From Hearing Aids to AI-Enhanced Cochlear and Assistive Technologies

The use of AI systems as mediators for communication and learning presents continuous issues. Service delivery Families of Speech Generating Devices (SGDs) users are placed in the dual role space as both 'users' and 'managers' of complex technological artefacts with their ability to interpret AI outputs, make technical adjustments and wordsmith output matched by the parental imperative to ensure that the child's changing communicative needs are accommodated. This technological activity increases the burden of care and is often based on unevenly distributed resources and levels of digital competence, raising issues with equality. Additionally, AI-enabled metrics and developmental dashboards provide data that parents and educators use to keep an eye on kids. While this data may help guide evidence-based action, it may also cause anxiety due to the pressure of normalization and the feeling of being continuously monitored. Ambivalence between empowerment and surveillance also highlights the ambiguous character of AI as both a supervisor and a facilitator in a child's learning process (Greenhagh et al., 2023).

Due to spoken language biases and auditory comprehension being preferred over alternative modes (e.g., sign languages, tactile signing, visual cues), AI-mediated devices can inadvertently support normative views of successful communication. These psychosocial factors highlight the need for incorporating ethical, culturally sensitive and trauma-informed AI systems in development and implementation (Palavi et al., 2025).

At all levels of development and in parallel with research outcomes, the authors propose multi-stakeholder efforts that bring technologists, educators, healthcare workers, families and Deaf communities together to contribute to technology design will be necessary. Design co-research approaches insist on the involvement of DHH [(deaf and hard-of-hearing)] users in forming technologies that value their communicative choices, cultural norms and everyday practices. Policy must also promote open infrastructure, equitable resource allocation and protection from abusive data practices or biased algorithmic decisions. Pedagogical training of educators should raise awareness about advantages and limitations of AI tools and should supports pedagogies that are flexible so as to leave sufficient space for plural ways of communication (Eyuboglu et al., 2021). Only by grounding AI-augmented systems in integrative-justice can deaf childhoods be disenfranchised of homogeneity and replaced with the recognition that they are 'valuable differently'.

AI-assisted systems have changed the way deaf and hard-of-hearing children perceive sound, language, learning, and communication; providing powerful aids for breaking through tradition-based hearing barriers. However, these technologies also create additional levels of complexity regarding cultural participation, normative expectations, care labor, and psychological well-being (BeForte et al., 2020). New ways of understanding success and contribution that are intimately related to inclusion, relational care, and cultural competence may be generated through critically destabilizing these relationships. AI and deafness As we forge ahead, AI's role in the lives of deaf and hard-of-hearing children will be shaped by reaching into these frameworks to shape what technologies and practices we create that augment human dignity, connection, and flourishing (Singh & Singh, 2024).

3.2 Educational Platforms, Speech Recognition, and Algorithmic "Benchmarks"

AI-based education is also showing more and more promise in helping deaf or hard-of-hearing children learn, with educational platforms that are both interactive and accessible now becoming personalized. The platforms, which sometimes use speech recognition technology to transcribe spoken language into real-time captions or text, allow deaf children to follow along and study with hearing peers. This enhanced speech-to-text accuracy is achieved by other advanced AI architectures filtering out background noise and supporting a variety of accents, although — tremendously – you are providing improved access to the classroom (Ching et al., 2018). Additionally, some tools have AI-based sign language tutors or avatars that provide interactive and personal experience in learning the sign language at the child pace–which is very important since many deaf children are born to hearing parents who might not immediately communicate using the linguistic signs (see media1.png). In addition to contributing to language learning, these tools span communication divides between deaf children and their families. Artificial benchmarks are built into such educational technologies to monitor development by examining linguistic outputs, comprehension and engagement measures (Billen et al., 2023).

3.3 Datafied Childhoods: Surveillance, Metrics, and Developmental Dashboards

Datafied childhoods, in which continuously produced fine-grained developmental data are re-mobilized for further analysis via dashboards at the parent, educator, and clinician levels, are becoming an increasingly important component of AI-integrated systems in D/HH children's everyday activities. Metrics including language acquisition progress, social interactions, speech quality, and learning engagement are monitored via these development dashboards. According to experts, these data-driven technologies create a kind of surveillance that may cause more stress and worry even while they provide parents immediate feedback and personalized intervention plans to help their kid learn and grow (loh et al., 2025).

The risk of constantly quantifying our child's development is that it could render the intricate process of growing up and developing into data-points and overly specific milestones, which risks side-lining other types of communication about, or progress in meeting, this vast array of potential. This datafication raises ethical issues concerning privacy, autonomy, and the psychological effect on children and families of being constantly scrutinized for success through algorithmic measurement. It is therefore crucial to also mitigate the potential harmful effects on these children of AI-assisted activities.11 Weighing the positives of data-informed support against sensitivities around them, will be a key factor in ensuring equitable childhood neuro-phenotype AI augmentation (Chen & Liu, 2021).

4. PARENTING UNDER THE GAZE OF ALGORITHMS AS INTENSIVE PARENTING, EXPERT SYSTEMS AND THE PRESSURE TO OPTIMIZE

In today's society, the practice of parenting becomes more and more indwelled by mediating and formative algorithms, AI-enhanced systems, as well as expert knowledge constructions particularly in case of parents being responsible for children with hearing loss (Gilliver et al., 2013). Algorithmically driven "systematic" intense parenting is a double-edged sword providing parents with the knowledge and resources to be smart, but possibly making them feel more observed as parents, anxiety, nervousness, self-doubt based in "asks," not demands (Ching et al., 2010).

Expert systems provide normative ways of responding to your input, or in plain English, actions you should take or guidance on how to "best" manage your child's hearing loss. One example of this is the AI-augmented decision-support tool for parents in medical (or educational or social care) settings with a hearing-impaired child. To help give tailored interventions or corrections, these solutions, for instance, are used to analyze automated speech recognition results, educational attainment information, and the kind of equipment (hearing aid) used (Hall & Tomblin, 1978). In addition to acting as a caretaker, this kind of monitoring puts the parent under continual scrutiny as an algorithmically "membrane" performance (in which one becomes a high-res human).

Family relationship and power may be reconfigured (re)defined by the algorithm parents deploy. The offloading of agency and judgment to AI systems should also free up capacity and duty, which may impact on trust between parents, teachers and clinicians (Fellinger et al., 2009). These encounters underscore the importance of just and accountable design and participatory governance structures in AI decision-making systems that intervene in family life and parental autonomy (Meinzen-Derr et al., 2008).

All ironing is forgotten once the imperative to be perfect in a world of algorithmic scrutiny emerges, which fragments care into merely an end-point divorced from its contextual, emotional and human aspects (Topol et al., 2011). Yet, the more one focuses on being aware of other peoples needs and developing an emotional intelligence, which understands the logic behind (social) interconnectedness opposed to logical self-centered motives for "success", it challenges this reductionism. This entails encouraging designs and norms in such AI-influenced settings to be more flexible and pluralistic, allowing parents to contribute to their children's well-being in a variety of ways, rather than just socially optimizing them. Along with it, there should be consideration of how our social and technical structures might reinforce exclusion or inequality by giving preference to a certain kind of speech, information, or resource (Hornsby et al., 2017).

The answer to these problems is interdisciplinary. Cultural customs, family values, and caregiver variety. No Assistance as Technologists, medical professionals, educators, legislators, and disabled communities should all be involved in the development of AI-assisted parenting supports. They can co-design an approach to this type of support that strikes a balance between the algorithmic advice that would be produced or summarily programmed for imperative generation by algorithms and respecting the diversity of caregiving (including families with multiple members from different generations at the same time) and cultural norms for parents/caregivers in various childrearing spaces around the world without converting offensive remarks or sensitive personal information into simple numerical metrics (Stevenson et al., 2010).

Policies must protect against the dangers of monitoring and algorithmic overreach in order to prevent the increased stress of intense parenting from worsening mental health or further marginalizing low-tech households (Wake et al., 2005). Parents may be educated to effectively interact with the expert systems for their children via digital literacy and awareness, giving them the ability to exercise power over rights as much as care. Developing AI with an inclusive, transparent, and equitable foundation may empower parents rather than ensnaring them in a limited optimality regime (Chen et al., 2021). This crucial step makes it possible for new networks and dialogues to engage families in electronically mediated places and frames the endeavor as one of social justice, autonomy, and care rather than merely innovation (van der Spuy & Pottas, 2008).

4.2 Algorithmic Norms and the Pathologizing of "Deviations"

We are concerned that normative assumptions about acceptable or typical conduct and skills are expressed in algorithmic systems used in social services, health, and education (Ravi et al., 2016). By reifying diversity as a deficit or disease, such algorithmic standardizations run the possibility of creating pathologizing measures for handicapped bodies and subjects (like those declared for toddlers with hearing impairments). Through the identification of non-normative forms of communication, behavior, or development as disordered and need repair, AI-tech that is trained on data that supports ableist worldviews and prevailing cultural norms may promote exclusion. More than just reification or classification according to abled norms, this pathologization of disability is not neutral; it determines who has access to resources, services, and figures in the absence of humanizing, putting disabled people outside because they are biomedical possessions rather than complete human beings (Levinger & Alhuzail, 2018).

This results in a type of digital surveillance and control where algorithmic rulings, which increasingly act as "courts of last resort" for "normal" (acceptable) functioning versus "deviant" (unacceptable) behavior, replace the feudalist approach (Yoshinaga-Itano, 1999).

4.3 Emotional Labour, Care Burden and Moral Judgement of Parents

The care of children with HL is hard and stressful, which may be burdensome for the parents and result in social disapproval. Parents who do emotional labor are constantly negotiating their own and their kids' emotional lives, trying to see the bright side of things and control everything that can be controlled while also pleading for help and for accommodations. Mothers experience considerable psychological and physical strain to provide, 24-hours-a-day help in planning treatment sessions, maintaining assistive technology and preparing educational materials. It's the responsibility of mothers who carry most of the caregiving burden that is hidden and exacts a toll on women. Mo of hers are more likely to be stressed and burned out, and to experience social isolation (Matthijs et al., 2012).

Parents today may be morally condemned more harshly for not adequately promoting the welfare of their child, in both social and algorithmic terms. Any divergence from the socially supported or algorithmically determined norms for language proficiency, progress in communication development, and attainment could result in internalized shame toward or blame for themselves. Besides mediating between social and technological expectations, these pressures produce a fragile landscape where parents are buffeted and questioning themselves in both practical and emotional terms by the norm of intensive parenting. Supportive policies, and empathic practices recognize and reduce this hidden labor (Alkahtani et al., 2025).

5. IMPOSTER SYNDROME IN PARENTS AND CHILDREN: IMPOSTER FEELINGS IN PARENTS OF CHILDREN WITH HEARING IMPAIRMENT

For both parents of deaf or HH children and the children themselves, impostorism a chronic doubt that one will be exposed as a fraud even in the absence of evidence to the contrary is a major psychological challenge. The phenomenon of impostorism is a manifestation of this complex when external normative demands, usually delivered to the individual through technology-mediated expert systems, fixate and prescribe specific goals in relation to social integration success or communication skills (Schmulian & Lind, 2020).

Imposter syndrome is only a subset of the struggles many parents of children who are deaf or hard-of-hearing experience. These struggles are only compounded when students find themselves trying to learn square-by-multipedal device or system maintenance and troubleshooting as they fight for the right under the watch of educators and doctors to be able what's good. Parents by contrast hate to be put upon in this way and also are reticent to ask for emotional help because they would then be seen as "incompetent".

Deaf and hard of hearing students may also be susceptible to impostor syndrome, which is the uneasiness that results from a discrepancy between their own life narrative and what may not seem to be an ideal of "normal" accomplishment. Students may feel like phoney failures in both the hearing and Deaf worlds because value-based AI in language-integrated educational settings or mixed-normative social scenarios may have emphasized the auditory-feasible spoken word as the indicator of competence (Shott et al., 2001). Particularly vulnerable to marginalization are those whose only form of communication in a spoken language-focused setting is sign language. Neoliberalism's demands for parental responsibility, techno-optimist aspirations for AI-enacted optimization, and ableist normativities come together to create a high-stakes environment where parents and/or children are held to very low, if not outright, standards (Swanepoel & Almec, 2008).

To treat impostor syndrome in parents and kids with hearing loss, multifactorial therapies are required. Additionally, sharing experiences, normalizing difficulties, and strengthening your own resilience all depend on support, which may be found in the form of therapy and peer connections, including community organizations. Psychotherapies that concentrate on the interaction of disability, identity, and culture might help to demilitarize norms of perfection and remove internalized stigma. Imposter syndrome may be countered at a broader systemic level by enhancing health and education systems that are inclusive, adaptable, and culturally embedded rather than based on rigid measures of "what does success look like?" In order for AI and expert systems to assist rather than penalize users, operate from pluralistic conceptions of success, and recognize many forms of communication and achievement, they must be developed transparently, with impacted families as partners (Hindley, 1997).

5.2 Children's Internalization of "Deficits" in AI-Mediated Environments

Imposter syndrome of hearing-impaired parents and children as intricate, multi-layered phenomena whose effects are exacerbated by the effects of cultural intersects at the intersections of normativity, technology mediation and structural injustice. Seeing the syndrome of this injustice as arising from larger cultural and system level dynamics, as opposed to purely moral failing in individual people can lead to more humane, inclusive, justice-oriented responses.

Against this negative impact of imposter syndrome, it can work against it with policies for the support of parents (Marie's case) without burning out, access to psycho-social resources and expanding what framing who does AI via inclusive policy reform such as cultural shift towards rewarding family life, where space is given and praise due diverse identities and contributions. Parents and children who are DHH thus offer an important challenge to normative imaginaries of success, value, and belonging in AI-enhanced politics today. By examining the psychological, sociological, technological and policy-related aspects of this challenging issue to help drive research, advocacy and practice for people living with hearing loss in today's modern family (Persson et al., 2022).

6. RETHINKING SUCCESS, CONTRIBUTION AND HUMAN WORTH: BEYOND PRODUCTIVITY: CARE, INTERDEPENDENCE, AND COMMUNICATIVE PLURALISM

In attunement to entanglement perpetrates violence against the notions of autarky that are ingrained in liberal Western discourse. People are surrounded by networks of material, cultural, and social relationships that influence their possibilities and capacities. Deaf communities, technological scaffolding, and linguistic coconstructions that mediate modalities of accessibility and belonging for those who are Deaf and hard of hearing (Bratu et al., 2024). This paradigm highlights the reciprocity that underpins care and communication rather than portraying reliance as a weakness. It promotes social interactions based on solidarity and justice by supporting inclusive policies and technology that meet a variety of needs without spreading stigma around vulnerability.

A polyphony of communication is significant when extending categories of contribution to include more than just spoken language as well as dominant linguistic systems. It attests to the legitimate and riches co-existence of varied modes of communicative action, spoken language and sign languages, visual gesturing and tactile signing, writing systems and digital media as sites where meaning ostensively presents itself or is produced for social life. AI-enhanced edu/social-systems who welcome communicative pluralism in which deaf and hard of hearing kids/families can articulate identity/authenticity, connect as they would like, not adapt to assimilationist forces. Pluralistic communication practices legitimize diversity, attend to cognitive and emotional accessibility, and reassert non-normative epistemologies grounded in embodied, community knowledge (da Silva Nunes et al., 2019).

It would suggest that assistive technology and artificial intelligence are digitally shaped to represent plurality and caring. In order to foster contextual flexibility, AI systems should be co-designed by and with members of the Deaf community, offering a combination of language-driven input and feedback (Vohr et al., 2008).

The justice-oriented alternative to prevailing paradigms by reconsidering the success, contribution, and human worth in care, interdependence, and communicative diversity. It focuses on interpersonal relationships, alternative expressions, and the moral significance of caring as a foundation for thriving (Abo Zed & Metwally, 2024).

6.1 Valuing Non-Normative Modalities: Sign, Silence, and Embodied Communication

"Non-standard" modalities, such as physical communication, silence, and sign language, are significant, multi-layered forms of interaction that should be recognized on par with speech. The same information that spoken language conveys to hearing people is conveyed via sign languages, which are complete, sophisticated natural languages with their own syntax and vocabulary (Fowler et al., 1997). They are agents of communication and contribute to artistic performance, social cohesion, and cultural identity. Messages That Are Silenced Written by Jami Lobpries Body language, particularly amongst censured or hearing-impaired populations when communication transcends spoken words, is a manner of expressing relationship meanings and what it means to be human.

The ableist mindset is so deeply ingrained that it's hard to develop a taste for these ways of knowing and being. This distirbance upsets the conventional wisdom of a deficiency or delay in relation to variance from standard spoken language. It does, however, recognize all human language as mediums of communication and this is a good tendency and a source of diversity. Promoting these forms of communication leads to more inclusiveness that lowers or even eliminates obstacles for individuals with hearing loss. Learning other ways (both spoken and not spoken) that language is communicated multimodally in and on the body outside of the larynx can form a basis for recognizing embodied, physical communication (embodied cognition) versus silent forms of (nonsounded) communication. This expansive view can only result in the best improvement for our overall system of communication practices and a more respectful and dignified existence for all deaf people (Mathos & Broussard, 2005).

7. TOWARDS JUST AI-AUGMENTED FUTURES IN PARENTING AND DISABILITY

For families with children with disabilities, such as hearing loss, the introduction of the latest generation of AI-enabled parenting tools poses entirely new and serious ethical concerns. If such conceptions of success, caring and worthiness are grounded if it will maintain any more elementary commitments to equality and decency, cultural diversity or democratic governance it will be because we recognize that a better common future is possible for ourselves, with AI. For AI technologies to lean toward enabling instead of constraining, celebrating rather than denigrating, and honouring rather than corroding relational and cultural diversity, attention must be paid to how such technologies are designed, implemented and regulated within parenting as well as disability landscapes. Imaging AI to be a vehicle for autonomy and inclusiveness rather than as an apparatus of normative sensitivities, user involvement throughout the technology life cycle from conception into iteration ensures sustainability, meaning and moral agility.

REFERENCES

Abo Zed, N. N., & Metwally, A. H. S. (2024). Stress coping strategies and their relationship to family adjustment for mothers of hearing-impaired children. *Egyptian Journal of Social Work, 18*(18), 103–122.

Alkahtani, R., Bakry, H., Al Hawi, L. M., Alshehri, J. D. A. O., & Elbeltagy, R. (2025). Quality of life of mothers of children with Down syndrome: A study comparing those with and without hearing loss. *Frontiers in Psychiatry, 16*, 1611074. PMID: 40950766

Asta, B., Satekin, M. Ç., Uzdil, N., & Yilmaz, S. T. (2024). The effect of having a child with hearing impairment on parents. *International Journal of Pediatric Otorhinolaryngology, 177*, 111864. PMID: 38237356

Billen, R. M., Sams, J., & Nordquist, V. M. (2023). A conceptual model of parenting children with disabilities. *Journal of Family Studies, 29*(4), 1781–1803.

. Bratu, M., Ciolan, L., Nedelcu, A., Stan, S., Bologa, R., Mironov, C., ... & Avarvare, D. (2024). The Influence of Technology-Based Pedagogy in Vocational Education on the Motivation and Emotional State of Students with Hearing Impairments. *Informatica Economica, 28*(3).

Chen, P. H., Lim, T. Z., Chang, S. T., & Cho, M. Y. (2021). Developing new scales for assessing parents' aural and oral rehabilitation skills to interact with children with hearing loss. *International Journal of Audiology, 60*(10), 797–807. PMID: 33401986

Chen, P. H., & Liu, T. W. (2021). Does parental education level matter? Dynamic effect of parents on family-centred early intervention for children with hearing loss. *International Journal of Disability Development and Education, 68*(4), 457–478.

Ching, T. Y., Crowe, K., Martin, V., Day, J., Mahler, N., Youn, S., & Orsini, J. (2010). Language development and everyday functioning of children with hearing loss assessed at 3 years of age. *International Journal of Speech-Language Pathology, 12*(2), 124–131. PMID: 20420353

. Ching, T. Y., Dillon, H., Leigh, G., & Cupples, L. (2018). Learning from the Longitudinal Outcomes of Children with Hearing Impairment (LOCHI) study: Summary of 5-year findings and implications. *International journal of audiology, 57*(sup2), S105-S111.

Continisio, G. I., D'Errico, D., Toscano, S., Maldonato, N. M., De Falco, R., Nunziata, F., & Malesci, R. (2023). Parenting stress in mothers of children with permanent hearing impairment. *Children (Basel, Switzerland), 10*(3), 517. PMID: 36980075 da Silva Nunes, A. D., de Lima Silva, C. R., Balen, S. A., de Souza, D. L. B., & Barbosa, I. R. (2019). Prevalence of hearing impairment and associated factors in school-aged children and adolescents: A systematic review. *Brazilian Journal of Otorhinolaryngology, 85*(2), 244–253. PMID: 30555026

Dharanidharan, D., & Kuruveettissery, S. (2025). Stress and coping among parents of children with hearing impairment: A scoping review. *British Journal of Guidance & Counselling*, ●●●, 1–18.

. Erbasi, E., Scarinci, N., Hickson, L., & Ching, T. Y. (2018). Parental involvement in the care and intervention of children with hearing loss. *International journal of audiology, 57*(sup2), S15-S26.

Eyuboglu, D., Caner Mercan, G., & Eyuboglu, M. (2021). Psychosocial difficulties and quality of life in children with hearing impairment and their association with parenting styles. *Early Child Development and Care, 191*(6), 952–962.

Fellinger, J., Holzinger, D., Sattel, H., Laucht, M., & Goldberg, D. (2009). Correlates of mental health disorders among children with hearing impairments. *Developmental Medicine and Child Neurology, 51*(8), 635–641. PMID: 19627335

Fowler, K. B., McCollister, F. P., Dahle, A. J., Boppana, S., Britt, W. J., & Pass, R. F. (1997). Progressive and fluctuating sensorineural hearing loss in children with asymptomatic congenital cytomegalovirus infection. *The Journal of Pediatrics, 130*(4), 624–630. PMID: 9108862

. Gilliver, M., Ching, T. Y., & Sjahalam-King, J. (2013). When expectation meets experience: Parents' recollections of and experiences with a child diagnosed with hearing loss soon after birth. *International journal of audiology, 52*(sup2), S10-S16.

Hall, P. K., & Tomblin, J. B. (1978). A follow-up study of children with articulation and language disorders. *The Journal of Speech and Hearing Disorders, 43*(2), 227–241. PMID: 661261

Hindley, P. (1997). Psychiatric aspects of hearing impairments. *Journal of Child Psychology and Psychiatry, and Allied Disciplines, 38*(1), 101–117. PMID: 9232460

Hornsby, B. W., Gustafson, S. J., Lancaster, H., Cho, S. J., Camarata, S., & Bess, F. H. (2017). Subjective fatigue in children with hearing loss assessed using self- and parent-proxy report. *American Journal of Audiology, 26*(3S), 393–407. PMID: 29049623

Ioannou, A., & Andreva, A. (2019, August). Play and learn with an intelligent robot: enhancing the therapy of hearing-impaired children. In *IFIP Conference on Human-Computer Interaction* (pp. 436-452). Cham: Springer International Publishing.

Kim, S., & Yim, D. (2021). The effects of parent training on narrative interaction for parents with hearing loss who have children with normal hearing: A case study using AI speakers. *Journal of Speech-Language & Hearing Disorders*, *30*(1), 89–101.

Kushwaha, A. (2024). AI and non-verbal communication: Enhancing understanding of emotional cues for hearing impairment children. *As the editors of Transforming Learning. Power and Education*, ●●●, 13.

Levinger, M., & Alhuzail, N. A. (2018). Bedouin hearing parents of children with hearing loss: Stress, coping, and quality of life. *American Annals of the Deaf*, *163*(3), 328–355. PMID: 30100590

Li, Y., Wang, H., Hossain, E., Mann, M., Yu, J., Newman, K. S., & Bai, Z. (2025). Leveraging Usefulness and Autonomy: Designing AI-Mediated ASL Communication Between Hearing Parents and Deaf Children. In *Proceedings of the 24th Interaction Design and Children* (pp. 512-526).

Loh, D. S., Packer, R. L., & Scarinci, N. A. (2025). Navigating childhood hearing loss: The experiences of parents, grandparents and siblings. *Disability and Rehabilitation*, *47*(11), 2846–2857. PMID: 39316779

Mathos, K. K., & Broussard, E. R. (2005). Outlining the concerns of children who have hearing loss and their families. *Journal of the American Academy of Child and Adolescent Psychiatry*, *44*(1), 96–100. PMID: 15608549

Matthijs, L., Loots, G., Mouvet, K., Van Herreweghe, M., Hardonk, S., Van Hove, G., & Leigh, G. (2012). First information parents receive after UNHS detection of their baby's hearing loss. *Journal of Deaf Studies and Deaf Education*, *17*(4), 387–401. PMID: 22960753

Meinzen-Derr, J., Lim, L. H., Choo, D. I., Buyniski, S., & Wiley, S. (2008). Pediatric hearing impairment caregiver experience: Impact of duration of hearing loss on parental stress. *International Journal of Pediatric Otorhinolaryngology*, *72*(11), 1693–1703. PMID: 18819718

Molchanova, L. N., & Chekanova, A. V. (2018). Development of parental competence through psychological and pedagogical support for families in the upbringing of hearing-impaired children. *Psychology in Russia : State of the Art*, *11*(4), 223–238.

Paghandeh, M., Hassanzadeh, S., & Ghasemzadeh, S. (2019). Effectiveness of parent-child interaction program on parenting stress and parent-hearing impaired child relationship. *Journal of Research in Psychological Health*, *13*(1), 99–124.

Palavi, L. A., Holt, E. A. L., & Nosa, V. (2025). A scoping review on the nature of parental involvement among Pacific and minority populations with hearing loss. *Journal of the Royal Society of New Zealand*, *55*(3), 721–753. PMID: 39989647

Persson, A., Marklund, U., Lohmander, A., & Flynn, T. (2022). Expressive vocabulary development in children with moderate hearing loss–the impact of auditory variables and early consonant production. *Clinical Linguistics & Phonetics*, *36*(6), 547–564. PMID: 34231440

Quittner, A. L., Barker, D. H., Cruz, I., Snell, C., Grimley, M. E., & Botteri, M., & CDaCI Investigative Team. (2010). Parenting stress among parents of deaf and hearing children: Associations with language delays and behavior problems. *Parenting, Science and Practice*, *10*(2), 136–155. PMID: 20607098

Rakovac Bekes, E., Galzina, V., & Berbić Kolar, E. (2024). Using Human-Computer Interaction (HCI) and Artificial Intelligence (AI) in Education to Improve the Literacy of Deaf and Hearing-Impaired Children. In *2024 47th ICT and Electronics Convention (MIPRO)* (pp. 1624-1629).

Ravi, R., Gunjawate, D. R., Yerraguntla, K., Rajashekhar, B., & Lewis, L. E. (2016). Knowledge and attitude of parents/caregivers towards hearing loss and screening in newborns–a systematic review. *International Journal of Audiology*, *55*(12), 715–722. PMID: 27686575

Schmulian, D., & Lind, C. (2020). Parental experiences of the diagnosis of permanent childhood hearing loss: A phenomenological study. *International Journal of Audiology*, *59*(1), 54–60. PMID: 31566461

Sheng, H., Shen, X., Du, H., Zhang, H., Huang, Z., & Yu, X. (2024). AI empowered Auslan learning for parents of deaf children and children of deaf adults. *AI and Ethics*, *4*(4), 877–887.

Shott, S. R., Joseph, A., & Heithaus, D. (2001). Hearing loss in children with Down syndrome. *International Journal of Pediatric Otorhinolaryngology*, *61*(3), 199–205. PMID: 11700189

Singh, S., & Singh, M. (2024). Impact of Resilience, Optimism and Socio-economic Status on Coping in Parents among Visually and Hearing-impaired Children. *Journal of Scientific Research and Reports*, *30*(12), 698–707.

Stevenson, J., McCann, D., Watkin, P., Worsfold, S., & Kennedy, C., & Hearing Outcomes Study Team. (2010). The relationship between language development and behaviour problems in children with hearing loss. *Journal of Child Psychology and Psychiatry, and Allied Disciplines*, *51*(1), 77–83. PMID: 19686333

. Swanepoel, D., & Almec, N. (2008). Maternal views on infant hearing loss and early intervention in a South African community. *International journal of audiology, 47*(sup1), S44-S48.

Tang, X., & Ji, Y. (2024, December). Design of infant monitoring products for hearing-impaired parents. In *2024 17th International Symposium on Computational Intelligence and Design (ISCID)* (pp. 93-96). IEEE.

Topol, D., Girard, N., Pierre, L. S., Tucker, R., & Vohr, B. (2011). The effects of maternal stress and child language ability on behavioral outcomes of children with congenital hearing loss at 18–24 months. *Early Human Development, 87*(12), 807–811. PMID: 21745720

. van der Spuy, T., & Pottas, L. (2008). Infant hearing loss in South Africa: Age of intervention and parental needs for support. *International Journal of Audiology, 47*(sup1), S30-S35.

Vohr, B. R., Jodoin-Krauzyk, J., Tucker, R., Johnson, M. J., Topol, D., & Ahlgren, M. (2008). Results of newborn screening for hearing loss: Effects on the family in the first 2 years of life. *Archives of Pediatrics & Adolescent Medicine, 162*(3), 205–211. PMID: 18316656

Wake, M., Poulakis, Z., Hughes, E. K., Carey-Sargeant, C., & Rickards, F. W. (2005). Hearing impairment: A population study of age at diagnosis, severity, and language outcomes at 7–8 years. *Archives of Disease in Childhood, 90*(3), 238–244. PMID: 15723906

Ying, L. W., & Ai, J. T. T. (2025). Perspectives of hearing parents and their deaf children: Exploring needs and support systems in Ipoh, Malaysia. *International Journal of Child Welfare and Development, 22*, 125–131.

Yoshinaga-Itano, C. (1999). Benefits of early intervention for children with hearing loss. *Otolaryngologic Clinics of North America, 32*(6), 1089–1102. PMID: 10523454

Chapter 20
Regulating Algorithmic Bias and Global Legal Approaches in Gender, Diversity, and Intersectional Equity in AI-Driven Professional Systems

Divya S. Khurana
https://orcid.org/0009-0000-4367-1742
CLC, Chandigarh Group of Colleges, Jhanjeri, Mohali, India

Dev Parbhakar
University Institute of Legal Studies, Chandigarh University, India

Ravinderjeet Kaur
University Institute of Legal Studies, Chandigarh University, India

ABSTRACT

Algorithmic discrimination takes many shapes, each amplifying bias in AI-powered career platforms. AI tools used for hiring, promotions, performance ranking and workplace monitoring can inscribe and amplify instead of erasing gender and racial inequality. There is a potential for bias due to unrepresentative training data, the use of proxy variables rather than protected characteristics in decision making, design trade-offs that favour system efficiency over equity and feedback loops that keep

DOI: 10.4018/979-8-3373-6618-0.ch020

into the data "successful" profiles from minority groups. When researchers have looked more closely at AI hiring systems, they have seen intricate interactions among multiple categories, where the model might favor some women overall while being particularly biased against certain groups of Black men or particular communities of women from a given ethnic background an insight that reveals discrimination to be not something that emerges cleanly along individual axes like gender and race.

1. INTRODUCTION

The phenomenon of algorithmic bias is emerging as a significant problem in today's fast evolving landscape of artificial intelligence (AI), particularly in practical systems such as hiring systems, performance review tools, and predictive analytics for workforce management. Definition: Algorithmic bias refers to systematic and repeatable errors in a computer system that create unfair or otherwise negative impacts, such as disadvantaging certain individuals or groups, users or customers. And in the workplace, these biases can widen the inequality gap by influencing decisions on hiring, promotions or pay negotiations and even layoffs.

This dialogue includes classifying biases, examining the effects of biases and efforts to counter them in international legal systems as well as some of the challenges they face or can pose which draws form most recent scholarship and policy interventions arguing for a more equitable AI governance. Mitigating and regulating algorithmic biases in AI driven professional systems is going to need a mix of technical interventions with anti-discrimination laws that actually work on the ground, which systematically recognise gender, diversity and intersectional harms in workplaces. And if a solution exists, the legal runner-up to fighting bias in AI is no longer simply an issue of data cleanliness anymore but instead can be understood as one about equality, labor rights and compliance with human rights (Ihua-Maduenyi & Okongwu, 2025).

An intersectional approach recognises that gender bias in AI is combined with race, class, disability, migration status and sexuality and other identities to compound multiple injustices for women of colour or trans workers when they are tested by recruitment and promotion algorithms. Gender data gaps) and partial labour information (missing data on the varied experiences of women, men and non-binary workers, such as career breaks, informal work or time spent providing care) can lead AI tools to interpret these paths as negative signals with regard to productivity or engagement. International labor and human rights standards have evolved so that discrimination in employment is understood to include not just explicit exclusion but also more indirect and structural practices that effectively disadvantage historically marginalized groups, a formulation readily applied to opaque algorithmic tools for recruiting or managing workers.

The other type of discrimination is feature selection bias, in which factors such as education level or where you live are given undue weight in ways that indirectly work against various types of people ZIP codes could be a proxy for race when determining whether candidates from minority neighborhoods will get approved for loans. There is also the problem of proxy discrimination, whereby neutral-seeming factors correlate with the protected features in question, such as punishing resumes with gaps due to maternity leave as disproportionately affecting women (Yu, 2024).

A related company to Bastion, Textio, sexually identified words and phrases to be avoided as well in its tech brainchild that purports to minimize the biases of language used on applications for jobs or funding from Venture Capitalists/investors. Job ads overlooking older women due to implied demographics) also demonstrate the possibility for targeted advertising in professional networking sites to exclude groups. They intersect with the diversity-related issues where teams don't have gender or race representation and so don't experience those types of flaws, thus self-reinforcing bias.

1.1 Evolution of Anti-discrimination Principles in Digital Era

Anti-discrimination norms that evolved out of post-World War II human rights instruments such as the Universal Declaration of Human Rights (1948) and domestic civil rights legislation like the U.S. Civil Rights Act (1964), were initially concerned with ending conscious bias and unjustifiably differentiated impacts in human exercise s of discretion such as in employment, housing, or service provisionEarly waypoints were the U.S. DOJ's 2022 settlement against Facebook's housing ad algorithms, as baselines for example that showed how machine learning could bake in segregation and revealed it so regulators have retooled disparate impact doctrines systems.

This change was intensified by international soft law: the OECD AI Principles (2019) and UNESCO's Ethics of AI Recommendation (2021) embedded non-discrimination in trustworthy AI, which was balanced with fairness, transparency, and bias audits. At the mid-point, enacting classification in this way as "high risk" and obliging equity audits, explainability and human oversight (as AI regulation does) is instrumentalised to operationalise intersectional protections which are rooted in data protection by design under GDPR. In the Global South, scholar interests in algorithmic harms influenced by ILO Principles on Digital Work Rights are being debated in conjunction with India's nascent data protection regime and constitutional non-discrimination mandates (Art 14-15).

Paradigm shift is terms of recognizing/understanding intersectionality, along with compounded biases (eg gender/race) via inclusive data sets (including participation audits and the strict scrutiny that will withstand a doctrinal challenge under the laws per Ricci v. DeStefano). But the challenges remain: AI can be opaque, eluding the intent required to activate requirements; output rules are also susceptible to claims of "reverse discrimination." This is the emerging direction, toward hybrid rules that mix process (transparency, oversight), and outcome (equity metrics) that steer digital equity toward closer alignment with the universality of human rights (Baerjee & Bhat, 2025).

2. AI-DRIVEN PROFESSIONAL AND WORKPLACE SYSTEMS

The impact of algorithmic bias in AI for professional systems: gender and intersectional equality. Some gender bias is baked into training data that reflects patriarchal values, meaning algorithms end up implicitly undervaluing the work of women and buttressing stereotypes like that taking on caregiving roles make people less reliable workers. In such policy AI tools, for example, gender-neutral prompts lead to recommendations based on male norms such as workplace temperatures at levels benefiting men only or even suggestions that do not take into account the more specific needs of women and their potential effects on productivity and health in workspaces.

This same can have implications for racial and ethic groups, if such individuals are much less commonly seen in data then any duty machine learning product won't perform well on non-whites; similar to their resume screening tool that favored anglo-saxon names over all other and discriminated against non-anglo fantastic candidates multiplied. Intersectional fairness is about the intersection of these biases, for example being a disabled trans person means double or quadruple or more-hurting in AI performance reviews that do not take into account your othered identities and it is an epistemic injustice against you because you become unintelligible. The price of that in the corporate environment drives up marginalized employee turnover and diminishes innovation, among other things. For example, AI in credit scoring for freelancers could discriminate against women of color by relying on proxies such as patterns of online activity that are associated with social and economic conditions. The only way to reverse this is representation: there are levels of outrageousness, and we need feminist lenses with which to view these machine- originating narratives as that vision becomes multi-perspectival.

3. ALGORITHMIC BIAS AND STRUCTURAL INEQUALITY CONCERNING IMPOSTER SYNDROME

Imposter syndrome is tied very closely with kind of algorithmic bias and structural inequity in really deep ways that I want to engage and reckon with, but somehow it's like more broken of a cycle between you feeling terrible about yourself and the law just being casually unjust (Amalia et al., 2025). We have to be careful that we don't contribute or make imposter syndrome for algorithmic bias and structural inequality worse than it already is, which can continually signal underrepresented people that they are not actually members (with their hard work deserved), and the system "knows better" believes they're less capable/real. Imposter feelings, in turn, are internalised response to historical patterns of discrimination that have become somewhat automated and scaled by algorithmic networks (Lopez Belloso, 2022).

That doubt is further confirmed by structural problems like wage gaps and promotion differences the average woman and person of color get paid less and promoted more slowly respectively, all of which support the story that they really don't fit in (Vijeyarasa, 2023). There are also algorithmic tools used to grade, or even admit (the latter use of the tech leading to admission-related racial bias since said admissions-tech frequently factors in projected student success that can be prejudiced, through tests) that tend to bake-in racial and economic bias by design a number rely one aforementioned test-scores that historically favor privileged white-students who have been able to afford prep-material (Ahmad et al., 2025).

Even if a low-income student of color clears these hurdles and attends college, they may experience impostor syndrome the sensation that they don't actually belong there for fear that, because the odds were against them from the beginning it's just by chance that they arrived this far which lead to higher dropout rates and mental health burdens (Kashyap & Mitra, 2025). Social media algorithms that are programmed to optimize engagement commonly serve up content that reinforces stereotypes, silences the oppressed and raises voices of privilege, eroding users from vulnerable populations' self-esteem as they struggle to gain a place online or in their career (Ounia, 2023).

More broadly, algorithms used by criminal justice systems to predict recidivism, the likelihood that someone will commit another crime, have been shown in studies to wrongly flag Black defendants as future criminals at twice the rate of white defendants and displace flawed historical data on recidivism with data reflecting biased policing practices from the past: over-policing of Black neighborhoods (mergen et al., 2025). That kind of across-the-board problem is endemic across financial systems, as credit-scoring algorithms that are trained on information larded with redlining hangovers refuse to lend to people in historically excluded places and trap their residents into second-rate economic outcomes — creating a stigma for those who do make it out (Dhar et al., 2025).

Women enterprisers are penalized when they submit business plans due to gendered language score models by the algorithms. But it's mostly from those that the system benefits -- and imposter syndrome is a product of, but not to blame on, the person or ourselves (ul Haq, 2024). Public service announcements about the havoc wrought by drugs have been shown to exacerbate negative perceptions of drug users, while psychological counseling or mentorship programs tailored toward marginalized populations might help, they are band-aids on a gaping wound if we don't unwind the algorithms and structures that contribute to inequality (Mustaq et al., 2025).

In the medical industry as well, diagnostic algorithms that were developed on white patients fail to recognize the symptoms in diverse communities, with disastrous outcomes that exacerbate structural injustices by preventing access to insurance. Since there is a chance of professional consequences in a field where even the most pro-diversity companies use diversity merely for show, a minority doctor may also feel more impostor syndrome as long as they are speaking out against these techniques (Karagianni, 2025). In addition to undermining the confidence of unseen creators targeted by those recommendations, this directive from entertainment recommendation algorithms to pull even tighter on beauty standards and narratives confirms the signaling between algorithmic bias and cultural structural inequalities that leads to imposter syndrome (Monko & Mjahidi, 2025).

Therefore, in order to stop the trend, society must concentrate just as hard on developing a more moral foundation for AI—using techniques like bias audits and inclusive design—as it does on enacting legislative changes meant to address underlying disparities in housing, education, justice, and other areas (Vassilopoulou & Kyriakidou, 2025). In the end, rethinking impostor syndrome as a result of systemic injustice and algorithmic prejudice will alleviate the pressure on people to be "good enough" when their own "otherness" contributes to systemic oppressions that create environments where various abilities may flourish without any suspicion. This is how technology would benefit everyone, not just a (fortunate) select few: an all-hands strategy designed to alleviate personal suffering while advancing equality (Su, 2025).

3.1 From Structural Injustice to Imposter Syndrome

Structural inequality indicates the long-standing patterns by which institutions distribute the material and cultural conditions of life in ways that are biased upward along lines of identity such as race, gender, class, caste/religion or ability. These inequities manifest themselves in who is admitted to elite programs, who gets hired or promoted, whose work is cited and whose voices are amplified in public discourse. As members of under-represented groups walk into spaces that are not designed with them in mind, they become more vulnerable to biases/scrutiny/ stereotype judgments that can undermine their sense of belonging and confidence over time (Deckker & Sumanansekara, 2025).

Imposter syndrome or, more precisely, "imposter phenomenon" consists of a persistent pattern in high-achieving people to doubt their abilities and accomplishments, have difficulty internalizing success and believing that they are competent; often attributing their success to luck or external factors. Research suggests the pattern is not just some private psychological weaknesses but instead, that it has a strong connection to discrimination, racialised or gendered stereotypes and minority stress. Imposter feelings are highly correlated with depression, anxiety, low self-esteem and even suicidal ideation among racial and ethnic minoritised groups, suggesting what appears on the surface to be personal doubt is also a response to hostile or exclusionary environments.

3.2 Algorithmic Aspects

The important aspect of imposter syndrome involves a kind of "algorithmic gaslighting," in which biased output does not correspond to a person's lived experience of their own ability but is taken as authoritative anyway. "People can personalise these algorithmic verdicts, questioning whether they were accepted to a school or hired for a job only because of the stated "diversity balance" at play – or conversely complaining that they didn't make the cut due to (implicit) quotas – underlining classic imposter narratives about having 'slipped through the cracks.'" By consistently misclassifying, under-recommending and/or invisibilising groups of people, platforms create an environment in which a state of being invisible and unbelonging is pervasive, contributing directly into imposter feelings (Kim & Lee, 2025).

3.3 Feedback Loops of Bias, Exclusion and Imposter Syndrome

Structural inequality and algorithmic bias create feedback loops that further perpetuate imposter syndrome. Due to a systemic lack of representation in training data, some historically marginalised groups are classified incorrectly or with less accuracy, or are predicted of performing worse systematically. These skewed outputs in turn become the rationale for less investment, fewer opportunities, and more aggressive monitoring, depressing performance indicators even further for those communities providing fresh "evidence" to retrain the next generation of biasing models (Mokofe, 2025).

Instead of wondering why certain people "lack confidence," this view inquires into the design of workplaces, universities and platforms so that they send loud messages all the time about who doesn't belong (now "helpfully" amplified by automated systems). It even acknowledges that interventions around personal resilience or coaching can tend to pathologise the individual who, in any event, then still faces all those mechanisms of discrimination and technologies of marginalisation that led them to doubt themselves in the first place (Ahmed, 2024).

This will entail a redesign of algorithmic systems with explicit commitments to equity, transparency and contestability, as well as ongoing efforts to transform organisational cultures, representation and accountability. Designing spaces where people can interrupt, trace and govern patterns of harm and exclusion is essential to challenge the silent normalization of bias. Within such a framework, mitigating imposter syndrome is indistinguishable from undoing systemic unfairness and bias in algorithms, understanding that feelings of being an impostor among minorities or women are often rational responses to unjust systems as opposed to signs of individual failure.

4. MECHANISMS, SOURCES OF ALGORITHMIC AND DATA BIAS IN GENDER, RACE AND INTERSECTIONAL DIMENSIONS IN AI MODELS IN RECRUITMENT, PROMOTION AND EVALUATION SYSTEMS

The algorithmic and data biases in AI-based technology for recruitment, promotion, and evaluation derive from interlocked technical These are systems trained on historical data, model architectures and feature engineering decisions that encode the culture and power dynamics of organizations into code; when previous hiring or promotion patterns favour white, male, cisgendered, able-bodied or upper class candidates AI tools trained on them tend to "learn" these profiles signal merit as well as leadership potential while seeing deviations from this baseline norm as statistical noise or risk. Bias acts on many levels: in the definition of the problem in choice of data and labelling performance ratings, promotion to date that already are tainted by discrimination in who gets included or not women, racial/caste minority & non-binary people, migrants & those with discontinuous careers all systematically under-sampled and in proxy variables like university pedigree, post code, employment gaps or prior salary which correlate strongly with gendered and racialised stratification (Cuesta, 2025).

Even when protected attributes are explicitly omitted, models feed on unstructured text (cv, cover letter, reference note), metadata (name, pronoun, picture) and behavioural signal (application time, device used, excluding trace on last social platform visited), which all effectively acts as ad hoc markers of a person's identity triggering discrimination through an opaque channel. In hiring, automated

CV screening tools can down-rank applicants from women's colleges, historically Black institutions or regional universities because historical hires are biased toward elite-representative institutions, while keyword-based scoring advantages more masculine-coded language and penalizes career breaks for caregiving (guilty of both: filtering out disproportionately many women and caregivers of all genders).

Video-interview analysis using facial recognition and voice analysis often operates with lower accuracy when faced with darker skins, women's voices, non-native accents meaning the 'employability', 'engagement', or 'confidence' scores will be lower for racialised and intersectional minorities; worse still, these models are typically trained on predominantly white male faces and speech (Noschis, 2024). Promotion and performance-rating systems have their own biases: algorithmic "potential" or "leadership" scores often start with earlier ratings, billable hours, or sales numbers influenced by access to high-visibility assignments, informal sponsorship, and client networks that historically benefit dominant strength in the workplace; as a result women of colour or other intersecting subordinate groups are algorithmically recoded as lower potential despite holding equal (or even greater) aptitude (Tiwari, 2025).

Feedback and engagement analytics measuring email response times, time spent talking in meetings, or collaboration patterns can conflate social exclusion and marginalisation (being invited to fewer things, talked over more frequently, or assigned excess "office housework") with personal disengagement or low leadership levels1-2 – strengthening a deficit narrative about those who have already been marginalized. At the data level, label bias occurs when a set of "successful" employees is picked out from an historical cohort that also structurally excluded women, racial minorities, LGBTQIA+ people or disabled workers from senior roles; consequently, the model internalises quite a narrow archetype of success and punishes candidates whose career path follows alternative routes through caregiving, migration or chronic illness. Measurement bias appears when supposedly neutral targets, such as "cultural fit," "executive presence" or "communication style", encode white, male, Western and neurotypical norms; when evaluation rubrics incorporate imprecise criteria that managers interpret more harshly for minoritised employees, creating biased ground truth for model training.

The logic and origin of the bias in AI and data among algorithms and models for recruitment, promotion or assessment systems are even so into a great extent ingraining gendered, racialized population individuals with all their intersectional dimensions through systematic reproduction of inequalities along more stealthy but equally pervasive path (Latorre & Perez Sedeno, 2023). At the root of these biases are bad sources of information, with training sets often mirroring historical societal bias. For instance, scoring algorithms on resumes may have been trained predominantly from historical records of hiring decisions made by a whole lot of white dudes in industries full of white dudes; such a background is likely to result in unfavorable scores for applicants of female or underrepresented minority status (since tokenism doesn't really count as diversity), with the application not recognizing diverse candidates — due, among other reasons, that legacy discriminatory input went into factors like unequal access to education and networking.

This temporal prejudice, and also results to that end, is embedded mechanically in the form of surface-like but extremely-correlateting components — for example zip codes or school prestige or historical tracking of extracurricular participation — strongly related to either race or gender will lead AI to discriminate inadvertently; a Black applicant from a poor neighborhood might be rated similarly as less not solely on account of their skin color but because it proxies onto lower "success" rates by relation to biased history in which these have witnessed association with detrimental outcomes (Priyadarshini & Priyadarshini, 2024). In promotion systems, evaluation AI might rely on performance statistics that are fucked by workplace subcultures favoring "aggressive" behaviours usually code-male; if these disadvantage women pursuing collegial workstyles, the gender-bias could be baked-in through algorithmic amplification (small numbers off at the start grow exponentially in iterative decisionmaking). Racial discrimination seeps in, too, through data left skewed: Training sets that power AI models in assessment tools like these gauging a worker's level of performance, say often include over-represented people of color employed in low-level roles because of structural racism; the system forecasts lower propensity for promotion among racial minorities based on patterns that bear out segregation not skill (Zallio et al., 2025).

4.1 Role of Data Representation, Training Sets and Socio-Technical Contexts

Algorithm design choices, particularly the focus on optimizing for predictive accuracy or time-to-hire, incentivize exploiting any strong correlation in the data (even when that correlation is a product of structural racism, sexism, casteism or classism) and fairness constraints are generally added as an afterthought at best. Intersectional harms arise when model predictions interact with combinations of overlapping identities: valid data and legitimate representatives (e.g., Black women or Dalit women) could be missing from training examples for senior roles, resulting in higher uncertainty, misclassification and/or risk-averse recommendations that hold back such candidates from career paths to leadership positions compared with both white women or men from their sub-caste; conversely, trans or non-binary prospective employees might be misgendered, policed into binary categories or rendered invisible altogether making them difficult to discriminate against.

Feedback loops propagate these biases: if AI tools continue to promote those who already look like existing leaders, then the next generation of training data consolidates the profile of "success," so that fewer marginalised candidates produce performance metrics a system is geared to favour, and statistical proof of differences becomes self-perpetuating (Alberngues & Lu, 2025). Finally, the institutional and regulatory context counts: opaque proprietary systems, weak audit requirements and limited rights to explanation or contestation can result in biased rankings or risk scores quietly determining who is shortlisted, interviewed, promoted or placed under performance review even as organisations parade AI in public as being objective and efficient. Understanding these mechanisms and bias sources historical, representational, measurement, proxy-based, design-level damage is therefore imperative if recruitment, promotion and evaluation systems are to be transformed from devices that replicate inequality into tools deliberately engineered for substantive workplace justice informed with a gendered, racial and intersectional look.

4.2 Ethical theories and fairness metrics in decision-making systems

Intersectional aspects exacerbate the problems when biases intersect multiplicatively: for instance, a video or audio based AI recruitment tool double-penalising Black women by virtue of gender-biased language analysis concluding that "nurturing" language appears less leadership-oriented and racial proxies (such as recognition-using name algorithms to flag names that sound ethnic racist assumptions based on such sources) thereby appearing increased risk from being racist indicators (Shin, 2025). Whether through, for instance, sampling bias in the data collection process (only "successful" individuals from a certain class or race are sampled), or feedback loops in adaptive AI systems that iterate on our decisions: they remember that we made those same choices once before and then some inflates this manefestation of social exclusion even further if success is correlated with an initial underrepresentation of minority components in the inputs.

Human-in-the-loop sources of bias further reinforce entrenched hierarchies as developers from homogenous backgrounds (frequently white, male, and affluent) unconsciously perpetuate the creation models that include implicit assumptions in criteria design, preferring for example "cultural fit" which emphasizes candidates meeting a particular norm rather than paying attention to intersectional experiences such as LGBTQ+ people of color. In evaluation settings, natural language processing models trained on web-scraped data introduce bias by alternating the score given to feedback about Two randomly selected Asian employees is "team player" and "innovator," which connects to racialized stereotypes that can be amplified by large unregulated internet sources (Alam, 2025).

Near the peripheries, where minorities bear a greater share of errors, algorithmic tools that optimize towards the majority accuracy usually do not display the desired fairness. For example, facial recognition models in remote proctoring software may fail to register darker skin tones, giving racial minorities incorrect attendance or engagement scores. Biases, such the sexism of annotators permeating the ground truth—for instance, women's contributions being judged as less significant in peer evaluations that train promotion AI—have also been reported by sources (Muralidhar et al., 2025). Due to the fact that traditional training data does not include individuals who structurally carry multiple-tiered memberships that intersect, a Latina woman may be subject to both gender bias in communication style scoring and racial bias in the assessment of transcribing across cultural cues and how they interact with holistic scoring criteria itself. These biases occur concurrently and exacerbate harm. They also exacerbate social inequalities and function as obstacles to fair hiring, advancement, and performance assessments; hence, they need extensive, multi-layered changes to ensure AI promotes justice.

5. GLOBAL LEGAL AND POLICY FRAMEWORKS ON ALGORITHMIC DISCRIMINATION

Worldwide, regulators are testing out a spectrum of models to regulate AI bias at work, from one-size-fits-all horizontal AI laws to sectoral labour and equality rules that have been repurposed for algorithmic contexts (Martinez et al., 2024). The AI Act of EU categorizes AI systems utilized in employment, worker management and access to self-employment as "high risk", with companies needing to show safeguards for non-discrimination data governance, human oversight and post-deployment monitoring; there would be invoked equality laws and data-protection laws like the EU's non-discrimination directives and GDPR. By contrast, in the U.S. much relies on pre-existing civil rights and employment laws to litigate disparate impact or disparate treatment when it comes to algorithmic tools, though with support from evolving guidelines that enforcement bodies have been issuing on automated hiring and assessment technologies.

Outside Europe and the US, as lawmakers debate whether to introduce standalone AI statutes, a range of softer policy or sector-specific approaches are followed in many jurisdiction on an ethics basis. For instance, India has proposed a comprehensive data protection law and various AI ethics and governance frameworks, but continues to rest heavily on equality guarantees in its constitution, labour regulation and sectoral policy to tackle algorithmic bias with others suggesting that the country should transition towards a more explicit rights-based auditable regime for algorithmic decision-making. International organisations, such as the OECD, UNESCO, and ILO have published soft laws with respect to trustworthy AI that ought to be rights-respecting there is a cross-cutting commitment across these documents to fairness, non-discrimination and gender equality which informs domestic strategies and corporate governance directives. Localised legal paradigm approaches to regulating AI-based professional systems and the algorithmic chasm in gender, diversity and intersectional equity priorities across the globe (Barqawi & Al-Rashdan, 2025).

The four-fifths rule regulating disparate impact in AI hiring in the USA is inspired by pre-existing legislations such as Title VII of the Civil Rights Act. The rates of protected groups such as women and minorities are noticed, moreover if one rate is 80% or less than another rate discrimination may be inferred. Proposed bills such as the Algorithmic Accountability Act target audits of high-risk systems, whereas the FTC employs Section 5 to reach unfair acts. New York City's Local Law 144 requires automated recruiting systems be independently audited for bias, specifically whether the system promotes racial and gender fairness. A GBA+ approach to impact assessment, where consideration of intersectionality can be used to understand impacts on people at intersections between factors/credentials etc, is a component of Canada's Directive on Automated Decision-Making. While China prioritizes interpretability in the professional space, Australia's AI Ethics Framework links justice and diversity to non-mandatory principles (de Silva de Alwis, 2024).

Internationally, country members are encouraged to consider non-discrimination as their first priority and pay attention to gender where it intersects with AI vulnerabilities in the UNESCO policy guide on Ethics of AI. Requirements for diverse development teams and democratic processes to deal with bias at its source are standard parts of those models. But the EU's aggressive approach seems worlds apart from the US's litigation based enforcement, and deficiencies in global harmonization are brutally exposed. Other projects launched to help ensure that professional systems will further equality globally as developments included multinational coalitions aimed at defining measures of fairness and a repository for AI impact reports.

6. EMERGING TRENDS IN GLOBAL AI LAW HARMONIZATION

Regulating for bias in algorithms is complicated, especially when it comes to setting up gender and diversity (or intersectional) protections for AI-based professional systems. One significant challenge is algorithm opacity; as companies increasingly rely on proprietary "black box" models, it's difficult to prove bias under laws that demand evidence of intent or impact. That proving a disparate impact case is difficult, means that one way the statute does not take into account how people are harmed is by recognizing the ways in which e.g., Indigenous women are harmed and so underprotect "multiply-marginalized" classes (McClure et al., 2024).

Historical data is biased, bolstering social inequalities and feedback loops are strengthening them, but it's hard to enforce the EU AI Act due to a shortage of resources — from legal expertise to how individual national implementations pan out. Internationally, differences in jurisdiction result in uneven enforcement; the US favours self-regulation whereas the EU is more aggressive, so biased systems can thrive in less regulated countries. By baking in intersectionality, these solutions could turn AI into a tool for liberation, ushering in more equitable office spaces (Imam et al., 2025).

7. GOVERNANCE, ACCOUNTABILITY AND REMEDIES FOR ALGORITHMIC HARMS

Good governance of algorithmic systems will need multi-level approaches that engage oversight bodies, mandatory auditing, and enforceable remedies to alleviate bias-driven and discriminating harms in domains such as hiring, lending and legal justice. A dedicated regulatory body (such as proposed AI certification / investigation houses) need to have a power to investigate, should have public complaint channels and be able to enforce established systems, perform bias audits and issue fines for non-compliance (Malja & Afrasiabi, 2025). Algorithmic impact assessments (AIAs) before deployment, regular third-party audits in particular for public sector tools all aimed at fore-stalling the discovery of adverse impacts will help rebuild trust in algorithmic decisionmaking by signaling responsiveness to exploring disparate impact, with results publicly reported.

Accountability mechanisms move responsibility for opaque automation from itself to its human overseers and deployers, requiring them to provide human review for decisions with harm potential, transparent documentation of decision pipelines, and traceability back to failure points. Enterprises need to create cross-functional teams for bias impact statements, inclusive design and continuous model monitoring, and regulatory sandboxes can enable safe experimentation with anti-bias techniques without hampering innovation. Self-regulatory best practices, such as protections for whistleblowers and routes to public interest litigation, act as a complement to hard law by enabling marginalised claimants to contest harms and by ensuring that no automated decision is final without redress.

Remedies to algorithmic harms favour substantive justice, through rights of individuals to challenge outputs and class injunctions against discriminatory systems as well compensatory redress such as backpay or retraining opportunities. Updating nondiscrimination laws to govern digital practices and creating safe harbors for the use of sensitive data in efforts to mitigate bias, can help strike a balance between reducing harm and fostering innovation. Given ongoing sectoral gaps in India, It is the place-based and context-based framework oriented toward safety, fairness and contestability in its inaugural instantiation (through institutional support for audits and oversight) that work to mitigate power asymmetries that are built into algorithmic infrastructures (Nwokocha et al., 2025). They are also anchored in international good practice, as contained in the OECD guidelines which have been designed to promote good governance by encouraging soundness, transparency and stakeholder participation.

Now and into the future, go by a rubric that governance is achieved when ethic A(I) principles (fairness, non-discrimination and minimisation of harm) are part of life cycle management paths (design through to decommission), which allows deployers to own outcomes instead redirecting blame onto code neutrality. This turns the reputational and legal risk liability of what's being experienced into opportunities for more sensible, less lethal systems that are responsively adapting through civil society feedback loops. The governance of algorithmic systems includes designing institutions that control the creation, deployment and influence of AIs to ensure that they comply with social values and are structured in a way that is engineered to limit harms. There are many varieties of algorithmic harm: all the way from bias amplification and privacy invasion to economic displacement and bodily harm (ISLAM, 2025).

Additional avenues are provided by human rights-based strategies, such as grievance procedures that would enable individuals to contest AI system choices. For example, data audits, system redesigns, or penalties might be used as remedies for biased recruiting algorithms. The creation of ethical evaluations in corporate due diligence, together with monitoring and public reporting, was recommended by policy responders (Sharma et al., 2025). For example, the National Telecommunications and Information Administration (NTIA) in the United States opposes a liability framework that results in a "all covering safe harbor," which gives companies justification to reduce damages.

8. CONCLUDING REMARKS TOWARDS INCLUSIVE AND EQUITABLE AI GOVERNANCE

Across systems, certain regulatory approaches are emerging as crucial: ex ante risk assessment of high-impact AI; mandates to test and document models for disparate impact across intersecting protected groups; and requirements that employers be transparent about when and how automated tools influence employment decisions. The legal regimes are starting to require human oversight, explainability rights of access and effective redress mechanisms towards algorithmic decision systems and to do so as a way of implementing equality norms in the design and governance AI-based professional systems. For gender, diversity and intersectional equity the most promising approaches are those that combine binding non-discrimination duties, participatory design with affected communities, inclusive databases and data sets which adequately represent all relevant groups as well as independent audits or impact assessments explicitly taking into account outcomes for multiple overlapping identities, not just single-minded categories

9. FUTURE DIRECTIONS

The way forward for just AI and sustainable digital justice is in creating, deploying, governing systems where bias and structural inequality are intentionally designed out, with long-term social inclusion and fairness the goal. At its heart is the inclusion of multi-disciplinary dimensions – such as social science, law, ethics and community voices – at all stages in designing and building AI, to ensure AI systems are shaped by contextually grounded policy considerations that can respect these values across gender, race, ethnicity and socio-economic status. Beyond reactive bias mitigation, the future of AI research is oriented towards proactive design principles such as fairness-by-design and participatory AI, where those affected by technologies are not only consulted but co-create models to ensure representation and outcomes are fair.

REFERENCES

Ahmad, R., Saleem, S., & Hussain, S. (2025). Ethical and Legal Challenges of Artificial Intelligence: Implications for Human Right. *Journal of Law. Social Policy Report*, *2*(01), 10–25.

Ahmed, U. (2024). Feminist Perspectives on AI: Ethical Considerations in Algorithmic Decision-Making. *Journal of Gender, Power, and Social Transformation*, *1*(3), 1–10.

Alam, A. (2025). Ethical challenges and bias in ai-driven marketing: Educational imperatives and policy perspectives. In *Impacts of AI-Generated Content on Brand Reputation* (pp. 55–108). IGI Global Scientific Publishing.

. Amalia, A. R., Pitaloka, D., & Mujtahidin, S. (2025). Gender Discrimination in Artificial Intelligence: An International Human Rights Law Perspective and the Quest for Binding Regulation. *Unram Law Review, 9*(2).

Barqawi, L., & Al-Rashdan, S. (2025, May). The Impact of AI on Women's Roles in the Workplace: A Legal Gender Perspective. In *2025 12th International Conference on Information Technology (ICIT)* (pp. 631-634). IEEE.

Cuesta, J. (2025). Gender bias in Artificial Intelligence. *Journal of Economic Policy Reform*, •••, 1–25.

de Silva de Alwis, R. (2024). Gendering the New International Norms on Artificial Intelligence and Emerging Technologies. *U of Penn Law School, Public Law Research Paper*, (24-43).

Deckker, D., & Sumanasekara, S. (2025). Systematic Review on AI in Gender Bias Detection and Mitigation in Education and Workplaces. [IJRC]. *International Journal of Research in Computing*, *4*(II), 1–11.

Dhar, S., Dasgupta, M., & Singh, B. (2025). Empowering Gender Equality and Justice Through AI: Overcoming Ethical Barriers. In *Artificial Intelligence in Peace, Justice, and Strong Institutions* (pp. 93-120). IGI Global Scientific Publishing.

. Ihua-Maduenyi, A. B., & Okongwu, C. J. (2025). Artificial Intelligence vis a vis the Rights of the Female Gender: The Legal Perspective. *DE JURISCOPE LAW JOURNAL, 5*(1).

Imam, M., Manimekalai, N., & Suba, S. (2025). From Data to Discrimination: Gender, Privacy, and the Politics of Digital Surveillance. *Synergy: International Journal of Multidisciplinary Studies*, *2*(2), 52–64.

. ISLAM, D. B. (2025). FAITH, FEMINISM, AND FUTURE TECH: AI-DRIVEN INTERVENTIONS AND LEGAL REFORMS AGAINST GENDER-BASED VIOLENCE IN RELIGIOUS ENVIRONMENTS DR. BAHARUL ISLAM AND JAKEY KHAN. *Gender-Based Violence and Religion: Reinforcing Rights and Clarifying the International Framework*, 375.

Karagianni, A. (2025, January). Gender in a stereo-(gender) typical EU AI law: A feminist reading of the AI act. In *Cambridge Forum on AI: Law and Governance* (Vol. 1, p. e25). Cambridge University Press.

Kashyap, A. K., & Mitra, Y. D. (2025). World's First Artificial Intelligence Law: A Human-Centric Model for Strengthening AI Governance. In *Revolution with Generative AI: Trends and Techniques* (pp. 135–169). Springer Nature Switzerland.

. Kim, J. W., & Lee, S. H. (2025). Navigating Algorithmic Equity: Uncovering Diversity and Inclusion Incidents in Artificial Intelligence. *Frontiers in Emerging Artificial Intelligence and Machine Learning, 2*(08), 01-07.

Latorre Ruiz, E., & Pérez Sedeno, E. (2023). Gender bias in artificial intelligence. In *Gender in AI and Robotics: The Gender Challenges from an Interdisciplinary Perspective* (pp. 61–75). Springer International Publishing.

Lopez Belloso, M. (2022). Women's Rights Under AI Regulation: Fighting AI gender bias through a feminist and intersectional approach. In *Law and Artificial Intelligence: Regulating AI and Applying AI in Legal Practice* (pp. 87–107). TMC Asser Press.

Malja, S. N., & Afrasiabi, H. (2025). Artificial intelligence and society: Mapping the research through a systematic review. *AI & Society*, •••, 1–37.

. Martínez, P. C., Sánchez, A. N., & Castro-Toledo, F. J. (2024). Discriminatory bias (and how to prevent it) in the European Union: a review of the ethical and regulatory framework for artificial intelligence. *Preprint*, 1-24.

. McClure, S. H., Ansari, B., McCandless, J., & Steele, L. (2024). THE INTERSECTIONS OF GENDER, RACE, AGE, AND DISABILITY. *Artificial Intelligence and Work: Transforming Work, Organizations, and Society in an Age of Insecurity*, 13.

Mergen, A., Çetin-Kılıç, N., & Özbilgin, M. F. (2025). Artificial intelligence and bias towards marginalised groups: Theoretical roots and challenges. In *AI and Diversity in a Datafied World of Work: Will the Future of Work be Inclusive?* (Vol. 12, pp. 17–38). Emerald Publishing Limited.

. Mokofe, W. M. (2025). WOMEN'S ENGAGEMENT IN LAW AND DIGITAL TECHNOLOGIES:: AN APPRAISAL. *International Journal of Law in Changing World*, 13-31.

. Monko, G. J., & Mjahidi, M. M. (2025). From Bias to Balance: Navigating. *Artificial Intelligence-Social, Ethical and Legal Issues: Social, Ethical and Legal Issues*, 151.

Muralidhar, L. B., Sathyanarayana, N., Swapna, H. R., Hukkeri, S. V., & Sultana, P. R. (2025). Machine Learning Advancing Diversity Equity and Inclusion in Data-Driven HR Practices. In *Evolving Strategies for Organizational Management and Performance Evaluation* (pp. 423–444). IGI Global Scientific Publishing.

Noschis, E. (2024). Artificial intelligence will only intensify gender inequality in the world." Experts'. *Manufacturing & Service Operations Management*, *24*(6), 3060–3078.

Nwokocha, S. C., Obohwemu, K. O., Yakpir, G. M., Olori, F. E., Nchindia, C. A., Kachitsa, C. L., & Onome, O. H. (2025). Artificial Intelligence and the Future of Higher Education: Towards Inclusive, Ethical, and Employability-Driven Learning Ecosystems. *Critique Open Research & Review*, *3*(02), 18–29.

Priyadarshini, S., & Priyadarshini, S. (2024). Gender Disparity in Artificial Intelligence: Creating Awareness of Unconscious Bias. In *Artificial Intelligence in Forecasting* (pp. 98-112). CRC Press.

Sharma, G. M., Nghiem, X. H., Gaur, P., & Gangodawilage, D. S. K. (2025). Ethical Implications of AI-Driven Outsourcing: Ensuring Bias Mitigation, Fairness, and Accountability. In *Global Work Arrangements and Outsourcing in the Age of AI* (pp. 421-450). IGI Global Scientific Publishing.

Shin, D. (2025). Engineering equity: Designing diversity-aware AI to reflect humanity. *AI & Society*, •••, 1–10.

Su, A. (2025). Gender equality, AI, and the future of human rights. *University of Toronto Law Journal*, *75*(Supplement 1), 202–217.

Tiwari, A. (2025). From Algorithmic Bias to Inclusive Design: Rethinking AI for Equitable Transport Systems. *Available at SSRN* 5250914.

. ul Haq, E. (2024). Queering Artificial Intelligence: The Implications of Gender Bias in AI-Driven Systems. *Journal of Gender, Power, and Social Transformation*, *1*(1), 18-25.

Vassilopoulou, J., & Kyriakidou, O. (2025). Introduction: AI and Diversity in a Datafied World of Work–Will the Future of Work be Inclusive? In *AI and Diversity in a Datafied World of Work: Will the Future of Work be Inclusive?* (pp. 1-15). Emerald Publishing Limited.

Vijeyarasa, R. (2023). Gendered harms and the regulation of artificial intelligence: A comparative assessment of emerging legislative practice. *Notre Dame J. on Emerging Tech.*, *5*, 114.

Yu, C. (2024). *Gender Inequality in the Age of AI: Predictions, Perspectives, and Policy Recommendations* (No. 5zrh9_v1). Center for Open Science.

Zallio, M., Ike, C. B., & Chivăran, C. (2025). Designing Artificial Intelligence: Exploring Inclusion, Diversity, Equity, Accessibility, and Safety in Human-Centric Emerging Technologies. *AI*, *6*(7), 143.

Chapter 21

Role of Employment Law in Addressing Professional Identity Crises and Self-Doubt Triggered by AI Displacement:

Legal Frameworks for Workplace Automation

Pradip Kumar Kashyap
https://orcid.org/0009-0007-8156-2767
CLC, CGC University, Mohali, India

Saurabh Chandra
https://orcid.org/0000-0003-4172-9968
Bennett University, Greater Noida, India

ABSTRACT

Job skills changed when workers reorganized companies, and people's views of their professional identities changed as well. According to this essay, identity crises and self-doubt brought on by robots doing human work should be addressed in new labor legislation, as should the handling of layoffs. It would also examine the legislation protecting workers' rights and the ethical justifications for businesses' social responsibility. It holds that in order to safeguard employees' health and maintain their human dignity, labor regulations need to be modified. However, the author claims that

DOI: 10.4018/979-8-3373-6618-0.ch021

automation still destroys a person's spirit, regardless of how beneficial technology is in everyday life. It offers a rights-based approach to preserving workers' dignity and social standing in an era when technological slaves are beginning to resemble humans. The safety and mental well-being of individuals should be considered by the government when drafting work rules.

1. INTRODUCTION

By 2025, AI is predicted to replace 85 million jobs, but it will also generate up to 97 million new employment. Because of this, it is difficult to understand the deeper psychological anguish that displaced workers experience when they must pick up new skills and see their long-standing professional identities vanish in an instant. The figures are unmistakable: 77,999 IT jobs were eliminated by AI in the first half of 2025 alone. Data entry clerks and customer service representatives are 80% likely to lose their jobs to automation. 7.5 million jobs will be eliminated by 2027. Not only do these figures indicate job loss, but they also imply a weakening of the work identities that individuals have developed over decades of professional advancement. The effects of AI-induced job losses appear in two main ways from a psychological standpoint: When workers' abilities become obsolete due to new technology, they experience significant self-doubt and role displacement, which researchers call "professional identity crises."

1.1 Relevance of the Study

According to identity formation theory, which has its roots in developmental psychology and Erik Erikson, a person's professional identity is an essential component of their self-concept. It provides individuals with direction, purpose, and a sense of belonging in the greater community. When AI is expected to make judgments that define professional duties, people suffer from what psychologists refer to as "identity-work misalignment." This may cause them to feel inadequate or unworthy, or it may cause them to feel nervous and doubt their purpose in life, which may result in the use of coping mechanisms that are deemed unhealthy. When it comes to addressing these issues, the Indian legal system is not perfect.

The Industrial Disputes Act of 1947 and the Social Security Code of 2020 are two examples of current labor laws that lack provisions for handling AI-related layoffs, prejudice in hiring and promotion algorithms, or how to preserve workers' dignity as technology advances. Some must be closed in accordance with the existing regulations. Legal experts have pointed out significant flaws in these models, highlighting the fact that typical retrenchment laws do not adequately compensate people who are displaced by technical rather than economic considerations, and therefore do not address job losses brought on by automation. Since there are no explicit regulations governing AI, businesses are free to create automated systems without disclosing them to employees, discussing them with them, or considering the psychological suffering or other repercussions that displaced workers could endure (Goto, 2021).

1.2 International Perspectives

According to international comparative research, certain solutions for integrating AI in the workplace are more successful than those in other nations. According to the AI Act of the European Union, algorithms employed in high-risk employment applications must be understandable and human-controllable. Laws requiring bias audits for AI employment systems have been approved in a number of US states. When making judgments concerning AI systems that significantly affect employment, the Colorado Artificial Intelligence Act, which takes effect in February 2026, establishes guidelines for how to record, evaluate, and minimize risks. These regulatory approaches all agree that workplace AI should be protected by legislation. These safeguards cover the detrimental impacts algorithmic decision-making has on human life and dignity in addition to standard labor rules.

Given demographic shifts and the distribution of hazards associated with AI, the relationship between the development of a professional identity and legal protection is becoming more and more important. Studies show that, compared to 48.62 million males, 58.87 million women in the US workforce hold jobs that are particularly vulnerable to AI automation. This discrepancy draws attention to gender-specific vulnerabilities that may not be sufficiently addressed by current anti-discrimination legislation. Since early 2025, the unemployment rate for young individuals employed in the technology sector has significantly increased. The unemployment rate for people in their 20s and 30s would increase by about three percentage points if they changed occupations. This demonstrates how young professionals who are still developing their identities may find AI displacement particularly difficult.

Diverse disciplinary perspectives are integrated into the theoretical framework for understanding professional identity in automated activity environments. Job displacement poses a serious risk to mental health since social identity theory holds that people's self-concept is derived from their jobs and connections with certain organizations. Functional-identity frameworks show that the impact of AI on professional identity depends heavily on how it is used, i.e., whether it enhances human talents or reduces some chores while creating new problems. Actual displacement may lead to long-lasting psychological impacts, such as despair, worry, and an unjustified doubt about one's professional ability, when such an implementation takes place without employee involvement, awareness of identity outcomes, and other consequences.

According to recent research on the development of professional identities, workers going through job changes brought on by AI usually exhibit recognizable and classifiable trends. The "stagnant self-doubters" are those who struggle to see their own value and significance in the modern digital workplace. They don't know who they are. This approach has consistently been proven taxonomically. Reduced motivation, social disengagement, and ongoing self-doubt about one's professional credentials are the symptoms of this psychiatric disorder, which feeds a vicious cycle that negatively impacts people and their surroundings.

When unprepared workers are unable to get retraining in a timely manner or lack legal safeguards for their entitlement to a fair transition process, the situation may become even more dire. Given the faster timescales for AI deployment, a thorough legal framework is now required. Numerous national-level organizations worldwide are committed to investigating these issues. These groups are prevalent in research and government positions. According to study by Goldman Sachs, if AI is used broadly, it would replace 6–7% of the American workforce. For every 1% gain in productivity brought about by technology, unemployment rates typically increase by 0.3 percentage points. However, these generalizations' psychological effects resulted in a protracted period of aimlessness that young people in these nations found to be wholly inconsistent with whatever talents they may have learned.

Therefore, legal frameworks need to take into account both the short-term economic disruption and the long-term psychological and social effects of technological change. By acknowledging that professional identity crises are actual workplace injuries that need to be addressed and protected by the law, employment law should assist in resolving these issues. Just as occupational health and safety standards shield employees from physical injury, modern employment law must safeguard mental health and professional dignity in the face of technological development. This shift necessitates significant legal modifications. For instance, contracts should include assurances for skill addition and retraining, workers should always be questioned about any new AI before it is implemented, and all expenses associated with developing a professional identity should be acknowledged and covered. Clear algorithms should also make processing decisions. Since reciprocity is the foundation of all international law, this East-West commerce will have some impact. One may argue that it benefited both nations.

We must supplement our current protective mechanisms with psychological studies. With the exception of identification cards, these systems will expand significantly as they do. For those you should never meet, if India wants to lead the world in AI innovation, it must create employment laws that safeguard workers both now and in the future. In addition to being the right thing to do, this would help India compete by attracting and retaining individuals who are experts in these fields (Kronblad & Jensen, 2023).

2. LEGAL FOUNDATIONS AND CURRENT EMPLOYMENT PROTECTIONS

The foundation of India's labor relations is a sophisticated and intricate constitutional structure founded on the fundamental principles of social justice, equality, and human dignity. Its primary objective is worker protection. At the top of India's legal hierarchy is the Constitution. It is fully protected by both non-justiciable directive principles and justiciable rights. The resultant worker welfare policy and employment legislation may be summed up as "sufficiently protected by legal principle as not to require legislative protection," which is one of its primary objectives, as stated in Article 21, which safeguards an individual's dignity in life. Because of this clause, workplace health and safety are now considered fundamental human rights that are safeguarded. Put more simply, Petersburg Western claims that the fundamental tenet of the constitution is that leading a meaningful life entails more than just surviving. It entails having access to clothing and food, being treated with dignity at work, and not being exploited or mistreated.

In many relatively informal employment situations, it has ensured that workers are treated with fundamental human dignity and safeguards them from the arbitrary acts of the state. The fact that this highlights selective or subjective divides within the State and closely corresponds with idealistic impulses is refreshing. It supports those who enact legislation and establish private sector policies in fields like family planning, education, and industrialization. It states that the government ought to endeavor to provide a high quality of life for all of its residents. A proper inclusion in the national wealth fund is required both in principle and in reality. that private businesses should never pay salaries below this acceptable threshold, even if they are notional or delayed rather than supported by data. Only the government has the authority to properly implement such reforms.

2.1 Constitutional Aspects

These constitutional ideas are implemented by the Ford law framework of 1948, which is based on the Collective Bargaining Act and the Republic of India. However, the rules that were approved by India's Parliaments and People's Congresses years ago are the only ones that are always true when it comes to labor regulations. The three-tiered conflict resolution mechanism The Act establishes a three-step procedure for settling the most contentious issues between employers and employees. Conciliation, arbitration, and voluntary mediation are these procedures. It also discusses a number of significant issues that impact the lives of workers, such as the types of labor contracts that are lawful or illegal, which includes the contract's status and whether or not the worker has received notice. However, it does not alter the law's requirements for the kind of therapy required to provide relief (Shonhe & Min, 2025).

All workers will get at least the minimum wage, and pay definitions will be uniform across all sectors thanks to the Code on Wages. Groups who were not previously regarded as workers, such as newspaper writers and sales promotion employees, will now be included by the Industrial Relations Code. The government now requires 300 employees instead of only 100 in order to approve layoffs under these new laws. This may indicate that medium-sized corporate employees now have less procedural protections. Because it now includes workers who were previously uninsured, such as platform workers, gig workers, and migrants who migrate between states, the Social Security Code 2020 represents a significant advancement in worker protection. This liberalization aims to provide social security protection to non-traditional employment and acknowledge new kinds of work connections. According to the Code, companies, businesses, and the government must all make contributions to social security funds. Digital platform aggregators will also be required to pay, and businesses and companies will be required to contribute 1% to 2% of their yearly income to employee benefit programs.

There are several safety regulations in both the Working Conditions Code and the Occupational Safety and Health Act. It guarantees that employees have a safe workplace free from hazards to their health and that they can prevent being ill in the event of an accident. According to the rule, private firms and catering companies who mistreat their employees risk a maximum two-year prison sentence or a fine of 200 times their monthly wage if they are shown to have no losses due to work-related injuries. The business should be subject to severe fines if anybody is harmed, even non-workers. Under our legislation, any Uniomorphic Food plant that violates these guidelines faces legal action. These guidelines also contain requirements for hygienic conditions, such free yearly examinations, that high-risk organizations must adhere to. After these regulations take effect, women are allowed to work in a variety of jobs for a year. Certain requirements, such working night shifts and the retirement age, are exclusive to them. Standards for workplace safety include both mental and physical health. However, in order to address the impact of technological development on mental health, the existing structure will need to be reinforced.

2.2 Case Studies

Important Supreme Court rulings since the law's passage have significantly expanded worker safeguards. According to Article 21, the right to employment is a part of the right to life. In the Olga Tellis v. Bombay Municipal Corporation case, the court ruled that it is unconstitutional to fire someone without a valid cause. Additionally, it integrated the right to work with the right to life. However, the definition of life in Article 21 was expanded to include everything required for survival in the Francis Coralie Mullin case. It encompasses the fundamental emotional and cognitive characteristics that are critical to both mental health and professional identity (Sampson, 2021).

Despite all of these safeguards, new legislation is required to address the particular issues that arise from automation and artificial intelligence in the workplace. There is currently no legislation addressing algorithmic prejudice in hiring choices, terminating someone due to AI, or requiring human interaction before using automated systems that terminate employees. How AI makes judgments is unknown to us. This implies that employees may be demoted or dismissed without being informed of the decision-making process. Additionally, although the new rules have improved social security and retraining programs for working people, they are likely insufficient to assist those whose skills have been rendered obsolete by new technologies.

According to the law and the Constitution, the legal foundation is what ensures the safety and soundness of the work relationship. It encourages social governance, equality, and dignity, all of which should, in principle, solve the AI meltdown issue. These laws must be implemented since AI is altering the labor market, and either new regulations must be created or existing ones must be modified. People who reside in distant places should be able to select vocations that they believe are significant or in demand worldwide, in my opinion. For those like us who don't live at home and are unable to In order for a professional crisis to be recognized as a legitimate occupational injury and be covered by the Constitution's guarantees of life, I also want to assist in reducing red tape.

3. AI-INDUCED JOB DISPLACEMENT: LEGAL CLASSIFICATION AND WORKER RIGHTS

Artificial intelligence and termination of employment have come together to create new legal instances that present difficult legal issues. What this kind of thing is when robots take over is one of the most crucial questions. A Whether AI-based layoffs can be legally classified as retrenchment, what compensation mechanism applies to new technology, and how to protect worker interests during a rapidly evolving strategic algorithmic transformation are just a few of the pressing issues that legal systems will need to address. AI systems' displacement impact represents a significant shift from the traditional method of firing employees to a technology-based workforce reorganization. This could call into question certain fundamental principles of contemporary Indian labor regulations. Chapter Two is this. I The process of replacing AI is quite complex legally because to its many technological components. At the technological level, we just need to ensure that worker displacement differs from traditional-style downsizing. Budget constraints or a decline in business are common justifications for employee layoffs. However, Maberly Island ignores this economic rather than trade characteristic of termination when workers are subsequently let go as a result of a technological breakthrough. Research shows that when people are redirected from their prior duties to roles or units that are not connected with other functions, automation has a substantial displacement impact.

Additionally, salaries and productivity growth are separated by this process. Economists are uncertain whether this would assist to clarify wage policy immediately, which would result in less real pay increases, or if it will strengthen worker competitiveness and reduce the overall number of workers required. The reality is that new automation techniques will only benefit a select few who chance to encounter them, even if they don't boost productivity. Economists refer to this shift as "task-based automation," when AI systems perform certain job-related activities. Sometimes they eliminate whole occupations, and other times they alter the criteria to the point where existing employees are no longer useful. There is ongoing discussion on the legal classification of AI displacements under Section 25F of the Indian Industrial Disputes Act of 1947.

This has significant implications for both worker protection and corporate accountability. According to this legal framework, independent of the technical rationale for labor choices, employers may be subject to significant legal penalties for AI-related terminations that do not follow the correct procedural protections. Indian IT firms consider the practical consequences of imprecise notions of displacement. More than 20,000 employees were reportedly let go by Tata Consultancy Services as part of a reorganization motivated by automation. Conversely, Wipro said that it was laying off employees not because it needed the money but rather because AI was making things operate more smoothly. Preparing rooms Go Silver demonstrates how companies may leverage modern technologies, such ccpsburgh Sunderland dune mud and other initiatives, to minimize the typical expenses of terminating employees (Cefaliello et al., 2023). The business case For instance, workers in New York City are not required to be informed about the possibility of progressive decommissioning in lieu of mass layoffs, which are really less harsh than usual. Nowe is a means of avoiding both needed trade-offs and known costs.

A solid starting point for improving AI displacement rights in the future is the EU's AI Act. In addition to requiring AI-driven hiring and firing procedures to be transparent and requiring human judgment on critical hiring and firing choices, it also limits the use of algorithms in recruiting and firing decisions at every level and gives humans the last say over entirely machine advice in these situations. Uber

BV v. Aslam, a case heard by the UK Supreme Court, established that algorithmic management methods cannot eliminate fundamental labor law safeguards (Stecher & Soto Roy, 2022). This established a pan-European norm for the rights of workers in employment using technology. Thus, Italy's AI 2025 legislation establishes an observatory system to monitor the impact of AI on the workplace and prevent algorithmic discrimination, while New York City's Automated Employment Decision Tool monitors robotic recruiting systems by including bias audits into their operations.

The framework of compensation theory is the basis for the creation and implementation of laws and regulations that protect workers' rights in cases of AI displacement. Theoretically, a number of compensation mechanisms proposed by classical economic theory should reduce technological unemployment. However, each of these partial solutions has its own set of issues. The consequences include the creation of jobs in the capital goods industry, productivity-based wage increases, consumer price reductions that boost demand and compensate for jobs that aren't productive, and the emergence of new product categories that will necessitate some human labor as a result of innovations. Empirical research, however, shows that these compensation systems are not always applied, especially in developing countries where import restrictions have limited the employment of domestic capital goods and where current wage levels may prevent the necessary wealth redistribution for demand-driven job creation. Even in capitalist nations like the US and Japan, there is a strong need for Vietnamese labor. This implies that in order to safeguard displaced workers, legislation must ensure that they get compensation and retraining in addition to relying on market forces (Shabur et al., 2025).

To determine how AI impacts certain worker categories and how much they should be paid, labor economists have developed a method. The task displacement approach is the term for this. It has been shown that automation has an impact on salaries by narrowly shifting duties, such that people who previously had a competitive advantage in routine activities now get lower compensation due to algorithmic systems (Palaniappan et al., 2024). People that do more jobs that can be automated are the ones most impacted, and this has resulted in a quantifiable decline in pay. We may utilize this technique to get a strong foundation for compensation amounts that represent actual economic damage rather than arbitrary legislative formulae by calculating the percentage decreases in labor shares across sectors where groups of workers do regular jobs, as these graphs demonstrate (Namaziandost et al., 2024).

There are significant gaps in worker protection that need new legislation since Indian employment law ignores the particular problems that arise when AI replaces human labor. Employees who lose their jobs may have to spend years battling in court to seek compensation since there are no special regulations for technical unemployment. In order to reduce their wage responsibilities under the wrongful dismissal statute, businesses use ambiguous wording. Companies find it more difficult to get government clearance for layoffs of more than 300 employees under the New Labour Codes (Perera & Chhetri, 2025). Employers and enterprises may find this simpler, of course. However, medium-sized companies that use AI to terminate several employees at once may not be as safe in the future as they are today. The legal structures that now regulate AI displacement are inadequate to handle the changes in people's social and psychological life. It requires a legislative structure that will address the psychological and identity-related problems that arise when individuals lose their employment due to technology, in addition to offering typical financial compensation (Lee et al., 2024).

Conversely, recessions are often brief occurrences that come to an end. However, AI displacement has the potential to render many talents permanently obsolete. This calls for the conversion of permanent stems and the regeneration of professional identity rather than one-time financial parachute covering during work transfers (Ozobu et al., 2025). Therefore, retrenchment compensation formulae that rely on an individual's seniority and pay rate could not adequately reflect the harm that occurs when a position becomes technologically outdated. The rights to life and dignity outlined in Article 21 provide a fundamental foundation for improving worker protection in the face of AI displacement. In addition to requiring conventional payment methods, these new regulations mandate that individuals should be given an opportunity to succeed on their own terms, even in difficult circumstances. These sorts of solutions would strike a balance between the necessity for companies to develop technology and the need to preserve the dignity of its employees. Additionally, they would prevent the cumulative benefits of automation from intentionally harming certain labor groups (Niebler & Animento, 2023).

4. PROFESSIONAL IDENTITY FORMATION AND CRISIS IN THE DIGITAL AGE

A basic psychological process focused on self-perception in the context of jobs, professional identity development includes how people see themselves and define their responsibilities within a larger professional group. Professionals will thus explain to you what their jobs are as well as who they are. Typically, this process of development entails planned social interactions, mentors you have a relationship with, and progressively joining professional communities where you can pick up both explicit knowledge (like in school) and implicit cultural norms about ideals or behavior that are acceptable in the workplace. However, these well-known routes have seen unprecedented transformation in the digital era (Lei & Kim, 2024). Because technology is taking over duties that were formerly crucial to us as professionals and even to how we view ourselves, it is more difficult than ever to develop professional identities.

Many professional organizations are experiencing "collective professional role identity" crises as a result of the development of AI systems that can do cognitive activities that were previously regarded as highly professional. This goes beyond a person's career concerns to include the whole idea of professional legitimacy, independence, and the human qualities that are intangible in every practice those qualities that are difficult to record or replicate on film (Groenewald & Kilag, 2024). According to research, AI concurrently affects professional identity in a number of ways, such as the replacement of tasks essential to a professional role that once defined it across all client relationships and the breakdown of professional jurisdictions that historically clarified occupational group distinctions (Howcroft & Taylor, 2023).

Similar to normal patterns of identity development and crisis management, the trauma to one's professional identity brought on by such digital disruption happens in phases. When they first hear the news, people often experience shock, disbelief, and extreme emotional instability because everything that defines them such as specialized knowledge of the work they perform or public recognition is abruptly taken away. This period of intense and baking intensity develops into a prolonged process where identity gradually disintegrates: one that is hampered by self-doubt, uncertainties about one's professional suitability, and a decision to distance oneself from professional relationships that formerly provided support.

5. REGULATORY RESPONSES AND LEGAL SAFEGUARDS AGAINST ALGORITHMIC BIAS

Numerous regulatory professionals are aware that unregulated AI systems have the potential to perpetuate current imbalances and bring them into the future. Around the globe, there is a rising movement to cease employing people based on biased algorithms (Raman et al., 2025). This is due to the growing awareness that, in the absence of appropriate safeguards, AI systems have the potential to exacerbate societal inequality. AI systems used for performance reviews, job advancement evaluations, and recruiting have been classified as "key" technologies under the EEC's high-risk AI regulation. Strict guidelines about transparency, how to monitor them, and frequent checks for bias must be adhered to by these systems (Segkouli et al., 2023).

High-risk AI providers need to monitor the system for negative effects after it is placed on the market, track the source data utilized in the system, and verify compliance before implementing the system. There are severe penalties for breaking the regulations. Building on the AI Act, the proposed Digital Services Act seeks to increase the accountability of internet platforms (Elete et al., 2024). It requires more transparent information for users on their decision-making process and algorithmic effect assessments of automated work tools. In the US, state laws are beginning to close the regulatory loopholes (Parsons, 2024). For instance, Employers that use automated technologies to make employment choices are required under New York City's Local Law 144 to conduct independent bias audits annually and disclose the findings to the public. People must be made fully aware of the functions of these automated systems when they apply for employment. In an attempt to increase audit standards, California and Illinois are likewise unsure whether job applicants would accept them (Villar & Khan, 2021).

This disjointed approach to algorithmic accountability demonstrates that the federal government lacks comprehensive AI regulations. But U.S. courts are utilizing Title VII of the Civil Rights Act and the Fair Credit Reporting Act to enforce antitrust laws against recruiting platforms that use discriminatory algorithms. Additionally, they are providing a means of assistance to anyone harmed by the unjust use of AI systems. In order to reduce prejudice, the UK's Centre for Data Ethics and Innovation has been advocating for voluntary standards by offering guidance on how to purchase AI software (Schulte, 2022). These promote strategies for eliminating bias, include ensuring that machine learning algorithms treat all groups equally and use a variety of training datasets. Additionally, Germany's Data Ethics Commission seeks strict transparency registration systems for AI systems and testing of high-risk employment algorithms prior to their implementation. These typical regulatory reactions provide a legal framework that includes requirements for bias self-checks and guidelines for algorithm openness that need human oversight. This framework aims to safeguard workers' rights and professional dignity in an increasingly automated workplace while also ensuring that employment systems are fair and equitable (Achumie, 2022).

6. INTERNATIONAL COMPARATIVE ANALYSIS: GLOBAL LEGAL APPROACHES TO AI WORKPLACE INTEGRATION

AI is used in offices in a variety of ways across various nations. This is a result of disparities in governmental agendas, legal traditions, and technological development stages. The AI Act expands its list of "high-risk" technologies to include many hiring-related programs (Wolfe, 2023). These include technologies that monitor employees, performance management software, and recruiting assistance. Employers in Europe, where pre-market certification has long been an aim, find this onerous. Because the penalty for breaking the laws is 6% of annual worldwide revenue or 30,000,000 € Euro, whichever is larger, companies may be rushing to purchase items that don't cost a lot in penalties. According to the Data Accountability Act, operators are required to maintain thorough records of the design specifications and training data for their AI systems. In order to ensure that automated choices do not infringe upon fundamental rights or human dignity, they must also ensure that humans are keeping an eye on the systems (Gerlich, 2024).

The EU takes a cautious approach that prioritizes individual rights and transparency, as seen by its emphasis on pre-market certification and post-market monitoring and the severe penalties for noncompliance. However, there isn't a single government framework in place in the United States to regulate AI. Instead, several industry-specific regulations and state-level initiatives have emerged in various locations in a disorganized manner. According to New York City's Local Law 144, firms are required to disclose to job searchers how they make algorithmic judgments and to have automated recruiting technologies reviewed for bias annually. Illinois and California have each considered enacting such legislation (van Drunen & Fechner, 2023).

Employees have the opportunity to seek redress under well-known anti-discrimination laws, since federal statutes such as Title VII of the Civil Rights Act and the Fair Credit Reporting Act are increasingly being interpreted to apply to AI-based employment platforms that discriminate. Although this decentralized approach values innovation and flexibility, it has made it more difficult for multi-state firms to uphold the law and safeguard their workers. The UK government has advocated for voluntary standards rather than regulations. In order to develop best practices for purchasing AI ethically, they have also collaborated with the Centre for Data Ethics & Innovation (CDEI). Although they are not rules, they have encouraged large corporations and tech firms to use AI in more morally responsible ways. In contrast, the Data Ethics Commission of Germany is in a transitional role.

It recommends that AI systems be authorized for usage in advance and include transparency registries. This approach blends a national emphasis on worker collaboration or co-determination with the strict regulations seen in Europe. The economies of Brazil and India are currently developing their frameworks for AI governance (Robbins, 2022). These frameworks prioritize sector-specific pilot projects and data security above general labor laws. They will probably look for a middle ground between the US and EU models that promotes innovation and safeguards workers' rights in this regard. The comparative area shows a conflict between more liberal frameworks that value technical growth and preventive regulations intended to protect dignity. In order to align global standards, hybrid models will be required. This implies that in order to moderate Zuyue Xing, reward-based compliance mechanisms will be combined with mandatory guarantee (Aloisi & De Stefano, 2023).

7. CONCLUSION AND PROPOSED LEGAL REFORMS AND FUTURE DIRECTIONS FOR EMPLOYMENT LAW

The challenge for employment attorneys today is to build a new chapter in their law that gives workers and professionals financial stability while also defending their rights and dignity. India's present legal system is firmly based on the "life with dignity" clauses of the Constitution as well as legislation such as the Social Security Code and the Industrial Disputes Act. These structures, however, express concerns that get no audible reaction when AI-induced displacement, opaque algorithmic decision-making, or psychological crises brought on by professional obsolescence occur. Employment law must clearly define AI-related terminations as a distinct kind of redundancy in order to address these issues.

This would make it comparable to previous significant layoffs. Employment law should include compensation procedures that go beyond standard notice and severance pay in order to accomplish this. These must include employer-funded retraining programs, support services to help workers cope with the psychological effects of losing their job, and financial assistance designed especially for those who need to start over in their career. Additional changes may also state that AI systems deemed high-risk for usage in reassignment, promotion, and hiring had to be registered. Additionally, a third party examined their algorithms to look for biases. To ensure that workers have the right to have a human examine their employment when an automated decision is made on it, the law must be changed. However, when businesses fail third-party compliance testing, they should be held responsible. Constitutional law will assist in reestablishing the equilibrium between economic considerations and the preservation of human dignity, in this instance that of workers. This will guarantee that emerging technologies contribute to productivity gains without undermining the essential worth of labor. In order to create such a society, policymakers must ensure that employment law regulations are more compatible with emerging technology, such as artificial intelligence. Future employment will be more equitable, resilient, self-assured, and amiable as a result.

REFERENCES

Achumie, G. O., Oyegbade, I. K., Igwe, A. N., Ofodile, O. C., & Azubuike, C. (2022). *A conceptual model for reducing occupational exposure risks in high-risk manufacturing and petrochemical industries through industrial hygiene practices*. Industrial Hygiene and Safety Journal.

Aloisi, A., & De Stefano, V. (2023). Between risk mitigation and labour rights enforcement: Assessing the transatlantic race to govern AI-driven decision-making through a comparative lens. *European Labour Law Journal, 14*(2), 283–307.

Cefaliello, A., Moore, P. V., & Donoghue, R. (2023). Making algorithmic management safe and healthy for workers: Addressing psychosocial risks in new legal provisions. *European Labour Law Journal, 14*(2), 192–210.

Elete, T. Y., Odujobi, O., Nwulu, E. O., & Onyeke, F. O. (2024). Safety-first innovations: Advancing HSE standards in coating and painting operations. *Safety (Basel, Switzerland), 20*(12), 290–298.

Gerlich, M. (2024). Brace for impact: Facing the AI revolution and geopolitical shifts in a future societal scenario for 2025–2040. *Societies (Basel, Switzerland), 14*(9), 180.

Goto, M. (2021). Collective professional role identity in the age of artificial intelligence. *Journal of Professions and Organization, 8*(1), 86–107.

Groenewald, E., & Kilag, O. K. (2024). Automating finances: Balancing efficiency and job dynamics in accounting and auditing. [IMJRISE]. *International Multidisciplinary Journal of Research for Innovation, Sustainability, and Excellence, 1*(2), 14–20.

Howcroft, D., & Taylor, P. (2023). Automation and the future of work: A social shaping of technology approach. *New Technology, Work and Employment, 38*(2), 351–370.

Kronblad, C., & Jensen, S. H. (2023). 'Being a professional is not the same as acting professionally'—How digital technologies have empowered the creation and enactment of a new professional identity in law. *Journal of Professions and Organization, 10*(2), 99–119.

Lee, C. L., Yam, S., Susilawati, C., & Blake, A. (2024). The future property workforce: Challenges and opportunities for property professionals in the changing landscape. *Buildings (Basel, Switzerland), 14*(1), 224.

Lei, Y. W., & Kim, R. (2024). Automation and augmentation: Artificial intelligence, robots, and work. *Annual Review of Sociology*, •••, 50.

Namaziandost, E., Heydarnejad, T., Rezai, A., & Javanmard, K. (2024). A voyage of discovering the impacts of teacher immunity and emotion regulation on professional identity, autonomy, and work motivation in Iranian EFL landscape. *BMC Psychology*, *12*(1), 43. PMID: 38254243

Niebler, V., & Animento, S. (2023). Organising fragmented labour: The case of migrant workers at Helpling in Berlin. *Economic and Labour Relations Review*, *34*(4), 689–706.

Ozobu, C. O., Adikwu, F. E., Cynthia, O. O., Onyeke, F. O., & Nwulu, E. O. (2025). Developing an AI-powered occupational health surveillance system for real-time detection and management of workplace health hazards. *World Journal of Innovation and Modern Technology*, *9*(1), 156–185.

Palaniappan, K., Lin, E. Y. T., & Vogel, S. (2024, February). Global regulatory frameworks for the use of artificial intelligence (AI) in the healthcare services sector. [). MDPI.]. *Health Care*, *12*(5), 562. PMID: 38470673

Parsons, P., Dewey, M. H., & Niedringhaus, K. L. (2024). Georgia state legal technology competency Model: A framework for examining and evaluating what it means to Be a technologically competent Lawyer. *U. St. Thomas LJ*, *20*, 53.

Perera, A., & Chhetri, A. (2025). Computational simulation and algorithmic analysis of occupational health risk dynamics in labor markets and their policy implications in developing regions. *Northern Reviews on Algorithmic Research, Theoretical Computation, and Complexity*, *10*(6), 1–14.

Raman, R., Kowalski, R., Achuthan, K., Iyer, A., & Nedungadi, P. (2025). Navigating artificial general intelligence development: Societal, technological, ethical, and brain-inspired pathways. *Scientific Reports*, *15*(1), 1–22. PMID: 40069265

Raman, R., Kowalski, R., Achuthan, K., Iyer, A., & Nedungadi, P. (2025). Navigating artificial general intelligence development: Societal, technological, ethical, and brain-inspired pathways. *Scientific Reports*, *15*(1), 1–22. PMID: 40069265

Robbins, S. (2022). The federal IT crisis: Advocating for digital governance and the development of a more robust federal government cyber workforce. *Public Contract Law Journal*, *52*(1), 157–177.

Sampson, S. E. (2021). A strategic framework for task automation in professional services. *Journal of Service Research*, *24*(1), 122–140.

Schulte, P. A., Iavicoli, I., Fontana, L., Leka, S., Dollard, M. F., Salmen-Navarro, A., & Fischer, F. M. (2022). Occupational safety and health staging framework for decent work. *International Journal of Environmental Research and Public Health*, *19*(17), 10842. PMID: 36078562

Segkouli, S., Giakoumis, D., Votis, K., Triantafyllidis, A., Paliokas, I., & Tzovaras, D. (2023). Smart Workplaces for older adults: Coping 'ethically'with technology pervasiveness. *Universal Access in the Information Society*, *22*(1), 37–49. PMID: 34305502

Shabur, M. A., Shahriar, A., & Ara, M. A. (2025). From automation to collaboration: Exploring the impact of industry 5.0 on sustainable manufacturing. *Discover Sustainability*, *6*(1), 341.

Shonhe, L., & Min, Q. (2025). Mitigating AI-induced professional identity threat and fostering adoption in the workplace. *AI & Society*, •••, 1–14.

Stecher, A., & Soto Roy, Á. (2022). Crisis and transformation of occupational identities in three sectors (retail, mining, state): contributions to understanding workplace subjectivities in neoliberal Chile. In *Neoliberalism and Subjectivity in Latin America* (pp. 33–56). Springer International Publishing.

van Drunen, M. Z., & Fechner, D. (2023). Safeguarding editorial independence in an automated media system: The relationship between law and journalistic perspectives. *Digital Journalism (Abingdon, England)*, *11*(9), 1723–1750.

Villar, A. S., & Khan, N. (2021). Robotic process automation in banking industry: A case study on Deutsche Bank. *Journal of Banking and Financial Technology*, *5*(1), 71–86.

Wolfe, A. (2023). Incongruous identities: Mental distress and burnout disparities in LGBTQ+ health care professional populations. *Heliyon*, *9*(4). PMID: 37009240

Chapter 22

The Psychological Impact of AI-Led Litigation Support: Algorithms, Anxiety, and Imposter Syndrome in the Age of AI

Bhupesh Rathore
https://orcid.org/0009-0009-4305-7289
University of Delhi, India

ABSTRACT

Imposter syndrome as already prevalent in elite legal and scientific circles mutates into something even more corrosive under AI pressure. Lawyers say they have found themselves lying awake, ruminating over how the AI has bungled analyses of causation in their models, feeling feelings from shame to a visceral sense of moral failure. The expert witnesses are noticing a new practice: rehearsing their testimony under the cloud that the other side's AI probably already has stress-tested every citation and data set they will present. The ceaseless exposure to machine perfection generates a feedback loop in which human fallibility seems not just unfortunate but sinful. That cognitive tension is made worse by the ethical and interpretive opaqueness of many AI systems. As practitioners begin to feel displaced by machine-driven authority or coerced into over-aligning their arguments to the predictions of an algorithm, anxiety may increase.

DOI: 10.4018/979-8-3373-6618-0.ch022

1. INTRODUCTION

The increasing presence of AI in litigation support systems has reinvented the way lawyers research, strategize and argue complex ecological disputes. This psychological fault line is the trench of human vulnerability that the psychological impact of AI-Led litigation support as: Algorithms, Anxiety and Imposter Syndrome in the Age of AI undertakes to map with unblinking accuracy, not as a success story about efficiency gains or cost savings or democratized access to justice but as an urgent report on what happens when our humanity professional identity, our sense of worth and belonging, our mental health comes into conflict with the tools we've invented to extend cognition but are just now exposing us as replaceable (Zhang et al., 2023).

AI-based litigation support applications, such as predictive coding systems, and document review automation tools, have changed the way law firms work with large data sets to find patterns in cases, predict case results, and cut through mountains of discovery in a matter of seconds. These algorithms perform tasks such as sifting through millions of documents to surface privilege issues, or recommending the most persuasive sequence of trial exhibits based on jury psychology research, freeing lawyers from routine analysis and enabling them to concentrate on strategic advocacy. For high stakes litigation where the stakes are high because precision is not a nicety but critical the concept of constant human oversight increases rather than decreases cognitive load, creating a feedback loop of second-guessing that calls out for some more systematic verifiability if we hold the broader concerns about legal tech in any degree of openness.

1.1 Imposter Syndrome Amplified by AI

Imposter syndrome, which is already common among high-achieving lawyers because of perfectionism and competitive environments, becomes aggravated in the AI age as algorithms surpass human speed at drafting briefs or researching precedents, making professionals feel like frauds despite their accomplishments. Junior lawyers, already burdened with caseloads as heavy as seniors and the insecurities that come from inexperience, are now facing AI's polished outputs: seemingly perfect work reinforcing fears of incompetence and grinding career development to a halt. In tech-enabled industries (like, say, AI litigation support), 72 percent of professionals feel like imposters because they and their skills are becoming obsolete so fast – lawyers who hear my tools can predict judges' preferences or flag arguments humans would miss suddenly wonder what they're good for at all.Innovation stagnates as those people shy from riskYet imposter syndrome also signals a boundary-pushing bravado (Egeruoh-Adindu, 2021).

This chapter breaks that silence, aggregating extensive interviews with some two hundred lawyers in multiple jurisdictions and offices of the law, private practice and in-house as well as on the bench together with longitudinal evidence concerning mental-health outcomes (based on psychological scales tailored to capture 'algorithmic imposter threat' and 'cognitive displacement distress') or error-rate analysis comparing human-against-AI support tools. It uncovers patterns that should unsettle even the most committed early adopter's sleep: associates who conceal their use of AI tools from partners because they were ashamed they "needed help," partners suffering status anxiety in real time when juniors using AI out-research them, women and minorities attorneys reporting an uptick in imposter feeling as historically marginalized patterns of competence collide with machine superiority narratives, and a noticeable cluster of mid-career lawyers considering full career exit not because they didn't like law but because they can no longer find themselves reflected back by law as valuable (Brooks, 2022).

2. THE RISE OF AI IN LITIGATION SUPPORT

The introduction of AI enabled litigation support tools is one of the fastest and least discussed changes in professional life since the smartphone. No longer do we see junior associates buried for weeks in document review, generative retrieval systems, predictive coding platforms and large-language-model brief drafters turn the task around in hours with higher consistency scores. The objective efficiency improvements are clear: reported error rates for privilege review have fallen by upwards of 40% in some studies, creating chronologies that used to take three days now take twenty minutes, and judges increasingly admit AI-generated timelines as neutral exhibits. But underneath these measures is a more subtle corrosive effect: an entire profession being forced to face up to the notion that much of what it considered skilled craftsmanship was in fact expensive pattern-matching.

Junior lawyers see this and internalize a new rule: the real power now belongs to those who control the algorithm, not to those who mastered the doctrine. All the expertise in the world will only compound in real time the silent crisis exploding among us slow-motion humans still expected to put our names, and consciences, to what comes out next. This is a book that for the first time doggedly dedicates itself to illuminating this crisis with as much so rigor, as much empathy and no inclination to look away, which is why in an era of AI-driven litigation support it remains not just relevant but absolutely essential.

2.1 AI tools for case analysis, predictive outcomes, and evidence synthesis

Litigation support AI tools are changing the way cases are analyzed, aiding rapid understanding and relationship mapping across vast amounts of legal information. Learning algorithms can be fed patterns from past judgments, statutes and paraphrased legal arguments to build predictive models of case success. For example, services such as Lex Machina and Blue J Legal use outcome prediction engines that determine how certain fact patterns and styles of argument influence judges' decisions. In the same way, case mapping technology, based on natural language processing (NLP), uses intelligence to identify relevant case law and then ranks it according to how closely related the two cases are contextually for more targeted legal reasoning (Bernstein et al., 2025).

One of the cruel ironies of legal A.I. is that it makes the job both easier and harder. "Easier because the grunt work is now eliminated; harder because what's left are exactly those things that require judgment, taste and emotional resilience — skills many lawyers aren't confident they have after the algorithmic crutches disappear," she writes. When 80% of document review goes away, the other 20% feels really critically important — and every call you make feels heavy. Just that the lawyer clears a little bit more time — and not a lot more cognitive bandwidth, since as soon as you save some of it in querying, you spend at least the same amount on meta-questions: Was I asking exactly right? Should I have requested more examples? Is this line of reasoning really novel, one that isn't merely a clever reworking of the training data? The cognitive load lessens; the emotional load spreads.

It is not equitably distributed, psychically. Law students joining the work force in 2025 will treat AI like prior generations treated Westlaw: as a given, trivially neutral aspect of the landscape. Many have never declassified anything by hand, and can't even picture why someone would. Mid-career associates who were mentored in the old paradigm feel like theirs was a bait-and-switch; partners whose reputations were made by pre-AI excellence often oscillate between Luddite panic and passive-aggressive sabotage ("I want to see the cases in full, not just the summary spit out by AI"). The result — which, more than anything since word processing came on the scene in the 1980s is a generational three-way fracture that is even more emotionally charged because feelings are existential now rather than merely clerical.

Among mental health professionals who treat overachievers, there is a new diagnosis in the air: It is called "AI comparison syndrome," and likely someday it will be in the DSM, which lists psychiatric disorders (though that could be because all of our jobs are eventually going to be replaced by robots). Some lawyers say that they experience physical symptoms — racing heart, nausea — when asked to file a brief without stating the level of AI help received, like academic integrity panic but in reverse. The syndrome is fueled by the fact that most firms still do not have clear policies regarding attribution, allowing individuals to police their own ethical boundaries in an environment where "everyone is doing it" is both true and impossible to prove.

3. COGNITIVE DISSONANCE AND IMPOSTER SYNDROME IN THE AI-ERA LEGAL PROFESSION

The advent of AI in legal praxis left devastating psychological effects on lawyers manifested as cognitive and imposter syndrome upon a radical tech shift. What may be at work is cognitive dissonance; on the one hand, lawyers believe that their traditional expertise based in part upon mastery of doctrine and interpretive skill as much or more than the scope of a document search, matters more to some extent compared with certain AI technologies like document review, precedent analysis and predictive modeling (Ejjami, 2024).

Senior partners used to be able to draw on authority as the firm's living library of institutional memory, but now they see associates equipped with Claude or Harvey outdo their own decades' worth of pattern recognition. The assault to the psyche the sense of having prided oneself on loftier philosophy that turns out to be bullshit, coupled with feelings of a rushed decision slammed through without near sufficient fictitious pomp and circumstance for such swift judgment is especially wounding for those whose careers are built on the mystique of judgment itself: the being able to "read" a judge, discern which way he thinks or she will jump; feel one's way through the emotional temperature in mediation; make that one argument that changes everything.

When predictive programs show that 87% of such motions, no matter how they are framed appear before Judge X as a similar motion which were denied then the romantic image of coutroom art turns out to be childish. Many resist by denying what AI generates dismissing its outputs as "missing nuance" or "not having soul," even as they quietly use those same outputs in their own work.

Midlevel associates are bearing an even more brutal iteration of the same crisis. They came into the profession at the tail end of the old paradigm, putting in 80-hour weeks to master skills that are now automated. Their psychological contract was "suffer now, achieve mastery later"; that has been retracted unilaterally. Where they hoped to emerge from the crucible of law as the kind of respected expert that writing thoughtful judicial opinions brings into being, they instead discover a world in which mastery is more and more measured by one's success at prompt-engineering rather than thinking like a lawyer. The imposter phenomenon, driven largely by a previously unheard of group of people women and minorities at elite institutions is actually democratized, because now even the most pedigreed Harvard Law Review editors feel slightly fraudulent: their best work product more likely than not was co-authored with a stochastic parrot. For many, the solution is more overwork chasing those diminishing returns of human-only value (the frilliest footnotes! Still others drop out altogether, coasting along quietly on AI-generated work while losing a sense of professional mission (Schmitz & Zeleznikow, 2021).

The most striking victims are the young lawyers who never knew practice without AI. They have no pre-automation base level of performance to measure their own competence against, so every task they perform with heavy AI support contributes to the narrative that they are not real lawyers. They see partners take credit for AI-drafted briefs, win praise for predictive insights that were in fact surfaced by Lex Machina and leave college convinced the whole profession is a performance (Zisaru et al., 2021). Their cognitive dissonance is "as radical disenchantment: they hold, at the same time that law is an intellectually demanding profession and that its central activities are now routine pattern-matching better done by machines". Many panic and engage in existential questioning of their career choices before earning enough to pay back loans, wondering if they picked a profession whose prestige was always an illusion propped up by scarcity. Even judges are not immune as life-tenured judges, the alleged summit of legal sophistication, more and more face briefs which are orders of magnitude more sophisticated than anything human advocates could generate on their own (Simshaw, 2022) Imposter syndrome fades into a quieter, stronger sort of confidence: the awareness that one is not valuable in so far as one knows more than the machine, but simply because a person is something the machine can never be responsible (Gupta, 2025).

4. DESIGNING PSYCHOLOGICALLY ADAPTIVE AI INTERFACES IN LITIGATION

An ideal for litigation is to create psychologically intelligent AI interfaces in which cognitive science adaptation is seamlessly structured into the technology that mitigates dissonance, lowers cognitive load and fosters trust, and empowers lawyer judgment under uncertain conditions: where much of what is controlling a high-stakes context remains unknown but can nevertheless be controlled. The values are dynamically changed by these parameters, which depend on users' experience and tension status, as well as task urgency and needs in this paper, human-centered design is considered in that automation is balanced with human control.

Conventional AI systems often inundate users with black-box decisions, ultimately exaggerating imposter syndrome and decision paralysis; adaptive approaches mitigate this by personalized explanation, complexity scaling and real-time feedback loops. In litigation, where success is based on precision and ethical reasoning, an interface must lead with explainability surface techniques such as interactive counterfactuals and case-based reasoning to show how predictions are unstitched from precedents, statutes, and patterns of evidence. For example, in e-discovery, adaptive systems observe cognitive load through interaction while complexifying visualization for beginners and offering multidimensional analysis for experts to avoid overload and focus tactics. This is modelled by cognitive load theory, which breaks down tasks and introduces two different types of automation: low-stakes ones such as initial document triage are supported using System 0 automation (lead-machine processing), freeing up cognitive resources for system thinking on arguments or motions (Seroja, 2022).

The key agreed design pillars include as- adaptive dissonance management, inspired by Cognitive Dissonance AI (CD-AI) frameworks that maintain 'productive' uncertainty without alienation. In the case method, interfaces resist premature resolutions, forcing lawyers to dupe scholars into reconciling rival precedents by way of guided synthesis for e.g., pitting constitutional pro/con arguments against empirical outcomes and scaling difficulty up or down according to user capacity.

There are ethical safeguards to protect fairness such as transparent algorithms which have been audited for bias in predicting judi cial trends a response to resolutions like the ABA Resolution, demanding oversight of AI vendors (Namvarpour et al., 2025) or the general product policy a tinker model proposed by Walrand and Varaiya can bend in. Multimodal interface Manifest in gestalt-effect, multimodal interfaces such as text, visuals and speech may foster usability for evidence synthesis as by 'stacking habits', they support verification rituals which act as a failsafe against the bad impact of overreliance (Jones et al., 2023).

Developing AI interfaces that are psychologically supportive, rather than bells and whistles, for litigators is less about bells and whistles, as it is mitigating the same cognitive dissonance and impostor syndrome that has become a corrosive force within the profession (Fang et al., 2025). They seek to design systems that increase, rather than decrease, the lawyer's feelings of being in control, of being competent and of really having legitimate expertise despite their performance relies on massive amounts of processing power from today's AI (Androff & Mathis, 2022). It is this that necessitates a friction controlled in places, radical transparency in others and constant vigilance to the fact that every pixel onscreen or within the chips either consoles the human professional or silently gnaws at their identity (Beg et al., 2025).

The uses willful cognitive dumping while requiring human checkpoints. Pure automation renders us helpless; pure manual work degrades us (Chu et al., 2022). Adaptive interfaces thus create "islands of control" that require the lawyer to make a choice to continue. The click is a record of audit, ethics and malpractice but it is also reparative of agency. The lawyer is never the rider; and the client is not to be treated as a beast of burden, or dumb driven cattle (Saurebrei et al., 2023).

There has to be room for sorrow in the interface. There is no getting around the very real loss that so many lawyers feel when they realize certain tasks they used to find pride in are nothing for machines. As a result, adaptive systems will feature noninvasive "legacy mode" views which display how long it would have taken the same output to be produced five or ten years ago with only Westlaw and no human associates (Balcombe, 2023). It's simultaneously wrenching and satisfying to see "This research plan would have required 185 billable hours in 2018," but it confirms the long-standing strain of what was once asked of the profession (Cheong et al., 2024). Some firms are even dabbling in private "reflection channels" where lawyers can write never shared, completely encrypted about feeling obsolete; the system will only acknowledge receipt and provide appropriate psychological help without retaining or reopening the correspondence. These minor concessions to grief make a brutal transition less so (Nadarzynski et al., 2024)

5. INTEGRATING ETHICS, EMPATHY AND EXPLAINABILITY IN LITIGATION SUPPORT TOOLS

Building truly ethical, empathetic and explainable AI into litigation support tools can no longer be an exercise in academic abstraction; it is the only path to avoiding what could be a moral hazard that slowly erodes the soul of the legal profession while also exposing lawyers, clients, and the courts to catastrophic risk (Terblanche et al., 2022). So ethics, empathy, explainability must be structural, non-negotiable, from the very architecture (working up to the level of operating system and beyond), not add-on compliance checklists or user-configurable "ethics modes" people can switch off under deadline pressure (Dahan & Liang, 2020).

Begin with ethics as obligatory memory (Egeruoh-Adindu, 2021). Every serious litigation AI would need to be accompanied by an immutable cryptographically signed audit trail of not only what the model output, but why it chose each non-deterministic decision (Brooks, 2020). If one line of cases is favored over the other, it must maintain all of the specifications for weighting – including a description of how weights are assigned, fiscal year data come from and are calibrated, with when its authority was actually down-ranked (Aleesa, 2022). It is never erasable, not even by the firm's global administrator, and automatically attached to final work product in a machine-readable format that courts or bar investigators or malpractice carriers can parse in seconds (Engstrom & Gelbach, 2021). It follows that the object is no longer a matter of private virtue, but rather a forensic quality of the artifact (Tung, 2019). Attorneys who attempt to present raw model output as their own independent work are required effectively to strip or falsify the ledger in doing so, which they must do actively itself a compelled disclosure under recently proposed Rule 3.3 and 8.4 amendments that are already circulating in several jurisdictions. The psychological impact is liberation: the tool takes on the risk of non-revelation, allowing the human lawyer to think judgment rather than cover-up (Zidaru et al., 2021).

It is this latter that should be radically human-centered, and not the machine-centric technical meaningfulness. Existing 'show your work' features that dump token probabilities or attention heatmaps are useless to 99% of practicing lawyers, and actively incentivize blind deference (Nadarzyuski et al., 2019). Rather than drawing on its own intuitive powers, the litigation tools would have to express each material inference in terms of natural-language reasoning chains that look more like what a fastidious junior associate's memo might generate the model preferred the broader reading of 'occurrence' in the insurance policy because 41 out of 47 post-2018 Delaware Chancery decisions with similar 'related acts' provisions adopted that construction (Tapalova & Zhiyenbayeva, 2022). The model down-weighted the three opposing cases as in each a criminal fraud exclusion was at issue (McStay, 2020). This is not condescension it is the least of what candor to the tribunal requires once machines are co-authors. Importantly, what is required here is for there to be a bright red banner whenever the model is extrapolating out of dense training data "less than five factually similar cases nationwide; so, the following analysis will be speculative and requiring especially careful human review." Attorneys who disregard such warnings do so at their peril, and the warning becomes part of the duty of competence (Bhargava et al., 2021).

The system denies requests altogether if the potential load is greater than some multiple of the estimated relevance; instead, it proposes narrowing options based on Rule 26(b)(1) and its most recent sanctions rulings through the utilization of guidelines in that regard. In pro bono or criminal defense modules, these defaults are reversed: rather than being finicky enough to flag large troves of materials that exhausted humans might gloss over, the system is aggressive toward likely exculpatory material, generating Brady letters when those thresholds have been hit. And these are not "fairness packs" that you can add on to the software; they are hard-coded into binary distributions so companies cannot fork unethical editions (Peters et al., 2020).

Yet the ethics, empathy and explainability integration should be self-reinforcing in a never-ending feedback loop of stakeholders. When a lawyer clicks past one of the moral-injury prompts or accepts a high-burden discovery offer, the system contributes that interaction to a pooled dataset held by the consortium but stripped of details identifying the case and client; when taken together, these data contribute to training future models that can help find even better interventions. Confronted with such reports by the thousands, bar associations and courts can see which firms are repeatedly de-activating empathy features and establish a sort of soft reputational pressure well before formal discipline. These playful reflections transform abstract duties into a lived professional subjectivity (Mingotto et al., 2021).

6. POLICY AND EDUCATIONAL INTERVENTIONS FOR SUSTAINABLE HUMAN-AI COEXISTENCE IN AI LED LITIGATION

The regulatory frameworks should aim at enhancing the coexistence of human beings with AI in AI-lawful litigation, which is bound to be characterized by principles of accountability, transparency and fairness. Public-private partnerships develop certified platforms, subsidizing small firms' access through grants, reducing disparities in a legal landscape where Big Law is already adopting AI (Glikson & Woolley, 2020).

Elite law was already suffering from imposter syndrome; AI is a gasoline shower. When a machine can draft a perfectly competent research memo in eight minutes, the human whose eight-hour work product is deemed merely adequate because it is overwhelmed by the superior work of AI —starts to sense that their skills are not much longer necessary. The issue is made worse by the black-box quality of many tools: associates are instructed to "check the work" but often they aren't computationally literate enough to tell whether AI hallucinated a case or artfully gerrymandered the holding. No longer "will a partner find out I'm not as bright as he or she thinks?" but 'will a machine show I was never as smart as I suspect? Some lawyers deal with the uncertainty by obsessively footnoting every AI-assisted output with caveats; others lurch in the opposite direction and present entire drafts of AI-generated text as their own, new moral hazard emerging. Both of which are symptoms of the same deep fear: That the profession's traditional signifiers of excellence were always modified somewhat theatrically, and now that the curtain has been lifted.

Lawyers have long drawn meaning from the sense that they practise a craft demanding uniquely human attributes: judgment, empathy, moral imagination, persuasive storytelling. AI wears away this story around the edges first — contact review, due diligence, deposition summaries — and then progresses toward what feels like the core: brief writing, oral argument preparation, settlement evaluation (Gado et al., 2022). Every incursion demands a renegotiation of the meaning of "a lawyer," as opposed to "someone who knows how to deploy legal A.I." For many, the psychological contract they signed with the profession ("I will cede my twenties for the privilege of mastery and esteem") feels unilaterally rewritten. The result is a kind of grief: denial (this will blow over), anger (why didn't they teach us this in law school?), bargaining (perhaps I will specialize in one of the few areas where AI can't field), depression (nothing I do matters anymore), and, for a tiny minority, acceptance (I am now a prompt engineer who happens to have a JD). Many are still trapped in the mire of anger and depression.

Court filing schedules don't stop for existential crises. Read More A lawyer who is having AI write a summary-judgment motion now has a different sort of performance anxiety: the understanding that, in all likelihood, the other side is doing it, too — and maybe with a superior tool or amped-up prompting strategy. Discovery fights that used to be fought based on "human error" are now increasingly fought based on whose algorithm failed to spot the smoking-gun email. Clerks describe lying awake practicing prompts the way they used to practice arguments, tortured by fear that a single badly worded instruction could cost the case.

6.1 Education Sustaining Human-AI Competitive Coexistence

Educational programs give lawyers the hybrid skills that change from view of AI-powered litigations as enemy to collaborative environment by means of modelled curriculum and ongoing education (Topol, 2019). Law schools induce AI literacy express NLP, bias mitigation, and appeal to ethics though simulations through which students evaluate computer generated motions training them to critique what they judge as one of the most important skills needed by overseers. These official CLE programs regarding new dumbness prioritize what might be called "techno-legal reasoning," with case studies of when the AI got it wrong in some high-profile picture issues, teaching verification rituals and dissonance management to minimize over-dependence.

Mentorship models introduce AI-conversant juniors to their co-pilots, AI-fluent seniors, equipping humans with judgment-habit-stacking and feedback. Micro-credentials in XAI and cognitive ergonomics combat imposter syndrome while interactive environments gamify ethical gray areas to increase empathy when advocating. Firm-wide academies use VR to simulate litigation experiences, while training on intelligent interfaces that grow to meet the user. So, three intertwined reforms are essential and nonnegotiable.

First, law schools need to let go of the fantasy that "thinking like a lawyer" can be taught without reference to an AI-driven universe. By 2027, every accredited program would require a yearlong skills-based course titled "Human Judgment in the Age of Machine Prediction," which integrates traditional legal reasoning with prompt engineering, statistical literacy, model-limitation analysis and applied ethics. Students learn to draft three ways: fully manually; AI-first with significant human editing and improvement; or human-first with A.I. polishing, then argue for their positions on all three in a simulated argument. They drill down into genuine sanctions orders based on hallucinated citations and run red-team exercises to force models to generate precedent. The bar exam itself needs to change; the MBE should cover some tasks that call for you to identify slight AI mistakes, and the MPT should show a pile of work product (some prepared by an AI, others by people) out of which test-takers must audit and certify. Mandatory CLEs should dedicate no less than one quarter required credits to technology competence and ethical oversight of non-human agents, with malpractice carriers discounting the premium for proven completion.

Second, regulators and courts should adopt safe harbors and bright-line requirements for disclosure that reward transparency rather than penalizing early adopters. It could model an "AI Candor Rule"(already on the table in various state bar task forces)under which any brief, memo or discovery response containing non-trivial machine-generated text carried a one-sentence affidavit as "Some of this filing was composed with the aid of undersigned has read and vetted every assertion and citation herein (Boukherouaa et al., 2021)." Filing the certificate achieves immunity from sanctions for good-faith hallucinations as long as the lawyer can demonstrate that reasonable verification steps were taken. "AI provenance" cover sheets on submissions, like corporate disclosure statements, to encourage transparency and mitigate the stigma that drives underground use.

Third, firms and public-interest employers should create "human-in-the-loop" structured apprenticeship programs that slow specific tasks down deliberately to ensure the transmission of skills. Junior attorneys, for instance, could be required to complete their first 500 billed hours work on core tasks (issue spotting, synthesizing authority, framing arguments) both with and without AI while mentors compare the outputs side by side and in real time (Chalmers et al., 2021)

7. CONCLUSION AND FUTURE ASPECTS

The triad appears when AI tools produce better first drafts, causing panic about skills atrophying and imposter syndrome around the question of whether we are justifying human fees in an era when clients want AI-level efficiency. When the model is down or a new legal issue not in the training distribution arises, these lawyers may feel a kind of learned helplessness: they know that answer exists but don't have internal machinery to rebuild it from first principles.

None of this is inevitable. Some firms are even testing out purposeful friction — for example, having associates do some of the work by hand before turning to AI, treating it more like a sparring partner than a ghostwriter. Can we or should we redefine professional identity in terms of humanly unique strengths: client counselling, negotiation, ethical judgment, creative advocacy for the yet uncharted areas of law? The mentally healthiest lawyers seem, according to Mr Holden-Smith's findings, to make-believe that rather than putting on a command performance every day, they are managing a stringently talented but emotionally-autistic junior associate who is capable of learning and sometimes needs overruling. They don't worship the algorithm, and they don't rage against it; they absorb it the way an earlier generation absorbed Lexis and Westlaw — without giving up faith that law is still, at root, a human drama played out in human minds. The psychological toll of AI-led litigation support isn't the loss of employment so much as it's the loss of purpose. Yet in a profession that has long drawn its esteem from the arduousness of its work, and the alleged irreplaceability of its judgment capable machines threaten an identity crisis as much as anything economic.

REFERENCES

Androff, D., & Mathis, C. (2022). Human rights–based social work practice with immigrants and asylum seekers in a legal service organization. *Journal of Human Rights and Social Work*, *7*(2), 178–188. PMID: 34722859

Balcombe, L. (2023, October). AI chatbots in digital mental health. [). MDPI.]. *Informatics (MDPI)*, *10*(4), 82.

Beg, M. J., & Verma, M., M, V. C. K., & Verma, M. K. (2025). Artificial intelligence for psychotherapy: A review of the current state and future directions. *Indian Journal of Psychological Medicine*, *47*(4), 314–325. PMID: 40831472

. Bernstein, M. H., Sheppard, B., Bruno, M. A., Lay, P. S., & Baird, G. L. (2025). Randomized Study of the Impact of AI on Perceived Legal Liability for Radiologists. *NEJM AI*, *2*(6), AIoa2400785.

Bhargava, A., Bester, M., & Bolton, L. (2021). Employees' perceptions of the implementation of robotics, artificial intelligence, and automation (RAIA) on job satisfaction, job security, and employability. *Journal of Technology in Behavioral Science*, *6*(1), 106–113.

Boukherouaa, E. B., Shabsigh, M. G., AlAjmi, K., Deodoro, J., Farias, A., Iskender, E. S., & Ravikumar, R. (2021). *Powering the digital economy: Opportunities and risks of artificial intelligence in finance*. International Monetary Fund.

. Brooks, W. (2022). Artificial bias: the ethical concerns of AI-driven dispute resolution in family matters. *J. Disp. Resol.*, 117.

. Brooks, W. (2022). Artificial bias: the ethical concerns of AI-driven dispute resolution in family matters. *J. Disp. Resol.*, 117.

Chalmers, D., MacKenzie, N. G., & Carter, S. (2021). Artificial intelligence and entrepreneurship: Implications for venture creation in the fourth industrial revolution. *Entrepreneurship Theory and Practice*, *45*(5), 1028–1053.

Cheong, I., Xia, K., Feng, K. K., Chen, Q. Z., & Zhang, A. X. (2024, June). (A) I am not a lawyer, but...: engaging legal experts towards responsible LLM policies for legal advice. In *Proceedings of the 2024 ACM Conference on Fairness, Accountability, and Transparency* (pp. 2454-2469).

Chu, C. H., Nyrup, R., Leslie, K., Shi, J., Bianchi, A., Lyn, A., & Grenier, A. (2022). Digital ageism: Challenges and opportunities in artificial intelligence for older adults. *The Gerontologist*, *62*(7), 947–955. PMID: 35048111

Dahan, S., & Liang, D. (2020). The case for AI-powered legal aid. *Queen's Law Journal*, *46*, 415.

Egeruoh-Adindu, I. E. (2021). Technology and the Law: The Impact of Artificial Intelligence (AI) on Litigation and Dispute Resolution in Africa. In *Nigerian Yearbook of International Law 2018/2019* (pp. 413–436). Springer International Publishing.

Egeruoh-Adindu, I. E. (2021). Technology and the Law: The Impact of Artificial Intelligence (AI) on Litigation and Dispute Resolution in Africa. In *Nigerian Yearbook of International Law 2018/2019* (pp. 413–436). Springer International Publishing.

Ejjami, R. (2024). AI-driven justice: Evaluating the impact of artificial intelligence on legal systems. *Int. J. Multidiscip. Res*, *6*(3), 1–29.

Engstrom, D. F., & Gelbach, J. B. (2021). Legal tech, civil procedure, and the future of adversarialism. *University of Pennsylvania Law Review*, •••, 1001–1099.

Fang, C. M., Liu, A. R., Danry, V., Lee, E., Chan, S. W., Pataranutaporn, P., . . . Agarwal, S. (2025). How AI and Human Behaviors Shape Psychosocial Effects of Extended Chatbot Use: A Longitudinal Randomized Controlled Study. *arXiv preprint arXiv:2503.17473*.

Gado, S., Kempen, R., Lingelbach, K., & Bipp, T. (2022). Artificial intelligence in psychology: How can we enable psychology students to accept and use artificial intelligence? *Psychology Learning & Teaching*, *21*(1), 37–56.

Glikson, E., & Woolley, A. W. (2020). Human trust in artificial intelligence: Review of empirical research. *The Academy of Management Annals*, *14*(2), 627–660.

Gupta, N. (2025). The Rise of AI Copilots: Redefining Human-Machine Collaboration in Knowledge Work. *International Journal of Humanities and Information Technology*, *7*(03).

Jones, C., Thornton, J., & Wyatt, J. C. (2023). Artificial intelligence and clinical decision support: Clinicians' perspectives on trust, trustworthiness, and liability. *Medical Law Review*, *31*(4), 501–520. PMID: 37218368

McStay, A. (2020). Emotional AI and EdTech: Serving the public good? *Learning, Media and Technology*, *45*(3), 270–283.

Mingotto, E., Montaguti, F., & Tamma, M. (2021). Challenges in re-designing operations and jobs to embody AI and robotics in services. Findings from a case in the hospitality industry. *Electronic Markets*, *31*(3), 493–510.

Nadarzynski, T., Knights, N., Husbands, D., Graham, C. A., Llewellyn, C. D., Buchanan, T., & Ridge, D. (2024). Achieving health equity through conversational AI: A roadmap for design and implementation of inclusive chatbots in healthcare. *PLOS Digital Health*, *3*(5), e0000492. PMID: 38696359

Namvarpour, M., Pauwels, H., & Razi, A. (2025). AI-induced sexual harassment: Investigating Contextual Characteristics and User Reactions of Sexual Harassment by a Companion Chatbot. *Proceedings of the ACM on Human-Computer Interaction*, *9*(7), 1–28.

Peters, D., Vold, K., Robinson, D., & Calvo, R. A. (2020). Responsible AI—Two frameworks for ethical design practice. *IEEE Transactions on Technology and Society*, *1*(1), 34–47.

Schmitz, A. J., & Zeleznikow, J. (2021). Intelligent legal tech to empower self-represented litigants. *Colum. Sci. & Tech. L. Rev.*, *23*, 142.

Seroja, T. D. (2022). Technological Advancement In The Society 5.0 Era For Notary In Indonesia: Glory Or Obsolete? *Legal Brief*, *11*(3), 1589–1597.

Simshaw, D. (2022). Access to AI justice: Avoiding an inequitable two-tiered system of legal services. *Yale JL & Tech.*, *24*, 150.

Tapalova, O., & Zhiyenbayeva, N. (2022). Artificial intelligence in education: AIEd for personalised learning pathways. *Electronic Journal of e-Learning*, *20*(5), 639–653.

Terblanche, N., Molyn, J., de Haan, E., & Nilsson, V. O. (2022). Comparing artificial intelligence and human coaching goal attainment efficacy. *PLoS One*, *17*(6), e0270255. PMID: 35727801

Topol, E. J. (2019). High-performance medicine: The convergence of human and artificial intelligence. *Nature Medicine*, *25*(1), 44–56. PMID: 30617339

Tung, K. (2019). AI, the internet of legal things, and lawyers. *Journal of Management Analytics*, *6*(4), 390–403.

Zhang, W., Shi, J., Wang, X., & Wynn, H. (2023). AI-powered decision-making in facilitating insurance claim dispute resolution. *Annals of Operations Research*, •••, 1–30. PMID: 37361057

Zidaru, T., Morrow, E. M., & Stockley, R. (2021). Ensuring patient and public involvement in the transition to AI-assisted mental health care: A systematic scoping review and agenda for design justice. *Health Expectations*, *24*(4), 1072–1124. PMID: 34118185

Zidaru, T., Morrow, E. M., & Stockley, R. (2021). Ensuring patient and public involvement in the transition to AI-assisted mental health care: A systematic scoping review and agenda for design justice. *Health Expectations*, *24*(4), 1072–1124. PMID: 34118185

Chapter 23

Workplace Automation Laws and the Rise of Imposter Syndrome Among Employees

Gayatri Choudhary
https://orcid.org/0009-0009-4305-7289
Apex University, Jaipur, India

Pranjal Mishra
Government Law College, Bundi, India

Sunita Meena
Government Law College, Bundi, India

Suman Surela
Government Law College, Bundi, India

ABSTRACT

Workplace automation powered by artificial intelligence, robotic process automation (RPA), and advanced machine learning has shifted from back-office trial balloons to a central operational strategy. AI systems that remove routine work from manufacturing, IT services and gig platforms by no: it technological displacement clauses. This development is in line with a broader trend towards proactive measures against such practices, involving bias audits in AI hiring tools. This historical development illustrates a tension between technological determinism and worker protections. The primary legal reforms address automation risks through mandatory reskilling, compensation amendments and algorithmic accountability as India's labor codes

DOI: 10.4018/979-8-3373-6618-0.ch023

fall short of global standards such as the ban on opaque high-risk systems in EU AI Act. The lagging regulation creates a paradox in most jurisdictions automation races ahead unconstrained by law, while employees are assured that "humans remain in the loop," fostering an ambient that fuels imposter syndrome.

1. INTRODUCTION

Labor laws to protect automatons have transformed from "protective systems for the workers in industry" operated industrial machinery, work automation tools and techniques such as AI in India with a tradition of rapidly digitalizing system and also incorporating legacy laws like the Industrial Disputes Act (1947). For originally conceived to fatally restrict retrenchment with the help of notice and compensation as per Section 25F, these laws suddenly must handle with automation at scale (Tulshyan & Burey, 2021). The risk-based categorisation of high-risk employment AI by EU's AI Act seeks to make transparent the decisions made by algorithms; India: Industrial Relations Code, 2020 proposes reskilling fund for retrenched workers- credits each such worker with 15 days wages per year of service. Lack of specific AI labor laws in India creates voids and implications for the right to life under Art 21 comes into play where job loss endangers people work and calling for the consideration of classifying layoffs by AI as retrenchment. On the international level, the WARN Act (from the US) calls for advance notice for mass layoffs, applicable to AI contexts as well; NYC's AEDT Law110 mandates bias audits of hiring tools and shapes Indian policy dialogue around ethical automation. In India, while Social Security Code 2020 offers a mere lip service to gig workers in platform workers such as Uber and Swiggy, it does not have the same kind of enforcement for AI-deactivations with no appeal including human oversight mandates (Preston, 2025).

According to various sources such as McKinsey, the World Economic Forum and OECD reports up to 45-60 per cent of existing job activities in developed economies could be automated over the next 5-10 years. Unlike the first generation of automation, it is not just the dull, dirty and dangerous jobs that are at risk: so are those requiring cognitive and creative tasks like legal discovery, medical diagnostics, financial analysis, journalism and software development even middle management. This kind of speed is unprecedented; OpenAI's GPT series, Anthropic's Claude, Google's Gemini, and xAI's own models have exploded the cost of producing professional-quality text, code, images, decision-support from thousands of dollars a task to pennies.

At the same time, collaborative robots (cobots), autonomous warehousing systems deployed by companies such as Amazon and Ocado, and self-driving delivery vehicles have made physical automation potentially cheaper and less dangerous than human labor in many controlled environments (Spitko, 2024). Governments are responding with a haphazard patchwork of laws that aim to slow, nudge or tax the transformation. The EU's AI Act (2024) considers "high-risk" workplace AI systems such as tools for recruitment, performance assessment or task assignment as mandating human supervision, transparency and non-discrimination audits. California's Automated Decision Systems Accountability Act (2023, expanded in 2025) requires impact assessments and employee notice if A.I. has a significant impact on hiring, firing or promotion. France and Spain have adopted "right to explanation" clauses for algorithmic management, while Luxembourg and Estonia play with a robot tax to finance reskilling. But enforcement is weak; most companies self-certify compliance, and penalties are rarely imposed. Federal legislation has stalled in the United States, leaving a patchwork of state laws and executive orders.

Automation markets value add to expand at a projected $29.43 billion by FY2029, spurred on by labor-cost escalation and "digital" expectations, where laws need to strike efficiencies that preserve equity while including ILO Conventions 155 and 187 for twenty-first century facility safety. Ethical considerations catalyze this transformation privacy rights that finally include AI surveillance tools, such as Amazon's Time Off Task metrics "that cause undue stress with constant monitoring". Policy makers push for an amendment to make "retrenchment" under Section 2(oo) include automation and in all fairness it should also become applicable for severance and reporting while others argue the move will stifle innovation., where India's four labor codes provide some modernization but would need AI-specific riders to achieve comprehensive production.

2. GLOBAL FRAMEWORKS LIKE EU AI ACT AND US WARN ACT

The Industrial Relations Code's reskilling fund: the IR Code's reskilling fund is meant to address displacement by paying for training of retrenched workers but that will not be enough against projected 83 million global job losses by 2027 as per WEF estimates and a call for AI-specific allocations to supplement.

Reforms "Classify AI termination as retrenchment in Section 25F of the Industrial Disputes Act with one month's notice, 15 days' wages for every year of service and compulsory Government approval before any such action is taken" to stop how firms like TCS or Wipro play clever by putting their employees on "bench" during which they don't get much work (while not firing them); making section 25F a three-liner provision so that more public sector companies fall within its ambit; ensuring retrenchment doesn't serve as a convenient means to bypass other laws something 'erstwhile employers' are said doing by resorting to this falling under IDA-legal umbrella."

This reform mitigates wage polarisation, where high-skilled workers flourish and low-skilled become redundant and gender equality is achieved by focusing on female-dominated clerical positions. Challenges of enforcement continue, and proposed creation of AI labor tribunals to resolve disputes quickly will ensure that the reforms are not only the words but also being a positive change for everyone without stifling the Indian automation market growth (Georgescu et al., 2024).

3. KEY LEGAL REFORMS FOR AUTOMATION RISKS

Legal responses to impostor syndrome brought on by automation emphasize the need of integrating mental health into AI legislation by requiring awareness training and a clear strategy for human-AI partnerships. The inclusion of psychological risk from algorithmic management has also been suggested by OSH updates, which align with ILO guidelines on digital well-being and the "right to disconnect." Employer-funded therapy and bias-free upskilling are included in the policy, which uses skill affirmation programs similar to Germany's reskilling mandate to counteract syndrome. The ramifications of the EU AI Act also include required impact assessments before deployment and discriminatory liability for psychological damage.

Tax advantages encourage businesses to choose human augmentation over replacement, but public pressure on digital rights immunizes them. In order to promote equitable use of technology, these responses present symptoms as something that may be addressed under anti-discrimination legislation.

3.1 Overwork in Performance and the "Human-in-the-Loop"

The EU, California, and other theater automation rules require "meaningful human oversight" of high-risk AI systems, but they seldom ever specify what "meaningful" really means. In response, businesses have developed complex theater: even when AI-generated material is already 98% flawless, workers must electronically approve, evaluate, and make minor edits. Being paid six figures to serve as a rubber stamp for a system that is more intelligent than you is a weird sensation that results from this. Employees report "babysitting" models for hours on end checking for hallucinations, adding "human tone," or rewording words to seem less robotic tasks that seem more like busywork meant to maintain employment than to provide real benefit (Bowen & Botha, 2023).

Humble boasts about "orchestrating AI workflows" and "prompt engineering at scale," which are new euphemisms for "doing my job," abound on LinkedIn and corporate Slack channels. Extreme performative overwork is the outcome, with 70-hour weeks devoted to proving that one is still contributing the vital 2% that is purportedly only possible by humans. Knowledge workers in highly automated companies now devote 41% of their time to "impression management" tasks, such as recording their contributions, going to alignment meetings and making slide decks that highlight their "irreplaceable judgment," up from 12% in 2019, according to a 2025 Harvard Business Review study. The irreplaceability of human judgment makes employees feel like performers in a play with a script that everyone knows is fictitious. Because employees are fully aware that they are carrying out a position that exists only to please authorities and allay investor fears about mass layoffs, this arduous farce exacerbates impostor syndrome.

3.2 The Death of Expertise and Credential Hyperinflation

A credential arms race has been sparked by automation. A decade ago, most white-collar jobs only required a bachelor's degree and a few years of experience. In order to be evaluated for jobs that AI can currently accomplish at superhuman speed, job ads nowadays often need master's degrees, several certifications such as Google Cloud Professional, AWS Solutions Architect, CFA Level II, PMP, Six Sigma Black Belt, and prompt-engineering nanodegrees and more. Resumes have devolved into performative papers that include hundreds of acronyms that the majority of hiring managers no longer comprehend, and the signal-to-noise ratio in labor markets has collapsed. Because their certification portfolio is already out of date, employees live in fear. Traditional indicators of skill, such as bar examinations, CPA exams, and medical board certificates, are now essentially passable thanks to large language models trained on the whole corpus of human knowledge.

Professionals who have spent ten years learning those areas suffer terrible psychological effects when Claude 3.5 scores in the 99.8th percentile on the SAT or Grok completes International Math Olympiad tasks in a matter of seconds. Workers start to suffer from what philosopher Byung-Chul Han refers to as "the burnout society doubled by the obsolescence society": in addition to being worn out from excessive effort, the skill that caused the weariness has been commoditized. When the outward validation system (degrees, titles, corner offices) that formerly guarded against internal doubt is automated away, imposter syndrome reaches catastrophic proportions.

3.3 Persistent Uncertainty and the Transparency Paradox

Transparency-requiring automation regulations have psychologically backfired. These days, businesses send yearly alerts to staff members about which systems are tracking productivity or influencing promotions, as well as publishing "AI impact assessments." However, the real weighting of AI against human judgment in performance appraisals is seldom ever revealed, and the records are buried in complex legalese. While coworkers with excellent AI-generated performance metrics are given raises and promotions, employees are given ambiguous assurances "Your manager makes the final decision, with AI as one data point among many." Because they are unable to see the yardstick, employees are aware that they are being evaluated against unseen machine criteria, creating a panopticon effect without resolution.

According to Microsoft's 2025 Work Trend Index, 68% of knowledge workers currently feel that their performance reviews are more impacted by how successfully they "collaborate with AI tools" than by the quality of their own output (Marder et al., 2024). However, no one can pinpoint the ideal human-AI cooperation. Chronic ambiguity taints one's perspective of oneself as a consequence. People alternate between crushing impostor anxiety ("I'm just a meat puppet the lawyers require") and grandiose fantasies. SSRI prescriptions, therapy visits, and anxiety problems have increased among the same groups most exposed to cognitive automation: college-educated professionals between the ages of 25 and 45.

3.4 The moral injury of training your replacement

There is the betrayal of forced "AI upskilling," in which employees are obliged to teach the very systems that will diminish their prospects for work. Posing as "AI-augmented superworkers," staff spend weeks labeling data, tuning prompts and generating feedback loops that immediately help improve models' performance on their own tasks. A radiologist corrects an A.I.'s misdiagnosis, a copywriter rates which versions of an ad are most compelling, a paralegal flags hallucinations in contract reviews each is an action that makes the next version of the tool more accurate and thus more likely to automate a head count.

Companies justify this with reference to EU AI Act requirements for "continuous training on real workflows," but employees experience it as a form of moral injury: being ordered to participate in their own obsolescence or they risk livelihood. This form of moral injury, previously observed primarily in military and healthcare settings, has been recognized more broadly in the psychological literature as "automation complicity stress". Workers report disassociation, rage and a distancing of emotional response, "I just click the buttons they tell me to click." Imposter syndrome grows into something even nastier: not that I'm a fraud, but rather "that I'm an eager accomplice in my own erasure."

Older workers see their lifetime of tacit knowledge suddenly devalued; younger ones are gaslit with speeches about "lifelong learning" from leaders who seem to be eagerly automating as much as they can. Midcareer professionals are walloped by imposter syndrome as they watch juniors less credentialed, less seasoned, but more AI-fluent leapfrog them on projects and promotions. The employees being left out to dry are not failing to adapt, they are adapting all too well in a game that was rigged from the get-go. The true pretenders are the stories of "augmentation," "upskilling" and "human-AI collaboration" that perpetuate a dying economic deal on life support, out there under the ghosts in the machine.

4. IMPOSTER SYNDROME IN AUTOMATED WORKPLACES

Imposter syndrome a term that psychologists Clance and Imes first used in 1978 to describe high-achieving individuals who, despite external evidence of their competence, constantly fear being exposed as frauds has become a shape-shifter in the automation age. Where past generations were afraid of being outed as short on talent, now we face being outed as economically obsolete yet somehow still hanging around. This effect can be measured to some degree in industries where AI is rapidly spreading.

A meta-analytic comparison between Dark Camp- Service industries Why not all automatons were created equal Journal of Occupational and Organizational Psychology, 98% models Cybernetics why researchers who present model Cyber System reference for this study themselves as diligent and altruistic are specials likely to model internal file their claims with a single endpoint. The logic is simple as when an employee sees a giant language model draft a contract, generate a market report or debug code in seconds tasks that used to justify six-figure salaries and decades of credentialing the natural conclusion.

The new variant of imposter syndrome has a particularly toxic twist: It is based in reality; the fear of being 'exposed' as incompetent or not smart enough is now being statistically confirmed by data about wages for millennials and technological displacement curves. Workers start suffering from what researchers at MIT's Initiative on the Digital Economy call "preemptive obsolescence trauma" a steady, low-level panic that one can never stop proving one's usefulness in an economy that demands ever more speed and efficiency (Bodislav & Georgescu, 2025).

5. TRIGGERS FROM AI OUTPERFORMING HUMAN TASKS

In automated workplaces, imposter syndrome is no longer a private whisper of self-doubt but instead a rational, collective scream. Government workers watch as colossal language models, robotic process automation systems and fully automated analytics tools perform the basic functions of their jobs but faster, more accurately and at nearly zero marginal cost and then are told in surreal fashion that they must "review and approve" what those machines produce, as if their judgment still matters.

The effect on mentality is brutal, of course: when your freshly minted $400k-a-year associate's job can be robotically executed in thirty seconds by something that the firm pays $20 a month for model access as far it's concerned it's difficult not to view continued employ as being either highly ephemeral, an act of charity or just due to plain old legal friction. Managers add insult to infection as they bless "productivity gains of 40–70%" in all-hands meetings, and insist, with the kind of dead-faced sincerity that makes you wonder if you're the delusional one, that "no one is getting replaced only augmented.

Workers are shamed into an exhausting display of irreplaceability: vampire shifts of "human insight" documentation, on-the-spot-engineering theatrics, 70-hour weeks demonstrating to all that they still contribute the mythical 2 percent nobody else can provide but is nonetheless their staple wage. Mandatory "human-in-the-loop" oversight under the EU AI Act and similar laws constitutes a daily humiliation: signing one's name to work that isn't one's own, knowing that the signature exists only to appease regulators. This is compounded by the moral injury of being asked to train one's own replacement, all in the name of "upskilling," categorizing data and correcting hallucinations so a subsequent version requires even fewer humans (Cooke et al., 2025).

5.1 Linking Automation to Rising Imposter Syndrome and Job Insecurity and Skill Obsolescence Fears

Automation is a primary driver of "imposter syndrome" due to job insecurity, fears of skill obsolescence, and AI-human performance gaps, as evidenced by 2025 polls finding over half of workers felt undervalued following the integration of AI. The higher speed and accuracy exhibited by AI in some tasks, such as coding or diagnosis, reduces confidence among workers who now attribute the output of a task to tools and not knowledge resulting in self-doubt that makes them retreat from strategic tasks.

IT industry layoffs in India at TCS and Wipro due to automation efficiencies raise concern, with jobless workers finding re-employment prospects slim if they're AI illiterate. Surveillance magnifies this; real-time metrics yield pressure cooker settings in which small latency leads to feelings of inadequacy on the model of Amazon warehouse worker complaints about making stress-induced errors. Gig platforms worsen this state by wielding algorithmic opacity in deactivating drivers in the dark, imbuing chronic imposter syndrome in being forever "unreliable" despite the messiness of being human such as traffic.

6. LEGAL AND POLICY RESPONSES TO PSYCHOLOGICAL IMPACTS

Legislation is starting to require employers to provide routine training on demystifying AI, while explaining that the technology can be registered as an enhancement tool rather than a replacement for workers. "In doing so, not only is anxiety reduced, but with this level of expertise and confidence in your abilities, you are more like to challenge -and beat - the imposter syndrome that afflicts millions of people on a daily basis. Tax credits for re-skilling are becoming a more popular tool in policy circles to incentivize employer engagement in these types of programs.

Almost no jurisdiction viewed the psychological damage caused by workplace automation as a regulatory matter in its own right. The risk of displacement was accepted, the mental health toll nodded to in passing, but the very particular harm of being paid to watch a machine do your job better than you could day after day was dismissed as an unfortunate but unstandardized side effect of progress. That began to change in 2025 when the three converging forces of skyrocketing workplace mental-health claims, a series of class-action suits framed around "algorithmic emotional distress," and politically embarrassing leaks of internal Slack messages in which executives joked about "keeping the meat peripherals busy until the lawyers let us fire them" forced a course correction. Its provisions include making employers of high-risk AI systems carry out annual "psychological impact assessments" conducted by independent occupational psychologists, not the consultancies that introduced the automation (Arora et al., 2024).

Progress has been slower and more piecemeal in the United States. California's Workplace Psychological Safety Act 2025 is the most far-reaching state-level attempt. It decouples the Fair Employment and Housing Act from employer driven technological redundancy, defining "severe and pervasive imposter syndrome or existential job insecurity based on enforced technological redundancy" as a defined mental disability that substantially limits major life activities. Now, employers with 50+ employees who have AI- automatability in roles must undertake the interactive process and provide reasonable accommodations including (1) transfer to non-AI-automated tasks, (2) lowering the level of AI-validation work to less than 30% of typical working time, or (3) paid mental-health leave up on request of upto 12 weeks. The law firms and consultants immediately challenged the law on First Amendment grounds, as they said that truthful productivity metrics are protected speech; but as of November, 2025, the California Supreme Court has declined to take any appellate challenge from parties without a record made before intermediate appellate courts.

The legal solutions are beginning to integrate anti-discrimination norms in order to protect people of weaker social statuses that are disproportionately harmed by the psychological effects of automation. And given the greater prevalence of imposter syndrome among women and minority communities, laws that focus on bias prevention are now aimed at AI systems and workplace cultures. Anti-discrimination laws are being reinterpreted to include algorithmic fairness, and unchecked bias that exacerbates mental health issues carries penalties.

Collectively, legal and policy responses to the psychological impacts of automation are unsystematic in nature, encompassing occupational health safety, transparency, training and mental health services; worker participation; and antidiscrimination. The aim is to develop a regulatory environment that nurtures the mental health of workers as an essential dimension in technological advancement, since responsible automation calls for comprehensive attention to productivity and human dignity (Crawford, 2021).

The inclusion of workplace mental health protections in AI regulation is a significant step forward for the regulation of digital labor spaces. Historic AI legislation and guidance have been mostly concerned with fairness in algorithms, data privacy, and economic effects, but newer laws are building a shared understanding that protecting workers' mental health is necessary to ensure the ethical roll out of automated tech. These protections are designed to reduce risks to mental health from AI-generated stress, surveillance, job insecurity and what Musk and others call "imposter syndrome," so that the fruits of technological progress don't compromise how workers feel.

Transparency and explainability mandates also directly further mental health protections. Informing employees about when and how AI is employed in employment decisions decreases employee uncertainty and fears of being treated unfairly, which are key drivers of psychological stress. The legislation requires not only transparency of AI use but also access to explainable decisions, as well as the ability to challenge outcomes, which increases employee empowerment and creates psychological safety. Such mechanisms also help to avoid the alienation and disorientation that underlie imposter syndrome in automated work environments.

7. WORKPLACE MENTAL HEALTH PROTECTIONS IN AI REGULATIONS

A mental health protections is that of training and workforce empowerment. Employers are increasingly required by law to ensure AI tools training is provided across all parts of their organisations in order to increase comfort with and reduce fear of and resistance against the technology. By enabling workers and agents to have the information they need, BPI initiatives close the delta between human and machine performance and this closing of the gap has a great deal to do with impostor syndrome as it relates to automation. Second, such training fosters perceptions of collaboration rather than combat with AI, encouraging employees to see automation as complementary to their skillset (Badawy & Shaban, 2025).

A key aspect of mental health protections in AI governance is the formal acknowledgement that algorithmic management can lead to profound psychosocial risks. Automatic performance-monitoring systems, predictive scheduling algorithms, and AI-based task management, for example, have been linked to increased worker anxiety and reduced feelings of autonomy that contribute to burnout and imposter syndrome. Regulations are therefore developing to specify norms that demand such risks be evaluated and mitigated before deploying AI. For example, impact assessments under laws such as the EU AI Act have to explicitly include mental health implications and so strategies are needed now to ensure that all adverse effects on workers are minimized.

Many workplaces have a statutory duty to provide human resources support in the area of mental health. Counseling, stress management and peer support programsin the workplace funded or supported by employer are often required or promoted. These services deliberately and directly tackle the particular stressors of automation transitions, such as imposter syndrome; and they work to make psychological care an integral part of occupational health structurally. Some AI guidelines embed mental health as a requirement rather explicitly, linking it to certification of AI for example in terms that evidence employer support for employee well-being.

There are also regulations which relate employment security and fairness to the body of mental well-being. Automation-caused economic displacement and algorithmic shutdowns in the gig economy, amongst other things, leads to significant psychological fallout. There are also mental health protection in AI law, such as notice periods, severance pay and appeal rights against decisions of AI that help mitigate the fear and insecurity resulting in imposter syndrome. These safeguards ensure stability and predictability, which are essential to psychological safety.

When the EU AI Act became law in August 2024, mental health appears only once in a recital of the act and even then it says that high-risk AI systems "may" have an impact on workers' psychological well-being. By mid-2025, that single recital became the legal hook for the most major expansion of worker mental-health rights in decades. A game-changer was the European Commission's Interpretive Notice 2025/847 of May 2025. It stipulated that AI systems deployed at work to accomplish tasks, evaluate performance or monitor workflow are high-risk not just for discrimination and privacy but also when there is "significant evidence" that they lead to "severe psychological strain, including chronic impostrer feelings, learned helplessness or burnout, and suicidal ideation." Deployers are now required to consider what mental-health impacts their deployment will have and how they can be minimized in their fundamental rights impact assessments, with failure punishable by fines of up to 6% of global annual turnover (Gander, 2024).

In practice this has stopped a number of planned rollouts at Siemens, Deutsche Bank and SAP until the human-centered redesigns were reviewed. Spain passed Royal Decree 729/2O25 which established a new legal right called the desconexión algorithmic algorithm disconnection. Workers can also decline to engage with AI workplace systems after hours, and all employer surveillance (keystroke logging, sentiment analysis, attention tracking) must end at the conclusion of a shift. Any breach is considered a violation of the basic right to sleep.

The United Kingdom, after Brexit, was initially reluctant to adopt EU-like regulation; however in September 2025 the HSE publish PSYRISK-AI as a binding code of practice. And a violation of the code is admissible evidence in personal-injury claims. It would compel employers to manage "exposure to one's own technological redundancy" as a foreseeable risk of psychiatric injury in the workplace no different than asbestos or repetitive strain. One of the most promising solutions, perhaps, is Luxembourg's pre-emplotive AI Well-Being Levy to be introduced in 2025. Firms using AI that eliminates or diminishes >20% of meaningful jobs are taxed 1.5% of what they save in labor costs and these funds go instead into a National Mental Health Resilience Fund that supports therapy, career transition coaching and universal basic services for displaced workers. The tax has generated €340 million ($377 million) in its first year and is being considered by France and the Netherlands.

Critics of these protections say that they slow down innovation and produce bureaucratic drag. The evidence so far is that the opposite is true: businesses forced to grapple with the psychological cost upfront are redesigning deployments in order to value actual human roles, leading not just to more sustainable productivity gains. At the Volvo Cars factory in Ghent, for example, an AI-powered system for quality inspection was redesigned so that human workers handle only the edge cases requiring empathy and contextual reasoning error rates fell 31% while taking out the soul-crushing 'babysitting' effect.

Enforcement remains the weak link. Only 9 percent of E.U. companies required to submit psychological impact assessments in 2025 had done so on time, and national authorities are short-staffed. Trade unions have begun training hundreds of "AI mental-health delegates" who perform spot audits and file collective complaints. The new global norm is plain and has a right to mental health in the workplace, which now includes not receiving money to watch a machine outperform you at your life's work (Newman et al., 2025). Whether enforcement keeps up with the letter and spirit of the law will determine whether this epochal extension of worker dignity is sustained against whatever emerges from the next wave of automation.

8. TRAINING MANDATES TO FOSTER HUMAN-AI COLLABORATION

Training requirements which encourage the collaboration between human and AI has surfaced as a foundational element of modern AI regulation, born from the understanding that employees must be armed with sufficient prior knowledge to effectively interact with (and trust) an automated system in their workplace. These requirements cover more than mere technical competency and stress a fluency in terms of AI's ethical, legal, and operational implications that will allow workers to exploit the benefits of AI rather than fear it. The new EU AI Regulation, which became law in February 2025, illustrates this trend by mandating for the first time that businesses using AI offer full role-based training to their employees (Maithili et al., 2023).

Article 4 of the EU AI Regulation Andrus Reinsalu reported as the training obligation set out by Article 4 of the EU AI Regulation is wide in scope, and covers employees who work with AI systems in an operational capacity, be it in HR, customer service, sales or any other relevant business unit. The ultimate objective is to guard against misuse - and manage risks such as algorithmic bias, errors or ethical shortcomings - through AI literacy for everyone in the organization. The regulation does not lay out specific training curricula, but it places a demand that the training content is adapted based on employees' technical knowledge, the context of AI application and riskiness profile. For example, workers engaged with "high-risk" AI systems recruitment algorithms, employee evaluation tools or performance monitoring dashboards also require a more sustained deeper level of training because of the potential for profound implications for the terms and dignity of employment that could follow.

The cutting edge of workplace regulation is no longer about slowing or paying the victims of automation it is about requiring instruction in real human–AI collaboration as a fundamental job skill, coupled to enforceable training commitments. Starting in 2025, more and more of us will be in a porridge: If workers are expected to coexist with superhuman tools, companies can't get away with just dumping the tools on the desk and calling it "augmentation." Rather, companies should methodically educate their employees to conduct, question, criticize and humanely direct AI systems in a manner that foregrounds personal agency and professional identity while also taking ethical responsibility. Not providing that training is now considered a regulatory infraction on par with neglecting to instruct someone in how to safely operate heavy machinery.

The EU took the lead in Article 29(4) of the AI Act as further specified by Commission Delegated Regulation (EU) 2025/1123: any type of employer using a high-risk workplace AI must provide at least 40 hours certified human–AI collaboration training in the first year after which there would be an obligation to have an annual minimum. The ethical override procedures and crucially psychological resilience modules that teach workers how to retain self-worth when the model proves more capable at measurable tasks. Providers are approved to offer training, and records of completion are auditable. In France and Spain, the cost is part-funded with existing professional-training levies, making no financially painful.

Workers learn to describe their unique contributions (contextual judgment, stakeholder alignment, moral imagination) with a syntax that performance-review algorithms have no choice but to treat as equivalent in weight to raw output metrics. Early results are encouraging: companies that take the full curriculum saw imposter-syndrome scores plummet 38% dealing with knowledge-related experiences and voluntary attrition slashed in half, compared with control groups who completed only technical prompt-engineering training. Both Luxembourg and British Columbia have linked training requirements to the continued licensing of the AI system itself. A company is also not allowed to renew its annual AI-deployment permit if 90% of its affected workers have expired collaboration certifications. This has spawned a thriving world of specialized training providers many as co-ops with the folks who used to work in knowledge roles and immersive simulations, where humans and multiple AI agents haggle over ambiguous real-world test scenarios (legal gray zones, medical edge cases, creative strategy). Participants are made to rehearse multiple scenarios in which the best possible outcome requires them deliberately refusing or miscreative with the AI's top choice, drilling home that human authorhood is still supreme (Park et al., 2025).

Perhaps the most radical of all is the phenomenon of "collaboration sabbaticals." Denmark's 2025 Collective Agreement for Finance and Consulting gives every worker who comes into contact with generative AI six paid days off a year just to train in advanced human–AI collaboration, off-site and free from the distractions of normal KPIs. Participants come back ready to treat AI not as an enemy or a crutch but as a sparring partner, which can do much to soften the psychic violence of imposed obsolescence.

9. PROPOSED RIGHTS TO SKILL DEVELOPMENT AND ANTI-DISCRIMINATION MEASURES

Even more forward-looking policymakers and labor coalitions have stopped treating reskilling as corporate charity, and started drafting it as an enforceable civil right. Since submitted as the main shelf bill to both the E.U. Parliament, the Califorina State Legislature, and the Canadian House of Commons, it can be boiled down into three basic rights entwined and repeating throughout –The Right To Continuous

Skills Mobility (RTCS)The Right To Skills Portability (RTSP)The right Not to be Discriminated Against For Being "Merely Human"

The Right to Lifelong Learning requires any employer that automates 20% or more of the core tasks in a job to invest in 120 hours per year of paid, on-the-job training in new, future-proof skills determined by workers not employers (Hoang et al., 2025). The curriculum cannot be proprietary ("learning the company's new AI tool") and must be accredited. Choices may include advanced data science, systems thinking, ethical AI governance, creative synthesis or nothing take class in ceramics or psychotherapy or climate modeling. Failure to provide those hours, or trying to only guide workers toward internal tools are considered unfair labor practices. In Sweden's pilot program (2025–2027), participants, who spent the hours retraining to become AI ethics auditors or human–machine team designers, had wage gains 2.8 times higher than those who were merely given their employer-sponsored prompt-engineering classes.

The right to Portability of Skills All training funded by the scheme, is available as portable digital credentials bound into a worker-controlled lifelong learning passport (analogous to the European Skills, Competences, Qualifications and Occupations framework but blockchain-verified and nonrevocable). Companies cannot tack on non-compete agreements or loan-repayment stipulations that recoup the value if the employee leaves before five years. This directly undermines the current system of reskilling's being linked to corporate retention a system that has kept millions trapped into psychologically corrosive roles.

The most incendiary plank is the Right Not to Be Discriminated Against for Being "Merely Human." Based on existing frameworks of age and disability anti-discrimination, it bans adverse employment actions (i.e. demotion, failure to promote, constructive dismissal) because a workers' performance metrics stand lower than an AI baseline while the human is working in empathetic endeavors or moral judgment calls or relationships that require long-term development or radical creativity domains not yet fully automated. Performance reviews will now have to use dual-track scoring: one axis for efficiency where AI often wins and another for uniquely human contribution where humans, by definition, cannot lose to machines.

Cumulatively, these new rights reverse the psychological script. As opposed to the current race in which workers frantically flee obsolescence, it becomes a legal burden on employers to demonstrate they are investing in human futures rather than simply postponing layoffs. Early data from the pilot regions have voluntary attrition rates dropping and internal innovation rising because workers, feeling secure enough to be honest and open, are treating AI as a junior colleague rather than an executioner (Miville et al., 2024).

Rapid technological advancement, driven by automation in the workplace and advances in artificial intelligence, has thrust the issue of fair skills development and anti-discrimination to the fore of legal and policy discussion. The proposed rights to skills are a response to the need to lay down guidelines that prevent workers being made redundant due to replacement with technology in routine tasks and 're-skilling' of what their job now would be. Together with strong anti-discrimination provisions, these rights seek to ensure that inclusion, fairness and autonomy are fostered in an increasingly automated labour market.

The entitlement to training is conceived as a formal right for employees to lifelong learning financed or initiated by employers and supported by government structures. Anti-discrimination protections work in tandem with the Right to skills development, to prevent marginalized groups such as women, minorities and people with disabilities from being left behind or disproportionately negatively impacted by systems of automation and labour market change (Rao et al., 2026). Discriminatory hiring algorithms, biased performance evaluations and opaque AI management tools have magnified workplace disparities and in many cases echoed or widened systemic social biases. Legislation is being proposed that would require mandatory algorithmic bias audits, transparency requirements, and penalties for failing to prevent unfair treatment. There are increasing efforts to extend antidiscrimination laws to make them apply clearly against decisions that involve AI, making clear the idea that the vision of protecting workers should scale up from human biases to algorithmic ones.

They are also vital, as they tackle the psychological aspects of automation by removing certain points that contribute to when or how those more vulnerable in society develop or exacerbate feelings of imposter syndrome through affirming fair treatment and equal opportunities. In the world of work, intersectional labor law frameworks would enshrine new fine-grained protections that recognize how race, gender, age and disability intersect with the effects of automation. For instance, policies could mandate that AI tools must be tested for disparate impacts before being used in hiring or promotion decisions, and require proactive outreach and training programs that enable underrepresented populations to meaningfully participate in the automated economy.

The rights to skill and anti-discrimination offer a holistic legal ecosystem designed to empower workers in the age of AI. They reinforce the idea that the benefits of automation should be broadly shared, and that human dignity and equality are still part of technological progress (Gonzalez-Morales, 2025). Hinging these rights in our labor codes, regulatory regimes, and corporate governance can help us chart a path through employment transition that allows societies to be more adept at transition complexity; more effective in shielding vulnerable workers; rewarding of resilient and fair labor markets integrating machines with humans qualitatively as comrades rather than adversaries.

10. CONCLUSION

The age of automation has not just reinvented what we do for work; it's set out to redefine why we ever thought work mattered. For the first time in history, there are tens of millions of people who are well-informed and conscientious and educated, who wake up every morning knowing that a machine can do their job better or faster and so they will have to return to work all day again tomorrow to serve their boss's interests. The resulting crisis of purpose is not individual failure, it is the inevitable depression of an economy that measures human worth in dollars saved rather than dignity retained.

Everything regulatory theater, moral injury at training one's successor, credential hyperinflation, and the daily humiliation of checking in with the overseer follows from this one unspoken pact: society will permit exponential technological replacement so long as it happens slowly enough to disguise it by a slowed rate of increase in headline unemployment numbers. That agreement is now breaking. The laws, the court decisions and the collective agreements that surging wave represented in 2025 were the first time governments had formally acknowledged that mental health, professional identity and indeed access to meaningful work were not sentimental luxuries but public goods of a foundational nature that markets would not automatically supply. What's coalescing psychological impact assessments and caps on AI-babysitting duties, a right to enforceable training, anti-bias measures in place for "merely human" competencies is the first real bid to civilize the transition instead just managing its body count.

AI and workplace automation will transform global labor markets, bringing with them both enormous potential and formidable problems. Policies and regulations are emerging to manage these shifts, balancing technology advancements with the prevention of labor exploitation, enhancing mental health, and advancing social justice. A thorough response to the economic, psychological, moral, and universal human rights consequences of automation lies at the heart of this shift. The lawmakers, technologists, businesses, and employees must continue to discuss how workplace automation laws connect with psychological reactions like impostor syndrome. Society can capitalize on AI's promise while protecting workers' rights, mental health, and humanity by implementing human-centered policies and comprehensive legal frameworks. This comprehensive approach demonstrates that automation is not just a job killer but also a chance to reimagine work for more creativity, inclusivity, and prosperity for all in the digital age.

REFERENCES

Arora, G., Yadav, T. P., Tomer, A., Tewari, P., Sharma, H., & Malik, S. (2024, November). Secure Cloud-based Process on Innovations with AI: Legal, Psychological and Managerial Implications. In *2024 International Conference on Intelligent & Innovative Practices in Engineering & Management (IIPEM)* (pp. 1-6). IEEE.

Badawy, W., & Shaban, M. (2025). The impact of imposter syndrome on ego integrity and gender dynamics among aging nurses: A mixed-methods study. *Geriatric Nursing*, *65*, 103467. PMID: 40616923

Bodislav, D. A., & Georgescu, R. I. (2025). New Organization Heights—The Impostor's Impostor Syndrome. *Encyclopedia*, *5*(1), 21.

Bowen, T., & Botha, P. A. (2023). Assessing the Influence of the Imposter Phenomenon on Critical Leadership Competencies: Conceptual Framework Proposal. *Journal of Research Initiatives*, *8*(2), 2.

. Cooke, C. D., Hastings, J. F., Hastings, C. M., & Quezada-Horne, N. M. (2025). Behind the mask of Black women social workers: Workplace integration, code-switching, and the silent struggles. *Journal of Social Work Education, 61*(sup1), S161-S176.

Crawford, J. T. (2021). Imposter syndrome for women in male dominated careers. *Hastings Women's Law Journal*, *32*, 26.

Gander, M. (2024). Antagonistic identity discourses in career transitions: An autoethnographic study in higher education. *Studies in Higher Education*, *49*(12), 2656–2667.

. Georgescu, R. I., Bodislav, D. A., Andrei, I. V., & Co ocariu, A. (2024). Workplace economics--How does the Impostor Syndrome affect organisational output?. *Theoretical & Applied Economics, 31*(4).

Gonzalez-Morales, M. G. (2025). From toxic to brave organizations: Transforming power cultures into relational cultures. *Organizational Dynamics*, •••, 101203.

Hoang, T. H., Nguyen, T. T., Bui, T., Binh, A. D. T., Truong, H. Q., & Asif, M. S. (2025). Employee ambidexterity and adaptive resources in the face of digital HRM changes: Evidence from frontline banking staff. *International Journal of Productivity and Performance Management*, *74*(11), 46–67.

Maithili, P., Pooja, M., & Pujakaleeswari, N. (2023, June). Women in science and technology: issues, problems, solutions, policies. In *2023 2nd International Conference on Advancements in Electrical, Electronics, Communication, Computing and Automation (ICAECA)* (pp. 1-4). IEEE.

Marder, B., Javornik, A., Qi, K., Oliver, S., Lavertu, L., & Cowan, K. (2024). Does LinkedIn cause imposter syndrome? An empirical examination of well-being and consumption-related effects. *Psychology and Marketing*, *41*(3), 492–511.

Miville, M. L., Vera, T., & Bensmiller, N. (2024). Education and Career Development. In *Counseling and Gender: Intersectional Approaches for Practice, Research, and Advocacy* (pp. 145–163). Springer International Publishing.

Newman, K., Snay, S., Endres, M., Parikh, M., & Begel, A. (2025, October). Disclosure of Neurodivergence in Software Workplaces: a Mixed Methods Study of Forum and Survey Perspectives. In *Proceedings of the 27th International ACM SIGACCESS Conference on Computers and Accessibility* (pp. 1-17).

Park, J., Damaske, S., Choi, J., McHale, S., Rosenberger, J., & Yin, J. (2025). Job Tenure and Gendered Perception of Workplace Challenges in Gendered Organizations: Computer Science, Engineering, and Mathematics Fields. *Socius: Sociological Research for a Dynamic World*, *11*, 23780231251376456.

Preston, E. E. (2025). *Navigating Shifts: Black Women in Higher Education and the Intersection of Imposter Syndrome, Remote Work, and Office Reintegration During the COVID-19 Pandemic* (Master's thesis, Azusa Pacific University).

Rao, D. N., & Rajeshwari, B., & RAO, S. U. M. (2026). Intersectionality and Competency Mapping: An Industrial Psychology Perspective on the Experiences of Under-represented Groups in the Indian IT Sector. *Journal of Cortex Explore*, *1*(1), 13–22.

Spitko, E. G. (2024). Workplace AI and Human Flourishing. *Connecticut Law Review*, *57*, 231.

Tulshyan, R., & Burey, J. A. (2021). End imposter syndrome in your workplace. *Harvard Business Review*, *14*, 4729.

Compilation of References

Abilash, K., Kamini, P. S. M., & Joshi, R. (2025). Navigating Post-Pandemic Mental Health Challenges: Unleashing the Potential of Artificial Intelligence. In *Healthcare Informatics Innovation Post COVID-19 Pandemic* (pp. 55–64). Auerbach Publications.

Abo Zed, N. N., & Metwally, A. H. S. (2024). Stress coping strategies and their relationship to family adjustment for mothers of hearing-impaired children. *Egyptian Journal of Social Work, 18*(18), 103–122.

Achumie, G. O., Oyegbade, I. K., Igwe, A. N., Ofodile, O. C., & Azubuike, C. (2022). *A conceptual model for reducing occupational exposure risks in high-risk manufacturing and petrochemical industries through industrial hygiene practices.* Industrial Hygiene and Safety Journal.

Advocate, T. H., & Advocate, S. A. (2025). THE ROLE OF ARTIFICIAL INTELLIGENCE IN JUDICIAL DECISION-MAKING: A COMPARATIVE LEGAL ANALYSIS. *Contemporary Journal of Social Science Review, 3*(1), 1–6.

Afroogh, J. J. S., Atkinson, K. C. A. M. D., & Dhurandhar, A. (2025). LLMs and Childhood Safety: Identifying Risks and Proposing a Protection Framework for Safe Child-LLM Interaction. *arXiv preprint arXiv:2502.11242*.

Ahmad, R., Saleem, S., & Hussain, S. (2025). Ethical and Legal Challenges of Artificial Intelligence: Implications for Human Right. *Journal of Law. Social Policy Report, 2*(01), 10–25.

Ahmed, U. (2024). Feminist Perspectives on AI: Ethical Considerations in Algorithmic Decision-Making. *Journal of Gender, Power, and Social Transformation, 1*(3), 1–10.

Ajiga, D., Okeleke, P. A., Folorunsho, S. O., & Ezeigweneme, C. (2024). Navigating ethical considerations in software development and deployment in technological giants. *International Journal of Ethics and Research Utilization, 7*(1).

Al Lawati, A., Al Rawahi, N., Waladwadi, T., Almadailwi, R., Alhabsi, A., Al Lawati, H., & Al Sinawi, H. (2025). Impostor phenomenon: A narrative review of manifestations, diagnosis, and treatment. *Middle East Current Psychiatry*, *32*(1), 18.

Alam, A. (2025). Ethical challenges and bias in ai-driven marketing: Educational imperatives and policy perspectives. In *Impacts of AI-Generated Content on Brand Reputation* (pp. 55–108). IGI Global Scientific Publishing.

AlAshry, M. S., & Al-Saqaf, W. (2024). Constraints on AI: Arab Journalists' experiences and perceptions of governmental restrictions on ChatGPT. *Journal of Information Technology & Politics*, •••, 1–21.

Aldosari, N. M., Alqahtani, A. F., Almutairi, Y. M., & Alsubaie, O. M. (2024). A Comprehensive Review of Mental Health Challenges and Interventions for Healthcare Workers. *Clinical Epidemiology & Public Health*, *2*(1), 1–13.

Al-Hadrawi, B. K., Al-hadrawi, K. K., Ezzerouali, S., Al-Hadraawy, S. K., Aldhalmi, H. K., & Muhtar, M. H. (2024). Mind Intruders: Psychological, Legal, and Social Effects of Human Parasites in the Age of Technological Progress. *Pakistan Journal of Life and Social Sciences*, *22*(2).

Ali, K. A. R., & Somu, C. S. (2025, May). Artificial Intelligence in Detecting and Mitigating Online Child Sexual Abuse: Approaches and Solutions. In *2025 2nd International Conference on Intelligent Computing and Robotics (ICICR)* (pp. 464-471). IEEE.

Alkahtani, R., Bakry, H., Al Hawi, L. M., Alshehri, J. D. A. O., & Elbeltagy, R. (2025). Quality of life of mothers of children with Down syndrome: A study comparing those with and without hearing loss. *Frontiers in Psychiatry*, *16*, 1611074. PMID: 40950766

Almohammadi, I. A., Hamad, E. O., Alqarni, B. A., Alzahrani, M. A., & Aljohani, J. A. (2025). Graduate Students' Use of Artificial Intelligence Applications in Scientific Research: Prevalence and Association with Perceived Impostor Syndrome. *International Journal for Research in Education*, *49*(2), 123–188.

Almomani, A., Alâãšqerem, A., Alauthman, M., Aldweesh, A., Aoudi, S., & Salloum, S. A. (2025). Ethical Foundations of AI-Driven Avatars in the Metaverse for Innovation and User Privacy. *IEEE Access : Practical Innovations, Open Solutions*.

Almulaifi, R., W. (2025). The hidden ethics of competence: Why impostor syndrome must be named in teacher education. *International Journal of Ethics Education*, *10*(2), 373–388.

Aloisi, A., & De Stefano, V. (2023). Between risk mitigation and labour rights enforcement: Assessing the transatlantic race to govern AI-driven decision-making through a comparative lens. *European Labour Law Journal, 14*(2), 283–307.

Alparslan, G. (2024). The adequacy of global legal norms on legal issues related to digitalization and artificial intelligence. *International Journal of Law and Politics Studies, 6*(1), 68–75.

Alruwaili, T. F., & Mgammal, M. H. (2025). The impact of artificial intelligence on accounting practices: An academic perspective. *Humanities & Social Sciences Communications, 12*(1), 1–18.

Alshdiefat, A. A. S., Lee, A., Sharif, A. A., Rana, M. Q., & Abu Ghunmi, N. A. (2024). Women in leadership of higher education: Critical barriers in Jordanian universities. *Cogent Education, 11*(1), 2357900.

Alter, A. (2017). *Irresistible: The Rise of Addictive Technology and the Business of Keeping Us Hooked.* Penguin Press.

Al-Zahrani, A. M. (2024). Unveiling the shadows: Beyond the hype of AI in education. *Heliyon, 10*(9). PMID: 38737255

Amerini, I., Barni, M., Battiato, S., Bestagini, P., Boato, G., Bruni, V., & Vitulano, D. (2025). Deepfake media forensics: Status and future challenges. *Journal of Imaging, 11*(3), 73.

Amin, M. R. M., Ismail, I., & Sivakumaran, V. M. (2025). Revolutionizing education with artificial intelligence (AI)? Challenges, and implications for open and distance learning (ODL). *Social Sciences & Humanities Open, 11*, 101308.

Amoroso, M. P. (2024). Intelligent borders: Exploring the suitability of artificial intelligence systems in refugee status determination under international law. *Refugee Survey Quarterly, 43*(4), 410–426.

Andira, D. P., & Daulay, A. A. (2025). Understanding the Impostor Phenomenon among Active Student Organization Members in Indonesian Universities. *Journal of Mathematics Instruction. Social Research and Opinion, 4*(3), 739–748.

Androff, D., & Mathis, C. (2022). Human rights–based social work practice with immigrants and asylum seekers in a legal service organization. *Journal of Human Rights and Social Work, 7*(2), 178–188. PMID: 34722859

Ang, C. S., & Lee, K. F. (2025). Ethical Considerations in AI-Powered Health Communities to Promote Good Health and Wellbeing: A Narrative Review. *Navigating Health Information in the Age of Artificial Intelligence*, 67-94.

Arbani, T. S. (2025). Ethics of Artificial Intelligence Usage in the Judiciary to Uphold Efficiency and Justice. *Journal Governance Bureaucratic Review*, *2*(1), 1–12.

Arora, G., Yadav, T. P., Tomer, A., Tewari, P., Sharma, H., & Malik, S. (2024, November). Secure Cloud-based Process on Innovations with AI: Legal, Psychological and Managerial Implications. In *2024 International Conference on Intelligent & Innovative Practices in Engineering & Management (IIPEM)* (pp. 1-6). IEEE.

Ashraf, B. (2024). AI and Human Rights: Navigating Technological Responsibility. *UCP Journal of Law & Legal Education*, *2*(2), 54–72.

Assefa, Dr. E. A. (2024). The Double-Edged Sword of Artificial Intelligence (AI) in Education: Maximising benefits while mitigating risks. *The Journal of Quality in Education*, *14*(24), 154–176. DOI: 10.37870/joqie.v14i24.450

Asta, B., Satekín, M. Ç., Uzdîl, N., & Yilmaz, S. T. (2024). The effect of having a child with hearing impairment on parents. *International Journal of Pediatric Otorhinolaryngology*, *177*, 111864. PMID: 38237356

Australian Human Rights Commission. (2008, December 1). *The Elimination of All Forms of Discrimination Against Women (CEDAW)*. https://humanrights.gov.au/our-work/sex-discrimination/publications/elimination-all-forms-discrimination-against-women-cedaw

Avery, J. J., Abril, P. S., & del Riego, A. (2024). Attributing AI Authorship: Towards a System of Icons for Legal and Ethical Disclosure. *Nw. J. Tech. & Intell. Prop.*, *22*, 1.

Ayhan, T., & Colpitts-Elliott, H. (2025). Radical care in displacement: Rohingya women's activism amidst neoliberal humanitarianism and repression. *Journal of Ethnic and Migration Studies*, *51*(9), 2415–2433.

Bachi, D. M. (2025). Impostor Syndrome and Self-Doubt Among High Achievers. *Indonesian Journal on Health Science and Medicine*, *2*(1).

Badawy, W. (2025). The ethical implications of using children's photographs in artificial intelligence: Challenges and recommendations. *AI and Ethics*, •••, 1–12.

Badawy, W., & Shaban, M. (2025). The impact of imposter syndrome on ego integrity and gender dynamics among aging nurses: A mixed-methods study. *Geriatric Nursing*, *65*, 103467.

Bailey, M., & Mobley, I. A. (2019). Work in the Intersections: A Black Feminist Disability Framework. *Gender & Society*, *33*(1), 19–40. DOI: 10.1177/0891243218801523

Bajorek, J. P. (2024). *Your AI Roadmap: Actions to Expand Your Career, Money, and Joy*. John Wiley & Sons.

Balan, A. (2024). Examining the ethical and sustainability challenges of legal education's AI revolution. *International Journal of the Legal Profession, 31*(3), 323–348.

Balcombe, L. (2023, October). AI chatbots in digital mental health. [). MDPI.]. *Informatics (MDPI), 10*(4), 82.

Banerjee, S., Agarwal, A., & Bar, A. K. (2024). Securing well-being: Exploring security protocols and mitigating risks in ai-driven mental health chatbots for employees. *American Journal of Computer Science and Technology, 7*(1), 1–8.

Barati-Ahmadabadi, H., Dalvi-Esfahani, M., & Ramayah, T. (2025). The interplay of cyberslacking, social isolation and social media addiction: A study of employees' introversion. *Asia-Pacific Journal of Business Administration*, •••, 1–31.

Barnes, T., Lee, K. J., Tavares, C., Rodríguez-Pérez, G., & Nagappan, M. (2024). Towards understanding barriers and mitigation strategies of software engineers with non-traditional educational and occupational backgrounds. *Empirical Software Engineering, 29*(4), 82.

Barqawi, L., & Al-Rashdan, S. (2025, May). The Impact of AI on Women's Roles in the Workplace: A Legal Gender Perspective. In *2025 12th International Conference on Information Technology (ICIT)* (pp. 631-634). IEEE.

Basty, R., Said, H., & Halse, S. (2025). The AI Art Paradigm: Disruptions in the Digital Art Ecosystem and Future Trends. *ACM Journal on Responsible Computing, 2*(4), 1–22.

Bavin, K. (2025). Working for nothing: the exploitation of postgraduate students. In *Embracing the Unknown* (pp. 135–144). Policy Press.

Bazargani, K., & Deemyad, T. (2024). Automation's impact on agriculture: Opportunities, challenges, and economic effects. *Robotics (Basel, Switzerland), 13*(2), 33.

Beg, M. J. K., & Verma, M. K. (2025). Revolutionizing Mental Healthcare Through Artificial Intelligence. In *Chatbots and Mental Healthcare in Psychology and Psychiatry* (pp. 21–54). IGI Global Scientific Publishing.

Beg, M. J., & Verma, M., M, V. C. K., & Verma, M. K. (2025). Artificial intelligence for psychotherapy: A review of the current state and future directions. *Indian Journal of Psychological Medicine, 47*(4), 314–325. PMID: 40831472

Bekbolatova, M., Mayer, J., Ong, C. W., & Toma, M. (2024, January). Transformative potential of AI in healthcare: Definitions, applications, and navigating the ethical landscape and public perspectives. [). MDPI.]. *Health Care, 12*(2), 125. PMID: 38255014

Belenguer, L. (2022). AI bias: Exploring discriminatory algorithmic decision-making models and applying possible machine-centric solutions adapted from the pharmaceutical industry. *AI and Ethics*, *2*(4), 771–787. DOI: 10.1007/s43681-022-00138-8

Benedict, D. S. M. (2024). 'Om Mani Padme Hum': Discovering the Spiritual and Psychological Dimensions of a Sacred Mantra from Tibetan Buddhism. *Available at SSRN* 4742637.

Bhargava, A., Bester, M., & Bolton, L. (2021). Employees' perceptions of the implementation of robotics, artificial intelligence, and automation (RAIA) on job satisfaction, job security, and employability. *Journal of Technology in Behavioral Science*, *6*(1), 106–113.

Bigler, C., & Pita, Y., & K.C., S. (2025). Are we leaving women with disabilities in the Global South behind? How the reinforcement of different forms of violence leads to unsustainable development. *Women's Studies International Forum, 109*, 103051. DOI: 10.1016/j.wsif.2024.103051

Billen, R. M., Sams, J., & Nordquist, V. M. (2023). A conceptual model of parenting children with disabilities. *Journal of Family Studies*, *29*(4), 1781–1803.

Biswas, S., Patil, B., & Bhattacharjee, S. (2023, December). An AI-Driven Multifaceted Approach to Mental Health: Leveraging Technology for Mental Well-Being. In *International Conference on Humainzing Work and Work Environement* (pp. 241-255). Singapore: Springer Nature Singapore.

Bjørn, P., Menendez-Blanco, M., & Borsotti, V. (2022). Equity & Inclusion. In *Diversity in Computer Science: Design Artefacts for Equity and Inclusion* (pp. 77–96). Springer International Publishing.

Block, N. (2024). Willful Wisdom: Harnessing insights from decision science toward wiser decision making on climate change and energy transition. *Tex. Env't LJ*, *54*, 1.

Bodislav, D. A., & Georgescu, R. I. (2025). New Organization Heights—The Impostor's Impostor Syndrome. *Encyclopedia*, *5*(1), 21.

Boine, C. (2025). *Unveiling Hidden Assumptions: How Underlying Beliefs Shape Legal Norms and Create Insufficiency in Artificial Intelligence Regulation* (Doctoral dissertation, Université d'Ottawa/University of Ottawa).

Boine, C. (2024). The AI Act Manipulation Gap. *Emory Int'l L. Rev.*, *39*, 417.

Bose, E., Kumar, C. A., & Meenakshi, N. (2025). AI-Driven Psychological Profiling on Social Media: Mechanisms, Ethical Breaches, and Regulatory Challenges in Data Inference. Recent Trends in Social Studies. 2025; 2 (1): 1–7p. *AI-Driven Psychological Profiling on Social Media Bose et al. STM Journals*, 2.

Boukherouaa, E. B., Shabsigh, M. G., AlAjmi, K., Deodoro, J., Farias, A., Iskender, E. S., & Ravikumar, R. (2021). *Powering the digital economy: Opportunities and risks of artificial intelligence in finance*. International Monetary Fund.

Bowen, T., & Botha, P. A. (2023). Assessing the Influence of the Imposter Phenomenon on Critical Leadership Competencies: Conceptual Framework Proposal. *Journal of Research Initiatives*, *8*(2), 2.

Bozkurt, A., Xiao, J., Farrow, R., Bai, J. Y., Nerantzi, C., Moore, S., & Asino, T. I. (Eds.). (2024). The manifesto for teaching and learning in a time of generative AI: A critical collective stance to better navigate the future. *Open Praxis, 16*(4), 487-513.

Brandao, P. R. (2025). The impact of artificial intelligence on modern society. *AI*, *6*(8), 190.

Brandusescu, A., & Sieber, R. E. (2025). Design versus reality: Assessing the results and compliance of algorithmic impact assessments. *Digital Society : Ethics, Socio-Legal and Governance of Digital Technology*, *4*(2), 64.

Brinkman, A. H., Rea-Sandin, G., Lund, E. M., Fitzpatrick, O. M., Gusman, M. S., & Boness, C. L., & Scholars for Elevating Equity and Diversity (SEED). (2023). Shifting the discourse on disability: Moving to an inclusive, intersectional focus. *The American Journal of Orthopsychiatry*, *93*(1), 50–62. DOI: 10.1037/ort0000653

Burrage, C. M. (2025). *A Hermeneutic Phenomenological Study of Complex Adaptive Leadership Among Black Leaders in Artificial Intelligence and Robotics* (Doctoral dissertation, The Chicago School of Professional Psychology).

Carneiro, L., & Gomes, A. (2025). Applications of Artificial Intelligence Use in Therapeutic Interventions: A Multidisciplinary Approach. In *AI in Mental Health: Innovations, Challenges, and Collaborative Pathways* (pp. 167-212). IGI Global Scientific Publishing.

Carroll, N., Holmström, J., Stahl, B. C., & Fabian, N. E. (2024). Navigating the utopia and dystopia perspectives of artificial intelligence. *Communications of the Association for Information Systems*, *55*(1), 32.

Castro, A. R., & Collins, C. S. (2021). Asian American women in STEM in the lab with "White Men Named John". *Science Education*, *105*(1), 33–61.

Cazzaniga, M., Jaumotte, M. F., Li, L., Melina, M. G., Panton, A. J., Pizzinelli, C., & Tavares, M. M. M. (2024). *Gen-AI: Artificial intelligence and the future of work.* International Monetary Fund.

Cefaliello, A., Moore, P. V., & Donoghue, R. (2023). Making algorithmic management safe and healthy for workers: Addressing psychosocial risks in new legal provisions. *European Labour Law Journal, 14*(2), 192–210.

Chakkour, S., & De Koning, A. (2023). Legal precarity, migrant mothering and the space of hesitation in Paris. *Ethnic and Racial Studies, 46*(2), 275–294.

Chalmers, D., MacKenzie, N. G., & Carter, S. (2021). Artificial intelligence and entrepreneurship: Implications for venture creation in the fourth industrial revolution. *Entrepreneurship Theory and Practice, 45*(5), 1028–1053.

Chang, X. (2023). Gender Bias in Hiring: An Analysis of the Impact of Amazon's Recruiting Algorithm. *Advances in Economics. Management and Political Sciences, 23*(1), 134–140. DOI: 10.54254/2754-1169/23/20230367

Charitonos, K., Khalil, B., Ross, T. W., Bonfini-Hotlosz, C., Aristorenas, M., & Webster, B. (2025). Crisis-prompted online language teaching: A qualitative inquiry into autonomy among teachers in refugee settings. *ReCALL, 37*(2), 250–266.

Chatterjee, D. (2025). An empire of artificial intelligence: Exploring an intersection of politics, society, and creativity. *International Journal of Politics Culture and Society, 38*(1), 81–110.

Chatterjee, S., Dindarian, A., & Rengaraju, U. (2025). Preserving Data Assessment, Privacy in Mental Healthcare: Ensuring Authenticity, Confidentiality, and Security in Data Integration from Diverse Source. In *Revolutionizing Youth Mental Health with Ethical AI: Transform Youth Mental Well-being by Exploring Responsible AI and GenAI Applications* (pp. 185–253). Apress.

Chavali, D., & Dhiman, V. K. (2024). The nexus of minds unveiling the significance of AI in mental health and viable remedie. *Open Access Research Journal of Biology and Pharmacy, 11*(1), 031-048.

Chawki, M. (2025). AI moderation and legal frameworks in child-centric social media: A case study of Roblox. *Laws, 14*(3), 29.

Chen, P. H., Lim, T. Z., Chang, S. T., & Cho, M. Y. (2021). Developing new scales for assessing parents' aural and oral rehabilitation skills to interact with children with hearing loss. *International Journal of Audiology, 60*(10), 797–807. PMID: 33401986

Chen, P. H., & Liu, T. W. (2021). Does parental education level matter? Dynamic effect of parents on family-centred early intervention for children with hearing loss. *International Journal of Disability Development and Education*, *68*(4), 457–478.

Cheong, B. C. (2024). Transparency and accountability in AI systems: Safeguarding wellbeing in the age of algorithmic decision-making. *Frontiers in Human Dynamics*, *6*, 1421273.

Cheong, I., Caliskan, A., & Kohno, T. (2025). Safeguarding human values: Rethinking US law for generative AI's societal impacts. *AI and Ethics*, *5*(2), 1433–1459.

Cheong, I., Xia, K., Feng, K. K., Chen, Q. Z., & Zhang, A. X. (2024, June). (A) I am not a lawyer, but...: engaging legal experts towards responsible LLM policies for legal advice. In *Proceedings of the 2024 ACM Conference on Fairness, Accountability, and Transparency* (pp. 2454-2469).

Ching, T. Y., Crowe, K., Martin, V., Day, J., Mahler, N., Youn, S., & Orsini, J. (2010). Language development and everyday functioning of children with hearing loss assessed at 3 years of age. *International Journal of Speech-Language Pathology*, *12*(2), 124–131. PMID: 20420353

Chua, S. M., Tan, I. Y. K., Thummachai, M. E., Chew, Q. H., & Sim, K. (2025). Impostor syndrome, associated factors and impact on well-being across medical undergraduates and postgraduate medical professionals: A scoping review. *BMJ Open*, *15*(7), e097858. DOI: 10.1136/bmjopen-2024-097858

Chu, C. H., Nyrup, R., Leslie, K., Shi, J., Bianchi, A., Lyn, A., & Grenier, A. (2022). Digital ageism: Challenges and opportunities in artificial intelligence for older adults. *The Gerontologist*, *62*(7), 947–955. PMID: 35048111

Chybis, L., Lamping, S., Dobinson, T., & Ford, K. (2025). Professional Transition in Australia: Ukrainian Migrant Teachers' Lived Experiences. *Journal of Intercultural Studies (Melbourne, Vic.)*, •••, 1–19.

Clance, P. R., & Imes, S. A. (1978). The imposter phenomenon in high-achieving women: Dynamics and therapeutic intervention. *Psychotherapy (Chicago, Ill.)*, *15*(3), 241–247. DOI: 10.1037/h0086006

Clarke, B. J., Hartley, M. T., & Button, C. (2025). Impostor phenomenon and counselor development: The critical role of self-compassion. *Journal of Counseling and Development*, *103*(2), 149–160.

Cobb, H. L., & Fox, K. S. (2025). Unmasking Imposter Syndrome Among Women in Academia: A Call for Systemic Change. In *Empowering Women in Academia: Improving Methods, Practices, and Approaches for Change and Transformation (IMPACT)* (pp. 89-122). IGI Global Scientific Publishing.

Coken, J. (2025). *Make Imposter Syndrome Your Superpower: The Ultimate Guide for Women in STEM to Lead with More Authority, Influence, and Impact*. Morgan James Publishing.

Colin, N., & Stamp, K. (2024). How Can We Address Challenges and Embrace Opportunities in Dancing for Health? In *Dancing* (pp. 97-112). Emerald Publishing Limited.

Compare, C., Lorusso, M. M., & Albanesi, C. (2024). The power of connection: Resource and responsibility in the virtual community experience of Italian trans and gender-diverse activists. *Journal of Community & Applied Social Psychology, 34*(4), e2859.

Consumer Protection Act, 2019 & CCPA Guidelines (2022). Government of India.

Continisio, G. I., D'Errico, D., Toscano, S., Maldonato, N. M., De Falco, R., Nunziata, F., & Malesci, R. (2023). Parenting stress in mothers of children with permanent hearing impairment. *Children (Basel, Switzerland), 10*(3), 517. PMID: 36980075

Convention on the Rights of Persons with Disabilities. (2006). OHCHR. https://www.ohchr.org/en/instruments-mechanisms/instruments/convention-rights-persons-disabilities

Cooper, Z. (2024). The AI Authorship Distraction: Why Copyright Should Not Be Dichotomised Based on Generative AI Use. *Available at SSRN* 4932612.

Craft, J. L. (2025). Self-Compassion and Law Student Professional Identity Formation. *The Journal of Law Teaching and Learning, 2*(1), 235.

Crawford, J. T. (2021). Imposter syndrome for women in male dominated careers. *Hastings Women's Law Journal, 32*, 26.

Cross, J. E., Pleasant, S. D., Snow, V., Cross, J. E., Gibson, B., Nixon-Jones, L., & McMurtry-Chubb, T. (2024). Panel Discussion: It's All Write: Teaching Legal Writing as Resistance. *Journal of Legal Education, 73*, 176.

Crutchley, J., Nahaboo, Z., & Rao, N. (2024). Precarious academic citizens: Early Career Teachers' experiences and implications for the academy. *Teaching in Higher Education, 29*(3), 789–809.

Cuesta, J. (2025). Gender bias in Artificial Intelligence. *Journal of Economic Policy Reform*, •••, 1–25.

Cynthia, S. T., & Roy, B. (2025, June). An Empirical Study on the Impact of Gender Diversity on Code Quality in AI Systems. In *Proceedings of the 33rd ACM International Conference on the Foundations of Software Engineering* (pp. 1540-1549).

da Silva Nunes, A. D., de Lima Silva, C. R., Balen, S. A., de Souza, D. L. B., & Barbosa, I. R. (2019). Prevalence of hearing impairment and associated factors in school-aged children and adolescents: A systematic review. *Brazilian Journal of Otorhinolaryngology*, *85*(2), 244–253. PMID: 30555026

Dahan, S., & Liang, D. (2020). The case for AI-powered legal aid. *Queen's Law Journal*, *46*, 415.

Das, A., & Santra, S. (2025). THEORIZING THE GHIBLI EFFECT: A CRITIQUE OF AI, AESTHETIC THEFT AND THE CRISIS OF AUTHORSHIP IN THE CORRIDORS OF POWER. *Journal of Dharma*, *50*(1).

Dasgupta, R., Mekala, S. H., Jaigirdar, F. T., Anwar, A., & Chang, L. Y. C. (2025). Unlocking Australia's AI usage in law enforcement from human involvement perspective: A systematic literature review. *AI & Society*, •••, 1–28.

Dastin, J. (2018). *Insight—Amazon scraps secret AI recruiting tool that showed bias against women | Reuters*. https://www.reuters.com/article/world/insight-amazon-scraps-secret-ai-recruiting-tool-that-showed-bias-against-women-idUSKCN1MK0AG/

De La Osa, D. U. S., & Remolina, N. (2024). Artificial intelligence at the bench: Legal and ethical challenges of informing—or misinforming—judicial decision-making through generative AI. *Data & Policy*, *6*, e59.

De Queiroz, H. J. D. S. (2025). Navigating Legal Barriers in Climate and Environmental Technologies. In *Navigating Law and Policy in STM Enterprises: Ethical Governance, Regulation, and Innovation Strategy* (pp. 225-260). IGI Global Scientific Publishing.

de Silva de Alwis, R. (2024). Gendering the New International Norms on Artificial Intelligence and Emerging Technologies. *U of Penn Law School, Public Law Research Paper*, (24-43).

Deckker, D., & Sumanasekara, S. (2025). Systematic Review on AI in Gender Bias Detection and Mitigation in Education and Workplaces. [IJRC]. *International Journal of Research in Computing*, *4*(II), 1–11.

Decosimo, H. (2022). A Taxonomy of Professional Identity Formation. *Louis ULJ*, *67*, 1.

Deshpande, S., & Rangaswamy, R. (2025). Minority Stress and Mental Health of Indian Non-binary Individuals. *Global Social Welfare : Research, Policy & Practice*, •••, 1–10.

Dey, D. N. C. (2024). Mental health of adolescents and youth in India: A critical analysis in the era of AI. *Available at SSRN* 5056368.

Dhar, S., & Sarkar, U. (2024). Safeguarding Data Privacy and Informed Consent: Ethical Imperatives in AI-Driven Mental Healthcare. In *Intersections of Law and Computational Intelligence in Health Governance* (pp. 197-219). IGI Global.

Dhar, S., Dasgupta, M., & Singh, B. (2025). Empowering Gender Equality and Justice Through AI: Overcoming Ethical Barriers. In *Artificial Intelligence in Peace, Justice, and Strong Institutions* (pp. 93-120). IGI Global Scientific Publishing.

Dharanidharan, D., & Kuruveettissery, S. (2025). Stress and coping among parents of children with hearing impairment: A scoping review. *British Journal of Guidance & Counselling*, •••, 1–18.

Dhinakaran, D., Raja, S. E., Jasmine, J. J., Kumar, P. V., & Ramani, R. (2025). The Future of Well-Being: AI-Powered Health Management with Privacy at its Core. *Wellness Management Powered by AI Technologies*, 363-402.

Dhrubo, A. M. (2025). Digital Dasein: A Heideggerian existential typology of digital human twins. *AI & Society*, •••, 1–15.

Diaconescu, L. V., Mihăilescu, A. I., Stoian-Bălăşoiu, I. R., Cosma, A. N., Drakou, A., & Popa-Velea, O. (2024). The predictive value of burnout and impostor syndrome on medical students' self-esteem and academic performance: A cross-sectional study. *Education Sciences*, *14*(12), 1318.

Díaz-Rodríguez, N., Del Ser, J., Coeckelbergh, M., López De Prado, M., Herrera-Viedma, E., & Herrera, F. (2023). Connecting the dots in trustworthy Artificial Intelligence: From AI principles, ethics, and key requirements to responsible AI systems and regulation. *Information Fusion*, *99*, 101896. DOI: 10.1016/j.inffus.2023.101896

Didier, N. (2024). Turning fragments into a lens: Technological change, industrial revolutions, and labor. *Technology in Society*, *77*, 102497.

Domínguez-Soto, C., Labajo, V., & Labrador-Fernández, J. (2025). Torture and blessing: The impostor phenomenon among Spanish female executives. *Equality, Diversity and Inclusion*, *44*(2), 209–227.

Doring, N., Le, T. D., Vowels, L. M., Vowels, M. J., & Marcantonio, T. L. (2024). The impact of artificial intelligence on human sexuality: A five-year literature review 2020–2024. *Current Sexual Health Reports*, *17*(1), 4.

Dries, N., Luyckx, J., & Rogiers, P. (2024). Imagining the (distant) future of work. *Academy of Management Discoveries*, *10*(3), 319–350.

Duenas, M. (2025). Imposter Syndrome's Impact on Latine College Students During Transformative Times. *Journal of Latinos and Education*, *24*(2), 349–361.

Dushi, D., Berdufi, N., & Karagianni, A. (2025). The legal framework and legal gaps for AI-generated child sexual abuse material. *Computer Law & Security Review*, *59*, 106205.

Dyer, A. M., & Starbird, L. I. (2024). Organizational Impostor Phenomenon: Theoretical Foundations and Practical Implications. *Journal of Library Administration*, *64*(8), 893–902.

Easterbrook-Smith, G. (2022). Skin in the Game: Imposter Syndrome and the Insider Sex Work Researcher. In *The Palgrave Handbook of Imposter Syndrome in Higher Education* (pp. 173–187). Springer International Publishing.

Eaton, S. E. (2025). Global trends in education: Artificial intelligence, postplagiarism, and future-focused learning for 2025 and beyond–2024–2025 Werklund Distinguished Research Lecture. *International Journal for Educational Integrity*, *21*(1), 12.

Ebadpour, Z., Nikghadam-Hojjati, S., & Barata, J. (2024, June). Human-Centric Principles for Computational Systems Supporting Collaborative Creativity. In *Doctoral Conference on Computing, Electrical and Industrial Systems* (pp. 61-81). Cham: Springer Nature Switzerland.

Ebrahimi, M., Rahimi, B., Sharifi, M., Sadat, D., Amiri, N., Khalil, S., & Quraishi, T. (2024). Empowering Women through Artificial Intelligence: Opportunities and Challenges. *Journal Electrical and Computer Experiences*, *2*(2), 38–46. DOI: 10.59535/jece.v2i2.346

Egeruoh-Adindu, I. E. (2021). Technology and the Law: The Impact of Artificial Intelligence (AI) on Litigation and Dispute Resolution in Africa. In *Nigerian Yearbook of International Law 2018/2019* (pp. 413–436). Springer International Publishing.

Ejjami, R. (2024). AI-driven justice: Evaluating the impact of artificial intelligence on legal systems. *Int. J. Multidiscip. Res*, *6*(3), 1–29.

Elete, T. Y., Odujobi, O., Nwulu, E. O., & Onyeke, F. O. (2024). Safety-first innovations: Advancing HSE standards in coating and painting operations. *Safety (Basel, Switzerland), 20*(12), 290–298.

Emas, R., Dolamore, S., Jones, P. A., Lovell, D., Whitebread, G., & Chordiya, R. (2024). Imposter phenomenon & belonging in master of public administration students in the US context. *Journal of Public Affairs Education, 30*(4), 560–587.

Emma, L. (2024). *The Ethical Implications of Artificial Intelligence: A Deep Dive into Bias, Fairness, and Transparency. Retrieved from Emma, L.(2024). The Ethical Implications of Artificial Intelligence: A Deep Dive into Bias*. Fairness, and Transparency.

Engstrom, D. F., & Gelbach, J. B. (2021). Legal tech, civil procedure, and the future of adversarialism. *University of Pennsylvania Law Review*, •••, 1001–1099.

Ergasheva, G., Khursanov, R., Bazarova, D., Altiyev, R., Tadjibaeva, A., Yusupdzhanova, G., & Madatova, Z. (2025). Integrating Digital Competencies into Legal Education: A Pedagogical Framework for the Future. *Qubahan Academic Journal, 5*(2), 446–478.

Ernst, K. P., Pagot, R., & Prá, J. R. (2024). Sustainable development goal 5: Women's political participation in South America. *World Development Sustainability, 4*, 100138. DOI: 10.1016/j.wds.2024.100138

European Union. (2022). *Digital Services Act.* [EU]. *Regulation.*

Evteeva, M., Burges, L., & Gelabert, T. S. (2024). Internalized misogyny: The patriarchy inside our heads. *Journal of Integrated Social Sciences, 14*(1), 82–108.

Eyuboglu, D., Caner Mercan, G., & Eyuboglu, M. (2021). Psychosocial difficulties and quality of life in children with hearing impairment and their association with parenting styles. *Early Child Development and Care, 191*(6), 952–962.

Ezeugwa, F. A., Olaniyi, O. O., Ugonnia, J. C., Arigbabu, A. S., & Joeaneke, P. C. (2024). Artificial Intelligence, Big Data, and Cloud Infrastructures: Policy Recommendations for Enhancing Women's Participation in the Tech-Driven Economy. *Journal of Engineering Research and Reports, 26*(6), 1–16.

Faiyazuddin, M., Rahman, S. J. Q., Anand, G., Siddiqui, R. K., Mehta, R., Khatib, M. N., & Sah, R. (2025). The impact of artificial intelligence on healthcare: A comprehensive review of advancements in diagnostics, treatment, and operational efficiency. *Health Science Reports, 8*(1), e70312. PMID: 39763580

Fang, C. M., Liu, A. R., Danry, V., Lee, E., Chan, S. W., Pataranutaporn, P., . . . Agarwal, S. (2025). How AI and Human Behaviors Shape Psychosocial Effects of Extended Chatbot Use: A Longitudinal Randomized Controlled Study. *arXiv preprint arXiv:2503.17473*.

Faraz, A., Ahsan, F., Mounsef, J., Karamitsos, I., & Kanavos, A. (2024). Enhancing child safety in online gaming: The development and application of protectbot, an ai-powered chatbot framework. *Information (Basel)*, *15*(4), 233.

Farooq, F., & Farhad, S. (2025). The unseen burden: Exploring the lived experiences of mothers caring for individuals with substance use disorder. *Addiction Research and Theory*, •••, 1–13.

Feldman, R. (2024). Artificial Intelligence and Cracks in the Foundation of Intellectual Property. *UC LJ*, *76*, 47.

Feller, G., & Burroughs, B. (2022). Branding kidfluencers: Regulating content and advertising on YouTube. *Television & New Media*, *23*(6), 575–592.

Fellinger, J., Holzinger, D., Sattel, H., Laucht, M., & Goldberg, D. (2009). Correlates of mental health disorders among children with hearing impairments. *Developmental Medicine and Child Neurology*, *51*(8), 635–641. PMID: 19627335

Ferrara, E. (2023). Fairness and Bias in Artificial Intelligence: A Brief Survey of Sources, Impacts, and Mitigation Strategies. *Sci*, *6*(1), 3. DOI: 10.3390/sci6010003

Ferri, D., Tekuchova, I., & Krolla, E. (2024). BETWEEN DISABILITY AND CULTURE: THE SEARCH FOR A LEGAL TAXONOMY OF SIGN LANGUAGES IN THE EUROPEAN UNION. *The International and Comparative Law Quarterly*, *73*(3), 669–706. DOI: 10.1017/S0020589324000253

Figueroa, C. A., Ramos, G., Psihogios, A. M., Ekuban, E., Bansie, P., de Haas, M., & Stiles-Shields, C. (2025). Advancing youth co-design of ethical guidelines for AI-powered digital mental health tools. *Nature Mental Health*, •••, 1–9.

Fine, A. (2025). *Judging AI: Exploring Professional Identity and Attitudes Toward Artificial Intelligence in the Legal System* (Doctoral dissertation, University of Nevada, Reno).

Fine, A., & Marsh, S. (2024). Judicial leadership matters (yet again): The association between judge and public trust for artificial intelligence in courts. *Discover Artificial Intelligence*, *4*(1), 44.

Fines, B. G. (2025). Picturing the Professional Identity of Law Professors. *The Journal of Law Teaching and Learning*, *2*(1), 301.

Flood, J., & Robb, L. (2025). Beyond Traditional Expertise: How AI and Blockchain Are Reshaping Legal and Accounting Professional Identity and Practice in the Fourth Industrial Revolution. *Available at SSRN.*

Flores, L. Y., & Rhames, A. (2025). Women of Color Psychologists as Leaders in Higher Education. *Women & Therapy*, *48*(1), 7–23.

Foley, A., & Melese, F. (2025). Disabling AI: Power, exclusion, and disability. *British Journal of Sociology of Education*, •••, 1–22. DOI: 10.1080/01425692.2025.2519482

Fortunato, J. R., Soares, L. R., Alves, G. S., Canedo, E. D., & Mendes, F. F. (2025, April). Enhancing Women's Experiences in Software Engineering. In *2025 IEEE/ACM 47th International Conference on Software Engineering: Software Engineering in Society (ICSE-SEIS)* (pp. 37-42). IEEE.

Foster, J. (2024). Pixelated Harm: An Analysis of the Impact of AI-Generated Images on CSAM Criminalization and Child Safety. *Okla. City UL Rev.*, *49*, 425.

Fowler, K. B., McCollister, F. P., Dahle, A. J., Boppana, S., Britt, W. J., & Pass, R. F. (1997). Progressive and fluctuating sensorineural hearing loss in children with asymptomatic congenital cytomegalovirus infection. *The Journal of Pediatrics*, *130*(4), 624–630. PMID: 9108862

Francisco, N. A. (2021). Bodies in confinement: Negotiating queer, gender non-conforming, and transwomen's gender and sexuality behind bars. *Laws*, *10*(2), 49.

Frie, E., Meier, M., & Kohl, T. (Eds.). (2019). *Dynamics of Social Change and Perceptions of Threat* (p. 156690). Mohr Siebeck., DOI: 10.1628/978-3-16-156690-5

Gado, S., Kempen, R., Lingelbach, K., & Bipp, T. (2022). Artificial intelligence in psychology: How can we enable psychology students to accept and use artificial intelligence? *Psychology Learning & Teaching*, *21*(1), 37–56.

Gaitis, K. K., Fakonti, C., Lonard, Z., Lu, M., Schidlow, J., Stevenson, J., & Fry, D. (2025). Legal challenges in tackling AI-generated CSAM across the UK, USA, Canada, Australia and New Zealand: Who is accountable according to the law? In *Searchlight 2025–Who Benefits? Shining a Light on the Business of Child Sexual Exploitation and Abuse* (pp. 50-59).

Gander, M. (2024). Antagonistic identity discourses in career transitions: An autoethnographic study in higher education. *Studies in Higher Education*, *49*(12), 2656–2667.

Garwood-Cross, L., Light, B., Cooper-Ryan, A. M., & Vasilica, C. (2024). Sex education against the algorithm: The algorithmically enforced de-platforming of YouTube sex edutainment. *Journal of Gender Studies*, •••, 1–13.

George, A. S. (2024). Automated Futures: Examining the Promise and Peril of AI on Jobs, Productivity, and Work-Life Balance. *Partners Universal Innovative Research Publication*, *2*(6), 1–17.

George, A. S. (2024). Bridging the digital divide: Understanding the human impacts of digital transformation. *Partners Universal International Innovation Journal*, *2*(3), 1–34.

Gera, A., Dhull, A., Singh, A., & Singh, K. K. (2025). Legal and regulatory issues related to AI in healthcare. In *Responsible and Explainable Artificial Intelligence in Healthcare* (pp. 259–283). Academic Press.

Gerlich, M. (2024). Brace for impact: Facing the AI revolution and geopolitical shifts in a future societal scenario for 2025–2040. *Societies (Basel, Switzerland)*, *14*(9), 180.

Ginsburg, J., Howell, M., Lincoln, E., Medepalli, V., Gentges, J., Courtney, D. M., & Milman, B. (2025). Curated Collection for Educators: Five Key Papers About Impostor Phenomenon. *Cureus*, *17*(7).

Glikson, E., & Woolley, A. W. (2020). Human trust in artificial intelligence: Review of empirical research. *The Academy of Management Annals*, *14*(2), 627–660.

Goktas, P., & Grzybowski, A. (2025). Shaping the Future of Healthcare: Ethical Clinical Challenges and Pathways to Trustworthy AI. *Journal of Clinical Medicine*, *14*(5), 1605. DOI: 10.3390/jcm14051605

Gonzalez-Morales, M. G. (2025). From toxic to brave organizations: Transforming power cultures into relational cultures. *Organizational Dynamics*, •••, 101203.

Goto, M. (2021). Collective professional role identity in the age of artificial intelligence. *Journal of Professions and Organization*, *8*(1), 86–107.

Government of India. (2021). *Information Technology (Intermediary Guidelines and Digital Media Ethics Code) Rules, 2021*. Ministry of Electronics and Information Technology.

Government of India. (2023). *Digital Personal Data Protection Act, 2023*. Ministry of Electronics and Information Technology.

Grenardo, D. (2024). What About Us? How Law Schools Can Help Historically Underrepresented Law Students Develop Their Professional Identities. *Mercer Law Review*, *75*, 24–07.

Grenardo, D. A. (2022). The phantom menace to professional identity formation and law success: Imposter syndrome. *University of Dayton Law Review. University of Dayton. Law School*, *47*(3), 2.

Grethel, M., Lewis, J., Freeman, R., & Stone, C. (2023). Discovery of unexpected paternity after direct-to-consumer DNA testing and its impact on identity. *Family Relations*, *72*(4), 2022–2038.

Groenewald, E., & Kilag, O. K. (2024). Automating finances: Balancing efficiency and job dynamics in accounting and auditing. [IMJRISE]. *International Multidisciplinary Journal of Research for Innovation, Sustainability, and Excellence*, *1*(2), 14–20.

Growiec, J., & Prettner, K. (2025). The Economics of p (doom): Scenarios of Existential Risk and Economic Growth in the Age of Transformative AI. *arXiv preprint arXiv:2503.07341*.

Guan, Y., Liao, H., Li, Z., Hu, J., Yuan, R., Li, Y., & Xu, C. (2024). World models for autonomous driving: An initial survey. *IEEE Transactions on Intelligent Vehicles*.

Guenes, P., Tomaz, R., Kalinowski, M., Baldassarre, M. T., & Storey, M. A. (2024, April). Impostor phenomenon in software engineers. In *Proceedings of the 46th International Conference on Software Engineering: Software Engineering in Society* (pp. 96-106).

Gupta, N. (2025). The Rise of AI Copilots: Redefining Human-Machine Collaboration in Knowledge Work. *International Journal of Humanities and Information Technology*, *7*(03).

Hajiheydari, N., Delgosha, M. S., & Saheb, T. (2025). AI in medical diagnosis: A contextualised study of patient motivations and concerns. *Social Science & Medicine*, *371*, 117850. DOI: 10.1016/j.socscimed.2025.117850

Halder, S., Samajdar, S., & Basak, S. (2026). Ethics in AI-Based Mental Health Care. In *Wearable AI in Psychotherapy* (pp. 213–236). IGI Global Scientific Publishing.

Hall, P. K., & Tomblin, J. B. (1978). A follow-up study of children with articulation and language disorders. *The Journal of Speech and Hearing Disorders*, *43*(2), 227–241. PMID: 661261

Haneman, V. J. (2025). The law of digital resurrection. *BCL Rev.*, *66*, 1569.

Hansen, J. M., Ferrell, O. C., Ferrell, L., Levin, M. A., Wilson, P., & Cloud, K. (2025). Pandora's Box Reopened: Can Generative AI Restore Hope or Result in a Decline in the Quest for Academic Integrity. *Journal of Macromarketing*, *45*(4), 831–862.

Harehdasht, Z. F., & Saki, R. (2025). Decoding the Gender Gap: Addressing Gender Stereotypes and Psychological Barriers to Empower Women in Technology. *arXiv preprint arXiv:2509.26332*.

Harris, F.III, Wood, J. L., King, T. M., & Essien-Wood, I. (2025). Racelighting Impact Theory. *Community College Journal of Research and Practice*, *49*(10-11), 638–652.

Harsch, K., Gilliland, B., & Gilliland, E. (2025). *Beyond Plagiarism: Transforming Pedagogy to Help Students Write with Sources*. University of Michigan Press.

Hartman, A., Hoessler, B., Tom, V., & Camman, C. (2022). Identity as a compass when navigating uncharted equitable spaces: Our queer evaluation practices. *New Directions for Evaluation*, *2022*(175), 53–73.

Hascalovitz, C., & Deonandan, R. (2025, August). Unmasking the Algorithm: Bridging Innovation and Ethics in AI-Enabled Psychological Care. In *International Conference on AI in Healthcare* (pp. 159-171). Cham: Springer Nature Switzerland.

Hazan, S. (2025, July). Promise or Peril: The dual edges of AI in cultural heritage and the Ouroboros effect. [BCS Learning & Development.]. *Proceedings of EVA London*, *2025*, 60–67.

Hernandez-Saca, D. I. (2025). Re-Framing the Master Narratives of Learning Dis/Abilities through an Emotion and Intersectional Lens. *Journal of Disability Studies in Education, 1*(aop), 1-33.

Herrick, S. S., Bennett, E. V., & Bundon, A. (2025). Feeling 'not enough'or 'too much': Exploring how LGBTQ+ adults experiencing disability navigate Canadian health contexts. *Journal of Health Psychology*, •••, 13591053251327263.

Hilliard, D. L. (2025). *Exploring the Underutilization of AI in Courtroom Decision-Making Processes* (Doctoral dissertation, Walden University).

Hindley, P. (1997). Psychiatric aspects of hearing impairments. *Journal of Child Psychology and Psychiatry, and Allied Disciplines*, *38*(1), 101–117. PMID: 9232460

Hine, E. (2024). Governing silicon valley and Shenzhen: Assessing a New Era of artificial intelligence governance in the United States and China. *Digital Society : Ethics, Socio-Legal and Governance of Digital Technology*, *3*(3), 50.

Hoang, T. H., Nguyen, T. T., Bui, T., Binh, A. D. T., Truong, H. Q., & Asif, M. S. (2025). Employee ambidexterity and adaptive resources in the face of digital HRM changes: Evidence from frontline banking staff. *International Journal of Productivity and Performance Management*, *74*(11), 46–67.

Hogan, A. J. (2019). Social and medical models of disability and mental health: Evolution and renewal. *Canadian Medical Association Journal*, *191*(1), E16–E18. DOI: 10.1503/cmaj.181008

Ho, J. Q. H., Hartanto, A., Koh, A., & Majeed, N. M. (2025). Gender biases within Artificial Intelligence and ChatGPT: Evidence, Sources of Biases and Solutions. *Computers in Human Behavior: Artificial Humans*, *4*, 100145. DOI: 10.1016/j.chbah.2025.100145

Holzer, L. (2020). What does it mean to be a woman in sports? An analysis of the jurisprudence of the court of arbitration for sport. *Human Rights Law Review*, *20*(3), 387–411.

HORNE, J. (2025). Does AI represent authentic intelligence, or an artificial identity? *Journal of Systemics, Cybernetics and Informatics*, *23*(7), 49–68.

Hornsby, B. W., Gustafson, S. J., Lancaster, H., Cho, S. J., Camarata, S., & Bess, F. H. (2017). Subjective fatigue in children with hearing loss assessed using self- and parent-proxy report. *American Journal of Audiology*, *26*(3S), 393–407. PMID: 29049623

Horton, K. B. (2024). Mentorship in the academy: Barriers and strategies for African American female faculty. *Journal of Ethnic & Cultural Diversity in Social Work*, *33*(5), 265–275.

Howcroft, D., & Taylor, P. (2023). Automation and the future of work: A social shaping of technology approach. *New Technology, Work and Employment*, *38*(2), 351–370.

Hsu, C. L., Liu, C. H., Huang, C. C., Chen, H. L., Chiu, Y. L., & Yang, C. W. (2024). The effectiveness of online educational interventions on impostor syndrome and burnout among medical trainees: A systematic review. *BMC Medical Education*, *24*(1), 1349.

Huecker, M. R., Shreffler, J., McKeny, P. T., & Davis, D. (2025). Imposter Phenomenon. In *StatPearls*. StatPearls Publishing., https://www.ncbi.nlm.nih.gov/books/NBK585058/

Husbands, D., Linceviciute, S., & Yetkili, O. (2025). The impostor phenomenon among racially minoritised university students: 'who knows how to get rid of this?'. *Race, Ethnicity and Education*, *28*(5), 670–688.

Ijaiya, H. (2024). Balancing Data Privacy and Technology Advancements: Navigating Ethical Challenges and Shaping Policy Solutions. *Journal homepage:* www. ijrpr. com *ISSN, 2582*, 7421.

Imam, M., Manimekalai, N., & Suba, S. (2025). From Data to Discrimination: Gender, Privacy, and the Politics of Digital Surveillance. *Synergy: International Journal of Multidisciplinary Studies*, *2*(2), 52–64.

Ioannou, A., & Andreva, A. (2019, August). Play and learn with an intelligent robot: enhancing the therapy of hearing-impaired children. In *IFIP Conference on Human-Computer Interaction* (pp. 436-452). Cham: Springer International Publishing.

Ishtaiwi, A., Al-Qerem, A., Aldweesh, A., & Alkasassbeh, M. (2025). A Framework for Addressing Cybersecurity Risks in the Metaverse Safeguarding Against Generative AI Threats. In *Examining Cybersecurity Risks Produced by Generative AI* (pp. 381–400). IGI Global Scientific Publishing.

Ivasiuc, A. (2020). Threatening the Social Order: The Security–Morality Nexus in the Crisis of Capitalism. *Journal of Extreme Anthropology*, *4*(1), 227–249.

Jackson, I., Jesus Saenz, M., & Ivanov, D. (2024). From natural language to simulations: Applying AI to automate simulation modelling of logistics systems. *International Journal of Production Research*, *62*(4), 1434–1457.

Jafar, A., Shabnam, S., & Khan, A. (2025). Artificial Intelligence in Mental Healthcare: Opportunities, Risks, and Regulations. In *AI in Mental Health: Innovations, Challenges, and Collaborative Pathways* (pp. 339-378). IGI Global Scientific Publishing.

Jang, S. J., Chang, S. J., & Lee, H. (2025). Intensive care nurses' impostor phenomenon: Associations with narcissistic personality, shame-proneness, and guilt-proneness. *Australian Critical Care*, *38*(2), 101110.

Jeffrey, A., Brickell, K., & McConnell, F. (2025). Geography and legal expertise: The transgressive nature of research at the boundary of geography and law-making. *Transactions of the Institute of British Geographers*, *50*(2), e12696.

Jeter, S. R. (2025). Leveraging the Outsider Within: A Composite Narrative of Black Women's Academic Success. *Journal of Women and Gender in Higher Education*, •••, 1–23.

Jha, A., & Mundhra, J. (2023). *HOW ACCOMMODATING IS REASONABLE ACCOMMODATION: ANALYSING INDIA'S RIGHTS OF PERSONS WITH DISABILITIES ACT, 2016*.

Jha, D., Durak, G., Sharma, V., Keles, E., Cicek, V., Zhang, Z., & Bagci, U. (2025). A Conceptual Framework for Applying Ethical Principles of AI to Medical Practice. *Bioengineering (Basel, Switzerland)*, *12*(2), 180. PMID: 40001699

Jiawei, Z., & Moreira, J. I. (2023). Promoting Trustworthiness in the Application of Artificial Intelligence in the Judiciary: The Intersection of Media Communication, Court Decisions, and Public Trust. *International Journal of Criminal Justice Sciences*, *18*(2), 481–496.

Johnson, C. M., & Plisco, M. (2025). Impostor phenomenon, self-compassion, and campus connectedness in Black female undergraduates. *Journal of American College Health*, *73*(3), 879–885.

Jones, C., Thornton, J., & Wyatt, J. C. (2023). Artificial intelligence and clinical decision support: Clinicians' perspectives on trust, trustworthiness, and liability. *Medical Law Review*, *31*(4), 501–520. PMID: 37218368

Jones, L. A. (2025). Guarding the Gates: Exploring a Theological–Philosophical Framework for Cybersecurity and Spiritual Discernment in the Digital Age. *Businesses*, *5*(4), 60.

Jones, M. O. (2025). Lessons from the Digital Coalface in the Post-Truth Age: Researching the Middle East Amid Authenticity Vacuums, Transnational Repression & Disinformation. *Daedalus*, *154*(2), 132–156.

Joseph, A., Sánchez Abril, P., & Del Riego, A. (2024). Attributing AI Authorship: Towards a System of Icons for Legal and Ethical Disclosure. *Available at SSRN* 5152508.

K.S. Puttaswamy v. Union of India, (2017) 10 SCC 1.

Kapartziani, C. (2025). Towards a Sustainable Digital Future: Exploring AI, Legal Frameworks, and Environmental Transformations in the Post-COVID Era? *ESI* Preprints *(European Scientific Journal, ESJ)*, *21*(8), 1-1.

Karagianni, A. (2025, January). Gender in a stereo-(gender) typical EU AI law: A feminist reading of the AI act. In *Cambridge Forum on AI: Law and Governance* (Vol. 1, p. e25). Cambridge University Press.

Karamchand, G. (2025). Detecting the Abuse of Generative AI in Cybersecurity Contexts: Challenges, Frameworks, and Solutions. *Journal of Data Analysis and Critical Management*, *1*(03), 1–12.

Kashyap, A. K., & Mitra, Y. D. (2025). World's First Artificial Intelligence Law: A Human-Centric Model for Strengthening AI Governance. In *Revolution with Generative AI: Trends and Techniques* (pp. 135–169). Springer Nature Switzerland.

Kawakami, R., & Venkatagiri, S. (2024, June). The impact of generative ai on artists. In *Proceedings of the 16th Conference on Creativity & Cognition* (pp. 79-82).

Kazi, J. (2025). Children and Deepfakes: Protecting Minors from Digital Manipulation and Exploitation. *Available at SSRN* 5389057.

Keles, S. (2025). Navigating in the moral landscape: Analysing bias and discrimination in AI through philosophical inquiry. *AI and Ethics*, *5*(1), 555–565.

Khalil, A. I., Alharbi, R., Al Qtame, H., Al Bena, R., & Khan, M. A. (2024). Investigating the association between resilience and impostor syndrome in undergraduate nursing and medical students: A cross-sectional study. *Journal of Medicine and Life*, *17*(9), 868.

Khawaja, Z., & Belisle-Pipon, J. C. (2023). Your robot therapist is not your therapist: Understanding the role of AI-powered mental health chatbots. *Frontiers in Digital Health*, *5*, 1278186.

Khor, E. T., & K, M. (2023). A Systematic Review of the Role of Learning Analytics in Supporting Personalized Learning. *Education Sciences*, *14*(1), 51. DOI: 10.3390/educsci14010051

Kieslich, K., Diakopoulos, N., & Helberger, N. (2024). Anticipating impacts: Using large-scale scenario-writing to explore diverse implications of generative AI in the news environment. *AI and Ethics*, •••, 1–23.

Kim, S., & Yim, D. (2021). The effects of parent training on narrative interaction for parents with hearing loss who have children with normal hearing: A case study using AI speakers. *Journal of Speech-Language & Hearing Disorders*, *30*(1), 89–101.

King, S. L. (2025). *An Exploratory Analysis of Automated Deception Detection for Mental Health Applications* (Doctoral dissertation, University of South Florida).

Kneese, T., Vecchione, B., & Marwick, A. (2025). A chatbot for the soul: Mental health care, privacy, and intimacy in AI-based conversational agents. *Communication and Change*, *1*(1), 15.

Kokolaki, E., & Fragopoulou, P. (2025). Unveiling AI's Threats to Child Protection: Regulatory efforts to Criminalize AI-Generated CSAM and Emerging Children's Rights Violations. *arXiv preprint arXiv:2503.00433*.

Kooli, C., & Chakraoui, R. (2025). AI-driven assistive technologies in inclusive education: Benefits, challenges, and policy recommendations. *Sustainable Futures : An Applied Journal of Technology, Environment and Society, 10*, 101042. DOI: 10.1016/j.sftr.2025.101042

Krishnan, D. R., & Manickam, D. S. (2024). Enhancing Accessibility: Exploring the Impact of AI in Assistive Technologies for Disabled Persons. *Nafath, 9*(25). Advance online publication. DOI: 10.54455/MCN2505

Kronblad, C., & Jensen, S. H. (2023). 'Being a professional is not the same as acting professionally'—How digital technologies have empowered the creation and enactment of a new professional identity in law. *Journal of Professions and Organization, 10*(2), 99–119.

Kumar Sharma, M., & Yadav, D. A. (2024). From Automation to Augmentation: Redefining Management in the Era of Artificial Intelligence. *Available at SSRN* 5075423.

Kumar, S., & Saxena, G. (2022). Child online pornography: Criminal methods and investigation. In *Research Anthology on Child and Domestic Abuse and Its Prevention* (pp. 639–660). IGI Global Scientific Publishing.

Kushwaha, A. (2024). AI and non-verbal communication: Enhancing understanding of emotional cues for hearing impairment children. *As the editors of Transforming Learning. Power and Education*, •••, 13.

Kuzmanov, I. (2025). The mind hunt: Criminal profiling before artificial intelligence. *Journal of Novel Research and Innovative Development, 3*(1), a71–a87.

Lane, A. M., & Mountford-Brown, V. G. (2025). Situating imposter syndrome in the experience of becoming and being an entrepreneurship educator. *Education + Training, 67*(4), 507–523.

Latorre Ruiz, E., & Pérez Sedeno, E. (2023). Gender bias in artificial intelligence. In *Gender in AI and Robotics: The Gender Challenges from an Interdisciplinary Perspective* (pp. 61–75). Springer International Publishing.

Lazarus, A. (2025). *Narrative Rx: A Quick Guide to Narrative Medicine for Students, Residents, and Attendings*. https://escholarship.org/uc/item/8z48215f

Lee, C. L., Yam, S., Susilawati, C., & Blake, A. (2024). The future property workforce: Challenges and opportunities for property professionals in the changing landscape. *Buildings (Basel, Switzerland)*, *14*(1), 224.

Lee, P. Y. K., Ma, N. F., Kim, I. J., & Yoon, D. (2023). Speculating on risks of AI clones to selfhood and relationships: Doppelganger-phobia, identity fragmentation, and living memories. *Proceedings of the ACM on Human-computer Interaction*, *7*(CSCW1), 1-28.

Lee, Z. (2024). Unveiling the Underbelly of Artificial Intelligence: The Inadequacies of the Legal System with Regard to Victims of Nonconsensual Sexual Deepfakes. *JL & Pol'y*, *33*, 182.

Lehman, K. J., Karpicz, J. R., Nakajima, T. M., Sax, L. J., & Rozhenkova, V. (2024). "None of This Happens in a Vacuum": The Impact of External Dynamics on Department Chairs' Efforts to Broaden Participation in Undergraduate Computing. *Computer Science Education*, *34*(1), 137–159.

Lei, Y. W., & Kim, R. (2024). Automation and augmentation: Artificial intelligence, robots, and work. *Annual Review of Sociology*, •••, 50.

Levesque, J. (2025). The AI-Enhanced Trafficking Threat: Examining the Technological Evolution of Trafficking in Persons Operations with AI Tools. *Journal of Human Trafficking*, •••, 1–21.

Levinger, M., & Alhuzail, N. A. (2018). Bedouin hearing parents of children with hearing loss: Stress, coping, and quality of life. *American Annals of the Deaf*, *163*(3), 328–355. PMID: 30100590

Lewis, M. (2025, June). Art, Identity, and AI: Navigating Authenticity in Creative Practice. In *Proceedings of the 2025 Conference on Creativity and Cognition* (pp. 916-930).

Li, Z. S., Arony, N. N., Awon, A. M., Damian, D., & Xu, B. (2024). AI tool use and adoption in software development by individuals and organizations: a grounded theory study. *arXiv preprint arXiv:2406.17325*.

Liang, Y., Zhang, J., Chen, J., Wu, J., Shen, H., & Liang, W. (2025). Generative large language models and academic integrity: Ethical risks, detection challenges, and Governance in the age of AI. *Ethics & Behavior*, •••, 1–19.

Liberman, A. (2025). Annotated Bibliography: Higher Education in Hostile Contexts. *American Association of Philosophy Teachers Studies in Pedagogy*, *10*, 258–316.

Little, C. (2025). Think, Reflect, Refine: Shaping the Modern Lawyer. *University of the District of Columbia Law Review*, *28*(1), 9.

Livingstone, S., & Stoilova, M. (2021). The datafication of childhood: Privacy risks, regulation and children's rights. *New Media & Society*, *23*(8), 2434–2451.

Li, W., Song, R., Zhang, B., & Yu, K. (2025). AI Creativity and Legal Protection for AI-Generated Works in Posthuman Societal Scenarios. *Sustainable Futures : An Applied Journal of Technology, Environment and Society*, •••, 100749.

Li, Y., Wang, H., Hossain, E., Mann, M., Yu, J., Newman, K. S., & Bai, Z. (2025). Leveraging Usefulness and Autonomy: Designing AI-Mediated ASL Communication Between Hearing Parents and Deaf Children. In *Proceedings of the 24th Interaction Design and Children* (pp. 512-526).

Loh, D. S., Packer, R. L., & Scarinci, N. A. (2025). Navigating childhood hearing loss: The experiences of parents, grandparents and siblings. *Disability and Rehabilitation*, *47*(11), 2846–2857. PMID: 39316779

Lopez Belloso, M. (2022). Women's Rights Under AI Regulation: Fighting AI gender bias through a feminist and intersectional approach. In *Law and Artificial Intelligence: Regulating AI and Applying AI in Legal Practice* (pp. 87–107). TMC Asser Press.

Luria, E., Cohen, R., & Ben-David, S. (2022). Digital reward systems and child attention development: A review of cognitive risks. *Journal of Child Psychology and Technology*, *14*(2), 115–132.

Luxton, D. (2025). AI-Powered Virtual Therapy: Toward a Responsible and Client-Centered Future. *Journal of Health Service Psychology*, •••, 1–9.

Maithili, P., Pooja, M., & Pujakaleeswari, N. (2023, June). Women in science and technology: issues, problems, solutions, policies. In *2023 2nd International Conference on Advancements in Electrical, Electronics, Communication, Computing and Automation (ICAECA)* (pp. 1-4). IEEE.

Maji, S., Shivhare, V., & Kumar, Y. (2025). Imposter Phenomenon, Social Comparison Orientation, and Mental Health: A Study of High-Achieving Indian College Students. *Roeper Review*, *47*(1), 47–59.

Malalla, B., & Al Mubarak, M. (2025). Ethical challenges in artificial intelligence technology: Business applications. In *Sustainable Digital Technology and Ethics in an Ever-Changing Environment* (Vol. 1, pp. 27–46). Springer Nature Switzerland.

Malja, S. N., & Afrasiabi, H. (2025). Artificial intelligence and society: Mapping the research through a systematic review. *AI & Society*, •••, 1–37.

Mandal, S., & Hawamdeh, M. M. K. (2025). Digital Well-Being and AI: Navigating the Intersection Between Technology and Mental Health. In *Digital Citizenship and the Future of AI Engagement, Ethics, and Privacy* (pp. 111-132). IGI Global Scientific Publishing.

Mansoor, M. A., & Ansari, K. (2024). Early detection of mental health crises through AI-powered social media analysis: A prospective observational study. medRxiv, 2024-08.

Mansoor, M. A., & Ansari, K. H. (2024). Early detection of mental health crises through artificial-intelligence-powered social media analysis: A prospective observational study. *Journal of Personalized Medicine*, *14*(9), 958.

Marder, B., Javornik, A., Qi, K., Oliver, S., Lavertu, L., & Cowan, K. (2024). Does LinkedIn cause imposter syndrome? An empirical examination of well-being and consumption-related effects. *Psychology and Marketing*, *41*(3), 492–511.

Margetis, G., Ntoa, S., Antona, M., & Stephanidis, C. (2021). Human-centered design of artificial intelligence. *Handbook of human factors and ergonomics*, 1085-1106.

Maroju, P. K., & Bhattacharya, P. (2025). Understanding emotional intelligence: The heart of human-centered technology. In *Humanizing Technology With Emotional Intelligence* (pp. 1–18). IGI Global Scientific Publishing.

Martinho, A. (2025). Surveying Judges about artificial intelligence: Profession, judicial adjudication, and legal principles. *AI & Society*, *40*(2), 569–584.

Martini, B., Bellisario, D., & Coletti, P. (2024). Human-centered and sustainable artificial intelligence in industry 5.0: Challenges and perspectives. *Sustainability*, *16*(13), 5448.

Martins, B. O. (2023). Security knowledges: Circulation, control, and responsible research and innovation in EU border management. *Science as Culture*, *32*(3), 435–459.

Mason, A., & Minerva, F. (2022). Should the Equality Act 2010 Be Extended to Prohibit Appearance Discrimination? *Political Studies*, *70*(2), 425–442. DOI: 10.1177/0032321720966480

Mathos, K. K., & Broussard, E. R. (2005). Outlining the concerns of children who have hearing loss and their families. *Journal of the American Academy of Child and Adolescent Psychiatry*, *44*(1), 96–100. PMID: 15608549

Matthijs, L., Loots, G., Mouvet, K., Van Herreweghe, M., Hardonk, S., Van Hove, G., & Leigh, G. (2012). First information parents receive after UNHS detection of their baby's hearing loss. *Journal of Deaf Studies and Deaf Education, 17*(4), 387–401. PMID: 22960753

Mayuranathan, M., Nahar, G., Vijayakumar, A., Mamodiya, U., & Babu, D. M. (2024). Sustainable Business Models for Smart City Using Artificial Intelligence Techniques. In *Navigating the Circular Age of a Sustainable Digital Revolution* (pp. 263–294). IGI Global.

McAlinden, A. M. (2022). Reconceptualising 'risk': Towards a humanistic paradigm of sexual offending. *Social & Legal Studies, 31*(3), 389–408.

McGrath, S. A., & Dye, M. H. (2023). Selected abstracts from the 48th Annual Mid-South Sociological Association meetings in Nashville, TN, October 12–15, 2022. *Sociological Spectrum, 43*(sup1), S1-S39.

McStay, A. (2020). Emotional AI and EdTech: Serving the public good? *Learning, Media and Technology, 45*(3), 270–283.

Meharunisa, S., Almugren, H., Sarabdeen, M., Mabrouk, F., & Kijas, A. C. M. (2024). The impact of artificial intelligence on women's empowerment, and work-life balance in Saudi educational institutions. *Frontiers in Psychology, 15*, 1432541. DOI: 10.3389/fpsyg.2024.1432541

Meinzen-Derr, J., Lim, L. H., Choo, D. I., Buyniski, S., & Wiley, S. (2008). Pediatric hearing impairment caregiver experience: Impact of duration of hearing loss on parental stress. *International Journal of Pediatric Otorhinolaryngology, 72*(11), 1693–1703. PMID: 18819718

Mergen, A., Çetin-Kılıç, N., & Özbilgin, M. F. (2025). Artificial intelligence and bias towards marginalised groups: Theoretical roots and challenges. In *AI and Diversity in a Datafied World of Work: Will the Future of Work be Inclusive?* (Vol. 12, pp. 17–38). Emerald Publishing Limited.

Mingotto, E., Montaguti, F., & Tamma, M. (2021). Challenges in re-designing operations and jobs to embody AI and robotics in services. Findings from a case in the hospitality industry. *Electronic Markets, 31*(3), 493–510.

Mirza, M., Esht, V., Verma, M., Bahadur, B., Jaiswal, A. K., Alagarajan, M., & Kakkar, R. (2025). Epidemiology of disability and access to disability support and rehabilitation services in India: A secondary data analysis of the National Sample Survey (2018). *BMJ Open, 15*(5), e090220. DOI: 10.1136/bmjopen-2024-090220

Mishra, R. (2024). Embracing a paradigm shift: Transitioning from traditional teaching methods to ai-based nlp education. *Research and Reviews in Literature. Social Sciences*, •••, 75.

Miville, M. L., Vera, T., & Bensmiller, N. (2024). Education and Career Development. In *Counseling and Gender: Intersectional Approaches for Practice, Research, and Advocacy* (pp. 145–163). Springer International Publishing.

Moassefi, M., Fennell, N., Yang, M., Gunter, J. B., Schmit, T. M. S., & Cook, T. S. (2025). Empowering Women in Imaging Informatics: Confronting Imposter Syndrome, Addressing Microaggressions, and Striving for Work-Life Harmony. *Journal of Imaging Informatics in Medicine*, *38*(3), 1291–1296.

Mohammed, I. A. (2024). Eliminating ghostwriters: How a federal right of publicity can save the music industry from generative artificial intelligence. *J. Intell. Prop. L.*, *31*, 212.

Molchanova, L. N., & Chekanova, A. V. (2018). Development of parental competence through psychological and pedagogical support for families in the upbringing of hearing-impaired children. *Psychology in Russia : State of the Art*, *11*(4), 223–238.

Montgomery, K. C., & Chester, J. (2019). Data protection for children and adolescents: Challenges of big data and artificial intelligence. *Pediatric Clinics of North America*, *66*(6), 1263–1275.

More, M., Shah, S., Shelke, A., & Behare, N. (2025). Ethical and Regulatory Considerations in AI Adoption Within Legal Systems. In *Exploration of AI in Contemporary Legal Systems* (pp. 163–186). IGI Global Scientific Publishing.

Moretti, V., & Pronzato, R. (2024). The emotional ambiguities of healthcare professionals' platform experiences. *Social Science & Medicine*, *357*, 117185.

Mosurinjohn, S., & Loewen-Colón, J. (2023). The Age of (the Algorithmic) Aquarius: How AI Meets Our Esoteric Needs. *American Religion*, *5*(1), 137–147.

Moustaghfir, S., & Chankob, A. (2025). Creativity in an AI-Driven World: What Do We Fear? *International Journal of Linguistics. Literature and Translation*, *8*(2), 89–100.

Muir, L. (2025). Prospecting for gold: finding your guide. In *The Guide to LGBTQ+ Research* (pp. 17–21). Emerald Publishing Limited.

Munawar, M. (2025). Ethical Considerations and Privacy in Metaverse. In *Unveiling Social Dynamics and Community Interaction in the Metaverse* (pp. 159–182). IGI Global Scientific Publishing.

Munoz, J. P., Hoyt, C., Hamed, R., Anvarizadeh, A., & Taff, S. D. (2023). Generative disruptive questions: Operationalizing diversity, equity, inclusion, justice, and accessibility in occupational therapy education. *Journal of Occupational Therapy Education*, *7*(4), 13.

Muralidhar, L. B., Sathyanarayana, N., Swapna, H. R., Hukkeri, S. V., & Sultana, P. R. (2025). Machine Learning Advancing Diversity Equity and Inclusion in Data-Driven HR Practices. In *Evolving Strategies for Organizational Management and Performance Evaluation* (pp. 423–444). IGI Global Scientific Publishing.

Mutambara, P. D. E. (2025). Deploying AI to achieve the UN SDGs. In *Deploying artificial intelligence to achieve the UN Sustainable Development Goals: Enablers, drivers and strategic framework* (pp. 117–136). Springer Nature Switzerland.

Muzingili, T. (2025). Navigating the Phenomenology of Adoption Disruption in Zimbabwe: Insights from Adoptive Parents. *Adoption Quarterly*, **•••**, 1–29.

Nabaskues Martínez de Eulate, I. (2025). On Transhumanism. A Socio-legal Approach beyond T-800 and The Replicant with Reference to Arendt and Aristotle: Über Transhumanismus. Ein rechtssoziologischer Ansatz jenseits von T-800 und The Replicant unter Bezugnahme auf Arendt und Aristoteles. *Zeitschrift für Rechtssoziologie*, *45*(1), 84–102.

Nadarzynski, T., Knights, N., Husbands, D., Graham, C. A., Llewellyn, C. D., Buchanan, T., & Ridge, D. (2024). Achieving health equity through conversational AI: A roadmap for design and implementation of inclusive chatbots in healthcare. *PLOS Digital Health*, *3*(5), e0000492. PMID: 38696359

Namaziandost, E., Heydarnejad, T., Rezai, A., & Javanmard, K. (2024). A voyage of discovering the impacts of teacher immunity and emotion regulation on professional identity, autonomy, and work motivation in Iranian EFL landscape. *BMC Psychology*, *12*(1), 43. PMID: 38254243

Namvarpour, M., Pauwels, H., & Razi, A. (2025). AI-induced sexual harassment: Investigating Contextual Characteristics and User Reactions of Sexual Harassment by a Companion Chatbot. *Proceedings of the ACM on Human-Computer Interaction*, *9*(7), 1–28.

Nascimento, P. V. M., de Siqueira, P. B. B., Chrispim, N., Chaves, R. M., Barbosa, C. E., & de Souza, J. M. (2025). The future of AI in government services and global risks: Insights from design fictions. *European Journal of Futures Research*, *13*(1), 9.

Naseviciute, L., & Juceviciene, R. (2024). Overcoming the barriers to women's career in information and communication technology business. *Equality, Diversity and Inclusion*, *43*(1), 23–40.

Nationen, V. (Ed.). (2014). *The Convention on the Rights of Persons with Disabilities: Training guide*. United Nations.

Nebeker, C., Parrish, E. M., & Graham, S. (2022). The AI-powered digital health sector: ethical and regulatory considerations when developing digital mental health tools for the older adult demographic. In *Artificial Intelligence in Brain and Mental Health: Philosophical, Ethical & Policy Issues* (pp. 159–176). Springer International Publishing.

Negi Advocate, C. (2023). In the era of artificial intelligence (AI): Analyzing the transformative role of technology in the legal arena. *Available at SSRN* 4677039.

Nelson, R. K., & Muse, V. A. (2025). Evaluating the Prevalence of Imposter Syndrome Among Community College General Biology Students. *Community College Journal of Research and Practice*, •••, 1–15.

Neufeld, A., Babenko, O., Lai, H., Svrcek, C., & Malin, G. (2023). Why do we feel like intellectual frauds? A self-determination theory perspective on the impostor phenomenon in medical students. *Teaching and Learning in Medicine*, *35*(2), 180–192.

New ILO working paper exposes significant 'disability wage gap' | International Labour Organisation. (2024, August 28). https://www.ilo.org/resource/news/new-ilo-working-paper-exposes-significant-disability-wage-gap

Newar, R., Gupta, R. K., Krishnan, R. G., Shekhawat, K., & Walia, Y. (2025). Self-esteem as a mediator of the relationship between imposter phenomenon and academic performance among college students. *International Journal of Adolescence and Youth*, *30*(1), 2496449.

Newman, K., Snay, S., Endres, M., Parikh, M., & Begel, A. (2025, October). Disclosure of Neurodivergence in Software Workplaces: a Mixed Methods Study of Forum and Survey Perspectives. In *Proceedings of the 27th International ACM SIGACCESS Conference on Computers and Accessibility* (pp. 1-17).

Niebler, V., & Animento, S. (2023). Organising fragmented labour: The case of migrant workers at Helpling in Berlin. *Economic and Labour Relations Review*, *34*(4), 689–706.

Nigar, N., Dovchin, S., Wilson, R., & Kostogriz, A. (2025). Hybrid professionalism: Multilingual cosmopolitan identities of immigrant English teachers. *Journal of Multilingual and Multicultural Development*, •••, 1–18.

Nikken, P., & Schols, M. (2015). How and why parents guide the media use of young children. *Journal of Child and Family Studies, 24*(11), 3423–3435. PMID: 26472932

Noble, S. U. (2018). *Algorithms of Oppression: How Search Engines Reinforce Racism*. NYU Press.

Noschis, E. (2024). Artificial intelligence will only intensify gender inequality in the world." Experts'. *Manufacturing & Service Operations Management, 24*(6), 3060–3078.

Nwokocha, S. C., Obohwemu, K. O., Yakpir, G. M., Olori, F. E., Nchindia, C. A., Kachitsa, C. L., & Onome, O. H. (2025). Artificial Intelligence and the Future of Higher Education: Towards Inclusive, Ethical, and Employability-Driven Learning Ecosystems. *Critique Open Research & Review, 3*(02), 18–29.

O'Connell, C., & McKinnon, M. (2021). Perceptions of barriers to career progression for academic women in STEM. *Societies (Basel, Switzerland), 11*, 27.

O'Connor, R. (2025). Working-class imposterism in the law school:"I always have this in the back of my head that I'm expected to fail". *The Law Teacher*, •••, 1–25.

O'Neill, C., Selwyn, N., Smith, G., Andrejevic, M., & Gu, X. (2022). The two faces of the child in facial recognition industry discourse: Biometric capture between innocence and recalcitrance. *Information Communication and Society, 25*(6), 752–767.

Obiefuna, P. (2025). The Integrity of Human Authorship: An Argument Against Artificial Fear. *Available at SSRN* 5234383.

Ochs, S. L. (2021). Impostor Syndrome & The Law School Caste System. *Pace Law Review, 42*, 373.

Odalonu, B. H. (2022). Worsening insecurity in Nigeria and its implications on governance and national development. *African Journal of Humanities and Contemporary Education Research, 5*(1), 31–49.

Ohu, F. C., Burrell, D. N., & Jones, L. A. (2025, October). Public Health Risk Management, Policy, and Ethical Imperatives in the Use of AI Tools for Mental Health Therapy. [). MDPI.]. *Health Care, 13*(21), 2721.

Olawade, D. B., Ayoola, F. I., Ebo, T. O., Asaolu, A. J., Egbon, E., & David-Olawade, A. C. (2025). Artificial Intelligence in Forensic Mental Health: A Review of Applications and Implications. *Journal of Forensic and Legal Medicine*, •••, 102895. PMID: 40441026

Olawade, D. B., Ayoola, F. I., Ebo, T. O., Asaolu, A. J., Egbon, E., & David-Olawade, A. C. (2025). Artificial intelligence in forensic mental health: A review of applications and implications. *Journal of Forensic and Legal Medicine, 113*, 102895.

Oliveira, A. L., Hernandez-Ramirez, R., & Ayanoglu, H. (2025, May). AI and Gender Perspectives in Startup Environments: Mitigating Bias, Challenging Stereotypes, and Design Implications. In *International Conference on Human-Computer Interaction* (pp. 396-418). Cham: Springer Nature Switzerland.

Oman, Z. U., Siddiqua, A., & Noorain, R. (2024). Artificial Intelligence and its ability to reduce recruitment bias. *World Journal of Advanced Research and Reviews, 24*(1), 551–564. DOI: 10.30574/wjarr.2024.24.1.3054

Osorio de Barros, G., & Severino Soares, O. (2025). AI and the Next Generation: Protecting Childhood in the Digital Age. In *Environmental, Social, Governance and Digital Transformation in Organizations* (pp. 103–133). Springer Nature Switzerland.

Ozmen Garibay, O., Winslow, B., Andolina, S., Antona, M., Bodenschatz, A., Coursaris, C., Falco, G., Fiore, S. M., Garibay, I., Grieman, K., Havens, J. C., Jirotka, M., Kacorri, H., Karwowski, W., Kider, J., Konstan, J., Koon, S., Lopez-Gonzalez, M., Maifeld-Carucci, I., & Xu, W. (2023). Six Human-Centred Artificial Intelligence Grand Challenges. *International Journal of Human-Computer Interaction, 39*(3), 391–437. DOI: 10.1080/10447318.2022.2153320

Ozmen Garibay, O., Winslow, B., Andolina, S., Antona, M., Bodenschatz, A., Coursaris, C., & Xu, W. (2023). Six human-centered artificial intelligence grand challenges. *International Journal of Human-Computer Interaction, 39*(3), 391–437.

Ozobu, C. O., Adikwu, F. E., Cynthia, O. O., Onyeke, F. O., & Nwulu, E. O. (2025). Developing an AI-powered occupational health surveillance system for real-time detection and management of workplace health hazards. *World Journal of Innovation and Modern Technology, 9*(1), 156–185.

Pacheco, E. M. (2025). Coping and Resilience: Strategies for Managing the Psychological Impact of Remote Exposure to Trauma. In *Remote Trauma Exposure* (pp. 155–190). Springer Nature Switzerland.

Packin, N. G. (2021). Disability discrimination using artificial intelligence systems and social scoring: Can we disable digital bias? *J. Int'l & Comp. L., 8*, 487.

Paghandeh, M., Hassanzadeh, S., & Ghasemzadeh, S. (2019). Effectiveness of parent-child interaction program on parenting stress and parent-hearing impaired child relationship. *Journal of Research in Psychological Health, 13*(1), 99–124.

Pagliara, S. M., Bonavolontà, G., Pia, M., Falchi, S., Zurru, A. L., Fenu, G., & Mura, A. (2024). The Integration of Artificial Intelligence in Inclusive Education: A Scoping Review. *Information (Basel)*, *15*(12), 774. DOI: 10.3390/info15120774

Palaniappan, K., Lin, E. Y. T., & Vogel, S. (2024, February). Global regulatory frameworks for the use of artificial intelligence (AI) in the healthcare services sector. [). MDPI.]. *Health Care*, *12*(5), 562. PMID: 38470673

Palavi, L. A., Holt, E. A. L., & Nosa, V. (2025). A scoping review on the nature of parental involvement among Pacific and minority populations with hearing loss. *Journal of the Royal Society of New Zealand*, *55*(3), 721–753. PMID: 39989647

Palimaru, A. I., Malika, N., Brown, R. A., Holmes, P., Dickerson, D. L., Rodriguez, A., & D'Amico, E. J. (2025). "Am I Not Native Enough?" A Qualitative Exploration of Experienced Discrimination Among American Indian/Alaska Native Emerging Adults. *Journal of Racial and Ethnic Health Disparities*, •••, 1–15.

Palmer, A., & Schwan, D. (2025). Digital Mental Health Tools and AI Therapy Chatbots: A Balanced Approach to Regulation. *The Hastings Center Report*, *55*(3), 15–29.

Pandey, H. M. (2024). Artificial Intelligence in Mental Health and Well-Being: Evolution, Current Applications, Future Challenges, and Emerging Evidence. *arXiv preprint arXiv:2501.10374*.

Para, E., Dubreuil, P., Miquelon, P., & Martin-Krumm, C. (2024). Interventions addressing the impostor phenomenon: A scoping review. *Frontiers in Psychology*, *15*, 1360540.

Parker, J. S., Haskins, N., Coleman-Chatman, T., Duru, C., Ramirez, D., Chae, N., & Nortey, A. (2024). Dismantling the imposter syndrome: A case study of early career women of color in school mental health fields. *Journal for Specialists in Group Work*, *49*(1), 3–24.

Park, J., Damaske, S., Choi, J., McHale, S., Rosenberger, J., & Yin, J. (2025). Job Tenure and Gendered Perception of Workplace Challenges in Gendered Organizations: Computer Science, Engineering, and Mathematics Fields. *Socius: Sociological Research for a Dynamic World*, *11*, 23780231251376456.

Parsons, P., Dewey, M. H., & Niedringhaus, K. L. (2024). Georgia state legal technology competency Model: A framework for examining and evaluating what it means to Be a technologically competent Lawyer. *U. St. Thomas LJ*, *20*, 53.

Parti, K., & Szabo, J. (2024). The legal challenges of realistic and AI-driven child sexual abuse material: Regulatory and enforcement perspectives in Europe. *Laws, 13*(6), 67.

Passalacqua, M., Pellerin, R., Magnani, F., Doyon-Poulin, P., Del-Aguila, L., Boasen, J., & Léger, P. M. (2025). Human-centred AI in industry 5.0: A systematic review. *International Journal of Production Research, 63*(7), 2638–2669.

Paul, F. A., Ali, A., Ganie, A. U. R., & Basistha, B. (2025). Imposter Syndrome in Higher Education: A Hidden Crisis-threatening Student Mental Health and Success. *Lebanese Journal of Mental Health, 1*(1), 49–51.

Perera, A., & Chhetri, A. (2025). Computational simulation and algorithmic analysis of occupational health risk dynamics in labor markets and their policy implications in developing regions. *Northern Reviews on Algorithmic Research, Theoretical Computation, and Complexity, 10*(6), 1–14.

Persson, A., Marklund, U., Lohmander, A., & Flynn, T. (2022). Expressive vocabulary development in children with moderate hearing loss–the impact of auditory variables and early consonant production. *Clinical Linguistics & Phonetics, 36*(6), 547–564. PMID: 34231440

Peters, D., Vold, K., Robinson, D., & Calvo, R. A. (2020). Responsible AI—Two frameworks for ethical design practice. *IEEE Transactions on Technology and Society, 1*(1), 34–47.

Plate, D., & Hutson, J. (2025). The intellectual bankruptcy of anti-AI academic alarmism: A rebuttal. *Teaching in Higher Education*, •••, 1–12.

Pozzi, T., Legg, E., McCullough, S., & Lubell, M. (2025). Transformative climate change education for graduate students: Developing a theory of change to increase equity in climate change science. *Environmental Education Research, 31*(11), 2351–2373.

Prabhakar, P., Pati, P. B., & Parida, S. (2024). Navigating Legal and Ethical Dimensions in AI, IoT, and Cloud Solutions for Women's Safety. In *Developing AI, IoT and Cloud Computing-based Tools and Applications for Women's Safety* (pp. 155-191). Chapman and Hall/CRC.

Prabhakar, P., Pati, P. B., & Parida, S. (2025). Navigating Legal and Ethical Dimensions in AI, IoT, and Cloud Solutions for Women's Safety. In *Developing AI, IoT and Cloud Computing-based Tools and Applications for Women's Safety* (pp. 155-191). Chapman and Hall/CRC.

Preston, E. E. (2025). *Navigating Shifts: Black Women in Higher Education and the Intersection of Imposter Syndrome, Remote Work, and Office Reintegration During the COVID-19 Pandemic* (Master's thesis, Azusa Pacific University).

Price, P. C., Holcomb, B., & Payne, M. B. (2024). Gender differences in impostor phenomenon: A meta-analytic review. *Current Research in Behavioral Sciences, 7*, 100155. DOI: 10.1016/j.crbeha.2024.100155

Priyadarshini, S., & Priyadarshini, S. (2024). Gender Disparity in Artificial Intelligence: Creating Awareness of Unconscious Bias. In *Artificial Intelligence in Forecasting* (pp. 98-112). CRC Press.

Priyadharshini, D., Muthuvel, I., Saraswathy, S., Kavitha, P. S., & Jegadeeswari, V. (2025). Precision to plate: AI-driven innovations in fermentation and hyper-personalized diets. *Frontiers in Nutrition, 12*, 1659511. PMID: 40977977

Purwanto, A. N. I. (2025). Human-Centered AI: Designing Intelligent Systems that Empower, Not Replace. *RIGGS: Journal of Artificial Intelligence and Digital Business, 4*(3), 3212–3221.

Pyae, A. (2025). What is Human-Centeredness in Human-Centered AI? Development of Human-Centeredness Framework and AI Practitioners' Perspectives. *arXiv preprint arXiv:2502.03293.*

Qiu, N., Jiang, Y., Sun, Z., & Du, M. (2023). The impact of disability-related deprivation on employment opportunity at the neighbourhood level: Does family socioeconomic status matter? *Frontiers in Public Health, 11*, 1232829. DOI: 10.3389/fpubh.2023.1232829

Quittner, A. L., Barker, D. H., Cruz, I., Snell, C., Grimley, M. E., & Botteri, M., & CDaCI Investigative Team. (2010). Parenting stress among parents of deaf and hearing children: Associations with language delays and behavior problems. *Parenting, Science and Practice, 10*(2), 136–155. PMID: 20607098

Rahman, M. A. (2023). Silhouettes of the Digital Minds: Exploring Emotional and Intellectual Interaction between Youth and Artificial Intelligence. *Available at SSRN* 5190217.

Rakovac Bekes, E., Galzina, V., & Berbić Kolar, E. (2024). Using Human-Computer Interaction (HCI) and Artificial Intelligence (AI) in Education to Improve the Literacy of Deaf and Hearing-Impaired Children. In *2024 47th ICT and Electronics Convention (MIPRO)* (pp. 1624-1629).

Raman, R., Kowalski, R., Achuthan, K., Iyer, A., & Nedungadi, P. (2025). Navigating artificial general intelligence development: Societal, technological, ethical, and brain-inspired pathways. *Scientific Reports*, *15*(1), 1–22. PMID: 40069265

Rao, D. N., & Rajeshwari, B., & RAO, S. U. M. (2026). Intersectionality and Competency Mapping: An Industrial Psychology Perspective on the Experiences of Under-represented Groups in the Indian IT Sector. *Journal of Cortex Explore*, *1*(1), 13–22.

Ravi, R., Gunjawate, D. R., Yerraguntla, K., Rajashekhar, B., & Lewis, L. E. (2016). Knowledge and attitude of parents/caregivers towards hearing loss and screening in newborns–a systematic review. *International Journal of Audiology*, *55*(12), 715–722. PMID: 27686575

Raymond, M. (2025). Our AI, Ourselves: Illuminating the Human Fears Animating Early Regulatory Responses to the Use of Generative AI in the Practice of Law. *Mary's J. on Legal Malpractice & Ethics*, *15*, 221.

Rea, E. A. (2021). Changing the Face of Technology": Storytelling as Intersectional Feminist Practice in Coding Organizations. *Technical Communication (Washington)*, *68*(4), 26–39.

Recommendation on the Ethics of Artificial Intelligence. (2024). UNESCO. https://www.unesco.org/en/articles/recommendation-ethics-artificial-intelligence

Reddy, G., & Amer, A. (2023). Precarious engagements and the politics of knowledge production: Listening to calls for reorienting hegemonic social psychology. *British Journal of Social Psychology*, *62*, 71–94.

Reichard, R. J., Pitichat, T., & Parker, K. K. (2024). Elevating aspiring diverse leaders through PsyCap: Individual sources and organizational support for developing HEROs. *Organizational Dynamics*, *53*(4), 101086.

Rice, A. J., Ogle, C. M., Martin, S. L., & Cozza, S. J. (2025). The impact of wartime child casualties on adult professionals. *Psychiatry*, *88*(3), 308–327.

Richardson, T. T., Mudathir, D., Hossain, S., & Cheatham, L. (2025). Intersectional Predictors of Mental Health Problems Among Black College Students: A Multi-Level Analysis Examining Individual, Institutional, and Societal Level Factors. *Journal of Evidence-Based Social Work*, •••, 1–25.

Robbins, S. (2022). The federal IT crisis: Advocating for digital governance and the development of a more robust federal government cyber workforce. *Public Contract Law Journal*, *52*(1), 157–177.

Roberts, K. T. (2025). wisible within the nvisib txola tersectic ci. *Human Rights (Chicago, Ill.)*, *50*(5).

Robinson, J. C. (2025). Unshackling Dreams from the Hacker's Digital Chains. In *Artificial Intelligence: Ethics and the New World Order* (pp. 95–171). Springer Nature Switzerland.

Rofi, I. B., & Eshita, M. M. (2025). *Exploring opportunities, risks, and resilience among young indigenous social media users in the Chittagong hill tracts through qualitative and quantitative lenses* (Doctoral dissertation, Brac University).

Romanishyn, A., Malytska, O., & Goncharuk, V. (2025). AI-driven disinformation: Policy recommendations for democratic resilience. *Frontiers in Artificial Intelligence*, *8*, 1569115.

Rosen, E., Garboden, P. M., & Cossyleon, J. E. (2021). Racial discrimination in housing: How landlords use algorithms and home visits to screen tenants. *American Sociological Review*, *86*(5), 787–822.

Rousseau, D. (1995). Psychological contracts in organizations: Understanding written and unwritten agreements. *Sage (Atlanta, Ga.)*.

Rubambiza, G., Sengers, P., Weatherspoon, H., & Liu, J. (2024, May). Seam work and simulacra of societal impact in networking research: A critical technical practice approach. In *Proceedings of the 2024 CHI Conference on Human Factors in Computing Systems* (pp. 1-19).

Ruffino, P. (2022). Seeking deep relations in a precarious industry: Addressing mental health through independent videogame development. *Television & New Media*, *23*(7), 761–776.

Sagert, S. J., & Christensen Pacella, K. A. (2025). Higher imposter syndrome symptoms associated with greater odds of eating disorders in college and university students. *Journal of American College Health*, •••, 1–6.

Saha, A. (2025). Human-centred innovation in Society 5.0. *Society 5.0: A Transformation towards Human-Centered. Artificial Intelligence*, •••, 143.

Salina, J. H. (2023). Humanizing the culture of technology teams: Strategies for creating healthier and more productive work environments. *Journal of Software Engineering and Applications*, *16*(12), 641–671.

Sampson, S. E. (2021). A strategic framework for task automation in professional services. *Journal of Service Research*, *24*(1), 122–140.

Schmager, S., Pappas, I. O., & Vassilakopoulou, P. (2025). Understanding Human-Centred AI: A review of its defining elements and a research agenda. *Behaviour & Information Technology*, •••, 1–40.

Schmitz, A. J., & Zeleznikow, J. (2021). Intelligent legal tech to empower self-represented litigants. *Colum. Sci. & Tech. L. Rev.*, *23*, 142.

Schmulian, D., & Lind, C. (2020). Parental experiences of the diagnosis of permanent childhood hearing loss: A phenomenological study. *International Journal of Audiology*, *59*(1), 54–60. PMID: 31566461

Schulte, P. A., Iavicoli, I., Fontana, L., Leka, S., Dollard, M. F., Salmen-Navarro, A., & Fischer, F. M. (2022). Occupational safety and health staging framework for decent work. *International Journal of Environmental Research and Public Health*, *19*(17), 10842. PMID: 36078562

Schweiger, G. (2025). The ethics of AI-assisted digital phenotyping in adolescent mental health: A framework for informed consent and trust. *AI and Ethics*, •••, 1–21.

Segkouli, S., Giakoumis, D., Votis, K., Triantafyllidis, A., Paliokas, I., & Tzovaras, D. (2023). Smart Workplaces for older adults: Coping 'ethically'with technology pervasiveness. *Universal Access in the Information Society*, *22*(1), 37–49. PMID: 34305502

Seroja, T. D. (2022). Technological Advancement In The Society 5.0 Era For Notary In Indonesia: Glory Or Obsolete? *Legal Brief*, *11*(3), 1589–1597.

Shabur, M. A., Shahriar, A., & Ara, M. A. (2025). From automation to collaboration: Exploring the impact of industry 5.0 on sustainable manufacturing. *Discover Sustainability*, *6*(1), 341.

Sharifi Poor Bgheshmi, M. S., Sharajsharifi, M., & Saeidabadi, M. R. (2025). Between exploitation and resilience: Reconciling AI's role in surveillance capitalism and disaster risk management. *Journal of Cyberspace Studies,* 1–31.

Sharma, G. M., Nghiem, X. H., Gaur, P., & Gangodawilage, D. S. K. (2025). Ethical Implications of AI-Driven Outsourcing: Ensuring Bias Mitigation, Fairness, and Accountability. In *Global Work Arrangements and Outsourcing in the Age of AI* (pp. 421-450). IGI Global Scientific Publishing.

Shen, A. (2025). Behind Our Masks: The Impact of Intersectional Identity on Neurodivergent Masking. *Backstory, 1*(1).

Sheng, H., Shen, X., Du, H., Zhang, H., Huang, Z., & Yu, X. (2024). AI empowered Auslan learning for parents of deaf children and children of deaf adults. *AI and Ethics*, *4*(4), 877–887.

Shen, J., Iandoli, L., & Aguirre-Urreta, M. (2022). Human-centered design for individual and social well-being: Editorial preface. *AIS Transactions on Human-Computer Interaction*, *14*(4), 446–460.

Shiels, T., Kenny, N., Shiels, R., & Mannix-McNamara, P. (2021). Incivility in higher education: Challenges of inclusion for neurodiverse students with traumatic brain injury in Ireland. *Societies (Basel, Switzerland)*, *11*(2), 60.

Shin, D. (2024). Conclusion: misinformation and AI—how algorithms generate and manipulate misinformation. In *Artificial misinformation: Exploring human-algorithm interaction online* (pp. 259–277). Springer Nature Switzerland.

Shin, D. (2025). Engineering equity: Designing diversity-aware AI to reflect humanity. *AI & Society*, •••, 1–10.

Shonhe, L., & Min, Q. (2025). Mitigating AI-induced professional identity threat and fostering adoption in the workplace. *AI & Society*, •••, 1–14.

Shott, S. R., Joseph, A., & Heithaus, D. (2001). Hearing loss in children with Down syndrome. *International Journal of Pediatric Otorhinolaryngology*, *61*(3), 199–205. PMID: 11700189

Shukla, S. (2024). Principles governing ethical development and deployment of AI. *Journal of Artificial Intelligence Ethics*, *7*(1), 45–60.

Shymko, V., & Babadzhanova, A. (2025). Ethical challenges and strategic responses to AI integration in psychological assessment. *AI and Ethics*, *5*(5), 5415–5423.

Simshaw, D. (2022). Access to AI justice: Avoiding an inequitable two-tiered system of legal services. *Yale JL & Tech.*, *24*, 150.

Singh, A., Kaur, S., & Sharma, R. (2025). Breaking Barriers: The Evolving Role of Women in Leadership. In *Enhancing Workplace Productivity Through Gender Equity and Intergenerational Communication* (pp. 397-426). IGI Global Scientific Publishing.

Singh, A. (2024). The Two Faced Lie: Regulation of Generative AI and Watermarking. *Available at SSRN* 5347736.

Singh, S., & Singh, M. (2024). Impact of Resilience, Optimism and Socio-economic Status on Coping in Parents among Visually and Hearing-impaired Children. *Journal of Scientific Research and Reports*, *30*(12), 698–707.

Singh, V. (2024). AI, women's health care, and trust: Problems and prospects. In *Artificial Intelligence and Machine Learning for Women's Health Issues* (pp. 235–254). Academic Press.

Sivaram, J., Narrain, J. M., Honnavalli, P., & Eswaran, S. (2023). Adversarial machine learning: The rise in AI-enabled crime. *Computer Fraud & Security, 2023*(2).

Siwale, K., & Mwalemba, G. (2023). Societal influences on career decision making: Perspectives of A frican women pursuing technology-related professions. *The Electronic Journal on Information Systems in Developing Countries, 89*(4), e12259.

Skolnick, K. R. (2025). A second look at second look: Promoting epistemic justice in resentencing. *NYUL Rev., 100*, 1.

Snyder, A. L., & Pallett, L. H. (2026). Mindfulness, Motivation, and Milestones: Facilitated Support for Doctoral Students During Dissertation Writing. In *Improving Doctoral Education and Research Development for Sustainability* (pp. 271-302). IGI Global Scientific Publishing.

Sommer, E. (2024). Real Concerns for an Artificial Threat: Artists, AI, and the Battle to Script Hollywood's Future. *Nev. LJ, 25*, 449.

Soomro, S., Fan, M., Soomro, S., Naseer, E., Shaikh, S. N., & Shaikh, S. N. (2025). Balancing AI and Human Interaction: Impact of AI Interaction on Well-Being. In *AI in Mental Health: Innovations, Challenges, and Collaborative Pathways* (pp. 141-166). IGI Global Scientific Publishing.

Spitko, E. G. (2024). Workplace AI and Human Flourishing. *Connecticut Law Review, 57*, 231.

Sriram, H. K. (2024). A comparative study of identity theft protection frameworks enhanced by machine learning algorithms. *Available at SSRN* 5236625.

St. John, V. J., Wilson, G. D., Tran, L., Applin, L., & Evans, D. (2025). Administrative Burden in Higher Education: Race, Criminal Records, and Street-Level Bureaucrats in College Admissions. *Public Administration Review*.

Stecher, A., & Soto Roy, Á. (2022). Crisis and transformation of occupational identities in three sectors (retail, mining, state): contributions to understanding workplace subjectivities in neoliberal Chile. In *Neoliberalism and Subjectivity in Latin America* (pp. 33–56). Springer International Publishing.

Stevenson, J., McCann, D., Watkin, P., Worsfold, S., & Kennedy, C., & Hearing Outcomes Study Team. (2010). The relationship between language development and behaviour problems in children with hearing loss. *Journal of Child Psychology and Psychiatry, and Allied Disciplines, 51*(1), 77–83. PMID: 19686333

Strachan, D. M. (2022). Among us: Imposter syndrome and barriers to Black success. *Cardozo J. Equal Rts. & Soc. Just., 29*, 319.

Su, A. (2025). Gender equality, AI, and the future of human rights. *University of Toronto Law Journal, 75*(Supplement 1), 202–217.

Sun, H. (2024). The Law and Ethics of AI Creativity. *John's L. Rev., 98*, 405.

Sun, Y., Sheng, D., Zhou, Z., & Wu, Y. (2024). AI hallucination: Towards a comprehensive classification of distorted information in artificial intelligence-generated content. *Humanities & Social Sciences Communications, 11*(1), 1–14.

Tabassum, A., Ghaznavi, I., Abd-Alrazaq, A., & Qadir, J. (2025). Exploring the Application of AI and Extended Reality Technologies in Metaverse-Driven Mental Health Solutions: Scoping Review. *Journal of Medical Internet Research, 27*, e72400.

Taghizadeh-Hesary, F. (2025). The impact of artificial intelligence adoption and financial accessibility on energy sustainability. *Energy Strategy Reviews, 59*, 101744.

Tahvanainen, L., Tetri, B., & Ahonen, O. (2024, May). Exploring and extending human-centered design to develop AI-Enabled wellbeing technology in healthcare. In *Nordic Conference on Digital Health and Wireless Solutions* (pp. 288-306). Cham: Springer Nature Switzerland.

Tang, X., & Ji, Y. (2024, December). Design of infant monitoring products for hearing-impaired parents. In *2024 17th International Symposium on Computational Intelligence and Design (ISCID)* (pp. 93-96). IEEE.

Tapalova, O., & Zhiyenbayeva, N. (2022). Artificial intelligence in education: AIEd for personalised learning pathways. *Electronic Journal of e-Learning, 20*(5), 639–653.

Tarvin, E., & Stanfill, M. (2022). "YouTube's predator problem": Platform moderation as governance-washing and user resistance. *Convergence, 28*(3), 822–837.

Terblanche, N., Molyn, J., de Haan, E., & Nilsson, V. O. (2022). Comparing artificial intelligence and human coaching goal attainment efficacy. *PLoS One, 17*(6), e0270255. PMID: 35727801

Thirupathi, L., Kaashipaka, V., Dhanaraju, M., & Katakam, V. (2025). AI and IoT in Mental Health Care: From Digital Diagnostics to Personalized, Continuous Support. In *Intelligent Systems and IoT Applications in Clinical Health* (pp. 271-294). IGI Global.

Thomaidou, A., & Limniotis, K. (2025). Navigating Through Human Rights in AI: Exploring the Interplay Between GDPR and Fundamental Rights Impact Assessment. *Journal of Cybersecurity and Privacy*, *5*(1), 7.

Thomas-Davis, S. (2020). Cloaked in Liminality. *Prison Stories: Women Scholars' Experiences Doing Research Behind Bars*, 51.

Tiwari, A. (2025). From Algorithmic Bias to Inclusive Design: Rethinking AI for Equitable Transport Systems. *Available at SSRN* 5250914.

Topol, D., Girard, N., Pierre, L. S., Tucker, R., & Vohr, B. (2011). The effects of maternal stress and child language ability on behavioral outcomes of children with congenital hearing loss at 18–24 months. *Early Human Development*, *87*(12), 807–811. PMID: 21745720

Topol, E. J. (2019). High-performance medicine: The convergence of human and artificial intelligence. *Nature Medicine*, *25*(1), 44–56. PMID: 30617339

Torkamaan, H., Tahaei, M., Buijsman, S., Xiao, Z., Wilkinson, D., & Knijnenburg, B. P. (2024). The role of human-centered ai in user modeling, adaptation, and personalization—models, frameworks, and paradigms. In *A Human-Centered Perspective of Intelligent Personalized Environments and Systems* (pp. 43–84). Springer Nature Switzerland.

Tran, N. (2023). From imposter phenomenon to infiltrator experience: Decolonizing the mind to claim space and reclaim self. *Peace and Conflict*, *29*(2), 184.

Tulshyan, R., & Burey, J. A. (2021). End imposter syndrome in your workplace. *Harvard Business Review*, *14*, 4729.

Tung, K. (2019). AI, the internet of legal things, and lawyers. *Journal of Management Analytics*, *6*(4), 390–403.

Uche, I. B., Uche, O. A., & Ene, J. C. (2025). Superstitions and criminal behavior: The role of witchcraft accusations in Nigerian rural communities. *Social Thought*, •••, 1–23.

Ugwudike, P., Lavorgna, A., & Tartari, M. (2024). Sharenting in digital society: Exploring the prospects of an emerging moral panic. *Deviant Behavior*, *45*(4), 503–520.

Ulum, O. G. (2025). Draw Me Your Name: Name-Based Discrimination and Identity in Turkey's Socio-Political Context and Beyond. *Race and Social Problems*, •••, 1–32.

Umucu, E., Vernon, A. A., Pan, D., Qin, S., Solis, G., Campa, R., & Lee, B. (2025). Health inequities among persons with disabilities: A global scoping review. *Frontiers in Public Health, 13*, 1538519. DOI: 10.3389/fpubh.2025.1538519

UNESCO. (2020). *Global Education Monitoring (GEM) Report 2020 | UNESCO.* https://www.unesco.org/en/articles/global-education-monitoring-gem-report-2020

Urbas, G. (2021). Legal considerations in the use of artificial intelligence in the investigation of online child exploitation. *ANU College of Law Research Paper,* (21.44).

Usmani, U. A., Happonen, A., & Watada, J. (2023, June). Human-centered artificial intelligence: Designing for user empowerment and ethical considerations. In *2023 5th international congress on human-computer interaction, optimization and robotic applications (HORA)*. IEEE.

Utami, L. S., Mandala, S., & Darwati, D. (2025). Legal Aspects of Moral Rights and Economic Rights in Music Creation Using AI Music Generators. *Jurnal Pendidikan Indonesia, 6*(7), 2925–2941.

van der Miesen, L. (2021, September). Simulacral Technologies and The Threefold Identity Crisis: Can deepfakes effectuate a society-wide increase of imposter syndrome and feelings of inadequacy? [BCS Learning & Development.]. *Proceedings of Politics of the Machines-Rogue Research, 2021*, 261–266.

van Drunen, M. Z., & Fechner, D. (2023). Safeguarding editorial independence in an automated media system: The relationship between law and journalistic perspectives. *Digital Journalism (Abingdon, England), 11*(9), 1723–1750.

Van Zyl, L. E. (2025). The Unintended Negative Consequences of Artificial Intelligence Use for Psychologists. *OSF pre-print. DOI, 10.*

Vargas-Murillo, A. R., Turriate-Guzman, A. M., Delgado-Chávez, C. A., & Sanchez-Paucar, F. (2024). Transforming justice: Implications of artificial intelligence in legal systems. *Academic Journal of Interdisciplinary Studies, 13*(2), 433.

Vassilopoulou, J., & Kyriakidou, O. (2025). Introduction: AI and Diversity in a Datafied World of Work–Will the Future of Work be Inclusive? In *AI and Diversity in a Datafied World of Work: Will the Future of Work be Inclusive?* (pp. 1-15). Emerald Publishing Limited.

Vecchietti, G., Liyanaarachchi, G., & Viglia, G. (2025). Managing deepfakes with artificial intelligence: Introducing the business privacy calculus. *Journal of Business Research, 186*, 115010.

Venkatachalam, S. (2023). *Exploring the Horizons of Access to Justice: An Analysis of Disabled Women Who are Subjected to Violence in India*. https://research-information.bris.ac.uk/en/studentTheses/exploring-the-horizons-of-access-to-justice

Verma, N. (2025). ETHICAL IMPLICATIONS OF AI IN PSYCHOLOGICAL INTERVENTIONS. *Shodhbodhalaya*, 187-205.

Verma, S., & Pathania, B. (2025, August). Review on: Ethical Consideration in the Integration of AI Technologies in Mental Health Care. In *2025 9th International Conference on Inventive Systems and Control (ICISC)* (pp. 20-27). IEEE.

Vicsek, L., Pinter, R., & Bauer, Z. (2025). Shifting job expectations in the era of generative AI hype–perspectives of journalists and copywriters. *The International Journal of Sociology and Social Policy*, *45*(1/2), 1–16.

Vijeyarasa, R. (2023). Gendered harms and the regulation of artificial intelligence: A comparative assessment of emerging legislative practice. *Notre Dame J. on Emerging Tech.*, *5*, 114.

Villar, A. S., & Khan, N. (2021). Robotic process automation in banking industry: A case study on Deutsche Bank. *Journal of Banking and Financial Technology*, *5*(1), 71–86.

Vivek, R., & Krupskyi, O. (2024). Breaking stereotypes, building inclusion: Blind hiring strategies as catalysts for a diverse and discrimination-free workplace. *Bulletin of VN Karazin Kharkiv National University Economic Series*, (107), 108–122.

Vogel, E., Moats, D., Woolgar, S., & Helgesson, C. F. (2021). Thinking with imposters: the imposter as analytic. In *The Imposter as Social Theory* (pp. 1–30). Bristol University Press.

Vohr, B. R., Jodoin-Krauzyk, J., Tucker, R., Johnson, M. J., Topol, D., & Ahlgren, M. (2008). Results of newborn screening for hearing loss: Effects on the family in the first 2 years of life. *Archives of Pediatrics & Adolescent Medicine*, *162*(3), 205–211. PMID: 18316656

Wachter, S. (2022). The theory of artificial immutability: Protecting algorithmic groups under anti-discrimination law. *Tul. L. Rev.*, *97*, 149.

Wagner, J. L., Boyle, J., Boyle, C. J., Choi, D., Ballou, J. M., Patel, N., & Malcom, D. R. (2022). Overcoming past perceptions and a profession-wide identity crisis to reflect pharmacy's future. *American Journal of Pharmaceutical Education*, *86*(7), 8829.

Wake, M., Poulakis, Z., Hughes, E. K., Carey-Sargeant, C., & Rickards, F. W. (2005). Hearing impairment: A population study of age at diagnosis, severity, and language outcomes at 7–8 years. *Archives of Disease in Childhood*, *90*(3), 238–244. PMID: 15723906

Wang, H., Feng, Y., Tian, Y., Wang, Z., Hu, J., & Tomizuka, M. (2024). Towards the next level of vehicle automation through cooperative driving: A roadmap from planning and control perspective. *IEEE Transactions on Intelligent Vehicles*, *9*(3), 4335–4347.

Wang, L. (2024). Blending in or Being Co-Opted: Reflecting on an Internship-Cum-Field Work at a New Town Government in China. *The Professional Geographer*, *76*(2), 239–247.

Wang, S. J., & Huang, H. C. (2025). To ask is human, to answer divine: How awe-inspiring generative AI leads to self-enhancement and imposter anxiety. *Information Technology & People*, •••, 1–32.

Wang, X., Zhou, Y., & Zhou, G. (2025). The Application and Ethical Implication of Generative AI in Mental Health: Systematic Review. *JMIR Mental Health*, *12*, e70610. PMID: 40577783

Whaley, B. A., Martinis, J. G., Pagano, G. F., Barthol, S., Senzer, J., Williamson, P. R., & Blanck, P. D. (2024). The Americans with Disabilities Act and Equal Access to Public Spaces. *Laws*, *13*(1), 5. DOI: 10.3390/laws13010005

Wickenden, M. (2023). Disability and other identities?—How do they intersect? *Frontiers in Rehabilitation Sciences*, *4*, 1200386. DOI: 10.3389/fresc.2023.1200386

Williamson, S. M., & Prybutok, V. (2024). The era of artificial intelligence deception: Unraveling the complexities of false realities and emerging threats of misinformation. *Information (Basel)*, *15*(6), 299.

Wolbring, G., & Nasir, L. (2024). Intersectionality of Disabled People through a Disability Studies, Ability-Based Studies, and Intersectional Pedagogy Lens: A Survey and a Scoping Review. *Societies (Basel, Switzerland)*, *14*(9), 176. DOI: 10.3390/soc14090176

Wolfe, A. (2023). Incongruous identities: Mental distress and burnout disparities in LGBTQ+ health care professional populations. *Heliyon*, *9*(4). PMID: 37009240

Wood, A. (2024). Dark echoes: the exploitative potential of generative AI in online harassment. In *Psybersecurity* (pp. 90–129). CRC Press.

Xu, J., Li, Z., & Li, S. (2024). Legal ethics and professional responsibility in the legal profession. In *SHS Web of Conferences* (Vol. 190, p. 02006). EDP Sciences.

Yadav, M., Kanwal, P., & Luu, T. M. N. (2025). Overcoming imposter syndrome: Exploring the challenges women leaders face in confronting self-doubt and internalized biases. In *Narratives on Defining Moments for Women Leaders in Higher Education* (pp. 65–90). IGI Global.

Yahaya, M. S., & Sokatsha, Z. (2025). Feminist artificial intelligence (AI) approaches for civic governance in Africa. In *Designing Artificial Intelligence for Public Policy and Governance in Africa* (pp. 89–101). Springer Nature Switzerland.

Yarosewick, G. V. (2025). Protect Authors Not Algorithms: The Rise of Artificial Intelligence and Its Interference with Copyright Law. *Widener L. Rev., 31*, 203.

Ying, L. W., & Ai, J. T. T. (2025). Perspectives of hearing parents and their deaf children: Exploring needs and support systems in Ipoh, Malaysia. *International Journal of Child Welfare and Development, 22*, 125–131.

Yona, L., & Milman-Sivan, F. (2025). The Prison-Identity Complex: Unravelling Labour and Law in Identity-Based Prison Worklines. *Laws, 14*(3), 37.

Yoo, D. W., Woo, H., Pendse, S. R., Lu, N. Y., Birnbaum, M. L., Abowd, G. D., & De Choudhury, M. (2024). Missed opportunities for human-centered AI research: Understanding stakeholder collaboration in mental health AI research. *Proceedings of the ACM on Human-Computer Interaction, 8*(CSCW1), 1-24.

Yoshinaga-Itano, C. (1999). Benefits of early intervention for children with hearing loss. *Otolaryngologic Clinics of North America, 32*(6), 1089–1102. PMID: 10523454

Yu, C. (2024). *Gender Inequality in the Age of AI: Predictions, Perspectives, and Policy Recommendations* (No. 5zrh9_v1). Center for Open Science.

Yu, H., & Ai, B. (2022). Experiencing "paragliding": A student-teacher perspective on doing qualitative research in a Chinese university. *International Journal of Qualitative Methods, 21*, 16094069211070443.

Yu, T. (2023). David Foster Wallace, Both Professional and Not. *English Studies, 104*(2), 305–328.

Yu, Y., Sharma, T., Hu, M., Wang, J., & Wang, Y. (2025, May). Exploring parent-child perceptions on safety in generative AI: concerns, mitigation strategies, and design implications. In *2025 IEEE Symposium on Security and Privacy (SP)* (pp. 2735-2752). IEEE.

Zallio, M., Ike, C. B., & Chivăran, C. (2025). Designing Artificial Intelligence: Exploring Inclusion, Diversity, Equity, Accessibility, and Safety in Human-Centric Emerging Technologies. *AI*, *6*(7), 143.

Zhang, H., Mao, Y., Lin, Y., & Zhang, D. (2025). E-mental Health in the Age of AI: Data Safety, Privacy Regulations and Recommendations. *Alpha Psychiatry*, *26*(3), 44279.

Zhang, S., Luo, J., & Guo, P. (2025). Technology, Innovation, and the Legal Profession. In *Technology, Legal Education and Legal Profession in China and Australia: Opportunities and Challenges* (pp. 97–113). Springer Nature Singapore.

Zhang, W., Shi, J., Wang, X., & Wynn, H. (2023). AI-powered decision-making in facilitating insurance claim dispute resolution. *Annals of Operations Research*, •••, 1–30. PMID: 37361057

Zhang, X., & Zheng, H. (2025). Psychiatry in the age of AI: Transforming theory, practice, and medical education. *Frontiers in Public Health*, *13*, 1660448. PMID: 41089865

Zhang, Z., & Wang, J. (2024). Can AI replace psychotherapists? Exploring the future of mental health care. *Frontiers in Psychiatry*, *15*, 1444382. PMID: 39544371

Zhao, Y., & Sun, P. (2025). Artificial intelligence in the promotion of human well-being: Current trends and future directions. *Well-Being Sciences Review*, *1*(1), 3–8.

Zidaru, T., Morrow, E. M., & Stockley, R. (2021). Ensuring patient and public involvement in the transition to AI-assisted mental health care: A systematic scoping review and agenda for design justice. *Health Expectations*, *24*(4), 1072–1124. PMID: 34118185

Zubir, A. H., & Azmi, I. M. (2025). AI and Access to Justice: Digital Gap Debunked? In *Advancements in Industry and Technology* (pp. 139–146). Springer Nature Switzerland.

Zuboff, S. (2019). *The Age of Surveillance Capitalism*. PublicAffairs.

About the Contributors

Laeeq Razzak Janjua holds a PhD in International Relations with a specialization in Political Economy from WSB University, Poland, and also holds a Postgraduate Diploma in Compliance. He is affiliated with TMF Group, Poland, where he works as a Compliance Officer. He also serves as a lecturer at WSB University, Poland. Dr. Laeeq Razzak Janjua is a finance professional working in compliance and academia, with a career marked by dedication, expertise, and a strong commitment to excellence.

Dorottya Edina Kozma Ph.D. is a certified economist (Associate Professor) with a professional background spanning academia and the private sector. She graduated as Economist, specialized in Applied economics and Accounting – diplomas are issued by University of Pannonia and Budapest University of Economics and Business. Her expertise in sustainable development, environmental accounting and practical experience in company management aligns with her active involvement in various projects and events. Her primary research areas include sustainable development goals, circular economy, climate change and environmental control management and ESG. She has participated in projects focused on environmental accounting, ESG, climate change. Additionally, she is highly engaged in professional and educational activities, including curriculum developments, ESG e-learning course.

Bhupinder Singh is faculty of North Bangkok University, Thailand. He has 50 books, 150 paper publications, 163 paper presentations in international/national conferences and seminars, participated in more than 40 workshops/FDP's/QIP's, 25 courses from international universities of repute, organized more than 59 events with international and national academicians and industry people's, editor-in-chief and co-editor in journals, developed new courses. He has given talks at international universities, resource person in international conferences such as in Nanyang Technological University Singapore, Tashkent State University of Law Uzbekistan; KIMEP University Kazakhstan, All'ah meh Tabatabi University Iran, the Iranian

Association of International Criminal law, Iran and Hague Center for International Law and Investment, The Netherlands, Northumbria University Newcastle UK, Taylor's University Malaysia, AFM Krakow University Poland, European Institute for Research and Development Georgia, Business and Technology University Georgia, Texas A & M University US name a few. His leadership, teaching, research and industry experience is of 16 years and 3 Months. His research interests are health law, criminal law, research methodology and emerging multidisciplinary areas as Blockchain Technology, IoT, Machine Learning, Artificial Intelligence, Genome-editing, Photovoltaic PV Glass, SDG's and many more.

***

Saurabh Chandra is an accomplished legal scholar and currently serves as an Associate Professor & Assistant Dean at the School of Law, Bennett University, India. With a robust academic foundation, he earned his Bachelor of Arts and Bachelor of Laws (B.A. LL.B.) from the prestigious Aligarh Muslim University (A.M.U.). He further specialized in Business Laws, completing his Master of Laws (LL.M.) at the renowned National Law School of India University (NLSIU), Bangalore. Dr. Chandra's academic journey culminated in a Doctorate in Law (Ph.D.) from the esteemed National Law University (NLU) Delhi. In addition to his impressive legal education from some of India's most prestigious institutions, Dr. Chandra also holds a master's degree in management with specialization in Human Resources in Management and another in Journalism and Mass Communication. With almost two decades of teaching experience, he has numerous publications to his credit. His expertise is complemented by a robust portfolio of scholarly publications.

Avinash Krishna Goswami is Ph.D. in criminal law from Sharda University. He has a wide research experience since 2016. Actively involved in many research projects. He has been an active member at Family Dispute Resolution Clinic, Knowledge Park, Police Station. In 2021 he was honored with letter of appreciation from Police Commissioner, G.B. Nagar for resolving disputes at Family Dispute Resolution Clinic. In 2020 he was honored with letter of appreciation from Chairman, National Commission of Women, Government of India, New Delhi. He is also an active member of Internal Complaints Committee on Sexual Harassment, Sharda University. Avinash has published more than 10 research papers in UGC CARE / SCOPUS and Peer reviewed journals of national and international repute.

Hind Hammouch holds a Ph.D. in Economics and Management from the Faculty of Legal, Economic, and Social Sciences (FSJES) at Sidi Mohamed Ben Abdellah University in Fez, Morocco. She is a Professor at the Institute for

Training in Offshoring Professions in ICT and Audiovisual Sectors (IFMOTICA) in Fez and a lecturer at FSJES Fez, teaching undergraduate and graduate courses. Her research focuses on corporate social responsibility (CSR), Environmental, Social, and Governance (ESG), management control systems, organizational and financial performance, and the integration of artificial intelligence in sustainable development. Dr. Hammouch has authored numerous peer-reviewed articles in Scopus-indexed journals and book chapters with IGI Global and other international publishers. She also serves on editorial boards and peer-reviews for reputable journals and conferences. Her multidisciplinary approach bridges theory and practice in management, sustainability, and digital innovation.

Rakesh Ranjan Kumar is an Assistant professor of Law specializing in constitutional law & Human Rights in age of Artificial Intelligence. His academic work includes work on the structure of constitutional institutions, the evolution of powers of legislative, executive & judicial powers in democratic countries, contemporary legal reforms, Artificial intelligence etc. Many of his research contributions' focus has been on engaging with emerging debates on state functioning, Human rights rights, feminist jurisprudence, and institutional processes to achieve justice and equality. Committed to public-oriented legal education, he continues to contribute to academic discourse through research, writing, and active participation in academic arena. His works have focused on examining the lacunas in the constitutional framework and the administrative functionalities of the governance structure along with new technological breakthrough.

Saurabh Kumar, Accomplished legal academic and practitioner with over 14 years of combined experience in legal practice and education. Supreme Court advocate turned Assistant Professor with a distinguished track record in human rights law, gender justice, and international law. Core Expertise: - Artificial Intelligence & Law - International Law & Criminal Law - Constitutional & Public Law - Space Law Academic Excellence: He is currently advancing his scholarly journey as a Ph.D. researcher at Chanakya National Law University. He holds advanced qualifications including an LL.M. from MUIT in Criminal Law, LL.B. (Hons.) from Banaras Hindu University. Dual NET qualified (2019 & 2025) with specialized training from The Hague Academy of International Law. Published researcher with peer-reviewed articles in leading law journals, focusing on women's rights and prison reform. Active participant in international legal discourse with certifications from prestigious institutions including WIPO, UNITAR, and the World Bank. Professional Distinction: - 7 years of Supreme Court practice (2012-2019) providing robust litigation experience - 5 years as Assistant Professor at GNSU

Suparna Kundu is pursuing Ph.D (Law) from Amity Law School, Amity University, Kolkata, India . She has completed Master in Laws from Symbiosis Law School Noida, Symbiosis International (Deemed University). She has completed Bachelor in Law from KIIT School of Law - KSOL I KIIT Deemed to be University.

Navonita Mallick, doctoral candidate in Law specializing in child rights, focuses on advancing legal frameworks to protect vulnerable children. Author of multiple law books and contributor to SCOPUS-indexed and international publications, her work explores intersections of criminal law, governance, gender, and technology. With professional experience in contract analysis and legal practice, she brings both academic depth and practical insight to her writing. Passionate about research and advocacy, her publications aim to simplify complex legal issues, inspire dialogue, and empower future generations through accessible and impactful knowledge.

Shashwata Sahu, a distinguished research scholar currently pursuing her Ph.D. in Law at KIIT University, Bhubaneswar, embodies an unwavering passion for the field of law. With a profound interest in Constitutional Law, she stands as a self-driven scholar, firmly rooted in the principles of altruism. With an impressive literary portfolio, Shashwata has authored nine impactful books, each delving into crucial aspects of law and society. Her works include "The Growing Significance of Artificial Intelligence," "The role of Indian media in covering crimes: a critical analysis," "The use of Amicus Curiae Briefs at the International Criminal Tribunals," "Assessing the legal landscape of bio-medical waste management in India," "Journey of Law: From Deities to Decrees," "Evolution of Local-Self Government in India", "The Invisible Manual Scavengers of India", "Law and Justice in a Globalizing World: An LL.M. Companion" and "Comparative Public Law: An LLM. Companion." Beyond her authored books, Shashwata's contributions extend to numerous publications in both international and national journals indexed in Scopus and Web of Science.

Sheersha Saxena is a distinguished Assistant Professor of Law at Vivekananda Global University, with a notable publication record of 8 works. Her expertise spans Bhartiya Nyaya Sanhita, Bhartiya Sakshya Adhiniyam, Constitutional Law, and Human Rights. Ms. Saxena's research focus on human rights, artificial intelligence, and data privacy law has led to presentations at prestigious national and international conferences, including the National Seminar on India's Digital Competition Bill and the International Colloquium on Future Proofing Human Rights in the Age of Artificial Intelligence. Her dedication to legal education and research has made her a respected voice in her field.

Arunima Shastri is a legal academic whose work explores the evolving intersections of law, technology, and social justice. She holds an LL.M. in Corporate and Commercial Law from the National Law University, Odisha, and is currently in the final stages of her Ph.D. at Gujarat National Law University. Her doctoral research critically examines the interface between intellectual property rights, visual art, deepfakes, and digital expression in contemporary society. Her academic interests span intellectual property law, data privacy, blockchain regulation, and human rights, with a particular focus on the rights of marginalized communities, including LGBTQ+ rights. Her teaching and research emphasize bridging legal theory with technological realities, promoting a nuanced understanding of how emerging technologies challenge traditional legal frameworks. Through her scholarship and pedagogy, she contributes to advancing discourse on digital rights, creative expression, and equitable access to justice in the evolving global legal landscape.

Pragya Singh is a distinguished legal academic and scholar currently serving as an Assistant Professor of Law at The Neotia University in Kolkata, West Bengal. With a comprehensive educational background spanning prestigious Indian institutions and over seven years of teaching experience across multiple universities, Dr. Singh has established herself as a dedicated educator and researcher in the field of law. Her academic journey reflects a deep commitment to legal education, research excellence, and the advancement of legal scholarship in contemporary India. Educational Background and Academic Credentials Dr. Singh's academic foundation is built upon a rigorous educational trajectory at some of India's most esteemed institutions. She completed her doctoral studies in Law at the University of Allahabad in 2025, marking the culmination of years of intensive research and scholarly inquiry. Prior to this, she earned her Master of Laws degree from Banaras Hindu University, Varanasi, in 2015, followed by her Bachelor of Laws degree from the same institution between 2009 and 2012. Her Undergraduate education includes a Bachelor of Arts with Honor's from Banaras Hindu University.

Abhishek Srivastava is a dedicated academician and legal educator at Amity University Rajasthan, where he serves as Assistant Professor in the domain of law and governance. With a strong foundation in legal scholarship and pedagogy, he is committed to nurturing critical thinking, ethical reasoning, and interdisciplinary engagement among students. His academic responsibilities extend beyond the classroom. As the Mentor-Mentee Coordinator, he plays a pivotal role in fostering student development and academic guidance. He is also an active contributor to the university's Alternative Dispute Resolution (ADR) Committee, where he organizes and oversees competitions, workshops, and training sessions that promote practical legal skills and collaborative learning.

Aditi Srivastava, Have a rich experience of 7 years in academic as Assistant Professor of Law after pursuing Masters in Laws from IMS Unison in International Comparative Law and than PhD from Sharda University in Cyber Laws in reference to Senior Citizens. Have a passion for research, technical writing on current issues of legal concern. Currently in SOL, DBUU have the responsibility as coordinator of Research, IQAC (NAAC 1) and Events apart from teaching International law, Constitution of India, Business and Labour Acts to LLB, BBA, BA and BCOMLLB specializations. Presently mentoring Navadhara inter disciplinary Legal project with Computer Science department of DBUU with 2 teams of law students. Orcid id 0000-0003-2398-3866

Namit Srivastava is a legal academic and researcher with strong focus on constitutional law, labour law and international space law. My main interests span labour law reforms, environmental liability, and technology-policy intersections. I have approx. 10 years of teaching and research experience. Presently I am with CHRISt (Deemed to be University) Bengaluru, India as an Assistant Professor.

Versha Vahini has vast experience of law teaching and research. Before joining Bennett University, she was the Associate Dean and founder Head of the Department of School of Law at Manav Rachna University. She has obtained her Ph.D from Indian Law Institute, New Delhi and LLM from National Law School of India University, Bangalore. Her Ph.D. thesis analysed the competition law regime in India in a comparative study with that of United States and European Union. She has more than 22 years' experience of Law teaching, research and administration of HEI, at various prestigious law schools including NLSIU, Bangalore, The Indian Law Institute, New Delhi, NUJS, Kolkatta, NLIU, Bhopal. She has successfully guided six Ph.D scholars and has published numerous articles in various journals of national and international repute and books authored and edited.

Index

A

B

C

D

E

F

H

I

J

L

M

P

S

T

W

www.ingramcontent.com/pod-product-compliance
Lightning Source LLC
LaVergne TN
LVHW061530290926
849162LV00004B/732